The General

Lieutenant General Robert Lee Bullard, 1919

ALLAN R. MILLETT

The General
Robert L. Bullard and Officership in the United States Army 1881–1925

Contributions in Military History, Number 10

GREENWOOD PRESS
Westport, Connecticut ● London, England

Library of Congress Cataloging in Publication Data

Millett, Allan Reed.
  The general :   Robert L. Bullard and officership in the United States
Army, 1881-1925.

  (Contributions in military history ;   no. 10)
  Bibliography: p.
  Includes index.
  1. Bullard, Robert Lee, 1861-1947. 2. United States. Army—
Officers.   3.   Military service as a profession.
I. Title. II. Series.
U53.B78M54   355.3'31'0924 [B]   75-68
ISBN 0-8371-7957-2

Library of Congress Catalog Card Number: 75-68
ISBN: 0-8371-7957-2

First published in 1975

Greenwood Press, a division of Williamhouse-Regency Inc.
51 Riverside Avenue, Westport, Connecticut 06880

Printed in the United States of America

Contents

Acknowledgments	ix
Introduction	3

I THE LIEUTENANT 1861-1891

1. Alabama Boyhood, 1861-1881	19
2. West Point, 1881-1885	32
3. Frontier Service, 1885-1889	47
4. Leaving the Line, 1889-1898	69

II WAR AND EMPIRE 1898-1904

5. The Third Alabama Volunteers, 1898-1899	91
6. Volunteers for the Philippines, 1899	111
7. Campaign in Southern Luzon, 1899-1900	121
8. Pacification in Southern Luzon, 1900-1901	135
9. Return to the Infantry, 1901-1902	154
10. Mindanao: The Road, the Lake, and the Moros, 1902-1904	165

III IN SEARCH OF THE NEW ARMY 1904-1912

11. In Search of the New Army, 1904-1909	189
12. California and Mexico, 1909-1911	205
13. The Army War College, 1911-1912	221

IV WATCH ON THE RIO GRANDE 1912-1917

14. The Second Division, 1912-1915   247
15. Pacification in the Lower Valley of
        the Rio Grande, 1915-1917   273

V THE WORLD WAR 1917-1919

16. Joining the American Expeditionary Force, 1917   301
17. The First Division: Introduction to War, 1917-1918   331
18. The First Division: Cantigny, 1918   353
19. The III Corps: The Second Battle of the Marne, 1918   377
20. The III Corps: The Meuse-Argonne Offensive, 1918   395
21. The Second Army, 1918-1919   417

VI AFTER THE WAR 1919-1947

22. Major General, United States Army, 1919-1925   439
23. Evening Parade, 1925-1947   458

Essay on Sources   475
Index   493

Illustrations

PHOTOGRAPHS

Lieutenant General Robert Lee Bullard, 1919   *frontispiece*
Robert Lee Bullard, 1885   239
Officers of the Third Alabama Volunteers, 1898   240
Troops of the Third Alabama, Camp Shipp, Alabama, 1898   240
Colonel Robert Lee Bullard, Thirty-Ninth U.S. Volunteers, 1899   241
Major Robert Lee Bullard, Infantry, 1906   242
Twenty-Eighth Infantry Assault on Cantigny, May 28, 1918   243
Traffic Jam at Esnes, Meuse-Argonne, September 28-29, 1918   243
Pershing and Bullard Inspect Second Army Troops, Toul, France,
April 11, 1919   244

MAPS

The Army in Apache Country, 1886   48
The Thirty-Ninth Volunteers in Southern Luzon, 1900-1901   136
Mindanao and the Lake Lanao District   166
The Lower Valley of the Rio Grande   274
The Western Front   300
The St. Mihiel Salient and the Ansauville Sector   330
The First Division at Cantigny   352
The Third Corps in the Aisne-Marne Counteroffensive   376
The Third Corps in the Meuse-Argonne Offensive, September 26-
October 12, 1918   394
The Second Army Sector, 1918   416

Acknowledgments

From the moment I started serious research in 1967 until The General *was* completed in 1972, literally hundreds of sympathetic historians, archivists, librarians, academics, and interested people contributed to this book. I cannot list all of them by name, but I want them to know that I remember who they are and thank them for their help. I only hope the book meets their expectations; certainly it would have been impossible without their collaboration.

I want to acknowledge the assistance of the staffs of The Ohio State University Library, especially Mrs. Clara Goldslager; the University of Missouri-Columbia Library; the Manuscript Division of the Library of Congress; the Old Military and New Military Records Divisions of the National Archives, especially Mr. Elmer O. Parker and Mr. John Taylor; the library of the National War College, Washington, D. C.; the United States Army Military History Research Collection, Carlisle Barracks, Pennsylvania; the library of the National Guard Association of the United States, Washington, D. C.; the United States Military Academy Library, especially Mrs. Marie T. Capps; the Princeton University Library; the Yale University Library; the State Historical Society of Wisconsin, Madison, Wisconsin, especially Miss Ruth H. Davis; the library of the University of North Carolina at Chapel Hill; the Duke University Library; Savery Library, Talladega College, Talladega, Alabama; the library of the University of Oregon; Case Western Reserve University Library, Cleveland, Ohio; Fort Union National Monument, Watrous, New Mexico; the State of Alabama Department of Archives and History, especially Mr. Milo B. Howard, Jr.; the public library of Harlingen, Texas; the Minnesota Historical Society, St. Paul; the Tennessee State Library and Archives; the Massachusetts Historical Society, Boston; the Adjutants-General of South Dakota, Oklahoma, and Louisiana; the Henry E. Huntington Library, San Marino, California; the George C. Marshall Research Foundation and Library, Lexington, Virginia, especially Dr. Forrest C. Pogue; the Center of Military History, Department of the Army; the library of the University of Texas at Austin; the United States Army Administration Center, St. Louis; the national headquarters of Alpha Tau Omega fraternity, Chicago; the Draughon Library of Auburn University, Auburn, Alabama, especially Mrs. Frances Honour; and the Service Historique de l'Armée de Terre, Vincennes, France.

My research also was assisted by the late Colonel Peter C. Bullard, USA, Atlanta, Georgia; Colonel Daniel W. Bender, USMC (Retired); Mr. Arthur L.

Chaitt, secretary of the Society of the First Division, Philadelphia; Miss Marjorie Andrews, LaFayette, Alabama; Mr. Alexander Nunn, Loachapoka, Alabama; Mrs. T. F. Yancey, Sr., Opelika, Alabama; Mr. James Noel Baker, Opelika, Alabama; Mrs. C. W. Canon, Opelika, Alabama; Mrs. Ruth Crump, Lanett, Alabama; Mr. Charles W. Edwards, Auburn, Alabama; Mrs. Rollo E. Harding, Raymondsville, Texas; Mr. A. A. Champion, Brownsville, Texas; Mr. Joseph P. Wiegers of the Bernarr Macfadden Foundation, New York City; Mrs. Dan Ingram, Lebanon, Tennessee; Professor Robert D. Ward, Georgia Southern College; and General Charles L. Bolté, USA (Retired), Alexandria, Virginia; Professor I. B. Holley of Duke University; Dr. Richard C. Brown, State University College at Buffalo, New York; and Colonel Elliott Johnson, USAF.

I also profited by the suggestions of those who read chapters of the book as I wrote them. If there are errors in fact and interpretation, they are mine, not theirs, and I want to thank them for their interest and patience. I profited from the advice of Professor Peter Karsten, University of Pittsburgh, who read the introduction. I am especially indebted to Mr. Charles W. Edwards, Auburn, Alabama, Lt. Col. and Mrs. T. F. Yancey, Sr., Opelika, Alabama, Mr. Alexander Nunn, Loachapoka, Alabama, Professor Allan Jones, Auburn University, and Mrs. Honour, who read the chapter on Bullard's Alabama background; to Mrs. Capps, Colonel Roger H. Nye, and Major Scott Dillard, all of the United States Military Academy, who read the chapter on Bullard's cadet years at West Point; to Mr. Robert M. Utley of the National Park Service and Dr. Don Rickey, who read the chapter on the frontier Army; to Dr. B. F. Cooling III, United States Army Military History Research Collection, Dr. Mabel E. Deutrich of the National Archives, Professor Edward M. Coffman of the University of Wisconsin at Madison, and Professor Jack C. Lane of Rollins College, who read the chapters on Bullard's peacetime service before and after the Spanish-American War; to Dr. Graham Cosmas, Professor Marvin Fletcher of Ohio University, and Professor John M. Gates of the College of Wooster, all of whom read the chapters on the Spanish-American War and the Philippine Insurrection; Colonel Clarence C. Clendenen, USA (Retired), who read the chapters on Bullard's service on the Texas-Mexico border; Professor Coffman, General Bolté, Dr. Pogue, and Professor Donald W. Smythe of John Carroll University, who fought through World War I with General Bullard; and the veterans of the First Division and Mr. E. O. Nigel Cholmeley-Jones of Westport, Connecticut, who also read the World War chapters. I admire the interest of those who read the entire manuscript—the editors of this series, Professor Russell F. Weigley, Professor Harry L. Coles, Captain R. H. Sinnreich, and my father.

I am also indebted to my colleagues of the Departments of History at the University of Missouri-Columbia and The Ohio State University who offered their expert and interested opinion at various stages of the study. I received the same support from my colleagues at the Mershon Center, The Ohio State University. I also want to thank the faithful typists of the Mershon Center for their patience with my manuscript and correspondence.

The cost of research travel, typing, and the collection of materials was borne by generous grants from the Research Council of the University of Missouri-Columbia; the National Endowment of the Humanities; the American Philosophical Society; and the Mershon Center. I am indebted by the grantors' financial assistance and confidence.

The project would have been impossible, of course, without the understanding and editorial skills of my wife Sally.

Columbus, Ohio
January 1974

The General

Introduction

Lieutenant General Robert Lee Bullard, United States Army, whose military career began in 1881 and ended in 1925, served during a formative period in the history of American military policy and the army. Most important, Bullard lived through the crucial phase of the professionalization of the United States Army officer corps. Bullard's career illuminates the process by which one man was integrated into the occupation of army officer and came to hold high responsibility in his profession. It also reveals the fundamental changes in officership which accompanied America's emergence as a self-conscious world power, industrial nation, and an occupationally specialized society.

1.

A profession is an occupation more "professionalized" than other occupations, that is, it is assuming attributes typical of all professions. While there may be no consensus about the exact number and character of these attributes, they include the following: (1) the occupation is a full-time and stable job, serving continuing societal needs; (2) it is regarded as a life-long calling by the practitioners, who identify themselves personally with their job subculture; (3) the occupation is organized for the control of performance standards and recruitment; (4) the occupation requires formal, theoretical education; (5) the occupation has a service orientation in which loyalty to standards of competence and loyalty to the clients' needs are paramount; (6) the occupation is tacitly granted a great deal of collective autonomy by the society it serves, presumably because the practitioners have proven their trustworthiness. Historically, professionalized occupations have been closely related to job specialization, economic development, and the expansion of knowledge about man's physical and social environment. The most differentiating characteristic of professions has been the accumulation and systematic exploitation of specialized knowledge applied to specialized problems.[1]

Professions are based on some system of knowledge which is continually enlarged by both academic research and experience. This knowledge tends to be esoteric and highly specialized with a language, methodology, and application beyond the grasp of the layman. Yet the layman needs the professional's knowledge and skill to solve common and important problems, although the particular problem may be narrow. The professional, however, asks that he, and

3

not his client, set the conditions under which his knowledge and skill are utilized and that the client accept the professional's definition of what the problem really is. In return for his professional authority, the professional enters a compact with the client not to go beyond the functional specificity which defines his profession. In return for his self-restraint in matters of material reward and emotional dominance over the client, the professional asks society to sanction his practice.

Professions expect to set their own ethical codes, establish their own educational systems, recruit their own members, and maintain a unique occupational culture. The latter is based on the assumptions that the professional's services represent social good, that the monopoly conditions which the professional wants represent human progress, and that the professional's fundamental commitment is to objective results from the application of his theoretical knowledge. The professional's competency will be judged by his peers and his conduct will be determined by the norms of his profession, but he will not abuse society's faith in his skill by ignoring either his client's needs or the regulating judgment of his colleagues. If society agrees with the practitioner's claims to "extraordinary trustworthiness," then it grants the high degree of autonomy which characterizes a profession, although the professional's freedom is conditional and ultimately depends on continuous social approval. Without constant self-policing and task success, a profession can narrow its own freedom and destroy public trust as rapidly as it gained its relative autonomy.[2]

Everett C. Hughes, a perceptive student of men's work, agrees that professions do define their work and have a broad social mandate, but the characteristic that separates them from other occupations is the reason for their autonomy. Professions do society's difficult and morally ambiguous jobs, make other people's mistakes for them, and salvage the pieces, so that ordinary humans can go on with their lives without guilt and a sense of failure. Because the professional is doing a difficult and unattractive task, the lay observer sees him as a charismatic hero, while the professional knows he is only playing statistical probabilities. The practitioner-client relationship is crucial in the professional's life, and his greatest frustrations and anxieties come when he and his public have conflicting conceptions "of what the work really is or should be, of what mandate has been given by the public, of what it is possible to accomplish and by what means, as well as of the particular part to be played by those in each position, their proper responsibilities and rewards."[3]

Individual and collective clients may be aware of a profession's formal code of ethics, but this understanding usually is limited to professional-client relations, not the peer relations that determine the very heart of professional life. Since a professional by definition must be peculiarly sensitive to peer-related awards of status and prestige and since peer relations are more ambiguous than client relations, professionals are particularly annoyed when public rewards and peer-granted rewards are not congruent. Yet a profession cannot afford for many of its members to express public dissatisfaction with their colleagues, for to do so throws the whole profession's credibility into doubt. If there is to be criticism and doubting, it must be internalized by formal peer-group action or subtle informal sanctions. Such sanctions often fall as heavily upon the complainant as they do upon the transgressor. The price of autonomy is collectively paid, and no individual practitioner dares attack his colleagues, however justified his charges, without risking his career. Thus the corporateness that preserves autonomy camouflages a system of discipline which often escapes the layman's attention.[4]

The aspiring professional, as he begins the arduous *rite du passage* of formal professional training, quickly learns that his apprenticeship contains more than learning basic techniques. He is confronted with the need to develop an occupational personality. His new identity is partially inherited, partially self-developed. He inherits the broadly defined characteristics of his career and the special institutional setting in which he finds himself. He must develop stable and lasting concepts of self which are compatible with his profession. This "professional socialization" is not taken lightly by the practitioners with whom he begins his career. Although the aspirant's training is likely to center on learning and applying his profession's special skills, the profession demands that the aspirant take positive pride in the problems he faces and the skills he uses to solve them, that he absorb the profession's current ideology, and that he willingly accept the profession's existing system of rewards, colleagueship, acceptable motives, and conditions of practice. The difficulty lies in the fact that the aspirant must conform to professional "absolutes" at the same time he discovers that his chosen work is intensely competitive, even at the individual level. He learns that his profession is made up of warring factions which have clustered around disputes over theoretical knowledge, experimental methods and techniques of practice, institutional missions, leadership, ethics, recruitment, and standards of competence. He discovers that his profession's internal frictions may be hidden from public view, but that they are real and play a critical role in shaping his own career. A major part of his professionalization is simply identifying all the current and impending conflicts in his profession and then deciding how he will cope with them. Just how well he chooses will probably influence the course of his entire career long after he has been formally admitted to his profession.[5]

Unless a professional practices alone and lives on fees from his individual clients, he customarily finds that some organization dominates his career. In twentieth-century America, professionals have progressively plied their skills within the organizational context of business corporations, governmental agencies, and other complex institutions like universities, research centers, and hospitals. The result has been that occupations often have become professional at the same time that they have become bureaucratized. This parallel process is not necessarily fatal to professionalization. If professionals or coalitions of professionals dominate the organization, or at least that part of its activities which intervenes upon their interests, they may find that they have the freedom, status, and client relations upon which their profession will thrive. The only real risk is that of alienating the public, but this danger is offset by the stability and permanence of their organization. Since their profession is already divided into competitive factions and informal hierarchies of skill and influence, a formal system of authority is not especially terrifying and often makes task organization and the identification of responsible leadership much easier, especially for new practitioners. As long as the organization values the professional's technique and rewards him on the basis of his performance, the practitioner is not likely to feel that his professional values have been compromised.[6]

For a professional working in an organization, however, especially one with a hierarchical rank structure like an army, the organization may become the client itself.[7] Loyalty to the organization becomes the primary responsibility. Such loyalty can obscure the profession's responsibility to society as well as cut it off from the sources of innovativeness and the public support upon which its effectiveness depends. For an individual professional, the fundamental challenge is to balance the demands of the organization and the ideals of the profession, because they may not be the same. The bureaucratized professional may have to function simultaneously as loyalist, advocate, and critic, roles whose inherent conflicts make professional life at once challenging and frustrating.

2.

Whether one considers military officership a profession or not depends to a large degree on one's views on the morality of war and the legitimacy of the national government that employs military officers. Since much writing on military affairs pivots on the issue of military subordination within a nation's political life, it is not surprising that the subject of professionalism is generally regarded as a subissue, relevant only as a weapon in arguments about theories of civil-military relations. If one has serious reservations about a society's need for armed forces or the degree of power military men wield, it follows that one will not admit military officers to professional status, for to do so would sanction their function and presumably increase their autonomy.[8] If, on the other hand, one recognizes a continuing need for expertly led armed forces and believes that ascribing professional status to officers will produce a proper balance of skill and political control, then officership will be judged a profession.[9] Given the occupational values of contemporary Western society, it is, of course, too much to expect officers themselves to deny that they are professionals. Since wars and armies antedate the occupation of full-time officership in Western culture, and since there is scant historical evidence that the status of officership makes much difference to the incidence of wars and coups, there is merit to military officers' pleas that their status be determined not as part of some argument about civil-military relations or "militarism," but by a nonprescriptive assessment of their skill, their degree of collegial corporateness, and their sense of responsibility to the society they serve, ideally to the point of sacrifice of life.[10]

There is considerable evidence that the officers corps in Europe and the United States developed professional attributes in increasing measure in the nineteenth century. Military officers sought professional status and worked assiduously to justify their occupation as a skill-oriented, theoretically based, socially useful, and culturally unique career. Although the process of professionalization differed in speed and degree from nation to nation, military professionalism was a common development in all the advanced industrial states of Europe and in the United States.

The general cultural conditions that stimulated the growth of military professionalism were several and of varying importance. The most important factors, however, were probably the differentiation of political leadership from military management and the subordination of the latter to the former; the institutional reforms of European armies in the Napoleonic and post-Napoleonic era; the adoption on the Continent of the cadre-conscript mass army; the growing body of specialized literature which emphasized the possibility of scientific military leadership; the increased popular sense of national identity and the transference of patriotism to the agencies of the nation-state, including the standing armed forces; and the increasing technological complexity of weapons themselves.

The thrust of professionalization produced a reasonably coherent rationale for professional status by World War I. The fundamental assumption was that nation-states would continue to settle some of their disputes by war and would maintain or create armies and navies for this purpose. The goals of military action and the character of the armed forces which a nation might use would undoubtedly vary, but the training of military forces in peacetime and their effective direction upon the land and sea battlefields of any war required men who had made officership a career. The development of large and complex military organizations, the adoption of progressively sophisticated weapons, and the increased ability of national governments to produce the resources for such armed forces provided strong arguments for specialized officership. Wartime mobilization had not yet become so total as to blur the lines between "civilian" and "military" in war-waging. Wars were to be decided on the battlefield by armed forces, and battlefield leadership was too important to be left to men who had not trained for such a role on a continuous basis.[11]

The most impressive argument for military professionalism, an argument created by officers and eventually accepted by most civilians, was that direction of armed forces was a learned skill, not a matter of innate genius. The organizational corollary to this assault on the idea of the "great captain" or "inspired amateur" concept of leadership was that military command was a collective effort that required a high degree of mutual trust and understanding between officers. Unless an officer had accepted the norms of his military organization and passed through its educational system (formal and informal), he would not be accepted by his colleagues as a fully competent peer. Unless he voluntarily adhered to the prevailing concepts of his officer corps on matters of strategy, tactics, discipline, organization, and training, he could not work effectively as a commander or a member of a commander's staff. The attribute that separated a military officer from other practitioners was his understanding of the theoretical constants in war, pretentiously labeled "military science." Although officers had written on the recurring problems of command before the Napoleonic Wars, the "lessons" of nearly twenty years of European war produced a revolution in military theorizing by career officers, theorizing which was then used as the basis of formal military education. Very little of this "military science" had anything to do with science and technology, but focused instead on decision-making and the nature of war. Predictably, the search for principles of war created a special language of command even though it did not produce immutable laws for battlefield victory. As important as the theories themselves was the fact that the language of strategic discourse was monopolized by military officers and served as the intellectual basis for professionalization. [12]

To what degree the process of professionalization created a unique philosophical outlook for officers ("the military mind") or alienated them from civil society is unanswerable with any precision. Obviously officers might stress the permanence of nationhood and war, the priorities of the organization over the individual's needs, the value of stable institutions and traditions, the need of discipline, and the virtues of duty, honor, and country. If there was anything approaching a "military mind" that all career officers shared, it was probably a product of the priorities of a particular military organization and the officer's role in some part of that organization. Officers closest to the "military ethic" in their attitudes were likely to be those whose careers were limited to regimental duty. They were not the professional leaders of their armies. The professional elite of nineteenth-century armies, especially in Germany, exhibited qualities of mind common to any manager of large-scale enterprise: loyalty to the organization and its mission, a commitment to rational planning, a continuing search for the most efficient use of available resources, and as much control as possible over an unstable and unpredictable external environment. Although the prerequisites of combat leadership (physical and moral courage, physical stamina, and competence in inspiring men and using weapons) did differentiate the officer from the civilian bureaucrat, it is doubtful that even long-term professional socialization produced a coherent philosophical point of view that was uniquely military. [13]

Of all the nineteenth-century European officer corps, the British were the least given to strategic speculation and professional study, presumably because they saw little need for it after Waterloo. The concept of scientific, highly organized and educated officership struck British officers as Continental pretentiousness. They felt no social compulsion to seek professional status since they were likely to come from the same social elite that managed the government, the economy, and the national institutions. Gentlemen officers of a nation enjoying geographic security and a strong navy saw little need to insist upon individual or collective privileges connected solely with officership. Had British officers militantly sought professional status (as did the Prussians), they would have been alienated from their portion of English society, which they certainly were not. The serious students of strategy and battlefield command made scant headway in the nineteenth-century Bristish Army, and military reform was more a product of sporadic ministerial interest than a grass-roots development from within the officer corps. Despite three generations of military fiascos scattered around the Empire from Afghanistan to the Transvaal, the British officer corps ended the century with its gallant amateurism intact.[14]

If it had not been for the Civil War, the same condition would have been true for their American cousins. Although the United States Military Academy served as a conduit for the French version of military science and European concepts of officership, the officer corps of the small standing United States Army was not even led by West Pointers until after the Civil War, and even then Academy graduates were not a numerical majority. Officership as an occupation was defined by American civil society, and the roots of its culture were in England, not France or Prussia. The American officer was not necessarily an evil influence, but his popular acceptance depended on his ability to play a socially defined role that had little to do with his competence as a battlefield commander. He was expected to be a military gentleman whose value was measured by his commitment to literary education, outdoor sport, republicanism, personal honor, and American egalitarianism. The ideal army officer was a man of few specialties and many general aptitudes: explorer, surveyor, canal-builder, Indian agent, diplomat, author (but not of military works), and artist. The American officer was certainly expected to be a heroic and successful leader in war, but the peacetime roles most related to wartime command (troop trainer, student of warfare, disciplinarian, expert in weapons and supply management) were those roles civilians found most alien and hence scorned. Americans preferred officers whose image combined the attributes of George Washington, Audubon, and the Deerslayer, not Napoleon or Clausewitz.[15]

The Civil War killed some six hundred thousand American military amateurs and the concept of amateurism, at least in part of the officer corps of the postwar United States Army. Between the Civil War and World War, the army officer corps became an institutionalized profession. Its teachers, writers, and thinkers, influenced by both Continental developments and their own experience, created an educational system for career-long formal training in the techniques of contingency planning and the management of large troop formations in war. At least two of the army's commanding generals, William Tecumseh Sherman and John M. Schofield, encouraged more rigorous evaluation of officer performance and attempted to curb active political partisanship. Unlike the officer corps of the United States Navy, army officers were not confronted with a new philosophy of national development, naval strategy, and war ("Sea Power") or bewildering disputes about technology and ship design. The "technological revolution" in land warfare was to come only with World War I; the changes in army ordnance and mobility before 1917 came slowly and were absorbed without crisis.

The army's concern was managerial: who would direct the nation's wartime armies on the battlefield and how would these generals be selected? The professionalist army reformers had an obvious answer: career officers with both practical field experience and theoretical training on the European model. To use any other criteria, particularly political influence, was nonprofessional. Unlike other professionals (including the navy's officers), army officers did not claim that generalship was a "scientific" matter which could be reduced to predictable formulas for human behavior or the performance of machinery. At the risk of being called romantic irrationals and of accepting "inspired" amateurs to their ranks, army officers insisted that their fundamental expertise was in the moral inspiration of fighting men. The professional officer was most capable of understanding and integrating both the rational and irrational characteristics of combat leadership. An army trained and organized by such officers would be the most efficient in war. The professionals recognized the value of the "scientific management" movement in business and other organizations; they recognized that technology would change the weapons of war; they appreciated the value of European military practices. But they insisted that the social environment of America and the unpredictable nature of war demanded that the professional officer be hero, gentleman, student of men, and manager. He could not, however, learn or balance this set of occupational roles without long experience and formal education. This was the professionals' argument, and by 1918 they had won it with the American people.[16]

3.

Lieutenant General Robert Lee Bullard, United States Army, was born before the Civil War and died after the end of World War II. His active army career began at the age of twenty and ended with his mandatory retirement at sixty-four. His service in the army covered much of the crucial period of the professionalization of the American officer corps, and his career is an admirable vehicle for examining that process. Bullard himself was not an active professionalizer, that is, part of the elite of officers who influenced the process of professionalization as teachers like Arthur L. Wagner, polemicists like Emory Upton, or policy-makers like William Tecumseh Sherman or Leonard Wood. Bullard never held a position of high influence or authority until World War I when the process was largely complete. He made no major contribution as an author, and he never held a teaching or staff post which would have allowed him to influence his peers or assist in drafting the military legislation of his era. To deny that Bullard had no particular impact on the institutional life of the United States Army does not mean that he was either an unimpressive person or a mediocre officer who gained high rank simply by staying alive. Bullard's claim to attention is that he was a successful officer by the army's standards and that he was an intelligent and articulate student of his own career and officership in his army.

This study assumes that the significant and identifiable influences upon Bullard's life were produced by his social environment, specifically his occupation as officer in the United States Army. To phrase it baldly, one can understand more about Bullard by examining his relationship with his Academy classmates and his first company commander than by discussing his relationship with his mother or wife. Essentially, this study deals with the professional socialization of one army officer. It focuses on his relations with other officers (superiors, peers, and subordinates) and the enlisted men under his command. It looks at the challenges of forty-four years of officership, challenges defined not simply by war, but by the demands of the army. By examining the process of professional socialization, the changing nature of officership (professionalization) in the United States Army comes into clearer focus.[17]

If Bullard is to serve as a model for an experience hundreds of other officers shared, he must in some way be typical of his "generation" of officers. He was, in several important ways. Of the army's general officers appointed between 1898 and 1920, the typical officer was a native-born Anglo-American whose family came to North America before the Revolution. The typical general grew up on a farm or in a small rural town, was reared a Protestant, and had a father who was either a farmer, small businessman, professional man, or public official. The majority of the generals came from the Northeast or Northcentral part of the country, but the South was proportionately overrepresented with 27 percent of the generals from 23 percent of the white population. The typical general was a graduate of the United States Military Academy. Bullard was born in Alabama, reared in a Methodist farm family, and graduated from West Point in 1885.[18]

Bullard meets more subtle measures of typicality. In the course of this study, I reconstructed the careers in detail of fifty-four army officers commissioned between 1870 and 1900. Forty men in this group served primarily as line officers, and of this group thirty-two became generals. Fourteen had staff billets, ten of them as generals. Making allowances for the rich individuality of these men, Bullard's career was typical of twenty-nine line officers who became generals. The careers of those two giants of Bullard's army, Leonard Wood and John J. Pershing, and of the maverick Frederick Funston were not typical, for they became general officers while still in their forties and skipped the normal ascent through the rank structure. Bullard and his peers did not escape the long gauntlet of service and survival which led to colonel and, for some, general. Bullard held every officer rank, commanded every tactical formation in his arm (infantry) from platoon to field army, and seldom served away from troops. When he did, however, his assignments and experiences conform with Morris Janowitz's theory that the army's generals often have unconventional opportunities which dramatize their adaptability and intellectual sophistication.

Although there are strong continuities in the officership experience, Bullard's career varies substantially when contrasted with those of officers commissioned in the 1870s and with those of officers commissioned in the 1890s, suggesting that there were four or five different "generations" of officers in the period of professionalization, 1870-1918. For example, the officers of the 1870s spent far less time in school and staff assignments than the officers of the "generation of 1890." When Bullard's career is compared with those of American generals and admirals who reached flag rank in 1969, the changes in career patterns are pronounced. Bullard was promoted to brigadier general after thirty-two years of commissioned service during which he had twenty-one different assignments, less short periods of detached duty. He spent twenty-two years with troops, four years, on colonial service, four years in educational assignments, one year on staff duty, and one year on detached service. The new general of 1969 averaged twenty-four years of service. He had twenty-one different assignments (like Bullard), but spent substantially less of his career in command assignments. The modern brigadier had eight years in operational assignments, five years in service schools and other educational assignments, and eleven years in staff assignments.[19] With so little time spent, comparatively, in positions of command, one wonders less whether the modern brigadier general's choice is between "heroic" or "managerial" leadership styles (to use Janowitz's model) than whether he develops any leadership style at all.[20]

There are aspects of Bullard's career that directly reflect the officer corps' increasing professionalism. For example, Bullard became a serious student of European military literature, while older officers read English novels. Yet he questioned the value of academic soldiering and avoided school and staff assignments until it was obvious that his career would wither without such experiences. Another dominant theme in his career was his concern for his reputation. He valued the approval of his peers, but he recognized that the most talented of his associates were fierce competitors and that he could not count on the army's good wishes alone for advancement. Bullard thought his career depended on his public reputation, and he cultivated civilian attention through his writings, his political activity as an active Democrat, his work with the National Guard, his public speaking, and his cooperation with friendly newspapermen. Convinced as he was that America's military strength depended on the mutual trust and understanding between the officer corps and the civilians who were the nation's wartime soldiers, he reduced the ambiguity of his activities to tolerable proportions. Bullard did not condemn civil society—the essence of professionalism to some officers like Sherman and Upton. His liaison with civil life played a major part in his successful command experiences in the Spanish-American War, the Philippine Insurrection, the border troubles with Mexico, and World War I. Conversely, he antagonized his peers by actively lobbying for appointment to brigadier general.

Having lived with General Bullard for seven years, I cannot think of him, finally, as simply an example of a social process. He was an appealing man, tall, athletic, and picturesque in manner and language. Even before his promotion to general, he had become (consciously so) an army "character" whose adventurous spirit and love of soldiering impressed all but his most dogmatic enemies. His ambition and professional competitiveness did not destroy his sense of humor, modesty, and his sensitivity to others. He often feared he was too generous with subordinates and too obsequious with his superiors, but his successes suggest that he usually found the right combination of personal example, firm authority, and persuasion in his handling of men. Robert Lee Bullard lived and served close to the ideal of officer and gentleman.

NOTES

[1]Wilbert E. Moore and Gerald W. Rosenblum, *The Professions: Rules and Roles* (New York: Russell Sage Foundation, 1970), pp. 3-22, 54; Talcott Parsons, "Professions," in Daniel L. Shils, ed., *International Encyclopedia of the Social Sciences*, 17 vols. (New York: Macmillan, 1968), XII, pp. 536-47.

[2]Ernest Greenwood, "Attributes of a Profession," *Social Work* 2 (July 1957), pp. 45-55; Howard S. Becker, "The Nature of a Profession," *Education for the Professions, Yearbook of the National Society for the Study of Education*, Vol. LXI (Chicago: University of Chicago Press, 1962), pp. 26-46.

[3]Everett C. Hughes, *Men and Their Work* (Glencoe, Ill.: Free Press, 1958), pp. 8-9, 76, 90-91.

[4]Moore and Rosenblum, *The Professions: Roles and Rules*, pp. 66-83; Harvey L. Smith, "Contingencies of Professional Differentiation," and T. H. Marshall, "Professionalism and Social Policy," in Sigmund Nosow and William H. Form, eds., *Man, Work, and Society* (New York: Basic Books, 1962), pp. 219-35; William J. Goode, "Community Within a Community: The Professions," *American Sociological Review* 22 (April 1957), pp. 194-200; Rue Bucher and Anselm Strauss, "Professions in Process," *American Journal of Sociology* 62 (January 1961), pp. 325-34.

[5]Howard S. Becker and James W. Carper, "The Development of Identification with an Occupation," *American Journal of Sociology* 61 (January 1956), pp. 289-98. See also the essays in Howard M. Vollmer and Donald L. Mills, eds., *Professionalization* (Englewood Cliffs, N.J.: Prentice-Hall, 1966).

[6]Richard H. Hall, "Professionalization and Bureaucratization," *American Sociological Review* 33 (February 1968), pp. 92-104; Harold L. Wilensky, "The Professionalization of Everyone?" *American Journal of Sociology* 70 (September 1964), pp. 137-58; Daniel Katz and Robert L. Kahn, *The Social Psychology of Organizations* (New York: John Wiley & Sons, 1966), pp. 171-98, 336-89.

[7]Anthony Downs, *Inside Bureaucracy* (Boston: Little, Brown, 1967), pp. 25-6, 49; Peter M. Blau and W. Richard Scott, *Formal Organizations* (San Francisco: Chandler, 1962), pp. 60-74; Bengt Abrahamsson, *Military Professionalization and Political Power* (Beverly Hills, Calif.: Sage Publications, 1972), pp. 64-6.

[8]For examples of this point of view, see the following classics in the literature of civil-military relations: Alfred Vagts, *A History of Militarism*, rev. ed. (New York: Free Press, 1959) and Stanislav Andreski, *Military Organization and Socity*, rev. ed. (Los Angeles and Berkeley: University of California Press, 1968).

[9]See especially Samuel P. Huntington, *The Soldier and the State* (Cambridge, Mass.: Harvard University Press, 1959); Morris Janowitz, *The Professional Soldier: A Social and Political Portrait* (Glencoe, Ill.: Free Press, 1960); and S. E. Finer, *The Man on Horseback* (New York: Frederick A. Praeger, 1962).

See also R. D. McKinlay, "Professionalization, Politicization and Civil-Military Relations" and Maury D. Feld, "Professionalism and Politicalization: Notes on Military and Civilian Control": in M. R. Van Gils, ed., *The Perceived Role of the Military* (Rotterdam: Rotterdam University Press, 1971), pp. 247-76.

[10]General Sir John Winthrop Hackett, *The Profession of Arms* (1962 Lee Knowles lectures at Trinity College, Cambridge University), reprinted as Department of the Army Pamphlet 360-302 (1966); Colonel Robert N. Ginsburgh, "The Challenge to Military Professionalism," *Foreign Affairs* 42 (January 1964), pp. 255-68.

[11]Kurt Lang, "Military," in Shils, ed., *International Encyclopedia of the Social Sciences* X (1968), pp. 305-11.

For a basic discussion of the history of warfare in the nineteenth century, see Theodore Ropp, *War in the Modern World*, rev. ed. (Durham, N.C.: Duke University Press, 1962), pp. 125-217.

For the increase in professional characteristics and the politics of professionalization in European armies, see the following institutional histories: Gordon A. Craig, *The Politics of the Prussian Army, 1640-1945* rev. ed., (New York: Oxford University Press, 1964); Karl Demeter, *The German Officer Corps in Society and State, 1650-1945* (New York: Frederick A. Praeger, 1965); Herbert Rosinski, *The German Army*, rev. ed. (New York: Frederick A. Praeger, 1966), Samuel F. Scott, "The French Revolution and the Professionalization of the French Officer Corps, 1789-1793," in Morris Janowitz and Jacques van Doorn, eds., *On Military Ideology* (Rotterdam: Rotterdam University Press, 1971), pp. 5-56; Paul-Marie de la Gorce, *The French Army* (New York: George Braziller, 1963); and O. A. Ray, "The Imperial Russian Army Officer," *Political Science Quarterly* 26 (December 1961), pp. 576-92.

[12]On the science of strategy, see especially Michael Howard, "Jomini and the Classical Tradition in Military Thought"; Peter Paret, "Clausewitz and the Nineteenth Century"; Gordon A. Craig, "Command and Staff Problems in the Austrian Army, 1740-1866"; and Jay Luvaas, "European Military Thought and Doctrine, 1870-1914"; all in Michael Howard, ed., *The Theory and Practice of War* (New York: Frederick A. Praeger, 1966), pp. 3-93. See also James D. Hittle, *The Military Staff* (Harrisburg, Pa.: Stackpole Press, 1961), pp. 50-165.

[13]Morris Janowitz and Roger W. Little, *Sociology and the Military Establishment*, rev. ed. (New York: Russell Sage Foundation, 1965), pp. 20-27, 31-76.

For attempts to generalize on the existence of a unique "military mind," see Huntington, *The Soldier and the State*, pp. 7-18, 59-79; Maury D. Feld, "Professionalism, Nationalism, and the Alienation of the Military," in Jacques van Doorn, ed., *Armed Forces and Society* (The Hague: Mouton, 1968), pp. 55-70, and "The Military Self-Image in a Technological Environment," in Morris Janowitz, ed., *The New Military* (New York: Russell Sage Foundation, 1964), pp. 159-88; Bengt Abrahamsson, "Military Professionalism and Estimates on the Probability of War," in Jacques van Doorn, ed., *Military Profession and Military Regimes* (The Hague: Mouton, 1969), pp. 35-51; and Jacques van Doorn, "Ideology and the Military," in Morris Janowitz and Jacques van Doorn, eds., *On Military Ideology* (Rotterdam: Rotterdam University Press, 1971), pp. xv-xxix.

[14]E. S. Turner, *Gallant Gentlemen: A Portrait of the British Officer, 1600-1956* (London: Michael Joseph, 1956), pp. 220-53, 256-93; Correlli Barnett, *Britain and Her Army, 1509-1970* (New York: William Morrow, 1970), pp. 272-349; Jay Luvaas, *The Education of an Army: British Military Thought, 1815-1940* (Chicago: University of Chicago Press, 1964), pp. 7-247; C. B. Otley, "Militarism and the Social Affiliations of the British Army Elite," in van Doorn, ed., *Armed Forces and Society*, pp. 84-108.

[15]Marcus Cunliffe, *Soldiers and Civilians: The Martial Spirit in America, 1776-1865* (Boston: Little, Brown, 1968) and "The American Military Tradition," in H. C. Allen and C. P. Hill, eds., *British Essays in American History* (London: Edward Arnold, 1957), pp. 207-24; Charles R. Kemble, *The Image of the Army Officer in America* (Westport, Conn.: Greenwood Press, 1973), pp. 17-94; Russell F. Weigley, *History of the United States Army* (New York: Macmillan, 1967), pp. 117-96.

Huntington in *The Soldier and the State* (pp. 143-221) attempts to equate Southern "conservatism" with a regional sympathy for military professionalism, but Cunliffe found little special interest in the South for European-style military professionalism. Allen Guttman, "Political Ideals and the Military Ethic," *The American Scholar* 34 (Spring 1965), pp. 221-37, finds little classical conservatism in any American region or epoch.

[16]For basic discussions of the process of professionalization between the Civil War and World War I, see Huntington, *The Soldier and the State*, pp. 222-269; Robert D. Miewald, "The Stability of Military Managerial Doctrine: The United States Army, 1866-1941," (unpublished Ph.D. dissertation, University of Colorado, 1966), pp. 85-244; and Weigley, *History of the United States Army*, pp. 265-354.

No reliable survey data exists on the status of military officers in the United States until 1925, but a series of studies done since then indicates that officers enjoy occupational prestige comparable with other professions and business managers. See Charles H. Coates and Roland J. Pellegrin, *Military Sociology* (College Park, Md.: Social Science Press, 1965), pp. 43-47.

On the parallel professionalization of the naval officer corps, see Peter Karsten, *The Naval Aristocracy: The Golden Age of Annapolis and the Emergence of American Navalism* (Glencoe, Ill.: Free Press, 1972).

[17]For the use of biography as a mode of sociological research, see Norman K. Denzin, *The Research Act: A Theoretical Introduction to Sociological Methods* (Chicago: Aldine, 1970), pp. 3-28, 219-59.

[18]Richard C. Brown, "Social Attitudes of American Generals, 1898-1940," (unpublished Ph.D. dissertation, University of Wisconsin, 1951), pp. 1-39.

[19]Gilbert W. Fitzhugh *et al.*, *Report to the President and the Secretary of Defense on the Department of Defense by the Blue Ribbon Defense Panel, 1 July 1970* (Washington: Government Printing Officer, 1970), pp. 137-8.

[20]Janowitz, *The Professional Soldier*, pp. 40-46.

I *THE LIEUTENANT*
1861-1898

I have often needed a diary, an experience case record for reference. It is late to start at 38-1/2 years, but I shall have some spare moments in the next ten days between here and Manila and I set my memory to work. Many things worthy of remembrance and reference have happened to me, especially in the last two years. To write them is to learn my lessons of experience anew. It will do me good. To live them over in memory will be like the review of a hard-studied study. It ought to polish the fixed and fix some floating principles in me, and help arrange knowledge and experience for convenient use.

Robert Lee Bullard, Diary entry,
November 26, 1899, aboard the army
transport *Pennsylvania*.

1

Alabama Boyhood
1861-1881

From the ridges covered with long-leaf pines and oaks to the sandy loams and red clay of the bottomlands covered with gum, poplar, pine, and maple, the land of eastern Alabama was verdant. It was well watered, the streams falling away to the west to the Tallapoosa River and to the east to the Chattahoochee. Blanketed by the heavy forests, the fertile and unspoiled land looked good to the Georgia pioneers along the east bank of the Chattahoochee. But before 1832 the land belonged to the Creek Indians.[1]

Among the whites eyeing the Creek lands, either as land speculators or squatters, was a young man named Daniel Bullard, late of Robeson County, North Carolina. His background was unexceptional. Since the first Bullards, sons of an English seaman, had settled in North Carolina around 1760, the family had lived as solid, industrious farmers on the edge of the Carolina piedmont. The family must have treasured memories of England, for Daniel's grandfather, James Bullard, was a reluctant rebel in the Revolution. James Bullard served sporadically in the Carolina militia and was relieved to see the war end. Born in 1778 while his father was farming and harrying Tories without enthusiasm, Daniel's father Robert grew up in his father's furrow and farmed. Having married Katherine McLean, Robert Bullard raised nine children, among them Daniel, born in 1811. But the Bullard holdings were too small to support all of Robert Bullard's children, so Daniel, the youngest son, left home at the age of twenty-one. He headed for the Georgia frontier, arriving at Columbus, Georgia, on the Chattahoochee about the time the Creeks ceded their lands to the United States government.[2]

In 1835 Daniel Bullard, following the leadership of three brothers named Edwards, set out across the river to settle in the Creek lands. It was a risky venture, for the remaining Creeks were sullen in the face of the white invasion. The Edwards acquired lands southeast of the modern city of Opelika and established themselves as planters near Spring Villa creek and mill. A farm boy with little more than quick wits and muscle, Daniel Bullard followed the fortunes of the Edwards family, trailing them to the Spring Villa area. In his travels Daniel became acquainted with the Reverend William Mizell, a Methodist circuit-rider, and his daughter Susan. Daniel and Susan were married and became another farm family. In 1836, however, the Creeks attacked the white farmers and travelers along the Chattahoochee. With their neighbors, Daniel and his wife fled back to Georgia. The Creeks let them go, but burned their farms; in Bullard family legend the piety and honesty of William Mizell in dealing with the Creeks persuaded the Indians to spare the Mizell family. What part Daniel Bullard played in the punitive expeditions against the Creeks is uncertain. In any event the uprising was smothered by eleven thousand Alabama and Georgia militiamen and a handful of soldiers. Daniel Bullard was thereafter called "Captain" Bullard, although it is doubtful that he commanded any of the local ad hoc militia companies that rounded up the Creeks and sent them to the Indian Territory. As the Creek menance ended, Daniel Bullard and his wife were again homesteading in Russell County, Alabama.[3]

Daniel and Susan Bullard grew old with Russell County, farmed, and raised a family of twelve children, eleven of whom reached maturity. Their farm was near a resort called Yongesborough, the site of a lime quarry and plantation built in the 1850s by a wealthy Georgian, William Penn Yonge. In contrast to the rich, sporting Yonge the Bullards were typical, unpretentious antebellum Alabama gentry. Daniel Bullard remained a hardworking farmer who became a slave owner and claimed the occupation of "planter." He was not politically active nor did he become a civic leader in nearby Opelika. His greatest achievement was raising funds and supervising the construction of the county's first Methodist church. Daniel Bullard, in addition to running his small plantation with the help of a white overseer, also sold cotton gins for Brown and Company of Columbus, Georgia, and his business trips took him as far west as Texas. A large, handsome man, he enjoyed both his family and his business acquaintances, accepting both with tolerance, good humor, and affection. His wife, Susan, was more temperamental, pious, lighthearted, artistic, and strict with her children. In her husband's absence she ran her household and slaves firmly, her actions always guided by what she thought was her Christian duty. There was little time for frivolity in the Bullard household as the first nine children arrived, all girls. The Bullard girls grew up happily and married well into the solid, upright East Alabama middle class; their husbands included a lawyer, a banker, several well-to-do farmers, a doctor, and the manager of the Chewacla Lime Kiln.[4]

Working his small plantation through good times and bad, handling his slaves with kindly firmness, Daniel Bullard aged with equanimity and prospered. He and his wife were part of a church-going, mutually reinforcing community which included their own brothers, sisters, kin, fellow pioneer families, and their daughters' husbands. In the comfortable Bullard log and frame home, dinner served as many as twenty. And in 1857 Daniel Bullard at the age of forty-six had his first son, Daniel Walter.

In 1859, however, the Bullard family and most of Russell County began to take the talk of secession and war seriously after John Brown's raid on Harper's Ferry. Bordering the northeast corner of Alabama's "Black Belt," Russell County was cotton country, although its farmers primarily grew grain and raised livestock. In

1860 the county had 10,936 whites and 16,656 slaves, not a population balance in which talk of servile insurrection could be dismissed easily. When Opelika's political elite tested local sentiment, they found the Russell County middle class to be firm Southerners, ready to fight for their way of life. The Bullards stood prepared with their friends and neighbors to go to war.

Amid the political confusions of the winter of 1860-1861, the Bullards had a second son, named William Robert, on January 15, 1861. This second son was upstaged, however, by the birth of the first Bullard grandchild, a boy, to Martha Ann Greene. This child, James Benjamin Greene, was born February 18, the inaugural day of Jefferson Davis as president of the Confederacy. This historical coincidence made "Ben" Greene's birth a bigger family event than the birth of his month older uncle, William Robert.[5]

1.

Born into the Civil War, William Robert Bullard's boyhood was shaped as much by the mythos of the Lost Cause as by the realities of Southern rural life. For Russell County the war was a severe blow, disrupting the economy, creating shortages of food and clothes, shattering race relations, and killing and maiming the county's young men. Russell County's patriotism was real, its sacrifices considerable, its "bombproofs," "mossbacks," and "featherbed" citizens few in number. Opelika and Russell County raised three companies of volunteers, one of which, Company H of the Sixth Alabama Infantry, was commanded by Captain R. M. Greene, Martha Ann's husband. As his son Ben and infant brother-in-law William Robert crawled together at home, Captain Greene fought and survived in Confederate campaigns in Virginia. Twice wounded, he was with the Sixth Alabama, a remnant of eighty men, when the Army of Northern Virginia surrendered at Appomattox. In the Sixth Regiment, formed in East Alabama, more than six hundred men died and another six hundred were disabled. Wreathed in valor and suffering, Captain Greene came home in uniform and impressed young William Robert: "This first vision of a soldier has stuck to me through life. His live, keen looks, bearing and manner were burnt upon my memory."[6]

At home in Russell County the war touched the Bullard family in many ways. Daniel Bullard spent a great deal of time traveling in pursuit of dwindling business and in the summer of 1863 was trapped in besieged Vicksburg. Susan, giving birth to her last child, a son, in June 1863, thought her husband dead. But in late July Daniel Bullard returned to his distraught wife and daughters. Moreover, the war forced the family to abandon its modest gentility. For the first time, Susan Bullard made clothing for her family and slaves, raised indigo for dye, and cultivated okra, which she substituted for unobtainable coffee. The family's wealth dwindled, wiped out by inflation. Yet the war did not actually reach Russell County until 1864 and then not seriously until the spring of 1865. The Yankees came as cavalry raiders, destroying the railroads and some rolling stock near Opelika in July 1864. In April 1865, with the Confederacy collapsing, Union cavalrymen rode into

Opelika. Opposed by nothing more devastating than the insults of young girls and old men, they burned Confederate military stores, railway depots, and more railroad cars. Their greatest impact was on Russell County's blacks. Hearing of the Union Army's protection, the slaves, including the Bullard's, fled the county's farms. Freedom for the Negroes plunged the county into deeper economic distress.[7]

Yet, for young William Robert the war was more a powerful symbol than a personally experienced reality. His vision was of staunch womenfolk and valiant young men. His small world was further colored by the war when the state of Alabama in 1866 created a new county which included the Bullard farm, and named it for Robert E. Lee. Sometime thereafter young William Robert asked his parents if he could change his name, too. He was baptized Robert Lee Bullard, "Lee" to his family for the rest of his life.

Isolated by his large and attentive family from the upsets of the war and postwar readjustment, young Lee had a secure and normal childhood. He was not, however, a robust and adventuresome boy. Plagued from youth with a congenital urethral defect and pampered by his aging mother, he spent much time indoors, working with his sisters and learning to sew, cobble shoes, and play the piano. His mother and sisters taught him to read, write, do sums, and translate simple pieces in Greek and Latin. He grew flowers. He did not work hard on his father's farm, doing such chores as tending stock, cutting wood, weeding the vegetable garden, and occasionally "chopping" cotton and corn. Even if he had been strong, his father did not need his labor, for after a brief fling at freedom the Bullards' Negroes returned and worked for wages. Thus Lee's forays into Lee County were for pleasure. He and Ben Greene and a gaggle of cousins played old English children's games and hunted birds with rocks. At ten he learned to shoot and hunted rabbits and doves.[8]

Robert Lee Bullard was anything but a strong and aggressive child. Among his cousins, the slight, fine-featured, sensitive little boy was called "Babe" or "Momma's Boy." Once when he went to Opelika to stay overnight in the Greene household, he fled to a corner and cried so uncontrollably that he was immediately taken home. Only when he became a teenager did he travel much about Lee County, and he never spent a night away from home until he went to college. However, in a home where he was surrounded by cousins, nephews, and nieces of the same age, he did not escape the abrasive experience of childhood peer competition, ridicule, and reinforcement. By the time he was ten, Lee had a family reputation for industry and determination.[9]

In addition to piety and love, Daniel and Susan Bullard provided their children with some formal education. After the end of the war Daniel Bullard's fortunes improved rapidly as the cotton market recovered. Around 1868 he purchased a second farm and larger house known as the "Bryant Place." Lee remembered the move as "a tremendous rise in the world for the whole family."[10] To the boy's world of gins, cotton fields, mules, dogs, Negroes, and relatives, Daniel Bullard added schoolteachers, bringing young men from Opelika to board with his family and to teach the farm children. Daniel built a rude schoolhouse on his property and paid the teachers. Lee learned to read, write, spell, and do mathematics beyond the level of ability he reached under his family's tutoring. He himself later thought that he had little talent for learning, but around Opelika he was known as a prize student. His intellectual achievements must have given him some satisfaction, for he referred to himself as "Engineer" Bullard and called his brothers "shoemaker" and "straggler." Another product of his reading was a growing sense of nationalism and duty; the Great Centennial of 1876, enthusiastically celebrated in Lee County, impressed the imaginative young man.[11]

Another part of Robert Lee Bullard's Alabama heritage was his troubled attitude toward Negroes. From his earliest memory, Bullard was aware of the complicated and tension-filled relations of whites and blacks on his father's farm. The presence of Negroes, was, first of all, an economic necessity, for they provided the manual labor and housekeeping skills that kept the Bullard household and farm functioning. But the Bullard family was not entirely happy about their black charges, troubled in part by their intense Christianity and bothered by the degree of responsibility and supervision they had to assume for their blacks. While the Bullards were upset by the holiday their former slaves took in 1865, they were relieved by the end of slavery and the social pressure that forced them to be responsible masters. When the freedmen returned to work as hired hands, Daniel and Susan Bullard continued to be humane employers, and the Bullard farm never lacked for help.

A troubling aspect of race relations on the Bullard farm was the blurred lines between black and white personal relations, including sex. As an infant, Robert Lee was nursed by a young black girl, who was probably a mulatto and who through her entire life had the irritating habit of addressing the Bullards as equals. Pete Christian, a black farm hand who was largely responsible for teaching Lee the skills of woodsmanship and farming, was the son of a white overseer. Aware how deep his relationship with blacks had been, Robert Lee Bullard blamed their influence for many of his own shortcomings. Raised in a family of the strictest probity, Bullard thought that his most unattractive character traits could be traced to the fact that he "grew up . . . absorbing negro." He believed "the associations were bad for me. I feel it to this day." The Negroes' worst offense was their influence on his speech, for he was embarrassed by his inability to conquer his Southern accent and his rural colloquialisms. Bullard once admitted that he could not pronounce a "g" on the end of a word if his life depended on it. Yet for all his resentment toward Negroes, he also admitted that many of those who had given him skills, love, and encouragement as a child had been the black folk in his parents' household. This confluence of personal experience, Southern mores, and anxiety gave Bullard an ambiguous attitude, noblesse and distaste toward non-whites which he never resolved.[12]

2.

In 1876 the aging Daniel Bullard decided to move his family nine miles north of Opelika to the hamlet of Oak Bowery in Chambers County. Though the elder Bullard had again been financially hurt by the Depression of 1873, he had held on to enough money to buy a two-story Greek revival home known as "Oak Grove." He also retained ownership of eighty acres in Lee County. Bullard's reasons for moving were personal and cultural. At sixty-five, he may have thought of becoming semiretired and devoting more time to his three young sons. In addition, Oak Bowery, though in decline, was still a haven of antebellum Methodist gentility. Opelika, on the other hand, was much too modern and tumultuous for a proper family like the Bullards. By the 1870s Opelika had a reputation for financial chaos, rowdyism, public drunkenness, brawling, racial clashes, and intense political feeling. Opelika had lost its "tone." Daniel Bullard's primary motive, however, was to find more education for his children, especially his academically inclined son, Lee. Oak Bowery residents once had maintained several private primary schools and two "institutes," one for girls, one for boys. While these schools had closed, the town still had an educated elite, and their sons and daughters were private tutors. At a time when people were leaving the exhausted land about Oak Bowery for the West or Opelika, when the antebellum aristocratic families were selling their property and abandoning plantation life in Chambers County, the Bullards retreated to their new home, "Oak Grove."[13]

The Bullards had no difficulty fitting into their new home, for "Oak Grove" was large and solid. The house had eight large rooms, four columns along the front portico, a front balcony and four chimneys. Built above ground on brick posts, the house was landscaped with oaks and cedars. Although it had deteriorated somewhat in twenty-six years, it was still an Oak Bowery landmark and a suitable residence for a retired pioneer planter like "Captain" Bullard. The town of Oak Bowery was equally attractive to the Bullards, for its social life revolved about the activities of the Oak Bowery Methodist Church, a prestigious combination of several hundred solid citizens and a well-appointed Greek revival church. Shortly after moving, Daniel and Susan Bullard, their daughters Emma, Winnifred, Sarah, and their sons Daniel, Robert Lee, and Clarence became part of the congregation.[14]

For fifteen-year-old Robert Lee Bullard, the move to Oak Bowery started a coming-of-age. He was pleased by his new home and female friends, but he was even more impressed by his family's declining wealth and the economic implications of his father's retirement. While he had always been a good student, he had excelled for the personal satisfaction of learning and because his parents expected excellence. In Oak Bowery he apparently saw that education was his only hope of preparing himself for a respectable occupation, since he would have no inherited wealth. He was especially impressed when Ben Greene returned to Opelika in 1879 as a graduate of Emory College in Georgia and quickly started his climb from cashier to president with the Bank of Opelika. Robert Lee turned his considerable determination upon his school books.[15]

Under the supervision of the minister of the Oak Bowery Methodist Church, Robert Lee spent the better part of four years in study. At nineteen he wanted to go to college, but his family did not have the money. To earn his tuition he taught school to some hill children, force-feeding his pupils for five months on Greek, Latin, geometry, and trigonometry. Although he had overcome much of his boyish diffidence and shyness, he found teaching the rough boys and girls, some as old and tall as he, a trying experience. The students he learned to cope with, even to enjoy, but "to satisfy the pride, whims and fancies of loving but ignorant and unreasonable parents is next to impossible." When his school disbanded in June 1880, he was ready to continue his own education.[16]

In September the nineteen-year-old ex-teacher packed a few belongings and struck out to attend the new Agricultural and Mechanical College of Alabama at nearby Auburn. According to family tradition, he walked to his brother Daniel's farm, borrowed a mule and linen duster, and with $100 set out for college. For a young man who had never spent a night away from home it was a momentous occasion, made more so by his awareness that his $100 would probably see him through only four months in Auburn.

The Agricultural and Mechanical College at Auburn had been created under the provisions of the Land Grant College Act of 1862, but its name did not describe its curriculum or character. In 1880, almost a decade after its founding, the college was still the direct academic descendant of its institutional father, the East Alabama Male College, a Methodist-sponsored school in the classical-pious tradition. The faculty was still largely that of East Alabama Male College, and the curriculum emphasized English, Latin, Greek, modern foreign languages, mathematics, physical science, history, political economy, and "mental and moral science." Engineering and agronomy programs were offered and degrees granted in both, but many of the students (182 in 1880) were in the literature and science curricula, the standard liberal arts courses for a bachelor's degree. According to the provisions of the Morrill Act, the college had a compulsory course in military science and engineering and its student body was organized as a corps of cadets. The military instruction was rudimentary, no more than drill, physical exercise, and simple tactics. While the college regulations bristled with strict behavior codes and punishments, the students were not especially regimented.[17]

While the Agricultural and Mechanical College was still struggling to find both its academic identity and institutional stability, it had several appeals. The first was that it did not charge tuition, and $10 met all the incidental fees. The college thought a student might get by on $200 for an entire academic year. A student could save clothes money because he was required to wear a gray cadet uniform to all classes and the boys simply wore their uniforms at all times.

Still an introspective and serious youth as he turned twenty, Robert Lee managed to survive an entire school year at the Agricultural and Mechanical

College. Admitted to the "second" (junior) class in the literature curriculum, his work in English, mathematics, classical languages, and physics was the best in his class. Much of his study, however, was a repetition of the subjects he had read and studied with his tutors, and by his own account the only class that really stimulated him was the course in military tactics. Taught by R. A. Hardaway, a former Confederate colonel and later president of the University of Alabama, the class mixed military history, army regulations, and drill. Bullard remembered Hardaway's class as the colonel's memories of the principles of war, for "he made his own enunciations and discussion of principles giving us as vouchers his own rich experience in the Confederate army."[18] Compared to the Military Academy, Bullard remembered the college's military training and discipline as lackadaisical despite the uniforms and military organization of the student body. Nevertheless, Bullard took the military training and regulations seriously.

Although Bullard was one of the few students at the college who went to drill without grousing, neither he, his family, nor his classmates thought of him as a potential career officer. He himself regarded his military training as a gentlemanly and patriotic diversion, and he preferred his academic work. But the prospect of leaving school when his money ran out probably made him sensitive to any opportunity that allowed more schooling. In May 1881, Bullard saw a notice from Congressman William J. Samford of Alabama's Third District that a competitive examination would be held in June for an appointment to the United States Military Academy. Wanting to finish college and reluctant to return to rural teaching, he decided to take the examination. Colonel Hardaway probably influenced him to do so, for the colonel was a member of the examining board. In any event Bullard placed first on the examination, besting two other college students. He again checked with his family and found that they could not support him for his last year at the Agricultural and Mechanical College. "I decided that the cadetship offered my best chance and I took it." In June 1881, he packed for West Point.[19]

3.

While there is a certain internal logic to Robert Lee Bullard's path to West Point, his admission to the Military Academy was shared by sixty-three Alabamans between the Civil War and the end of the century, and their collective portrait suggests some social factors that predisposed these men to go to West Point. There are also the substantive experiences of Bullard's contemporaries at the Academy. What reasons did they remember for attending West Point? Although the evidence is fragmentary and limited, one can still draw a partial social profile of the type of young man from Alabama who shared the West Point experience with Bullard in the latter part of the nineteenth century.

The number of Alabamans who were appointed to the Military Academy between the Civil War and the War with Spain was probably around one hundred twenty. Alabama, like the other states, was allowed one appointment at the Military Academy for each representative; a member of Congress could have only one appointee at the Academy at a time. Until the appointee graduated or left the Academy without graduating, no new appointment could be made. If an appointee failed any of his preliminary examinations before his class began its academic work, he could be replaced by an alternate for the same year. If an appointee flunked out in his first year (as many did), he could not be replaced until the succeeding class assembled. Between 1870 and 1890 Alabama had eight congressmen; after 1890 it had nine. If every congressman had made appointments without a break and if every appointee had lasted four years (which they did not), as few as eighty Alabamans might have gone to West Point. If all Alabama's nominees had failed either their preliminary examinations or their first year and had then been immediately replaced, around two hundred young Alabamans might have been appointed. Neither of these things happened. But by using the records of the West Point Alumni Association, one can identify sixty-three Alabamans who were accepted at the Military Academy between the Civil War and 1899. Thirty-two of this group graduated; thirty-one did not.[20]

Using the "Who's Who" of nineteenth century Alabama, Thomas M. Owen's *History of Alabama and Dictionary of Alabama Biography*, one can construct a collective portrait of the family backgrounds of thirty-two of the Alabamans who attended West Point. For twenty-seven of these men, Owen provides data on their fathers. For two, Robert Lee Bullard and Frank McIntyre (both of whom became generals), family data is provided as part of the son's biography, and three had brothers listed in Owen. Of this group there are twenty graduates, twelve nongraduates. For this group, the "typical father" was a city or small-town lawyer whose career included service as a public official from judge to congressman (sixteen fathers) or a man whose occupation was a mix of business ventures, mercantile and agricultural (thirteen fathers). Two fathers were doctors, another a university professor. Twenty held public office. Nine of the fathers had some college education. In terms of religion, the families who had identifiable church affiliations included seven Episcopalians, four Methodists, five Presbyterians, two Baptists, and one Catholic. Twenty-two fathers had seen military service, nineteen in the Confederate army, serving in ranks from private to lieutenant general. Thirteen became officers. The other three were a pre-Civil War enlisted man, a Union officer, and a post-Civil War Alabama National Guard officer. Of the seventeen fathers who had postwar political careers, there were eleven Democrats and six Republicans.[21]

Collectively, the families with West Point sons portrayed in Owen's biographical dictionary represent Alabama's political and economic elite. What is more significant, however, is that there were nearly as many West Point graduates (fourteen) whose fathers were not prominent enough to be included in Owen as there were West Point graduates (eighteen) from Alabama's elite. For those Academy graduates whose families made Owen's biography, it is not difficult to speculate about the impact of social origins upon the decision to go to West Point. The appointees came from families with an established reputation for civic leadership, individual achievement, and political activity. They had access to the congressmen who made appointments to the Academy. Economically as secure as middle-class Southerners could be after the Civil War, the families could maintain an Anglo-American tradition which emphasized formal education, and, more important, they could afford to give their sons some schooling. In the case of those sons who became army officers, there was a solid foundation of family accomplishment upon which to build, even if this family success was limited to local prominence. But what of the thirteen West Point graduates whose families were not important enough to make the *History of Alabama and Dictionary of Alabama Biography*? Obviously their lack of social prominence was not a bar to admission to the Academy or a factor in their ability to graduate. That these "nonelite" graduates (a relative term since they were not the sons of illiterate marginal farmers or blacks) were appointed at all reflects in part the nature of the appointment process. The system of congressional selection meant that sons of farmers at least partially escaped competition with the candidates from "elite" families who tended to live in cities like Birmingham, Montgomery, and Mobile. More important, Alabama congressmen had begun to use competitive academic examinations for selecting nominees, although this policy was not universal or even followed consistently by individual congressmen.

The central factor in influencing young Alabamans to seek and win appointment to the Military Academy appears to be family emphasis upon the access to academic education. The family emphasis might, as in Bullard's case, be motivated by a combination of genteel Anglo-American tradition and a realization that occupational success outside Alabama's decaying white rural society meant having formal education. One of Bullard's contemporaries, William L. Sibert of Gadsden and a West Point graduate in 1884, had a representative experience. The son of a former Confederate officer and displaced farmer notable enough to be included in Owen's "elite," Sibert worked as a farm laborer and received a sporadic education despite his demonstrated academic ability. His family's financial status was precarious, and his father held a number of mercantile jobs, including managing a hotel. Sibert, however, spent enough time with a tutor and with books to win a two-year scholarship to the University of Alabama. In order to finish this education, he accepted an appointment to the Military Academy in 1880, becoming the first nominee from his congressional district to graduate from West Point.[22] Sibert, who became a major general and whose career crossed Bullard's on at least two significant occasions, followed a path to the Military Academy much like Bullard's, but it was not the only one. Another Alabaman, Major General Frank McIntyre (class of 1886), could not have had social roots much more dissimilar to those of Bullard and Sibert. McIntyre's parents were both Irish Catholic immigrants who settled in Montgomery. McIntyre was educated in that city's parochial schools and also won a scholarship to the University of Alabama, which he attended between 1880 and 1882. He, too, went to West Point more to finish college than to become a career officer or to fulfill some social destiny.[23]

The limited testimony of Bullard's West Point generation (the Academy classes of the 1870s, 1880s and 1890s) suggests that an appointment to West Point was not so much the positive selection of a military career as a flight from farming, rural teaching, or low-economic/low-status urban occupations. Even in those cases where a nominee's father was a practicing professional man or businessman (especially in the Midwest and South), family size and limited income often put a university education out of reach. The young men who went to the Military Academy had little personal commitment to a military career. Their notions of army officership were vague, romanticized versions of family experience in the Civil War or the even more superficial caricatures of the occupation they read in nineteenth-century fiction and American history. The most reasonable conclusion about family influence is that there was no active hostility to a son going to the Academy and so considering a military career. In fact (although evidence on this matter is limited), the doctors like Fred Ainsworth and Leonard Wood and older men who sought commissions and were appointed directly from civil life seem to have given more thought to a military career than the youths of academic bent who trekked to West Point for a free college education.[24]

NOTES

[1]W. Brewer, *Alabama: Her History, Resources, War Record, and Public Men from 1540 to 1872* (Montgomery, Ala.: Barrett and Brown, 1872), pp. 510-16, 160-4, 315-17; Marie Bankhead Owen, *Our State-Alabama* (Birmingham, Ala.: Birmingham Printing Company, 1927), pp. 630-32, 688-89.

[2]Lt. Gen. Robert Lee Bullard, USA (Ret.), "Derivation and the American Part of my Direct Line of the England-North Carolina-Georgia-Alabama Bullard Family from Which I Come," August 31, 1930, Robert Lee Bullard Papers, Manuscript Division, The Library of Congress, hereafter cited as BP.

[3]Florence Weldon, "History of Opelika from 1836 through 1900," (unpublished MS thesis, Alabama Polytechnic Institute, 1939); Rev. L. L. Cherry, "The History of Opelika and Her Agricultural Tributary Territories," published in the *Opelika* (Ala.) *Times* in 1883 and 1885 and reprinted in the *Alabama Historical Quarterly* 15 (1953), pp. 176-339, 383-537; Thomas M. Owen, *History of Alabama and Dictionary of Alabama Biography,* 4 vols. (Chicago: S. J. Clarke, 1921), I, 434-36, and II, pp. 861-64 (hereafter cited as Owen, *History of Alabama*).

[4]Bullard, "Derivation and the American Part of My Direct Line of the England-North Carolina-Georgia-Alabama Bullard Family. . . ," previously cited; R. L. Bullard, Diarybook autobiography, written November and December 1899, Diarybook 1, pp. 4-5, BP; Sarah Jane Bullard Richards, "My Memories of the Old South" (written in 1927), copy furnished the author by Mrs. T. F. Yancey, Sr., of Opelika, and "Spring Villa," copy furnished the author by Mrs. Frances M. Honour, Ralph Brown Draughon Library, Auburn University.

Bullard's detailed 1899 autobiography was written while he was en route to the Philippines. It is hereafter cited as Diarybook autobiography.

[5]Sarah Jane Bullard Richards, "My Memories of the Old South," p. 2.

⁶Robert Lee Bullard, manuscript autobiography (1930), pp. 2-3, BP. It is hereafter cited as Bullard autobiography.

⁷Sarah Jane Bullard Richards, "My Memories of the Old South," pp. 3-6; Walter Fleming, *Civil War and Reconstruction in Alabama* (New York: Columbia University Press, 1905), pp. 15-60, 78, 181, 254.

⁸Diarybook autobiography, p. 10-12, BP.

⁹Winnifred Phillips Yancey, "Robert Lee Bullard as His Family Saw Him," *Trails in History* (official newsletter of the Lee County Historical Society), Vol. I; J. B. Greene, "Robert Lee Bullard: A Sketch," and Emma Bullard Davis, "Robert Lee Bullard," *mss.* written circa 1925, both provided the author by Mrs. T. F. Yancey, Sr.

¹⁰Diarybook autobiography, p. 7, BP.

¹¹Winnifred Phillips Yancey, "Robert Lee Bullard as His Family Saw Him," previously cited; J. B. Greene, "Robert Lee Bullard: A Sketch," previously cited; Florence Weldon, "History of Opelika from 1836 through 1900," pp. 66-67; Diarybook autobiography, p. 7, BP.

¹²Diarybook autobiography, pp. 4-7, 21; Bullard autobiography, p. 3; and Robert L. Bullard, "Some Experiences with Backward Peoples or Savages," speech, n. d. (circa 1910), all BP; Sarah Jane Bullard Richards, "My Memories of the Old South," pp. 4-8.

¹³E. G. Richards, "Reminiscences of the Early Days of Chambers County," *Alabama Review* 4 (Fall 1942), pp. 417-445; Anne Elizabeth Newman, "A Historical Sketch of LaFayette, Alabama," *Alabama Review* 4 (Fall 1942), pp. 446-451; will of Daniel Bullard, Book of Wills #3, p. 661, November 27, 1899, Chambers County Probate Court, Chambers County Courthouse, LaFayette, Alabama.

¹⁴Bessie Thomas Love *et al.*, "Old Oak Bowery," in *War Was the Place*, Chattahoochee Valley Historical Society Bulletin No. 5 (Alexander City, Ala., 1961), pp. 124-158; Jean Cameron Agnew, "Oak Grove: Boyhood Home of General Robert Lee Bullard," pamphlet written in 1919-1922 with marginal notes by General Bullard, BP; Oak Bowery Church Register, *Alabama Historical Quarterly* 19 (Spring 1957), pp. 111-29.

¹⁵Diarybook autobiography, pp. 23-24, BP; J. B. Greene, "Robert Lee Bullard: A Sketch."

¹⁶Diarybook autobiography, pp. 26-27, BP.

¹⁷Willis G. Clark, *History of Education in Alabama, 1702-1889*, Publication No. 8, in Herbert B. Adams, ed., *Contributions to American Educational History* (Washington: Government Printing Office, 1889), pp. 139-146; Agricultural and Mechanical College of Alabama, *Catalogue 1880-1881* (Auburn, 1880).

¹⁸Bullard autobiography, p. 8, BP. Bullard's record at the Agricultural and Mechanical College is based on research in the Register of Students and minutes of faculty meetings by Mrs. Honour.

¹⁹Diarybook autobiography, pp. 28-29; J. B. Greene, "Robert Lee Bullard: A Sketch."

²⁰The Alabamans (defined as those born or raised in Alabama and appointed to the Military Academy from Alabama) are culled from the West Point Alumni Association, *Register of Graduates and Former Cadets of the United States Military Academy, 1902-1964* (West Point, N.Y.: Association of Graduates, USMA, 1964).

²¹The biographical data is from Owen, *History of Alabama and Dictionary of Alabama Biography*, Vols. III and IV, which lists its profiles alphabetically.

The Alabama profile of fathers' occupations is not radically different from the national profile compiled by the Military Academy for cadets admitted 1842-1886 which lists farmers and planters (827), merchants (495), lawyers and judges (455), physicians (271), mechanics (263), army officers (246), "no occupation" (179), and clergymen (102). All other occupations had less than a hundred representatives. *Army and Navy Journal,* October 9, 1886.

²²Edward B. Clark, *William L. Sibert: The Army Engineer* (Philadelphia: Dorrance & Company, 1930), pp. 17-24.

²³"Frank McIntyre" in Owen, *History of Alabama* IV, pp. 1119-1120.

²⁴On contemporary West Point graduates, I've relied on the following substantive descriptions of family backgrounds: Frank Parker (1894) from Ellen Parker, comp. and ed., "Record of the Parker Family of the Parish of St. James, Goose Creek and Charleston, South Carolina," 1930, copy in the Major General Frank Parker Papers, Southern Historical Collection, The University of North Carolina at Chapel Hill; Beaumont Buck (1885), *Memories of Peace and War* (San Antonio: The Naylor Company, 1935), pp. 1-24; Johnson Hagood (1896), *The Services of Supply* (Boston: Houghton, Mifflin, 1927), pp. 1-4; Thomas Cruse (1879), *Apache Days and After* (Caldwell, Ida.: Caxton Printers, 1941), pp. 20-24; Donald W. Smythe on John J. Pershing (1886) in "John J. Pershing: Soldier" (unpublished Ph.D. dissertation, Georgetown University, 1960), pp. 1-22; George O. Squier (1887), autobiography written in 1884 in "A Literary Notebook," Major General George Owen Squier Papers, Michigan Historical Society Collection, Ann Arbor, Michigan; Frederick Palmer on Tasker H. Bliss (1875) in *Bliss, Peacemaker* (New York: Dodd, Mead, 1934), pp. 1-18; Hugh S. Johnson (1903), *The Blue Eagle from Egg to Earth* (Garden City, N.Y.: Doubleday, Doran, 1935), pp. 1-72; John McAuley Palmer (1892), "An Old Soldier's Memories" I, pp. 1-67, Brigadier General John McAuley Palmer Papers, Manuscript Division, Library of Congress; David A. Lockmiller on Enoch H. Crowder (1881) in *Enoch H. Crowder* (Columbia, Mo.: University of Missouri Press, 1955), pp. 1-23; Edward M. Coffman on Peyton C. March (1888) in *The Hilt of the Sword: The Career of Peyton C. March* (Madison, Wisc.: University of Wisconsin, 1966), pp. 3-6; Hugh L. Scott (1876), *Some Memories of a Soldier* (New York: Century Company, 1928), pp. 3-12; George B. Duncan (1886), "Reminiscences, 1882-1905," pp. 1-11, copy in the possession of Dr. Edward M. Coffman, University of Wisconsin; T. Bentley Mott (1886), *Twenty Years as Military Attaché* (New York: Oxford University Press, 1937), pp. 19-25.

On the social origins of the Army surgeons appointed after the Civil War with careers similar to the West Pointers, see L. N. Wood, *Walter Reed* (New York: Julian Messner, 1943), pp. 3-141; John M. Gibson, *Physician to the World; The Life of General William C. Gorgas* (Durham, N. C.: Duke University Press, 1950), pp. 14-55; Mabel E. Deutrich, *Struggle for Supremacy: The Career of General Fred C. Ainsworth* (Washington: Public Affairs Press, 1962), pp. 1-5; Herman Hagedorn, *Leonard Wood,* 2 vols. (New York: Harper and Brothers, 1931), I, pp. 1-47. Gorgas, An Alabaman, was unable to muster the influence to go to West Point, although (or because) his father had been a prominent Confederate general and a West Pointer. In this case the family appears to have been hostile to both West Point and a military career.

An example of a civil appointee with high career motivation was Hugh Drum, the son of an officer killed in Cuba in 1898. See the memorandum, "The Military Service of Major General Hugh A. Drum," June 15, 1938, Lieutenant General Hugh A. Drum Papers in the possession of Col. Elliot H. Johnson, USAF. Another appointee from the ranks with high career commitment was James G. Harbord.

2

West Point
1881-1885

From the stately paddle-wheeler pushing up the Hudson River, the Military Academy must have looked like an enchanted fortress to twenty-year old Robert Lee Bullard. From Alabama he had traveled by train to Washington, the first large city he had ever seen, to pick up his certificate of appointment from Congressman Samford. Again he boarded a train for the north, this one for New York City. From the rail station on Manhattan island, Bullard, following the path of hundreds of nineteenth-century cadets, found the steamer *Mary Powell* and rode it up the Hudson River. The boat ride was spectacular, for on both sides of the river the wooded hills dipped to the water. Then, set on a plateau below Storm King mountain, wrapped in green and looking like a gray medieval fortress, the Military Academy, the womb of Lee, of Jackson, of Longstreet, of the despised Grant and Sherman, became visible.[1]

The stunning beauty of the Hudson Valley, the eternal quality of the Academy's stone buildings, and the air of calm and order that surrounded the Plain were a facade built by nature about a self-satisfied institution. The West Point of Thomas Jefferson, of Sylvanus Thayer, of Dennis Hart Mahan had by 1881 fallen into the hands of an officer-faculty and army bureaucracy that had made the Academy a monument to tradition and academic conservatism. Created at the beginning of the century as a model of scientific and engineering training, the Academy had produced graduates capable of exploring, mapping, and developing the continent. In the Mexican War those graduates still in uniform also proved they could fight and win a war in the vastness of North America. In the Civil War West Pointers dominated the high command of both the Union and Confederate armies. For West Point the Civil War was its zenith. In the peace that followed it lost its educational leadership to civil institutions and mortgaged its capacity to progress to the delusion that it had found a secret formula for producing great generals from striplings.[2]

The faculty, alumni, and cadets of the Military Academy in 1881 lived with the sentimental yoke of the Civil War about their collective neck. Under the jealous eyes of William Tecumseh Sherman, the Commanding General of the United States Army, and the Association of Graduates, West Point's traditions, curriculum, and routine were as carefully preserved as the captured cannon on Trophy Point. The Academic Board, dominated by Academy graduates serving as either temporary instructors or tenured professors, killed even the mildest suggestions for curriculum reform and defended the Academy's capricious customs which passed for leadership training. The "tactical" officers, seasoned lieutenants and captains responsible for the military training of the Corps of Cadets, were omnipresent inspectors and drill-masters, ready to punish the cadets for the slightest violation of Academy regulations. The Academy's regime was severe, and graduates recalled their experiences at West Point with the somber nostalgia characteristic of the survivors of some long-ago disaster. Colonel T. Bentley Mott (USMA, 1886), a cosmopolitan soldier-diplomat, never found in all his travels a like institution, though he imagined the Academy might fairly be compared with one of Frederick the Great's military schools, a Jesuit seminary, and a Tibetan lamasery.[3]

To the casual visitor's eye, the Academy was an impressive sight. The main buildings—the library, the academic building, the messhall, the chapel, and the two cadet barracks—were clustered at the south edge on the Plain. Built of heavy gray stone, they were the romantic era's version of a medieval fortress with Greek revival flourishes. The newest of the two four-story cadet barracks had crennelated towers and sallyports for entranceways. West of the barracks along a main road were the homes of the faculty and the military staff. Across the Plain was the hotel, social center of the Academy's visitors, set among the accumulated batteries and fortresses of a century of military garrisoning. Along the edge of the Plain but still above the bluffs of the Hudson were a riding hall, the hospital, stables, and ordnance laboratory. From the Plain, roads led down to the South and North Landings, and a single road ran south from the military reservation to the patrician resort town of Highland Falls.[4]

Whether Robert Lee Bullard realized it or not, he had begun a process of selection by attrition by simply appearing at West Point to take the preliminary physical and academic examinations. In the thirty years after the Civil War, the Military Academy seldom graduated more than a quarter of the young men appointed in any given year. For Bullard's class (1885), two hundred men received appointments, but forty-eight either declined or never reported to West Point. Of those who took the examinations for admission, sixty failed the written tests in English, mathematics, writing, and American history. Four others did not pass the physical examination. Of the eighty-five men admitted, thirty-nine eventually graduated.[5] There were other odds working against Bullard, for he came from a region notorious for its inability to produce West Point graduates. Appointees from the former Confederacy between 1867 and 1884 failed to be admitted at the rate of 42 percent, a casualty rate at least 10 percent higher than that of every other region in the United States. Only fifteen Alabamans appointed over the same period survived to graduate, although sixty-six appeared for the examinations and thirty-four were admitted.[6] The only odds running in Bullard's favor were those created by the fact that he had won his appointment by competitive examination.

Of those admitted in June with his class, fifteen of the thirty-three cadets chosen by competition survived, while only ten of the fifty-two men appointed directly by a congressman passed the preliminary examinations.[7]

Aware as he must have been of his educational limitations, Bullard may have feared that he would survive neither the preliminary examinations nor his first academic year. Whether he knew it or not, he was nearly as well prepared as the best in the class of 1885 and no worse than his companions who survived to graduate. He was, in fact, part of an elite group of eighteen who had had some schooling at the high school and college level.[8] The Military Academy did lag behind the best universities of the 1880s, but, given the sort of cadets it received, the Academic Board's complacency becomes more reasonable. Besides, the faculty argued, the formal West Point curriculum was only a part of the Academy education, and some of the most educational experiences West Point offered in 1881 did indeed lie outside the classroom.

1.

Deeply rooted in the Military Academy's culture was its stern system of discipline. The Academy's control over the cadets fell basically into two categories, the hazing of plebes (Fourth Classmen) by the upper three classes and the rigid enforcement of cadet regulations by the officers of the tactics department ("tacs") assigned to command each cadet company.

Hazing was extralegal. Superintendents in succession attempted to end hazing, modestly proposing that since the cadets' inhumanity to other cadets was against regulations, it ought to be stopped. Moreover, the hazing occasionally resulted in public scandals when a cadet was dismissed or injured, producing the sort of attention the Academy did not need. But the Association of Graduates and the Academic Board rallied in each hazing crisis and successfully defended the practice as an essential orientation to army life. In defense of hazing, Academy graduates insisted that the experience was essential to their success as combat officers—without ever being very specific about hazing's benefits. Hazing was West Point tradition, the initiation ritual for all plebes, and it was sanctified custom in 1881. It was a dubious system, for it placed the initial military experience for the plebes in the hands of the callow and revengeful Third Class ("yearlings") rather than under the close supervision of the "tacs." Thus the plebe's initial impression of army discipline must have been that it was based on a mixture of sadism, petty tyranny, and personal whim.[9]

From the plebes' arrival in June until the beginning of classes in the fall, hazing was a major part of the Academy's "orientation" program. When the new class arrived at the Academy, it was greeted by the Third and First Classes, who immediately began a barrage of name-calling and "bracing" at attention. In the week a new class took to finish its preliminary examinations, draw uniforms and equipment, and be processed, it was segregated in "Beast Barracks," the hazers' domain. While the upperclassmen used this week and two more to teach the plebes the school of the soldier and eight-man squad drill, they also issued out large portions of harassment. There were formations at any hour and a succession of "clothing drills" in which the cadets raced back and forth from their rooms to formations, hurriedly changing their uniforms for the yearlings' amusement.

After "Beast Barracks," the plebes moved into a tent camp along the northern edge of the Plain where they lived the rest of the summer with the Third and First Classes. For the upperclassmen the camp was a welcome relief from their academic work, a gala round of dances, socializing, and games. The biggest camp entertainment was hazing the plebes. Along with the scheduled drills and inspections, the plebes were initiated to "yanking" (being pulled suddenly from one's bed), "dragging" (being pulled along a street), "chewing" (gnawing at rags), singing any printed matter an upperclassman wanted to hear, and doing endless rounds of exhausting calisthentics. The "tacs" usually turned a blind eye to the whole business unless there was a serious incident.

Robert Lee Bullard quickly learned that anonymity and passivity were the escape routes from hazing, and after seventeen years, he thought that the "large doses" of hazing were good for him: "It was the best training I have ever received." When he arrived at West Point, $200 in debt and homesick for his family and a sweetheart in Oak Bowery, he was shocked from his reveries by the cadets. Without any suitable traveling clothes, he wore his Agricultural and Mechanical College cadet uniform, a decision that immediately singled him out for intense "jumping." He was shocked to learn that West Point cadets found him a "tin soldier" and "gross cadet." No doubt he was relieved to trade his Confederate gray for the summer whites of Academy cadets. By the end of summer camp, as he recalled, he had learned the value of self-discipline, promptness, and alertness from the hazers. While Bullard believed that the hazing stripped him of his "inordinate conceit," he had never been an arrogant or rebellious youth, so it is hard to believe that the hazing produced any significant changes in his behavior or personality. To a youth raised in a large family, the hazing was probably an anxious, irritating, but not traumatic experience.[10]

While the hazing of plebes stopped at the end of the summer camp, the Military Academy's formal behavior code, the Cadet Regulations, remained in force throughout the year and applied to all classes. Enforced by the faculty and "tacs," the Cadet Regulations made the Academy a model total institution. From the time a cadet put his foot ashore for his preliminary examinations until the time he put on army blue with shoulder-straps, he was supposed to live within the confines of behavior specified by the published *Regulations, U.S. Corps of Cadets* and *Orders, U.S. Corps of Cadets*. His ability to learn and to accept the Academy's regulations was viewed as essential instruction in the moral prerequisites of officership: "promptness and precision in obedience to and execution of orders; manliness, self-reliance, and truth in every position and relation of life."[11] To inculcate such military virtues and some Victorian ones as well, like abstinence from strong drink and tobacco, the Academy laid out rules to govern every conceivable phase of cadet life: the arrangement and cleanliness of rooms;

movement about the Academy grounds; relations with all Academy personnel; rigid time schedules for all meals, classes, and formations; the performance of military duties; dress; the upkeep of uniforms and equipment; travel away from the Academy; and general deportment.[12]

To see that the cadets obeyed these regulations the Commandant of Cadets and his six or seven assistants in the Department of Tactics patrolled the barracks and Academy grounds. For minor infractions of the Cadet Regulations, the "tacs" awarded demerits or "skins." The "skins" were assigned according to an elaborate system which prescribed the number of demerits to be awarded in each of eight different categories of infractions. Many violations of the Cadet Regulations carried immediate penalties such as extra tours of guard duty or restriction. Each day the "skin list" was read to the cadets at an evening formation, and the demerits officially recorded by the Academy adjutant. Each month a cadet got a written report on his standing in "discipline" or, more accurately, how many "skins" he had for the month and year. If a cadet accumulated more than 125 demerits between June 1 and December 31 and more than 90 between January 1 and May 31, he would be "found" or judged unsatisfactory in military deportment and dismissed. The Academy, however, could not implement all its disciplinary dismissals because the president, secretary of war, and the Congress often intervened to void such dismissals and set aside convictions by courts-martial. Therefore, the Academy preferred that a cadet resign voluntarily or accept a "set back" or assignment to a class less advanced than his own.

For the cadet whose conduct and memory of the regulations was exemplary, there was a meager reward system. If he received fewer than eight demerits a month, the difference between his demerits and eight was subtracted from his semiannual total. If he had no outstanding demerits, he received a four-day Christmas vacation in his Second Class year. The highest reward for military deportment and skill in drill and military duties was appointment to cadet rank. If the tactics department thought a cadet showed a high combination of attention to duty, leadership ability, and intelligence, it could appoint him a corporal as a Third classman, sergeant as a Second classman, and lieutenant or captain as a First classman. Cadet officers carried some of the responsibility for the governance and discipline of the Corps of Cadets, although in Bullard's era their powers and influence were limited. Nevertheless, cadet rank was prized by the militarily ambitious cadets (especially the position of First Captain) since the appointments were limited, carried a few privileges, and were supposed to be an augury for a successful military career. If a cadet did not perform to the "tacs' " satisfaction, the high black chevrons could come off after a "skin." To win and hold cadet rank a cadet had to be an ardent supporter of the Academy's ways.[13]

For all the talk about "modest demeanor" and "manly tone" which characterized the Academy's system of discipline, its actual workings produced some questionable lessons in truthfulness and obedience. For a youth of literal outlook and strict upbringing, the Academy must have produced considerable anxiety, for even the simplest cadet could see his peers daily skirting the regulations. Many of the cadets played a constant game of cat-and-mouse with the "tacs," the lesson being that what one did was not so important as not getting caught. For the rebellious and libertine spirits, the game was to sneak from the post to drink, wench, gamble, and smoke, all dangerous diversions. The cadets' more common insurgencies involved the violation of curfew regulations to study, smoking while hiding inside one's fireplace covered by a blanket, or smuggling illegal food into one's room for a clandestine snack.

Bullard made a successful adjustment to the Academy's disciplinary system and developed the subtlety of mind to cope with a code that extolled mature behavior and patronized the cadets at the same time. As a plebe his infractions were many, but of the minor sort: oil on the rear sight of his rifle, not writing his name on the blackboard, gazing and laughing in ranks, not having his chair against his desk in inspection, slouching at drill, marching out of step. In plebe camp, he received twenty-four "skins," about average for his class. After his plebe year he rarely received more than ten "skins" a month. He did not, however, get to the stage where he received no demerits as many of his classmates did. As a plebe he seems to have tried hard to soldier and to obey the regulations, and he stumbled constantly. As an upperclassman his transgressions came from inattention and casualness in class, drill, and guard duty. In four years he never quite became a spit-and-polish cadet. His only serious clash, however, with the regulations was an argument he had with a drawing instructor, an incident for which he was badly "skinned."

Although he continued to accumulate "skins" right through his last year, Bullard was never in serious disciplinary trouble and his deportment was good enough to win cadet rank. Appointed a sergeant as a Second classman, he became one of the sixteen cadet officers for the Corps in the class of 1885, being selected a lieutenant in his company. He had no trouble getting his Christmas furlough in 1883. He seems to have seen little of the "secret life" enjoyed by some of his peers. Troubled by the possibility of academic failure or disciplinary dismissal, he took the regulations seriously. He had no independent funds or civilian friends outside the post. Already twenty when he became a plebe, he had sufficient maturity to accept group discipline even though he did not think he had any special talent for soldiering. Bullard's deferrence to authority is not surprising. He was just the sort of pliant youth the Academy wanted to train when it was shaped by Sylvanus Thayer years before the Civil War.[14]

2.

By 1881 the Military Academy's curriculum had become a relic of what had once been the nation's finest technological education program. The first year courses were designed partially as remedial training but were also designed to weed out the least competent cadets: algebra, geometry, trigonometry, French and English grammar, and occasional lectures on ethics and "universal history." In the second year the emphasis was on more mathematics, French, and mathematical drawing and topographic sketching. The third year was heavily scientific: "natural and experimental philosophy" (physics and astronomy), chemistry, mineralogy, geology, and more drawing. The final year included a smattering of Spanish, a dash of world history, a brush with military and civil law, and a great deal of military engineering and ordnance. Most of the professional military training which the cadets received came in the two upperclass years. In addition to engineering, this training consisted of learning the tactical manuals for all arms of the army, military signaling, and some exposure to the strategic theories of Dennis Hart Mahan. The largest part of the military training was tactical drill, the cadets performing with as much speed and precision as possible the evolutions of Emory Upton's tactics for infantry, cavalry, and artillery.[15]

By 1881 former graduates of the Academy had an iron grip on the teaching positions; most of them had no further education beyond their cadet days. The permanent professors and heads of departments (the elite Academic Board) were nearly all West Pointers who saw their mission as preserving the prewar curriculum of natural and experimental philosophy (physics), modern languages, mathematics, military science and engineering, drawing, and a mixture of chemistry, mineralogy, and geology. The Academy chaplain taught history, geography, and ethics while officers on temporary assignment headed the departments of ordnance, law, and "practical" military engineering. For assistants the tenured department heads relied on officers whose qualifications were limited to academic achievement in their specialties as cadets. Most served one tour as instructors, although some returned for subsequent tours as assistant professors. Dedicated as they were, these officers saw their primary job as guiding the cadets mechanically through the prescribed texts—books also often written by West Pointers.[16]

The method of instruction at the Academy was nearly as old as the institution itself. Each class of cadets was divided into sections in each of the prescribed courses. Each section had eight to ten cadets; the academic leaders were placed in the first section of each course and the other cadets were arranged downward into additional sections by academic standing. This system had the virtue of forcing competition among peers and was a useful way of judging performance. The instructor assigned a daily lesson from the prescribed text. On the following day, the instructor would first ask if there were any questions on the lesson. Few cadets responded. The instructor then passed out questions over the lesson on slips of papers. Each cadet would march to the blackboard in rotation, write his name and then write explanatory notes, formulas, or diagrams. Prefacing each recitation with "I am required to discuss . . ." or "I am required to solve the following problem. . . ," the cadet would recite, without any participation by the class or the instructor. When he was finished, the instructor would grade him on his ability to match the solution in the text and then another cadet would recite. Except for occasional lectures and experiments and practical work in drawing, this was West Point teaching, day in and day out.[17]

The instructors' primary function was to grade the work of their sections and each cadet received regular evaluations. Both the instructors and cadets kept track of scores down to the decimal point, and cadets were moved from section to section on the basis of their performance. To slip down a section was a traumatic experience. Twice a year there were comprehensive exams on the coursework which determined the cadets' academic standing in their class.

Such was the education of Robert Lee Bullard, and about the best that can be said of it is that it did not entirely deaden his interest in learning and his love for language and history. From the day that he learned he had passed the preliminary exams to the day he graduated, he persevered without academic distinction. Like his fellow cadets of limited educational background who were sound enough to be admitted, he started well and then slipped back between the bottom half and third of his class. He quickly learned that the routine at West Point was a stultifying grind of recitation and study, study and recitation, broken only by meals, inspections, and drills. He was in class seven hours a day or studied from 7 A.M. until lights out at 11 P.M. Although some of his fellow cadets, especially those in academic trouble, often studied clandestinely after lights out, Bullard does not seem to have been a midnight student; at least he was never caught. In his plebe year, his academic standing was quite respectable, seventeenth in a class of fifty-eight. He stood eleventh in English, twelfth in French, and twenty-fourth in mathematics. His academic work was probably more meaningful than his standing indicates, for it saved his self-respect while he adjusted to Academy life.

After his plebe year, Bullard began his slide into academic mediocrity. At the end of the Third class year, his standing of eighth in French, twenty-second in mathematics, and thirty-third in drawing placed him twenty-second in a class of forty-three. As a Second classman, drawing remained his bane (thirty-fourth), and he added two other academic disasters, chemistry (thirty-second) and "natural and experimental philosophy" (twenty-fifth). Even in military instruction he managed only a ranking of thirtieth, and he ended the year thirtieth in a class of forty-one. In his last year he stood thirteenth in Spanish, twenty-third in law, twenty-seventh in ordnance and gunnery, and thirty-first in engineering. He graduated twenty-seventh in a class of thirty-nine. As he himself admitted, his academic record at West Point was unexceptional, although he was never in any danger of being "found" in any subject. His low academic standing did not particularly concern him since he knew the West Point tradition that scholarship bore little relation to military success. While Bullard was sorry he hadn't done better, he thought that he had done as well as his background and intelligence permitted, and his academic record seemed almost irrelevant to his prospects in the army.[18]

3.

The one thing that the Military Academy did exceedingly well was to socialize the cadets to army life, however unique the West Point form. That the Academy was successful in producing career army officers is undeniable. Between 1802 and 1896 only eleven of the 3741 graduates did not take a commission, although they were under no obligation to do so and often had to lobby with the government for a position. The Academy's attitude toward officership, however, was ambiguous. While the Corps of Cadets relished the fame of its graduates, it frowned on individual cadets who took soldiering seriously. Excellence in mathematics, engineering, and chemistry and graduating as one of "The Five" was the cadet definition of success. Neither the Academic Board nor the tactical officers did much to counter this denigration of officership in the United States Army, and the Board of Visitors wondered if the Academy was really fulfilling its responsibility of producing troop leaders. The purpose of the Academy, as the Board of Visitors reported in 1884, was "the proper technical education of officers and their preparation in all mental, moral and physical qualities for the important duties which they are to perform." The Board expected West Pointers to be the leaven of the officer corps in any future war, the leaders and organizers of a volunteer army. It found, however, precious little instruction in the skills such officers would need: American history, supply matters, sanitation, leadership, and troop training.[19]

Aside from the interminable tactical drills, parades, guard mounts, and inspections, the Academy's military training was limited. When a cadet graduated he knew cavalry and infantry tactics at the company level and how to serve both field and seacoast artillery. He learned the names of a great deal of equipment and the trajectories of many types of ordnance. The only two military skills the cadets truly enjoyed learning were fencing and riding. The Master of the Sword from 1858 to his death in 1885 was Antone Lorenz, a smoothshaven former French officer, respected by the cadets for his fencing skill and his casual attitude toward "skins." Lorenz, who adored physical competition and aggressiveness, made fencing a welcome release from classroom drudgery, but he taught only swordplay. Riding was the cadets' favorite class. For most of Bullard's years at the Academy, the riding instructor was Captain Edward S. Godfrey (USMA, 1867). Unlike his fellow Academy staff members, Godfrey gloried in the warrior role and talked to the cadets about soldiering. He was an authentic fighter. A troop commander in the Seventh Cavalry, he survived the Little Big Horn fight and won a Medal of Honor the following year for gallantry in action against the Nez Percés. A superb horseman, he always rode a large black mount and wore his stained cavalry campaign hat inside the Riding Academy. With piercing dark eyes and a mustache that enwreathed his face, he was an impressive sight.[20]

Bullard, like most of his classmates, knew how to ride before he arrived at West Point, but military horsemanship was something apart from urging some mule along a dusty Alabama road. From the earliest exercises the cadets went to riding at all gaits, mounted drill, jumping, and trick riding. Part of their equestrian education included cavalry tactics, and often the high point of an entire month was pulling on yellow gauntlets, buckling on saber and pistol, fixing one's chinstrap, and galloping about under a swallow-tailed guidon. For youths raised on Sir Walter Scott and the Civil War this was real soldiering, and Bullard loved it.[21] Except for the riding and fencing, however, the cadets learned few individual skills, since rifle practice was limited and pistol training nonexistent.

There was more to the process of military socialization than learning to handle a sword and steed like a knight-errant in cadet gray. A harsh but loving master, West Point wrapped the cadets into an ordered and secure world in which the army provided their basic needs. From Beast Barracks to graduation day, the cadets followed a secure and stubborn ritual as predictable as the waxing and waning of the moon. Though they were well paid ($500 a year), the cadets were either issued the uniforms and equipment they needed or bought their books, personal items, and sundries on credit. Each cadet carried a detailed account book in which he kept his records of credits and debits (''39¢ for haircut . . . 5¢ for damage to cup in messhall''); $4 each month went into a fund to purchase his uniforms upon graduation. Each cadet got a $2 allowance at the Academy confectionary shop. West Point did not recognize family affluence, for all cadets were equal in the paymaster's ledgers, as they were equal on the ''skin'' list.

To feed the cadet's body the Academy served unspectacular but nourishing food and to feed the cadet's soul (with much less success) it marched him off to chapel each Sunday morning for the compulsory Anglican service. Each Sunday afternoon the cadets slept—gladly. There were few other sanctioned amusements. Occasionally the Dialectic Society would have the sort of overblown recitation of poetry or prose that passed for Victorian culture. Less often, some enterprising and self-righteous cadets would hold extra prayer-meetings or temperance lectures.[22]

After a cadet's second year, he was allowed to leave West Point for two and a half months. Following the annual ritual, Bullard's class bought civilian clothes (''cits''), stored their uniforms, and scattered throughout the country for a summer of freedom in 1883. For many cadets the furlough was a watershed. Returning home they found themselves regarded as mature men of the world by their kin. The cadets with rural origins usually were appalled by the parochial and captive way of life they found at home. Many recognized with sadness and clarity that they had broken with their family past and local culture forever. Bullard had such an experience. Although he visited Oak Bowery, he spent most of his furlough with his classmate Edward P. Lawton at Lawton's home in Savannah, Georgia. For Bullard, Oak Bowery had memories, but little else. After he had left for West Point, his mother had died, and he returned home two years later to find his father badly aged. The homecoming was painful for the young cadet. Old Daniel Bullard was irritable during his son's visit but Bullard recognized that the old man cared for him. It was not an emotion Daniel Bullard had often shown for his second son, and it made the reunion that much more awkward. Bullard gladly returned to Savannah, but when he and his class returned together to West Point in August, he was depressed by his rootlessness and lack of identity. Although such despondency was chronic with West Point furloughmen, Bullard was especially shocked by the recognition that his home was now the army.[23]

In its unconscious way, the Military Academy gave its cadets a new and growing sense of loyalty to the nation and the army. For the Southerners it was an especially significant experience, for they came to West Point with rich memories of the Civil War and expected to be discriminated against by the army that had conquered their homeland. Instead they learned that among West Pointers there were no enemies, just heroes in different colored uniforms. For West Point the Civil War was something to be cherished in the traditions of the Academy. When the Academy band played for the cadet parades, one was as likely to hear "Dixie" as "Rally 'Round The Flag."[24] One particular episode dramatized the reconciliation for Bullard. In June 1883, the Association of Graduates dedicated a monument to the Academy's greatest superintendent, Sylvanus Thayer. Among the more than one hundred graduates who came to the June Week ceremonies were a scattering of former Confederates, but for Bullard the most impressive visitor was Ulysses S. Grant. Seated on the superintendent's porch the "lone, calm, silent, brooding" general watched the ceremonies. Looking at Alabama's archvillain, Bullard was awed by Grant's presence. He later joined the line of cadets that filed by the superintendent's porch to shake Grant's hand. Puffing a cigar and talking to other generals, Grant simply dangled a limp hand over the railing, which each penitent quickly grasped and moved on. Grant paid no attention to his admirers. But for the Southern cadets the act was supreme reconciliation and a pledge of national loyalty.[25]

For Bullard, West Point symbolized not just a college education, but an experience representing the very meaning of American life. At his "stern but just" alma mater he found a highly competitive system which rewarded individual merit and rejected "partiality, favor or affection." Instead of hating the faculty's impersonality or the strict regulations, Bullard believed that they simply demonstrated the Academy's egalitarianism. Nowhere else, he thought, could young men from across the country so quickly slough off their class ties and regional prejudices and take up new loyalties to army and country. Where else could the top graduates be the son of an immigrant German blacksmith in Kansas and the son of an Irish storekeeper? By graduating from West Point, Bullard became part of a new, national, college-educated elite based on academic merit, not family affluence or favoritism. Yet he regarded his experience as essentially egalitarian and West Point's policies as "leveling," not elitist.

His own friends at the Academy had diverse backgrounds, academic abilities, and temperaments: Charles H. Muir from Michigan, Willard Holbrook from Wisconsin, Robert A. Brown of Pennsylvania, Austin H. Brown of Illinois, John Little from Tennessee, John Barrette from Iowa, his roommate Henry McCain from Mississippi, and Ed Lawton from Savannah, Georgia. Muir was graduated eighth, Lawton last, and the rest of Bullard's friends in between. Bullard believed that the class of 1885 arrived as callow, intolerant, self-centered youths and departed four years later as a band of brothers. Such social alchemy was the American way.[26]

While the class of 1885 was memorable neither for its escapades nor its exceptional military record, the careers of its thirty-nine members testify to the Academy's effectiveness as a socializing agency. West Pointers stayed with the army until the army could no longer use them. Of Bullard's classmates eleven became at least temporary generals, seven retired as colonels without ever wearing stars, and one quit as a lieutenant colonel after thirty years. Six retired prematurely because of physical disabilities and nine died in uniform from disease or injury. Only four men voluntarily resigned from the army, and one was forced to resign "for the good of the service." Interestingly, not one was killed in action, although Apaches, Sioux, Spanish, Filipino insurgents, Moros, Mexicans, and Germans all got a shot at the members of the class of 1885.[27]

For all the bonds of sentiment and experience that forged West Point friendships that endured over a lifetime, Bullard's career did not depend upon the support and intervention of his classmates. The duties of officership were too unpredictable, the army too large and scattered for classmates to help one another. Only once might Bullard's classmates have helped him. In the spring of 1917, as the War Department struggled to send at least one division to France for symbolic purposes, Brigadier General Joseph Kuhn, president of the Army War College, and Brigadier General Henry McCain, acting adjutant general of the United States Army, might have felt the tug of class comradeship when they assigned Bullard to that division as a brigade commander. But there is no record that they did, nor would their friendship have been a satisfactory substitute for a lifetime of command experience. If professional judgments made at West Point were of crucial importance in Bullard's career, the impression Bullard made not on a classmate, but on a humorless, ambitious, hypermilitary Missourian who was the first sergeant of Company A when Bullard was a lieutenant of that cadet company probably had greater effect on his future. Like all cadets, Bullard was most aware of the cadets in the classes ahead of him, not behind him. But to the members of the class of 1886, the personalities of Bullard's class were part of their cadet lore. The first sergeant of Company A must have formed some opinion of his lieutenant's abilities, and his opinion eventually counted because he was John J. Pershing.[28]

4.

June Week 1885 was not much different from June Weeks past and those to come except that it was abnormally rainy. As always, the Academy was a conquered fortress, invaded by the Board of Visitors who listened to the final examinations and gently probed the Academy's management. The West Point Hotel was occupied by families, friends, vacationers, and young ladies drawn by the pageantry. As always there was a dinner held by the Association of Graduates and a class reunion or two, and near the end of the week the new class of candidates began to struggle up from the South Dock. For the graduates of the class of 1885, the week meant arranging their new "cits" and uniforms by Hatfield for departure after graduation.[29]

There was, no doubt, much discussion about the graduates' military assignments, although there could have been few surprises. According to the rhythm of the Academy the top students went into the engineers or the artillery, since those branches seemed to need their mathematical skills and because an engineer and artilleryman might expect a more stable domestic life. Of the top ten graduates only Michael O'Brien, Haydn Cole, and Charles Muir were appointed to infantry regiments and that by choice. The top two graduates became engineers, the other five of the top ten went to the artillery. All ten of the artillery officers from the class of 1885 graduated in the top half of the class. For the average cadets, regardless of their cadet rank, there were only two choices, limited by the War Department according to officer needs. Was it to be cavalry or infantry? Bullard thought about applying for the cavalry, but concluded that riding was hard on his sensitive bladder and that promotion to first lieutenant might be faster in an infantry regiment where resignations were greater than in the cavalry.[30] That he had a choice may have been a matter of self-delusion because only four classmates below him in standing were assigned to cavalry regiments and three of these went to the Negro Ninth and Tenth Cavalry, units of low prestige among West Pointers. As always the "good of the service" prevailed and nearly half the class of 1885 went by choice or not into the infantry.

For the class of 1885, June Week passed rapidly. There were the customary riding exhibitions, gunnery drills, dress parades, fencing and gymnastics demonstrations, and quick flirtations with the bedazzled girls who hovered about the cadet formations. Then suddenly it was graduation day and Governor Hoadley of Ohio, a member of the Board of Visitors, was making another tiresome speech and Superintendent Wesley Merritt was handing out diplomas. Then the caps went flying, and it was over. Usually there was time for one last stroll about the grounds, then it was off for New York City and the traditional class dinner at some posh restaurant like Delmonico's. After a night of mild ribaldry and many stanzas of "Army Blue," the class scattered on to their homes. While on graduation leave at Oak Bowery, Bullard received both his commission and his orders to the Tenth Infantry regiment from the War Department.[31] Somewhere between Alabama and Fort Union, New Mexico, Second Lieutenant Robert Lee Bullard probably put on his blue uniform for the first time, but he did not record the event. Forty years, two wars, and many skirmishes later, he took it off for the last time as a major general.

NOTES

[1]Diarybook autobiography, p. 31, BP.

[2]Stephen E. Ambrose, *Duty, Honor, Country: A History of West Point* (Baltimore, 1966), pp. 191-237; Sidney Forman, *West Point* (New York: Columbia University Press, 1950), pp. 110-74; and Thomas J. Fleming, *West Point: The Men and Times of the United States Military Academy* (New York: William Morrow, 1969), pp. 209-50.

[3]T. Bentley Mott, *Twenty Years as Military Attaché* (New York: Oxford University Press, 1937), pp. 24-45.

[4]"Report of the Board of Visitors to the Military Academy," *Annual Reports of the War Department, 1880* (Washington: Government Printing Office, 1880), I. pp. 541-60; "Report of the Board of Visitors to the United States Military Academy at West Point," *Annual Reports of the War Department, 1882* (Washington: Government Printing Office, 1882), I, pp. 531-36.

[5]Appendix C, *Report of the Board of Visitors to the United States to the United States Military Academy, 1895* (Washington: Government Printing Office, 1895), p. 14.

[6]"Report of the Board of Visitors of the Military Academy," *Annual Reports of the War Department, 1885* (Washington: Government Printing Office, 1885), I, pp. 855-57.

[7]*Annual Report of the Board of Visitors to the United States Military Academy, Made to the Secretary of War for the Year 1886* (Washington: Government Printing Office, 1886), p. 29.The class was filled with alternates appointed to fill the June vacancies.

[8]Entry, "Bullard, Robert L.," *School History of Candidates No. 1*(1880-1899), United States Military Academy (USMA) Archives, USMA Library, West Point, N. Y.

[9]The discussion of hazing in the 1880s and cadet life is drawn primarily from the following sources: Charles D. Rhodes (USMA, 1889), "Diary of a Cadet at the United States Military Academy, 1885-1889," *mss* in the Major General Charles D. Rhodes Papers, USMA Library; Charles F. Crain (USMA, 1894), letters to his parents, May 1890-June 1894, 4 vols., USMA Library; Mott, *Twenty Years as Military Attaché*, pp. 24-25; Wirt Robinson (USMA, 1887), journals, 1883-1887, USMA Library: Frank Parker (USMA, 1894) to Mr. and Mrs. A. M. Parker, May 1890-June 1894, Frank Parker Papers; George B. Duncan (USMA, 1886), "Reminiscences, 1882-1905," pp. 1-11, *mss* in the possession of Professor E. M. Coffman, University of Wisconsin; John McA. Palmer, "An Old Soldier's Memories" I, pp. 68-144, Palmer Papers; Eben Swift (USMA, 1876), "West Point, 1872-1876," in *mss* autobiography, Eben Swift Papers, USMA Library; Beaumont Buck, *Memories of War and Peace*(San Antonio: The Naylor Company, 1935), pp. 24-38; George O. Squier (USMA, 1887), "The United States Military Academy at West Point," *mss* written 1888-1892, George O. Squier Papers; Williston Fish (USMA, 1881), *Memories of West Point, 1877-1881*, 3 vols. (Batavia, N.Y.: Josephine Fish Peabody, 1957); and Hugh T. Reed (USMA, 1873), *Cadet Life at West Point* (Chicago: Hugh T. Reed, 1896).

[10]Diarybook autobiography, pp. 31-35, BP.

[11]"Report of the Board of Visitors of the Military Academy," *Annual Reports of the War Department, 1880*, p. 544.

[12]*Regulations, U. S. Corps of Cadets, 1884* and *Orders for the U. S. Corps of Cadets, 1884*, copies in the USMA Archives.

[13]This description is based on the Board of Visitors' reports and cadet narratives previously cited as well as the author's examination of the *Registers* of 1880-1886.

[14]Bullard autobiography, p. 9, BP; entries, "Bullard, Robert L.," *Register of Delinquencies No. 22*, pp. 8, 132, 217, USMA Archives; Special Order 204, December 21, 1883, and Special Order 101, June 14, 1884, both in *Post Orders*, Vol. 10, USMA Archives.

[15]The curriculum is printed in the *Registers* for 1881-1885 and in the U.S. Military Academy, *Staff Records* (1882-1887), No. 12, USMA Archives.

[16]Fish, *Memories of West Point* III, pp. 787-872.

[17]Mott, *Twenty Years as Military Attaché*, pp. 35-36.

[18]Diarybook autobiography, p. 36, BP. Bullard's academic record is extracted from the *Registers* of 1881 to 1886 and from U.S. Military Academy *Staff Records* (1882-1887), No. 12, USMA Archives.

[19]*Report of the Board of Visitors on the Part of the House of Representatives upon the Discipline, Instruction, Police Administration, and Fiscal and Other Affairs of the Military Academy at West Point* (Washington: Government Printing Office, 1884), pp. 6-7.

[20]The description of Lorenz and Godfrey is from Fish, *Memories of West Point* I, pp. 1-9, and III, pp. 810-813.

[21]Diarybook autobiography, p. 40, BP.

[22]For the details of cadet life, I have relied primarily on Rhodes, "Diary of a Cadet at the United States Military Academy, 1885-1889"; George O. Squier, "The United States Military Academy at West Point"; and the letters of Hiram M. Chittenden (USMA, 1884) to Mr. and Mrs. Chittenden, June 1880-June 1884, United States Military Academy Library.

[23]Diarybook autobiography, p. 38, BP.

[24]Buck, *Memories of War and Peace*, pp. 24-28; Simeon Dinkins to Williston Fish, May 10, 1931, in Fish, *Memories of West Point* II, p. 488.

[25]Bullard autobiography, p. 11, BP; Duncan, "Reminiscences, 1882-1905," p. 5.

[26]Diarybook autobiography, pp. 42-43, BP. *Cf.* John P. Lovell, "The Professional Socialization of the West Point Cadet," in Morris Janowitz, ed., *The New Military* (New York: Russell Sage Foundation, 1964), pp. 119-157.

[27]The careers of the class of 1885 are extracted from Edward S. Holden and Wirt Robinson, eds., *General Cullum's Biographical Register of the Officers and Graduates of the U.S. Military Academy; Supplements, 1890-1900* (Cambridge, Mass.: Riverside Press, 1901), *1900-1910* and *1910-1920* (Saginaw, Michigan, 1910 and 1920), and West Point Alumni Association, *Register of Graduates and Former Cadets of the United States Military Academy*, pp. 276-277.

[28]Although both Pershing and Bullard mentioned their acquaintance at West Point in their post-World War I memoirs, there is no evidence that they had any special relationship during their cadet days. See Robert L. Bullard, *Personalities and Reminiscences of the War* (Garden City, N.Y.: Doubleday, Page, 1925), pp 41-43, and John J. Pershing, *My Experience in the World War*, 2 vols. (New York: Stokes, 1931), I, p. 81.

[29]*Army and Navy Journal*, June 6, 1885.

[30]Diarybook Autobiography, p. 40, BP.

[31]2d Lt. Robert Bullard to the Adj. Gen., USA, July 13, 1885, 4482 ACP 1885, Appointments, Commissions, and Personal Branch Document File, Records of The Adjutant General's Office, 1780s-1917, Record Group (RG) 94, National Archives of the United States (NA). Hereafter cited as Bullard AGO File.

3

Frontier Service
1885-1889

Over one hundred years old, the United States Army was ending an epoch in 1885 when Lieutenant Bullard joined it. Like the nation it served, the army was watching the closing days of continental expansion and the settlement of the national domain. Created in the wake of the American Revolution in order to police the trans-Appalachian lands ceded to the national government by the states, the regular army had moved West with America's trappers, herdsmen, miners, and farmers. Only twice in the nineteenth century had the army's westward movement been reversed, once to fight the Seminoles in Florida and again to be swallowed up in the Civil War. In 1885 the regular army had for twenty years been performing its traditional mission, serving as a federal constabulary in the trans-Mississippi territories.[1]

Although the majority of the army's garrisons and the bulk of its troops were stationed west of the Mississippi, the institutional character of the army was not solely dictated by the demands of frontier service. In fact, there were "four armies" that a new officer might join, and his career and his understanding of what the army was might vary considerably, depending on which army he joined.

For the academic elite of each West Point class, the army was the Corps of Engineers, a small and prestigious group of one hundred and twenty officer-civil engineers whose service was linked to the physical conquest of the continent. Since early in the century the Corps of Engineers had served as the federal government's technical agent for the exploration and development of the national domain. In addition to lending its skill to railroad builders, the Corps of Engineers supervised federally funded engineering projects designed to increase the economic usefulness of the nation's major rivers and harbors. In 1885, for example, the Corps of Engineers was responsible for $10.6 million in harbors and rivers projects and for only $4.6 million in coast defense construction. Spiritually and intellectually, the Corps of Engineers was closer to its civil engineering brethren than it was to the Indian-fighting army, and its political ties with the Congress, built upon decades of congressional interest in the local economic benefits of government projects, gave it considerable autonomy within the War Department. For the individual engineer officer, an army career was a succession

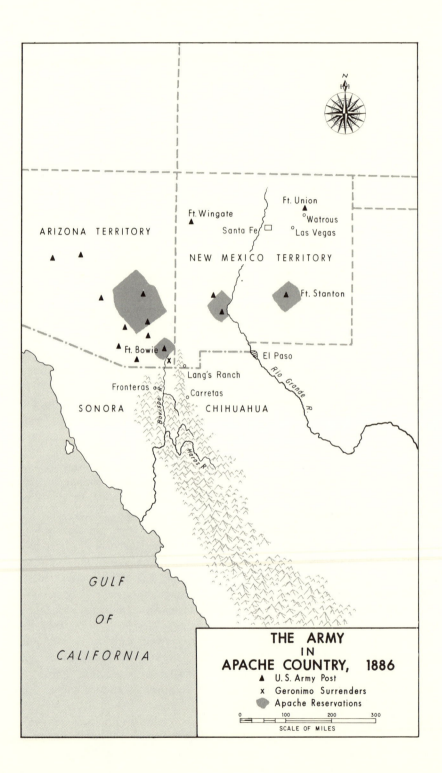

THE ARMY
IN
APACHE COUNTRY, 1886

▲ U.S. Army Post
x Geronimo Surrenders
⬡ Apache Reservations

0   100   200   300
SCALE OF MILES

of assignments to public works projects. His work contacts and social life were within civilian society; his values were as shaped by the profession of civil engineering as by the army; his life-style was more analogous to that of a civil servant than to that of the majority of the army's officers.[2]

Another army that a new officer might join was one of the five regiments of artillery. After the Civil War the army's artillery was parceled out to the coast defense batteries along the Pacific and Atlantic oceans and the Gulf of Mexico. Unless an officer joined a field artillery battery (each regiment was supposed to have two) on the frontier, he was likely to spend his career in a world dominated by problems of ordnance design, casement and barbette engineering, and fire-control systems. His mission was to see to it that hostile naval powers (the only conceivable one was Great Britain) would not be tempted to attack and hold the nation's seaports for ransom. But beyond the sand and marsh grass he never saw an enemy fleet. Yet it was an interesting time for a coast artillery officer, for the War Department had just recommended the modernization of the seacoast batteries, laying out an ambitious program for engineering and ordnance reform. The artillery officer could be a participant in the growing world of science and technology. In addition to his concern for the emplacement of the most modern coast artillery pieces, he might easily interest himself in the basic development of electronic communications, photography, physics, and chemistry. Like his contemporary in the Corps of Engineers, the artillery officer in his world of mathematics and science, in his intellectual and physical proximity to civilian life, had little in common with the frontier officer.[3]

The third army was composed of the War Department staff agencies which performed the army's housekeeping functions. Just whose interests this bureaucratic army served had not been satisfactorily resolved in 1885, although a decade before there had been a rich debate on the subject. The army had two masters, the secretary of war, a civilian political appointee, and the commanding general, the army's senior officer. Unhappily for the commanding general, tradition and bureaucratic politics vested control of the army in the secretary of war. The transient secretaries of war seldom interested themselves in either the broad debates on military policy or the routine administration of the War Department. Therefore, the real power of the War Department was exercised in fragments by the bureaus, the quasi-military, quasi-civilian housekeeping agencies. In 1885 these agencies were the Office of the Adjutant General, the Office of the Inspector General, the Ordnance Department, the Quartermaster Department, the Subsistence Department, the Medical Department, the Pay Department, the Bureau of Military Justice, the Signal Corps, and the Bureau of Pensions and Records.[4]

Often acting at cross-purposes with one another and generally insensitive to the needs of the frontier army, the bureaus acted in the name of the secretary of war and the civilian virtues he represented. In addition, the central offices of each bureau, located in Washington, were attuned to the individual and collective concerns of the Congress. In personnel matters congressional concern meant personal favoritism in matters of officer assignment and in the promotions of general officers. In fiscal matters, the Congress decreed that the War Department was answerable to the Treasury Department for its appropriated funds and property with a high degree of accountability. Even without this policy, the War Department's civilian appointees brought the values of the accounting firm and law office to Washington, and they expected the officer-bureaucrats to be the soul of accuracy, honesty, predictability, and orderliness in all transactions.

The power which the War Department bureaus held over the Line stemmed not from the long tenure of the bureau chiefs (nearly fifty different generals held such posts between 1865 and 1900) nor from the size of the staff corps, which, excluding the Medical Department, numbered only around 250 of the army's 2,100 officers. The staff corps' rivalry with the Line did not arise because the staff officers were inexperienced political appointees. Except for twelve men appointed to the Pay Department between 1865 and 1884, the bureau staffs were composed of former line officers, many with distinguished records in the Civil War and Indian warfare. While the bureaus' informal alliances and personal friendships in Washington added to the staff officers' authority, the bureaus' ultimate control rested on the administrative assumptions they shared with the secretary of war and the Congress: that the army must be managed according to the rigid, highly detailed War Department regulations. For the bureaus the ultimate test of the army's effectiveness was not whether the West was won or the Line was happy, but whether the Congress accepted the secretary's annual report and legislative requests in the name of statistically proven efficiency.[5]

When the bureau officers looked beyond their regulations, they tended to follow their parochial occupational interests in officer management methods, experimental weaponry, equipment inventions, medical research, and the creation of new rations. Noble or trivial, these projects reflected a narrowness of focus that blinded these officers to the larger problems of military training and planning. Line officers, drawing their inspiration from the leadership of General Sherman and Colonel (Brevet Major General) Emory Upton, had attacked the War Department bureau system in the 1870s on precisely this issue: that no one in the War Department was systematically studying the problems of wartime high command and manpower and supply mobilization. The army was being run like a business by businessmen in uniform. Instead of considering the merit of these criticisms, both the Congress and the War Department bureaucrats viewed the line officer reformers as jealous malcontents, and in 1885 the businessmen in blue were still running the whole army unreformed and unchastened.[6]

For the majority of the officers of Bullard's generation, the "real" army was the frontier constabulary garrisoning some one hundred and twenty posts beyond the Mississippi. This was the army of ten cavalry regiments, twenty-five infantry regiments, and the field artillery which composed the army's field service troops. In the mid-1880s the vast majority of the army's officers ad twenty-four thousand enlisted men served in these thirty-five skeletonized regiments. As a group, these long-serving career soldiers were experienced and hardened by the Civil War and frontier service. The officers were nearly all native-born and middle-aged; when

Bullard was commissioned there were only about 450 officers under thirty in the army. Above the rank of second lieutenant, the officers were predominantly Civil War veterans; comparatively few were also West Point graduates. The weathered and mustachioed captains and lieutenants spent years in grade and accepted it. The troopers and infantrymen of the frontier army were five-year enlistees, the majority of whom were rural youths or wandering aliens between the ages of twenty and thirty. Most of them served but one enlistment, and many deserted before then. More than ten thousand enlisted men in 1885 were foreign-born, mostly Irish and German.[7]

The Tenth Regiment of Infantry, United States Army, was born and raised for the West. Created in 1855 for frontier service, its companies garrisoned posts in Minnesota and Kansas before going to the New Mexico territory in 1860 to fight the Navajos. In the Civil War small battalions of the regiment fought Confederates in New Mexico and in the eastern theater. The war destroyed the Tenth Infantry, for by 1863 it was but a remnant of three officers and one hundred men. In 1865, however, the second Tenth Infantry was organized, again for frontier service. Until 1869 its companies manned posts in Minnesota and the Dakota territory. For the next ten years the Tenth Infantry was stationed along the Rio Grande and guarded settlements from raids by the Lipan Apaches. In 1879 the War Department rewarded the regiment by transferring it to four comfortable posts along the Great Lakes. In 1884 the War Department sent the Tenth Infantry back to the frontier, ordering it to garrison two posts in Colorado, one in Texas and Fort Union in the New Mexico territory. Nineteen men promptly deserted. The rest of the Tenth packed their families and property and went back to the West.[8]

For the officers of the Tenth Infantry, the return to the frontier was unwelcome but expected. As a group they were service-hardened. In 1885 the regimental commander was fifty-nine-year-old Henry Douglass, an 1852 West Point graduate from New York who had served in the West with other regiments before and after the Civil War. Contrary to the mythology of the "old army," Douglass and his officers were not defrocked Civil War generals; Douglass had spent the entire war as a regular and had been breveted for gallantry but once, to major. A mild commander, the heavy, bearded Douglass was well-liked. Knowing the conditions of frontier service, he contented himself with his duties as post commander at Fort Union. The regiment's lieutenant colonel, major, and nine of its ten captains were also Civil War veterans, three of whom had been colonels in the Volunteers and the rest junior officers and enlisted men in either the Volunteers or regular army. They had been with the regiment since its reorganization. Only in 1884 when John F. Stretch (USMA, 1867) was promoted did the regiment have a company commander who had missed the war and was a West Pointer. Of the twelve first lieutenants, four were Civil War veterans and only two West Point graduates. All had been with the regiment at least eight years. The seven second lieutenants had been commissioned after 1877 and four were West Pointers.[9]

Built on the eastern slope of the Sangre de Cristo mountains in northeastern New Mexico, Fort Union, the home of the Tenth Infantry's headquarters, was older and more service-worn than its new garrison. The first Fort Union was built by the army in 1851 to protect the freighters on the Sante Fe trail. Until the late 1870s the Fort Union garrisons had more military missions than they had the troops to perform. There were campaigns against the Jicarilla Apaches, the Mescalero Apaches to the south, the Utes to the north, Comanches and Kiowas to the east, and Navajos to the west. During the Civil War the fort was the major base for the Union troops which repulsed the Confederate invasion of New Mexico in 1862. Rebuilt after the Civil War, Fort Union was really three army installations: a post for four companies of line troops, a quartermaster depot, and an ordnance depot. Geographically, the fort was isolated from the civilian inhabitants, a melange of Mexican farmers and herdsmen, wandering Indians, and pioneer Anglo-American ranchers and tradesmen. Built on a treeless grassy plain, Fort Union sat along the mountain branch of the Santa Fe trail, seven miles north of the main trail, which ran through Watrous. Other civilian towns were no closer, and the only substantial one, Las Vegas, was twenty-eight miles distant.

By 1884 Fort Union had outlived its usefulness, but the War Department was reluctant to close the post. The Indians were on reservations in other regions, and the Santa Fe trail traffic had withered after the arrival of the railroad in Watrous in 1879. The duty the garrison performed was spending its money in the Fort Union area and guarding federal prisoners, primarily Indians. The most savage experiences on the post were imposed by nature and human error—blizzards, flooding rains, and an occasional fire. Yet the environment's challenge was substantial enough to keep the garrison busy, for wood had to be cut and hauled from seven miles away, the fort's water pumps and primitive sewage facilities had to be maintained, the forage for the animals cut, and the eroding brick and adobe buildings constantly repaired. At Fort Union the essential mission was to survive and perhaps find some comfort.[10]

For Bullard the assignment to Fort Union was not banishment from civilization, but a thrilling chance to be part of the Wild West. In September 1885 he left Oak Bowery and headed for the frontier by train, carrying his valise, trunk, and two favorite books, a dictionary and *Don Quixote*. At El Paso the rails ended, and Bullard rode north by stage until he reached Watrous. From Watrous he and his luggage were loaded unceremoniously into an army wagon and driven the seven miles to the post and his awaiting regiment.[11]

To Bullard's eyes, Fort Union, a sprawl of low buildings and rutted wagon tracks on its treeless plain, was not a backwater garrison of bored soldiers but the home of a society of gallant officers, their charming ladies, and their loyal enlisted men. Everything was new and slightly mysterious—the one room bachelor quarters and its army issue furniture, the offices and barracks, the ream of special regulations for the garrison's routine, the officers' personalities, and Fort Union's web of social conventions and informal associations. As a new lieutenant he himself was a subject of curiosity, a new character to be weighed and absorbed into the life of the Tenth Infantry and the post. So conventional was his background and training that he probably was quickly judged and then ignored, the mark of acceptance for second lieutenants. Bullard was probably viewed by his new comrades as a pleasant young man who could join the rotation as post officer of the day and provide a new face at dinner parties.

There was little at Fort Union for Bullard to do except carry on his personal reconnaissance of the post's buildings and its officers' eccentricities. Assigned to Company F, he learned that his unit was four hundred miles away on the Mexican border under its commander, Captain John Stretch. Since Stretch had only eighteen men available for duty, the company was hardly beyond the capacity of one seasoned officer to manage. There was no hurry for Bullard to leave Fort Union, so both he and the company's first lieutenant, handsome, polished Stephen Y. Seyburn, remained at the regimental headquarters. Bullard set up his meager room, learned the routine of a lieutenant in garrison, and enjoyed a round of visits and dinners with his new comrades. Among those he met were the post surgeon, Major Peter J. A. Cleary, and his attractive young stepdaughter, Rose Douglass Brabson, whose father had been a congressman from Tennessee. The person who attracted him most, however, was a young widow living on the post. Bullard, sporting a new mustache, became her ardent companion. "I was so constantly with her that—well, I grew very tired so that when an order came about the end of Nov. for me and Seyburn to join our company, I was glad to go."[12] In two months of frontier service Bullard sampled army life in the Wild West, but there was still one experience which eluded him. He had not been in the field on an Indian campaign. Far to the south an Apache named Geronimo would give Bullard the opportunity.

1.

For longer than men living in 1885 could remember, the control of the Southwest had ebbed and flowed between four distinct cultures, locked in reciprocated hatred, violence, and deceit. Viewed historically, the first two warring cultures were Indian. On one side there were the herders and cliff-dwellers, the Zuni, Pueblos, Pimas, Papagos, and eventually the Navajos, after the latter developed a pastoral culture. The other Indian claimants were the Apache, a tribal group who called themselves simply *Dine* or *Tinde*, "The People." The Zuni gave them their alien name, Apache, which meant "The Enemy." Late migrants from northern North America, the Apaches carved out a homeland which ran west to western Arizona, south into Mexico, east to the Staked Plains of Texas, and north into western Kansas and the high Rockies. In this domain of desert, pine-covered mountain, red mesa, and rocky canyons, the Apaches traveled at will and lived by hunting and raiding upon the other people of the Southwest.[13]

The third culture was Mexican, a blend of Spanish and Indian, and it first touched the Apaches in the eighteenth century. At first the Spanish colonial government in Mexico tried to pacify the Indians with Christianity, but the Apaches proved reluctant converts. The Spanish and Mexican armies then tried both war and bribery. The Apaches won the wars and accepted the gifts and continued to raid the Mexicans for slaves and booty. By the 1830s the warfare had become genocide beyond any official control.

For the first fifteen years in which the Southwest was part of the territory of the United States, the scattered American miners, lumbermen, and ranchers lived in an uneasy peace with the Apache. By the Civil War, however, American irregulars had joined the Mexicans' Apache-hunts, and the territorial government and army joined the Apaches' foes. The lure of transportation routes to the Pacific, of mines of gold and silver, of ranches and farms and the towns to serve them, drew another culture into the battle for *Apachería.*

From the opening days of the Civil War until 1886, the American-Apache war swept back and forth throughout the Southwest Territory. The Mexican-Indian-Apache war went on as well. In the American-Apache war two general approaches to the Apache problem developed. For white settlers the emerging consensus, born of seemingly endless death and destruction, was that the Apaches must either be reduced to degraded peonage or exterminated. For the United States government, attuned to more humane (and remote) impulses and without the military capacity or stomach for genocide, the policy was to stop the raiding, to restrict by force and negotiation Apache tribal life to a series of reservations, and to make the Apaches wards of the federal government.

The army officer who found the right mixture of war, diplomacy, and administrative control to pacify the Apaches was Brigadier General George Crook, an intelligent, sensitive, dogged soldier of much frontier service. Crook understood the Apaches' love of their land and tribal life. While he was untroubled by the necessity of hunting down and killing the most hostile Apache bands, he also assumed that honest administration of the Indian reservations, scrupulous respect for treaties, and the preservation of at least part of tribal culture might bring an end to the Southwest's Apache war. In addition, Crook took command of the Department of Arizona when the Grant Administration was ready to oppose extermination. Crook used his mandate wisely. First, he recognized that among the Apaches there were individual and tribal rivalries which might be exploited by a policy of conciliation, and by honestly administering the reservations and protecting the reservation Apaches from both whites and hostiles, Crook won over several important Apache leaders and their bands. Crook also recognized that his regular troops could not match the hostiles' speed and endurance. Therefore, he organized companies of Indian scouts, particularly friendly Apaches, and put them under the command of a select group of army officers and seasoned frontiersmen. These scouts carried the battle to the hostiles, supplemented by cavalrymen and supported by mule trains. In his own department Crook subdued the Apaches by 1875 and departed for further service against the Sioux.[14]

At the time of Crook's departure, the focal points of Apache affairs were the San Carlos and Fort Apache agencies in southeastern Arizona. Even under the most able Indian agents and effective Apache police, the change to reservation life would have been difficult and marked by violence. Instead, the Apaches' adjustment was damaged by tribal feuds, Indian Bureau frauds, and continuous white pressure to eliminate the Apaches and seize their agency lands. From 1875 until 1882, the Apache agencies were racked by illness, malnutrition, murder, treachery, and a series of breakaways by irreconcilables. Among the latter was a Chiricahua warleader, Geronimo, who for personal and tribal reasons saw no future in becoming a permanent agency Apache.

Crook's officers and Indian agents could find little to admire in Geronimo. In his fifties by the 1880s, Geronimo had, by force of personality, cruelty and cunning as a warrior, and bottomless hatred for whites and Mexicans, made himself the natural leader of the San Carlos malcontents. Those who knew him, white and Apache alike, recognized his bravery, physical endurance, and intelligence; they also agreed that he was vicious, untrustworthy, and psychologically incapable of living without violence until survival dictated surrender. Physically, he was the model hostile, a squat, powerful man with a face that might have been designed by a writer of Wild West dime novels. Emotionally, he had been blighted by years of warfare with Mexicans and American settlers, years of violence that included the massacre of his own family by Mexican militiamen. Growing old in war, he had learned to survive and kill by studying the ways of his enemies and perfecting the tactics of the ambush and quick withdrawal. Although no better armed than his enemies, he and his followers could move faster afoot than mounted men, live on much less than whites, and knew the deserts and mountains far better than their pursuers.[15]

Moved from agency to agency, harried by and harrying Indian agents, contemptuous of agency Apaches, and periodically threatening to kill the peaceful chiefs, Geronimo was a constant menace. In May of 1885 he led some forty warriors and ninety women and children off the San Carlos agency and onto the warpath. In 1881 he had done the same thing, and it had taken two years to negotiate his surrender. As he had in 1882 upon his return to Arizona, General Crook formed his team of army officers, civilian scouts and packers, and Apache scouts and went after the hostiles. In the meantime, Geronimo's band splintered and raided through Arizona and New Mexico and into Mexico, killing scattered whites and Mexicans and ambushing or avoiding cavalry patrols. To quiet the hysterical civilians, Crook deployed some four thousand troops between the Atlantic and Pacific railroad, which connected Flagstaff and Albuquerque, and the Mexican border. The border itself was no longer a barrier, for after 1882 United States and Mexican troops ignored the line in hot pursuit of the Apaches. Yet for all Crook's efforts and eleven months of chase and diplomacy, Geronimo did not come in. Upset, peeved, his reputation in tatters, Crook asked to be reassigned in April 1886.

To replace Crook, the War Department sent another proven frontier campaigner, Brigadier General Nelson A. Miles, an officer who was as militarily theatrical as Crook was affectedly inconspicuous. Like Geronimo, Miles would have been an incredible fictional character but for his real existence. A youthful New Englander who had done little but clerk in a dry goods store, Miles found a home in the Civil War. Commissioned a lieutenant at twenty-two, he was a brigadier general of Volunteers at twenty-six. Handsome, powerful, utterly fearless, arrogant, intelligent, Miles was a legend in the Army of the Potomac, an army with its share of heroes. At the end of the war he was given a regular commission as a colonel of infantry and then commanded his regiment, the Fifth Infantry, in a series of successful Indian campaigns. In 1880 he again became a general officer, his frontier career a conspicious success. Moreover, he had married into the Sherman family, and Philip H. Sheridan, the commanding general, was his active patron. His next goal was promotion to major general, a rank for which George Crook was a competitor.

Nelson Miles was too astute not to recognize that the chances of winning fame in the Southwest were slim. General Sheridan was sour on Crook's Apache scouts and the idea of negotiating with the hostiles. Sheridan wanted complete subjugation. President Grover Cleveland was attracted to the idea of treating the hostiles as common criminals and turning them over to civil authorities for trial. As he traveled to Fort Bowie, his headquarters near the Arizona-Mexican line, Miles knew he had a delicate assignment which promised little but frustration. His career hung on his ability to catch forty Apaches who had all of the Southwest in which to hide.[16]

General Miles was not without some ideas about how to catch Geronimo, and there were plenty of civilians and officers who were eager advisers. Miles' own contribution was to order all his patrols which cut the hostiles' trail to hold the pursuit as long as physically possible. In a second effort to track the Apaches, Miles erected a series of heliograph stations, throughout Arizona, New Mexico, and Sonora. Information of the Apaches whereabouts could then be flashed from garrison to garrison, and patrols could be directed toward their assumed path. Miles' measures, however, did not answer the question of continuous pursuit. If Apache scout units were not to track and capture Geronimo, who would? The officers of the Fourth Cavalry at Fort Bowie and a new assistant surgeon, Leonard Wood, had an answer: a picked group of American soldiers, chosen scientifically for their endurance, could catch Geronimo. They would need Indian trackers, pack mules, supply support, and occasional replacements, but Wood thought that the picked force could match the Apaches' pace. Miles approved the idea and selected Wood's friend, forty-three-year-old Captain Henry W. Lawton and his Troop B, Fourth Cavalry, as the nucleus of the elite unit. To it were added a detachment of mounted infantry, Apache scouts, and a packtrain.[17]

In May 1886 Lawton's command picked up the trail of Geronimo's band, then raiding in Arizona, but could not close with the Apaches. Geronimo disappeared once more into Mexico. Behind him, though neither close nor sure of the trail, came Captain Lawton, Surgeon Wood, three other army officers, and their mixed command. The last army expedition into the Apache refuge in the Sierra Madre was under way.

2.

For Second Lieutenant Bullard, the Geronimo campaign was an open-air classroom in which he learned a little about Apaches and a great deal about the United States Army. The first thing he learned was that the infantry in the Apache wars had the boring and never glorious role of protecting settlers and supporting the cavalry. The reason Company F was not at Fort Union when he arrived was that it was stationed at Lang's Ranch on the Mexican border; its mission was to guard a base used by General Crook's pack-trains as they hauled supplies to the scouts in the Sierra Madre. It was not romantic duty, but it was field service and a novel experience for Bullard. He and Seyburn made their way to the border without incident, Bullard enjoying the ride and the spectacular scenery. He was entranced with the Southwestern desert, its flora and fauna, its colored rock formations, its hidden gorges and secret mountain streams, its pines, joshua trees, and stunted junipers.

It was well that Bullard appreciated the beauties of New Mexico, for he had little to do at Lang's Ranch. To amuse himself when his minimal duties were complete, Bullard often went hunting, studied law and Spanish, and talked with the packers and scouts about Indian lore. From November 1885 until August 1886 his world was Lang's Ranch. When a large pack-train went into Sonora to another basecamp at Carretas ranch, Seyburn commanded the escort, not Bullard. After December there were no more Apache raids into New Mexico. For amusement Company F was reduced to marching the eleven miles to the dusty crossroads of Cloverdale and back. Like hundreds of similar detachments scattered throughout Arizona and New Mexico, Company F watched and waited for the Geronimo campaign to develop some drama.[18]

In the meantime, Lawton's expedition had made an epic march into the Sierra Madre, weathering scorching heat, thunderstorms, jagged terrain, poisonous insects, Mexican threats, the despondent rages of its commanding officer, and the optimism of its surgeon. It had not, however, caught Geronimo and by July it had run out of fresh trails. Although the Apache scouts remorselessly tracked their brethren, the white soldiers were wearing out and let Lawton know it by getting drunk and insubordinate. Since Miles kept couriers, replacements, and supplies shuttling to and from Lawton, the expedition's condition was no secret.[19]

Miles probably assumed that Lawton's expedition was worn out and that others would have to join the hunt. He also had heard that Geronimo was near Fronteras. The Fourth Cavalry had several officers anxious to attach their own and their regiment's reputation to Miles and reap the publicity of capturing Geronimo. The most persuasive was the regimental adjutant, First Lieutenant James Parker. A tall, gangling, stoop-shouldered West Pointer, Parker was an adept army politician and most ambitious officer. As the son of a New Jersey congressman, he recognized the advantages of personal relationships and persuaded Miles to give him a command. On July 16 Parker formed another Mexican expedition, built around Troop H, Fourth Cavalry. Parker's ninety-man force also included an infantry detachment, pack-train, white and Yaqui Indian scouts, and two other army officers, Second Lieutenant Wilds P. Richardson and Assistant Surgeon William B. Banister. Since he himself had written Lawton's orders, Parker knew exactly what sort of mission he wanted and got it—an independent command which would not join Lawton's force, but would "cooperate" with it in Mexico.[20]

On its way into Mexico, Parker's expedition passed Lang's Ranch, and Bullard got his chance to chase Geronimo. Parker wanted an officer to lead his mule train and two wagons to Carretas ranch, and Bullard was the only one available, since Seyburn was on leave. The mounted column moved on rapidly, because Parker had heard from smugglers that Geronimo's band was in the mountains northeast of Fronteras.

As acting quartermaster and commissary for Parker's expedition, Bullard followed the cavalry into Mexico on the eighty-mile ride to Carretas ranch. It was a hot march, and the detail was plagued by duststorms and dry water holes. At one point Bullard's Mexican guide got confused, and Bullard had to decide which way to head for himself. Fortunately, he guessed correctly, a mighty victory for his self-confidence. Like other American columns, Bullard's supply train drew Mexican militiamen. When he arrived at Carretas ranch, Bullard found it surrounded by *rurales* of questionable friendship.[21] From the base of Carretas, Parker's scouts searched the mountains while the troops dealt with the perils of Carretas—scorpions, tarantulas, mescal, and some Mexican girls "who made up for their lack of beauty by their generosity."[22] With such a range of choices, Lieutenant Bullard preferred scouting, although once he was almost shot by some jumpy Mexicans who took him and his men for Geronimo's band. The Apaches remained will-o'-the-wisps.

While Parker's expedition was camped at Carretas, First Lieutenant Charles B. Gatewood, Sixth Cavalry, joined the search. A former commander of Apache scouts and an agency official, Gatewood had been serving, reluctantly, as Miles' adviser on the Chiricahuas. Unlike most of his contemporaries of the Fourth Cavalry, the thirty-three-year-old officer did not see the Geronimo campaign as a golden opportunity for individual glory or as a last chance to refurbish the army's reputation as Apache-fighters. Rather, he was irritated by Crook's relief, was sick of nursemaiding the Apaches (whom he disliked), and was suffering from a bladder infection which made riding painful. Gatewood, however, knew Geronimo and his followers and was trusted by them. This circumstance made him invaluable to Miles because the department commander wanted to try another tactic against the hostiles: a negotiated surrender arranged by two agency Chiricahuas. These men, Martine and Kayitah, had once been Geronimo's followers, and Miles had persuaded them to try to talk their leader down from the Sierra Madre. Gatewood, with three civilian frontiersmen, would be their co-negotiator and escort into Mexico.[23]

Riding through Stretch's camp at Lang's Ranch, Gatewood learned the location of Parker's force and reached Carretas on July 21. With Gatewood in tow, Parker scouted south up to the divide between the Bavispe river and Nacori creek for a week without success. On August 3 Parker, some scouts, and Gatewood's party ran into Lawton's camp on the Haros River. Neither column had fresh information on the Apaches' location, and Lawton, Parker, and Gatewood were discouraged. The three officers conferred, and Gatewood decided to attach himself to Lawton's party, though Lawton was unenthusiastic about escorting the peace mission. However, since Miles had told Gatewood that the peace mission should have an escort, Lawton accepted Gatewood's party. Parker returned to his own camp a few miles north of Lawton's.[24]

Bullard thought that Parker had been foolish to surrender Gatewood's party since Lawton's command was exhausted and on a cold trail. But after four more days of futile scouting, Bullard was ready to leave when Parker started his command for the border. For the next ten days, he helped scout the Torres mountains east of the Bavispe river valley as the column struggled north. He saw spectacular gorges, small Mexican villages, awesome cliffs, but no Apaches.[25]

In the meantime Lawton and Gatewood had also turned northward, seeking their supplies and couriers. On August 14 Lawton learned from Miles and from the officer in charge of his pack-train that the enemy were north near Fronteras. On August 16 they again came upon Parker's party, camped near the town of Huepari with a group of Sonoran militiamen. Parker then moved eastward, while Gatewood's party, reinforced by six troopers, went ahead for Fronteras and, eventually, a rendezvous with Geronimo on August 24.

Geronimo and his band were indeed near Fronteras. Then Miles heard rumors of an Apache-Mexican agreement which would allow Geronimo to use Sonora as a sanctuary for raids into the United States, provided the Apaches would leave the Mexicans alone. Miles ordered Lieutenant Colonel George A. Forsyth and four more troops of the Fourth Cavalry into Mexico. One of Forsyth's officers made contact with Geronimo's agents and put Gatewood on the trail. At the same time, however, the prefect of Fronteras was outraged at the American intervention because he and his militia had planned to lure the Apaches into an ambush with promises of a truce. Lawton arrived at Fronteras on August 23, found that Gatewood had not yet contacted Geronimo, and promptly turned himself into a mean drunk. Wood saved the situation by calming Lawton and persuading the petulant Gatewood to take his two Apache peacemakers to Geronimo's camp.[26]

On August 24 and 25 Gatewood successfully persuaded Geronimo and Natchez, hereditary chief of the Chiricahua, to place themselves in Miles' custody. It was a delicate business, as Geronimo vacillated between joviality, seriousness, bellicosity, and contempt. Miles' terms were not appealing: imprisonment in Florida with the rest of the agency Chiricahuas or a fight to the finish. Geronimo preferred the sort of terms he always got from Crook—to return to the reservation and live in peace. The next issue became Miles' good faith, and it took two more days of parley with Gatewood and Lawton to convince Geronimo that Miles could be trusted and that the army would protect the Apaches from both the Mexicans and American vigilantes.[27]

Still armed and unpredictable, the Apaches trekked north with Lawton's command to the border to meet Miles. At Guadalupe canyon on the San Bernadino river, Bullard joined the caravan. When Geronimo surrendered, he had been fifteen miles away to the east, but he and Parker then joined Lawton's march north. They celebrated Geronimo's surrender and shared the delicious anguish that the still-armed Apaches might make one more break.[28] As a bona fide veteran of the chase, Bullard accompanied the Apaches to their meeting with Miles and then to Fort Bowie. There he saw Geronimo's band loaded on wagons and driven to the train which took them to Florida. The Apaches were not returned to the reservation, but they did not end up shredded by Mexican bullets or dangling from Arizona rope either. For the United States Army, Geronimo's exile ended a guerrilla war which offered little more than health-breaking field service and professional ruination. Though the Fourth Cavalry band played "Auld Lang Syne" as the Apaches left, the army didn't really want Geronimo back, even though it lost a mission with his departure.

For Second Lieutenant Robert Lee Bullard, the Geronimo campaign was his first and last taste of Indian fighting. He shared the reflected glory of the surrender, and he had proven himself an able campaigner. In a minor way he had become acquainted with Henry Lawton and Leonard Wood, both future generals, and he and Jim Parker became friends for life. As a veteran of the last Geronimo pursuit, Bullard inadvertantly was admitted to the clique of officers who led the chase. Able or not (and most of them were), this group's sheer persistence earned them army-wide notice. Until their deaths, these officers kept alive the Geronimo epic by arguing in print and before meetings of the Order of the Indian Wars about details of the campaign, about who should get the greatest credit for Geronimo's surrender. For Bullard the real hero was Leonard Wood, though he did not reveal this judgment until both Lawton and Gatewood were dead and Wood a brigadier general.

3.

With the Geronimo campaign concluded, the army in the Department of Arizona relaxed and turned once again to garrison routine. With the exception of an occasional renegade who jumped the reservation to raid, the several thousand Indians in the department remained pacific, though rightfully unhappy about the Indian Bureau's governance of their reservations. But there were no more major outbreaks. General Miles' chief concern became the efficient management of his command and the field training of his troops. Once the Geronimo campaign ended, he knew that the War Department would look closely at his expenses, and after Geronimo's surrender, he began to shuffle and concentrate his troops, saving $1 million in the transportation costs of men and supplies to his remote posts. While Fort Union was not remote, it had outlived its usefulness, and as part of the department reorganization Miles shifted part of its garrison elsewhere as a preliminary to closing the fort.[29]

Accompanying the Tenth Infantry's regimental headquarters, Company F moved to Fort Bliss, Texas, near El Paso, where Bullard rejoined it in October, 1886. Four months later, the Tenth Infantry was back in Fort Union, for the War Department had decided to keep the post open. The Fort Bliss interlude was marked by nothing more memorable than its band concerts and the fact that Bullard commanded his company temporarily while Captain Stretch took leave.

Back at Fort Union, Bullard settled into the casual routine of post life and the social life of his regiment. Like the typical lieutenant of his day, he was "ambitious for his regiment as well as for self," but found his military ardor softened by his enjoyment of hunting and the officers' social life. As one of his contemporaries mused, "the life of an officer under such conditions would have been ideal but for existence of soldiers and Indians."[30] At Fort Union, the Indians were far away and the soldiers were not especially trying. The Tenth Infantry's companies had light duty and much free time, for the army in 1887 was in the middle of one of its spasmodic attempts to cut desertion by liberalizing enlisted life. The military duties of the men consisted primarily of standing guard, riflery, drill, and inspections. For the ambitious enlisted man, there was the post library and school to attend (and a few did). For the energetic there were baseball games, boxing, theatricals, and foot and horse races. Most of the men, however, preferred poker and cribbage, barracks debates, getting drunk on payday, and making the pilgrimages to the Mexican hamlet of Loma Parda and its bordellos.[31]

For the officers, duty at Fort Union was monotonous but not very demanding. The most onerous thing the lieutenants did was to stand duty as officer of the day, a twenty-four hour long chore which required an inspection of sentry posts every two hours. An officer's normal work day, however, seldom went to noon. Often, after the morning guard mount and drill, the officers adjourned either to the shaded tennis courts or the billiard room at the sutler's for the latest army gossip. There was ample time for riding, hunting, fishing the nearby trout streams, and exploring, and most of the officers saw themselves as bona fide country sportsmen, forever wrangling about the merits of their horses, dogs, and equipment. A few of them read, though seldom anything more weighty than the *Army and Navy Journal*. In the late 1880s target shooting was the rage, and the Tenth Infantry officers spent many hours on the post rifle range.

The officers' rustic passions were tempered by their wives, daughters, and female relatives who turned Fort Union into a genteel middle-class community. While the army did little to encourage marriage, it had accepted decades before that American officers were not going to forego the family life that was the very foundation of their social class. Unlike European officers, American officers raised families on their posts, and the bachelor officer found himself subject to many subtle and unsubtle pressures to pair up quickly. While the center of social life in a European regiment was the officers mess, it was a family dinner, band concert, or post hop at Fort Union. And a European officer, no doubt, would have been horrified to see Fort Union wake up in the morning—pigs and chickens scratching in the fenced backyards, cows wandering across the parade field, privates hauling wood and water and shoveling manure, gaggles of children skipping off to the school, and the cacaphony of voices, male and female, Anglo and Mexican, ordering households about. Except for the regimented architecture and uniforms, it might have been any prosperous frontier town in the West.

For diversion, the post ladies cajoled their husbands into the usual late-Victorian middle-class amusements: whist, tennis, bicycling, picnicking, and amateur musicales. The height of status at Fort Union was to have an oyster dinner and show up in the latest eastern dress. All the national and Christian holidays meant a round of parties and dances, either at the old armory or in the breezeway between the duplex married quarters. If a family sought refuge from their quarters' leaking tin roof or the oily smoke of their stoves, they could flee twenty-eight miles to Las Vegas, a town of eight thousand which boasted lawns, sidewalks, trolleys, a variety of stores, gas and water systems, and telephones. Fort Union and its environs was the West, but in 1887 it was the civilized West. Army life for an officer had its hardships, but there was no slide into primitivism at Fort Union. The post culture of the Tenth Infantry was not so much a tale told by James Fenimore Cooper as it was a romance by Booth Tarkington or an illustration by James Montgomery Flagg.[32]

"Mister" Bullard received the normal assignments for his rank: shepherding recruits for the Sixth Cavalry at Fort Wingate in the northwest part of the territory, general court-martial duty, minor jobs as assistant engineering officer and assistant signal officer for Fort Union, and range officer at Fort Wingate at the district and departmental rifle matches. He hunted, rode, and fished. An amiable and articulate young man with good manners and breeding, he swam smoothly around the rocks and shoals of the post's personal rivalries and frictions. He avoided the quarrels between Colonel Douglass and Peter Cleary over whether the post surgeon should be called major or doctor. He was not a passionate gambler, hard drinker, or strong swearer as some of the older officers were. He was not one of Douglass' favorites. Nevertheless, he made friends and fit into the Tenth Infantry family.

In the spring of 1888 Bullard married Rose Brabson. His quiet, convenient romance with Rose had grown after his return from Fort Bliss. For a young officer with no income or attachments outside the army, Rose was a perfect wife: frugal, already accustomed to post life, socially adept, unassuming, and loyal to the army. Pleasant but shy, attractive but not vivacious, Rose Brabson had only one striking personal trait: she was a devout Catholic. In the cosmopolitan and generally agnostic frontier army officer corps, such religious devotion, especially to a faith as suspect as Catholicism, was unusual. Nevertheless, the Bullards never suffered any discrimination because of Rose's religious faith, although she herself, blighted by illness and family separations in later years, became increasingly withdrawn.

Married at Fort Wingate where Doctor Cleary was then stationed, the Bullards set up housekeeping with Rose's stepfather, for Bullard stayed at Fort Wingate as a competitor in the department rifle matches. In an army in which marksmanship was the rage, he became an excellent rifle shot. In August the Bullards took leave and visited Oak Bowery to see Daniel Bullard and his kin. Then Bullard and his pregnant wife returned to Fort Union, anticipating a quiet and comfortable winter together. Instead, barely settled, they had to move to Fort Marcy, the garrison in Santa Fe, because the War Department had finally decided to close Fort Union. With the regimental headquarters, band, and another company, Company F arrived at Fort Marcy on Christmas Eve 1888. Quarters were not available, and the Bullards had to live with another couple. Insecure and uncomfortable, they suffered a personal tragedy when Rose miscarried and nearly died in the hands of an incompetent surgeon, an experience which broke Rose's health and emotional stability for five years. In the spring of 1889 Rose went East to live with her mother, the first of many lengthy family separations for the Bullards. Army life began to pale for the young officer.[33]

The months in Santa Fe rolled by without event, and Bullard went about his duties with Company F. Month after month the regimental returns bore the monotonous entries: ". . . on duty with company . . . the companies performed the normal garrison duties at their respective stations during the month." Again Bullard spent the summer shooting and became a member of the department team which went to California to fire in the division matches. Rose rejoined him, and the summer was pleasant. Then it was time to move again. Company F was ordered to Fort Leavenworth, Kansas, site of the Infantry and Cavalry School, to become part of the demonstration troops. It was not an unwelcome change of station, for Fort Leavenworth was an old, large, and comfortable post near Kansas City. The Bullards were leaving the frontier.

Nearly four years to the day on which he came to Fort Union, Bullard rode eastward with his company and his wife. He was now a full member in the Tenth Infantry society; he was an integral part of the tight mesh of personal relations that shaped the life of a frontier regiment. His company life and his relations with the Tenth's other officers were his army. Occasionally he had made friends outside the regiment, either in the rifle matches or by sharing a post with troops from other regiments. He had in this way gotten to know two cavalry majors, Samuel and Edmund V. Sumner, Jr., both of whom gave Bullard "the encouragement of their confidence, friendship and favor." Sons of a Civil War general and veterans themselves of that war, the Sumner brothers were widely known in the army as excellent officers and sympathetic superiors. To be their friend was acknowledgement of a love of soldiering equal to theirs.[34] But beyond these personal examples—the Sumners, Seyburn, John Stretch—and the memories of West Point, the army was still largely unknown to Bullard. Some things he knew: that promotion was slow and unpredictable since it depended on vacancies within one's own regiment; that army record-keeping and personal accountability for funds and property were strict; that army regulations were numerous, inconsistent, and often bewildering; that duty and a stable family life often conflicted. These things he learned and accepted in Company F.

But his own destiny and that of the army's were not yet the same. While he had not become apathetic or cynical about army life, he had not become utterly wedded to his career. Instead he had spent four valuable years simply learning about himself and the nature of officership. The closed society of post life had been a useful arena for this education, for his relations with his fellow officers and their wives gave him a daily measure of his maturity and military efficiency. Their mild esteem fed his own self-respect and confidence. But his socialization and search for self-knowledge had little bearing on even his company. Since his duties after the Geronimo campaign put so few demands on him, his personal contributions were equally limited. The army expected nothing from its second lieutenants beyond the conscientious performance of duties long defined by custom and tradition.

Bullard's frontier service did nothing to damage his growing nationalism. In the New Mexico territory, the army was the most obvious representative of national interests and needs. In a culture still marked by violence, rampant individualism, racial intolerance, and material gain, the United States Army represented order, stability, personal sacrifice, and the coming of civilized government. That this symbolic role was a creation of the officers' imaginations is undeniable, but it gave many of them a powerful sense of purpose that chasing Indians did not. Too often, the officers believed, the civilians who demanded their services were too narrow and self-seeking to recognize that they were part of an American nation. The army, however, was the living symbol of the Republic. At no time was this more obvious or moving than at Fort Union's evening dress parade and retreat. Every evening at 5:45 the infantrymen, seldom more than two hundred men at the post, marched onto the parade ground, led by their officers in dress frock coats and swords. Each evening the ritual was the same: the stentorian commands, the slap of hands on weapons, the wheeling, pivoting, foot-stamping movements of the drill, the martial airs of the band. Then with the crash of the evening gun, the band struck up the National Anthem. Backs rigid, eyes narrow under their spiked dress helmets, the soldiers watched the colors drop slowly down the flagstaff. To the west the sun dropped behind the mesa, perhaps gilding a cloud or two drifting across the pale sky. As the last notes of the Star Spangled Banner faded and the troops passed in review, it was hard not to believe that one might share some collective destiny with the Republic and the army.

NOTES

[1]For the general description of the army between the Civil War and the War with Spain, see Russell F. Weigley, *History of the United States Army* (New York: Macmillan, 1967), pp. 264-92. See also the *Annual Reports of the War Department, 1885* (Washington: Government Printing Office, 1885).

[2]For the pre-Civil War period see Forest G. Hill, *Roads, Rails and Waterways: The Army Engineers and Early Transportation* (Norman, Okla.: University of Oklahoma Press, 1957), and William H. Goetzmann, *Army Exploration in the American West, 1803-1863* (New Haven: Yale University Press, 1959); and for the entire nineteenth century, see W Stull Holt, *The Office of the Chief of Engineers of the Army* (Baltimore: John Hopkins Press, 1923).

For descriptions of the life-style of army engineers, see Edward B. Clark, *William E. Sibert: The Army Engineer* (Philadelphia: Dorrance and Company, 1930); Joseph Bucklin Bishop and Farnham Bishop, *Goethals: Genius of the Panama Canal* (New York: Harper and Brothers, 1930), pp. 53-270; and the letters of Brigadier General Jay Johnson Morrow (USMA, 1891) to Mr. and Mrs. James E. Morrow, 1891-1918, Manuscript Division, Duke University Library.

'For an excellent description of coast defense artillery, see Emanuel Raymond Lewis, *Seacoast Fortifications of the United States: An Introductory History* (Washington: Smithsonian Institution Press, 1970), pp. 66-100. See Also William E. Birkhimer, *Historical Sketch of the Organization, Administration, Material and Tactics of the Artillery, United States Army* (Washington: Chapman, 1884), and A.C.M. Azoy, "Great Guns: A History of the Coast Artillery Corps," *Coast Artillery Journal* 84 (1941), pp. 426-34.

For my characterization of the life of a coast artillery officer, I used George O. Squier, "Artillery Notes," "Personal Orders and Letters, 1895," and "Biographical Sketch of Major General George Owen Squier, Chief Signal Officer of the Army," all in the Squier Papers, Michigan Historical Collections, and the diaries of Wirt Robinson for 1887-1898, USMA Library.

'There are sketches of the departments and bureaus in Theophilus F. Rodenbaugh and William L. Haskin, eds., *The Army of the United States: Historical Sketches of Staff and Line* (New York: Maynard, Merrill & Co., 1896), a compilation of articles which appeared in the *Journal of the Military Service Institution (JMSI)* in the 1890s. See also The Adjutant General's Office, *Legislative History of the General Staff of the Army of the United States* (Washington: Government Printing Office, 1901), and L. D. Ingersoll, *A History of the War Department of the United States, with Biographical Sketches of the Secretaries* (Washington: Francis D. Mohun, 1880).

'Erna Risch, *Quartermaster Support of the Army: A History of the Corps, 1775-1939* (Washington: Government Printing Office, 1962), pp. 452-514; P. M. Ashburn, *A History of the Medical Department of the United States Army* (Boston: Houghton Mifflin, 1929); Leonard D. White, *The Republican Era: 1869-1901* (New York: Macmillan, 1958), pp. 134-153.

For excellent descriptions of careers in the bureaucratic army, see Mabel E. Deutrich, *Struggle for Supremacy: The Career of General Fred C. Ainsworth* (Washington: Public Affairs Press, 1962), and Russell F. Weigley, *Quartermaster General of the Union Army: A Biography of M.C. Meigs* (New York: Columbia University Press, 1959). Representative of post-frontier medical service is John M. Gibson, *Soldier in White: The Life of General George Miller Sternberg* (Durham, N. C.: Duke University Press, 1958).

'The Staff-Line imbroglio is synthesized in Stephen Ambrose, *Upton and the Army* (Baton Rouge: Louisiana State University Press, 1964), pp. 85-135; Bernard L. Boylan, "The Forty-Fifth Congress and Army Reform," *Mid-America* 41 (July 1959), pp. 173-186; Lester D. Langley, "The Democratic Tradition and Military Reform, 1878-1885," *Southwestern Social Science Quarterly* 48 (September 1967), pp. 192-200; and Richard A. Andrews, "Years of Frustration: William T. Sherman, the Army, and Reform, 1869-1883" (unpublished Ph.D. dissertation, Northwestern University, 1968).

'For descriptions of soldier life in the frontier army, see Don Rickey, Jr., *Forty Miles a Day on Beans and Hay: The Enlisted Soldier Fighting the Indian Wars* (Norman, Okla.: University of Oklahoma Press, 1963), and Jack D. Foner, *The United States Soldier between Two Wars: Army Life and Reform, 1865-1898* (New York: Humanities Press, 1970).

The statistics are from "Report of the Surgeon General," *Annual Reports of the War Department, 1885,* I, pp. 588, 593.

[8]1st Lt. Stephen Y. Seyburn, *History of the Tenth United States Infantry* (Santa Fe, N. M., n. p., 1890), and "The Tenth Regiment of Infantry," *JMSI* 13 (March 1892), pp. 415-428; "Returns of the Tenth Infantry Regiment, January, 1880-December, 1890," reel 116 in "Returns from Regular Army Infantry Regiments, June 1821-December 1916," Microcopy 665, National Archives. Hereafter cited by month and Returns, Tenth Infantry.

[9]"Tenth Infantry," The Adjutant-General's Office, *Official Army Register, 1885* (Washington: Government Printing Office, 1885), pp. 136-38.

The most detailed picture of the personalities and duties of the regiment's officers is in the manuscript memoir of Colonel William Paulding, Paulding Papers, U.S. Army Military History Research Collection, Carlisle Barracks, Pennsylvania (USAMHRC). See also E. H. Plummer, "Henry Douglass," in Association of Graduates, *Annual Reunion, June 9th, 1893,* USMA Library.

[10]Leo E. Oliva, *Soldiers on the Santa Fe Trail* (Norman, Okla.: University of Oklahoma Press, 1967), pp. 167-201; Chris Emmett, *Fort Union and the Winning of the Southwest* (Norman, Okla.: University of Oklahoma Press, 1965); Herbert M. Hart, *Old Forts of the Southwest* (Seattle: Superior Publishing Company, 1964), pp. 122-26; and Robert M. Utley, *Fort Union National Monument, New Mexico,* National Park Service Handbook Series No. 35 (Washington: Government Printing Office, 1962).

[11]Diarybook autobiography, p. 44, and Bullard autobiography, p. 14, BP; September, 1885, Returns, Tenth Infantry, Reel 116, MC 665.

[12]Diarybook autobiography, p. 45, BP.

[13]For the background of the Apache wars, I have relied primarily on Dan L. Thrapp, *The Conquest of Apacheria* (Norman, Okla.: University of Oklahoma Press, 1967). See also Ralph H. Ogle, *Federal Control of the Western Apaches, 1848-1886* (Albuquerque, N. M.: New Mexico Historical Society, 1940).

[14]Crook's approach to Apache pacification is explained in Martin F. Schmitt, ed., *General Crook, His Autobiography* (Norman, Okla.: University of Oklahoma Press, 1960); John G. Bourke, *On the Border with Crook* (New York: Scribner's, 1891); and Britton Davis, *The Truth About Geronimo* (New Haven: Yale University Press, 1929). See also Joyce E. Mason, "The Use of Indian Scouts in the Apache Wars, 1870-1886" (unpublished Ph.D. dissertation, Indiana University, 1970).

[15]Davis, *The Truth About Geronimo,* pp. 142-143; Jason Betinez as edited by W. S. Nye, *I Fought with Geronimo* (Harrisburg, Pa.: Stackpole Press, 1959).

[16]See Virginia Johnson, *The Unregimented General: A Biography of Nelson A. Miles* (Boston: Houghton Mifflin, 1962), pp. 225-257, and Nelson A. Miles, *Personal Recollections and Observations of General Nelson A. Miles* (Chicago: The Werner Company, 1896), pp. 432-532, for Miles' account of the Geronimo campaign.

[17]The organization and tribulations of Lawton's command are best reconstructed in Lawton's letters to his wife May, June 21-September 2, 1886, Henry L. Lawton Papers, Manuscript Division, Library of Congress, and the Leonard Wood journals, May 4, 1886-September 8, 1886, Wood Papers. The latter is reproduced in Jack C. Lane, ed., *Chasing Geronimo: The Journal of Leonard Wood, May-September, 1886* (Albuquerque, N. M.: University of New Mexico Press, 1970). For the organization of the command, see Lane, *Chasing Geronimo,* pp. 25-46. See also Hermann Hagedorn, *Leonard Wood* (New York: Harper and Brothers, 1931), I, pp. 48-103. Maj. H. C. Benson, "The Geronimo

Campaign," *Army and Navy Journal* (July 3, 1909), pp. 1240-1241, is another participant's account.

[18]Diarybook autobiography, pp. 44-46, BP; November 1885-August 1886, Returns, Tenth Infantry, Reel 116, MC 665; "Report of Colonel Bradley" (Commanding Officer, District of New Mexico), *Annual Reports of the War Department, 1886* (Washington: Government Printing Office, 1886), I, 181-84.

[19]Entries, Wood Journal, June 11-July 13, 1886, in Lane, *Chasing Geronimo*, pp. 49-72; "Report of Captain Lawton," *Annual Reports of the War Department, 1886*, I, pp. 176-181.

[20]James Parker, *The Old Army: Memories, 1872-1918* (Philadelphia: Dorrance and Company, 1929), pp. 149-90; *Army and Navy Journal*, (July 17, 1886); and Brig. Gen. James Parker, "The Geronimo Campaign," *Proceedings of the Annual Meeting and Dinner of the Order of Indian Wars of the United States* (Washington: n. p., 1929), pp. 32-44.

[21]Diarybook autobiography, pp. 51-53, and Bullard autobiography, pp. 16-17, BP.

[22]Parker, *The Old Army,* p. 176.

[23]Charles B. Gatewood, "The Surrender of Geronimo," *Proceedings of the Annual Meeting and Dinner of the Order of Indian Wars of the United States* (Washington: n.p., 1929), pp. 49-61.

[24]Parker, *The Old Army*, pp. 177-78; Entry, Wood journal, August 3, 1886, in Lane, *Chasing Geronimo*, pp. 87-89.

[25]Diarybook autobiography, pp. 54-55, BP.

[26]Lane, *Chasing Geronimo*, pp. 136-137; Col. R. L. Bullard to Brig. Gen. Leonard Wood, February 13, 1901, Wood Papers; and Maj. Gen. L. Wood to Capt. F. R. McCoy, July 20, 1909, General Correspondence, Frank R. McCoy Papers, Manuscript Division, Library of Congress: *Army and Navy Journal*, September 1, 1886.

[27]Charles Byars, ed., "Gatewood Reports to His Wife from Geronimo's Camp," *The Journal of Arizona History* 7 (Summer 1966), pp. 76-81.

[28]Parker, *The Old Army*, pp. 180-181; Entry, Wood Journal, September 1, 1886, in Lane, *Chasing Geronimo,* p. 109.

[29]"Report of Brigadier-General Miles," *Annual Reports of the War Department, 1887* (Washington: Government Printing Officer, 1887), I, pp. 158-163; Miles, *Personal Recollections and Observations*, pp. 533-544.

[30]William H. Carter, *Old Army Sketches* (Baltimore: The Lord Baltimore Press, 1906), pp. 107, 130.

[31]Dale F. Giese, "Soldiers at Play: A History of Social Life at Fort Union, New Mexico, 1851-1891" (unpublished Ph.D. dissertation, University of New Mexico, 1969); reminiscences of Charles N. Jansen, J. E. Rouk, Henry Backes, and George Neihaus, all enlisted men in the Tenth Infantry, to Dr. Don Rickey, Jr., in 1954, transcripts in the USAMHRC.

[32]In addition to Giese, "Soldiers at Play: A History of Social Life at Fort Union," previously cited, I have relied on the following sources: Bullard diarybook autobiography, pp. 54-56, BP; Genevieve LaTourrette, "Fort Union Memories," *New Mexico Historical Review* 26 (October 1951), pp. 277-286; George B. Duncan, "Reminiscences," pp. 15-18; Thomas Cruse, *Apache Days and After* (Caldwell, Ida.: Caxton Printers, 1941), pp. 235-237.

For other accounts of post life in the Southwest, see Beaumont Buck, *Memories of War and Peace* (San Antonio: The Naylor Company, 1935), pp. 38-46; Alice B. Baldwin, *Memoirs of the Late Frank D. Baldwin, Major General, U.S.A.* (Los Angeles: Wetzel Publishing Company, 1929), pp. 12-17; Frank D. Reeve, ed., ''Frederick E. Phelps; A Soldier's Memoirs,'' *New Mexico Historical Review* 25 (July-October 1950), pp. 37-57, 109-135, 187-221, and 305-327; Frances A. M. Roe, *Army Letters from an Officer's Wife, 1871-1888* (New York: D. Appleton, 1909); Martha Summerhayes, *Vanished Arizona*: *Recollections of My Army Life* (Chicago: Lakeside Press, 1939). Critical of the influence of wives on official army matters is Duane M. Greene, *Ladies and Officers of the United States Army*: *or, American Aristocracy* (Chicago: Central Publishing Company, 1888).

[33]Diarybook autobiography, pp. 56-58, PB.

[34]Bullard autobiography, p. 19, BP; Reeve, ''Frederick E. Phelps; A Soldier's Memoirs,'' pp. 116-117, 308-311.

4

Leaving the Line
1889-1898

When the German General Staff published a comprehensive survey of the world's military forces in 1897, it excluded the United States Army from its study. The American army was not sufficiently important to describe, although the armies of Spain, Portugal, Switzerland, and Montenegro were. Indeed, the analysts of the *Grosser Generalstab* may have decided that, by European standards, the United States did not have an army. However slighted American officers might have felt, they would have agreed that the military posture of the United States was hardly worth serious note by Europeans.

Certainly in the sense that a Prussian officer understood it, the United States had no military system to provide either the professional leadership or mass trained manpower which war between industrialized nations demanded. American officers served a nation which flaunted its defenselessness for land warfare in innumerable ways; the United States spent only 13 percent of its small federal budget on the army, had only one West Point graduate per 1.28 million people, boasted more senators than colonels of the Line, paid its privates one-third the wage of a city policeman, and had proportionately fewer organized militiamen than it had before the Civil War. American officers probably would have agreed with General Nelson A. Miles that the nation should give thanks for a broad ocean and the friendship of Great Britain.[1]

For the line officers of the United States Army the last decade of the century was a period of intellectual crisis. The end of the Indian wars dramatized the fact that the combatant forces of the army were unprepared for any mission outside their Indian-police role. Few mourned the end of the Indian wars, and few would have characterized the last serious fighting, the destruction of the Ghost Dance movement in 1890, as a major military accomplishment. Only an officer as hyperbolic as Miles could have described the suicidal rebellion as "the most gigantic Indian conspiracy and threatened uprising that has ever occurred in the history of this country—far surpassing in magnitude the conspiracies of Pontiac, Tecumseh or Red Jacket."[2] Brigadier General Anson Mills on the eve of his retirement in 1897, on the other hand, could not believe that frontier service had profited either the army or the nation. Isolated in the West, the army was not and never had been "organized in its own interest, the interests of the people, nor in harmony with the other institutions of the Republic."[3] As Brigadier General Wesley Merritt pointed out in *Harper's Monthly*, the closing of the frontier would allow the Line to match the engineers and staff departments in useful service.[4]

Just what service the Line would perform was a matter of debate. Against a background of rising labor violence and ethnic strife, some officers suggested that the army concentrate on becoming a national police to stop political violence. While the army should not align itself with the interests of "capital," wrote First Lieutenant William Wallace in an 1895 essay, it should clearly be committed to constituted authority and opposed to any interest which subverted "the principles of liberal government." Wallace recognized that the federal government had no effective enforcement agency except its marshals, whose service in riot duty was like "meeting a lawless mob with a lawful crowd." By quick, impartial law enforcement, the army might regain popular prestige and contribute to domestic tranquillity.[5] But someone else had the riot duty mission, the National Guard of the states, and there was little in the National Guard's experience that made the mission attractive. As one National Guard general pointed out, the armed suppression of civil disobedience was a political and military nightmare. While riot duty had brought some increase in state support to the National Guard, it had done nothing to make military service more respectable.[6] The regular army's own limited experience, especially in the Pullman strike of 1894 and mine strikes in the Rockies, had taught similar lessons. Few army officers and National Guardsmen were enthusiastic about suppressing labor violence.[7]

The line officers' preferred mission was sanctioned by American society and international professional military thought: defense of the nation's geographic borders against foreign invasion. Although the army's regiments had seldom been stationed to perform this mission, the regular army of the nineteenth century never quite forgot that it might have to fight to throw back an invader. The role of coast and border defense, however, was the responsibility of the navy, the coast artillery, and the organized militia, not the infantry and cavalry. In the 1880s the federal government, stimulated by an awareness of the rapid developments of weapons and naval design, conducted several investigations of the defenses against invasion. The War Department's major inquiry was performed by a board of army and navy officers and two congressmen whose chairman was Secretary of War William C. Endicott. The Endicott Board's findings matched those of earlier studies by the Navy Department and Major General John M. Schofield, commander of the Division of the Atlantic: the United States was virtually helpless in the face of invasion. This conclusion was no comfort to the Line, however, for the Congress' attention then focused upon providing the navy with a modern battlefleet. Only secondarily did the federal government provide funds for new coastal fortifications and ordnance. By 1895, ten years after the Endicott Board's findings, the Congress had appropriated only one-ninth of the $127 million expenditure the Board recommended. The actual improvement of coast defenses was even more limited.[8]

The renewed interest in coast defense brought immediate change only to the artillery regiments. Much of the reform remained theoretical since the Congress seldom provided the money for much gunnery practice. Each round cost between $21 and $64, and the War Department's budget could not absorb such expensive fireworks displays.[9] Nevertheless, Schofield remained convinced that coast defense priorities were critical, and when he became commanding general of the army in 1888, he established a permanent agency, the Board of Ordnance and Fortification, to push reform.[10]

Schofield, however, was not satisfied that the army had done all it could to defend the nation's borders and coasts. The end of the Indian wars and the continued pressure from the secretary of war to economize provided a rationale for concentrating the scattered cavalry and infantry regiments on large posts, suitable both for maneuvers and rapid railroad travel to the nation's edges. By 1890 the consolidation of regiments and the closing of frontier posts was well underway, and it was continued by Schofield's successor, Nelson Miles. Although many infantry and cavalry officers were untouched and thus insensitive to the gradual redeployment, the frontier army was headed East for the first time since the Civil War and back into the national consciousness.[11]

Reiterating the reforms proposed by General Sherman in the 1870s, a few officers flooded the professional press in the 1890s, a symptom of intellectual ferment. In a decade in which every major American institution met severe challenge, the War Department received its share of criticism, but in this case the muckrakers wore blue. The voice for the officer-reformers was the *Journal of the Military Service Institution*, established by officers in 1878 as a conduit for foreign military information and professional articles, and the newspaper *Army and Navy Journal*, a semiofficial weekly managed by the army's ardent champion in Washington, William C. Church. By and large the authors were line officers, and their reforms assumed that the Line's highest duty was the army's highest priority—the preparation for war with another modern nation.[12]

In an intellectual sense the line officer-reformers, which included men of all ages and ranks, called for a reordering of the army's organizational assumptions and values. They called for the adoption inside the officer corps of a uniquely military professional ethic: that the essential mission of all officers was to cultivate the values, attitudes, and organizational forms best suited for the systematic study and scientific conduct of war. They viewed civilian intellectuals' belief in the indestructibility of the Republic as frivolous optimism. As one lieutenant put it in an essay which won a Military Service Institution prize in 1893: "we find that civilization has not advanced to the point of making arbitration universal and war obsolete, and that a nation's only safety against imposition lies in being able to enforce and defend its rights by might."[13] Watching the government's diplomacy in the 1890s, these officers echoed much of the expansionist rhetoric of the decade. By and large they were not imperialists, but they felt that the competition of American and European trade in Latin America and American construction of an isthmian canal might very well bring war. An obscure lieutenant of cavalry named

James Guthrie Harbord wrote that "at no distant day the possession of Cuba and the adjacent isles will be essential to the protection of our interests in the canal across the Isthmus," and Captain Arthur Williams asserted in 1897 that "if we are to maintain our place among nations, we must enlarge and extend our intercourse with Central and South America. In doing so we are likely to come in conflict with other nations, and should be so prepared as, if possible, to avoid war, or if compelled to take up arms to do so promptly and effectively."[14] In a decade that saw the government consider punitive action against Chile in 1891, threaten Great Britain in 1895 over European intervention in Venezuela, and debate intervention against Spain in Cuba after 1895, such views were neither jingoistic nor naive.

With future war assumed, the reformers argued that the army must be reorganized for combat readiness. Drawing upon the European military practices as interpreted and popularized by Emory Upton in an earlier era, the reformers urged that the War Department be run primarily by line officers, who would put mobilization readiness and tactical matters first. As Brigadier General John Gibbon observed, the prevailing pattern of administration had been both too fragmented by the staff departments and overly centralized in Washington; the army was rapidly becoming "a mere *paper* machine."[15] The line officers' solution was the creation of a General Staff on the Prussian model, a collaborative body of peacetime planners and wartime managers who would shape policy to meet the Line's conception of wartime needs.

The Line's search for a new identity affected the reformers' vision of how the nation should provide for a large wartime army. Again following the writings of Upton, the reformers proposed that the federal government have sole responsibility for raising and officering the citizen-soldiers who would volunteer for wartime service. The most extreme reformers flirted with the idea of peacetime conscription, but most officers advocated a volunteer reserve trained to the Line's standards. The actual authorization and funding of such a reserve by Congress was an unobtainable ideal, and most officers knew it.

The only viable alternative was to increase the Line's influence on the National Guard and the cadets of the land-grant colleges created by the Morrill Act of 1862. By 1890 the pattern of increased army interest in both the National Guard and the student-cadets was well established. Working with the Congress and the National Guard Association, the War Department lobbied for federal subsidies for civilian rifle clubs and a doubling of the National Guard's federal funding to $400,000 in 1887. As the line regiments took garrisons in the East and Midwest, joint summer training camps with the National Guard were arranged and officers were detailed as temporary inspector-instructors for National Guard encampments. The Adjutant General collected inspection reports on the National Guard and lobbied for another increase in federal subsidy, but the Congress was not yet ready to sanction the army's growing influence on the National Guard. Nevertheless, informal persuasion and liaison with reformist National Guard officers convinced some army officers that the National Guard might be an able reserve in wartime.[16]

For all their logic and passion, the reformist officers were frustrated by public apathy, congressional economizing, and the absence of a menacing foreign invader. Whatever reforms worked their way from print into the army's daily life had to be worked in the existing army. The 1890s did bring change. In 1890 Secretary of War Redfield Proctor, a self-proclaimed expert on personnel management, sponsored a series of reforms in the regulations governing the promotion of line officers. Before he left office the next year he had gotten legislation passed which required examinations for advancement to first lieutenant and captain, promotion of lieutenants and captains by seniority within a branch rather than within a regiment, and the annual submission of efficiency reports on all officers. It was a modest attempt to equalize promotion and to weed out the grossest incompetents, but without expansion of the officer corps or the adoption of some form of promotion by selection system, these reforms were insignificant. Line officers might be promoted a year or two earlier, but they still spent over fifteen years as lieutenants; the number of officers eliminated for failing their examinations was inconsequential; and the efficiency reports had no bearing on promotion. Proctor himself was not especially moved by professional reform motives anyway, for he cut the number of cavalry troops in each regiment from twelve to ten and the companies in each infantry regiment from ten to eight, doing so because he thought he could eliminate a number of officer billets in each regiment.[17]

The major reform which affected the officer corps was the growing stress on formal professional education. Before the Civil War, the War Department recognized the need for additional technical training for engineers and artillery, but not until 1881 was a similar school created to instruct cavalry and infantry officers. Founded by General Sherman at Fort Leavenworth, Kansas, the School of Application for Infantry and Cavalry became a focal point of Line ferment. A decade after its founding, the Infantry and Cavalry School had partially evolved into an agency for training junior officers for high command or important staff positions in a large wartime army. Under the influence of First Lieutenant Arthur L. Wagner, the instruction at Leavenworth was shaped by the methods of the German officer-training system, primarily the historical study of campaigns and the use of wargames, either on maps or with troops. After 1888 the curriculum included problems teaching tactical problem-solving and the command of forces of all combatant arms. In 1890 Schofield, a patron of the school, ordered that the top three graduates in each class be recognized in the *Army Register*. Though its coursework was limited to lieutenants, the Infantry and Cavalry School became the institutional base for many of the Line's reformers.[18]

Since each class at the Infantry and Cavalry School included only one officer from each regiment, the school did not solve the Line's officer-training problems as General Sherman saw them. Sherman's primary concern was that so few of the Line's junior officers were West Point graduates. Sherman had some reason for his concern, for despite an increase in the proportion of West Point graduates in the officer corps after the Civil War, nearly half of all the army's officers had not attended the Academy. At the rank of captain (commanders of companies, troops, and batteries), non-West Pointers outnumbered West Pointers three to one in

1891.[19] Without formal Academy training, Sherman feared, officers would not have the motivation or intellectual standards necessary for professional excellence. In an article written shortly before his death, Sherman spelled out his credo for officers:

> As for the subaltern . . . he must devote his whole time to his daily duties and to his studies, which will better prepare him for the accidents of war that always come suddenly and unexpectedly, especially in this country; and, above all, he must never harbor a thought of doubt as to the allegiance due to his government and the officers appointed to administer it. With its politics he had nothing to do whatever.[20]

Officer education then had its ethical purposes; it was to keep officers from meddling in commerce and politics as well as to extend the officers' military knowledge.[21]

In 1891, Schofield extended Sherman's program to each post by ordering the creation of post lyceums. At every post the officers would educate themselves by presenting papers on military subjects or by reading and discussing the books used at West Point and Leavenworth. As an educational device, the lyceums were of limited value because the senior officers (and many junior) treated them as a farce. One captain, for example, gave the same paper every year, changing only the title.[22] In addition, the whole phenomenon of academic soldiering embarrassed some senior officers; one colonel of infantry thought that an order to each his officers the principles of fire discipline meant that he had to instruct his command in fire-fighting.[23] In such an unencouraging environment, the only serious students were usually junior officers who were self-motivated and who wanted to attend Leavenworth. The idea that officership meant continuing education in professional matters was not a concept that seized the officer corps.[24] Sometimes it was hard for line officers to remember the thunderous words of the dead Sherman which graced the masthead of the *Journal of the Military Service Institution*:

> I cannot help plead to my countrymen, at every opportunity to cherish all that is manly and noble in the military profession, because Peace is enervating and no man is wise enough to foretell when soldiers may be in demand again.

1.

Built on wooded bluffs above the Missouri, Fort Leavenworth was a small city of brick and frame buildings, barracks, and officers' quarters. As the headquarters of the Department of Missouri, an ordnance depot, the army disciplinary barracks, and the Infantry and Cavalry School, the post was home for sixty officers, six hundred enlisted men, and one hundred and ten military prisoners. The line garrison, assigned for tactical training to the school, included a light artillery battery, four troops of cavalry, and four infantry companies. A model post in appearance and management, Fort Leavenworth was commanded by one of the army's most respected senior officers, Colonel (Brevet Major General) Alexander McDowell McCook. The officers' social life at Fort Leavenworth was extremely pleasant. Except in the deep of summer, the post had a continuous stream of eastern visitors, card parties, dances, theater and musical productions, lectures, and "at homes." There were so many bachelor officers that the post had an officers' mess, and Fort Leavenworth was a favored hunting ground for young ladies. High-ranking and retired officers and congressmen streamed in and out of the post on business and pleasure. In addition the post had ample facilities for boating and baseball. For officers fresh from the frontier, Fort Leavenworth was a military mecca.[25]

Arriving at their new station in September 1889, the two officers, twenty-nine men and assorted wives and children of Company F, Tenth Infantry, quickly adjusted to Fort Leavenworth's routine. Bullard was most impressed with the rigor of the Infantry and Cavalry School's training and the students' competitiveness. The officers' work opened a vista of army life beyond the routine paperwork and social life. Here "was an army school whose teachings were turning the army from a mere Indian police to its true function, the art of war."[26] Although only a troop officer, Bullard attended lectures and problems and read the texts. Moreover, he made friends with many other lieutenants, went to the meetings of the post branch of the Military Service Institution, and rekindled his interest in the study of law, Spanish, heliography and telegraphy, surveying, and military history. But his ultimate goal, formal assignment to the school as a student, was denied him. Twice he requested assignment, since his company was already there. Twice the major general commanding replied that such an assignment was impossible since the Tenth Infantry's quota was filled by other officers.[27] While Bullard was stationed at Fort Leavenworth, he saw three other lieutenants from the Tenth Infantry arrive and graduate. His frustration was considerable, for all three were his juniors.[28]

Bullard's regular duties were little different from those at Fort Union. His most challenging assignment was serving as range officer for his friend, Major Edwin V. Sumner, who was inspector of small arms practice for the department. For three long summers Bullard's world was a montage of bucking Springfields, acrid smoke, hot cartridges, and punctured targets. Other than an occasional assignment to a court-martial, Bullard conducted the routine inspections and drill for Company F and helped Captain Stretch with his reports. Only once in three years did the company leave Leavenworth, going to nearby Fort Riley in December 1890 for a short field exercise.[29]

Though he performed his regular duties with competence, Bullard got little pleasure from them and found his family life a positive trial. While stationed at Fort Leavenworth, he and Rose were constantly "ranked" out of quarters by other married officers; each class of lieutenants had more married men than bachelors and the quarters merry-go-round caused severe morale problems on the post.[30] In addition, the Bullards had their first two children, both sons, Robert Lee, Junior, and Peter Cleary, at Fort Leavenworth. Going in and out of childbirth, Rose was constantly bedridden and ill, which both irritated Bullard and made him feel guilty about his irritation. His own health was not good. Socially, the Bullards made no impression on a socially conscious post, and Bullard made the newspapers only when his setter pup was stolen and when he left Leavenworth. His major recognition was that he had ably managed the enlisted mens' canteen.[31]

Perhaps his discontent with his duties and family life made him more philosophical. For the first time in his career, he started jotting down notes. His initial observation was that his experiences at Fort Leavenworth had convinced him of his inability to control his own career. It was difficult, he thought, to recognize opportunities and he had missed many which he had seen only in hindsight. Even when he had seen opportunities for useful service, he had been unable to act. He vowed that in the future he would seize every opportunity immediately.[32] His major problem, he concluded, was that he had no self-confidence because he did not know himself well enough, a thought which came to him while reading Shakespeare and Thackery. He concluded that his first job must be to develop self-discipline through self-denial, "the mother of independence and self-reliance." Once in command of himself, he could command others with confidence. He also decided to keep his own ambitions silent so his peers would not recognize and ridicule his failures. Above all, he would learn to cope with change and to adjust quickly. "Change is not disorder. Many people make it so, but needlessly in most cases and often to their own confusion. Learn order in change and you thus acquire one of the principles of rational life."[33]

If he doubted himself, Bullard's superiors did not. His efficiency reports characterized him as an officer of professional accomplishment and excellent conduct and habits. His regimental commander called him a "remarkably good company officer," a model of energy, studiousness, and initiative. When Bullard was examined on all phases of the duties of an infantry officer for promotion to first lieutenant, the three line officers of his promotion board judged his answers "excellent" or "very good." In 1892, he got the new shoulder-straps of a first lieutenant.[34]

His promotion, however, created new problems, for it meant transfer to another regiment. Apparently, he was considered too valuable an officer for the Tenth to lose, for while he and Rose visited Oak Bowery on leave, his colonel arranged his transfer back to the Tenth to fill a new vacancy in Company G. The assignment, however, meant Bullard's return to the frontier, for his company was stationed at Fort Reno in the Oklahoma Territory. His orders were delayed only long enough for him to be present when his second son was born. Leaving his family at Fort Leavenworth, he joined his new company.[35]

2.

Upon arriving at Fort Reno, Bullard learned the reason for his assignment: the company commander was on medical leave awaiting disability discharge and Company G was about to change stations. Under Bullard's command, the thirty-eight men of Company G left Fort Reno and moved to Fort Stanton, New Mexico Territory, a post established near the Mescalero and Jicarilla Apache reservation in the southern part of the territory. Bullard was again an Indian policeman.[36]

Set on a small reservation of sixteen square miles, Fort Stanton was eight miles from the town of Lincoln and one hundred miles from the nearest railroad. The department commander regarded the post as useless since the agency was actually run by Indian agents and Apache police. The post itself was pleasant enough, an open, shaded village of frame and stone barracks built beside the Rio Bonito, a mountain stream that brought trout onto the post. Since the post had been built for four companies and now held only E and G companies of the Tenth Infantry, there was ample room for the officers and men. But in 1892 the post was an anachronism.[37]

For the Bullard family, the Fort Stanton years began badly and did not improve. After getting Company G settled, Bullard went back to Leavenworth for Rose and his infant sons. On the trek from the railroad, Bullard's ambulance was caught in a blizzard, and only when he found a draw could he get his wailing and shivering family out of the wind.[38] For the next two years the Bullard household was characterized by misery and anarchy as Rose was sick and despondent; her state of mind was not improved by the birth of another child, a girl, "Little" Rose, in August 1894. The post's social life was both limited and unpleasantly dominated by the post commander, an abrasive martinet. Only the presence of Stephen Seyburn, commanding Company E, and his family made the post bearable and gave the Bullards social companions.[39]

Bullard's duties as an acting company commander were routine enough, and when he relinquished them in May to a captain, he had even less to do. Over the two year period, however, he assumed the duties of post quartermaster, commissary, treasurer, adjutant, ordnance officer, engineer officer, and range officer. He took the company on hikes, checked the telegraph lines, and dabbled in coal properties without financial gain or loss. He read, and he participated in the post lyceum where the subjects of study were the *Drill Regulations* and Wagner's *The Service of Security and Information*. He stayed busy as best he could.[40]

Despite his consistently excellent performance of duty, Bullard was not satisfied with himself. In his notebooks he wrote contemptuously of his unreadiness for field service, his weary domestic life, and his lack of a plan to get a command more important than a platoon of infantry. He was convinced that preparation inspired oneself and others and led to opportunity. He was sure that his greatest challenge was to find the moral courage for success: to make "a systematic, practicable plan" and pursue it industriously, applying "an unforgetting determination that even, in the midst of distracting and deflecting influences, returns to the aim." In doing his duty, he would have to stop worrying about whom he might offend or upset, for to change one's decisions was "displaying a weakness totally unworthy of one who has the strength to do right. . . . Critics are not due tender treatment but may be disregarded without compunction or regret."[41]

In 1894, the War Department finally closed Fort Stanton and ordered Companies E and G to join two other companies of the Tenth Infantry at Fort Sill in the Oklahoma Territory. The change of station meant another miserable winter journey with Rose sick and three children howling their way northward by wagon and train. Bullard reflected that moving a family was "more difficult than to march an Army Corps the same distance."[42] The living conditions at Fort Sill were adequate enough. The post's buildings were surrounded by lawns, gravel walks, and pleasant shade trees. Fort Sill was, however, eight days by wagon to the nearest railroad and its garrison had little to do but drill and do the post housekeeping. Although the post was maintained to watch the Comanche and Kiowa reservation, Indian police and two companies of Indian soldiers did all the constabulary duties necessary. It was a military backwater.[43]

In the ten months the Bullards lived at Fort Sill, Bullard served as post quartermaster and commissary, fighting his way through the account ledgers, requisitions, and the obstruction of his two "drunken, thievish" sergeant-assistants. His home life did not improve, for Rose was either sick or despondent and often both. Bullard regarded the Fort Sill period as the nadir in his marriage.[44] Bullard himself continued his self-analysis. He decided that he would have to trust his own judgment as well as seek principles and great truths. He formed a set of priorities for himself; he would concentrate on his family's financial well-being, his "official duty and professional advancement and improvement," and his own health. He was certain that he would have to progress by his own effort, not as "the tail to someone else's kite." He had tried that and had not "risen an inch." Day in and day out he doggedly carried out his duties and increased his reputation as a painstaking, careful, and efficient officer. While his superiors judged that he had no outstanding or special talents, they valued his versatility and sound judgment. Lieutenant Bullard, at the age of thirty-five, was judged a solid candidate to be either a general's aide, quartermaster, or professor of military science and tactics at some university.[45]

3.

As did other army officers, Bullard sought escape from the monotony of troop duty on the western posts by arranging a period of detached service from his regiment. There were limited opportunities for detached duty, and the competition was keen. A lieutenant might be one of the officers assigned to Leavenworth; he might receive a recruiting assignment in an eastern city; if an Academy graduate, he might return to the Military Academy as an instructor or tactical officer; and, lastly, he might be assigned to one of the one hundred-odd colleges which required a professor of military science and tactics to manage the colleges' corps of cadets. Officers eagerly sought college duty for several reasons. A successful tour as a professor of military science and tactics brought individual recognition in the army and might be used to cultivate civilian contacts in the National Guard and, possibly, a high command in the National Guard in case of war. As members of the solid middle class, army officers valued the social life of a college community, and some used the assignment to do academic work or investigate business opportunities. Married officers especially liked college duty, for often their families needed both the educational opportunities and better health conditions a college assignment promised. It is not surprising, then, that Bullard applied for duty as early as 1888 at either the University of Alabama or his alma mater, the Agricultural and Mechanical College of Alabama.[46] Seven years later, while he was stationed at Fort Sill, the War Department finally sent him east, but not to Alabama. His school was the North Georgia Agricultural College at Dahlonega. At the same time another officer of his own regiment got the assignment to the University of Alabama even though he was three years junior to Bullard and came from Massachusetts.[47] The War Department worked in wondrous ways.

The tour at Dahlonega was a mixed blessing. Arriving in the north Georgia hilltown, the Bullards found their new home "unattractive and undesirable beyond our worst expectations or conceptions." It was a farm town, and it took considerable imagination to call it (as one Georgian did) a community of "fine moral tone and culture." Bullard saw it as old, mudstained, and dilapidated and without much genteel social life. The only positive thing he saw about Dahlonega was that its climate was good, but his first impression was that he could not possibly survive a full four-year detail in such cultural isolation.[48]

North Georgia Agricultural College was little more impressive than the town, selected for the college because it was "away from the allurements of a great city." Opened in 1873 and housed in an abandoned United States branch mint building, the college in 1895 had 126 male and 64 women students. Endowed by the Land Grant College Act, it received an annual subsidy of $6000 from the state, did not charge tuition, and had a faculty of nine. The curriculum was the usual confusion of classics and the arts and science classes. The courses it was supposed to be teaching in engineering and agriculture were conspicuously absent or marginal. The faculty was spread so thin that the professor of military science and tactics was also the professor of French—regardless of his background.

Bullard's primary duty, however, was not to intimidate the Georgia hill children with French verbs, but to drill the male students into some semblance of military proficiency. It was not an easy task. The trustees at North Georgia Agricultural College were timid about allowing him to discipline his cadets (whose discipline the War Department judged poor in 1895) because they were afraid to lose a single student. Faculty support was no more impressive. Frustrated, Bullard threatened to quit teaching both French and military science. If he had done the latter, the college would have been in serious financial trouble with the federal government. The trustees relented and agreed to support his authority, and in 1896 the War Department's inspector judged Bullard's classes "on a firm foundation and . . . more than ordinarily progressive in its class of agricultural colleges." Bullard's two small companies of cadets were well-drilled as infantry and one-gun artillery. "The battalion is very much improved over last year," the inspector reported, and he felt that the cadets' attitude was excellent. Some of the boys might indeed be suitable officers in wartime. Bullard had been a most effective instructor, "well suited" for his assignment.[49]

While he again did a creditable job with his reluctant warriors, Bullard tired of the staid life in Dahlonega. He was grateful for the chance to study, and he was pleased that his own health (a touch malarial) and Rose's improved. He also valued the chance to be an attentive father for his three small children. The expense of living off an army post was burdensome on a salary of $2000 a year, however, and Bullard did clerical work for the college after working hours to earn an extra $15 a month. The extra job did little for his disposition. Therefore, in the spring of 1897 he again asked for the assignment he really wanted—to be a student officer at the Infantry and Cavalry School. To his amazement the War Department ordered him to join the class assembling in September.[50]

Once again Bullard's ambitions were crushed, for his eyes started to go bad in the summer of 1897 and, despite the fact that he got glasses, he found he could do no reading. Reluctantly he wrote the War Department that his eyes had developed "much weakness" from too much reading. He requested sick leave to see a civilian specialist. Since he was unable to study, he also asked to be relieved from his orders to report to Leavenworth. It was a bitter decision.[51] The Adjutant General sent him back to his regiment at Fort Reno, Oklahoma Territory, but gave him sufficient leave to go to Nashville, Tennessee, to be treated by Rose's brother, a physician. Bullard's brother-in-law diagnosed his trouble as a combination of blocked sinuses and infected tear ducts; a quick but painful "reaming" and Bullard's eyes returned to normal, but too late to get to Leavenworth.[52]

In addition to restoring his eyesight, the trip to Nashville opened an opportunity for temporary service with the Tennessee National Guard. Through his wife's relatives, Bullard was introduced to several prominent Nashville politicians and businessmen, including Governor Robert L. Taylor and former general James Longstreet. Taylor asked him to join his personal staff, a detail the War Department approved. This assignment was primarily social. Bullard arrived too late to play any role in the National Guard's sketchy training, which was being arranged by officers from the Sixth Infantry and Third Cavalry. Bullard, nevertheless, was impressed by the militiamen's high spirits, obvious intelligence, and decent arms and equipment. While he recognized that the Guardsmen were far from being tactically proficient, he recognized their hidden soldierly potential, an insight not all Bullard's peers found in their National Guard details.[53] The major benefit he got from his Nashville service, however, came from his personal acquaintance with Taylor, Longstreet, and several other Tennessee leaders. Unlike his tour at Dahlonega, Bullard had the opportunity to make "some good friends who afterward, in the Spanish-American war and post-war days of raging politics, were to prove valuable."[54] By the time he returned to the Tenth Infantry in November 1897, Bullard was once again confident that he could do something about his stale career.

4.

For the line officer of 1897 there was only one way to improve his military career immediately, and this single alternative reflected the army's inverted value system. The way a line officer capitalized on his efficient field service was to leave the Line, to transfer to one of the army's departments. Such transfers were difficult to arrange, for the competition was stiff and the positions limited. In the Adjutant General's, Inspector General's and Judge Advocate General's offices, there were only eleven positions to which a line officer might be appointed and, since the billets carried the rank of major, the selections were normally awarded to captains of the Line. The greatest opportunity for a staff appointment was in the Quartermaster's Department, which had a total staff of fifty-nine officers, thirty of whom were captains. Legislation restricted the selection of captain-quartermasters to first lieutenants of the Line; similar laws governed the selection of new captains in the Department of Subsistence, but there were only eight such billets in this department. For both departments there were seldom more than four new appointments each year.

The benefits of a staff appointment were several. There was a promotion of one rank and a substantial increase in pay, about $500 a year. The promotion meant better quarters, and the staff billet itself usually guaranteed an officer assignment either to Washington or to a substantial army post in the populated part of the country. The staff position released an officer from the drudgery of troop duty and from being a subordinate, for the staff officers had great personal freedom in doing their duties. A staff officer's work was seldom physically demanding, and ailing line officers found it good recuperation.

The officers who left the Line for the staff bureaus were neither young nor cast-offs. The army found some of its most influential generals of the early twentieth century in the 1897 staff: Arthur MacArthur, Henry C. Corbin (who served first as Adjutant General), Theodore Schwan, William H. Carter, Thomas H. Barry, Robert P. Hughes, Henry W. Lawton, and Tasker H. Bliss. In the Quartermaster Department, the captains of 1897 averaged eighteen years service in the Line before their appointment as quartermasters. Twenty of the thirty quartermaster captains were graduates of West Point, and eight were graduates of the Artillery School or the Infantry and Cavalry School. Some of the officers had had twenty-four years service in the Line, and the shortest line service was ten years. In the Subsistence Department, six of the eight captains were Academy graduates, and they averaged seventeen years line service before their appointment as commissaries.[55]

The battles for staff transfers were fought in the White House and in the Senate's chambers. Despite some adhesion to party lines in 1897, the Senate (which had to approve staff transfers) judged staff appointments as personal patronage matters. Generally, both the president and individual senators regarded the appointments to the bureaus as suitable rewards for long service in the Line, thus recognizing military efficiency in an offhand manner. No one, however, was likely to sponsor an officer for transfer unless that officer had mighty friends in the army and civil life.[56]

Dissatisfied with his duties and rank in the Line, encouraged by his civilian friends in Alabama and Tennessee, Bullard made his break with the frontier army in January 1898. Settling his family at Fort Reno, he took leave and went to Washington to lobby for a transfer to the Quartermaster Department. Visiting his old friends, Captain and Mrs. Stephen Seyburn and Colonel and Mrs. Samuel S. Sumner, he enjoyed the gala life of the army-government socialites in Washington. He found the new contacts dazzling and met "many influential men who seemed somehow to take a fancy to me and who rendered me very ready assistance."[57] Handsome, still slender at thirty-seven, good-humored and articulate, Bullard probably impressed the Fort Myer coterie favorably, but it remained to be seen whether his acquaintances were anything more than party-polite.

To sponsor his transfer, Bullard sought out the junior senator from Alabama, Edmund W. Pettus. Pettus was a Senate character, a lawyer-gold miner-Confederate brigadier who still wore boots, long planter's coats, and broad-brimmed hats and carried a large red bandana. Elected to the Senate by the Alabama legislature when he was seventy-six, Pettus was admitted to the Senate's inner circle as much for his quaintness as for any intrinsic qualities of power or intellect. His colleagues especially admired his oratory on the floor, spiced as it was with biblical allusions, humorous stories with an "Elizabethan" flavor, and ancient rural colloquialisms. A large, florid man with flowing hair, mustache, and Vandyke beard, Senator Pettus enjoyed the fellowship of Senate leaders of both parties and was in the midst of the favor-trading that made the Senate operate.[58]

Under Pettus' guidance, Bullard put together his package of endorsements for the president and secretary of war. His letters included notes from Senator John T. Morgan and Representative Oscar W. Underwood, two of Alabama's most influential politicians, and letters from a scattering of Republican and Democratic congressmen, the latter from Georgia, Tennessee, and Alabama. In addition, Bullard's application was endorsed by federal marshals, customs collectors, revenue collectors, postmasters, and Democratic party officials from these three states. The letters themselves said little except that the author was acquainted with Bullard, that he had an excellent reputation as an officer and gentleman, that he would be an able staff officer, and that the administration owed Alabama such an appointment in the army.[59]

There were, however, other officers who had letters and wanted an appointment as a quartermaster or commissary, even other Alabamans. Secretary of War Russell A. Alger, the focal point of the lobbying, found the field crowded with able candidates. To one lobbyist interested in a transfer for Captain Hunter Liggett, Alger wrote that "you know these places are much sought for. There are probably thirty or forty applicants for each position with all the political influence that can be mustered to carry them through."[60] To most inquiries, Alger could do nothing but answer that the officer would be considered when a vacancy occurred. Filling a January vacancy in the Subsistence Department with a Sixth Cavalry officer from Kentucky, he had to tell lobbyists that another position would not be open until June. There were no vacancies in the Quartermaster's Department. Bullard was among the disappointed aspirants, and his chances for the June transfer were not even good since the ''Alabama appointment'' was also sought by First Lieutenant Walter A. Thurston, an Alabaman and West Pointer eight years senior to Bullard in rank. Thurston was backed by Representative Joseph Wheeler, the ex-Confederate lieutenant-general and living legend in the Congress and Alabama.[61] Senator Pettus, however, was a very determined man and he did not let Bullard's application die. When the commissary opening came in June, he went straight to President McKinley and got him to agree that Alabama did indeed rate a new staff billet.[62] Since the nation was then at war with Spain and the opportunities for ambitious line officers had changed radically, Pettus' persistence became an embarrassment to Bullard. Just as he was to leave the Line, the infantry was the very place he wanted to be. The timing could not have been more awkward or more ironic. The ''real'' army had suddenly become the fighting regiments again.

5.

For Robert Lee Bullard, middle-aged first lieutenant of infantry, the first thirteen years (seventeen, if one counts West Point) of his military career were not lost or insignificant. Though he attempted to leave the Line in 1898, Bullard was not rejecting the army. Yet, by deciding to leave the infantry, he was admitting that troop duty in peacetime had no more challenges or lessons for an officer of his experience.

Of his two basic military experiences up to 1898, Bullard's service in the Tenth Infantry was far more formative than his cadet days at West Point. The Academy years were important, but not crucial. Without the appointment to West Point, Bullard probably would not have entered the army. Perhaps he did develop mental discipline at the Academy, but the specific academic subjects he learned had little relevance to his career. Perhaps the standards of military deportment and personal responsibility which Bullard learned at West Point were indispensable, but they could be learned after commissioning, and many officers did so. The personal skills of officership (drill, riding, shooting) were equally learnable on the frontier. Being a West Pointer might be essential for an officer in the Corps of Engineers, and it apparently helped men get staff appointments, but in the Line it was not proof positive of military promise. An Academy graduate, simply by virtue of his graduation, was no more or less careerist than his brother officers, for the officer corps was all careerist. In Bullard's case, the Academy was a decent place to leave his youth and to cultivate his growing sense of nationalism. The Academy's social egalitarianism also led Bullard to believe, justly so as it turned out, that the army would not reject him for being Southern and without private income. Being a West Pointer in the frontier army was not particularly crucial in the first years of

Bullard's military career, but without the Academy appointment he would not have been in the army.

Far more critical to Bullard's later career was his extended duty with troops. That this duty was on the frontier was incidental since it was essentially peacetime service. During his seven years as a second lieutenant, Bullard learned all the fundamentals of troop-leading. He developed tactical sense—an appreciation of the effect of terrain, weather, weaponry, and physical conditions upon mens' performance in battle. All he lacked was real combat experience, although the Geromino campaign had intimations of warfare. More important than tactical sense, he learned to live and function within the army's organizational system. In the posts where he served, he was exposed to a wide range of responsibilities in supply, communications, engineering, ordnance, training, and personnel administration. These duties might not have been very challenging or very impressive in scale, but they were invaluable to an apprentice officer. Bullard's mastery of particular administrative skills was probably not as important as the fact that the process of mastery gave him confidence and self-satisfaction. By the time he went to the North Georgia Agricultural College, he was a finished company grade officer, ready to apply his military knowledge without a second thought. He believed that he possessed all the skills needed to command more than a company. He saw the problems of command not as qualitatively unique (as a National Guard officer might), but simply as a matter of scale. Ten men or a thousand men—they still had to be drilled, trained, taught to shoot, fed, clothed, counted, medically treated, and inspired. Simply understanding how the army worked, being accepted by other officers as an experienced peer, instinctively knowing which regulations to follow and which to bend—these were things acquired in the long apprentice-ship.

Beyond the occupational skills Bullard learned as a troop officer in the Tenth Infantry were the social lessons of officership. If he had for some reason deviated from the unwritten rules of the army officer corps, his career would have been as dead as an unarmed Mexican in the Sierra Madre. If, for example, he had been a liar or a gambler who did not pay his debts, he'd have found himself ostracized and driven to resignation. Deviant social behavior, however, was never Bullard's problem. Yet the code of the officer corps had to be learned, and there were no books to guide a lieutenant. The lessons of peer relationships had to be assimilated by daily experience. Certainly by 1898 Bullard knew the importance of personal reputation, of the need to be known and approved of by his fellow officers. He recognized that his peers' judgments could be ungenerous and perverse, but he was willing to accept this measure of professional worth. He was willing to play the army's game by the army's rules and to deviate only when the rules were absent or ambiguous. And he learned to tell the difference between what was inviolate in the officers' code and what was not.

The most significant development of Bullard's early career was his development of a professional personality. By 1898 his self-knowledge had advanced to the point where he could confidently assume the role of officer and accept all the demands of duty without feeling that his very individuality was menaced. He understood his own strengths and weaknesses and coped with both. He felt no need to call attention to himself by eccentric behavior. By demonstrating his competence in all the small matters of garrison life, he learned to subordinate personal whim and convenience to the demands of his job. Regardless of each task's ultimate significance (and he recognized much of the triviality in his duties), he came to regard each job, each day as the most important task he had to do.

Yet Bullard's patience with the specific conditions of officership in the infantry in the 1890s was not inexhaustible, and in 1898 he tried to leave the Line. His desire to transfer tells nothing about his self-esteem as an officer or his vision of himself as a wartime commander. For officers of the post-Civil War army, the opportunities for high rank and important commands were the products of war and the creation of a mass, wartime army, not simply a reward for long service. In a military system that made commanding generals of officers who had left the peacetime army in frustration, one might reasonably conclude that there was no assurance of military greatness for any officer. The Republic would find its generals as it always had—by chance in the throes of war.

NOTES

[1]Nelson A. Miles, *Military Europe* (New York: Doubleday, 1898), *passim*.

[2]Maj. Gen. N. A. Miles to Rep. J.A.T. Hull, April 7, 1898, Vol. 35, "Letters Sent, The Commanding General," Records of the Office of the Commanding General of the Army, Record Group 108, National Archives.

[3]Speech, "The Organization and Administration of the United States Army," January 22, 1897, in Anson Mills, *My Story* (Washington: Byron S. Adams, 1918), pp. 361-381.

[4]Brig. Gen. Wesley Merritt, "The Army of the United States," *Harper's Monthly* 80 (March 1890), pp. 493-509.

[5]1st Lt. William Wallace, "The Army and the Civil Power," *Journal of the Military Service Institution* 17 (September 1895), pp. 235-266. Hereafter cited as *JMSI*. See also Maj. George S. Wilson, "The Army; Its Employment during Time of Peace, and the Necessity for Its Increase," *JMSI* 18 (May 1896), pp. 1-30.

[6]Letter on army reorganization by Brig. Gen. G. W. Wingate, president of the National Guard Association of the United States, *JMSI* 15 (January 1894), pp. 112-122.

[7]Jerry M. Cooper, "The Army and Civil Disorder: Federal Military Intervention in American Labor Disputes, 1877-1900" (unpublished Ph.D. dissertation, University of Wisconsin, 1971); Jim Dan Hill, "The National Guard in Civil Disorders," in Robin Higham, ed., *Bayonets in the Streets* (Lawrence, Ka.: University Press of Kansas, 1969), pp. 61-84; Louis Cantor, "The Creation of the Modern National Guard: The Dick Militia Act of 1903" (unpublished Ph.D. dissertation, Duke University, 1963), pp. 43-110.

[8]Edward Ranson, "The Endicott Board of 1885-1886 and the Coast Defenses," *Military Affairs* 31 (Summer 1967), pp. 74-84; John M. Schofield, *Forty-Six Years in the Army* (New York: The Century Company, 1897), pp. 458-460.

[9]1st Lt. George O. Squier, "Artillery Notes" (1892-1893), Squier Papers.

[10]Schofield, *Forty-Six Years in the Army*, p. 460.

[11]Schofield, *Forty-Six Years in the Army*, pp. 526-528; Nelson A. Miles, *Serving the Republic* (New York: Harper and Brothers, 1911), p. 261; Theodore A. Dodge, "Needs of Our Army and Navy," *Forum* 12 (October 1891), pp. 247-261.

[12]For a concise discussion of army reform literature, see Russell F. Weigley, *Towards an American Army: Military Thought from Washington to Marshall* (New York: Columbia University Press, 1962), pp. 100-176).

[13]1st Lt. Sidney E. Stuart, "The Army Organization, Best Adopted [sic] to a Republican Form of Government, Which Will Insure an Effective Force," *JMSI* 14 (March 1893), pp. 231-278.

[14]2d Lt. James G. Harbord, "The Necessity of a Well Organized and Trained Infantry at the Outbreak of War, and the Best Means Adopted by the United States for Obtaining Such a Force," *JMSI* 21 (July 1897), pp. 1-27; Capt. Arthur Williams, "Readiness for War," *JMSI* 21 (September 1897), pp. 225-256.

[15]Brig. Gen. John Gibbon, "Needed Reforms in the Army," *North American Review* 156 (February 1893) pp. 212-218.

[16]Cantor, "The Creation of the Modern National Guard: The Dick Militia Act of 1903"; 1st Lt. S. M. Foote, "Based on Present Conditions and Past Experiences, How Should Our Volunteer Armies Be Raised, Organized, Trained and Mobilized for Future Wars," *JMSI* 22 (January 1898), pp. 1-49; Brig. Gen. John Gibbon, "The Danger to the Country from the Lack of Preparation of War," *JMSI* 11 (January 1890), pp. 16-28; 2d Lt. Frank Eastman, "The Military Instruction of Our Youth and Citizen Soldiers," *JMSI* 11 (March 1890), pp. 255-270.

[17]"Redfield Proctor," *Dictionary of American Biography* (New York: Scribner's, 1935), XV, pp. 245-246; *Army and Navy Journal*, June 2, 1890; Capt. J. H. Dorst to Capt. A. Rodgers, February 19, 1890, Joseph H. Dorst Papers, USMA Library; memos, Lt. Col. H. Hodges, Secretary to the C/S, to Adj. Gen., December 16 and 26, 1913, Leonard Wood Papers.

[18]Elvid Hunt and Walter E. Lorence, *History of Fort Leavenworth, 1827-1937*, 2d ed. (Fort Leavenworth, Ka.: General Service Press, 1937), pp. 131-155.

[19]Peter Smith Michie, "On the Increase of the Number of Cadets," *JMSI* 12 (March 1891), pp. 246-265.

[20]William T. Sherman, "Our Army and Militia," *North American Review* 151 (August 1890), pp. 129-145.

[21]Richard A. Andrews, "Years of Frustration: William T. Sherman, The Army and Reform, 1869-1883," pp. 244-276.

[22]George Van Horn Moseley, "One Soldier's Journey," *mss* autobiography, I, pp. 55, 70, Major General George Van Horn Moseley Papers, Manuscript Division, Library of Congress.

[23]George B. Duncan, "Reminiscences, 1882-1905," pp. 49-50, *mss*. autobiography, Dr. E. M. Coffman, University of Wisconsin.

[24]Headquarters of the Army, "Memorandum for General Order," February 18, 1897, Vol. 34, "Letters Sent, The Commanding General of the Army," RG 108, NA.

[25]This paragraph is based on the "Fort Leavenworth" notes (mostly items from the Kansas City *Times*) published in the *Army and Navy Journal*, November 1889 to December 1892.

[26]Bullard autobiography, pp. 20-21.

[27]2d Lt. R. L. Bullard to the Major General Commanding, August 25, 1891, and the

Major General Commanding to 2d Lt. R. L. Bullard, September 4, 1891, Bullard AGO File.

[28]Diarybook autobiography, pp. 62-63, BP.

[29]September 1889-November 1892, Returns, Tenth Infantry, Reels 116 and 117, MC 665; *Army and Navy Journal*, December 7, 1889.

[30]Diarybook autobiography, pp. 62-62, BP.

[31]*Army and Navy Journal*, June 14, 1890 and January 7 and 21, 1893. Bullard's sons were Robert Lee Bullard, Jr. (March 2, 1891-March 26, 1955) and Peter Cleary Bullard (November 8, 1892-May 16, 1972).

[32]Scrapbook 28, Notes, 1890, BP.

[33]Scrapbook 28, Notes, January 1891, BP.

[34]"Efficiency Record of Bullard, Robert L.," 1890 and 1891, Bullard 201 File; "Examination for promotion to first lieutenant; Bullard, R. L.," January 28, 1892, Bullard AGO File.

[35]1st Lt. R. L. Bullard to Adj. Gen., May 20, 1892, Bullard AGO File; April-November 1892, Returns, Tenth Infantry, Reel 117, MC 665.

[36]Diarybook autobiography, p. 64, BP; November 1892-January 1893, Returns, Tenth Infantry, Reel 117, MC 665.

[37]Herbert M. Hart, *Old Forts of the Southwest* (Seattle: Superior Publishing Company, 1964), pp. 101-102; "Report of Brig. Gen. A.M'D. M'Cook," *Annual Reports of the War Department, 1894* (Washington: Government Printing Office, 1894), I, pp. 132-144.

[38]Diarybook autobiography, p. 65, BP.

[39]Diarybook autobiography, pp. 66-67, BP.

[40]January 1893-October 1894, Returns, Tenth Infantry, Reel 117, MC 665.

[41]Scrapbook 28, Notes, October 1893, BP.

[42]Diarybook autobiography, p. 69, BP.

[43]The description of Fort Sill is from W. S. Nye, *Carbine and Lance: The Story of Old Fort Sill*, 3rd ed. (Norman, Okla.: University of Oklahoma Press, 1969), pp. 243-295; Hugh L. Scott, *Some Memories of a Soldier* (New York: The Century Company, 1928), pp. 141-145; and memoir of Mrs. William Paulding, 1894-1913, pp. 1-22, *mss.*, 1956, Paulding Papers, USAMHRC.

[44]Diarybook autobiography, pp. 70-71, BP.

[45]Scrapbook 28, Notes, January 1895, BP; "Efficiency record of Bullard, Robert L.," 1894 and 1895, Bullard 201 File.

[46]2d Lt. R. L. Bullard to Adj. Gen., May 3, 1888, Bullard, AGO File.

[47]October 1895, Returns, Tenth Infantry, reel 117, MC 665.

[48]Diarybook autobiography, p. 72-73, BP. The optimistic description of Dahlonega and North Georgia Agricultural College is from G. R. Glenn, *Report of the State School Commissioner of Georgia for 1896* (Atlanta: n.p., 1897), pp. 51-73.

[49]Diarybook autobiography, pp. 74-75. The inspection notes are from Glenn, *Report of the State Commissioner*, pp. 65-66, and "Annual Report of the Adjutant General to the Secretary of War," *Annual Reports of the War Department, 1896* (Washington: Government Printing Office, 1896), I, pp. 226-27.

[50]Diarybook autobiography, pp. 76-77, BP; 1st Lt. R. L. Bullard to Adj. Gen., April 17, 1897, Bullard AGO File; July 1896, Returns, Tenth Infantry, Reel 117, MC 665.

[51]1st Lt. R. L. Bullard to Adj. Gen. July 22 and August 11, 1897; AGO Special Order 201, August 28, 1897, Bullard AGO File.

[52]Diarybook autobiography, pp. 78-79, BP; 1st Lt. R. L. Bullard to Major General Commanding, November 1, 1897, "Letters Received, Commanding General of the Army, 1897," I, p. 3327, RG 108.

[53]Diarybook autobiography, p. 79, BP; The Adjutant General's Office, *Organized Militia of the United States, 1897* (Washington: Government Printing Office, 1898) pp. 293-296.

[54]Bullard autobiography, p. 24, BP.

[55]The. Adjutant General's Office, *Official Army Register, 1898* (Washington, Government Printing Office, 1897), pp. 14-19.

[56]For the politics of a staff appointment and Senate-army relations, see Thomas Cruse, *Apache Days and After* (Caldwell, Ida.: Caxton Printers, 1941), pp. 253-256; Col. S. M. Whitside (on the appointment of 1st Lt. J. G. Harbord) to the Adj. Gen., February 15, 1900, Vol. I, "Private Papers," Major General James G. Harbord Papers, Manuscript Division, Library of Congress; Marie D. Gorgas and Burton J. Hendrick, *William Crawford Gorgas* (Garden City, N.Y.: Doubleday, Page, 1924), pp. 92-93; John M. Gibson, *Soldier in White: The Life of General George Miller Sternberg* (Durham, N. C.: Duke University Press, 1958), pp. 159-167; Adj. Gen. to Capt. H. L. Scott, June 24, 1897, General Correspondence, Scott Papers; Frederick Palmer, *Bliss, Peacemaker* (New York: Dodd, Mead, 1934), p. 36.

[57]Diarybook autobiography, pp. 80-81, BP; *Army and Navy Journal*, January 22 and 29, 1898.

[58]"Pettus, Edmund Winston," *Dictionary of American Biography* (New York: Scribner's, 1934), XIV, pp. 519-520; Thomas B. Owen, *Dictionary of Alabama Biography* (Chicago: S. J. Clarke, 1921), pp. 1351-1352; Charles W. Thompson, *Party Leaders of the Time* (New York: G. W. Dillingham, 1906), pp. 139-141.

[59]Senator E. W. Pettus, memorandum with enclosures, "Application of R. L. Bullard, 1st Lieut. 10th Infantry, for Appointment and Transfer to Subsistence and Quartermaster's Department, U.S. Army," January 20, 1898, Bullard AGO File.

[60]Secretary of War R. A. Alger to G. H. Russel, November 10, 1897, and Alger to John A. Porter, November 11, 1897, Vol. V, "Semi-Official Letters," Russell A. Alger Papers, William C. Clements Library, Ann Arbor, Michigan.

[61]Alger to Rep. J. Wheeler, January 10, 1898, Vol. V, "Semi-Official Letters," Alger Papers.

[62]R. A. Alger memo, May 27, 1898, Vol. V, "Semi-Official Letters," Alger Papers.

II   *WAR AND EMPIRE*
1898-1904

. . . we are determined to fight somebody. This generation has had no war. It must have one if anyone will fight us.

1st Lt. R. L. Bullard, diary
entry, January 11, 1898.

5

The Third
Alabama Volunteers
1898-1899

Among the pressures that harried the McKinley Administration into a war with Spain, military bellicosity was conspicuously absent. Looking back at the war, General Hugh L. Scott remembered with irony that he and his fellow officers knew that "our army was organized for peace and not war," but that this realistic assessment did not chill the war sentiment of 1898. Instead, enraged and titillated by the news of Spain's war of pacification in Cuba, "the people . . . took the bit in their teeth and ran away."[1] While Scott accurately recalled the War Department's relative lack of preparation for expeditionary service beyond the United States, the McKinley Administration conducted its diplomacy on the assumption of military strength. It and the Congress were not concerned about America's ability to cleanse the Caribbean of Spanish colonialism. Part of this confidence was blissful ignorance, part a spread-eagle faith in the power of American arms, especially the navy. But an equally important part of this martial self-confidence rested on a logical analysis of the purposes of the war, Spain's limited military capacity, and the military strategy necessary to bring American victory.[2]

Although it lagged behind the navy in considering the problems of a war with Spain, the War Department rapidly thought through its probable role with a sound understanding of the administration's diplomatic aims and its own capacities. First, the planners assumed that the major weapons to free Cuba would be the United States Navy and the Cuban Revolutionary Army. The strategic importance of a naval blockade of Cuba and of the isolation of the entire Caribbean was never challenged. With its fleet repulsed and its troops cut off from reinforcements and supplies, Spain presumably would sue for peace. The War Department's role would be modest and match the limited resources of the regular army. The first priority was defensive: to ensure that the harbor defenses of the Atlantic seaboard were sufficiently strong to deter or defeat any effort by the Spanish navy to panic the American public or upset the American naval effort. When the Congress voted $50 million for military purposes in March 1898, the War Department's appropriation, therefore, went largely to coast defense. The army's role in the isolation of the Caribbean was equally prudent. First, it would use the navy's control of the sea to ferry supplies to the Cuban insurgents, who were supposed to be long on manpower but short on arms and equipment. If the rebels could not defeat the Spanish, the army would dispatch an expeditionary force (perhaps fifty thousand men) to Cuba to deliver the *coup de grâce*. If this expedition successfully landed and survived the notorious Cuban fevers, it would force the Spanish army to concentrate for battle and thus turn over most of the Cuban countryside to the insurgents. In their more optimistic moments, the army planners and Nelson A. Miles, the major general commanding, envisioned a successful siege of Havana, the nexus of Spanish power in Cuba. This vision was encouraged by the Navy Department as was the idea that Puerto Rico should be occupied as well.[3]

To carry out its strategic role, the War Department decided that an army of 100,000 would suffice, and it further concluded that the majority of these men would be absorbed into the existing structure of the regular army. In essence, the War Department, in legislation developed by the House Military Affairs Committee, proposed the sort of "expansible army" popularized within the officer corps by the Civil War experience and the writings of Emory Upton. Presumably the War Department understood what had happened to such plans in 1846 and 1861: they had been overwhelmed by the speedy mobilization of Volunteers and the speedier granting of commissions. Perhaps it thought that the wastefulness of mass volunteering by state-organized troops was now well understood by the public. That was its first mistake. Specifically, the manpower legislation made no provision for service by the existing units of the Organized Militia or National Guard of the states, who numbered some 114,000 men in 1898. That was the War Department's second error. When the Congress, stimulated by the "On to Havana" cries of its constituents and the press, considered the War Department's proposals, it decided that the National Guard should have the first chance to serve. Even before the formal outbreak of war on April 19, the Congress decreed that the National Guard would get the first opportunity to volunteer. In addition, if the National Guard units volunteered for federal service *en masse* they would retain their state identities, and, more important, choose their own officers without meaningful army screening.[4]

To preserve the existence and local identification of the National Guard, the congressional opponents of the "expansible army" plan compromised with the War Department. With President McKinley's firm backing, the War Department made clear that most Volunteer general officers would come from the ranks of the career officer corps, and most of them did. Staff appointments outside the state regiments would also be the War Department's domain, although the secretary of war would see to it that each state got its share of commissions. Similar agreements were made for the commissioning of additional wartime officers for the expanded regular regiments. There was also a provision that each state regiment could include one career army officer, and that this officer did not give up his regular commission to assume Volunteer rank. This particular provision cost the regular regiments some two hundred officers, but given the Volunteers' pitiful state of training, discipline, and hygiene, this proved a wise measure.

The major cost of the manpower policy compromise was, however, more dead Americans at home than Spanish bullets and tropical diseases killed outside the United States. Even with 20 percent of the career army officers serving in state regiments and staffs, the flood of Volunteers overwhelmed the army's capacity for troop organization and supply. The military impotence and high mortality of the Volunteers came as no surprise to the War Department (indeed, it sometimes appeared as a self-fulfilling wish), for the bureau chiefs were aware that the army did not have the arms, equipment, transport, and camp facilities to make the Volunteers a quickly useable force. The hardest pressed departments (Quartermaster, Subsistence, Ordnance, and Surgeon-General) compounded their dilemma by their own fatuous assumption that somehow American industry would conjure up the special supplies they needed and that the Volunteers and the public would not notice the meager production of the army's logistical system in the mobilization's early stages. To officers enured to hardship by the Civil War and frontier service and by their subsequent bureaucratic service, the Volunteers' complaints about their rations, the quality of uniforms, their lack of blankets and tents, and their medical care were the ignorant wailings of unwanted amateurs.[5]

The lack of a supply system that could provide for more than the regular army did not prevent over two hundred thousand Americans from joining up to take a lick at the ''Spics.'' With a haste and confusion that exceeded that of the opening days of the Civil War, the Volunteers came to their camps. Working from the congressional manpower authorizations of April 22 and May 11, 1898, President McKinley called for 125,000 state Volunteers (presumably National Guardsmen) as well as three regiments of cavalry, ten regiments of infantry, and a brigade of engineers to be raised directly by the national government. In an actual mobilization the Guardsmen proved reluctant warriors, for less than half of the enlisted men in Organized Militia units answered the call. With each infantry regiment raised to a wartime strength of over a thousand men, this meant that a federalized National Guard regiment would be three-fourths raw recruits. Of raw recruits, however, the Volunteer Army had no shortage. Six weeks after the war began, there were 125,000 men in camp, if not under arms and in uniform.

Even where the equipment existed for the Volunteers, it took an exceptionally energetic and influential amateur soldier like Theodore Roosevelt or an equally determined and skilled regular army officer to pry supplies from the army's bureaus. It also took professional competence to muster a regiment correctly. Until a regiment was mustered into the federal service, the War Department would not provide pay, arms, clothing, food, and equipment, or transportation to the Southern camps where the expeditionary force was forming. Thus the state governors were anxious to have a regular army officer in their Volunteer regiments, if for no other reason than because he could unravel the mysteries of the War Department's requisitions and muster rolls. Presumably the regular officer would also discipline and train his regiment, and perhaps even command it or least one of its battalions.

The competition for efficient officers was keen. For one thing, the president had a thousand Volunteer commissions to give; half of the most coveted positions (those on generals' staffs) went to two hundred regular officers. Other officers went on mustering duty, and more went on temporary duty with the administrative and logistical bureaus. In the rush to arms, ambitious regular officers became as caught up in the Volunteer commission sweepstakes as the thousands of civilians who sought rank.

The roads to Volunteer rank were varied, and luck, availability, and political influence were as crucial as professional reputation to those army officers who went to the Volunteers. For Captain Walter S. Schuyler the matter was relatively simple, for he went from duty as a major of Volunteers and mustering duty in New York to the colonelcy of the Two-Hundred-Third New York Volunteers. But First Lieutenant John McAuley Palmer mustered in Illinois troops and did not get a Volunteer appointment, although his family was politically prominent. He also had the appalling experience of seeing his younger brother move from his clerk to a captaincy. Captain Lyman W. V. Kennon wrote letter after letter asking for a field grade appointment in a New England regiment, but had to settle for a Volunteer majority as an assistant adjutant general, arranged by a friendly senator. First Lieutenant Harry Bandholtz worked both the Governor of Michigan and his regimental commander with stunning success. He accepted a majority in the Thirty-Fifth Michigan, but only on the condition that he go on to Cuba with his regular regiment, the Seventh Infantry. First Lieutenant Beaumont Buck, a classmate of Bullard, was just as persistent. When his regiment departed from Fort Sherman, Idaho, he was left behind because he was ill. Bitterly disappointed, he contacted friends in his home state of Texas and became major of the Second Texas Infantry.[6] Similar experiences happened to four hundred other career officers. And one of them was First Lieutenant Robert Lee Bullard of the Tenth Infantry.

1.

Amid the hubbub of the mobilization and Admiral Dewey's victory in Manila Bay, the regular army regiments boxed their equipment, stuffed their packs, and entrained for ports on the Gulf of Mexico. From Fort Reno, the Tenth Infantry rolled south with nineteen other regular infantry regiments. Aboard one train was First Lieutenant Bullard, a battalion adjutant. Since his visit to Washington the winter before he had considered war a possibility: ". . . we are determined to fight somebody. This generation has had no war. It must have one if anyone will fight us." He had followed the news, brushed up on his Spanish, and read about Cuban geography and history. Yet he was not especially excited by the prospect of service with the Tenth Infantry, for his real ambition was to command Volunteers as a field grade officer. At thirty-seven and with seventeen years in uniform, he felt prepared for duties more demanding than being adjutant for a two hundred man battalion. On April 6, 1898, when the Tenth Infantry received orders to be ready to move on short notice, he was uninspired, especially since he had just recovered from diarrhea. On April 20 the Tenth was on its way to Cuba. The garrison wives sadly watched as the troops marched from Fort Reno to the railroad at Rush Springs. As Lieutenant Bullard departed, his wife pressed a sack lunch into his hand. Much less enthusiastic than the crowds which cheered them at each town along their route, the Tenth Infantry rode to war.[7]

The Tenth Infantry's first stop on its on-again-off-again journey to Cuba was Mobile, Alabama, one of the three points of concentration for the regular regiments. As part of the extemporized Fourth Corps, the Tenth drilled a little and talked a lot about its future. The officers filled their day with reunions with friends in other regiments and gossiped about the flood of new promotions and assignments. Should an officer take a Volunteer commission and risk missing the expedition to Cuba? But would there be an expedition in the near future? Even if the regulars went first, perhaps one's volunteer regiment might join an even bigger expedition, perhaps an attack on Havana itself and a decisive battle with the Spanish army. The officers of the Tenth Infantry had quick decisions to make. Two lieutenants never joined the regiment in Mobile, for they both quickly took volunteer commissions. Another went back to become a major in the Third Kentucky Infantry. Captain Stephen Seyburn left to be an inspector general with the rank of major and then colonel of the Two-Hundred-Second New York Volunteers. Bullard also cast his lot with the Volunteers. Before he left Mobile, he offered his services to the governor of Alabama.[8]

The Tenth Infantry moved on April 30 to Ybor City, Florida, a ramshackle town of blacks and Spaniards near the port of concentration at Tampa. Camped among the palmettos and loblolly pines, the Tenth routinely set up camp and drilled while the officers savoured the fine weather, the news of the victory in Manila Bay, and the War Department's generosity in getting regulars Volunteer commissions. With the McKinley Administration debating naval strategy and the best way to use its Volunteer host, there was little else to do but talk army news. The one diversion was to ride to Tampa, a wooden city bleached by sun and sand, and head for the Tampa Bay Hotel, a colossus of brick and wooden arabic gingerbread and Major General William R. Shafter's Fifth Corps headquarters. In the rocking chairs along the wide veranda the talkers monotonously came back to the big questions: when would the army's war start and would taking a Volunteer commission mean missing the big chances for professional recognition?[9]

In the meantime the mobilization was creating problems for the state governments, and Alabama was no exception. In its first call for troops, the War Department, using a quota system based on state populations, asked Alabama to provide two full infantry regiments and a separate infantry battalion, a force of about three thousand men. Theoretically this force would be built around the Alabama National Guard, some twenty-four hundred men in 1898. The Alabama Guard had three infantry regiments, a cavalry squadron of 180 men, and an artillery battery of 149 men. It also had a two-company battalion of Negro infantry, the "Gilmer Rifles" of Mobile and the "Capital City Guards" of Montgomery. Created in 1884 or 1885, these companies had black officers and a black battalion staff. Like the Negro units, the rest of the Alabama National Guard was really a collection of local companies: "Blues," "Greys," "Light Infantry," "Volunteers," and "Warrior Guards." When these companies arrived at the state's mustering camp at Mobile, the realities of the mobilization caused immediate concern. First of all, only 65 percent of the Guardsmen volunteered for federal service, although there were plenty of officers and officer-candidates willing to serve. To meet the War Department's requirement that each company have a minimum of eighty-one men before mustering, the Alabama National Guard had to do some hard recruiting. The manpower pinch was complicated by the fact that the Adjutant General and the Medical Department applied the regular army's recruiting standards to the volunteer army.

The big difficulty was the Medical Department's physical exams. Besides being free of disease and deformities, the recruits had to be at least 5'4" and weigh between 120 and 190 pounds. In addition, each recruit had to fit a rather rigid physical profile. Medical officers were allowed to accept variations of only "a few pounds" and a "fraction of an inch." The result was that the Alabama Guardsmen failed their physicals at percentages that ran as high as 50 percent a company and averaged 30 percent of all the Volunteers examined, new recruits included. And until each company was filled with fit men, there would be no federal pay or supplies for anyone, including regimental colonels. "Scouring the woods" for men, it took the Third Regiment of the Alabama Guard (which became the First Alabama Volunteer Infantry) four weeks to muster. The Second Alabama Volunteer Infantry (absorbing men from the other two National Guard regiments) took even longer. And Alabama had still not met its War Department quota.[10]

Running short of patriotic and fit white Alabamans, Governor Joseph F. Johnston began to listen to the suggestion that he form his missing separate battalion from black Volunteers. Similar appeals were reaching other governors and the McKinley Administration as well, but under the first call black militia units had been rejected by the War Department. This refusal, rooted in race prejudice and the fear that armed Negroes and whites would not mix in the volunteer camps, was countered by the Negro press and white liberals, who insisted that the black man had proven his fighting qualities in the Civil War. The champions of the black volunteer mounted an impressive array of arguments: the black regiments of the regular army were excellent soldiers and black Volunteers could be also; black troops would be more energetic and less disease-prone in the tropics; the federal government needed more troops wherever it could find them. For black Americans, federal military service had two appealing features. There was, first, real sympathy for the Cuban cause, for many black men were fighting in the rebel army. In addition, Negro military service, as it had in the Civil War, encouraged race pride and forced white Americans to recognize the full manhood of Negroes and the depth of racial discrimination in the United States.[11] In 1898, however, the issue was not whether Negro enlisted men could fight, but whether black officers, chosen by their own men as white National Guard officers were, would lead the Negro units to war. The initial War Department reaction, reflecting a long-standing army prejudice against the professional and social implications of black officership, was that black Guardsmen could not have officers of their own race. It dodged the issue initially by simply not accepting any black militia units from the states that had them.[12]

Governor Johnston had reasons for sympathizing with the Negroes' request for service. Another battalion meant patronage, and the governor was an energetic job-giver. Moreover, Johnston, a leader of the progressive wing of the state's Democratic Party and about to run for a second term, probably saw the black battalion as an easy way to please black voters, not yet disenfranchised and impotent. He may even have been moved by the plea of black community leaders that military service was the right of every American and that whites had no monopoly on patriotism. Although he was a white supremicist, he believed Negroes could progress through education, hard labor, and sympathetic white guidance. While Johnston's motives for raising a black battalion are not entirely clear, he seems to have been interested in filling Alabama's unit quota, cheaply appeasing the politically alert black middleclass of Mobile and Montgomery, and satisfying white candidates for Volunteer commissions. He seems to have been confident that black Alabamans would spring to arms. The officers of Mobile's "Gilmer Rifles" alone promised to raise at least five hundred men, and other black leaders promised additional Volunteers.[13]

Though he decided to build a full battalion upon the foundations of Alabama's Negro militia battalion, Johnston was not enthusiastic about entrusting the unit to its commander, Major R. R. Mims, or any other Negro militia officer. He wanted a white commanding officer for his new unit. The solution of the black officer issue rested in part on the selection of the battalion's commander, so Johnston quickly searched for a white major with impeccable military credentials. In early May he had written the War Department to ask the detail of "a recent West Point graduate" to drill the white regiments in the Volunteer camp at Mobile. The War Department replied that it had no suggestions or nominees, and that four officers had declined assignment to the Alabama state troops.[14]

If he insisted on a West Pointer, especially an Alabaman, Johnston limited his choices. Of the six Alabamans who had graduated from the Military Academy in the 1870s and were still in the army, one was a captain in the Quartermaster Department, one was an Indian agent in Utah, one was already a major of Volunteers, one was mustering officer for the state of Minnesota, and another had just been promoted to captain and had gone to Cuba with his infantry regiment. Of this group only Captain Walter Thurston (USMA, 1879) chose state service as the lieutenant colonel of the Second Alabama. Another regular, First Lieutenant John B. MacDonald (USMA, 1881), became lieutenant colonel of the First Alabama. Next in seniority was First Lieutenant Matthew F. Steele, an experienced cavalryman but already aide to Alabama's own brigadier general of Volunteers, Joseph Wheeler. Next was Captain William L. Sibert, an engineer officer with limited troop-leading experience. A year behind Sibert at West Point was First Lieutenant Bullard of the Tenth Infantry.[15]

Before he formally announced the creation of the First Battalion (Colored), Alabama Volunteers, Johnston investigated Bullard's willingness to command it. He also asked Bullard's opinion about having black officers, for Alabama's Negro leadership insisted that the battalion should at least have black company officers. Bullard replied that he would command the battalion if it was equipped for immediate field service and if it had a white adjutant and quartermaster. Unless the battalion could take the field quickly, he did not want the command. He told Johnston that if the unit was assigned to expeditionary duty in the Caribbean, all the other officers could be black. If the battalion remained in a camp of instruction, he wanted a white staff, although company officers could be black. If the battalion was to be deployed to garrison duty in the Gulf Coast forts, he needed all white officers.[16] On May 19 Johnston offered him the command and wired the War Department that he had appointed Bullard a major of Volunteers. Despite divided counsel from his friends, Bullard accepted the majority.[17] Three days later Johnston announced that the battalion would form at Mobile.

There was much still unsettled about the status of Major Bullard, U.S. Volunteers, and his First Battalion of Alabama Volunteers, and for another six days he thought about resigning his Volunteer commission and not leaving the Tenth Infantry. There was the matter of his application for a staff position in the regular army. In Washington the Adjutant General, learning of his Volunteer commission, called Senator Pettus and asked whether Bullard still wanted to be a captain in the Quartermaster or Subsistence departments. There was now a permanent opening in the Subsistence Department and Senator Pettus could have it if Bullard was interested. Pettus, apparently without consulting Bullard, said yes. Thus Bullard learned on May 20 that he had been nominated to be a captain and commissary, although he was not sure whether the captaincy was in the regular or Volunteer army. Even though he finally found that the captaincy was not in the Volunteers and that he would not be nominated for any position in the Volunteers raised directly by the War Department, he still had to decide whether to take the staff position. The officers of the Tenth Infantry said that he should take it, but he thought that the commissary appointment would kill his career. But following the prudent course, he wired his acceptance, since the appointment would not interfere with his Volunteer majority and command. On May 25 he was committed to the First Battalion and left Florida.[18]

For Major Bullard the next week must have been a trying experience, and for a time he must have bitterly regretted his decision to command the First Battalion. When he arrived in Montgomery to confer with Johnston and the Adjutant General of Alabama, he learned that his unit existed only on paper and that the state government had given all its scanty military supplies to the First and Second Alabama Volunteers. Obviously the First Battalion would not be going anywhere in the near future, for it could not draw War Department supplies until it was mustered and that would take time. Then there was the matter of officers. When Johnston announced the formation of the battalion, he had implied that it would have black company officers. In their conference, however, he and Bullard must have concluded that it would benefit both of them if all the battalion's officers were white. In any event, Bullard left Montgomery knowing that he would have white officers, all of them selected personally by Johnston from among Alabama's energetic and educated gentlemen. Bullard was satisfied with the decision, since it was obvious that his battalion would be in Alabama for some time to come. Whether he knew it or not, excluding black officers slowed his recruiting effort. Johnston did not make his task easier when he announced that the exclusion policy was not his, but the War Department's. Even the conservative white Mobile *Daily Register* knew this was no longer true, and Mobile's black community was outraged. The First Battalion was not off to a very auspicious start.[19]

2.

Facing the greatest challenge of his military career, Major Robert Lee Bullard arrived at the Mobile mobilization camp knowing little more than that he would have white officers and that his four companies would be raised in Montgomery, Mobile, Huntsville, and Troy. The first assembly of the First Battalion was a camp meeting attended by the forty-four men of Captain Francis G. Caffey's Montgomery company who had passed their physical examinations. They had no weapons, no uniforms, and no military experience, but they had enthusiasm. Borrowing tents from the First Alabama and commandeering a shed built for the white troops, Bullard got his men under shelter, arranged rations, and began building an infantry battalion from scratch.[20]

From the start, Bullard was pleased with his white officers. While only a handful had any military training as Civil War veterans, Guardsmen, or university cadets, they were just the sort of men Bullard wanted—quick to learn, conscientious in their duties, and loyal to their troops. Of the more than forty who eventually served in the Third Alabama, Bullard relieved only four. Their relationship with their black troops was all Bullard wanted, for they were fatherly, strict, patient, hard-working, and understanding. Apparently they accepted Bullard's central policy: building unit esprit by demanding rigid professional standards and appealing to the men's race pride and sense of mission. Emulating Bullard's attitude toward both his officers and men ("kindly superiority"), the battalion's officers applied their colonel's theory for building discipline: "Along with the usual military means of discipline and control, constant appeal was made to the negroes upon race and color. This of all means proved the most successful."[21]

The initial recruiting went well. The four companies, however, were raised in their hometowns, so Bullard had little direct influence on them. In addition to Caffey's Montgomery company, the battalion included a company from Troy, commanded by a local insuranceman, Thomas E. Hill, a Civil War veteran. The Huntsville company was sponsored by the Chamber of Commerce and Negro leaders, especially Wade H. Blankenship, who became its quartermaster sergeant. In Huntsville the men actually elected their captain, E. H. Bone, a realtor and former officer of Ohio Volunteers in the Civil War. His first lieutenant was the son of the company's most influential sponsor, Mr. W. S. Wells. All three of these companies received Negro support in their home towns. Such was not the case in Mobile, home of the "Gilmer Rifles." Angered by Johnston's exclusion of officers, the "Gilmer Rifles" refused to volunteer unless their commander, Charles T. Holbert, was accepted as their captain. Johnston and Bullard announced that there would be a Mobile company, the "Gilmer Rifles" or no, and sent Captain Robert Gage into the city to recruit. Gage presented Holbert with an order to turn over his state-owned weapons, uniforms, and equipment, which Holbert did. The "Gilmer Rifles" disbanded, Gage recruited a new company, and on June 3, preceded by the Eureka Brass Band, the Mobile unit marched into camp. The skeleton of the First Battalion was complete.[22]

After the initial rush of volunteering, organization of the First Battalion slowed, but the unit showed promise. When Bullard worked himself into a state of exhaustion and a case of measles, Captain Caffey and the battalion quartermaster, Lieutenant William T. West, carried on the work efficiently. Bullard thought that his battalion would be completely mustered before the first week of June, but it was not formed until June 21. There were officer vacancies to fill, one of them created by Captain Bone's failure to pass his physical. But the enlisted men of Companies A, B, C, and D were exceptional. In the Huntsville contingent, eighty-two of the one hundred twenty-five recruits passed their physicals with no trouble and 85 percent of them could read and write. The Montgomery company had only three illiterates. Governor Johnston, Major Bullard and Captain Caffey publicly praised the men's soldierly qualities. On June 6 a detachment of recruits joined from Talladega College, a south Alabama black school. Responding to a call from Johnston, the student detachment furnished six noncommissioned officers for Company B, the regimental sergeant major, and the regimental quartermaster sergeant. To assist his two white doctors, Bullard staffed his battalion hospital with black physician volunteers. His chief hospital steward was Dr. William E. Shaw of Montgomery who was aided by Dr. James C. Abrams, a graduate of Meharry Medical College, and Dr. John R. Wood, head of Talladega's dispensary. The regiment's good health owed much to their tireless efforts.[23]

Equipment for the First Battalion arrived as rapidly as the War Department's centralized requisition system and divided bureau authority would allow, and the battalion's preparations were not slowed because of crucial shortages. By June 14 half the battalion had uniforms, blankets, and equipment. Weapons were slower to arrive, but neither the First nor Second Alabama received rifles until June 19, so there seems to have been no discrimination in the distribution of arms. When he later testified to a presidential commission investigating the War Department's management of the Volunteer camps, Bullard had no major complaints about his organization's treatment. What shortages existed were caused not by a lack of supplies, but by the requirement that a company be mustered before federal equipment could be issued.[24]

While the First Battalion formed, however, there were developments in Washington and Montgomery which complicated Bullard's task and made it even more unlikely that he would get to the war. On May 26 McKinley, concerned that Caribbean operations and an expedition to the Philippines might strain his manpower resources, called for an additional 75,000 Volunteers. Most of these men were to fill understrength regiments already in existence, but under this call sixteen new regiments also were created. Alabama's quota was another 1,500 troops, which the War Department translated as two more infantry battalions. Rather than risk the time needed to raise two more white battalions (assuming there would even be volunteers) and then joining them with his black battalion, Johnston decided to expand the First Battalion into a full regiment. In effect, his decision was a compliment to Bullard's work and the Negro response to the governor's first call, but it meant that the black troops were stuck in Mobile for the indefinite future. The First Battalion drilled and watched the last of the regulars and six white Volunteer regiments leave Mobile for Florida.

In expanding the First Battalion, Johnston announced that he had received offers of at least four more black companies. The regiment was to have West Pointers as field grade officers and the company officers would be white men "of good character and fitted by education and training to render efficient services." He added that "all officers must be acceptable to the privates." For colonel, the newspapers speculated that the governor would appoint Louis V. Clark, a National Guard brigadier general and a former state adjutant general, but neither Clark nor the War Department was enthusiastic about the idea. The governor's choice was then rumored to be Captain Sibert of the engineers as colonel, Lieutenant Steele as lieutenant colonel, and Lieutenant Samuel Jones and Bullard as the majors. The officers of the First Battalion thought Bullard deserved the colonelcy.[25]

On June 21 the First Battalion entered the federal service, its ailing major the last man to be mustered, according to regulations. With talk of an entire Negro regiment growing, the muster was anticlimactic. Five days later Johnston announced that Alabama would meet the second call with the creation of the Third Alabama Volunteer Infantry, built around the foundation of the First Battalion. The recruiting began all over again, while Companies A, B, C, and D drilled.

To raise eight more companies for the Third Alabama, Johnston followed the same system he had used in calling for other black volunteers, but it did not suffice. The first additional troops were organized by prominent white citizens in their home communities: Mobile, Montgomery, Auburn, Anniston, Birmingham, and a couple of rural districts. But instead of coming to Mobile, the new companies were physically examined and mustered at home before being ordered to Bullard's Camp Joseph F. Johnston. It was a slow process, and recruits dried up. Concerned, Bullard detached several of his officers to scour not only Alabama but other parts of the South. Before it mustered, the Third Alabama had found volunteers in Meridian, Nashville, Pensacola, Louisville, and New Orleans. The level of education and motivation of the men in the second and third battalions did not match that of the First Battalion. Although the second-call recruits made good soldiers, they included a large percentage of black vagrants and petty criminals, illiterate field hands, and a scattering of Jamaicans, Cubans, and Mexicans. The only requirement was that the volunteers not be mulattoes. It took five more weeks to put together an entire regiment of 1,200 men, and by August 6, when the Third Alabama was finally mustered, the war in the Caribbean was virtually over. It looked as if the Third Alabama would disband just after it came into existence.[26]

Turning over most of the mustering responsibilities to Captain Caffey, Bullard concentrated on training his black Volunteers. It was an exhausting but rewarding experience, for the officers had to learn along with the men, and the non-commissioned officers were neither experienced soldiers nor leaders. Stripes came and went with great rapidity in the Third Alabama. From reveille at 5:15 A.M. until taps at 9:30 P.M., the black Volunteers drilled, practiced infantry tactics, had inspections, drew equipment, cooked their meals, held parades, and drilled some more. To build unit esprit, Bullard demanded, first, total dedication from his officers. In the Third Alabama the officers were always on duty, for Bullard wanted them to win the total trust and obedience of their men. Bullard's conception of the perfect company commander was a man who would act as banker, counselor, exemplar, and teacher for his troops. If the troops were training, the officers would train. When the troops had a formation, the officers would also attend.

To his black soldiers, Bullard was hard but fair. He quickly learned that neither the threat of formal disciplinary punishment nor appeals to individual honor were adequate motivators. Scarred by their heritage of slavery and discrimination, his troops responded to neither approach. Instead, Bullard learned, soldierly behavior had to be built by an obvious system of reward: quick promotions (he made two exemplary privates in Company D the regimental sergeant major and regimental quartermaster sergeant), special privileges and leave for those who excelled in drill and inspections, and personal compliments by the officers for duty well done. In all matters, he and his officers emphasized that the men of the Third Alabama carried with them the hope and pride of their race.[27]

Whenever he believed his troops needed collective disciplining, Bullard himself talked to them. On the night of July 14 he held a formation and scolded the men for excessive fighting in camp, petty thievery, sloppy camp hygiene, and too much talking in ranks and horseplay. He put them on their honor to discipline themselves and their comrades. On another occasion he had a company of stone-throwers carry rocks about camp for a day, much to the amusement of the other men. The stone-throwing was stopped by peer ridicule. Although the regiment's relations with the people of Mobile were generally excellent, Bullard used the same approach to stop a feud between his troops and some white streetcar conductors who abused the black Volunteers. Worried by his mens' habit of carrying pistols and knives off-duty, Bullard issued strict regulations for control of weapons, after one shooting affray with a conductor. He also had every man publicly swear to obey the law and "to better and use your influence to maintain the good name of your regiment." But he also promised that he and the officers would support the men in their just grievances, and he had the streetcar company fire one conductor who threatened to shoot "the niggers" from Camp Johnston. The incidents stopped.[28]

Life in the camp of the Third Alabama reflected the troops' basic good humor and growing esprit. Bullard's staff saw to it that the men got the best food and clothing the army could offer, and the men lived well on army rations and the extras they could buy with excess ration funds. On two occasions the regimental quartermaster refused shoddily made shoes and trousers and tried to ensure that every man got shoes and overcoats that fit. Bullard saw to it that company records were properly prepared so that the men were paid on time and in full. He sponsored a regimental canteen and recreation tent run by black YMCA workers. He encouraged public parades and ceremonies and religious services, the last directed by his Negro chaplain, J. J. Scott of Montgomery. Company D provided grim humor by adopting a wounded crow which they named "Jim" and had mustered in. Another source of amusement was Company C's Private "Doctor Lighthall," a stump-speaker who convulsed his comrades with sermons on "ticktacks" (tactics) and "hardtacks" (staples) in the Third Alabama.[29]

By the end of July, the First Battalion had made the successful transition to the Third Alabama Volunteer Infantry, and its major had become Colonel Bullard, justly rewarded by Johnston for his work in organizing the regiment. The other field officers came from the regiment; the able Captain Caffey was made lieutenant colonel, and Captains Thomas Hill and John Sheffey received majorities. Bullard mused with some irony that he was now also a captain and commissary of subsistence in the regular army at the peak of his career as an infantryman. When he tried to have his transfer to the Subsistence Department cancelled, he learned that the staff appointment was permanent and irrevocable.[30]

Well-disciplined, adequately trained, eager, and federalized, the Third Alabama awaited orders from the War Department. Bullard told the Mobile newspapers that he thought his regiment would go to Cuba for occupation duty. On August 18 he finally learned (from the Washington press) what the War Department had in mind for the Third Alabama: it was to be disbanded along with 100,000 other men in the Volunteer army. Bullard and his officers, many of whom had spent their own money on their companies, were thunderstruck. Led by Majors Hill and Sheffey, the officers contributed enough money to send a delegation to Washington to get the orders changed. Bullard was to lead the group. That night the colonel called a regimental formation. The men assembled in the middle of a thunderstorm, the water cascading from their sodden campaign hats and black ponchos. Bullard addressed the men: how many of them would volunteer to go to Cuba or Puerto Rico? The response was a sea of waving arms. How many wanted to be mustered out? Again, the response was unanimous. Confused, the dramatic moment wounded, Bullard found that no one could hear him in the driving rain. This time he asked the same questions from atop a packing crate, and the men understood. Cheering hoarsely, the majority voted to keep the Third Alabama alive.[31]

Bullard's mission to Washington was successful. Arranging a Third Alabama lobby from among Alabama's congressmen, he led a delegation to confer with Secretary of War Alger and Adjutant General Henry C. Corbin. In his interview he stressed the Third Alabama's superior qualifications for occupation duty: it was well-behaved, well-trained, completely equipped, and physically very healthy, having only one disease death since May. In an army in which white Volunteers were clambering to go home, the Third Alabama had voted six-to-one to remain in the service. Either overwhelmed by Bullard's enthusiasm or worried about another appointment, Alger quickly promised the Third Alabama lobby that the regiment would stay in the federal service and would be sent to Cuba. Bullard's mission returned to Mobile, where the colonel announced the good news and praised the troops for their esprit and military excellence.[32]

Believing they were finally bound for the Caribbean, the Third Alabama enthusiastically prepared for embarkation. All the signs were good. After Bullard's return from Washington, the regiment received generous shipments of tropical clothing, individual field equipment, and new .30 caliber Krag-Jorgenson rifles, the issue weapon of the regular army. It drew thirty days rations. Proud of his regiment's appearance, Bullard invited Johnston to review the Third Alabama before it left. The governor accepted, praising the regiment's willingness to serve, excellent discipline, and soldierly appearance. But what was supposed to be a gala farewell turned into a bitter leave-taking from Mobile, despite Johnston's presence and gracious remarks. The day before the governor's inspection, the War Department, to the "consternation" of the Third Alabama, ordered the regiment not to Cuba, but to Anniston, Alabama. The Third Alabama was never to leave its home state, but that did not mean that its mettle was not tested or its men safe from danger. As it turned out, the Third Alabama did not go to the Caribbean, but it did go to a combat zone.[33]

3.

The military cantonment at Anniston was more a convalescent home for peevish white soldiers than a point of concentration for regiments assigned to expeditionary duty. Built in the northern Alabama hill country, Camp Shipp was just two miles from the city, itself a recent creation of the Woodstock Iron Company and the Southern Railroad. A melange of squad tents, shacks, and wooden service buildings perched on raw cleared land, the camp had free clean water, good rail connections, and adequate sewage arrangements, all prerequisites for decent winter quarters. The first troops assigned to Camp Shipp were either Volunteer regiments transferred from Camp Thomas, Chickamauga Military Reservation, Georgia, or service-worn regulars from Cuba. For both groups Camp Shipp was a welcome change. The Fourth Corps and the citizenry of northern Alabama, however, did not make Anniston a hospitable locale for the black Volunteers.[34]

Completing its three hundred and fifty mile train ride, the Third Alabama set up its regimental camp and continued its training. Its physical needs were provided for, and the men had adequate shelter and food. If the army ration was monotonous and limited, the Subsistence Department ran a grocery store for the troops, and the men could trade what they didn't eat with civilians. The tents had wooden floors, and the men had hay-filled bedsacks and two blankets. For warmth and safety, three squad tents were attached to a central shack with a stove. The Third Alabama camp was neat and clean; the number of sick at any time was twenty or thirty men, a low figure. In its entire service, the Third Alabama lost only seven men to disease, a compliment to its discipline and the skill of its white and black physicians. The regiment's equipment and transport (mules and wagons) were adequate; only the fact that the Third Alabama did not receive its national colors irked its colonel. Superficially, since it was busy with its military duties and well-administered, the Third Alabama should have been a happy regiment at Camp Shipp. It was not, at least not entirely.[35]

First of all, the Third Alabama was a regiment without a military mission, despite its high state of training. For a while it looked as if the War Department would keep its promise to send it overseas, since it was reassigned to another expeditionary force preparing to sail for Havana in November. When no anarchy followed the Spanish evacuation, the movement was cancelled. It was then assigned to a force of regulars and Volunteers that was supposed to go to the Philippines. The movement was cancelled. The white Volunteer regiments went home, and the regulars alone were filled with recruits and sent to Manila. At a time when the white Volunteers were near mutiny in their desire to leave the army, Bullard, his officers, and at least four hundred of the enlisted men lobbied for duty in Cuba, Puerto Rico, or the Philippines. Among the regiment's petitions to the War Department was an offer to volunteer *en masse* as federal Volunteers for Philippine service. While no one questioned the Third Alabama's ability or the competency of its colonel, the War Department could find nothing for it to do but endure a winter in Anniston.[36]

There was much to endure. Within their first week at Camp Shipp, the men of the Third Alabama began to be harrassed by the townspeople and the Volunteers of the Second Arkansas, Fourth Kentucky, and Third Tennessee. The last regiment was especially vicious, its morale punctured by idleness, illness, and drunkenness. When they had provost duty in Anniston, the men of the Third Tennessee found sport in vilifying and beating up off-duty soldiers of the Third Alabama. They also encouraged the civilians to cheat and abuse the black soldiers. One trick was for hackmen to drive through the Alabama camp at full speed, scattering soldiers from the streets; only when a sentry bahoneted a horse did the harrassment halt.[37] The race-baiting was so bad by October that Bullard had to send officers with every detail going to Anniston. In November Bullard's sentries had shots fired at them. On the night of November 24 men of the Third Tennessee (including the provost guard) attacked a party of seventy-five black Volunteers, only three of whom were armed. The crowd of whites numbered several hundred and had weapons from the local militia armory. In the riot the Third Tennessee's provost guard shot and killed

Private James H. Caperton, a regimental clerk and former Talladega student. Two other blacks were wounded. All three were shot in the back. Only the desperate efforts of five Third Alabama officers prevented more bloodshed, for they got the men into a disciplined formation and marched them from Anniston despite a continued shower of rocks and taunts.[38]

Two nights later there was firing between the camps of the Third Alabama and Third Tennessee, separated only by the tracks of the Louisville and Nashville Railroad. When two black soldiers took some official papers to headquarters, they were stopped by a white sentry who raised his loaded rifle, aimed it at them, and announced to the assembled civilians that he would shoot the "damned, mother-fucking black sons of bitches."[39] Again only the intervention of an officer stopped the incident.

Bullard was angered by the treatment his men received and proud of the way they bore their torment. To keep the regiment intact and cohesive, however, he cracked down on all infractions of his strict orders about uniforms and weapons. He also refused to allow his Corps commander to punish his men without taking disciplinary action against the Third Tennessee. No charges were made against either regiment. But only when the Third Tennessee was mustered out in January 1899 did the camp calm down. In the Third Alabama's records Private Caperton was listed as "murdered."

The race-baiting in Anniston was the major cause of Bullard's greatest worry: desertion. Although he gave many furloughs in December after the movement to Havana was cancelled, he found that he could not keep his men in camp or get them to return from leave. Before it mustered out, the Third Alabama had eighty-eight deserters, the worst record in the Volunteer army. Bullard did what he could. Chaplain Scott and some college-educated enlisted men established a school; the regiment ran its own canteen in Camp Shipp; there was ample training and planned entertainment. To deter the most casual absentees, those soldiers who overstayed their leave and then turned themselves in to get their return trip at government expense, Bullard conducted a regimental ceremony in January to discharge six deserters. He personally read and explained the meaning of a dishonorable discharge and stripped the men of their buttons. The example helped somewhat, but not much. The sleet, mud, snow, and cold of the severe winter of 1898-1899, the feeling of purposelessness, the monotony of the food and training, all eroded the morale of the Third Alabama. The regiment was unraveling each day under its colonel's angry but understanding gaze.[40]

Despite his eleventh hour effort to get the War Department to use part of his regiment as the nucleus for a Volunteer regiment in the Philippines, Bullard received orders to disband in February 1899. He and his officers took so much time closing their records (the Philippines still beckoned) that the Secretary of War issued Bullard a direct order to dissolve his regiment. On March 20 the Third Alabama, still a cohesive unit of 46 officers and 992 men, passed out of existence. Considering its disappointments, its unrewarded and unpublicized labors, its patience and fortitude in the face of the most virulent racism, the Third Alabama's survival as a trained and disciplined regiment at Camp Shipp was a worthy achievement by its troops and its colonel.

Bullard believed the Third Alabama's experience decisively demonstrated that Negro Volunteers could become able soldiers and then take back to their communities a new race pride and sense of community, both of which he thought black people needed. He believed his career as its colonel had brought him lessons in command and psychology that were irreplaceable. When he later served in the Philippines, he saw black soldiers with his picture on a string around their necks: "It was worth all the labor and trials the 3rd Ala. Vol. Inf. had cost me." The respect was mutual, for reflecting on his black soldiers six months later, Bullard wrote in his diary that his black soldiers' discipline was "as good as any I ever hope to obtain from any troops."[41]

The command also lifted Bullard from an obscure, middle-aged first lieutenant to an experienced and publicized Volunteer colonel. He had become the friend of another powerful politician, Governor Johnston. His file in the War Department now had the warm endorsements of several respected generals, one of whom said of Bullard that "no colonel is a more competent commander." These notices were the first he had ever received from general officers. In 1901 the *Journal of the Military Service Institution* printed an analysis of his black soldiers' service written by the former colonel of the Third Alabama. Bullard's article, his first in the *Journal*, received national notice when Oswald Garrison Villard, editor of the prestigious *The Nation* and a prominent racial integrationist, cited it as proof of the soldierly qualities of America's black citizens with wise commanders. Villard's praise was Bullard's first journalistic publicity outside Alabama.[42]

Unhappily, however, it seemed in March 1899 that Bullard had finally used his skills as an infantry officer only to find that the army no longer wanted him to wear crossed rifles. When the Third Alabama went home, he became a captain and commissary of subsistence.

NOTES

[1]Hugh L. Scott, *Some Memories of a Soldier* (New York: The Century Company, 1928), p. 218.

[2]For the background of the War with Spain, see H. Wayne Morgan, *William McKinley and His America* (Syracuse, N.Y.: Syracuse University Press, 1963); Margaret Leech, *In the Days of McKinley* (New York: Harper and Row, 1959); and Ernest R. May, *Imperial Democracy: The Emergence of America as a Great Power* (New York: Harcourt, Brace, 1961). For the military features of the war, see Graham A. Cosmas, *An Army for Empire: The United States Army in the Spanish-American War* (Columbia, Mo.: University of Missouri Press, 1971).

[3]Cosmas, *An Army for Empire*, pp. 69-110; Ernest R. May, "William McKinley," in Ernest R. May, ed., *The Ultimate Decision: The President as Commander in Chief* (New York: George Braziller, 1960), pp. 93-107.

⁴Graham A. Cosmas, "From Order to Chaos: The War Department, the National Guard, and Military Policy, 1898," *Military Affairs* 29 (Fall 1965), pp. 105-121.

⁵For the War Department's logistical problems, see James A. Huston, *The Sinews of War: Army Logistics, 1775-1953* (Washington: Government Printing Office, 1966), pp. 273-291, in addition to Cosmas, *An Army for Empire*, pp. 139-176.

⁶Journal entries, July 1, 1898-March 25, 1899, Schuyler journals, Brigadier General W. S. Schuyler Papers, Henry E. Huntington Library, San Marino, California; John McA. Palmer, "An Old Soldier's Memories" II, pp. 208-220, John McA. Palmer Papers; Capt. L.W.V. Kennon to Mrs. Anna B. Kennon, May 10-June 2, 1898, Col. L.W.V. Kennon Papers, Duke University Library; Brig. Gen. (Philippine Constabulary) H. H. Bandholtz to 1st Lt. E. K. Massee, April 29, 1909, Major General Harry H. Bandholtz Papers, Michigan Historical Collections, University of Michigan, Ann Arbor, Michigan; Beaumont Buck, *Memories of War and Peace* (San Antonio: The Naylor Company, 1935), pp. 53-58.

⁷Diarybook 1, pp. 81-82, and attached diary, entries, January 11-April 21, 1898, BP; TAGO, "Statement of the Medical History in the Case of Maj. Gen. Robert L. Bullard, USA," Bullard 201 File; Paulding Memoir, pp. 73-76, Paulding Papers, USAMHRC.

⁸Diarybook attached to Diarybook 1, entries, April 24-29, 1898, BP.

⁹Diarybook attached to Diarybook 1, entries, May 1-12, 1898, BP.

¹⁰The Adjutant General's Office, War Department, *The Organized Militia of the United States in 1898* (Washington: Government Printing Office, 1900), pp. 7-13; *Report of the Adjutant General of the State of Alabama to his Excellency E. A. O'Neal, Commander in Chief* (Montgomery: W.D. Brown, 1884), p. 6; *Biennial Report of the Adjutant-General of Alabama to Thomas G. Jones, Governor and Commander-in-Chief* (Montgomery: Brown Printing Company, 1894),p. 17; *Biennial Report of the Adjutant General of Alabama to Joseph F. Johnston, Governor and Commander-in-Chief* (Montgomery: Roemer Printing Company, 1898), pp. 12-15, 72; Mobile *Daily Register* May 1-20, 1898; "Report of the Secretary of War," *Annual Reports of the War Department, 1898* (Washington: Government Printing Officer, 1898), I, Part 1, pp. 3-299; R. A. Alger to Mustering Officers, April 22, 1898, Appendix to the "Report of the Adjutant General," *Annual Reports of the War Department, 1898*, I, Part 1, pp. 289-292; Headquarters of the Army, General Orders 31 (April 31, 1898) and 32 (May 5, 1898), *Ibid.*, pp. 293-294.

¹¹For the Negro viewpoint, see Theophilus G. Steward, *The Colored Regulars in the United States Army* (Arno Press edition, New York: Arno Press, 1969), pp. 282-294; Edward A. Johnson, *History of Negro Soldiers in the Spanish-American War* (Raleigh, N.C.: Capitol Publishing Co., 1899), pp. 91-112; W. Hilary Coston, *The Spanish-American War Volunteer* (Camp Meade, Pa.: W. Hilary Coston, 1899); and John Hope Franklin, *From Slavery to Freedom: A History of Negro Americans*, 3rd ed. (New York: Knopf, 1967), Chapter XII. For sympathetic white viewpoints, see W. Thornton Parker, "Evolution of the Colored Soldier," *North American Review* 165 (February 1899), pp. 223-238, and Charles J. Crane, *Experiences of a Colonel of Infantry* (New York: Knickerbocker Press, 1923), pp. 254-256.

¹²For War Department policy, I have consulted two excellent studies: Marvin Fletcher, *The Black Soldier and Officer in the United States Army, 1891-1917* (Columbia, Mo.: University of Missouri Press, 1974), and Gerald H. Early, "The Negro Soldier in the Spanish American War," (unpublished MA thesis, Shippensburg State College, Pa., 1970).

¹³For political background, see Jimmie F. Gross, "Alabama Politics and the Negro, 1874-1901" (unpublished Ph.D. dissertation, University of Georgia, 1969); Lorena D.

Parrot, "The Public Career of Joseph Forney Johnston," (unpublished MA thesis, University of Alabama, 1963); and Nellie M. B. Connell, "Alabama's Part in the Spanish American War," (unpublished MS thesis, Auburn University, 1941), I, pp. 682-753.

[14]Gov. J. F. Johnston to Adj. Gen. USA, May 4, 1898, and Adj. Gen. to J. F. Johnston, May 7, 1898, AGO 77614 (1898), General Correspondence of the Adjutant General's Office, 1890-1916, RG 94.

[15]The data about West Pointers from Alabama is from Edward S. Holden and Wirt Robinson, eds., *General Cullum's Biographical Register of the Officers and Graduates of the U.S. Military Academy: Supplement, 1890-1900* (Cambridge, Mass: Riverside Press, 1901).

[16]Diarybook attached to Diarybook 1, entry, May 13, 1898, with attached copy of telegram, BP.

[17]Diarybook attached to Diarybook 1, entry, May 19, 1898, BP; Gov. J. F. Johnston to the Secretary of War, May 19, 1898, Bullard AGO File.

[18]Diarybook attached to Diarybook 1, entries, May 20-25, 1898, BP; Adj. Gen. H. C. Corbin to Sen. E. W. Pettus, May 19, 1898; Adjutant General to 1st Lt. R. L. Bullard, May 24, 1898, both Bullard AGO File; Maj. Gen. N. A. Miles to the Secretary of War, May 11, 1898, Vol. 35, Office of the Commanding General, "Letters Sent, 1898," RG 108.

[19]Diarybook attached to Diarybook 1, entry, May 27, 1898, BP; Mobile *Daily Register*, May 26 and 31, 1898.

[20]The most detailed accounts of the history of the First Battalion and Third Regiment are Bullard's own writings, especially the Diarybook autobiography, pp. 85-98, BP. The regiment had no formal history written, but much can be reconstructed from the Caption and Record of Events Cards, Third Alabama Volunteer Infantry, 1898-1899, and the Regimental Letters and Orders, Third Alabama Volunteer Infantry, Spanish American War, both in the records of The Adjutant General's Office, RG 94. The Mobile *Daily Register* also carried almost daily stories about the "colored camp." Mobile *Daily Register*, May 31, 1898.

[21]Bullard autobiography, p. 27; Diarybook autobiography, pp. 83-84; Capt. R. L. Bullard, USA. "The Negro Volunteer," *JMSI* 29 (July 1901), pp. 29-39.

[22]Mobile *Daily Register*, May 31-June 4, 1898. Much of the newspaper's information came from interviews with Bullard and his officers.

[23]Mobile *Daily Register*, June 4, 6, 20, 22, and 26, 1898; *Talladega College Record* V (June 1898), No. 7, and VI (October 1898), No. 1.

[24]Mobile Daily Register, June 10, 19 and 26, 1898; Bullard testimony, October 24, 1898, to the Presidential Commission Appointed to Investigate the Conduct of the War Department in the War with Spain (the Dodge Commission) U.S. Congress, 56th Congress, 1st Session, *Report of the Commission Appointed by the President to Investigate the Conduct of the War with Spain*, 8 vols. (Washington: Government Printing Office, 1900), Senate Document 221, III, pp. 627-629. Hereafter cited as War Investigating Committee *Report.*

[25]Mobile *Daily Register*, May 30, and June 1, 8, 11, 18, 21, 22, and 25, 1898.

[26]Diarybook autobiography, p. 85-98, and Bullard autobiography, p. 27, BP; Capt. R. L. Bullard, "The Negro Volunteer: Some Characteristics," previously cited; Mobile *Daily Register*, July 2, 17, 21, and August 4-6, 1898, Military Department of the State of Alabama, *General Orders, 1899: Number 14: Muster Rolls of Volunteers in the Spanish-American War of 1898* (Montgomery: Roemer Printing, 1899), pp. 25-36.

[27]Capt. R. L. Bullard, "The Negro Volunteer, Some Characteristics"; Regimental

Orders 1 through 23, July 2-August 20, 1898, Regimental Letters and Orders, Third Alabama Volunteer Infantry, RG 94.

[28]Capt. R. L. Bullard, "The Negro Volunteer: Some Characteristics"; Mobile *Daily Register*, July 15 and August 17, 1898.

[29]Capt. R. L. Bullard, "The Negro Volunteer: Some Characteristics"; Mobile *Daily Register*, June 10 and 20, July 17, 1898.

[30]Col. R. L. Bullard to Adj. Gen. USA, September 14, 1898, Bullard AGO File.

[31]Mobile *Daily Register*, August 18 and 19, 1898.

[32]Diarybook autobiography, pp. 85-98, BP; Mobile *Daily Register*, August 21 and 28, 1898; Hilary H. Herbert to Secretary of War Alger, August 18,1898, AGO 118495 (1898), General Correspondence of The Adjutant General's Office, 1890-1916, RG 94.

[33]Diarybook autobiography, pp. 85-98, BP; Mobile *Daily Register*, September 2, 4, and 6, 1898.

[34]Conditions at Camp Shipp are drawn from the testimony to the War Investigating Committee, October 22-25, 1898, printed in War Investigating Committee *Report* III, pp. 534-666, and Lt. Col. O. L. Falk to the Quartermaster-General, USA, January 9 and 16, 1899, File 126269, 1899, General Correspondence of the Office of the Quartermaster-General, 1890-1914, RG 92, NA.

[35]Testimony of Bullard, Lieutenant West, Quartermaster Sergeant Fountain Ragland (Third Alabama), and Private Edward Simmons (Third Alabama), War Investigating Committee *Report* III, pp. 627-629, 649-656.

[36]Adjutant General's Office, U.S. War Department, *Correspondence Relating to the War with Spain . . . April 15, 1898, to July 30, 1902*, vols. (Washington: Government Printing Office, 1902), I, pp. 520, 528, 538, 539, 583 (hereafter cited as *CRWS*); Governor J. F. Johnston to Secretary of War, December 29, 1898, AGO 185116 (1899); Petition of the Officers and Men of the Third Alabama Volunteer Infantry, February 28, 1899, AGO 295510 (1899), both General Correspondence of The Adjutant General's Office, 1890-1916; Col. R. L. Bullard to Adj. Gen. USA, November 17, 1898 with endorsement by Brig. Gen. L. A. Carpenter, Regimental Letters and Orders, Third Alabama Volunteer Infantry, RG 94.

[37]Col. R. L. Bullard to Adj. Gen., Second Division, Fourth Corps, October 23, 1898, Regimental Letters and Orders, Third Alabama Volunteer Infantry, RG 94.

[38]Bullard autobiography, p. 27 and Diarybook autobiography, pp. 95-98, BP; Caption and Record of Events Cards (September-December 1898), Third Alabama Volunteer Infantry, 1898-1899, RG 94.

[39]Sgt. J. T. Cobb and Pvt. J. R. Miles to Colonel Bullard, November 28, 1898, Company G Letterbook, with favorable endorsement by Capt. J. J. Hunter, Regimental Letters and Orders, Third Alabama Volunteer Infantry, RG 94.

[40]Caption and Records of Events Cards (January-March 1899), Third Alabama Volunteer Infantry, 1898-1899, RG 94; Orders and Memoranda, Headquarters Third Alabama, January-March, 1899, Regimental Letters and Orders, Third Alabama Volunteer Infantry, RG 94.

[41]Bullard autobiography, pp. 27-28, BP; Diarybook autobiography, pp. 97-98.

[42]Diarybook autobiography, pp. 97-98; Brig. Gen. L. A. Carpenter to Adj. Gen., USA, November 17, 1898, Regimental Letters and Orders, Third Alabama Volunteer Infantry, RG 94; O. G. Villard, "The Negro as Soldier and Officer," *The Nation* 73 (August 1, 1901), pp. 85-86.

6

Volunteers for
the Philippines
1899

President William McKinley had great difficulty getting expert advice about what to do with the Philippines. It is said that he consulted with God. While such weighty instruction was no doubt necessary on so important a political decision as the retention of the Philippines, McKinley had little difficulty getting a precise and early estimate from the War Department about the number of men the United States would need to garrison its inadvertent island empire. On November 12, 1898, as the negotiations with the Spanish continued in Paris, Secretary of War Alger gave the president the substance of the army's estimates: it would take a minimum of 100,000 regulars to defend the United States and the annexed territories.[1]

The prospect of creating a 100,000 man army was acceptable to neither the president nor Congress. Alger shared McKinley's concern and tried to soften the estimate by suggesting that perhaps the United States Army could be expanded by native troops officered by Americans. Colonial troops would perform constabulary duties much more effectively than whites, for they would not be separated from the people by language, race, culture, and tropical diseases as Americans would. Alger also pointed out that the creation of a colonial army would bring the state Volunteers home from Manila, an idea pleasing to both the administration and the militiamen.[2] Knowing that he had a fight on his hands in the Congress over ratification of the Treaty of Paris, the president was not anxious to press army "reorganization," the euphemism which meant either an increase or reduction of troop strength. He asked for and received a steady flow of troop lists from the War Department. At the end of January 1899 the military picture had not changed; the United States had 129,000 soldiers on duty in the United States and in the wreckage of the Spanish Empire. Some twenty-nine thousand men were in the Philippines, more than half of them state Volunteers whose term of enlistment would expire with the ratification of the peace treaty.[3]

During the night of February 4-5, troops of the revolutionary government of the

Philippines and infantry of General Elwell S. Otis' Eighth Corps exchanged volleys, and the Philippine Insurrection began. Anguished as he was with another war, McKinley still sought some alternative to the 100,000-man army; someone in the War Department and a senator or two continued to talk about supplementing the American army with native levies. In the meantime the state and federal Volunteers in the United States would be mustered out and more regulars would be ordered to Otis' embattled army around Manila.[4]

While the administration tried to divine the course of the fighting from Otis' optimistic cables from Manila and to estimate the Eighth Corps' manpower needs, the Congress began work on military legislation. A War Department bill sponsored by the House Military Affairs Committee was drafted to create the 100,000 man United States Army proposed the preceding autumn. The bill passed the House by a comfortable margin, the vote split on party lines. In the Senate, the Army Reorganization Act of 1899 met sterner resistance, anticipating the narrow vote of ratification for the Treaty of Paris. When the Senate finished with the House bill, the antiimperialists and antimilitarists merely agreed to keep the regular army at its authorized 1898 wartime strength of 65,000 men, and the final draft provided that this force would be reexamined by 1901 for possible reduction. For the emergency in the Philippines, the Congress authorized the War Department to raise a Volunteer force of not more than 35,000 men "to be recruited from the country at large." This force would bring the army up to the 100,000 man War Department estimate, but it would have only a two year existence.[5]

Encouraged by Otis' confident accounts of combat with the Filipino insurgents, the McKinley Administration did not act to create its Volunteer army, even though it recognized that the state troops must be brought home shortly. It accepted the fact that Otis needed immediate reinforcements, and regiments of the United States Army, some of them still weakened by service in the Caribbean, entrained for the Pacific coast. The War Department hoped that patriotism and enthusiasm over the imperial adventure would spur individual enlistments in the regulars. General Miles suggested raising a force of 10,000 Negro troops for service in the Philippines, these regiments to be officered by the most experienced officers in the army.[6] By June the administration was still procrastinating. The chimera of an army of Filipino loyalists lingered, and the War Department did no more than to authorize General Otis to raise native troops and create three regiments of federal Volunteers from the militiamen in the Philippines. Otis advised the War Department that it would be unwise "to call into service in Luzon native organizations of any character at present," adding without amusement that the insurgents had that manpower market monopolized. He also noted that he could raise no more than two understrength regiments from among the state volunteers, all of whom wanted to come home.[7]

Reluctantly on June 20 McKinley accepted the War Department's proposal to proceed with the organization of Volunteer regiments for Philippine service. The mobilization proposed by Adjutant General Henry C. Corbin was partial; though as many as twenty-five regiments could be raised within the Act of March 2, the War Department would create only nine in the United States. Otis would proceed to organize three regiments in the Philippines, filling the ranks with recruits from the United States. The nine regiments would be recruited in relation to the total population of the existing military departments; six would be raised east of the Mississippi, three in the West. The recruiters—officers of the regular army and the Volunteers—could waive the usual requirements on citizenship and education, but were to be strict on physical condition and marital status—unmarried. The Volunteers were not going to be garrison soldiers, for there was plenty of war awaiting them across the mysterious Pacific.[8]

1.

The tardy decision to create the Volunteers and the Eighth Corps' imperative need for reinforcements forced the War Department to concentrate on the selection of officers. The *Annual Report* of the secretary of war put the problem clearly: "As the volunteer forces were designed for immediate deployment in the field, rapid organization and training were necessary. The field officers were according-ly in the main selected from officers of the Regular Army."[9] Moreover, all the officers commissioned would be career army or recently released Volunteers of 1898; the War Department announced that appointments would be made on the basis of experience and merit, not influence, a policy which would cut down the patronage pressure on McKinley and the secretary of war. Unlike those to whom shoulder-straps had been distributed in 1861 and 1898, these Volunteer officers would all have to be approved on professional criteria.[10]

Despite the pieties about merit, the selection of Volunteer officers in 1899 was a political process in which military experience was but one factor. To General Miles, military experience meant long service and command in combat; the Volunteers should be commanded by officers "of the greatest experience and ability and who have already made records for themselves by their ability to organize, discipline and command in the field troops, companies, regiments and brigades, either in the Civil War, the Indian wars or the late war with Spain . . ." His ten candidates for colonelcies met this standard: six were officers in the Civil War, four West Point graduates of the 1870s. Seven were field grade officers in the regular army; all had been at least lieutenant colonels in the Volunteers of 1898. Miles' other candidates were equally tested: all but four of the twenty career officers he recommended as lieutenant colonels and majors were commissioned in the 1870s. The exceptions were Captain Harry C. Benson and First Lieutenants Samuel Reber, Guy V. Preston, and John J. Pershing. On the whole, Miles' roster was an impressive list of talent, and eventually eleven of these officers were offered field grade rank in the Volunteer regiments.[11]

Given the antagonism between the McKinley Administration and the Major General Commanding, an endorsement from Miles may not have been the best thing for an officer's chances for a volunteer command. At any rate, the War

Department came up with another group of candidates, probably selected by Adjutant General Corbin and his assistants. This "List of Officers of the Regular Army Who Have Demonstrated Special Fitness for the Command of Troops and Who Are Regarded as Qualified Physically and Mentally for Duty in the Tropics" also accented age and experience. The twenty regular majors recommended averaged twenty-seven years service; only two were under fifty years old, the youngest was forty-seven. The ages of the forty-four captains recommended ranged from thirty-seven to sixty-three; only three officers were under forty. The same group's commissioned service ran from fifteen to forty-one years; only six men had less than twenty years as army officers. As did Miles' list, the War Department roster provided information on brevets and citations; more knowingly it also provided the candidates' home states.[12]

With time pressing the McKinley Administration, it took but two weeks to commission the officers of the first twelve Volunteer regiments; half of the new colonels and lieutenant-colonels came from either Miles' or the secretary of war's lists. The other colonels were long service regulars or field grade officers from the 1898 volunteers; officers of the latter type formed the two regiments created in the Philippines. Of the career officers only six had been commissioned as late as the 1880s; the most junior was First Lieutenant Robert L. Howze (USMA, 1888), who had distinguished himself in Cuba. The selections, however, were not made in a pristine professional environment, for former officers, governors, congressmen, friends, and a mother or two cabled suggestions to both McKinley and the War Department. For the appointments of company grade officers, state quotas were established; McKinley himself ordered the commissioning of several candidates and paid special attention to Ohio's quota.[13] But in selecting the two colonels for each regiment, the criterion of professional experience held up well.

The creation of the twelve Volunteer regiments had hardly begun when the War Department pried an admission from Otis that he still would not have enough troops. Six months of fighting had not ended the insurrection; much to his distress Otis saw that the Eighth Corps was facing a popular national revolt, not just a cabal from the Tagalog "tribe." He needed a force over 60,000.

The task of raising the Volunteer force to its statutory limit was inherited by a new secretary of war, Elihu Root. A brilliant lawyer and corporate organizer, Root's military experience was nonexistent when he took office. His singleness of purpose, his willingness to educate himself in the intricacies of army management, his mandate "to clean up the War Department" gave him the aura of a vigorous, efficiency-minded reformer, impatient with bureaucracy, political patronage, and old-fogyism in the army. Upon coming to office, so one popular journal reported, Root examined Miles' recommendations for field grade commissions in the Volunteers and found them "impossible," serving only Miles' personal interests. Instead, the dynamic secretary made his own selections, casting aside the recommendations of congressmen and army bureaucrats to produce a new list of youthful and accomplished officers:

One characteristic of the new field officers is their youth. The oldest among them is a young major, his commission in the regular army being of a few month's standing. There is no one who knows the regular army who will not rejoice in the selection of the officers for the new regiments from the young men of the establishment.[14]

Root showed no magic in raising twelve more Volunteer regiments and selecting their officers. Knowing nothing of the army's career officers, he consulted the president, Generals Miles and Corbin, the generals in the Philippines, and two New York acquaintances with military opinions, Governor Theodore Roosevelt and General Francis Vinton Greene, guardsman, politician and historian. Of the colonels Root selected (with McKinley's approval), nine appeared on the June lists. There was no additional concession to youth; only four of Root's twenty-four colonels and lieutenant colonels had been commissioned as late as the 1880s. All were regular officers and were selected, as Root assured McKinley, after a careful review of their efficiency reports. There was not one who had less than fourteen years service in the regular army.[15]

The most junior officer selected by the secretary of war was Colonel Robert Lee Bullard, late of the Third Alabama Infantry and on sick leave in August 1899. Although he had applied for a commission in the Volunteer army rather than go back to duty in his regular army rank of captain and commissary of subsistence, he was not optimistic about his chances. Whether he knew it or not, he was not getting any help from the Alabama congressional delegation, for Senators Morgan and Pettus and the state's representatives were busy nominating worthy civilian Alabamans for commissions. Root may have been confused about Bullard's status in the army. That he had raised and trained the Third Alabama was clear. His age and rank may have eluded the secretary. On August 15 Root telegraphed McKinley, vacationing on Lake Champlain, that he had proceeded with the organization of the second group of Volunteers. He asked permission to commission his selections for colonelcies, made by "a very careful canvassing of the entire list." For command of the Thirty-Ninth Infantry Regiment, U.S. Volunteers, the secretary of war had chosen "Major Bullard, 10th Infantry." When McKinley approved Root's selections, the secretary replied that he had appointed Captain Bullard of the Subsistence Department to the colonelcy of the Thirty-Ninth Volunteers with a date of rank of August 5, 1899.[16]

2.

Pleased and surprised by his second regimental command, Robert Lee Bullard, trim and as fiercely mustaschioed as a legendary Confederate colonel, entrained for his regiment's assembly point, Fort Crook, a large and comfortable post ten miles south of Omaha, Nebraska. The Thirty-Ninth Volunteers' colonel arrived on August 24 and immediately turned to the problem of preparing his troops for tropical service. It was not an easy task, complicated by the fact that four companies of the regiment were assembling at Vancouver Barracks, Washington, far from the supervision of the regimental commander.[17]

Bullard should have had ample assistance, but his officers were either serving in the Philippines, recruiting their companies, or slow in reporting. As a group the officers of the Thirty-Ninth Infantry were able and experienced, some in fact so able and experienced that Bullard may have been wary of challenges to his authority. His lieutenant colonel was Enoch H. Crowder, a West Point cavalryman turned judge-advocate who had fought the Sioux in the 1890s; Crowder, however, never joined the regiment, serving instead in the military government of the Philippines. The three battalion commanders were proven soldiers, and two were regular officers with blossoming reputations. The senior major was thirty-one-year-old George T. Langhorne, two years a cadet at Virginia Military Institute and four at West Point, graduated in 1889 as first captain of the battalion of cadets. Langhorne, a foppish, aristocratic Virginian, was a first lieutenant of cavalry; he had fired shots in anger on the Mexican border, served as aide to three generals, and had been military attaché in Belgium. His most recent duty had been in the military government of Puerto Rico. The second battalion commander was also an Academy graduate, thirty-two year old John Henry Parker, a first lieutenant of infantry. Graduated in 1892, Parker had gone to Cuba with the Thirteenth Infantry. On July 1, 1898, he had his own crowded hour by covering the assault on San Juan Hill with a battery of Gatling guns; thereafter he was "Machine Gun" Parker, writing books and articles and talking about his weapons at a cyclical rate of 500 words a minute. Short, pugnacious, and quick-witted, Parker had an important friend, Theodore Roosevelt. The third major, Henry B. Mulford, was a Volunteer officer who was learning about war in the Philippines first hand when Bullard was drilling at Camp Shipp. Former colonel of the First Nebraska Infantry, Mulford, a slender businessman of thirty-seven and East Omaha militia officer, had been with his regiment from the start of its service in 1898. Harry Mulford's portrait suggests no ferocity in looks or spirit; his face was boyish, the eyes and mouth soft, unhardened by a cavalryman's mustache. The record suggests that he was already war-weary when he joined the Thirty-Ninth Volunteers in the Philippines.[18]

Bullard's fifteen captains did not have the advantages of an army career, but they were hardly unseasoned. One, William L. Murphy, was regular army (USMA, 1898). The rest were Volunteer officers from the state and federal Volunteers of 1898; four had fought either in Cuba, Puerto Rico, or the Philippines. Captain Wallace C. Taylor, who was to become a motive force in the Thirty-Ninth Infantry, had commanded a battalion of the First Nebraska, was wounded near Manila, and breveted for gallantry. Among the captains was one future general, Edward A. Kreger, a recent graduate of Iowa Agricultural and Mechanical College and an officer of the Fifty-Second Iowa Infantry. Other key officers of the Thirty-Ninth were Charles H. Hilton, former captain in the First Colorado; Thomas Hardeman of the First Alabama and Bullard's quartermaster; Frank S. Long, an Iowa battery commander; and Noel Gaines, a captain of

Kentucky infantry who became the Thirty-Ninth's adjutant. Of Bullard's captains, all but two had been captains in 1898.[19]

The thirty-three first and second lieutenants were also veterans, twenty-two having worn shoulder-straps in 1898. Five had been in combat. As a group they came from as far east as Pennsylvania, as far west as Washington. Five were former sergeants of the regular army; the others were young businessmen, lawyers, and collegians. While a couple of them became slackers, Bullard's lieutenants turned out well in the stress of the campaigning to come.[20]

But in August of 1899, when the Thirty-Ninth Infantry existed only in the dreams of its colonel and the hopes of the War Department, these officers were not numerous, skilled, or forceful enough to please Bullard. The colonel was an anxious man, impatient to form his regiment and move it to the Philippines. The majority of his captains were enlisting men, and Bullard kept the Fort Crook telegraphers busy with admonitions to his recruiters. To the small cities and towns of Iowa, Missouri, Tennessee, Alabama, Illinois, Michigan, Washington, Minnesota, Nebraska, and Pennsylvania went his instructions: make no compromises on health and physical condition, enlist no married men except skilled artisans with their wives' written permission, fill the companies, and get back to Fort Crook.

Bullard's directions from the War Department gave him from August 17 to September 24 to form the regiment, a not overgenerous schedule. The colonel, much to his disgust, could not make the deadline. While he was ready to bend army regulations to get supplies and prepare administrative records, the post commander was not. Daily the trains dumped undisciplined, raucous, sometimes drunk recruits into the Fort Crook camp of the Thirty-Ninth; daily the trains took away men declared unfit after a close examination by Bullard's three surgeons. Gradually the ranks filled. By September 16 there were 6 officers and 450 men at Fort Crook, 6 and 424 at Vancouver Barracks. Camp life had assumed some order; the men moved by bugle call and marched to the command of their sergeants. Impatiently Bullard supervised the drill and instruction, often teaching the officers and sergeants himself. He watched the supplies arrive: khaki uniforms, shoes, blue shirts, canvas leggings, web ammunition belts, Krag-Jorgenson rifles, and enough khaki pith helmets to turn the regiment into a Pacific version of the British army. By September 25 the regiment was outfitted except for overcoats and band instruments, neither absolute necessities where it was going. Bullard must have envisioned his rookies as a pocket-brigade, for he asked that the War Department provide him with carbines for mounted service and with five mule-packed Hotchkiss mountain guns. He was anxious to get into the fight, and, though he was still enlisting and discharging men, he announced to the War Department on October 3 that the Thirty-Ninth was ready to move.[21]

To the unblinking eyes of Major Frank D. Baldwin, Civil War veteran, scourge of the Comanche and Kiowa, twice winner of the Medal of Honor, the Thirty-Ninth Infantry was not nearly so ready as it appeared to its colonel. As inspector for the Department of the Missouri, Baldwin examined the regiment on October 4 and

5. He noted that it had twenty-six officers present for duty, ten on leave, and three in the Philippines. There was no officers' school. The troops were fully equipped for field service, they drilled fairly well, and their camp was orderly. The behavior and military demeanor of the officers and men was "excellent." The regimental hospital, staffed by hospital stewards of the regular army, was excellent. The regiment, however, was not prepared to deploy, for the soldiers had not fired their weapons and were weak on field skills. In addition, the regimental and company records were not up to regulation accuracy and neatness. Baldwin judged the Thirty-Ninth Infantry unsatisfactory and, undeterred by Bullard's temporary rank, ordered the Thirty-Ninth's colonel to get on with his work.[22]

Scorched by Baldwin's report, Bullard pointed out to the department commander that the inspector had given the regiment insufficient credit for its progress. Moreover, most of the officers were newly joined and had just started tactical training. Bullard also suggested that Baldwin was jealous that he himself was not commanding the Volunteers and that the aging major had made the inspection in an alcoholic daze.[23] The department commander must not have been too impressed with Bullard's rationalizations, for he did not release the two battalions at Fort Crook for another ten days. No doubt Bullard kept the pressure on, and he eventually triumphed, assembling his entire regiment for the first time at Vancouver Barracks on October 19. The Thirty-Ninth's new home was more congenial than Fort Crook, for the post and departmental adjutant was Henry P. McCain, Bullard's West Point roommate. The regiment's administrative and supply records were quickly brought up to regulation standards. While the clerks labored, the Volunteers had target practice and ran field problems. By the end of the month the Thirty-Ninth Infantry, 49 officers and 1310 men, was ready to sail.

Despite the Thirty-Ninth's hasty organization and training, Bullard was pleased with his regiment. The officers had worked hard and effectively in the training period, and he had confidence in their leadership abilities. The enlisted men were first-rate. The majority were adventurous, patriotic, laboring men in their early twenties whose faith in America's righteousness was untarnished by experience. Ninety-five percent of the regiment was native-born. Their eagerness in the training period and their disciplined behavior had already impressed their officers. Just before sailing they again demonstrated their responsbility: given two months pay, the men soberly spent some and mailed most to their homes. There were no incidents of drunk or disorderly behavior. Instead the men, tense with anticipation, had their photographs taken and wrote a letter or two. Some bought insurance policies.[24]

At last the Thirty-Ninth was off for the exotic Philippines. On November 2 it went by rail to the Portland, Oregon, docks and the army transports, *Pennsylvania* and *Olympia*. As the men filed up the gangplanks, blanketrolls slung, creased campaign hats pulled low in affected ferocity, Bullard said goodbye to his family amid the crates and baggage along the wharf. Although family separations were part of the accepted price of officership, Bullard found the goodbyes difficult. It was no easier when his transport, *Pennsylvania*, swung out into the channel and ran aground on a mud-bar. Several hours later, when the transport hit the first Pacific swells, Bullard's sense of anomie changed to seasickness. The great adventure was not off to a very auspicious start. Perhaps before he turned to organizing shipboard drills and his professional reading, Colonel Bullard thumbed through a chapter or two of his *Don Quixote*.[25]

NOTES

[1]A. Alger to W. McKinley, November 12, 1898, Series 1/Reel 5, McKinley Papers. For general background, see Margaret Leech, *In the Days of McKinley* (New York: Harper and Row, 1959), pp. 323-409.

[2]*Ibid.*

[3]Memo, "Army Estimate," January 24, 1899, Series 1/Reel 5, McKinley Papers; Graham A. Cosmas, "Military Reorganization after the Spanish American War: The Army Reorganization of 1898-1899," *Military Affairs* 35 (February 1971), pp. 12-17.

[4]Memo for President McKinley, February 14, 1899, Series 1/Reel 5, McKinley Papers; *Army and Navy Journal*, February 25, 1899.

[5]The bill was printed in full with commentary in the *Army and Navy Journal*, March 4, 1899. See also "Report of the Secretary of War," *Annual Reports of the War Department, 1898-1899* (Washington: Government Printing Office, 1899), I, Pt. 1, p. 3.

[6]Maj. Gen. N. A. Miles to A. Alger, April 26, 1899, Vol. 38, "Letters Sent by the Major General Commanding, 1899," RG 108.

[7]Maj. Gen. E. S. Otis to the Adj. Gen., June, 1899, Series 1/Reel 7, McKinley Papers.

[8]Adj. Gen. H. C. Corbin, memorandum, June 20, 1899, Series 1/Reel 7, McKinley Papers, with endorsement by Acting Secretary of War G. D. Meiklejohn, June 24, 1899.

[9]"Report of the Secretary of War," *Annual Reports of the War Department, 1898-1899*, I, Pt. 1, p. 3.

[10]Elihu Root to Franklin Bartlett, October 24, 1899, General Correspondence, Root Papers.

[11]Maj. Gen. Nelson A. Miles to Secretary of War Alger, April 26, 1899, Vol. 38, "Letters Sent by the Major General Commanding, 1899," RG 108.

[12]Memo, "List of Officers of the Regular Army Who Have Demonstrated Special Fitness for the Command of Troops and Who are Regarded as Qualified Physically and Mentally for Duty in the Tropics," enclosure to memo, Acting Secretary of War G. D. Meiklejohn to McKinley, June 24, 1899, Series 1/Reel 7, McKinley Papers.

[13]Gov. Asa Bushnell (Ohio) to Secretary of War Root, August 15, 1899, Series 1/Reel 7; Elihu Root to McKinley, September 19, 1899, Series 3/Reel 68; George Cortelyou to McKinley, July 5, 1899, Series 2/Reel 40, all McKinley Papers.

[14]HLN, "Secretary-of-War Root and His Task," *Harpers Weekly* 43 (September 2, 1899), pp. 857-860.

[15]Root to McKinley, August 15, 1899, Series 1/Reel 7, McKinley Papers.

[16]*Ibid.*; McKinley to Root, August 16, 1899; Root to McKinley, August 17, 1899, Series 1/Reel 7, McKinley Papers; on the president and Alabamans, see George Cortelyou to Adj. Gen. H. C. Corbin, July 20, 1899, Series 2/Reel 41, McKinley Papers.

[17]Bullard autobiography, p. 30-31; Diarybook 1, entry, December 4, 1899, BP; The Thirty-Ninth Volunteer Infantry Association, *History of the Thirty-Ninth United States*

Volunteer Infantry (Elgin, Ill.: 39th U.S.V. Infantry Assoc., 1937); "History of the 39th Infantry U.S. Volunteers," Historical Sketches of Volunteer Organizations, AGO 396223, 1901, RG 94.

[18]The individual and collective sketches of the Thirty-Ninth's officers are drawn from "History of the 39th Infantry U.S. Volunteers," and The Adjutant General's Office, *Official Register of Officers of Volunteers in the Service of the United States* (Washington: Government Printing Office, 1900). For the sketch of Langhorne, I used Charles D. Rhodes, "Diary of a Cadet at the United States Military Academy, 1885-1889," Rhodes Papers, and Capt. Frank R. McCoy to Mrs. McCoy, October 15, 1903, Family Correspondence, McCoy Papers. For Mulford, see "History of the Operations of the First Nebraska Volunteer Infantry, U.S.V.," in Karl I. Faust, *Campaigning in the Philippines* (San Francisco: Hicks-Judd Company, 1899), pp. 48-49. On Parker, see his own writings and letters in the papers of Theodore Roosevelt, and Leonard Wood and Theodore Roosevelt, *The Rough Riders* (New York: Charles Scribner's Sons, 1899).

[19]"History of the 39th Infantry U.S. Volunteers," previously cited.

[20]*Ibid.*

[21]Headquarters, 39th Infantry U.S. Volunteers, "Letters Sent Book, August 28, 1899-February 28, 1900," RG 94; Diarybook 1, entry, December 4, 1899, BP; R. L. Bullard to Adj. Gen., September 3, 1899, No. 3245 "Letters Received, Commanding General of the Army, 1899," Vol. I, RG 108; "History of the 39th Infantry U.S. Volunteers."

For comparison, see Frederick J. Herman, *The Forty-Second Foot: A History of the Forty-Second Regiment of Infantry United States Volunteers* (Kansas City, Mo.: n. p., 1942); Capt. John L. Jordan (Thirty-Eighth Volunteers) to Mrs. Jordan, September 17-October 29, 1899, John L. Jordan Papers, Tennessee State Library and Archives; Schuyler journals, entries, August 23 to December 14, 1899, W. S. Schuyler Papers.

[22]Bullard autobiography, p. 31, BP; Major Frank D. Baldwin to Adj. Gen., Department of the Missouri, October 6, 1899, File 4950, Office of the Inspector General, "Reports, 1899-1900," RG 159. The sketch of Baldwin is from Alice Blackwood Baldwin, *Memoirs of the Late Frank D. Baldwin, Major General, U.S.A.* (Los Angeles: Wetzel Publishing Company, 1929).

[23]Bullard autobiography, p. 31; Diarybook 1, entry, December 4, 1899, BP; Bullard's endorsement, October 6, to Baldwin's inspection report, cited above.

[24]Interviews with officers, *The Daily Oregonian* (Portland), November 1, 1899; "Memoir of Arthur W. Orton" (1947), "Memoir of Dr. Harry Morris" (1950-1952), "Memoir of Robert L. McNair" (1968), and "Memoir of Curg Lewis" (1970), in Thirty-Ninth U. S. Infantry (Volunteers) file, Spanish-American War, Philippine Insurrection, and Boxer Rebellion Veterans Research Project, USAMHRC.

[25]"Caption and Record of Events Cards, 39th U.S. Volunteer Infantry, 1899," RG 94; R. L. Bullard to Rose Bullard, March 8, 1900, BP; Diarybook 1, entry, December 4, 1899, BP; *The Morning Oregonian* (Portland), November 2, 1899.

7

Campaign in
Southern Luzon
1899-1900

For the officers and men of the Eighth Corps of the United States Army, the War with Spain was a wonderous adventure which staggered the imaginations of every man from the Major General Commanding to the rawest private in the ranks. While the rest of the army sweltered in the Caribbean or languished in mobilization camps in the United States, the Eighth Corps headed across the Pacific to secure the victory of Dewey's Asiatic Squadron in Manila Bay. The Corps' mission in the summer of 1898 was comprehensible enough. It was to capture the city of Manila and to hold the colonial capital until a peace with Spain was negotiated. What complicated matters was that Dewey's victory (indeed, Dewey's assistance) had resurrected the Philippine nationalist movement which had been sporadically fighting the Spanish since 1890. As the American transports steamed into Manila Bay and unloaded the succession of expeditionary divisions which formed the Eighth Corps, another movement to Manila was under way. From the cities and towns of Luzon, the insurgent generals, led by Emilio Aguinaldo, assembled their own army of forty thousand with twelve thousand men deployed about Manila. Not only did the Philippine nationalists march on Manila, but they disarmed and imprisoned the Spanish colonials, harried the Catholic friars, and confiscated wealth and lands. At the same time, the rebels took control of the civil government.

While Spain remained the common enemy, the two armies were reluctant allies. Both participated in the opera bouffe assault which saved Spanish honor and seized Manila's inner city on August 13, 1898. American-Filipino cooperation was never better than tenuous. The Spanish generals had, in fact, arranged that the American troops would not only seize the city but hold back the Philippine rebels after the city fell. The Eighth Corps thus held an intermediate position between the walled city and the insurgent army entrenched around Manila's outskirts.

From August to February 1899 the Eighth Corps and Aguinaldo's army measured each other for the clash both forces came to regard as inevitable. This

121

was especially true in November after the terms of the Treaty of Paris reached Manila: the United States had annexed the entire archipelago. Aguinaldo's revolutionary government and army were thus transformed from allies to rebels against the sovereignty of the United States. For two months, however, there was no major fighting. The American inactivity was purposeful, for the treaty had not yet been ratified by the Senate. McKinley had no desire to start a war he still hoped to avoid, and General Elwell S. Otis, a cautious worrier, felt that his corps (mostly state Volunteers) was neither large nor trained enough for more fighting.

Aguinaldo began to plan an attack on the Eighth Corps as early as November, but he too was unprepared when the war with the Americans began on the night of February 4-5, 1899. His own control of the revolutionary government was not secure. He also doubted the theory of his leading general, Antonio Luna, that the Philippine army, an ill-organized mass of village militia, could win a conventional war. But Luna, a European-educated member of the Philippine elite, won the argument in the councils of the revolutionary government, thus committing the insurgent army to a series of disasters.

From February to November Otis' soldiers fought their way out of Manila, then turned north up the central Luzon plain, and eventually drove Aguinaldo's disintegrating army into the mountains of northern Luzon. American forces occupied the towns along the northern coast, while other expeditions landed at the most important towns in the Visayan islands to the south. Despite the efforts of the American generals and their assiduous staffs, the campaigns bore little resemblance to the neat maneuvers the officers planned. Trailing long trains of *carabao* (the Philippine water buffalo) carts, pack mules, and Chinese coolies, the American troops trudged up to the insurgent trenches. When the insurgents fought, the Americans blasted their positions with artillery and rifle fire, usually managing to work around to an exposed flank and thus enfilading the Filipino trenches. Their ranks shredded, the Filipinos would flee to the next town or river or mountain pass to try again—with the same results. Despite the disagreeable weather, an uncertain supply system, illness, and the tendency of its generals to fight their own wars, by December 1899 the Eighth Corps had reduced the Philippine army to refugees and smiling villagers.[1]

The Eighth Corps had fought its war north of Manila, but it was not because the countryside south of the capital was free of insurgency. Indeed, the provinces bordering the Pasig River and the great inland lake of Laguna de Bay had been a seat of rebellion against Spain since 1890. In 1896 and 1897 the Spanish army had made little headway in pacifying the southern provinces. In 1898 the Filipino rebels seized control of the countryside. Displacing Spanish officials and loyalist Filipino functionaries, the nationalists quickly established their administrative grip. The new officials, raised on the traditions of European bureaucratic values, turned out paper work with revolutionary zeal; from their pens came lists of court decisions, tax rolls, militia rosters, police reports, land titles, legal documents, census rolls for men and beasts, licenses, administrative decrees, decisions on private petitions, treasury accounts, and inventories of the papers and property confiscated from the Spanish. If the political power of the revolutionary province and local *presidentes* was only one-tenth as great as the amount of paper work, their grip on the people must have been considerable.[2]

The men of the southern provinces were also part of the Aguinaldo's military effort against the Americans. During the summer of 1898 the Filipinos armed themselves with Spanish weapons, mostly Remington and Mauser rifles and an occasional field gun. Weapons and ammunition, however, were scarce, and target practice for the Filipino militiamen was nonexistent. Moreover, the restricted southern approaches to Manila were sufficiently manned by the Americans to prevent the periodic attacks Aguinaldo planned for his southern army. The Filipinos, commanded by Aguinaldo's trusted aide, Lieutenant General Mariano Trías, entrenched and waited while their northern brethren took the brunt of the Eighth Corps' offensives.

Aware of the Filipino strength to the south, Otis occasionally mounted expeditions into Cavite province and to the towns along Laguna de Bay. None of these limited offensives or reconnaissances-in-force did much to dislodge the insurgents. In April Major General Henry W. Lawton landed fifteen hundred men at Santa Cruz at the eastern end of the lake. The confused landing was weakly opposed, Lawton's force stumbled through the abandoned town, and then the expedition sailed back to Manila.[3]

In June 1899 Lawton's entire division marched south into Cavite in order to break up a rumored Filipino offensive. After some sharp fighting and the heat had felled hundreds of American soldiers, Otis halted the advance at Imus, twenty miles south of Manila, and established new positions across the isthmus. In July he also occupied Calamba and Los Baños on Laguna de Bay, but these American garrisons were immediately besieged in their enclaves. Again in October there was a week-long offensive in Cavite, but this advance bogged down in the rains. The "conquest" of southern Luzon awaited the dry season and reinforcements.[4]

The American position along the lake in the fall of 1899 was not inspiring. Officers visiting the Calamba garrison, the Twenty-First Infantry of Colonel Jacob Kline, were depressed by the lassitude they found. The Twenty-First was an unhappy unit, its commander ill and happy with his orders to remain on the defensive. Having lost many of its old regulars in Cuba to bullets and fever, the Twenty-First's fortunes had not improved in the Philippines. Its transports had run a typhoon enroute, and many of its raw and weak soldiers had collapsed with heat exhaustion in Lawton's June offensive. Fearing attacks from the encircling Filipinos, Kline compounded his regiment's malaise by keeping his men overlong in the trenches. Like other American posts along Laguna de Bay, the Calamba garrison was a captive of Otis' timidity, its own apathy, and an exaggerated fear of the wild riflefire which peppered the city from the trenches of the undefeated Filipino levies.[5]

1.

After an uneventful voyage, the transports *Olympia* and *Pennsylvania* dropped
anchor in Manila harbor on December 7, and Colonel Robert Lee Bullard went
ashore to learn what mission the Eighth Corps had for his eager regiment. He
discovered that Otis' headquarters did not even expect the Thirty-Ninth, for
Washington had not cabled the news of its departure. To his dismay Bullard
learned that the army thought that the insurrection was over and that operations in
northern Luzon were now mere chases. The heroes of the hour in the Manila press
were the officers rescuing American and Spanish prisoners. The army and civilian
press seemed obsessed with the rescues, and patrols raced each other to find the
most important hostage in insurgent hands, Navy Lieutenant James C. Gillmore.
Manila itself was living a schizophrenic existence under the American occupation.
By day the city bustled with business as the troops came and went, supplies were
ferried to the warehouses from the fleet of transports in the harbor, and the city
population adjusted its commerce to the rich *americanos*. At night, however, the
American provost guard cleared the streets and patrolled the city under martial
law, for Otis still feared an uprising by the rebels' Manila militia.[6]

The officers and men of the Thirty-Ninth found life in the exotic Orient too
novel to share their colonel's concern that the war was over. The soldiers—looking
like a regiment of displaced homesteaders in their limp campaign hats—marveled
at the overpowering sights and smells Manila offered. While their officers
struggled to correct their record books and find more tentage, the troops learned
that they could easily afford Chinese coolies to do their dirty work and that the
Filipinos would trade eggs, bananas, and chickens for the despised army ration of
canned salmon or "goldfish." But hardly had the Volunteers become accustomed
to Manila when Otis' staff dispatched them to camps around the city's outskirts.
There the veterans would excite the newcomers with tales of imminent attack, and
often the power of suggestion became so strong that the Volunteers would fill the
night with riflefire. After a few self-inflicted casualties, Otis' headquarters considered them ready for the next expedition.[7]

Bullard accepted the Eighth Corps' initiation ritual, but he badgered Otis'
headquarters for a combat assignment. Fortunately, his arrival coincided with the
preparations for another expedition south of Manila. The Eighth Corps was
anxious to break up another rumored attack on the capital and to rescue the one
thousand Spaniards in Filipino hands. More important, the army was ready to
crush the Cavite army and to occupy all the southern provinces. The First Division
of Otis' corps was again assigned the southern Luzon offensive. Otis and his chief
of staff, Brigadier General Theodore Schwan, made the plans, for on December 19
Henry W. Lawton had found his fatal bullet at San Mateo. His successor, Major
General John C. Bates, did not assume command until January 4, the day the
offensive began. Although there was confusion in its organization, the division
was well supplied with troops. The Cavite offensive was assigned to two brigades
(commanded by Lloyd Wheaton and Schwan himself) composed of six in-

fantry regiments, two cavalry squadrons, four artillery batteries, Macabebe scouts, assorted support troops, and a massive wagon train. Four other infantry regiments were assigned to the division, but were not part of the two maneuver brigades. One of these was the Thirty-Ninth, for Otis wanted the "siege" of Calamba raised as well. Given this peripheral operation, Bullard, his regimental headquarters, and the Third Battalion went by boat to Calamba in mid-December. His other two battalions remained in Manila.[8]

As the First Division massed in Cavite, Bullard took a close look at the Calamba siege. Conferring with his old friend Lieutenant Colonel James Parker and a sturdy, drawling artillery lieutenant, Charles P. Summerall, he quickly recognized that the Twenty-First had been needlessly cowed. The Calamba situation was "ridiculous," for the enemy was nothing more than "a lot of bare-foot, shirt-tail, half-armed Filipinos!" He reconnoitered the rice paddies, roads, and low hills about Calamba and asked for the rest of his regiment. At the end of December the Thirty-Ninth took over the defense of Calamba. Its colonel had no intention of missing what appeared to be the last campaign of the Philippine Insurrection.[9]

During his reconnaissance on December's last three days, Bullard chose to make his first attack upon the Filipino trenches behind the San Cristobal river to the northwest of Calamba. Though the enemy force there numbered four hundred men and one cannon, the ground to the north was firmer than the rice paddies to the east and south. There were also excellent strategic reasons for an assault along the Calamba-Cabayo-Santa Rosa road. An attack in that direction, even if limited, threatened the insurgent positions in Cavite from the rear, especially at the town of Biñan. Biñan, in fact, was a crucial objective in Otis' plans, for at that lakeshore town Schwan's brigade was to turn west and cut off the insurgent army in front of Imus. Schwan's attack was to be the envelopment which trapped Trías' force while Wheaton's brigade held it in place with a frontal attack. How much Bullard knew of these plans is uncertain, but since Otis briefed him before he left for Calamba, he may have had some knowledge of Schwan's movement. But the Thirty-Ninth had no role in the main attack.[10]

The Thirty-Ninth welcomed the New Year by moving into position to attack the San Cristobal position. Under the concealment of darkness, Bullard arranged his minor Cannae. To the west he sent Captain Wallace C. Taylor and Companies E and F to envelop the insurgents' right flank; Major John Henry Parker embarked with Companies I and L and put out into the lake in native barges, with orders to come ashore at first light behind the Filipinos' left flank. Along the northern edge of Calamba Bullard deployed the main assault force: Companies G, H, K, M, and the four guns of Summerall's battery. As the sky lightened the colonel may have had disquieting moments, for, after fifteen years of service, he was about to go into combat for the first time.

At about six o'clock Summerall's battery opened fire and Bullard led his four companies across the mile of open ground between Calamba and the river. Though the Filipino fire was not accurate, the attack faltered enough to raise the colonel's ire. He found that bullets, however high and aimless, had a way of ruining the best plans and parade-ground discipline. Though he had criticized another colonel who had been killed leading a charge, he learned that only his and his officers' personal example kept the men firing and moving. The attack had its ludicrous moments as well as frustrations. At one point, a group of fleeing insurgents ran by Bullard as he emptied his .38 revolver at them without a hit; as the firing line closed on the trenches one soldier threw down his rifle and chased off after a monkey. Yet with a handful of casualties, the three columns of the Thirty-Ninth converged on the San Cristobal trenches after three hours firing. At last the Filipinos gave way and fled up the road to Cabayo, leaving behind twenty dead and their fieldpiece.[11]

Gathering his eight companies on the road, Bullard pursued the Filipinos the seven miles to Cabayo. At the outskirts there was a skirmish with an enemy rearguard. Again the artillery and Volunteers' rifles opened the road, and the column trudged on, arriving at Santa Rosa five miles farther north before nightfall. The next day (January 2), after one more brief fight, Bullard, with Summerall's guns and Parker's battalion, took Biñan. On January 3 Captain Frank S. Long and Company L reconnoitered the road west to Carmona and discovered an insurgent position at a bamboo bridge. Long's men drove the Filipinos away, killing thirty. Whether he recognized it or not, Bullard's command had opened the way for Schwan's flank march.

The First Division's offensive began slowly and in great confusion, for Otis still feared an attack on Manila and would not release troops for Schwan's brigade. There was much marching and countermarching before Schwan got his command in hand. In addition, the general was more generous with transport than the roads would bear. His original plans allowed each regiment forty wagons and provided twenty-five more wagons for the brigade quartermaster. Schwan did not want any looting and he issued orders that all foraged food be paid for. With the lakeshore road jammed with plunging *carabao* and balky mules while staff officers searched the countryside for additional cartroads, Schwan's brigade marched south on January 4, the day after Long's fight on the Silang road. The brigade arrived before Biñan the afternoon of January 6. Instead of meeting Bullard, Schwan found the town defended by six hundred uniformed Filipinos. In the short fight for the town, Schwan's brigade lost five men, though it inflicted much heavier casualties on the insurgents. Most of the insurgents faded to the west before the men of the Thirtieth Infantry entered Biñan.

The Thirty-Ninth Infantry was not in Biñan to greet Schwan's troops because Otis and Schwan did not want it there. When Bullard cabled Manila about his successful attack from Calamba to Biñan, he received mild censure: "You did right in attacking the insurgents' line around Calamba, but should not have pursued." Bullard was ordered back to Calamba to "watch" for insurgents to the south and east. "Do not move from the vicinity of Calamba without orders from superior authority."[12] Presented with developments beyond his capacity to absorb, Otis developed a penchant for the maneuver "halt." For Bullard's benefit, he refined "halt" to "withdraw." In any event, by nightfall of January 3 Bullard's command was back in Calamba, having killed two hundred insurgents at the cost

of fourteen wounded. The colonel and his Volunteers had weathered their first
fight with both the Filipinos and the army's generals.

2.

On January 9 the Thirty-Ninth Infantry officially joined the "conquest" of
southern Luzon. Seeing that Schwan's brigade was losing the footrace with Trías'
disintegrating army, General Bates ordered Bullard's command south from
Calamba to the city of Santo Tomás in order to force the Laguna rebels in front of
Schwan's troops. Somewhere in the Santo Tomás area, Bullard should meet the
Filipinos of Miguel Malvar, *jefe* of Batangas province, and American soldiers
marching east along the north shore of Lake Taal. Even if Malvar's force retreated,
the seizure of Santo Tomás and the neighboring city of Tanauan would open the
roads west to the city of San Pablo and south to Lipa.[13]

Given the fragmentation of Trías' forces, Bullard's assignment was not especially perilous. For the twelve-mile march up the valley of San Juan river, his
command included all three battalions of the Thirty-Ninth (some eleven hundred
officers and men), Summerall's mixed battery of a field gun, two Hotchkiss pack
howitzers and a Gatling gun, and a battalion of the Thirty-Seventh Volunteers.

Nor was the terrain and weather a handicap. As long as there was no rain the
Calambo-Santo Tomaś road could bear the traffic, while the San Juan river
protected the road's western flank. The mountains which formed the western edge
of the valley of the San Juan were too far away to be tactically significant; the hills
above the road to the east were close enough to the road to offer terrain for an
ambush, but were neither very steep nor heavily forested. The roadway itself could
be blocked at a series of cuts, but insurgent trenches there would present an
exposed flank to a well-deployed attacker. The tactical situation was not unlike a
hundred others American troops had already overcome with minimum casualties.

Bullard was not yet ready, however, to take liberties with the insurgents, and his
scheme of maneuver was both wise and effective. At 3 A.M. on January 9 he
himself left Calamba with the First Battalion and the Thirty-Seventh's battalion to
sweep the foothills along the base of Mount Maquiling west of the Santo Tomás
road. Captain Taylor then took two companies to march through the hills east of
the road. Up the road itself came three more companies of the Thirty-Ninth,
Summerall's battery, and the supply train, the whole force commanded by Major
Langhorne. Three companies of the Third Battalion of the Thirty-Ninth remained
in Calamba as a reserve.

Bullard's advance went as planned, an exhilarating experience for any commander new to combat. The First Battalion ran off the remnants of Calamba's
besiegers and marched west of the San Juan, meeting the insurgents once more
among the hills and *cogon* grass and putting them to flight. Taylor's column had
little more to do than march. Langhorne's column trekked up the Santo Tomás
Road, meeting only sporadic fire from snipers and three weakly defended road
blocks. Only as the Americans approached Santo Tomás itself was there serious

resistance, for here the terrain was favorable for a defense. About a mile north of the town a branch of the San Juan river ran east through a gorge which cut horizontally across the road. The only direct route to Santo Tomás was a wooden bridge across the forty-foot-deep canyon. Behind the bridge the road ran through a cut in two hills in which the Filipinos had entrenched themselves. Langhorne's force and Summerall's guns deployed and soon reduced the insurgent position to shattered bodies and debris. The survivors fled again, leaving four cannon, twenty-five rifles, and fifty-nine bodies. Fifty Filipinos surrendered. While Langhorne was skirmishing with Santo Tomás' defenders for about an hour, Bullard's column swept into the city from the west, meeting little resistance. With a loss of one killed and two wounded, Bullard took Santo Tomás and awaited Schwan's columns. The next day the advance party of the Thirty-Eighth Volunteers, detached from Wheaton's brigade, tramped toward Santo Tomás, then turned south to occupy the city of Tanauan.

In this fluid situation the restless commander of the Thirty-Ninth was not satisfied to settle down at Santo Tomás to direct traffic. While the Thirty-Eighth Infantry, commanded by Colonel George S. Anderson, a more senior regular army officer, marched toward him, Bullard returned to Calamba and ordered up Parker's battalion and the rest of his pack mules and *carabao* carts. In Calamba he learned that his regiment had been assigned to Schwan's brigade, but he received no further instructions. Back in Santo Tomás he and Anderson conferred and agreed to push south after the *insurrectos*. Bullard approved of General Wheaton's last instructions to Anderson: "to pursue and punish the enemy wherever found."

Early in the morning of January 13 the Thirty-Eighth headed south for Lipa, Malvar's "stronghold" ten miles away. Bullard's regiment marched in support. Halfway to Lipa, Anderson's advance guard ran into another forlorn roadblock and took it under fire with rifles and Summerall's guns. Bullard, "eager to get into the fight," offered to add the Thirty-Ninth to the attack. He also coached Anderson on tactics, giving "good" advice, but it took only two companies to scatter the Filipinos. Bullard then suggested that the Thirty-Ninth take the lead since it was rested. Again Anderson politely declined. In the early afternoon the Thirty-Eighth marched into one more deserted and shuttered town.

But from Lipa's plaza came jubilant shouts: "¡*Viva los americanos!*" At last the Americans had caught up with some prisoners, some two hundred Spanish soldiers and a handful of priests and civilians. Amid the confusion a Spanish soldier approached Anderson and Bullard. Did the *coroneles* know that in Rosario, only five miles away, the *insurrectos* held none other than *el teniente* Gillmore?

Riding a wave of euphoria, contemptuous of the Filipinos' fighting qualities, and fearful that the insurrection was dying before sufficient glory had been won, the American colonels organized an ad hoc cavalry troop for a dash to Rosario. The moving spirit in the extemporized rescue mission was Bullard. Arming themselves with borrowed rifles, mounted on Filipino ponies, the knights-errant included the two colonels, Bullard's old friend Lieutenant Colonel Charles J. Crane of the

Thirty-Eighth, his dour West Point classmate Major Charles H. Muir of the same regiment, three more of Anderson's officers, Bullard's four mounted orderlies, and a Spanish guide. Off the scratch troop galloped, meeting no more resistance along the ride than the moving, squalling roadblock of refugees. Pistols at the ready, Bullard's force clattered into Rosario. The town was in pandemonium, and a few shots cleared the streets of all but debris and a couple of bodies. The Filipino militia fled to the south, probably believing that the hostile handful was the vanguard of the United States Cavalry. Behind they left papers, baggage, ammunition, and military supplies. And amid the confusion seventy more Spanish soldiers eluded their guards. After hysterically thanking the Americans and their quick-witted comrade, one of them showed Bullard a chest containing twenty thousand Mexican dollars. Money in hand, the mounted men returned immediately to Lipa. There had been no Americans in the area, let alone the elusive Lieutenant Gillmore, but the troop returned as euphoric as it left.[14]

In the next twenty-four hours, Bullard learned that his ride to Rosario was not as inspired as he had thought. He soon learned that Schwan was not impressed with any part of the attack on Lipa and Rosario, which he called at best "a most venturesome enterprise . . . [it] may well be characterized as a notable affair."[15] It was not, however, what he had had in mind for the Thirty-Eighth and Thirty-Ninth Infantry. Upon getting these regiments on January 10, he had sent orders for them to halt at Santo Tomás. Before approving any movement, Schwan wanted Anderson and Bullard "to report and explain the military situation to me" when he arrived at Santo Tomás on the evening of January 13.[16] Schwan thought that his message, relayed from Manila to Calamba, had gotten through. Then he learned from Bullard's adjutant in Calamba that Anderson had brought up supplies for another advance. This time his orders went by mounted courier: halt "at the very earliest moment feasible" so that the brigade could get its supply lines rearranged and bring up the Thirtieth Infantry. A movement on Lipa would spoil Bates' plans for the envelopment from south of Lake Taal.[17] This message Anderson received as his men marched into Lipa. As he and Bullard explained to the general, their regiments had halted in Lipa—but not they themselves. Schwan was not amused.[18]

When Bullard galloped for Rosario, he left his flanks as well as his rear unprotected. Only one of these flanks was attacked by the Filipinos. In his absence the soldiers of the Thirtieth Infantry and Fourth Cavalry joined the Lipa garrison, bringing with them the Thirtieth's commander, Colonel Cornelius Gardener, a martinet with anti-imperialist impulses and strong political connections in Michigan. Gardener found the Thirty-Eighth and Thirty-Ninth Infantry dining happily on foraged fruit and roast yearling *carabao*, for the rations were gone. To Gardener the picnic looked like looting, and he scolded the Volunteers and put Anderson and Bullard on report for "heinous" offenses when Schwan arrived in Lipa. The colonels reminded Schwan that he had authorized foraging (as he had) and that quartermaster receipts had been issued.[19] Adding to the embarrassment was the fact that the insurgents were not so defeated as they seemed. On the afternoon of Bullard's ride, Schwan's supply train, escorted by two companies of the Thirty-Ninth, had to run a gauntlet of sniping from Tanauan to Lipa.

Sometime during January 14 Bullard had a stormy session with Schwan. For his pains he then saw two of his battalions march away with Schwan's brigade when the general continued his chase to the east. Schwan had had enough of Bullard, though he admitted the success of the Lipa-Rosario raid. Tall, gaunt, gentlemanly, his flowing hair and mustache bleached white in forty-three years service, the general had one last ambition. Nearing retirement, he wanted promotion to brigadier general in the regular army. As his campaign began, the general had learned that McKinley had just promoted Arthur MacArthur (a mere lieutenant colonel in the regulars) and Samuel B. M. Young, an honor he too coveted. Since the Civil War his forte had been selfless and anonymous service. The southern Luzon campaign might be his last. A sergeant in the Tenth Infantry before Bullard's birth, General Schwan had little sympathy for youthful adventurers who confused his plans and stole his glory.[20]

Annoyed by Bullard's élan and concerned about the guerrillas popping away from the mountains behind him, Schwan ordered Bullard and his Third Battalion back to Santo Tomás to guard the brigade's supply route and telegraph lines. Mulford's and Langhorne's battalions joined Schwan's brigade (under Colonel Gardener's supervision) and tramped away for another three weeks of glorious and near-bloodless campaigning. They marched without their seething colonel.

3.

Robert Lee Bullard, a colonel without a regiment, returned to Santo Tomás uncontrite, vowing to "run a little war of my own and be heard from."[21] His immediate actions were vigorous, but subordinate. The problems of establishing a permanent garrison in Santo Tomás and of getting supplies forward to San Pablo were not simple, for instead of being a peaceful rear area the Santo Tomás-San Pablo district was still a battlefield. For a few days it had seemed otherwise. As Bullard and his Third Battalion marched to Santo Tomás, they found the roads jammed with returning Filipinos. In Santo Tomás, the inhabitants came in from the hills, the marketplace reopened, and the town again swarmed with white-clad civilians going about their daily chores. The bucolic peace in the town was illusory; one of the participants in the nightly cockfight was Miguel Malvar himself, conducting a reconnaissance. Then on January 18 the *insurrectos* struck a pack-train guarded by a detail of the Thirtieth Infantry. When the train was strung out along the road near Alaminos, the Filipinos opened fire at close range. The surprise was complete, the ambushed soldiers falling or fleeing, and the entire train was lost to the *insurrectos*. When Captain Long's Company L brought in the survivors, the sobered colonel found them "pitiable." It was the first time he had seen beaten American soldiers, and it was an unpleasant experience. He immediately organized another supply train, this time using more manageable *carabao* carts and his own troops for escorts.[22]

Nor was the Thirty-Ninth safe from the embarrassments of an ambush. On February 2 a patrol of two officers and eight men was attacked southwest of Tanauan near Lake Taal. The officers and six men were able to fight free, but a sergeant was killed and a private captured. The *insurrectos* did not seem to understand that they had lost the war.[23]

Stirred by the Filipino's hostility, Bullard began going out with his own patrols. On February 9 he personally took two companies into the hills between Alaminos and Lipa to search for Malvar's rumored headquarters. Three days later he found an insurgent camp at the isolated *barrio* of San Francisco. His troops encircled the *barrio*, surrounding about one hundred Filipinos. Sensing the attack, the *insurrectos* fired and fled, but not before twelve died and money, arms, and provisions were abandoned. Four soldiers were wounded. Scouting west to Lake Taal before coming in, Bullard was pleased with the Volunteers' performance and became determined to continue the aggressive patrolling.[24]

In the meantime, Schwan's brigade was occupying the eastern towns of Tayabas province and breaking up the last organized resistance south of Manila. Schwan considered the fighting to his rear a simple matter of chasing down small bands of *insurrectos* bypassed in his offensive. Satisfied with the accomplishments of his brigade, he sent out congratulations to his regiments and their colonels. Schwan commended Bullard for his aggressive leadership, and Generals Wheaton and Bates concurred that the Thirty-Ninth indeed had been a most visible unit in the campaign. Flattered by their praise, Bullard began to toy with a new idea, that he might someday become a general, at least a wartime general of volunteers. He sat down one evening and drew up a memorandum for the Adjutant General and the assistant secretary of war in order to refresh their memories about his existence and to bring his service record up-to-date. Bullard thought the memorandum convincing, but feared that his rivals had too much political influence. Bullard despaired: "For political reasons both Anderson and Gardener are favored. Record and facts show, however, that I have done more than either of them to deserve appointment." Reflecting on his performance since the start of the new year, he could not defeat the thought that he—a captain in the Subsistence Department— should be a general.[25]

NOTES

[1] For the military operations of the Philippine Insurrection, see Captain John R. M. Taylor, "The Philippine Insurrection Against the United States: A Compilation of Documents with Notes and Introduction," Microfilm Publication 719, NA; John M. Gates, *Schoolbooks and Krags: The United States Army in the Philippines, 1898-1902* (Westport, Conn.: Greenwood Press, 1973); William T. Sexton, *Soldiers in the Sun* (Harrisburg, Pa.:

Military Service Publishing Company, 1939); and Uldarico S. Baclagon, *Philippine Campaigns* (Manila: Graphic House, 1952).

²The mass of their captured records testifies to the insurgents' Spanish heritage. See File 914 (Laguna Province, 1898), Selected Documents, Philippine Insurgent Records, 1896-1901, with Associate Records of the United States War Department, 1900-1906 (PIR), Microcopy 254, NA; and Packages 4 and 35/AGO 460166 (Batangas Province), New Series of Packages, PIR, NA. One insurgent general surrendered because "I found myself without a single gun or clerk. . . ." (File 902, Selected Documents, PIR.).

³George B. Duncan, "Reminiscences, 1882-1906," p. 157, *mss* autobiography in the possession of Dr. Edward M. Coffman, University of Wisconsin-Madison.

⁴The military operations in southern Luzon are described in Taylor, "The Philippine Insurrection Against the United States" II, chapters 4 and 5; Baclagon, *Philippine Campaigns*, pp. 113-130; and Sexton, *Soldiers in the Sun*, pp. 221-231.

⁵James Parker, *The Old Army: Memories, 1872-1918* (Philadelphia: Dorrance and Company, 1929), pp. 240-244; Thomas Cruse, *Apache Days and After* (Caldwell, Ida.: Caxton Printers, 1941), p. 284; Beaumont Buck, *Memories of War and Peace* (San Antonio: The Naylor Company, 1935), pp. 75-77.

⁶Diarybook 1, entry, December 8, 1899, and Col. R. L. Bullard to Rose Bullard, March 8, 1900, BP; Captain John L. Jordan to Mrs. Jordan, December 28, 1899, John L. Jordan Papers, Tennessee State Library and Archives. (Jordan's regiment, the Thirty-Eighth Infantry, arrived shortly after Bullard's.) The description of Manila is from contemporary articles in *Harper's Weekly* and *Frank Leslie's Illustrated Weekly* for December 1899.

⁷Diarybook 1, entry, December 8, 1899, BP; Frederick J. Herman, *The Forty-Second Foot* (Kansas City, Mo.: n. p., 1942), pp. 31-32, 61; James H. Blount, *The American Occupation of the Philippines, 1898-1912* (New York: G. P. Putnam's Sons, 1912), pp. 159, 192-194, 196-199; George B. Duncan, "Reminiscences," pp. 159-161.

⁸Diarybook 1, entry, January 3, 1900, and Col. R. L. Bullard to Rose Bullard, March 8, 1900, and Bullard autobiography, p. 34, BP; Taylor, "The Philippine Insurrection Against the United States," chapter VI; entries, December 23, 1899-January 4, 1900, Brig. Gen. W. A. Kobbé, "Diary of Field Service in the Philippines, 1898-1901," Brigadier William A. Kobbé Papers, USAMHRC; Frederick Palmer, "Cleaning Up Cavite Province," *Collier's Weekly* 24 (March 3, 1900), pp. 6-7; "Report of Major General E. S. Otis, U.S. Army, Commanding the Division of the Philippines, and Military Governor of the Philippine Islands, September 1, 1899, to May 5, 1900," in *Annual Reports of the War Department, 1900* (Washington: Government Printing Office, 1900), I, Pt. 4, pp. 368-393 (hereafter cited as "Otis Report"); Mariano Trías, memo, to commanders of divisions and columns, December 20, 1899, Folder 1140, Selected Documents, PIR, and Licero Gerónimo to Mariano Barroga, Modesto Victorino, and "Other Companions and Chiefs Serving Under Our Sacred Cause," December 14, 1899, *ibid.*

⁹Diarybook 1, entry, January 3, 1900, and Bullard autobiography, p. 34, BP. Parker's memoir agrees with Bullard's account as does "Historical Sketch of the Foreign Service of the 10th Battery Field Artillery," *mss* (n.d., n.p.), General Charles P. Summerall Papers, Library of Congress.

¹⁰Col. R. L. Bullard to Rose Bullard, March 8, 1900, BP; "Reports of Col. R. L. Bullard, Thirty-Ninth Infantry, U.S.V., of the Operations of the Thirty-Ninth Infantry, January 1 to September 1, 1900," in *Annual Reports of the War Department, 1900* (Washington: Government Printing Office, 1900), I, Part 7, pp. 393-396; Brig. Gen. T. Schwan to Brig.

Gen. H. C. Corbin, February 16, 1900, Corbin Papers; Maj. Gen. E. S. Otis to Adj. Gen., January 8, 1900, *CRWS* II, p. 1129; Sexton, *Soldiers in the Sun*, pp. 221-228.

[11]Bullard autobiography, pp. 34-38, BP; "History of the 39th Infantry U.S. Volunteers," "Historical Sketches of Volunteer Organizations," AGO 396223 (1901), RG 94; "Historical Sketch of the Foreign Service of the 10th Battery Field Artillery," Summerall Papers.

[12]Brig. Gen. T. Schwan, Chief-of-Staff, to Colonel Bullard, Calamba, January 3, 1900, in "Otis Report," p. 377. "Otis Report," Bullard's contemporary correspondence, the two histories of the Thirty-Ninth Infantry, the history of Summerall's artillery platoon, Bullard's 201 File, and the "Caption and Records of Events Cards, 39th U.S. Volunteer Infantry, 1899-1901," in the records of The Office of the Adjutant-General, RG 94, are in essential agreement about where and when the Thirty-Ninth fought from January 1 to 3, 1900. The Thirty-Ninth's march to Biñan is not clearly identified on the "Map Showing Operations January 4, February 8, 1900 by the First Division, Eighth Corps" in the General Staff Map Collection (1900) in the Cartographic Branch, National Archives.

[13]The following operational narrative is based upon "Reports of Col. R. L. Bullard, Thirty-Ninth Infantry, U.S.V., of Operations of the Thirty-Ninth Infantry, January 1 to September 1, 1900," previously cited; "History of the 39th Infantry, U.S. Volunteers"; Col. R. L. Bullard to Rose Bullard, March 8, 1900, BP; and "Report of Operations of Schwan's Expeditionary Brigade in the Provinces of Cavite, Batangas, Laguna, and Tayabas, January 4 to February 8, 1900, by Brig. Gen. Theodore Schwan, U.S.V., Commanding," in *Annual Reports of the War Department* (Washington: Government Printing Office, 1900), I, Part 5, pp. 387-564 with maps and appendices (hereafter cited as "Schwan's Report").

[14]Col. G. S. Anderson to Brig. Gen. T. Schwan, January 21, 1900, "Schwan's Report," pp. 522-533; Bullard autobiography, pp. 39-41; Col. R. L. Bullard to Rose Bullard, March 8, 1900, and Diarybook 1, entry, January 24, 1900, BP; "History of the 39th Infantry, U.S. Volunteers," previously cited; Charles J. Crane, *The Experiences of a Colonel of Infantry* (New York: The Knickerbocker Press, 1923), pp. 330-333; Col. R. L. Bullard to Adj. Gen., Department of the Pacific, Eighth Army Corps, January 16, 1900, "Letters Sent" book of the Thirty-Ninth Infantry, August 28, 1899-February 28, 1900, in the Records of The Adjutant General's Office, RG 94; Sexton, *Soldiers in the Sun*, pp. 221-231.

[15]"Schwan's Report," pp. 396-397; Brig. Gen. T. Schwan to Adj. Gen., Eighth Army Corps, January 15, 1900, "Otis' Report," p. 383.

[16]Lt. Col. S. D. Sturgis (Schwan's adjutant) to Col. G. S. Anderson, January 12, 1900, and Brig. Gen. T. Schwan to Col. R. L. Bullard, January 12, 1900, "Schwan's Report," pp. 444-445.

[17]Capt. N. Gaines (Bullard's adjutant) to Brig. Gen. T. Schwan, January 12, 1900, and Brig. Gen. T. Schwan to Col. G. S. Anderson, January 13, 1900, "Schwan's Report," p. 446.

[18]Brig. Gen. T. Schwan to Adj. Eighth Army Corps, January 12, 14, and 15, 1900 "Otis' Report," pp. 381-383.

[19]Col. G. S. Anderson to Brig. Gen. T. Schwan, January 21, 1900, "Schwan's Report," p. 522-523; Lt. Col. S. D. Sturgis to Capt. S. E. Smiley (Schwan's aide), January 14, 1900, "Schwan's Report," p. 453; Capt. J. L. Jordan to Mrs. Jordan, January 23, 1900, Jordan Papers; Bullard autobiography, pp. 41-43, BP.

[20]Brig. Gen. T. Schwan to Adj. Gen., Eighth Army Corps, January 16, 1900, "Otis'

Report," p. 383; Lt. Col. S. D. Sturgis to Col. G. S. Anderson, January 14, 1900, and to Col. R. L. Bullard, January 15, 1900, "Schwan's Report," pp. 449-500; Bullard autobiography, pp. 41-43, BP; Brig. Gen. T. Schwan to Col. R. L. Bullard, February 6, 1900, reprinted in "History of the 39th Infantry, U.S. Volunteers"; Maj. Gen. E. S. Otis to the Adj. Gen., January 15,1900, *CRWS* II, p. 1132; Schuyler journal entry, January 13, 1900, W. S. Schuyler Papers; Brig. Gen. T. Schwan to Brig. Gen. H. C. Corbin, February 16, 1900, Corbin Papers; Mark A. Hanna to W. McKinley, September 1, 1900, and H. C. Payne to W. McKinley, September 5, 1900, both Series 1/Reel 12, McKinley Papers.

[21]Bullard autobiography, p. 41, BP.

[22]Bullard autobiography, p. 44, and Diarybook 1, entry, January 24, 1900; "History of the 39th Volunteers," Special Order 12, January 28, 1900, in Regimental Orderbook in the records of The Office of the Adjutant-General, RG 94; Brig. Gen. T. Schwan to Col. R. L. Bullard, two messages, January 19, 1900, "Schwan's Report," pp. 464-465; Maj. Gen. E. S. Otis to Adj. Gen., January 19, 1900, *CRWS* II, p. 1135.

[23]Col. R. L. Bullard to Brig. Gen. T. Schwan, February 8, 1900, in the Regimental "Letters Sent" book (August 28, 1899-February 28, 1900), RG 94; "History of the 39th Infantry, U.S. Volunteers," pp. 18-19.

[24]Col. R. L. Bullard to Rose Bullard, March 8, 1900, Maj. J. H. Parker to Brig. Gen. Schwan, February 12, 1900, and Col. R. L. Bullard to Adj. Gen., Schwan's Brigade, February 16, 1899, in Regimental "Letters Sent" book (August 28, 1899-February 28, 1900); "History of the 39th Infantry U.S. Volunteers," p. 18.

[25]Brig. Gen. T. Schwan to Col. R. L. Bullard, February 16, 1900, "Schwan's Report," p. 500; Col. R. L. Bullard to Rose Bullard, March 8, 1900, and "Memoranda Urging Colonel Bullard by Appointed Brigadier Generals of Volunteers" (n.d.), copies to Major General Henry C. Corbin and Assistant Secretary of War George D. Meiklejohn, Bullard AGO File.

8

Pacification in
Southern Luzon
1900-1901

Although they did not fully realize it, Colonel Bullard and Major Parker's orphaned battalion had not been shunted to a rear area behind Schwan's offensive. The guerrilla warfare of February was not the desperate tactics of a defeated enemy, but a prelude to a two-year struggle for the control of Laguna and Batangas provinces. In this contest the Thirty-Ninth and its commander were more severely tested than they had been in the January campaign.

Schwan's expedition into Batangas, Laguna, and Tayabas provinces was not futile, since the Americans killed hundreds of insurgents, captured and destroyed substantial numbers of arms and supplies, and disrupted the insurgent organization. After Schwan's advance the larger towns of these provinces were permanently garrisoned. The collapse of the Filipino revolutionaries, however, was more superficial than the American officers suspected. In fact, the higher officers of the Philippine army were already implementing instructions drafted in November 1899 by Aguinaldo and his refugee council of war. Aguinaldo's message ordered the strategy he had probably always preferred: guerrilla warfare against the Americans and revolutionary control of the people. The American military victory would be reversed. The rebel officers would govern the Filipinos with persuasion and terror under the very eyes of the occupiers. While being frustrated in their efforts to rule, the American troops would be eroded by disease and guerrilla warfare. Disillusioned by the cost and failure of their colonial experiment, the voters of the United States would reject the McKinley Administration. Their Democratic successors, sympathetic to anti-imperialism, would then withdraw the American troops.

In this campaign to throw back Western imperialism, the Filipino leadership hoped to receive diplomatic and military assistance from the Chinese republicans and Japanese pan-asianists. Reduced to doctrine, the Filipino strategy was the classic prescription for a traditional, technologically backward society faced with the occupation of a European army:

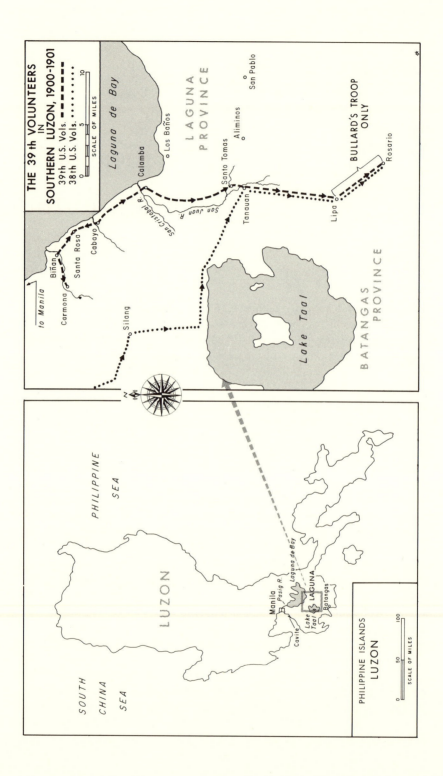

THE 39th VOLUNTEERS
IN
SOUTHERN LUZON, 1900-1901

39th U.S. Vols. ▬ ▬ ▬
38th U.S. Vols. ● ● ● ● ●

SCALE OF MILES
0   5   10

Laguna de Bay

LAGUNA PROVINCE

San Pablo

Aliminos

Santo Tomas

Los Baños

Calamba

San Juan R.

San Cristobal R.

Cabayo

Santa Rosa

Biñan

Carmona

to Manila

Silang

Tanauan

Lipa

Rosario

BULLARD'S TROOP ONLY

Lake Taal

BATANGAS PROVINCE

N

PHILIPPINE SEA

LUZON

SOUTH CHINA SEA

Manila

Pasig R.

Laguna de Bay

LAGUNA

Lake Taal

Cavite

Batangas

PHILIPPINE ISLANDS
LUZON

SCALE OF MILES
0   50   100

The object of the guerrillas will be to constantly fight the Yankees in the towns occupied by them, attacking their convoys, inflicting all the injury they can upon their patrols, surprising their detachments, destroying their columns when they pass places favorable to our attacks and inflicting exemplary punishment on traitors to prevent the people of the towns from unworthily selling themselves for the gold of the invader; but in addition they will protect the loyal inhabitants and will watch over their property and defend them from bandits and petty thieves.

Some 500 Filipinos will be enough for each province. We shall distribute them as guerrillas in every town with a base of operations giving strategic advantages hidden in the mountainous part of the province. These parties will be composed of few men in order to avoid attracting attention and to render their disappearance more easy when it is convenient for them to vanish. When the enemy attacks these small parties they will fall back to the base of operations so that when the enemy is most weary in their pursuit they may fall together upon him with all the advantage which will be given them by occupying a point prepared in advance for attack.

Let the exhausting climate decimate their ranks, and we should not forget that our object is only to prolong the war.[1]

In Laguna and Batangas, the insurgent hold on the population survived Schwan's offensive intact. Moreover, the geographic and demographic conditions in this part of southern Luzon gave the insurgents just the setting they needed for a successful resistance. The two provinces had a combined area of eighteen hundred square miles, which included, outside of the agricultural lowlands, extensive mountains, jungle and forests, and hill country broken by bewildering systems of canyons and streams. In dry weather the wagon tracks and trails were tortuous, and in the monsoon season they became virtually impassable. The terrain was, however, only part of the insurgents' tactical environment. More important, the two provinces were heavily populated (nearly half a million residents), and ethnically the people were homogeneously Hispanicized Tagalogs. Thus there was no latent ethnic hostility for the Americans to exploit. In fact, the area was politically cohesive, unified by its anticlericalism and racial antipathy for Europeans. The population was equally committed to its parochial way of life, to the web of family relationships, tilling, its mutant form of Catholicism, and its generations of identification with the land.

The army knew about inhospitable terrain. Its officers viewed the conditions in the Philippines as no more demanding than their prior campaigning on the American frontier or in the Caribbean. The prevalence of epidemic disease did not especially discourage them, for the army had also developed the sanitary doctrine, techniques, and equipment to frustrate disease, within the limits of contemporary medical knowledge. But the experience of living among such a large, hostile, and culturally alien people was a new experience. The Indian campaigns were not analogous. In the Philippines the army never had the railroads, buffalo hunters, and the push of white settlement to uproot and degrade their primitive foe. The Indian wars were amateur melees compared with the insurrection waged in 1900 by Mariano Trías, Miguel Malvar, and Juan Cailles in southern Luzon.[2]

1

By early February 1900 Colonel Bullard had the Thirty-Ninth Infantry back under his command, and he began establishing his permanent posts for the occupation of Laguna and Batangas provinces. While Bullard had not been impressed with the military problems of rounding up scattered guerrilla bands, he recognized the challenge of maintaining his troops in a hostile climate and of patrolling a vast area of responsibility. The American troops were none too numerous. In the early spring of 1900 there were only four regiments (perhaps four thousand men) stationed east of Lake Taal between Laguna de Bay and the south coast. Bullard's garrisons in Laguna and northern Batangas were concentrated at four towns. Major Langhorne's battalion was split between Calamba and Los Baños on Laguna de Bay. Langhorne himself commanded the Calamba garrison of two companies, while Captain Wallace C. Taylor managed the Los Baños garrison of two companies. The Thirty-Ninth was well deployed along the lake, for the two garrisons were close enough (six miles) to support each other and Langhorne and Taylor were able officers. They had to be, for their territory was unhealthy and heavily populated with insurgents.

Bullard's remaining two battalions were stationed in the interior on either side of a substantial range of mountains. The regimental headquarters and Companies L and M garrisoned Santo Tomás under Bullard's personal command. Two miles to the south, Parker held Tanauan with Companies I and K. Bullard's post was strengthened by a Gatling gun, and Parker's by a Hotchkiss howitzer; their impact was psychological, since they remained parked in front of the headquarters buildings.

Fifteen miles to the east, Major Harry B. Mulford's battalion occupied San Pablo, a city of strong adobe homes and seventeen thousand inhabitants. The countryside around it was low, well watered agricultural land and was heavily populated. Topographically, the San Pablo area was separated from Santo Tomás-Tanauan and the coast of Laguna de Bay by a complex range of volcanic peaks, forested hills, ravines, deep streams, and meandering foot-trails.

While Bullard's garrisons were not especially isolated from one another by many miles, the interpost line of communications was vulnerable. The roads were passable for wagons only in the dry season; in the rainy season even foot troops and mule trains found the going slow. While there were telegraph lines strung between the posts, they were bare to the insurgents' wirecutters. Of the five stations, San Pablo was especially isolated, and all three of the inland posts were surrounded by both inhospitable terrain and hostile Filipinos. Calamba and Los Baños were the most secure and easily supplied by boat, but neither qualified as a lakeside resort.[3]

As part of the Second District of the Department of Southern Luzon, Bullard's regiment was responsible for peacekeeping in the country from Calamba in the north to Lipa in the south. To the east, the Thirty-Ninth patrolled to the shore of Lake Taal north to Silang; the eastern border of its area ran from Laguna de Bay to the garrison town of Tiaon. Within this ill-defined area the Thirty-Ninth lived, marched, and fought, sharing the responsibility and hardship of watching the country *barrios* with patrols from the Thirty-Eighth and Thirtieth Volunteers, who were stationed to the south and east respectively.[4]

The Volunteers of the Thirty-Ninth settled into their garrison quarters (abandoned church or government buildings) reasonably certain that only a few bandits and guerrilla diehards would menace the growing tranquility of their district. The American soldiers watched the Filipinos come and go through the dusty streets and bustling marketplaces of the towns. For comfort, discipline, and sanitary reasons, the American soldiers lived within the circumscribed limits of their barracks and their military routine. Often the weather was too hot for much midday activity, but there were always records for the clerks to grapple with, requisitions to write, reports to forward, supplies to distribute, and a continual string of company punishments for petty offenses, most often drinking. While few doubted the antipathy of the Filipinos, the American soldiers found it increasingly difficult to believe that the insurrection was not over.

Certainly the Eighth Corps (renamed the Division of the Philippines) headquarters assumed that the army's major task was protecting the establishment of peaceful local Filipino governments. In addition it initiated public health and primary education programs. In Bullard's district, the post commanders held elections in February and March and each of the garrison towns soon had a mayor (*alcalde* or *presidente*) and a municipal council. These local officials functioned under the watchful eye of the army post commander and the district commander, an American officer who functioned as the provincial governor. The army garrisons did little to interrupt or change the Filipino way of life other than issue each citizen an identification card. Bullard, however, was not convinced that the benign army policy had reduced Filipino hostility. Even as he held elections, he had the post commanders organize a system of spies and informers to study the outwardly cooperative citizens of Calamba, Los Baños, Santo Tomás, Tanauan, and San Pablo. He suspected that the calm was superficial and the Filipinos' passivity was a tactic, not the dawn of an era of peace for Luzon. He did not, however, immediately guess how deeply the insurgent elite controlled the Filipino population.[5]

Bullard never assumed that the *insurrectos* had stopped fighting completely. There was ample evidence they had not. In March, for example, part of Juan Cailles' command in Laguna attacked Taylor's Los Baños garrison, but was easily driven off. But Bullard believed that the Filipino guerrillas were little more than small desperate bands living precariously in the mountains on limited supplies. To root out these bands, to destroy their camps *(cuartels)* and supplies, patrols of Thirty-Ninth took to the hills to end the guerrilla nuisance before the rains came.

The long patrols were by no means easy hikes through the hills. The Volunteers, sometimes staggering with heat exhaustion, fought their way through heavy vines, boulders, tangled gorges, and ubiquitous jungle. From head to foot they fought off worms, leeches, and insects. The threat of ambush was everpresent. The guerrillas themselves were hard to find when they did not want to be found. Actual combat dwindled. Occasionally a surprised Filipino soldier was killed; prisoners, taken in twos and threes, were disarmed and either paroled or placed on road-repair crews. The Third Battalion, for example, killed ninety *insurrectos* in January and February, but only two in March, April, and May. Yet even when there was no contact with the guerrillas, the patrols often had other successes: five American soldiers released; seven tons of rice destroyed; clusters of mountain shacks burned along with uniforms, bolos, ammunition, and a few rifles; bundles of Filipino documents found and analyzed for intelligence purposes. Calling themselves "Bullard's American Indians," the soldiers of the Thirty-Ninth tramped the hill trails and jungles of their district, convinced that they were about to destroy the last guerrilla band always one step ahead of them.[6]

The chief of the "American Indians" led his share of the patrols into the mountains. Unlike some of his fellow Volunteer colonels, he had the requisite ambition and energy to seek combat. When rooted to his headquarters in Santo Tomás, his problems with the regiment were depressingly constant: the growing sicklist, especially in the First Battalion at San Pablo; the lax discipline in this same battalion; the snarled state of the company records of the Third Battalion and Parker's apathy in administrative matters; the constant grappling with civil affairs and the *carabao* cart logistics system. The mountain patrols and mounted scouts between his garrisons gave the colonel a necessary release from the deadening routine of military administration. He too found the Filipinos elusive. In March he took a long patrol along the wild shore of Lake Taal, then in May led a force of twenty-five on a four-day scout through the mountains that ran from Laguna de Bay to south and west of San Pablo. The patrol penetrated the roughest terrain in his district, but found few signs of the guerrillas. Although the Americans found two small base camps and occasionally saw one or two Filipinos diving into the brush, Bullard's force could not scare up a fight, even though it set up many ambushes. Its captures were some wild pigs and chickens and a cache of fifty cartridges. Wearily reflecting upon his search after his return to Santo Tomás, Bullard reached a conclusion that was coming to many another army officer. The active insurgents were not hiding in the mountains in base camps, but were living in the towns and *barrios* among their own people and the American garrisons.[7]

2.

As Bullard surmised, the *insurrecto* leaders in his district ruled their countrymen through an "invisible government." Each cluster of huts had its military-political *jefe* in residence; often this official was also the civil leader recognized by the American military government. Sometimes the local officials were dedicated revolutionaries. More often they were terrorized trimmers, whose loyalties went to the side momentarily most threatening. Some officials, like Ramon Santos, *presidente* of Calamba, used the insurrection to strengthen their own petty tyrannies and extortion systems without giving political loyalty to either government, though pledging fealty to both.

In the spring of 1900 the *insurrecto jefes* in Laguna and Batangas, Juan Cailles and Miguel Malvar, were not pressing the American troops, but, instead, concentrated on maintaining their control of the people and organizing their guerrillas for a rainy season campaign. Bullard's raids on their base camps damaged their military position, especially when rifles and ammunition were lost, but did little to loosen the insurgents' grip on the villagers. Under the blind eyes of the American troops, the Filipino guerrillas operated a spy system to check on the loyalty of civil officials, recruited men for the sub rosa militia, and collected and cached supplies. The guerrillas used more than persuasion on countrymen whose behavior made them traitors or *americanistas*. Among the terrorist techniques were arson, mutilation, kidnapping, and execution, either by hacking a person to death or burying him alive. The power to execute rested with the local guerrilla officers; under Aguinaldo's decrees any Filipino who refused to serve in the revolutionary militia was a criminal subject to capital punishment. In addition, the terrorism was conducted for psychological effect, for the guerrillas surrounded their coercion with rituals and other mystical hocus-pocus in order to give their activities a supernatural character. Life, then, in Laguna and Batangas was dangerous for the unaligned villager. He had two governments, two military occupiers. As Bullard learned, his scouts had done little to make life more secure for the Filipinos. They obeyed those they feared most, and in May 1900, those were revolutionaries.[8]

The insurgent grip on the people was as tight in most of Luzon as it was in the area south of Laguna de Bay. As evidence accumulated in captured documents, the headquarters of the Division of the Philippines in Manila saw that the pacification had hardly begun. This assumption became official after General Otis returned to the United States in May. Major General Arthur MacArthur, his successor and an active field commander in the Philippines throughout 1899, did not accept Otis' conclusion that the insurrection had been broken. Yet the sporadic character of the insurgents' attacks on army detachments encouraged MacArthur enough that he continued Otis' benign military government. In June MacArthur carried Otis' conciliatory policy a step further and offered the guerrillas complete amnesty if they surrendered. The amnesty, by MacArthur's admission, was a failure, for only five thousand rebels took an oath of allegiance. Yet the effort had its educational value. Its very failure convinced the military governor of the enormity of the pacification yet to be done. MacArthur concluded that even after eighteen months of fighting that "every native, without any exception, residing within the limits of the Archipelago, owed active individual allegiance to the insurgent cause." The general's pessimistic assessment was shared by the Thirty-Ninth Volunteers. As Major Langhorne put it: "We are surrounded by traitors."[9]

Though the Division of the Philippines gave more attention to population control after MacArthur's assumption of command, the patrolling continued even after the June rains made it more difficult. The destruction of base camps and the killing or capturing of insurgent officers was still a crucial part of the pacification campaign. For Bullard's regiment, the war went on. As in the dry season, the patrols, usually an officer or two and twenty to thirty enlisted men, probed into the mountains, but now also checked the lowland *barrios* as well. The operations developed their own routine. A patrol would usually leave its barracks at night and march to an assigned village. There it would cordon off the huts and then, with daylight, part of the patrol would enter and demand the villagers' identification papers (*cédulas*). Suspicious villagers, especially of military age, were often detained and returned to Calamba, the district headquarters, for questioning. If a case could be made against a Filipino for active rebellion, he was held for trial by the military commission that sat in Calamba. Often the patrols would find caches of arms, ammunition, money, food, papers, and clothing. All but the papers were burned, along with the offending *nipa* hut. Less often a patrol would have a fight with the *insurrectos*. Most of these encounters were meeting engagements or ambushes which flared quickly and died out after a brief exchange of shots and bolo chops. The American soldiers then would find a brown body or two in the brush. They had their casualties as well: a private shot in the groin, another with a Mauser bullet through the temple, Captain William L. Murphy bleeding to death from a shoulder wound.[10]

Along with the patrols, the "American Indians" had equally demanding work simply maintaining their own garrisons. No wagon train or Signal Corps wiring party was safe without infantry guards. Soldiers escorted ambulances and paymaster parties from post to post. Others went on map-making expeditions. As the months rolled on, each company tallied its monthly marching mileage; each averaged between three hundred and five hundred miles in the summer of 1900. To handle patrols and escort duties the Volunteers created mounted detachments at each post with their colonel's active support.

The colonel of the Thirty-Ninth continued to lead his share of the patrols, and his taste for combat was undiminished. On July 30 Bullard took most of the Santo Tomás garrison into the mountains northwest of his post and, led by two Filipinos, found a major camp at the rear of a nearly impassable canyon. While his force could not surprise the insurgents there, it forced its way into the refuge and destroyed four thousand cartridges, medical supplies, blankets, uniforms, a complete apothecary shop, a headquarters building, and twelve other huts. On August 10 Bullard and a mounted patrol of eight men surprised fifty insurgents in a canyon camp southeast of Santo Tomás. Dismounting, Bullard's squad attacked the camp and drove the insurgents back up the canyon with rifle fire, killing two. With two Krags jammed and its ammunition nearly exhausted, the patrol retired. The next day Bullard returned with an entire company and destroyed sixteen buildings, some rice, and a lookout tower which had an excellent view of the roads to Lipa and San Pablo. One Filipino was captured.[11]

Bullard also labored to root out the insurgents' organization in his district and to comply with Manila's overambitious schemes for civic improvement. The headquarters of the Thirty-Ninth Infantry ran a spy system, collected documents, interrogated detainees, and made maps. Gradually Bullard uncovered the *jefes* in his area, both their identities and modes of operation. When Bullard was not chasing Filipino organizers, he was managing his regiment's program to improve the way of life in the garrison towns. The Thirty-Ninth Infantry established sixty-three schools in the summer of 1900, although it had trouble getting adequate supplies of books in English and Spanish, chalk, writing pads, pens, ink, and American flags. Throughout the summer, too, the Volunteers supervised the Filipino workers who built bridges and repaired roads. But much of the work was underfinanced, undermanned, and worked no revolution in Luzon's rural standard of living. If the Thirty-Ninth could honestly claim that it was not a gang of imperialist exploiters, it could not claim either that it had brought the blessings of Western civilization to Laguna and Batangas.[12]

Surveying the progress of pacification in his area, Bullard was discouraged. While he did not condemn the military government's attempt to win the people's loyalty by administrative justice and good works, he doubted that his own regiment would survive to see persuasion work. As the monsoon rains beat down, he watched his sick list soar. By midsummer his regiment was a collection of half-strength companies. Although the division headquarters in Manila continued to report the Thirty-Ninth's official (''paper'') strength to the War Department at forty-nine officers and twelve hundred thirty enlisted, Bullard had only twenty-four officers and seven hundred and twenty men fit and present for duty. His most afflicted unit was Mulford's First Battalion in San Pablo, which was wracked with typhoid. Although officers from the Inspector-General's department found Mulford complying with all the army's sanitary regulations, the First Battalion had half its officers and men in its hospital. Finally, in September, Bullard received permission to switch two of his battalions, and Langhorne's battalion replaced Mulford's in San Pablo. There was still great illness even when the seasons changed, and, in all, three officers and one hundred and eight men of the Thirty-Ninth died of assorted maladies during the regiment's service. Only thirteen were killed or died of wounds; thirty were wounded.[13]

The Thirty-Ninth's diminished strength gave it a reputation in Manila as a ''sick'' regiment, and, therefore, a problem. As rumors of its eroding reputation reached Santo Tomás, its colonel feared that he had not been strict enough with his ebullient Volunteers, especially with his battalion commanders. Officially, he pointed out to division headquarters that his regiment was stationed in a district that was ''horribly unhealthy,'' a condition which could not be changed immediately. He resented the charge that the Thirty-Ninth was somehow a demoralized and ineffective unit. ''Finally, we are not all sick nor all dying. Enough of us are left in good health and spirits and with sufficient stomach for a fight to have made this section very considerably more peaceful during the month of August that it was during the month of July.''[14] Privately, he hoped against all his professional impulses that the Thirty-Ninth Volunteers would be returned to the United States before 1901.[15]

The illness of his regiment increased Bullard's pessimism about the military government's policy of conciliation. As he learned of the cunning of the *insurrectos'* subversion, he doubted that order could be created in Laguna and Batangas without making the pacification very inconvenient for all the Filipinos. The war of patrols and cache-destroying seemed endless and futile. To challenge the insurgents it seemed ''that ultimately we shall be driven to the Spanish method of dreadful general punishments on the whole community for the acts of its outlaws which the community systemically shields and hides, *always.*''[16] Pacification would mean the summary imprisonment and execution of suspected insurgents, the resettlement of much of the rural population, and the destruction of the people's homes, crops, and livestock.

The sort of campaign Bullard and many other army officers regarded as a distinct possibility in the fall of 1900 was neither new nor novel in American military history. In the Philippines, however, the army's policy had been generous to the insurgents, for Filipino soldiers were accorded the status of prisoners of war and the general population that of noncombatants. The military government's judicial system rested on two agencies, the provost court of one officer and the military commission of a board of officers. Within Bullard's garrison towns, there was a provost court empowered to try criminal cases arising from violations of martial law. For minor offenses like curfew violation or disorderly conduct the provost courts were adequate, but they were not allowed to try capital cases. The heaviest sentence a provost judge could impose was one year's imprisonment and a fine of $1000 (Mexican), the fines going to the municipal treasury. For an insurgent arrested for a capital offense (killing an American soldier or an *americanista*, engaging in armed rebellion), the army required that a military commission hear the evidence and conduct a formal legal hearing. While a military commission might (and did) give an accused the death sentence or long term imprisonment, its sentences were often altered upon review in Manila by judge-advocates. Its psychological impact on the population was negligible. Procedural due process in the Philippines may have reassured the lawyers in Washington that American rule was justified, but it does not appear to have impressed the Filipinos except as a sign of weakness. It did not impress Bullard, either, for he systematically avoided cooperation with the military commission in Calamba.[17]

What Bullard most criticized, however, was not the form of justice but the tolerant attitude the military government took toward the guerrillas and the ''peaceful'' villagers who assisted them. To turn the people against the insurgents required a subtle mix of general coercion and a rapid improvement of the way of life of the common villager. In the latter category Bullard put freedom of religion, elementary education, improved roads and water supplies, secure marketplaces, youth programs, the physical security of person and property, and democratic, native local government. Sudden changes in the villagers' social behavior should not be demanded by the American government, which should, instead, govern the Filipinos by ''handling and governing them according to their genius and character.''[18]

The immediate problem, however, was to turn the people against the insurgent leaders and against their policy of armed resistance. Bullard, like many other officers, thought that the military government would have to be more strict in defining the legal status of the guerrillas and their village allies. The officers wanted the army's general statement on the customs and usages of land warfare (General Orders 100) widely publicized and strictly enforced. To do so would, the officers thought, rapidly break the back of the rebellion by destroying the terrorists' hold on the population.[19]

Written during the Civil War by the legal scholar Francis Lieber, General Orders 100 was the Lincoln Administration's answer to Confederate partisan warfare. Essentially, General Orders 100 proscribed any armed resistance other than that by uniformed soldiers fighting as conventional armies. Guerrillas, spies, terrorists, political organizers, false guides, and nonuniformed auxiliaries of any kind were neither recognized soldiers nor noncombatants. They were criminals, subject to immediate and harsh punishment for lawlessness. Under General Orders 100, however, the peaceful behavior of an occupied people had its rewards. It was the duty of a military commander to interfere as little as possible with the way of life of the people under his temporary jurisdiction. Only his mission and the basic welfare of his troops justified interference with the occupied people, and even decisions based on military requirements did not relieve a military governor from higher review or release him from his moral and legal responsibilities. Moreover, the military commander had to take positive action to prevent the murder, torture, rape, mutilation, robbery, intimidation, and exploitation of peaceful civilians and prisoners-of-war by his own soldiers.

If, however, a population persisted in assisting a guerrilla movement, it released a military governor from his responsibilities to govern in the community's behalf. In addition, he might justifiably order a number of measures to break an insurgency. Such measures ranged from martial law restrictions on personal behavior (curfews, identification checks) to harsh individual and group punishments, including the destruction of private property, starvation, and execution.[20]

In the Philippines, the United States Army found itself by 1900 in a profoundly ambiguous relationship with the Filipino people. For many junior officers and men, of course, there was little confusion. The Filipinos were ''goo-goos'' or ''niggers.'' Such people were racially incapable of anything but thievery, the foulest torture, murder, lying, and treachery. Treating them with any policy less than draconian was naive and futile. Yet the assumption of racial inferiority, especially as it was intellectually refined among the army's generals and the McKinley Administration, implied humane restraint and reformist government by the United States. The Filipinos did not yet understand their civic duties and could not be judged or punished for their ignorance, an ignorance based on both their colonial experience with Spain and their racial character. In addition, it would be hypocritical to spread democracy by the same methods which had led many Americans to want a war with Spain in 1898. And to wage an unchristian and "European"-style pacification campaign in the Philippines would only strengthen the anti-imperialists' position in the United States. Thus, in the fall of 1900 the military government shunned the strict application of General Orders 100 because of its fear of public reaction in the United States, because it was restrained by the War Department, and because many senior American officers still believed that friendly persuasion and good government would change the behavior of the Filipino people. But in the field, including the Second District of the Department of Southern Luzon, the officers were ready to accord the Filipinos full responsibility for all their acts. They had been well-educated by the sub rosa government, and they considered the Filipino rebel leaders a sophisticated and dangerous enemy. Their hope was that the wide publication and application of General Orders 100 would physically and emotionally alienate the common people from the insurgent officers.[21]

Despite the Thirty-Ninth Volunteers' reduced strength, there were signs in the fall of 1900 that, even without the application of General Orders 100, the regiment was winning converts to the American colonial government. The signs were no more than hopeful indicators of better times, but to the exhausted Thirty-Ninth they were welcome. In Tanauan, the *presidente* and his native police arrested an insurgent captain on a recruiting expedition in the city. When this captain was interrogated by Major Parker, he exposed much of the local revolutionary organization and admitted that Malvar's terrorism had alienated many of the insurgents. He also told Parker that he thought the rebels were beginning to recognize the benign character of American rule. On September 13 Captain Charles Hilton's Los Baños garrison easily repulsed a massed insurgent attack. The warning came from Filipinos. Furthermore, Bullard's constant patrolling was continuing to reduce the insurgents' supplies and to demoralize the village guerrillas. And in November William Jennings Bryan's presidential candidacy ended in defeat, a major blow to the insurgent cause and the anti-imperialist movement in the United States. The only setback in these months was self-inflicted by the Americans. In October the military government began to collect taxes in Laguna and Batangas, applying the Spanish revenue codes. The experience of having the Spanish taxes collected efficiently panicked the population, and for several days trade in Bullard's garrison town collapsed. Though Bullard at first thought that the tax collecting would help establish American authority, he also recognized the wisdom of lightening the tax burden when the military government quickly did so. It was not the time to alienate the pacific, property-holding Filipinos who were swinging behind the military government.[22] In all, the situation in Laguna and northern Batangas was improving by November 1900. But Bullard's regiment was not there when the insurrection broke apart the next spring. Illness and exhaustion forced the Thirty-Ninth to give up its district, and thus it missed the victory it had done much to create.

3.

Although Bullard learned that his regiment was to be shifted to another area in October, he did not curtail his patrols. He himself took an expedition along the shores of Lake Taal, making no contacts but finding small caches of rifles, cartridges, bolos, papers, and uniforms. The First and Second Battalions kept their soldiers out on scouts as well, despite the fact that the regiment's effective strength had now fallen to twenty-nine officers and six hundred and sixty-three men. What remained of the "American Indians" was, however, a hard and knowledgeable force. The regiment's problems were not tactical experience but the attrition of manpower and the constant demands of army administrative and supply routine. A sure sign that the insurrection was fading (or that Manila thought so, anyway) was the stream of orders from the Division of the Philippines demanding that the Thirty-Ninth Infantry improve its troop training, company record keeping, and compliance with army regulations.

After a couple of postponements, the Thirty-Ninth embarked for Manila in November and then was carried by army transports to its new stations along the southwestern coast of Batangas province. It went into posts formerly held by the Eighth Infantry: the regimental headquarters and First Battalion to Balayan, the Second Battalion to Nosugbú, the Third Battalion to Taal, Calaca and a post known as "Spanish Fort." Bullard assessed his new headquarters, a small seacoast town: "Balayan looks peaceful and filthy. There may be some mistake about peace; there is none about filth." He was glad to learn that the peacefulness was real too.[23]

The new year found the Thirty-Ninth back in the business of guerrilla-chasing, cache-destroying, and population control. Although the officers had to learn a new system of local politics, the regiment was able to build on the work of the Eighth Infantry, and its expeditions soon turned up weapons, ammunition, and food supplies in the isolated *barrios*. Actual fighting was limited. The population was hostile and the *insurrectos* still functioned by collecting taxes and terrorizing villagers, but the area was not especially dangerous to the Volunteers unless one wandered off by oneself. For Bullard, pacification was routine business: supervising local government and civil works, collecting intelligence on the insurgents' local leadership, arresting and replacing Filipino officeholders whose loyalty was compromised by captured documents, managing his system of provost courts, and dispatching expeditions to destroy reported caches. It was slow business, but the Thirty-Ninth kept at it, though without enthusiasm and without publicity. Many of the soldiers started to count the days before their return to the United States.[24]

The Thirty-Ninth did receive one welcome change of policy by the military government. On December 20, 1900, General MacArthur, reassured by McKinley's reelection and the creation of the anti-insurgent Federal Party, announced that henceforth his army would operate under a strict interpretation of General Orders 100. Any Filipino incriminated in any insurgent activity was subject to death, deportation, imprisonment, and the confiscation of property. If necessary, the army would retaliate against an entire community for insurgent activity. In practice, this meant burning homes and resettling the villagers in occupied towns.[25]

The insurgent officers' reaction to the army's application of General Orders 100 was to attempt to step up their terrorist campaign. To their dismay they found that the number of *americanistas* in their provinces was growing uncontrollably. Their militia was without weapons and was demoralized. Terrorism alienated the villagers and sent them to the Americans with information about the identity of nationalist leaders. In March 1901 the guerrillas were so disillusioned that they began to surrender in increasing numbers, taking advantage of the amnesty provisions offered by the military government. Throughout Luzon, American officers found themselves negotiating for the capitulation of the insurgent generals and their elusive bands. While there had been only 2,800 insurgents captured by September 1900, in the next six months 6,500 Filipinos were captured and 23,000 surrendered voluntarily.

In the Department of Southern Luzon there had been only thirty voluntary surrenders before December 1900. After the publication of General Orders 100 more than forty-five hundred Filipinos gave up, including six hundred officers. Exhausted and despondent, yet hopeful that they could work peacefully for the nationalist cause, Mariano Trías and Juan Cailles surrendered in the spring of 1901. Only Miguel Malvar continued the struggle, and his organization was destroyed in the next six months by a resettlement campaign in Batangas and Tayabas provinces.[26]

For the Thirty-Ninth Infantry, the collapse of the insurrection did not have dramatic impact. Bullard's territory was not heavily populated nor was its population among the most committed rebels. While the army garrisons in Cavite and Laguna accepted surrenders by the hundreds, the Thirty-Ninth rounded up less than a hundred rebels in Balayan and Nasugbú in March 1901. Rather, the Thirty-Ninth Infantry's main task was collecting its records and equipment for its return to the United States. On March 11 army transports began carrying the Volunteers back to Manila. After the regiment's officers got their accounts cleared by the headquarters staff in Manila, the Volunteers, under the command of Major Langhorne, sailed for San Francisco. There they mustered out of the service without incident. "Bullard's American Indians" ceased to exist except in the memory of its surviving veterans and its commanding officer.[27]

4.

The Thirty-Ninth Infantry Regiment, United States Volunteers, left the army with an honorable record for effective service, and its troops were proud of themselves and their commander. During its Philippine campaigns it had fought eighty-four engagements with the insurgents. Despite illness and the frustrations of a gentle pacification campaign, the Thirty-Ninth had killed insurgents at a ratio of ten to one, had suffered no major combat embarrassments, and had performed its civil duties with intelligence and efficiency. Each company estimated that it had marched more than two thousand miles on patrols. In the course of its Philippine service, half the regiment had been lost by death, injury, and discharge, most of the latter for illness. If the Thirty-Ninth never quite mastered the intricacies of drill, administration, and uniform regulations, it had the second lowest court-martial rate among the Volunteer regiments.[28] And its love affair with its commander survived to the end. The Volunteers respected their colonel's poise, aggressiveness, and concern for their welfare. They appreciated his casual approach to replacing lost equipment and his disregard for military ceremony. They told and retold the story of how the colonel had ignored General Schwan's orders to halt and how the general had demanded that Bullard check his "wild Indians." Even before the transports left Manila the volunteers had forgotten much of the heat, the strange rashes and malaria, the dull food, the long hikes, and monotony of garrison life. Their service was already transformed into sentimental memories. Over and over they sang the regimental song:

If you are sick or any way ill
Go to Major Wales and he will give you a pill
That will kill you or cure you,
He don't give a damn
For you are one of Bullard's Indians
And belong to Uncle Sam

Before departing the men of the regiment voted that Major Langhorne present Colonel Bullard the regimental colors as a mark of their esteem.[29]

Colonel Robert Lee Bullard, late of the Thirty-Ninth Infantry, remained in Manila when his regiment sailed. He watched the "American Indians" depart with great regret. He had developed a genuine affection for the regiment as a unit and as individuals. In the course of their service together, he had cited sixteen of his officers and eighteen enlisted men for decorations or certificates of merit. His promotion policy had been generous. His only disappointment was that the regiment had not been properly publicized in the Manila papers. Yet as a career officer, he could not help equating the regiment's record with his own professional reputation and advancement. As far as he could see, the end of the Thirty-Ninth Volunteers marked his own professional eclipse. He was amused that he had ever seriously thought of himself as a candidate for a brigadier-generalcy in the Volunteers. Reflecting on his own performance, he could see only one major failure—his inability to attract personal publicity. He envied other officers who had this talent. Without such a capacity an officer could hope for no preferment outside the normal seniority system in the American army. Perhaps, he thought, the regiment should have concentrated more on preparing for inspector generals' visits rather than field operations. Perhaps he should have made friends with the war correspondents in Manila or encouraged his officers to write accounts of the Thirty-Ninth's operations for the *Army and Navy Journal.* As he considered his return to the Subsistence Department, he found only one consolation. He was pleased that the Congress, which had permanently expanded the regular army in January 1901, had accepted the War Department's recommendation that all new officers be added as lieutenants. In the expansion of the Subsistence Department, he might become a major, a field grade clerk of beans and beef. "That's a joke." As far as he could see, he had finally used all the skills he had learned in the Tenth Infantry only to be denied both reward and an opportunity for further combat.[30]

NOTES

[1]Isabelo de los Reyes, Filipino junta in Madrid, "*Proclama*," published by P. García, Headquarters of the Captain-General, Philippine Republic, "Instructions for Guerrillas and Flying Columns," November 25, 1899, Exhibit 1020 to John R. M. Taylor, "The Philippine Insurrection Against the United States," Microfilm publication 719, National Archives; Lt. Col. Mariano Cabrera, "*Plan de Defensa de Batangas*," December 25, 1899, Folder 936, Selected Documents, Philippine Insurgent Records (PIR), National Archives.

[2]For background on the pacification of southern Luzon, see John M. Gates, *Schoolbooks and Krags: The U.S. Army in the Philippines, 1898-1902* (Westport, Conn.: Greenwood Press, 1973), pp. 128-247; Bonifacio S. Salamanca, *The Filipino Reaction to American Rule, 1901-1913* (New Haven, Conn.: Shoe String Press, 1968); Dean C. Worcester, *The Philippines Past and Present*, 2 vols. (New York: Macmillan, 1914); James A. LeRoy, *The Americans in the Philippines*, 2 vols. (Boston: Houghton Mifflin, 1914); *Annual Report of Major General Arthur MacArthur, U.S. Volunteers, Commanding Division of the Philippines*, 2 vols. (Manila: n.p., 1900); U.S. Congress, Senate, Committee on the Philippines, "Hearings: Charges of Cruelty, Etc., to the Natives of the Philippines" Vol. XV, Senate Document 205, 57th Congress, 1st Session; and "Hearings: Affairs in the Philippines," 3 vols., Senate Document 331, 57th Congress, 1st Session, both 1902.

Descriptive officer accounts of the pacification are Charles J. Crane, *Experiences of a Colonel of Infantry* (New York: Knickerbocker Press, 1923); Frederick J. Herman, *The Forty-Second Foot* (Kansas City, Mo.: n. p., 1942); James Parker, *The Old Army: Memories, 1872-1918* (Philadelphia: Dorrance and Company, 1929); U. G. McAlexander, *History of the Thirteenth Infantry United States Army* (Fort McDowell, Calif.: n. p., 1905), pp. 120-139; Schuyler journals, January 18, 1900-April 22, 1901, Brig. Gen. W. S. Schuyler Papers, Henry E. Huntington Library.

[3]Col. R. L. Bullard to Adj. Gen., First Division, Eighth Army Corps, March 2, 1900, 39th Infantry "Letters Sent" book (March 1 to November 22, 1900), Records of The Adjutant General's Office, RG 94.

[4]Col. R. L. Bullard to Adj. Gen., Division of the Philippines, August 29, 1900, 39th Infantry "Letters Sent" book, RG 94.

[5]Diarybook 1, entries for March-May, 1900, BP; Col. R. L. Bullard to Adj. Gen., First Division, Eighth Army Corps, March 2, 1900, 39th Infantry "Letters Sent" book, RG 94; "Report of Major General E. S. Otis, U.S. Army, Commanding the Division of the Philippines, and Military Governor of the Philippine Islands, September 1, 1899, to May 5, 1900," in *Annual Reports of the War Department, 1900* (Washington: Government

Printing Office, 1900), I, 448-561; Brig. Gen. T. Schwan to Brig. Gen. H. C. Corbin, May 12, 1900, printed in the *Army and Navy Journal*, May 26, 1900.

[6]On the patrolling, see Bullard autobiography, pp. 44-45, BP; "History of the 39th Infantry U.S. Volunteers"; Col. R. L. Bullard to Adj. Gen., Wheaton's Expeditionary Brigade, March 13, 1900, 39th Infantry "Letters Sent" book; Maj. J. H. Parker to Adj., 39th Infantry, May 31, 1900, Third Battalion "Letters Sent" book (April 26-September 20, 1900), RG 94; Col. R. L. Bullard to Adj. Gen., Second District, Department of Southern Luzon, May 26, 1900, 39th Infantry "Letters Sent" book; "Reports of Operations of First Battalion, Thirty-Ninth Infantry, U.S.V., January 14 to September 1, 1900, by Maj. H. B. Mulford, Commanding," *Annual Reports of the War Department, 1900*, I, Pt. 7, pp. 397-409.

[7]Col. R. L. Bullard to Adj. Gen., Second District, Department of Southern Luzon, May 12, 1900, 39th Infantry "Letters Sent" book.

[8]Captain John R. M. Taylor's "The Philippine Insurrection Against the United States: A Compilation of Documents with Notes and Introduction" is an invaluable and accessible source for the structure of the rebel infrastructure. Exhibits 1028 through 1035 are insurgent documents describing this appartus. In addition, I have used the following sources: Folder 914 (Laguna Province) and Folder 960 (Batangas Province), Selected Documents, PIR; Juan Cailles, "Acta," July 1900, and Juan Cailles to Vincente Reyes, July 12, 1900, Folder 631, Selected Documents, PIR; Package 35 (Batangas province records), AGO 460166, New Series of Documents, PIR; "Notes: Political Conference in Amaya between Lieutenant General Trias and the Japanese Consul in the Philippines, S. Hojo," October 11, 1900, File 622, Selected Documents, PIR; Maj. H. B. Mulford to Adj. Gen., Second District, Department of Southern Luzon, August 10, 1900, First Battalion "Letters Sent" book, 39th Infantry records, RG 94.

[9]"Annual Report of Maj. Gen. Arthur MacArthur, U.S.A., Commanding the Division of the Philippines and Military Governor in the Philippine Islands," *Annual Reports of the War Department, 1901* (Washington: Government Printing Officer, 1901), I, Pt. 4, pp. 88-114; Diarybook 1, entry, June 20, 1900, BP; Maj. G. T. Langhorne to Adj., 39th Infantry, appended to captured letter, August 18, 1900, Folder 602, Selected Documents, PIR.

[10]"Reports of Operations in the Second District, Department of Southern Luzon," Appendix B to "Operations in the Department of Southern Luzon," *Annual Reports of the War Department, 1901*, I, Part 5, pp. 266-278, 281-307, 309-311; "Caption and Record of Events Cards, 39th U.S. Volunteer Infantry, 1899-1901," Records of The Adjutant General's Office, RG 94; "History of the 39th Infantry U.S. Volunteers," previously cited.

[11]Col. R. L. Bullard to the Adj. Gen., Second District, Department of Southern Luzon, August 4 and 15, 1900, 39th Infantry "Letters Sent" book.

[12]Col. R. L. Bullard to Adj. Gen., Second District, Department of Southern Luzon, April 29, June 1 and 4, August 25, 1900, 39th Infantry "Letters Sent" book.

[13]Reports of Captain Frank B. McKenna on inspections of the 39th Infantry, June and July, 1900, appended to the "Annual Report" of Major W. D. Beach, Inspector-General, Department of Southern Luzon, Files 4904/0 and 4993/2, Records of the Office of the Inspector-General, U.S. Army, RG 159; Col. R. L. Bullard to Adj. Gen., Department of the Philippines, August 23, 1900, 39th Infantry "Letters Sent" book; "History of the 39th Infantry U.S. Volunteers," p. 28-32.

¹⁴Maj. Gen. A. MacArthur to Adj. Gen., July 7 and 9, 1900, *Correspondence Relating to the War with Spain*, 2 vols. (Washington: Government Printing Office, 1902), I, pp. 422-424; Col. R. L. Bullard to the Adj. Gen., Division of the Philippines, August 29, 1900, 39th Infantry "Letters Sent" book.

¹⁵Diarybook 1, entry, September 8 and 21, 1900, BP.

¹⁶Diarybook 1, entry, August 17, 1900, BP; Col. R. L. Bullard to Adj. Gen., Second District, Department of Southern Luzon, September 2, 1900, 39th Infantry "Letters Sent" book.

¹⁷Lt. Col. A. L. Wagner (AAG, Second District, DSL) to Col. R. L. Bullard, September 26, 1900, and Col. R. L. Bullard to Adj. Gen., Second District, Department of Southern Luzon, September 26, 1900, "Compiled Service File 264: Robert L. Bullard, 39th U. S. Vol. Inf.," RG 94.

¹⁸Robert L. Bullard, "Military Pacification," *mss* (1901); entries, 1900, Notebook 12; Robert L. Bullard, "Why Has the Philippine War Lasted So Long," *mss* (1901), appended to the Bullard autobiography, BP; Lt. Col. Robert L. Bullard, "Military Pacification," *JMSI* 163 (January-February 1908), pp. 1-24.

¹⁹Capt. John H. Parker, "The Last Phase of the Philippine Rebellion and the Problems Resulting Therefrom," *American Monthly Review of Reviews* 24 (November 1901), pp. 562-567; Capt. John H. Parker, "Conditions in the Philippines in October, 1900," enclosure to Roosevelt to E. Root, December 3, 1900, Root Papers; Major J. H. Parker to Adj. Gen., Department of Southern Luzon, October 5, 1900, Third Battalion "Letters Sent" book.

²⁰1st Lt. William E. Birkhimer, *Military Government and Martial Law* (Washington: James J. Chapman, 1892); Maj. Gen. G. B. Davis, "Doctor Francis Lieber's Instructions for the Government of Armies in the Field," *American Journal of International Law* 1 (January-April 1907), pp. 13-25; Frank Freidel, "General Orders 100 and Military Government," *Mississippi Valley Historical Review* 32 (March 1946), pp. 541-556.

²¹Taylor, "The Philippine Insurrection Against the United States," Chapter VI.

²²Diarybook 1, entries for October and November 1900, BP; Maj. J. H. Parker to Adj. Gen., Department of Southern Luzon, October 5 and 7, 1900, 39th Infantry "Letters Sent" book; "History of the 39th Infantry U.S. Volunteers"; Col. R. L. Bullard to Adj. Gen., Second District, Department of Southern Luzon, October (?) 1900, 39th Infantry "Letters Sent" book; Col. Juan Castaneda to Lt. Gen. M. Trías, December 13, 1900, Folder 631, Selected Documents, PIR.

²³Diarybook 1, entry, November 30, 1900, BP.

²⁴Col. R. L. Bullard to Adj. Gen., First District, Department of Southern Luzon, January 2 and 10, 1901, 39th Infantry "Letters Sent" book (November 28, 1900-May 5, 1901); Maj. G. T. Langhorne to Adj. Gen., First District, Department of Southern Luzon, February 9, 1901, 39th Infantry "Letters Sent" book; "History of the 39th Infantry U.S. Volunteers," p. 24.

²⁵"Annual Report of Maj. Gen. Arthur MacArthur, U.S.A., Commanding the Division of the Philippines and Military Governor in the Philippine Islands," *Annual Reports of the War Department, 1901*, previously cited; Robert L. Bullard, "Why the Philippine War Lasted So Long," *mss* (1901), BP.

²⁶Juan Cailles, "*Proclama*," April 1901, and Cuartel Central, "*Reorganisación de la Laguna*," August 1, 1901, File 1142, Selected Documents, PIR; Mariano Trias to Buenaventura Dimeguila, April 24, 1901, File 829, Selected Documents, PIR; Juan Cailles Letters to *presidentes local*, November 18-December 17, 1900, Folder 941, Selected

Documents, PIR, Juan Cailles, "*Manifesto,*" December 30, 1900, Folder 602, Selected Documents, PIR; Pedro Caballes to Juan Cailles, March 29, 1901, Folder 1240, Selected Documents, PIR; Brig. Gen. James F. Wade, "Operations in the Department of Southern Luzon," *Annual Reports of the War Department, 1901,* Vol. I, Part 5 with appendices, pp. 234-482.

[27]"History of the 39th Infantry U.S. Volunteers," p. 28.

[28]*Ibid.*; Report of the Office of the Judge Advocate, Headquarters Division of the Philippines, Appendix C to *Annual Report of Major General Arthur MacArthur, U.S. Volunteers, Commanding, Division of the Philippines* (Manila, 1900).

[29]"Memoir of Arthur Orton" (1947); "Memoir of Dr. Harry Morris (1950-1952); and "Memoir of Curg Lewis" (1970), all in the USAMHRC; "History of the 39th Infantry U.S. Volunteers," pp. 63-70; Maj. G. H. Langhorne to Adj. Gen., April 25, 1901, 39th Infantry "Letters Sent" book.

[30]Diarybook 1, entries, January 13, March 10 and 21, 1901, BP.

9

Return to the Infantry 1901-1902

While Colonel Bullard of the Thirty-Ninth Infantry was pacifying Laguna and Batangas, he had not been forgotten by the Subsistence Department. Criticized for maladministration during the War with Spain and embarrassed by the court-martial of Commissary General Charles P. Eagan, the Department, under Briga-dier General John F. Weston, was reluctant to allow its regular officers to continue serving as Volunteers. In 1900 only the intervention of Secretary of War Root had prevented the return of Bullard and Tasker H. Bliss to their commissary ranks and duties. In the spring of 1901, with the Volunteer regiments on their way home, the Adjutant General's Office ordered Bullard to Manila as assistant to the chief commissary of the Division of the Philippines.[1]

Commissary affairs in the Philippines were in some disarray. In March 1901 thefts of foodstuffs were uncovered by the chief commissary, who subsequently arrested several Volunteer commissary officers, sergeants in the regular army, and civilian employees. But after the challenge of command, Bullard found com-missary reform pale duty. Despite the responsibilities of chief commissary for the Department of Northern Luzon, he longed for the physical and intellectual stimulation he had enjoyed with the Thirty-Ninth Volunteers. As he reflected upon his experience, he concluded that whatever success he had had was attributable to his ability to free himself from regular army habits and customs and his lack of concern about his dignity as a colonel. He also believed that ceaseless mental activity had preserved his sense of initiative, the sine qua non for success and advancement.[2] As a commissary he felt himself stiffening in the arid routine of his work, his mind wandering, his ennui and physical condition limiting him to only six hours work a day. "Alas! I find in the staff that I am daily falling more and more deeply into the dreadful 'Indorsement Habit,' than which death itself is not more destructive of military efficiency."[3] Sometime in the summer of 1901, perhaps when he put the fourteenth endorsement on a paper debate on the merits of frozen beef compared with live cattle in tropical areas, perhaps as he considered the continual sickness in his newly-arrived family and the cost of living in Manila, Bullard began to think about trying to return to the infantry.

As far as the War Department was concerned, Robert Lee Bullard, whatever he had done since 1898, was now a manager of warehouses and accounts. On April 1, he had been promoted to major and commissary in the regular army. On May 6 he received his discharge as a colonel of Volunteers and removed the eagles and crossed rifles he had worn for three years from his uniform. He feared the parting was forever:

> Goodbye, birds, goodbye. It will be many a
> day before you will again hover about my
> shoulders. You were ever wild and migratory
> with me. You were hard to snare and never
> tamable. You had your wings always spread
> for flight and you were the most timid and
> uncertain things I ever knew.[4]

Again his career seemed to be at a dead end as Bullard ended twenty years in the army in June 1901. The fighting in the Philippines was now limited to Cebu and Samar; army officers and American civilians were daily returning to the United States. Depressed by his duties and annoyed by a recurrent case of prostatitis, Bullard reflected that he had once more missed success. He had deluded himself by thinking that he could substitute accomplishment for ''pull,'' for the army was no different from business. One must know how to collect for services as well as to render them. In August 1901 Bullard decided to try ''collecting,'' and asked and received sick leave to return to the United States. On September 5, 1901, the Bullards left Manila aboard the transport *Thomas*.[5]

1.

The month long ocean voyage to the United States and the eight months of sick leave that followed gave Bullard the leisure to read and reflect upon the sum of his experience in the Philippines. To the annexation of the islands and their pacification he gave little thought. As far as he could see, the islands were a strategic liability, indefensible in a war with another major power. The islands were so vulnerable that the only positive feature of their possession, Bullard thought, was that they would be a restraining influence on American diplomats contemplating war. Possession of the Philippines, then, might be a force for peace.[6]

Bullard believed that the great lesson of the Philippine Insurrection had been the military effectiveness of the hastily raised and deployed Volunteer regiments. There was no doubt in the mind of the colonel of the Thirty-Ninth Infantry that his troops had an élan and adaptability that more than overcame their ignorance of drill, sloppiness in bearing, and cavalier treatment of administrative rules and supplies. War was a matter of attack, to which the Volunteers brought the competitiveness of civilian life, a high degree of personal initiative and responsibility, and a tactical imagination undeadened by years of garrison routine. They were less resentful of officers than regulars, provided an officer treated them like grown men, explained his orders, and did not apply mechanical discipline. In fact, Bullard concluded, the indispensable skill for the career American officer was the scientific study of the type of inspirational leadership most suitable for Volunteers. The wartime inclusion of citizen-soldiers was not just a desperate expedient, but an important injection of new talent into both the officer corps and enlisted ranks. Only such men could give the army the decentralized leadership demanded by modern war.[7]

In the Philippines, Bullard had been surprised to learn how little regular officers knew about leadership. Invariably, troop commanders alienated their recruits by jamming drill and formal discipline into them "as we used to load an old field gun."[8] Instead, a commander should build esprit by making idealistic appeals to the recruits' patriotism, sense of manhood, sense of duty, and sense of honor. Bullard recognized that the experienced officer might feel a bit dishonest in making moral appeals, knowing that many deaths and much service would be futile. Yet only emotional preparation could ready the new soldier for the battlefield horrors, both physical and emotional, which had been created by modern firearms. No amount of coercive discipline and garrison comforts would sustain a soldier in modern war.[9]

Bullard, however, was not persuaded that expertise in troop psychology was the only skill an officer needed. Rather he saw that the army was becoming overspecialized with the several branches in "mad competition" to make themselves distinctive. If such specialization continued, "we shall soon come to the pass that we shall have nothing but sterile specialists; a general will be impossible."[10] He himself continued to read widely: Fritz Hoenig's *Inquiries into the Tactics of the Future*, General Jules Louis Lewal's *Etudes de Guerre*, Colonel Henry G. Sharpe's essay "The Art of Supplying Armies in the Field," and T. A. Dodge's histories of Roman warfare. Reading Spenser Wilkinson's *The Brain of an Army*, he approved of the Prussian system of professional education, especially since it mixed staff and line duty. His reaction to Ivan Bloch's *The Future of Warfare* was that "the author makes a very fair case for his contention" that war was a catastrophic way to settle disputes, but that his premises applied only to European nations, not to the strategic situation of the United States. Bullard thought Bloch's analysis of the effect of modern weapons a little exaggerated, and also doubted that the belligerents would be of equal strength, a condition "absolutely necessary to the logic of his deduction that war has become impossible or nearly so."[11]

His reading and reflection convinced him that the army needed to pay more attention to modern ordnance and logistics. The army needed lighter, more portable machine guns, capable of movement with the infantry in order to give continuous fire support in the attack; such weapons would also be invaluable on the objective to halt counterattacks.[12] In matters of supply, Bullard had learned that the army supply system was not responsive enough to troop needs and suffered from chronic overregulation. He believed that the army should procure whatever was necessary for combat and worry about the cost and accounting later. The commander could not give supply matters too much attention; as colonel of the Thirty-Ninth Volunteers, he had labored more on transportation problems and supply distribution than he had on tactics. He thought that future American officers would fail primarily because they did not appreciate the difficulties of supply.[13] That logistical training was possible seemed self-evident after Bullard had read the French military writers Lewal and deBrack. But a slavish acceptance of doctrine was dangerous, for systems, equipment, and transport were constantly changing; instead "principles, not details, progressiveness, broad general knowledge, a rational organization and brains, not bookishness . . . are the things that should be had in mind by Supply Officers."[14]

For all his reading, Bullard still remained hostile to the idea of an army devoted to the study of military science. Studying theory was easier than field service, and paper battles were an appealing substitute for maneuvers. He had seen the School of Application at Leavenworth "turn into a mere school of bookishness. A cloud no larger than a man's hand was enough to make such inclement weather that field exercises were necessarily called off, while the bare thought of the sun ran temperatures up to the point of prevention of all military work except with a book in a nice cool spot!" If this "aversion to practice" was spread to the other army schools, the United States Army would be an excellent training ground for professors of military science, but fighting officers would be in short supply.[15]

Because he had no other desire than to be a fighting officer, Major Robert Lee Bullard was headed to Washington to arrange a transfer back to the infantry.

2.

Turning north from Manila, the *Thomas* called at Yokohama and then plowed eastward across the northern Pacific route to San Francisco. The trip was not entirely happy for Bullard. His family was still ailing. Whenever he socialized with other army officers aboard the *Thomas*, he found "envy and jealousy" because he had held high rank in the Volunteers. His peers' resentment convinced him that other officers might try to ruin him; only mental alertness and harder work would protect him. Once he struck up a conversation with fellow passenger Senator Albert J. Beveridge, and, because he defended the American soldier against Beveridge's charges of barbarism, went away convinced that he had made a political enemy of no mean importance. Another passenger was none other than Commissary-General Weston, returning from a personal inspection in Manila. When Bullard approached him on the possibility of an interbranch transfer, Weston ignored him.[16] Sometime during the voyage, Bullard joined the Catholic Church. He had considered the conversion for almost two years, primarily to please his wife. The decision gave him great personal comfort, but he recognized that it might alienate many of his Protestant friends in the officer corps.[17]

Landing in San Francisco on October 1, Bullard wryly noted that his household goods were now scattered in six locations (Alabama, Fort Reno, Vancouver Barracks, San Francisco, Manila, and Fort Sam Houston) and got his family on a train for Texas. At Fort Sam Houston, with the Bullard family under the care of Colonel Cleary, Bullard's sense of desolation did not pass. The Philippines, he found, were barely known to Americans. He himself wanted to return to Luzon or Mindanao—wherever the troops were—but not as "an expert on soap, salt and pepper and pork and bacon." He had no taste or ability, he knew, for boring duty.[18]

In December Bullard went to Washington. Either before his departure from the Philippines or after his arrival in Washington, he created the strategem for the transfer: he and Major Frank F. Eastman, Twenty-Eighth Infantry, would exchange assignments. How Bullard learned of Eastman's readiness to accept a staff appointment is unclear, but Eastman's reasons were certain enough. Aged forty-seven and not in good health, Eastman was on his way to the Far East for the third time since 1898. He already had had two sick leaves in the United States. Promoted to major, he had returned again to the United States, joining his new regiment at Vancouver Barracks. He then returned with the Twenty-Eighth Infantry to Luzon in November 1901.

Building his case on the possibility of an exchange with Eastman, Bullard, accompanied by his old patron Senator Edmund W. Pettus, got a brief interview with President Theodore Roosevelt. Roosevelt politely but rapidly dismissed them with an order to see Secretary of War Root. Bullard's interview with Root went well but was inconclusive. To the secretary of war, Bullard confessed that he had erred in leaving the infantry in 1898. Now he wanted the exchange, not to find soft duty, but to seek hard field service, in which he had already proven his value. He wanted nothing more than an opportunity for more service as an infantry officer as a reward for his record in the Philippines. Root listened sympathetically and said he knew the quality of Bullard's service and respected his record. He was interested in any act that would tear "down the wall between line and staff." The secretary closed the interview by agreeing to give Bullard's request favorable endorsement if General Weston would, but Bullard left Root's office convinced that he had no "pull" and that he had talked too much.[19] Nonetheless, in the following days he saw Weston, Adjutant General Henry C. Corbin, and Lieutenant General Nelson A. Miles.

Carrying his request for transfer from office to office in the State-War-Navy building on Pennsylvania Avenue, Bullard stirred controversy which reached into the dark corners of army politics. He knew that if his transfer to the infantry should be approved and he retained the rank of major (as he intended), he would take lineal precedence over 162 infantry officers who had been senior to him when he left the Tenth Infantry. He argued that his record justified this dramatic improvement in his chances for future promotion and that there were precedents, as indeed there were.[20] To Assistant Adjutant General William Harding Carter, Bullard's request was bare-faced opportunism. Carter, a moving force in the creation of a General Staff, was conservative on the question of the morale of the officer corps. While he agreed that it was unfortunate that the vagaries of army assignments had sent Eastman back for a third Asian tour, Carter disapproved of the exchange, arguing that Bullard had arranged his original transfer to the Subsistence Department only through Senator Pettus' sponsorship. If President Roosevelt was serious that political influence would not determine promotion and assignment (as Carter reminded everyone Roosevelt had just said), granting Bullard's request would show Roosevelt's statement was "mere sham." More important, Bullard's transfer would give him rank over ninety-two older officers.[21]

Adjutant General Corbin, however, approved Bullard's request, saying that the interests of the army should be first, although he could not make up his mind what those interests were in this case. General Miles did not equivocate, disapproving of the transfer because it would work to the disadvantage of officers of longer service than Bullard. Weston said he had no objection to the exchange if the secretary of war was not worried about demoralizing the infantry officers Bullard would jump; as Bullard and others suspected, Weston, having won the president's favor in Cuba, was himself considering a return to the Line.[22]

Poorer by $300 and still uncertain what Root would do with his request, Bullard returned to Fort Sam Houston during the first week of January 1902. As far as he could see, his trip had bought him only some political experience, for he had been most impressed that "men who do things in this world" always had some goal for which they strove tirelessly. He was not sure that his transfer fell into the category of great lifeworks, but he was not yet ready to give up his request.[23] His determination would have been reinforced had he seen Root's final endorsement. The secretary wrote that he was unmoved by arguments based on the circumstances of Bullard's 1898 transfer or by the pattern of Bullard's promotion. Instead he thought "the transfer will be beneficial to the service, and any possible injury to individuals arising from the difference in age between Major Eastman and Major Bullard is too remote and problematic to furnish a just obstacle. The transfer is approved."[24]

As Bullard realized, Root's favorable endorsement was but one important step toward securing his transfer, but he could have hardly predicted that his case would become a minor cause célèbre for the Senate Military Affairs Committee. At the time Bullard's request went to the Military Affairs Committe for approval, Root, General Miles, and the committee were locked in conflict over military policy, most importantly the question of atrocities in the Philippines and the legislation for the creation of a General Staff. Aside from the policy issues, the senators were restive about Roosevelt's habit of nominating some comparatively junior officers for brigadier-generalships. The Military Affairs Committee tended to agree with Miles that promotions to general, transfers, and assignments should be determined by length of service (especially service in the Civil War) rather than by recent and romantic accomplishments in Cuba and the Philippines. Nine of the ten members of the committee were former Civil War officers themselves; they were not impressed by Roosevelt's shallow credentials as an expert on military leadership and administrative ability. Led by its chairman, Senator Joseph R. Hawley of Connecticut, and ranking Republican member, former Secretary of War Redfield Proctor of Vermont, the committee also was in the process of blocking Root's proposals to consolidate the staff bureaus and to make staff-line transfers a basic assignment policy.[25] Further, the committee viewed Roosevelt's and Root's nominations not as reforms to improve the leadership of the army, but as an effort to overwhelm senatorial patronage with presidential patronage.

The Senate Military Affairs Committee's skepticism about Bullard's transfer was reinforced by the reactions it received from other army officers. The *Army and Navy Journal* reported on February 22 that the committee had heard many complaints from army officers, all in the name of the officers Bullard would jump, now reported as one hundred and seventy-five. The *Journal* carried a public letter by Root to Senator Hawley defending the nomination for "the good of the service" and stating that Bullard had not planned the return transfer when he had left the infantry in 1898.[26] On March 1 the *Journal* printed an open indictment of Bullard's conduct by a West Point classmate, Captain Charles H. Muir. Muir pointed out that Bullard had finished behind him at the Academy, had transferred to the Subsistence Department through political influence, had been promoted in that department without serving in it, and would, if retransferred, block Muir's own highly deserved advancement. Echoing Muir, another officer testified that it was a crime to allow a healthy officer barely over forty to replace an ailing and older major of infantry. Such an act was certainly unjust if not illegal.[27]

The opposition to his transfer seemed widespread to Bullard as he followed the controversy from Fort Sam Houston. By March he was sufficiently distressed to make another trip to Washington where he found that his transfer was mired in the controversy over the General Staff Bill. He could see no hope for either: "The whole army seems like so many Chinamen in their [sic] aversion to reforms, changes, or reorganization of any kind." He had learned that Miles and the Senate and "all the preponderating mediocrities in the Army" were arrayed against the military changes suggested by the Administration. "The officers of the army kill any man who has an idea, as they would kill a mad dog."[28] With his sick leave extended, he returned again to Texas to sit out the crisis, leaving General Weston unconvinced that his anxiety and illness were not related: "I think if Major Bullard's transfer was approved by the Senate, his temperature would run from 105 to 98.5, which I believe is normal."[29]

Bullard's transfer request was still alive. Root, responding to pressure from Senator Proctor, pointed out that the exchange was not prohibited by law. In fact the secretary of war now thought he could make the decision legally by himself without the Military Affairs Committee's formal approval. In any event, the matter was too insignificant to provoke prolonged controversy: "I have never taken any special interest in the Bullard-Eastman transfer, nor do I think it makes very much difference to the service one way or the other."[30] The decision appears to have been left to the seventy-one-year-old senator from Vermont. It is doubtful that Proctor gave the transfer much thought. Proctor, however, had a reputation for expertise in War Department personnel policy, especially in patronage matters, and his power in the Senate and the Republican party made his approval necessary. With the Congress about to recess and the petty furor over the exchange dying, Proctor finally acquiesced, "rather against my better judgment but [I] could not refuse Judy [*sic*] Pettus."[31] On June 27, 1902, Major Robert Lee Bullard returned to the infantry with the advice and consent of Senator Redfield Proctor.

3.

Alone aboard the transport *Meade*, reading voraciously to keep from being depressed, Bullard was unaware of his good fortune. On June 4 he, Rose, and the children had left Texas for the long voyage back to the Philippines. Despondent over his apparent failure, weakened by a return of malaria, convinced that his military career was slipping away in purposelessness, Bullard made another hard decision on June 7 and left his family in San Francisco rather than expose them again to the sicknesses of Manila. Thus his return to his duty station meant another separation from his family.[32]

Upon arriving in Manila on July 16, he learned of his transfer to the Twenty-Eighth Infantry and was amazed at the admiration of other officers, who told him that he was "a shrewd, strong, rising man."[33] Bullard feared the admiration was insincere. He was sure that he had created resentment which would persist as long as he remained in the service, and he began to have recurrent nightmares for a period of several weeks. In two he single-handedly killed hordes of hissing rattlesnakes or a single monster snake which was attacking a dog he had owned in 1898. In another he was stationed in an isolated post in the Philippines with no other officer; in fact he seemed to be the entire garrison. Then another officer came, told him that he had been transferred to the Line and that he must now break up an insurgent band at a seacoast town. In a fourth dream he found himself behind a stone dam trying to brace it against a great flood of angry, muddy water. Desperately he tried to strengthen the dam with logs as the water chipped away at the masonry. The dam held. "Had it [the dam] gone down I would have been swept away without any doubt and I knew it." In the fifth dream he was in Washington and was visited by his old West Point roommate, Henry McCain, who told him a board of officers had told the Military Affairs Committee that he should not be transferred. He could not understand this board's authority or membership, but accepted its decision as final. "This was quite a disconnected illogical dream I thought on waking and so it never stayed in my mind like the others."[34]

In his waking hours, Bullard was acting commander of the Twenty-Eighth Infantry, garrisoned at the quiet post of San Francisco de Malabon. Fortunately, the routine was familiar and the duty light, for he was still disoriented by the sudden change in his status. At moments he wondered whether the price of the transfer was worth it: "How I wonder what is due to happen to me over here this time. One thing is certain; I have mortally offended many in running ahead of them *not in making a record* (none care if beaten in a record) but *in getting recognition of that record* which means running ahead of others in promotion.''[35] On the other hand, he could also see that the circumstances of his transfer had "not only benefited me directly but also indirectly helped my standing and general prestige in the army." He found himself the center of conversation at the Manila Army and Navy Club when he came to the city, and he messed with two brigadier generals. Bullard enjoyed the company of accomplished messmates. "These were men who stand for something, who represent something, whom it was a pleasure and advantage to meet, . . . I seemed also to represent something to them.''[36]

Bullard sensed that his return to the infantry was the turning point of his career, a judgment he never changed.[37] Certainly his good fortune marked him among his peers as a remarkably lucky officer whose ambition, opportunism, and strong political connections were as impressive as his ability. At the age of forty-one he had become the second of his Academy class to become a major and the first in the infantry. The other infantry officers of the class of 1885 would spend between four to six years more as captains, and some were still company commanders in their late forties when Bullard was promoted to lieutenant colonel in 1906. The price of the transfer was clear: it was the envy and contempt of many of his fellow officers. Notoriety became part of his army reputation, for Bullard's almost accidental preferment forced him away from his peers as his colonelcy in the Volunteers had not. As he himself knew, his reputation and accomplishments (or failures) would now be watched with special interest, and he was determined to be professionally beyond reproach. It was the only insurance for survival, given the jealousy of those officers he had jumped and would continue to lead with each successive promotion. Bullard's thoughts returned to one nagging question: what could he do to justify his superiors' confidence in him as the infantry's brightest young major?[38]

NOTES

[1]Acting Commissary General J. F. Weston to Maj. Gen. N. A. Miles, with endorsement by the Adjutant General and Secretary of War Elihu Root, June 8, 1900, Vol. 1, "Letters Received, Commanding General of the Army, 1900," RG 108; "Statement of Military Service," Bullard 201 File.

[2]Diarybook 1, entries for March 31, April 1-28, 1901, BP.

[3]Diarybook 2, entry, June 19, 1901; memos of Maj. R. L. Bullard, Office of the Chief Commissary, August 1901, Scrapbook 28, BP.

[4]Diarybook 1, entry, May 6, 1901, BP.

[5]Diarybook entries, June 12 and 13, August 13, 27, and 31, 1901, BP; "Statement of Medical History in the Case of Maj. Gen. Robert L. Bullard, USA," Bullard 201 File; Maj. R. L. Bullard to Adj. Gen., Dept. of Northern Luzon, August 17, 1901, Bullard AGO File.

[6]Notebook 2, entry, January 14, 1902, BP.

[7]This paragraph is based on the following writings: Robert L. Bullard, "The Volunteer,"

mss, 1902, and "The Military Study of Men," *mss*, 1901, both BP, and the entries for October 16, 1901, to April 3, 1902, Notebook 2, BP.

[8]Notebook 2, entry, April 4, 1902, BP.

[9]Notebook 2, entries, March 21, April 4, April 22, 1902, BP.

[10]Notebook 2, entry, January 19, 1902, BP.

[11]Book notes, February 26, 1902, Scrapbook 28, Box 14, and Notebook 2, entries for January 4 and February 4, 1902, BP.

[12]Notebook 2, entries for February 9 and March 21, 1902, BP.

[13]Notebook 2, entries for May 17, June 17-19, 1902, BP.

[14]Notebook 3, entries for June 26 and July 2, 1902, BP.

[15]Notebook 2, entry, January 19, 1902, BP.

[16]Diarybook 2, entries for September 17 and 19, and October 16, 1901; Notebook 2, entry, October 16, 1901, BP.

[17]Diarybook 2, entry, January 13 and October 8, 1901.

[18]Diarybook 2, entry, October 8, 1901, BP.

[19]Diarybook 2, entry, December 8, 1901, BP. Bullard's contemporaneous account is eight pages long. His brief for the exchange was "Exchange of Maj. R. L. Bullard, Commissary, U.S.A. with Major F. F. Eastman, 28th Infantry," appended to page 39 of diarybook 2 and part of his formal request, preserved with endorsements in the Bullard AGO File.

[20]"Exchange of Maj. R. L. Bullard" in Bullard AGO File, with memo, Maj. R. L. Bullard to Adj. Gen., December 13, 1901, RG 94.

[21]Lt. Col. W. H. Carter, AAG, memorandum, December 20, 1901, appended to "Exchange of Maj. R. L. Bullard" in Bullard AGO File.

[22]Corbin, Weston, and Miles endorsements on "Exchange of Maj. R. L. Bullard" in Bullard AGO File.

[23]Diarybook 2, entry, January 16, 1902, BP.

[24]Endorsement by Secretary of War Root, February 4, 1902, to "Exchange of Maj. R. L. Bullard," in Bullard AGO File.

[25]See Philip C. Jessup, *Elihu Root*, 2 vols. (New York: Dodd, Mead, 1938), I, pp. 243-264. Miles' position was consistently in favor of older officers. See, for example, Lt. Gen. Nelson A. Miles to Secretary of War Elihu Root, January 12, May 27, and November 22, 1901, in "Letters Sent, The Commanding General of the Army, 1901," Vol. 38, RG 108, and Lt. Gen. Miles to Acting Secretary of War William Cary Sanger, July 28, 1902 in the same volume bf correspondence; *Army and Navy Journal*, April 5, 1902.

The composition of the Senate Military Affairs Committee is from U.S. Congress, 57th Congress, 1st Session, *Official Congressional Directory*, 2d ed. (Washington, 1902).

[26]Root to Senator Joseph R. Hawley, February 18, 1902, reprinted with commentary, *Army and Navy Journal*, February 22, 1902.

[27]Capt. C. H. Muir to the Editor, *Army and Navy Journal*, March 1, 1902; *Army and Navy Journal*, March 29, 1902.

[28]Diarybook 2, entry, March 21, 1902, BP.

[29]Memo, Brig. Gen. J. F. Weston, April 18, 1902 attached to "Exchange of Major Bullard," Bullard AGO File.

[30]Elihu Root to Senator Redfield Proctor, March 6, 1902, Root Letterbooks, Vol. 175, Part 3, Root Papers.

[31]Redfield Proctor to Elihu Root, July 1, 1902, General Correspondence, Root Papers;

"Redfield Proctor," *Dictionary of American Biography* (New York: Charles Scribner's Sons, 1934) XV, pp. 245-246.

[32]Diarybook 2, entries June 4, 7, and 15, 1902, BP.

[33]Diarybook 2, entry, July 20, 1902, and Notebook 3, entry, August 5, 1902, BP.

[34]*Ibid.*

[35]Diarybook 2, entry, July 24, 1902, BP.

[36]Diarybook 2, entry, September 29, 1902, BP.

[37]Bullard autobiography, p. 56, BP.

[38]Diarybook, October 8, 1902; Notebook 4, entry, October 16, 1902, BP. At the time of his transfer Bullard became sixty-seventh on the majors' lineal list with a date of rank of April 1, 1901; the total number of majors of infantry was one hundred. At the age of forty-one, he shared the distinction of being the youngest major of infantry with Charles G. Morton (USMA, 1883), who was born on the same date as Bullard. Morton was ninty-sixth on the majors' list.

Bullard jumped twenty-three majors and between 116 and 129 captains. All but one of his West Point classmates in the infantry stood between numbers 122 and 131 on the captains' list with dates of rank as captains of March 2, 1899.

The above data was collected from The Adjutant General's Office, *Army Register, 1902* (Washington, 1902) pp. 190-311, and *1910* (Washington, 1910), which gives officers' birthdates, and from Edward S. Holden and Wirt Robinson, eds., *General Cullum's Biographical Register of the Officers and Graduates of the U.S. Military Academy: Vol. V, Supplement, 1900-1910*, (Saginaw, Mich.: Seeman and Peters, 1910), pp. 367-379.

10

Mindanao: The Road, the Lake, and the Moros 1902-1904

When the McKinley Administration annexed the Philippines, it purchased not only a rebellion but also about four hundred thousand Moslem warriors who, by European standards, definitely needed civilizing. Inhabiting the southernmost islands of the Philippine archipelago but concentrated on the large island of Mindanao and the islands of the Sulu Sea, these warriors called themselves simply "The People." The Spanish called them Moros.

The Moros were Malays converted to Islam in the spread of that faith from Borneo and Malacca in the fourteenth and fifteenth centuries. On Mindanao, as on the smaller islands to the southwest, they had established a feudal society which had beaten back the Spanish colonial army and terrorized the Christian Filipinos and Chinese who lived in the small seacoast towns. Moros who lived by the sea sometimes fished and traded; many lived more grandly as pirates and slavers. On Mindanao, the Moros settled two major inland areas, the valley of the Rio Grande de Mindanao on the south coast and the rimlands of Lake Lanao, forty square miles of water cradled in the center of the island amid unmapped volcanic mountains and primeval rainforest.

The Lake Lanao Moros were barely conscious of any world beyond the lake. Along its banks and the rivers that fed it, they had built fortified towns (*cottas*) where they dabbled in metal-working and weaving. Each *cotta* (and there were hundreds around the lake) was likely to have a rice paddy or two nearby, and the jungle and the lake provided roots, fruits, fish, and game.

Blessed by their natural environment, the Lake Lanao Moros could concentrate

165

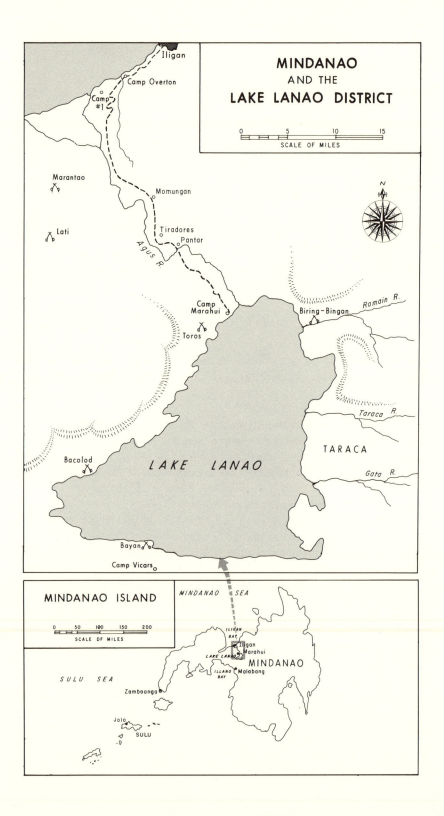

MINDANAO
AND THE
LAKE LANAO DISTRICT

0   5   10   15
SCALE OF MILES

Iligan
Camp Overton
Camp #1
Marantao
Momungan
Lati
Tiradores
Pantar
Agus R.
Camp Marahui
Biring-Bingan
Ramain R.
Toros
Taraca R.
Bacolod
TARACA
LAKE LANAO
Gata R.
Bayan
Camp Vicars

MINDANAO ISLAND

0   50   100   150   200
SCALE OF MILES

MINDANAO SEA
ILIGAN BAY
Iligan
Marahui
LAKE LANAO
MINDANAO
ILLANO BAY
Malabang
SULU SEA
Zamboanga
Jolo
SULU

on their preferred activity, feudal warfare. The ruling elite governed the *cottas* with a personalism only slightly softened by their religion. The business of the Moro leadership was war. Anyone who lived beyond the *cottas* ruled by a sultan or *datu* was the enemy, whether Moro or Asiatic or European infidel. War for the Moros was an indivisible blend of Allah's will, material gain, and personal prestige; it was a way of life which provided the warriors with women and slaves to support the tribe and with the psychic satisfactions of bloodshed and conquest. Their feudal set-piece melees, sieges, ambushes, and raids were waged with a high sense of competition. The Moros were not religious bigots in these matters, for, while they got a special satisfaction from raiding infidels, they hewed and hacked each other with nearly equal abandon.

Moro ferocity was enhanced by Moro appearance and demeanor. The Moro was abristle with edged weapons on all occasions. Moreover, dressed in turbans, loose jackets, and silk sarongs or anklelength trousers, the Moros were a riot of menacing color. The preferred combinations in stripes and solids were garish reds, oranges, and yellows, set off with greens, blues, browns, and purples. Betalnut chewing had an additional cosmetic effect, blackening the Moros' broken teeth and turning their lips blood red. Wealthier warriors also sported body armor, most often linked pieces of *carabao* horn, but occasionally chain mail and metal helmets. The Moros thought themselves impressive sights and reinforced their own visual impact with a broad repertoire of menacing gestures, looks, words, and body movements. A Moro warrior wanted to be taken seriously. He was.[1]

As its garrisons spread south through the seacoast towns of the Philippines, the army inherited "the Moro problem." The Spanish legacy was a bitter one: sporadic attempts at Christianization, bloodshed, and campaigns of reprisal. The European on Mindanao was feared and hated, feared only because of his modern firearms which the Moros craved, hated for his religion, appearance, manners, diseases, and interest in ending slavery, piracy, and polygamy. To a Moro, all white men looked alike, and he had no reason to assume that these new Europeans would be any less ruthless in ending the Moro way of life.

As the Philippine Insurrection faded, the Taft Administration in Manila began to worry more about bringing the blessings of modern civilization to the Moros as well as avoiding warfare with them. Only if one made policy some distance from Mindanao was this a credible goal. Fortunately, in Brigadier General George W. Davis, tactful former governor of Puerto Rico and Provost-Marshal-General of Manila, the American colonial government had an able commander in the Moro country. Davis generally agreed that whatever change came to Mindanao must be slow and not rely primarily on force. The army's role was to establish patrol posts throughout the island, to negotiate for the *datus'* allegiance, and to work slowly for the elimination of slavery, the nonnegotiable Moro habit. As Major General Adna R. Chaffee, commanding general of the Division of the Philippines, wrote his friend Henry C. Corbin, the army would govern the eighty thousand Moros of Lake Lanao with patience through an "understanding" with them that ". . . we will not interfere with their customs or religion and that we will keep out of that section the European population as much as possible."[2]

A key part of the army's plan to pacify the Lake Lanao Moros was opening a road from the port of Iligan on the north coast of Mindanao to the north shore of the lake. The Spanish had built such a road in 1890-1891 during one of their campaigns, but it had deteriorated. While American officers debated whether the major garrison on Lake Lanao should be stationed at Marahui at the terminus of this road or at Camp Vicars on the south end of the lake, none doubted that troops and supplies could best reach the lake over the Iligan-Marahui route. Even if Camp Vicars (strategically placed near the most hostile *cottas*) should be the major garrison, it should be supported by boat from Marahui rather than by a road from the Mindanao's south coast. Such a road would be longer and the terrain it had to conquer more severe than the Iligan-Marahui route.[3]

In the spring of 1902, the importance of the Iligan-Marahui road increased as it became apparent to Generals Chaffee and Davis that the Moros had their own ideas about the presence of American soldiers. Davis' first emmissary to the Lake *datus*, a middle-aged cavalry captain named John J. Pershing, had found the Moros sullen and dangerous. At first Chaffee thought Moro hostility was the product of either bureaucratic friction among the Americans or the misbehavior of patrols by the Fifteenth Cavalry. On March 9, 1902, the Lake Moros killed their first American soldiers, and it was apparent that at least some of the *datus* had interpreted the American policy of conciliation as a sign of weakness. Instead of opening the road from Iligan as he had been instructed, Captain Pershing found himself involved with a punitive expedition marching overland from the southcoast town of Malabang. Composed of 1,200 troops of the Seventeenth Infantry, Twenty-Seventh Infantry, and Fifteenth Cavalry and commanded by Colonel Frank D. Baldwin, this force mauled the Moros in a stand-up battle at Bayan on the lake shore on May 4, 1902.[4] While the Bayan fight impressed the *datus* temporarily that the Americans were serious about establishing their posts and ending slavery, it also ended the faint hope that Lake Lanao might be pacified without a much larger commitment of troops and money. It was this view General Davis brought with him from his headquarters at Zamboanga when he pinned on a second star and replaced General Chaffee as the army's senior commander in the Philippines in July 1902.

1.

No sooner had Major Robert Lee Bullard, Twenty-Eighth Infantry, returned to Manila than he began to look for infantry work, preferably fighting. In the summer of 1902 that meant Mindanao. Riding the wave of his new celebrity, Bullard lobbied for active service on his frequent trips to Manila from his regiment's station at San Francisco de Malabon. It is doubtful that the rest of the Twenty-Eighth Infantry shared his enthusiasm, for the regiment (newly formed in 1901 in the expansion of the regular army) had already seen extensive service in southern

Luzon. Many of its officers, regulars and former Volunteers alike, were already fighting the insurgents when the Twenty-Eighth, shedding deserters, sailed for the Philippines.[5]

By the end of September, pressed by unsettled conditions on Lake Lanao and apparently convinced that both Bullard and the Twenty-Eighth were up to the task, Davis ordered the Regiment's Third Battalion—with Bullard commanding—to sail for Iligan and to take up the construction of the road to Marahui. Davis made clear, however, that the mission was not to add to the tension by fighting the Moros. The battalion's job was construction, not combat. Nevertheless Bullard was delighted with the assignment. As his men prepared for embarkation, he wrote Senator Pettus of his good fortune. So excited was he on the day of departure that he left his written orders in Davis' office; they were delivered by launch to his steamer as it left Manila harbor. While the transport headed south, Bullard cursed his own stupidity and foolishness, the products of his vanity in getting the Mindanao assignment. His embarrassment added fire to his determination to drive the road through.[6]

The town of Iligan and the American troops which garrisoned it offered little encouragement to an ambitious officer. The town itself was a dilap-idated port on the Moro frontier. The Spanish had left a small fort near the harbor, a Catholic church roofed with thatch and decorated with garishly painted figures, and a plaza with a peeling, octagonal white bandstand. The rest of the town, inhabited by Moros, Christian Filipinos, and Chinese, was a crumbling collection of adobe or wooden buildings, most of them with grass roofs. Along the unpaved streets stood rows of palms, mango trees, and banana plants. The big attraction in Iligan was the grassy central plaza which unknown natives or Spanish soldiers had decorated by shoving *cerveza* bottles into the ground, the bases forming a mosaic. Until the spring of 1902, the Iligan garrison had been a single company whose major function had been to survive and hold colors each morning. Then the garrison had swollen in the wake of the fight at Bayan. It became the home of six companies of the Tenth Infantry, two troops of the Fifteenth Cavalry, two companies of Philippine Scouts, and a group of civilian clerks and teamsters. Commanded by Colonel Charles H. Noble, Tenth Infantry, and numbering more than eight hundred troops, the Iligan garrison lapsed into a routine schedule of drill and sporadic work on the Spanish road which ran south out of the town.[7]

Bullard spent most of the month of October setting up a tent camp outside Iligan, collecting equipment, scouting the road's right-of-way with his own officers and Captain Jay Johnson Morrow, commander of an attached company of engineers. The department commander, Brigadier General Samuel S. Sumner, visited his camp and praised the map-making and organization of the construction force. On October 27 the Third Battalion—six officers and three hundred forty-four men—began to work on the road to Marahui.[8]

At the beginning the road-building went well, probably because the route followed a Spanish railroad grade south from Iligan. While the work was not yet arduous, Bullard's resources were too few. Within a week Bullard had locked with

Noble over the use of the Iligan garrison's equipment. When Noble lent him some additional wagons, Bullard glowed in the thought that his new reputation as a "comer" could intimidate a colonel.[9] The work continued, but not rapidly. After the first three miles the route left the littoral of Iligan Bay and turned south into the volcanic hills and rainforest above the plunging Agus River. As the work became harder—lumbering, digging, and dynamiting—the troops dwindled from illness and expired enlistments. In less than six weeks the construction force fell to two hundred and seventy-six men. Bullard drove his troops, but even working all day in only twenty-minute shifts of work and rest did not prevent heat exhaustion, illness, and malingering. The soldiers of the Third Battalion did not share their major's urgency: "Taken altogether I believe this command of regulars is worse than any of the volunteers I ever had. Men and officers are harder to appeal to or get anything out of."[10] Bullard changed the routine: the entire command would work simultaneously, starting at sun-up but stopping at 11:30 A.M. Those that worked would have the afternoons to rest. Sick call dropped, morale picked up, and progress on the road improved. Bullard, however, was not satisfied by Noble's assistance, and he was anguished by the lack of progress seen by one of his visitors, Lieutenant General Nelson A. Miles. Problems mounted. The engineer assistance was reduced to a series of inexperienced engineer lieutenants who mismapped the right-of-way. Horses and wagons were few, and the manpower for the job was still too limited.[11]

By December Bullard was frustrated enough to go hunting Noble, whom he saw as an obstruction as challenging as the largest boulder in the Agus hills. He was confident that his reputation for industry and his personal ties to Davis would break open his deadlock with the Iligan commandant. In a letter to his old comrade of the Thirty-Ninth Volunteers, Captain George T. Langhorne, he charged that Noble had starved the construction force of manpower, transport, tentage, equipment, and supplies. He hoped Langhorne would use his position in Davis' headquarters to straighten Noble out or go right to Davis with the facts.[12] There was no immediate response from Manila and Bullard was sure that the army's endorsement "habit" and seniority system had again defeated him: "There is no stimulus to do anything except to hit on the least straining, least laborious way of living so as to hold out longer than one's neighbor and so acquire the highest rank by drawing one's pay and breath longest in the service."[13] In January 1903, as the work still flagged in the heavy jungle, he at last heard a rumor that Noble and his adjutant were to be reassigned and that the new commandant would be the colonel of the Twenty-Eighth, Morris C. Foote. And the rest of the regiment would join the construction force. Bullard was ecstatic: "If I never have another command in the world, I will at least have beaten my enemies here. I think they know who did it too."[14] But then he learned that while the rest of the Twenty-Eighth was indeed coming, Noble had been restored by General Sumner and that Colonel Foote would replace him as commander of the construction force. While not entirely unsuccessful, his ploy had made more enemies. His thoughts turned with self-pity homeward: "I wonder what compensation will ever come to me for my neglect of everything except official duty. My wife is living alone quietly and contentedly without me; my children are growing up without me.''[15]

With the coming of the rest of the Twenty-Eighth Infantry, the work on the Iligan-Marahui went on at a faster pace. Bullard's battalion, however, by January had blasted a path through the worst mile on the route. Emerging from the jungle, the road followed a relatively mild grade along a bluff above the Agus river, a route partially developed by the Spanish. The worst was over. By June, the road was complete to Pantar, a village at the gorge of the Agus five miles below the lake. Only the necessity of spanning the gorge with a suspension bridge too complicated for the infantrymen to erect delayed completion of the road. With its battalions stationed along the road at Momungan, Tiradores Hill, and Pantar, the Twenty-Eighth put the finishing touches on the road, the grading, ditching, surfacing, and brush-clearing along its shoulders. And in these tasks it had help from the Moros themselves.

In addition to his instructions to build the road, Bullard had been ordered by Davis to convince the Moros along the right-of-way that the army came in peace. If possible, Bullard was to enlist their labor, and for this purpose he had access to $20,000. For the first three months, the Moros avoided the soldiers, for the arrival of the Twenty-Eighth Infantry coincided with a cholera epidemic which swept the Lanao *cottas*. Bullard did not press for contact because it appeared to him that the Moros were hostile. Only careful study and diplomacy, he realized even before he left Manila, would keep his mission peaceful. To prepare himself, Bullard had collected what books he could find on Moro language and culture; between his scholarly reading and practical experience after reaching Iligan, he learned enough conversational Moro to eliminate the need for a translator. Bullard concluded that his ability to speak and read Moro, however limited, was crucial to his success as a peacemaker. His other major asset was American policy: the army would not force the Moros' conversion to Christianity.[16]

Occasional Moros sulked about Bullard's camps along the road as early as October, watching the army work and testing the security of the tent areas. Bullard did not chase them away. After three months, a formal delegation led by the *datu* of Alandug visited Camp No. 1 above the Agus. The most impressive moment of this first meeting, Bullard believed, was when he explained in Moro how boiling water rid it of the evil spirits of cholera. In addition, he passed out quinine and promised further medical aid. The talks proceeded on to favorite Moro topics: guns, food, and money. Bullard pointed out that the Moros did not need guns, for the soldiers had not attacked them. Money and food he would give to those who worked on the road. As a token of his friendship he gave the *datu* an American flag. The *datu* was pleased, telling Bullard he must be a white Moro sent to Mindanao by Allah. When Bullard talked with Davis, who visited his camp in January, he learned that he was doing "God's Work." If only all the Moros could see that their peaceful acceptance of American government was also Allah's Will.[17]

Shortly after these talks, the first group of Moro laborers showed up for work.

For such a hard task as the *datus* could clearly see American road-building was, they sent only slaves and boys. Bullard accepted their services, paying them in silver. When he was approached by the *datus*, angered by the money he had given their people, he said he paid only those who worked. He added that his "friends" were those who worked on the road. The *datus* understood the importance of friends with modern rifles. Simply the act of speaking directly and confidentially with the *"commandante"* was prestigious. Eventually three thousand Moros joined the road work, and while they were compulsive shirkers, their labor was useful and fulfilled Bullard's commitment to Davis to try peaceful pacification.[18]

Bullard was aware, however, that the Moros remained dangerous and that some *datus*, despite the marches of the indefatigable Captain Pershing and the Fifteenth Cavalry, remained hostile. Bullard did not know, though, that the cholera epidemic and a shortage of men and supplies had postponed a punitive expedition by Pershing's command in the fall of 1902.[19] No sooner had his battalion camped at Pantar in the spring of 1903 than he learned that Pershing was mounting a campaign to destroy an important *cotta*, that of the Sultan of Bacolod. Bullard's reaction was that General Sumner, a cavalryman of the "the only good Moro is a dead Moro" school, was provoking trouble, endangering Bullard's continuous negotiations with *datus* at the north end of Lake Lanao, and deviating from Davis' orders. Again Bullard challenged Sumner's authority by talking personally to General Davis about the bad judgment and timing of Pershing's campaign.[20] His appeal was to no avail. Pershing marched from Camp Vicars to Bacolod, rearranged the *cotta* with two days of fire from pack howitzers and Vickers-Maxim machine guns and then assaulted it. The Sultan of Bacolod lost over one hundred subjects, while Pershing's men emerged with a few wounded.

While Bullard still preferred negotiations to punitive expeditions, his criticism of the fighting on Lake Lanao was not from humanitarian motives. Rather Bullard thought that Pershing had stolen an assignment due his infantrymen. His own friction with General Sumner had doomed the Twenty-Eighth to the inglorious role of ferrying supplies to Pershing and maintaining the road while the cavalry fought.[21] Even as Pershing marched, the Iligan-Marahui road became an increasingly dangerous place. On May 1 a band of Moros attacked two infantry sergeants who were hunting. Two Moros went to Paradise, but one sergeant went to the base hospital to be sewn up. A patrol of the Fifteenth Cavalry could not find the culprit, the son of the Sultan of Birang-Birang. Shortly thereafter, the same Moros jumped a cavalry patrol led by Captain Clough Overton and killed Overton and one trooper. Six Moros died in the process. In June, as Bullard resumed command of the entire regiment in the absence of the colonel and lieutenant colonel, the incidence of sniping and thievery increased. Friendly *datus* told Bullard that the failure of the infantry to strike back debased both the Americans and the working friendly Moros. But still only patrols by the Fifteenth Cavalry were detailed to punitive attacks. In July the Moros ambushed two infantry privates on sentry duty, killing both, and jumped the first sergeant of Company I. The latter held off his assailants, killing one and wounding two, but he too had to be stitched together by the Twenty-Eighth's surgeons. By August Bullard and the Twenty-Eighth Infantry were more than ready to discard their shovels and their dollars and ply the Moros with Krags.[22]

2.

At the end of July Major Bullard returned to the shores of Lake Lanao with the Second and Third Battalions of the Twenty-Eighth and went into a tent camp near the *cotta* of Marahui, the terminus of the Iligan road. Behind him the road meandered like a muddy scar across the fields of *cogon* grass and through the jungle beside the plunging Agus to a new cantonment near the sea, Camp Overton. The regimental headquarters was at Camp Overton as well as the First Battalion, carpenters, mechanics, wheelwrights, stevedores, engineers, teamsters, and native working parties. The army had come to keep the northern route to the lake open and to support Camp Marahui and Camp Vicars. For Bullard, however, the supporting role was over, the road building and supply hauling chores done. His task now was to civilize the Lake Lanao Moros.

A sentry at Camp Marahui, looking south across the lake toward Camp Vicars, must have relished the view. His camp rested upon a hill above the lake and the army's boat docks. Behind him, the rainforest was draped with vines and blooming orchids. To the east and west, the land was hatched with meandering streams, peaceful *cottas*, rice paddies, and groves of bamboo, palm, and banana plants. To the east the lake shore was heavily populated, for there the mountains did not hug the shoreline. In the northeast the Ramain River knived into the hills, creating an enclave of *cottas*, then ran back four miles from the lake. South of the Ramain the hills closed in upon the shore, then fell back again to create the valleys of the Taraca and Gata rivers. This was the land of the Taraca and Maciu Moros, heavily populated, a region of many rice paddies, mangrove swamps, streams, gorges, and heavy vegetation. The trails through it were footpaths, impassable in the rain. At the long southern side of the lake the Butig Mountains cupped the land and the post at Camp Vicars, where Captain Pershing's garrison of the Fifteenth Cavalry and Twenty-Third Infantry watched the Moros and the rough cart path to Malabang on the south coast. When the sentry looked to the west from Marahui, he could see a littoral narrower, slopes steeper, and mountains higher than those to the east. Here the Moro *cottas* thinned out as one left Marahui. Along the west shore the land was relatively dry, there were fewer streams, and the many palms and meadows of *cogon* grass dominated the scattered rice paddies. Only the southwest corner of the lake was heavily settled, the domain of the Sultan of Bacolod.[23]

Coming up the road from Iligan, the new commander of the Department of Mindanao and Sulu found the view breathtaking. Brigadier General Leonard Wood, Rough Rider, Cuban governor-general, friend of the President, was much impressed by his first look at Lake Lanao and the camp of Marahui. In addition to

Wood's natural paradise, his vision included a future happy land of industrious, peaceful Moros providing wealth for themselves and wood, coffee, and cocoa for the outside world. He was no less impressed by the work of Major Bullard, remembered from the Geronimo campaign. "Major Bullard is Sultan of Sultans," one of Wood's bright aides noted. The welcome at Marahui on August 11 was just the sort of thing to impress the general: Bullard's troops lined up for inspection along with a reception committee of peaceful *datus*, each with his warrior retinue and American flag. As Wood arrived, Bullard's troops were firing a volley to satisfy the honor of a *datu* clubbed by an overzealous sentry. Wood could see, as he and his staff talked with him later, that Bullard was a Moro expert. And at some time before Wood continued his grand tour by launch to Pershing's post at Vicars, he approved Bullard's request to begin infantry expeditions against the Moros. These attacks were to be limited to those *cottas* which harbored known assailants. Indiscriminate shooting was not to be a substitute for diplomacy.[24]

In the four weeks after his conference with Wood, Bullard led four expeditions against hostile Moros. For the first, against the isolated hill *cotta* of Lati some twenty miles from the lake and west of the Agus river, Bullard developed what became his basic tactic: a night march followed by a quick dawn assault. At Lati (August 13) the Moros fled after a brief fight, leaving behind stolen army equipment and rifles. In the next expedition (August 20), Bullard took out three officers and one hundred ten men against the *cotta* of the Sultan of Baring-Bingan in the Ramain River valley. The objective of the attack was to kill or capture the sultan's son and his renegades. Again Bullard led the march, a tiring walk through a night-long rain and a disheartening series of swamps and bogs along the lakeshore. At dawn, however, the Americans again opened fire and assaulted the *cotta*. The surprised Moros rallied, and a few left the *cotta* for open combat. Seven of these died, but no soldiers fell. In the days following these attacks Bullard was busy receiving pledges of loyalty from many *datus*. On September 9, however, he led a platoon to the *cotta* of Toros near Marahui to break up a Moro war and chased the band which appeared with stolen arms. When one of the fleeing Moros surrendered, Bullard took him by boat to Marahui. On the return trip the captive pulled a *kris* and began to hack his way forward in the boat. When he fell at Bullard's feet with five .38 caliber bullets in him, he had killed one soldier and wounded another and a friendly Moro. The boat's deck was slippery with blood. In his last expedition in September, Bullard led a battalion of the Twenty-Eighth and a troop of the Fifteenth into the hills west of the Agus and destroyed the *cotta* of the Sultan of Marantao, another chronic troublemaker.[25]

The punitive expeditions drew the dividends Bullard expected, for the *datus* at the north end of the lake came marching in almost daily to pledge their loyalty to the United States. Each ceremony was a high state matter. The *datu* arrived in a procession led by his son, who carried an American flag, and a dancing warrior, who slashed the air with his *kris*. To the sound of drums and the discharge of weapons, the *datu* walked beneath a red parasol carried by a slave. Behind him came his warriors, all armed with spears, shields, and assorted cutlery. Before this

Lilliputian host and the American infantrymen, the *datu* would swear submission to the authority of the United States in the name of Allah and Mohammed the Prophet.[26]

Bullard learned that Moro diplomacy did not end with formalities. The Moros understood the power of Bullard's men and their rifles, not the abstraction of some far-off government or country. The *datus* wanted to talk with the *"commandante"* to find out where he stood in the Lake Lanao balance of power. Many made proposals for a military alliance, one *datu* even suggesting that his men and Bullard's attack Pershing's post at Vicars and so dominate the entire lake region. (In light of his envy of Pershing's publicity, one wonders what Bullard's first reaction to this plan was.) Not all the Lake *datus* felt the need to come to Marahui and instead sent messages. "I have important word," one wrote, "I think the President of America will name you for a high office and me also, because I am your friend. Your thoughts are mine." Some, like the powerful Sultan of Taraca, wanted to make sure that the visit to Marahui would demonstrate their power: "In the name of the Allah-ta-Allah, who has given everything, who rules this world and the next and who has many names: If you continue a good friend we wish to come and present ourselves. I wish [you] to write me if this suits you and if you will give me a salute. If you do not wish to be a good friend that is all right. If you do not wish to recognize me as a high datto, do not have any feeling on that account." To the *datus* the message was the same: swear allegiance, live in peace, do not wage war or slave under the American flag and you have nothing to fear from *"Commandante"* Bullard, his soldiers, and their rifles.[27]

As important as keeping the peace at Lake Lanao, Bullard had impressed General Wood. Their first conference had gone well, although Bullard became piqued when Wood got credit in the Manila newspapers for creating a new, successful Moro policy. In their second meeting in September, Bullard demonstrated his pacifying abilities by halting a civil war in front of the department commander. Two *datus* had their feudal hosts drawn up for combat. Bullard rode between the tribes to stop the war and to negotiate a settlement in his position of judge of the *datus*. Wood and his entourage were impressed with his gallant act, but also concluded that the pacification of the Moros was incomplete and that the Lake *datus* were "offish and ugly."[28]

More would have to be done to impress the Lake Moros, Wood reasoned. Pershing's expedition in the spring had not been sufficiently awesome since he had only leveled Bacolod and one other *cotta*. His subsequent show of force and negotiations had given the Moros an impression of weakness. Now, Wood wrote Roosevelt, he himself would use the soldiers he had concentrated at Marahui and Overton to march around the lake in October. The force would make the march "peacefully if possible, but if we are attacked by the hostile towns above mentioned . . . [we] shall clean them up with as little damage to ourselves as possible."[29] Wood's stubborn plan for a military parade around the lake disturbed Bullard. While he too had been touched by the magic of Wood's willpower and reforming zeal and was awed by the general's political connections, he believed that march was a poor idea. In September he told the general that a march would be interpreted as a military challenge by the *datus* and that it would ruin his negotiations. Wood was unmoved. Bullard despaired: "High authorities . . . want to do it all in one blow." He could not escape the conclusion that the march was also designed to publicize the martial virtues of the department commander. As the cables from Zamboanga confirmed that the big expedition was on, he tried to explain to the friendly *datus* that Wood's purpose was to gather intelligence and to negotiate with the most belligerent *cottas* along the proposed route.[30]

Wood assembled his expedition at Marahui at the end of October. By Lake Lanao standards it was a mighty host: eight companies of the Twenty-Eighth Infantry, four companies of the Twenty-Third Infantry, three troops from the Fourteenth Cavalry, an engineer detachment, and two pack howitzers of Captain George C. Gately's artillery battery. To support the expedition, Wood added a pack-train and a fleet of native boats, manned by soldiers, civilians, and a few Moros.

On November 4 Wood's column left Marahui in the midst of a driving rain, for the rainy season had come to Lake Lanao. While Wood personally took part of the force through the *cottas* at the lake's northwest corner and found all of them peaceful, Bullard led the two battalions of the Twenty-Eighth across the Agus and into the Ramain River district. Here too there was no fighting. The next day Wood rejoined Bullard, and the entire expedition inched its way south along the flooded eastern lakeshore. The march was entirely peaceful. At each major *cotta* there was a parlay and an exchange of gifts, but as the column staggered through the rain, plunging across swollen gullies and paddies, "a great many Moros" marched parallel to the troops "evidently very much exercised about our trip and wondering what we [were] there for."[31] On November 6 the weather worsened. A storm churned the lake, capsizing two boats in the five-foot waves. One American drowned, and 37,000 rounds of ammunition, twenty rifles, and five days rations went to the bottom. The column marched only four miles that day. As the rains continued, so too did General Wood, as if to prove that his will alone could master the weather and his troops' exhaustion. Bullard, glumly trying to negotiate with the Moros and despairing of ever being dry again, thought Wood's performance magnificent idiocy: "The general manifested no disposition to use guides but preferred to stagger around in the mud, marshes and brush and find his own way." Finally, one *cotta* resisted and Wood had his battle: a screeching bombardment and sodden charge in which one soldier died and five were wounded. The march continued. Then, on the evening of November 6, as if in answer to the prayers of the dispirited force, Wood received a telegram from Major Hugh Scott, his old friend and governor of Sulu, that a revolt was underway there by Datu Hassan of Look. Wood turned the column around. Rations nearly exhausted, it marched back through the rain sixteen miles to Pantar. The Lake Lanao force must now regroup and become the "Second Sulu Expedition."[32]

As the force prepared to leave Mindanao by steamer, Wood approached

Bullard: would the major accept the governorship of Lake Lanao province even though his regiment would return to the United States in December? They, the general and the major, were alike, Wood continued, for they were both outcasts in the army but heroes to the public. They should help each other; there was enough opportunity for service and reward in Mindanao for every officer capable of hard service. Flattered, Bullard agreed to stay. Wood then placed him in command of the two battalions of the Twenty-Eighth Infantry he had ordered to join the Sulu force.[33]

3.

Although Bullard later called his service as governor of Lake Lanao province "the most interesting work . . . of my whole life," his motives for staying in the Philippines beyond his regiment's service there were complex. Doubtless he received great satisfaction from bringing the rule of law to the Moros, but this psychic reward was largely retroactive, blossoming after his departure in 1904. At the time he was most impressed by the sheer challenges of the assignment and the opportunity to have almost complete freedom of command in the Lake province. Wood's favor was also worth cultivating, for the department commander combined in rare degree ability and political influence. By joining the Wood coterie, Bullard believed he was a member of the quarter of the officer corps which made the army go, the "inner corps" of the dedicated and active officers which Wood seemed to represent.[34] That he had paid a price for his Mindanao opportunity Bullard had no doubt:

> I have neither home nor family, neither the dear cares nor the thoughts for others that make life worthy. I have worked hard for the Moros and the U.S. and my own name. For the first two I feel that I've done something, for the last, but little. I've worked myself almost sick and have won a few words of commendation from the generals over me, letters. Truly to do anything great requires an amount of work and brains that seem wholly out of proportion to the results. I have neglected family, friends, business, everything and lived in the wilderness. And now it looks like another year of the same thing with health, I fear, broken too. I am certainly far from well. . . . I am just getting a start on being governor now.[35]

Bullard's willingness to extend his Lake Lanao assignment was also rooted in his conviction that his military reputation had not been sufficiently enhanced by his work on the Iligan-Marahui road or by his diplomatic work with the Moros. He had learned much by Pershing's experience at Camp Vicars. Pershing, Bullard thought, had been inordinately praised by the generals for killing a few Moros while he (Bullard) had been barely commended for his diplomacy. Now Pershing had left the lake for a choice assignment in Washington, wreathed in rumors that

Roosevelt would make him a brigadier general. There was a lesson here, Bullard mused: a career soldier should never forget that he has no other purpose but to fight.[36]

Wood, whose own reputation needed to be enhanced by combat, approved of aggressive and loyal subordinates, and Bullard proved he was both on the Second Sulu Expedition. Despite Scott's message that punitive action against Hassan should be swift, Wood mounted another "big show" for Sulu: two battalions of the Twenty-Eighth, one battalion of the Twenty-Third Infantry, two cavalry troops, and Gateley's battery. Disembarking on November 12, the Mindanao troops were joined by Scott's command: two more cavalry troops, three companies of the Seventeenth Infantry, and two more guns. Plowing through the swamps and *cogon* grass, the expedition engaged Hassan's Moros. Bullard's troops took the advance, skirmishing with Moro snipers throughout the day. The next day Wood again gave Bullard the choice assignment, attacking Hassan's entrenched tribesmen in a meadow and hill position west of Hassan's *cotta* near Lake Siet. Bullard's battalion drenched the Moro position with rifle fire and then charged it. The Moros fired a ragged volley and fled. Bullard's battalion began to pursue Hassan, but Wood checked them. Captain Frank R. McCoy, the most loyal of Wood aides, took the message and found Bullard reluctant to halt: "The active commandante didn't like being stopped one bit, and the order to get in touch with Ronayne's battalion on his left wasn't cheerfully received or obeyed. He is most ambitious, and was figuring on holding his advanced position, and rushing and taking Hassan, and his *cotta* before the arrival of the main body."[37] When Wood's main body came up, the general and Bullard led it into the abandoned *cotta* and then burned Hassan's village.

On November 14 Major Scott was able to persuade Wood to let him negotiate with Hassan, for the Moro *datu* had sent a message that he was ready to sue for peace. The parley was, instead, an ambush and Scott was gravely wounded. The pursuit continued along the shores of Lake Siet. Hassan's band attempted a stand in a tangle of mango swamps and volcanic rock. Bullard and Wood conducted a reconnaissance, and the next day Bullard's battalion assaulted the position after the Moros had been thoroughly raked with rifle and artillery fire. Eighty-two Moros died, and Hassan's band disintegrated. For the next week Wood's soldiers hunted down the fugitives. Only once more were Bullard's troops engaged when on November 20 Company E and Company F cornered a fleeing band in the hills and shot it to pieces. Though Hassan himself avoided capture, the Second Sulu Expedition had run out of Moros. On November 23 Bullard's two battalions returned to Mindanao, having killed one hundred sixteen Moros (by body count) and having established their commander in General Wood's favored circle.[38]

His regiment on its way to the United States, Bullard, surrounded by the alien faces of the Twenty-Third Infantry and the Moros, watched the days slide into 1904 without enthusiasm. Conditions on Lake Lanao had deteriorated after Wood's grand parade; on the day that the Sulu expedition had left, Moros had killed four boat guards at Marahui. The Moros had recovered the rifles and ammunition dumped overboard in November. Bullard found his troops single-minded in Moro affairs; "Any fool can fight and kill Moros but it takes a man of some sense to manage them without killing them yet without loss of prestige and dignity."[39] On New Year's Day he found little comfort in promising to himself to take more "care of my own soul," his family and business interests, health, diet, eyes, and "to steadily pursue some definite worthy object in life."[40] He knew, however, that Wood was depending on him to calm the Lake Lanao Moros, a job the department commander admitted he himself had botched. And his spirits rose when on January 10 he transferred to the governor's headquarters at Camp Vicars on the south shore. This post, neat and scenic, was nearer the most hostile Moros and was garrisoned by a battalion of the Twenty-Third and part of Gately's battery. Despite the loneliness and official isolation which were mitigated only by his duties and professional reading, Bullard felt his spirits lift: "I shall be able to do something here. I feel it. I am in command."[41]

He was, of course, still tied to the hyperactive general in Zamboanga. Service with Wood, Bullard was learning, had its interesting aspects. Hardly had Wood assumed command of the department than the general learned from a friend that his nomination for promotion to major general was in deep trouble in the Senate. President Theodore Roosevelt presented the situation unambiguously: the Senate Military Affairs Committee was blocking Wood's promotion because it was critical of his administration in Cuba and because it was angry about Roosevelt's aggressiveness in promoting general officers on the basis of merit rather than seniority and army popularity. Roosevelt thought that he had a sufficient number of Republican senators lined up behind Wood's nomination, but he suggested to the general that he mount a letter-writing campaign in his own behalf. The best kind would include other officers' approval of the general's military record and would influence prominent senators, particularly Democrats.[42] Wood acted on the problem with his customary directness: Major J. R. Kean lobbied with the senators from Virginia, Hugh Scott wrote Matthew Quay of Pennsylvania, and the general himself solicited recommendations from Francis Warren, William Howard Taft, Matthew Hanna, Joseph B. Foraker, Henry Cabot Lodge, Grover Cleveland, and General Fred C. Ainsworth, a list of luminaries which included some of Wood's most ardent supporters and enemies. One army officer with "pull" proposed a trade-off: Captain John J. Pershing, from his War Department staff post, wrote that he would be happy to back Wood's nomination since it showed that the administration was recognizing merit. He also thought it would be appropriate if Wood wrote the general's political friends, recommending Pershing's appointment as a brigadier general. Wood replied that his first choice was his colleague, Hugh L. Scott, but that he would write a letter to the Adjutant General since he believed Pershing was qualified.[43] In this battle of endorsements, Bullard's contribution was meager but willing. He wrote to Senator Pettus and at least one general that Wood was the best commander the department of Mindanao had had and that the general understood the Moro problem, that he was rapidly bringing civilization to Mindanao, and that he was "the livest man" in the army.

Bullard also offered a mix of first and secondhand testimony on Wood's crucial role in the pursuit of Geronimo. He made sure Wood got a file copy of the letter.[44]

Bullard served his general better on Lake Lanao than he did in Washington. Although feudal warfare had dwindled since 1902, there were still occasional Moro attacks on American soldiers, either to steal weapons or gain prestige by killing infidels. In December Moros had ambushed a duck hunting party which included the commander of the Twenty-Third Infantry; the next month two sentries were attacked and four rifles stolen. Every day Bullard talked with the *datus* cajoling them to keep the peace, end slavery, to turn in their firearms. Bullard continued to emphasize one theme: the *datus* must assert their authority to control their people; if they did not, they would be the ones arrested. Often the message sunk in, other times it did not. Then it became necessary to hit the reluctant *datu's cotta*, a quick raid with minimum forces and maximum psychological impact.

By now Bullard's expeditions had been reduced to arduous routine. On the night of January 21 he took his four companies and a machine gun from Vicars to the Ramain River. Bullard sent two companies by boat up the Ramain to flank the offending *cotta* while he himself took two companies on a two mile overland march through the swamps. At daybreak his force ran into an earthen fort built in a rice paddy a mile west of the *cotta*. The muddy battlements held two *latankas*, the Moro brass cannon. Bullard's force, however, surprised the ten defenders, who surrendered without a fight. Occupying the fort, Bullard parlayed an hour with the *datu*, asking him to surrender the men who had sniped at the Twenty-Third's colonel. The *datu* refused. As the boat force opened fire with rifles and its Vickers-Maxim, Bullard led his troops across the paddy. Joined, the four companies swept the *cotta*, killing thirty-two Moros. The only American casualties were two lieutenants wounded leading an abortive charge. Destroying the *cotta* and three forts, the force reembarked in its fleet of native *bancas*. On the return to Vicars a sudden storm swamped the boats, but by getting into the water and hugging the gunwales the soldiers saved their equipment and their own lives. With rowers in the most lightly loaded boats, the force was towed back to Vicars.[45]

In February Bullard took out two companies of infantry, thirty-five artillerymen, his one machine gun, and a pack train of one hundred and fifty animals for a ten day scout. Without a casualty the force captured six cannon, some rifles, and several *datus*. When it returned to Vicars it had marched one hundred and twenty miles.[46]

For Bullard the routine was becoming deadening. His thoughts turned more often to his family and kin in Alabama. He found that other army officers who came with their men to Lake Lanao regarded him as a permanent fixture in the Moro lands. Major-Governor Bullard—the thin, bearded man who spoke Moro and who had been made a *caliph* by his friends the Lake *datus*—seemed a man apart from the American officers who dined with him in his native bungalow at Vicars. His visitors told him how much they admired his handling of the Moros and how he surely would be General Wood's successor (complete with stars) at Zamboanga.[47]

In March of 1904 Wood began to plan another "big show" for the Lake Lanao Moros, the most punitive of all punitive expeditions to subdue those *datus* who continued to allow slaving, thievery, and warfare under the United States flag. Wood had developed a marked antipathy for the policy of governing through the *datus*, for he saw them as a despicable elite standing between their ignorant people and the blessings of civilization. To prepare his indictment of the *datus* he had Bullard prepare a list of Moro "lawlessness" on Lake Lanao from July 1903 to March 1904. The charge-sheet revealed a minor but consistently annoying pattern of violence: sniping, rifle snatching, Moro "riots," two jailbreaks, attacks on isolated sentries in which seven soldiers had died.[48] At the same time that he prepared the list of offenses, Bullard collected intelligence and maps and summoned the Lake *datus* to Vicars for a peace conference with General Wood.

As Wood suspected, Ami Binaning, the Sultan of Taraca, did not appear at the April 1 meeting but instead rallied his own warriors. That the sultan chose resistance came as no surprise, for the Taraca Moros had been the heart of the anti-Spanish resistance and had been the most hostile group on the lake since the army arrived. If the Taraca Moros had chosen peace, Wood would have been disappointed, for he believed that Pershing's 1903 expedition had left such an impression of weakness that the Moros needed a massive dose of American military might before capitulating. To this end he assembled at Vicars just such a force: six battalions of infantry, four troops of dismounted cavalry, Gately's pack howitzers, Vickers-Maxim machine guns, and a massive pack-train. In addition to the troops and civilian packers, the expedition included officers of the Philippine constabulary who were preparing to assume peacekeeping on the lake, the bulk of the general's staff from Zamboanga, and a touring Far Eastern expert from the University of Chicago.[49]

On April 3 Wood sent a force of two battalions of the Twenty-Third Infantry and two cavalry troops by boat to the mouth of the Taraca river. When this force got ashore, they were attacked by the Moros, but had little trouble discouraging the warriors. The main body of the Taraca expedition marched from Vicars immediately. Camping that night, Wood's troops were fired upon around their fires; two soldiers were wounded.

The next day, Easter Sunday, the column struggled single-file through a maze of high *cogon* grass, bogs, and gullies. Fortunately, not only was the march unopposed, but as the column progressed north it collected a host of Moro "volunteers." That night the column camped in a rice paddy a mile south of the Taraca river. Amid the braying of mules, the smoke of wet campfires, the chatter of the Moro "volunteers," and the occasional flash of a signalman's torch communicating with Vicars, Wood's chaplain held Easter services for the tired troops. Captain Frank McCoy thought the chaplain had trouble reconciling the Easter message with the expedition's purpose, for he kept muttering about Christian-Moslem wars. The assembly sang "America" and "Onward Christian Soldiers"— General Wood's voice prominent in the host—and then retired to the rice paddy dikes to find solid ground to sleep upon.[50]

Early the next morning Wood's united Taraca expedition began a week of pacifying the Taraca Moros. Most of the Taraca *cottas* chose resistance. Wood then opened fire at eight hundred yards with his pack howitzers, machine guns, and riflemen. After a short but violent bombardment each *cotta* was assaulted and destroyed. The surviving Moros fled. In a week the Taraca expeditions reduced more than a hundred *cottas* at a cost of two killed and eight wounded. Moro losses were unknown.

When Wood lead his bedraggled but happy troops back to Camp Vicars, he was satisfied that the Taraca Moros would no longer be a problem. He was, however, distressed that the Sultan of Taraca had not been apprehended. Instead Ami Binaning had fled to the west shore of the lake and the new *cotta* of his clansman, the Sultan of Bacolod. Bullard (who had remained at Vicars) and his garrison got the assignment. In a four-day march Bullard's troops marched along the west shore and assaulted the *cottas* of Bacolod and Canayan. At the loss of one man wounded, Bullard destroyed fifteen Moro cannon and ten muskets and recovered some stolen army property. He returned to Vicars with no prisoners but confident that the Lake Moros were ready for civil government, a judgment General Wood shared.[51]

With the Taraca expedition completed, Bullard, wan, ill, and living on bread, raw eggs, and malted milk tablets, went to Zamboanga for official business and unofficial leave. He did not return to Vicars until June 2. A week later he was out with the Vicars garrison on another patrol to the east shore of the lake to arrest still another belligerent *datu* Wood wanted punished. The expedition found the offending *cotta* deserted. On the return march, Bullard, tired and frustrated, sat down on the shore during a halt and wrote his resignation as governor. He had had enough of colonial duty; he wanted to go home. Wood tried to persuade him to stay, spinning tales about honor and indispensability. Bullard refused to reconsider.[52] Wood approved his request, and Bullard began to pack souvenirs, uniforms, and personal equipment. In his trunk were the articles he had written (all rejected) and fourteen letters of thanks from his superiors. As he prepared to depart his thoughts turned homeward to the healing ritual of garrison life:

> I think I would enjoy "straight duty" once more with troops. I think I'd like to see men on parade, drill and ceremony in full uniform and loaf about garrison and look at the guard mount and hear the band play and see the ladies on the sidewalk.
> I must begin to think of something about what I am to do when I reach the U.S., what new purpose to set myself, what work to take up. I imagine my family needs my thoughts and attention most.[53]

As his steamer cruised northward to Manila, he wondered what his transfer to the infantry and the Mindanao service had done: "I feel that I've added considerably to my military reputation in the last two years, but has it been worth the labor and pains and sacrifice. I doubt it.'' In Manila, however, he found his fellow officers most hospitable, and he received dinner invitations from two of the most ambitious officers he knew, a sure sign of his enhanced reputation.[54] He learned that the Manila papers had printed news of his work. When he left Manila on July 15 for San Francisco, he felt more confident that the Moro experience had added to his professional stature. When he arrived in San Francisco his thoughts were of the future. He never returned to the Philippines.

NOTES

[1]The description of the Moros of Lake Lanao is drawn primarily from Bullard's own studies of their language and culture, preserved in ''Moro Subject File,'' Box 10, BP, and his published writings ''Among the Savage Moros,'' *Metropolitan Magazine* 24 (June 1906) pp. 1-17, and ''Road Building among the Moros,'' *Atlantic Monthly* 92 (December 1903), pp. 818-826. See also Rev. Pio Pi, S.J., ''The Moros of the Philippines,'' Appendix VI to ''Report of Maj. Gen. George W. Davis, U.S. Army, Commanding Division of the Philippines,'' in *Annual Reports of the War Department, 1903* (Washington: Government Printing Office, 1903), III, pp. 365-378; and Najeeb M. Saleeby, *Studies in Moro History, Law and Religion* (Manila 1905).

[2]Maj. Gen. A. R. Chaffee to Maj. Gen. H. C. Corbin, April 30, 1902, Henry C. Corbin Papers, Manuscript Division, Library of Congress.

[3]*Ibid.*; Brig. Gen. Henry T. Allen to Gov. W. H. Taft, January 16, 1902, Henry T. Allen Papers, Manuscript Division, Library of Congress; Maj. Gen. A. R. Chaffee to Maj.-Gen. H. C. Corbin, February 28, 1902 and March 30, 1902, both Corbin Papers.

[4]Donald Smythe, ''John J. Pershing: Soldier,'' *mss*, pp. 118-182, and John R. White, ''Three Generals,'' *mss* in the John R. White collection, University of Oregon Library.

[5]Diarybook 2, entry July 24, 1902, BP; Returns of the Twenty-Eighth Infantry, March 1901-December 1902, reel 273 of ''Returns from Regular Army Infantry Regiments, June 1821-December 1916,'' Microcopy 665, NA.

[6]Diarybook 2, entries, September 29 and October 8, 1902; Bullard autobiography, p. 58-59, BP.

[7]The physical description of Iligan is from Sydney Adamson, ''What Shall We Do with the Moros?'' *Frank Leslie's Illustrated* (August 25, 1900); details on the garrison are from Returns, Iligan, Mindanao, P. I., April 1900-September 1903, reel 502 of ''Returns from U.S. Military Posts, 1800-1916,'' Microcopy 617, NA.

[8]Diarybook 2, entries for October, 1902, BP. For the details of the construction of the Iligan-Marahui road, I have used the following accounts: Maj. Robert L. Bullard, ''Road Building among the Moros,'' previously cited, and ''Preparing Our Moros for Government,'' *Atlantic Monthly* 97 (March 1906), pp. 385-393; C. C. Bateman, ''Military Road Making in Mindanao,'' *JMSI* 33 (September-October 1903), pp. 190-199; and 1st Lt. Andrew J. Dougherty, ''The Infantry Brings Civilization and Good Government to the Moro,'' *mss* (n.d.), attached to Bullard autobiography, BP. Bateman was the chaplain of the Twenty-Eighth and Bullard's ''intelligence officer''; Dougherty was a member of the Third Battalion. The participants' accounts are verified by the returns of the Twenty-Eighth Infantry and the post at Iligan (previously cited) and ''Annual Report of Brig. Gen. Samuel

S. Sumner, U.S. Army, Commanding Department of Mindanao," Appendix III to "Annual Report of Maj. Gen. George W. Davis, Commanding Division of Philippines," *Annual Reports of the War Department,* 1903 (Washington: Government Printing Office, 1903), III, pp. 297-353.

⁹Diarybook 2, entries, November 7 and 8, 1902, BP.

¹⁰Diarybook 2, entry, December 1, 1902, BP.

¹¹Batemman, "Military Road Making in Mindanao," previously cited.

¹²Maj. R. L. Bullard to Capt. G. T. Langhorne, December 17, 1902, and Diarybook 2, entry, December 24, 1902, BP.

¹³Notebook 4, entry, December 22, 1902, BP.

¹⁴Diarybook 2, entry, January 9, 1903, BP.

¹⁵Diarybook 2, entry, January 25, 1903, BP.

¹⁶Bullard autobiography, pp. 59-61, BP; Robert L. Bullard, "Road Building among the Moros" and "Preparing Our Moros for Government," previously cited; C. C. Bateman, "Military Taming of the Moro," *JMSI* 34 (March-April 1904) pp. 259-266.

¹⁷*Ibid.* Bullard's accounts are consistent over a thirty year period and match Bateman's.

¹⁸*Ibid.*

¹⁹Diarybook 2, entry, November 30, 1902, BP; "Annual Report of Brig. Gen. Samuel S. Sumner, U.S. Army, Commanding Department of Mindanao," *Annual Reports of the War Department, 1903*, III, previously cited.

²⁰Diarybook 2, entry, April 11, 1903, BP.

²¹Diarybook 2, entry, May 5, 1903, BP.

²²Diarybook 2, entry, July 15, 1903, BP; Bullard, "Preparing Our Moros for Government," previously cited. The events of April-August, 1903, are based on documents in "Returns of the Twenty-Eighth Infantry, January 1903-December 1905," reel 274 of "Returns from Regular Army Infantry Regiments, June 1821-December 1916," Microcopy 665, NA, and the returns from Iligan, Mindanao, P. I., April 1900-September 1903, previously cited.

²³The description is based on Bateman, "Military Road Making in Mindanao," previously cited; Captain John McA. Palmer, "Chapter Notes," Volumes IV and V, which describe Palmer's experiences as governor of the Lake province in 1906-1907, John McA. Palmer Papers, Manuscript Division, Library of Congress; and entry, August 11, 1903, Leonard Wood diary, 1902-1903, Leonard Wood Papers, Manuscript Division, Library of Congress. I also used maps of Lake Lanao made by the army in 1904.

²⁴Diarybook 2, entries, July 26-August 15, 1903, BP; entry, August 11, 1903, Wood diary, 1902-1903, Wood Papers; Capt. F. R. McCoy to Mrs. T. F. McCoy, August 16, 1903, Family Correspondence, Frank R. McCoy Papers, Manuscript Division, Library of Congress; Maj. H. L. Scott to Mrs. H. L. Scott, Family Correspondence, Hugh L. Scott Papers, Manuscript Division, Library of Congress; "Report Department of Mindanao," *Annual Reports of the War Department, 1904* (Washington: Government Printing Office, 1904) III, pp. 259-284; Hermann Hagedorn, *Leonard Wood,* 2 vols. (New York: Harper and Brothers, 1931) II, pp. 1-53.

²⁵Diarybook 2, entries, August 13-September 15, 1903, BP; returns, September and October 1903, Iligan, P. I. reel 502 of "Returns from U.S. Military Posts, 1800-1916," previously cited; returns, August and September 1903, Twenty-Eighth Infantry, reel 274 in "Returns from Regular Army Infantry Regiments, June 1821-December 1916," previously cited; "Report Department of Mindanao" in *Annual Reports of the War Department, 1904,* previously cited.

²⁶C. C. Bateman, "Military Taming of the Moro," previously cited.

²⁷C. C. Bateman, "Military Taming of the Moro"; Bullard autobiography, pp. 66-67, BP; Robert L. Bullard, "Preparing Our Moros for Government," previously cited.

²⁸Brig. Gen. L. Wood to Maj. Gen. J. F. Wade, August 23, 1903, Wood Papers; Diarybook 2, entry, September 12, 1903, BP; Capt. F. R. McCoy to Mrs. McCoy, September 19, 1903, McCoy Papers; H. Pollock to Maj. H. L. Scott, September 19, 1903, Scott Papers; Brig. Gen. L. Wood to T. Roosevelt, September 20, 1903, and Wood to Adjutant General, Division of the Philippines, September 21, 1903, Wood Papers.

²⁹Brig. Gen. L. Wood to T. Roosevelt, September 20, 1903, Wood Papers.

³⁰Diarybook 2, entry, October 22, 1903 and Notebook 4, entry, October 5, 1903, BP.; H. Pollock to Maj. H. L. Scott, September 19, 1903, Scott Papers.

³¹Entry, November 4, 1903, Wood Diary, 1902-1906, Wood Papers.

³²This reconstruction of the Lake Lanao "mud march" is based upon entries, November 2-10, 1903, Wood Diary, 1902-1906, Wood Papers; Capt. Frank R. McCoy to Mrs. McCoy, November 30, 1903, McCoy Papers; Bullard's own six-page narrative in Diarybook 2, November 29, 1903, BP; returns, November 1903, Camp Overton, Mindanao, P. O., reel 892 in "Returns from U.S. Military Posts, 1800-1916," previously cited; "Report Department of Mindanao" *Annual Reports of the War Department, 1904*, previously cited.

³³Diarybook 2, entry, November 29, 1903, BP; entry, November 8, 1903, Wood Diary, 1902-1906, Wood Papers.

³⁴Bullard autobiography, p. 67; Diarybook 2, entry, December 1, 1903; Notebook 4, entry, December 26, 1903, all BP.

³⁵Diarybook 2, entry, December 26, 1903, BP.

³⁶Notebook 4, entry, December 31, 1903, BP.

³⁷Capt. Frank R. McCoy to Mrs. McCoy, December 5, 1903, McCoy Papers.

³⁸The description of the Second Sulu Expedition is based on McCoy's letter and Brig. Gen. L. Wood to Adjutant General, Division of the Philippines, December 11, 1903, Wood Papers; entry, November 20, 1903, Wood Diary, 1902-1906, Wood Papers; return, November 1903, for the Twenty-Eighth Infantry, reel 274, "Returns from Regular Army Infantry Regiments, June 1821-December 1916," previously cited; Maj. R. L. Bullard to Adjutant, Infantry Force, Jolo Expedition, November 23, 1903, BP; Hugh L. Scott, *Some Memories of a Soldier* (New York: The Century Company, 1928), pp. 325-335; Brig. Gen. L. Wood to Col. O. J. Sweet, December 7, 1903, Wood Papers.

³⁹Diarybook 2, entry, December 31, 1903, BP.

⁴⁰Diarybook 2, entry, January 1, 1904, BP.

⁴¹On conditions on Lake Lanao and Wood's "mud march," see Diarybook 2, entry, December 1, 1903, BP, and entries, January 5-14, 1904, Wood Diary, 1903-1906, Wood Papers. On Camp Vicars, see Diarybook 2, entry, January 11, 1904, BP, and returns, Camp Vicars, Mindanao, P. I., June 1902-December 1907, reel 1328 of "Returns from U.S. Military Posts, 1800-1916," previously cited.

⁴²T. Roosevelt to Brig. Gen. L. Wood, August 1, 1903, Wood Papers.

⁴³Capt. John J. Pershing to Brig. Gen. L. Wood, September 8, 1903, and Brig. Gen. L. Wood to Capt. J. J. Pershing, January 9, 1904, Wood Papers.

⁴⁴Wood's papers for September, 1903-February, 1904 show the extent of the general's endorsement campaign. Bullard's effort is a letter to General (?), December 17, 1903; the letter's internal evidence suggests that it was sent to either General Corbin or General Weston or both. For the politics of Wood's nomination the best source is U.S. Congress,

Senate, Committee on Military Affairs, "Hearings before the Committee on Military Affairs concerning the Nomination of Brig. Gen. Leonard Wood to be Major-General, United States Army," Senate Executive Document "C", 58th Congress, 2d session (Washington, 1904).

[45]Maj. R. L. Bullard to Adj. Gen., Department of Mindanao, January 26, 1904, Wood Papers.

[46]Return, February, 1904, Camp Vicars, Mindanao, P. I., in "Returns from U.S. Military Posts, 1800-1916," previously cited; Capt. F. R. McCoy to Mrs. McCoy, February 14, 1904, McCoy Papers.

[47]Diarybook 3, entries, March 20-30, 1904, BP.

[48]Maj. R. L. Bullard to Governor of the Moro Province, March 31, 1904, General Correspondence, McCoy Papers.

[49]Telegram, Maj. R. L. Bullard to Capt. G. T. Langhorne, March 29, 1904, and Wood to Adj. Gen., Philippine Division, April 15, 1904, Wood Papers. Langhorne had become Wood's aide.

[50]The description of the Taraca expedition is based on two graphic letters: Capt. F. R. McCoy to Mrs. McCoy, April 12 and 20, 1904, McCoy Papers.

[51]Maj. R. L. Bullard to Adj. Gen., Taraca Expedition, April 15, 1904, and Maj. Gen. L. Wood to Adj. Gen., Philippine Division, April 16, 1904, Wood Papers.

[52]Diarybook 3, entry, June 9, 1904, and Bullard autobiography, p. 67, BP; returns, June 1904, Camp Vicars, Mindanao, P. I., reel 1328 in "Returns from U.S. Military Posts, 1800-1916," previously cited.

[53]Diarybook 3, entry, June 21, 1904, BP.

[54]Diarybook 3, entries, July 3 and 12, 1904, BP.

III

IN SEARCH OF
THE NEW ARMY
1904-1912

DEFENSIVE POLICY of the U.S.—Does not alter PACIFIC POLICY of U.S. Be as pacific as you please but do not let the other fellow catch you unprepared.

Lt. Col. Robert L. Bullard (1911).

11

In Search of
the New Army
1904-1909

Major Robert Lee Bullard, Twenty-Eighth Infantry, late governor of the Lake Lanao district of Mindanao, returned to the United States in 1904 to find "the real" army and his place in it. He was concerned that his long Philippine service had taken him away from the mainstream of army life. He felt that he might have lost his capacity to do his duty efficiently because he had been free from his superiors' direct observation for too long. Without a sense of communal identity, without a flow of approval and positive reinforcement from his fellow officers, Bullard believed he, as other men, would "yield to the calls of every passion and weakness." To restore his sense of identity, he wanted to return to the social environment of the army of continental defense and military science. Only in this army could he progress: "Man advances or holds his own only in the society of his equals and superiors; he loses when surrounded only by his inferiors."[1]

From his conversations with other officers, from his reading in the *Army and Navy Journal* and the *Journal of the Military Service Institution*, and from his brief trip to Washington, Bullard was aware that the army was changing. He had watched the parade of military legislation and executive action begun in 1899 with keen interest. He understood and approved of the rationale for army reform: that the regular army must be transformed from a confederation of frontier constabulary regiments and administrative bureaus into a unified force, regular and Volunteer, for the defense of the continental United States and its insular possessions from the armed forces of other industrial states. He had witnessed the first manifestations of this change in the 1890s, had seen the need for reform vindicated in the mobilization of 1898, and had identified himself with the reformers. From the Philippines he had watched with interest while Secretary of War Root guided the War Department through a series of structural changes. Bullard knew of these changes: the creation of a General Staff and a Chief of Staff, the formation of the Army War College, interchangeable and temporary assignment of line officers to the staff bureaus, and greater federal supervision of the National Guard. Since these reforms might improve the United States' military posture, Bullard approved of them. But in a personal sense this "new" army was an unknown, and before he could feel completely at ease, he had to rediscover the army he had served in nearly twenty-five years.

In the first two years after his return from the Philippines, Bullard found the garrison life he thought he needed. He got the leisure he sought to restore his health and family life. In August 1904 he rejoined the Twenty-Eighth Infantry, his wife Rose, and his children at the Presidio. When the regiment was then ordered to garrison Fort Snelling, an old post near Minneapolis, he took sick and regular leave to avoid the Minnesota winter. He did not report to Fort Snelling until April 1905, and his family joined him there in June. In comfortable quarters befitting the regiment's senior major, the Bullards had their fourth child, a boy, Keith, in September.

Bullard's duties at Fort Snelling were not taxing, for his regimental commander, Colonel O. J. Sweet, ran the Twenty-Eighth like an old two-company command. The regiment, barely five hundred men, had the conventional round of in-spections, target practice, athletic contests, parades, and hikes. Even with the additional courts-martial, garrison school duties, and boards that came his way, Bullard found ample time to write magazine articles on hunting and the Moros, to speak to the students at St. Paul's St. Thomas College, and to make friends in the Minnesota National Guard. He did a lot of reading, primarily about the Russo-Japanese War, field artillery, coastal fortifications, and German military training.[2]

Beneath the surface tranquillity of his military duties, duties which he performed ably enough for Sweet to call him an "excellent, zealous and most efficient all round officer," Bullard became restless and bored. When he took leave in San Francisco, he thought his health would improve and that he could give his children the paternal guidance they had lacked for nearly five years. His health, however, was still not good, and he concluded that his family got along better without him because the idleness "made myself and all about me miserable." He quickly tired of social conversation: "sitting around and having my time con-sumed by other people who have nothing to do doesn't suit me and that's what I'm doing." Occasionally he considered applying for service in the Canal Zone, even if it meant resigning his commission. Even when the Bullards were settled in the Fort Snelling garrison, the major doubted that he would find much stimulation. Rose's conservatism and shyness, compounded by ill health and the new baby, limited their social contacts on the post, and his own diffidence and cosmopolitanism made his contacts with the Minnesotans unsatisfying.[3]

In the summer of 1906 Bullard and the Twenty-Eighth Infantry joined the Indiana National Guard at Fort Benjamin Harrison near Indianapolis for joint maneuvers. It was his first direct contact with citizen-soldiers since the muster out of the Thirty-Ninth Volunteers, and the experience shook him from his ennui. On the eve of the encampment, he had been busy and had begun to recover his sense of worth. By the spring of 1906 his magazine articles had appeared in the *Journal of the Military Service Institution, Atlantic Monthly, Cosmopolitan, Field and*

Stream, and *Sports Afield.* His light pieces on hunting in the Philippines and life among the Moros were personally rewarding. He went to Indianapolis with a more positive attitude, but he still hoped that he could leave regimental duty as soon as possible.

The maneuvers were appalling, for both Sweet and the National Guard officers were incompetent and the Guardsmen still unreformed in matters of camp police and discipline. The regular officers carped at their colonel and the National Guard, the Indianapolis press praised the National Guard and criticized the criticisms of the regulars, and the Guardsmen enjoyed their pleasant camp-out. Bullard watched all with detachment. His meditations were interrupted only by a visit with some Indianans who had served in the Thirty-Ninth Volunteers, a reunion he thoroughly enjoyed but which saddened him as well. After talking with "American Indians," who already discussed the Philippines as if their service was as far distant as the Civil War, Bullard concluded that he had better "pull himself up" and apply himself to his profession. His dissatisfaction, his disappointments, the successes of others at his expense had been his own fault, the product of "defects in me, as lack of ability or foresight or strength or skill." His successes had ultimately been not the result of "unfair advantage" or "pull" but the application of military skills he was now letting erode. Unless he adjusted himself to the army of now and the future, he would lose whatever opportunities lay ahead:

> I have in this camp just had renewed reminder that one can never take up the past. Once gone, the past and the things of the past—all its conditions— are gone beyond recall or resumption. The "days of the empire" (Philippine war times) can never come back. The days when I was a colonel and the conditions when I was a colonel can never be brought back even in SIMILITUDE. My Moro experience and conditions can never be duplicated or simulated even. Now, I say I am now learning a like lesson. I wanted in this camp to deal with the state troops or the irregular troops as with my old volunteers. I am wholly unable to reproduce any like conditions to those I have heretofore passed through. The past is beyond recall in everything.[4]

1.

While he was meandering through his duties as a major of the Twenty-Eighth Infantry, Bullard began an intellectual journey. This inquiry into the character of the United States Army eventually allowed him to understand and live in peace with his institutional environment. His observations about the regular army, insights not especially unique and in fact shared by reformist officers like J. Franklin Bell and Leonard Wood, were not only accurate but represented an intellectual assimilation critical to Bullard's career. If he had not correctly analyzed the army's strengths and weaknesses, if his analysis had deviated markedly from those of the creative core of the army's officers, he might have missed the opportunities that lay ahead for challenging service. Without this systematic reflection upon his experiences since 1898 and the nature of the army, Major Bullard would have been professionally dead.

Bullard's thinking on military affairs stemmed from one basic premise self-evident to army reformers but obscured until 1898 by the army's frontier service. The fundamental problem with the United States Army, Bullard thought, was it lived under one system of promotion, supply, and administration and fought under another. For most soldiers, the transition from one system to another was both demoralizing and confusing, especially since many expected peacetime methods to work in wartime. They never did, but not because most soldiers did not doggedly try to force the demands of war into a mold created by army regulations. As with European armies, there was but one solution: *"have but one system for both peace and war and let that be the system worked out in war."*[5]

The greatest barrier to creating an army ready for war, Bullard thought, was not public apathy, congressional niggardliness, or the lack of a trained reserve. It was the officer corps of the regular army. Looking back on his experiences in the Philippines, Bullard was amazed at how ill-prepared his peers and superiors had been for actual war. The problem had been more than mediocre officers' natural timidity and fear for their careers. Rather he had seen officers who had built enviable reputations before 1898 as scholars, teachers, and administrators fail in combat because it had seldom occurred to them that field command was an art in itself. Some officers had been incompetent in the Philippines simply because the insurrection did not conform to their expectations of what war should be like, that somehow the enemy should have conformed to the maxims they had learned in military texts. Bullard remembered one officer, a "book soldier" of great reputation, who told him that "this war ruined me." Such failures were not because of a lack of physical courage or motivation. Rather it was because most officers developed a peacetime working pace and a fascination for thoroughness inappropriate for wartime conditions. The essence of war, Bullard found, was speed, speed in decision-making and execution. Time was both the commander's greatest resource and greatest enemy. Yet in war he "who hurries disorganizes them [most officers] . . . another war will cause as much confusion as the last." The result of officers' confusion and bewilderment was a command system most notable for its rigidity, inefficiency, and inertia.[6]

The merit system of promotion inherent in granting Volunteer commissions and the government's subsequent policy of making some relatively junior officers brigadier generals in the regular army helped change the values of the officer corps, Bullard thought. Despite officers' cries of "political influence" whenever such promotions were made, the value of this system of reward outweighed its evils. Bullard thought that a greater application of the merit system, even to promotions in the peacetime army, would improve the officer corps by stimulating competition. In the one place where personal competition was encouraged—in the army school system—the professional effort of student-officers provided a striking contrast with the lethargy of the rest of the officer corps. In fact, Bullard thought that the competition was too keen, almost destructive, because it did not exist anywhere else in the army.[7]

In assessing why some officers had been successful in combat and others had not, Bullard was convinced that war created its own ethic of officership. In one's relations to one's superiors, he found that too rigid adherence to orders was neither wise nor necessary. The most successful officers, he observed, were those who executed orders with "loyalty, judgment and goodwill," but who fought whenever possible, whatever their orders. Moreover, the effective officers led by personal example. "Obedience and subordination are better secured when an officer shows his men . . . that he is ready to do and to bear all that his men do and bear. This suggests discipline be made to apply to officers as well as men and that officers become not as in many cases they undeniably have become, a sort of privileged class, allowed to spare themselves all labors, hardships and restrictions." Personal example, however, was no substitute for personal supervision. The successful commander developed the efficiency of his subordinates by creating "a thorough system of supervision" and then checked on all the work, conduct, and reports of his subordinates. "Stringent supervision," wedded with quick reward or censure, created the highest standards of performance in junior officers.[8]

Bullard thought the officer corps had to create new standards of professionalism because the American enlisted man, regular or Volunteer, was hopelessly unmilitary. Bullard did not believe that this condition stemmed solely from the army's economic unattractiveness or from the physical softness of American youth. Rather the enlisted man's lack of motivation was a cultural attribute, pandered to by the army that accepted him. The enlisted man came from a society hostile to military service. The only military virtues that society recognized were patriotism and intelligence, qualities not especially valued in the regular army. Instead, the American soldier expected to have all his civilian "rights" remain intact in the army, the right to idleness, the right of wastefulness, the right to grumble, the right to avoid all routine labor, and the right to question all authority. His ultimate right, the soldier thought, when the army did not meet his expectations, was the right to desert.

To handle such a "modified, complicated, intellectual being the soldier is today," career officers yearned for the sort of discipline that characterized the German army, despite the fact that "we are not Germans." When soldiers failed to respond to arbitrary discipline, the usual response was a flight of fantasy—that the army could make life as comfortable for the enlisted man as he might enjoy as a middle-class civilian. Few officers tried to encourage their men with persuasion and praise for military duties done well. Yet this approval was the soldier's best reward. "There is no other. There must be a system within the army to recognize performance. Superiors must praise success, disparage lack of success to keep soldiers at their duty. Praise will not kill high officers, will get better job out of subordinates."[9]

Upon his return from the Philippines, Bullard observed one improvement in the army's policies. This was the new emphasis on field training. Yet he had serious reservations about the tactical training he saw. The greatest weakness was the fascination with large maneuvers held jointly with the National Guard. These maneuvers might have publicity value and give a few officers the experience of handling brigades and divisions, but most often they revealed how little officers and men knew about tactics, terrain appreciation, leadership, map-reading, and supply. Bullard was not sure about the source of the army's fascination for grandiose troop movements. He thought that it might come from an American predilection to do everything big or from the German-style strategic studies which had fascinated some officers since the 1890s. In any event, the troops seldom benefited from large scale maneuvers and the officers concentrated on order-writing and paperwork rather than the problems of command. The American army, he observed, fought one day and took a week to write reports about it.[10]

When the troops went into the field, Bullard believed, they should concentrate on small-unit training. This training might not be especially physical, but it would be educational. The men would develop efficiency in squad and company tactics, military skills "especially suited to our people" because they demanded individual initiative and intelligence. For the officers, "small maneuvers" quickly demonstrated the facts of war: how much the men could carry, how far and fast they could march, what equipment was adequate and what was not, which men could lead and which could not. Only small-unit tactics illustrated "the vast gulf that separates theory from practice, knowledge from its application, to show how well an officer may be instructed, however perfectly he knows and however glibly can state theory, he can nevertheless surely be relied upon, is absolutely certain to make mistakes on the field, not trifling ones but gross, unmistakable, glaring blunders that any neophyte can see . . . mistakes and failures teach more than success . . . and small maneuvers are the best place to learn lessons."[11]

There was nothing wrong with the United States Army, Bullard concluded, that couldn't be solved by some honest soldiering.

2.

In the autumn of 1906 the Roosevelt Administration interrupted Bullard's reveries by once again occupying Cuba. Growing out of electoral frauds, the Cuban civil war of 1906 drew Roosevelt into intervention under the terms of the Platt Amendment, which committed the American government to guarantee stable constitutional government in Cuba. In August 1906 a junta of former Cuban guerrillas known as the Liberals protested President Tomás Estrada Palma's rigged reelection with open rebellion. Both the Liberals and Palma's clique, the immoderate Moderates, asked for intervention, the first group demanding American-supervised elections, the second urging support for the Palma government. Although Roosevelt did not want to intervene, he wanted even less to fight the Liberals or sanction the violent overthrow of a constitutional government. He hoped that the Cubans, threatened with an American military occupation, would settle their differences. He was badly mistaken. The Moderates wanted American troops on the island to support their feeble military effort and neglected nothing that would attract an American expeditionary force, including allowing their own government to collapse in "anarchy." The rebels had no objection to an occupation, for they were confident that the Americans would again withdraw after holding free elections, which they would win. The Liberals' strategy worked, but not until the United States Army again occupied the island and had another opportunity to reform and pacify the Cubans.[12]

Bullard, in command of his regiment's second battalion, began the Second Intervention still frustrated by his routine duties. While he was impressed by the efficiency with which the General Staff arranged and dispatched the expeditionary force to Havana in October 1906, he was not excited by more foreign service and another family separation. Neither he nor his fellow officers thought that they would have to fight, since Secretary of War Taft had already assumed control of the Cuban government by the time they embarked at Newport News, Virginia. Upon arriving in Cuba, Bullard took his battalion to Matanzas on Cuba's northern shore and settled into a peaceful occupation while the Roosevelt Administration debated about how to withdraw the troops that had barely arrived. Bullard looked for something more interesting than guard mounts and tropical siestas: "I *must* begin to think about some plan to *do* something on this Cuban business."[13]

Debating the opportunities for prestigious service in an occupation they considered a fool's errand, Bullard and a colleague from Moro days, Captain Andrew J. Dougherty, decided they'd try for positions with the Provisional Government. For Bullard there was added incentive. In the fall of 1906 he was promoted to lieutenant colonel and transferred to the Eighth Infantry, a regiment then stationed in the Philippines. Another Asian tour would have been inopportune just as he was getting reoriented to the mainstream of army life. Anxious to avoid the humdrum of garrison life and a transfer to the Philippines, Bullard pressed the commanding general of the Army of Cuban Pacification, Army Chief of Staff J. Franklin Bell, for a detail to the Provisional Government. Stressing his ability to speak Spanish and his administrative experiences in the Philippines, Bullard convinced Bell that he should be among the officers assigned to the Provisional Governor's staff. His acquaintance with Leonard Wood and with Wood's aide, Captain Frank McCoy, probably strengthened his case, for McCoy was helping Taft put together an administration filled with Wood's subordinates from the earlier occupation. While Bullard had not been a member of the Military Governor's coterie, he was known and available. In less than a month after arriving in Cuba, he became a special political agent for Charles E. Magoon, the Provisional Governor. Bullard believed he had found a "worthy" job. "This gives me a chance, a real opportunity. There is much room for failure; also much for advancement and success."[14]

Bullard at first found his work for Magoon both challenging and educational. Throughout November and December he traveled about Cuba, negotiating with

Liberal *jefes* and investigating the island's general condition. His specific task was to get the rebels to work, a job he accomplished by organizing unemployed Cubans as highway laborers. Whereever he went, he found the Cubans still armed and ready to leap at one another's throats for jobs and personal prestige. His reports to Magoon stressed the shallowness of republicanism in Cuba, the pervasive influence of poverty and violence, and the ethnic and racial fragmentation of Cuban society. Occasionally he suggested that American annexation was the only realistic way to achieve a peaceful Cuba, but he admitted to himself that annexation was unpopular with all but the Cuban business elite. He thought that the Cubans lived on the border of chaos and hysteria, incapable by race and culture of achieving stable republican institutions. Yet American policy seemed to be based on every consideration but the character of Cuban life, and the Provisional Governor did not appear interested in learning these realities. For the United States, the Cuban "problem" had "not even begun."[15]

As he traveled through Havana on his way to other Cuban towns, Bullard could not help contrasting his peripatetic duties with the staid existence of the Army of Cuban Pacification. Visiting the Twenty-Eighth Infantry, he found that most of the officers had brought their families to Cuba and were thoroughly enjoying their tropical winter without a thought about future Cuban-American relations. He himself missed his family ("Living as I do seems like throwing life away almost") and doubted that his labors would have any influence upon the Provisional Government. While he was satisfied that he and Magoon were on cordial terms, he disapproved of the Governor's conciliatory policy toward the Liberals. The only thing that pleased him was that the American soldiers in Cuba avoided conflict with the population and did not meddle in civil affairs. At least the army would escape the occupation with honor.[16]

Bullard's duties allowed enough personal freedom and leisure to worry about his family, to hunt, to study Spanish and French, to read military literature, and to travel about the island. Purposely avoiding the company of American officers, he sought the company of civilians, Cuban and foreign, in order "to get a bit closer connection with the world everywhere." As he learned more about the island, he began to write articles for American periodicals about Cuban culture and United States foreign policy, essays which were intelligent comments upon Cuban life and intellectually satisfying to the author.

In articles published by *Army and Navy Life* and by the *North American Review*, Bullard emphasized that the Cubans were not prepared for self-government because of the nature of their cultural and colonial heritage. The Cubans were caught in a fundamental contradiction, being "a people of monarchical habit, tradition, customs . . . even genius and with republican, constitutional ideals and aspirations. Time, time will be needed for adjustment here." The Cubans' Hispanic heritage and the violence of their war for independence had psychologically handicapped the contemporary generation of *políticos* and the general population. Wavering between despair and euphoria, antagonized by American economic and cultural influence, the Cubans were incapable of stable self-government.[17]

At first, Bullard had thought that Cuban political instability had a racial basis, but he was surprised to learn that the population was largely white and that Cuban blacks had both more freedom and more just grievances than he supposed. In assessing Cuban race relations, he thought that Cuban Negroes were among the most patriotic and ambitious people he met on the island. By their contribution to the war for independence, they had won substantial rights, but still suffered from discrimination. Yet he thought that Cuba offered America an important lesson in race relations, "that Negroes may perhaps without danger of social equality be better treated than we are treating them at present in the U.S."[18]

Although his relations with Magoon had been satisfactory, Bullard learned that the governor did not fully appreciate his journalistic efforts. Magoon, a walrus-like Nebraska lawyer who had risen through the War Department's extemporized colonial service, believed that Bullard's assessment of the Cubans was indiscreet and damaged American policy. When his first article appeared, Magoon censured him for disloyalty to the Provisional Government. Bullard offered to be relieved, but Magoon typically avoided a crisis by asking that he wait before seeking reassignment. Angered, but not unhappy, Bullard then realized to his horror that the *North American Review* was publishing a second article even more critical of the Cubans. Cabling New York, he learned that the offending article was on the newsstands. He then rushed to the Havana magazine distributor who handled the *North American Review* and bought the seventy-five copies sent for Cuban sellers. While tracking down the magazines, he again saw Magoon and requested both leave and reassignment. Miffed, the governor denied his request, and Bullard was convinced that Magoon was trying to destroy him by making him suffer the "ill effects" of his essays. But when he finally took leave and visited Washington, he learned that he had become one of the army's noted authorities on Cuba from no lesser men than Roosevelt himself, General Bell, and Brigadier General Clarence Edwards, the chief of the Bureau of Insular Affairs. He was pleased that the administration was encouraging army officers to stir public interest in military affairs and foreign policy, and he left with no regrets about his articles. Magoon might be an enemy, but his friends of 1908 were far more influential.[19]

The occupation of Cuba dragged on while the Roosevelt Administration waited for Magoon's government to nourish economic recovery and constitutional reform. Among the Provisional Government's chores was to supervise honest elections and to improve the functioning of Cuba's governmental agencies. Working with Colonel Enoch H. Crowder in the Department of State and Justice, Bullard realized that the occupation would last at least a year longer, so he brought his family to Havana. It was not a happy decision because Rose, young Rose, and Keith all became ill, and he had to nurse all three of them as well as go to work. In two weeks the Bullard family was back in the United States where Rose entered a Georgia nursing home. The colonel doubted that his wife would ever again be well or happy. "I really hardly again expect to have a home." To control his anguish, he once again took up his solitary, disciplined life of work, study, and exercise.[20]

In August 1908, in an effort to reduce corruption, Magoon appointed Bullard Acting Secretary of Public Instruction for Cuba. Initially pleased by the prestige and challenge of his civil commission, Bullard soon learned that Magoon did not want reform as much as he wanted the peace bought "by dealing out the pie." Bullard's task was to hide the grossest frauds in the Department of Public Instruction, which meant primarily dismissing those women whose sexual expertise qualified them for the payroll. As he learned of the depth of the department's incompetency and corruption, he called it "the rottenest thing I have ever touched." From the National University to the primary schools, Cuba's educational system was turning out "degreed, diplomaed ignoramuses" among the elite and leaving the common people without the skills and ideals to create a better life. But Bullard's analysis was not accompanied by action, for Magoon stopped any reforms that might upset the elections of 1908 and Cuba's fragile political parties. Most of Bullard's work was limited to balancing patronage appointments and to curbing the worst graft. If his experience in the Department of Public Instruction was representative of the Provisional Government's "reforms," as he knew it was, Bullard could not see that the American occupation had changed the quality of Cuban life.[21]

When the Provisional Government and the Army of Cuban Pacification began to go home in the winter of 1909 after having held another set of elections, Bullard surveyed the impact of the American intervention. From the start, he thought, American policy had been naive and superficial. For the moment, political violence had subsided and the Cuban government was functioning, but Bullard doubted that the new Liberal regime would survive "because with the domineering, grandee spirit of the Spanish blood, no Cuban in power can abstain from squeezing his fellows, from making them feel his power and authority. . . ." While serving in Cuba, he had read several studies of the Reconstruction in the South and he had been again impressed at how difficult it was to work fundamental changes in any society. He was sure the American occupation in Cuba had not worked such changes and that the conditions which encouraged political violence had not changed. "The U.S. will have to go back. It is only a question of time." Personally, he was glad to see the intervention end. From his reading in army newspapers and conversations with other officers, he felt certain that colonial service was not the place to look for the "new army." His Cuban service, while it enhanced his reputation for versatility, was only an interlude in his personal search for a modern definition of the army, the military policy of the United States, and war.[22]

3.

Reflecting upon his reading of history, Bullard decided that the cause of war in the twentieth century was commercial competition between the world's great industrial powers. Because economic expansion was crucial to all great nations and greed was a universal phenomenon, he feared that modern wars would be more frequent and bitter than those fought for territorial gain and religious reasons. "Love of gain is the lowest, most conscienceless of all human passions in the individual." That this materialism would breed war he had no doubt. "We may expect as many and more fearful, cruel, far reaching, all-involving, unsparing wars than ever in the history of the world. The life of the world is daily growing denser; its struggle will therefore be harder, sterner."[23]

In a world of war and threatened war, a nation could preserve itself only by being prepared for war. Military preparedness, he thought, was all that kept the peace in Europe. Since war seemed to accompany all great social change and the growth of nations, it was not likely to disappear. The only way a single state might avoid continual conflict or destruction, "the one thing possible and reasonable, however hard and difficult," was to be well armed:

> Armament preserves nationality and national characteristics. Until, therefore, men come to be less set in their ways, care less for the preservation of their own national customs and ways, armament will continue to be kept up. There is as yet no indication that any nation is willing to have its laws, customs, and ways changed by passing under an armed conqueror and taking on the latter's ways. Just the opposite.[24]

Bullard was unimpressed by the contemporary argument that the rapi growth of modern technology would make war so horrible that no rational government would choose to fight. Reading the predictions of futurists, both optimistic and pessimistic, that the invention of the airplane would end either warfare or all civilization, he doubted that the potential destructiveness of aerial warfare would inhibit nations. Aerial weaponry would mean only that nations would transfer their emphasis in military spending from one weapon to another, "from battleship to the air ship, from the land soldier to the air soldier." No mechanical invention, he thought, would eliminate the causes of war. Through history man had changed weapons many times without bringing lasting peace. The cost of weapons, as they became more complex and destructive, did not deter nations. Aerial warfare would be no different. "Aerial navigation will only add a new device and will entail the added cost of providing and learning to use it." If the airplane proved cheaper and more effective than existing weapons, nations would rapidly develop more and better airplanes. The airplane "may wipe out big guns, it may wipe out big battleships," but it would not end "that struggle between men which is the law of nature," the human competition and conflict that brought war. "The aeroplane and dirigible will not wipe out war."[25]

It was ironic, Bullard thought, that at a time when war and preparedness were so crucial to national survival, modern nations were hostile to the martial virtues. The love of gain and personal liberty which marked modern nations and caused wars denied soldiers the social approval their services warranted. This was especially so in the United States, where civil society had become progressively more self-indulgent, materialistic, and democratized. Because it represented traditional virtues, "the views and customs of former ages," the regular army was viewed as anachronistic. Moreover, it did not show an annual profit, the ultimate American value. America's business and political elite, especially those who were lawyers and journalists, unthinkingly stimulated antimilitary sentiment. Rather than reexamine their English-based intellectual roots, these national opinion-shapers still talked about the chief of staff as if he were Oliver Cromwell and regarded regular officers as the inner circle of a militaristic conspiracy. Outside the army, there was little appreciation of the fact that a modern military force was a sure sign of progress and a high degree of civilization.[26] The irony was that Americans believed they were peaceloving, that the United States' world image was nonbelligerent. American foreign policy in both Asia and the western hemisphere was provocative; the Monroe Doctrine was "the most aggressive and presumptuous policy the world thinks it has as yet met with in any nation."[27] As the war scare with Japan in 1907 had demonstrated, however, the United States' military weakness was a national scandal and provoked future aggression. In a military sense, despite its great wealth, population, and technological superiority, the United States was virtually a protectorate of Great Britain.[28]

Bullard's realistic assumption that the American people would never surrender their culture values to military needs led him to think about the changes the army must make in order to protect the nation. For one thing, career officers, especially those who became wartime generals, must reconcile themselves to civilian control of the army. Both American history and the more recent wars in Asia and South Africa suggested that civilians would play an increasing role in military affairs. Rather than wail about this development, as he thought many of his peers were doing, the American officer should develop the skill to command in the environment of civilian control:

> We must always look to see the general have his course laid out for him by some authority who knows less than the general what the latter should do, by some person perhaps who has no military training at all, and it is worse than useless, it is folly for the military man or for the general to complain of this or to expect, as many do in the U.S. Army, anything else. If the general cannot win in spite of this, if he cannot circumvent or overcome this without complaint, he may as well throw up the sponge at once. Such interference has always taken place with generals in America, and only those generals who wasted no time or worry or useless complaint but who *somehow* managed to circumvent or overcome it without arousing hostility by open opposition have ever been able to succeed. . . .[29]

Moreover, if officers limited their reforming vision to the regular army alone, they would miss the central fact of American military policy: that national defense demanded a great army of citizen-soldiers, "half a million men to begin with." All other issues were peripheral to the creation of such an army. To Bullard, the first step was to close the gap military professionalism had created between the officer corps and the American public. It was the duty of officers to make the army "*part of the people*," to make the nation aware of "its rut of neglect, indifference and ignorance of its own weakness. . . ." The great task of the United States Army in the twentieth century was to bridge the gap between itself and the nation, for the modern army was a popular one, an army part of the mainstream of the national life. To bring about this reconciliation of army and people, the officer's fundamental duty was to discuss military affairs in the public press.[30]

Like his better known contemporaries Leonard Wood, John McAuley Palmer, and the leadership of the National Guard Association of the United States, Bullard turned publicist in order to propagate the gospel of preparedness. He, too, hoped to soften the army's hyperprofessionalism and the public's hyperantimilitarism. In the *Overland Monthly* in 1906, he pointed out that the essence of military policy was to prepare for war. Because the army did not contribute directly to the nation's economic growth, it should not be dismissed as either useless or amateur. Soldiering, Bullard argued, meant constant study, training, and the development of qualities of mind and body which should not be taken lightly by civilians. In a speech to the Minnesota National Guard and in two articles for the *National Guard Magazine*, Bullard pointed out that the United States would have to fight its future wars with the same force of citizen-soldiers it had used in the past. Whether regular officers liked it or not, wartime volunteers were America's army. To believe, however, that volunteers could spring to arms and fight effectively in the twentieth century was a romantic illusion. To defend itself, the United States must both increase its standing forces and establish a stronger National Guard. To do both or either, however, the public would have to overcome its unthinking antipathy for military life. It would have to learn that preparedness deterred war, that military service also spread virtues which America's pluralistic society needed: group discipline, social cohesion, and patriotism, "the highest human virtue." It would take the efforts of all Americans—soldiers, citizen-soldiers, and patriotic civilians—to create such an army.[31]

Assessing the role of the army officer in America's military policy, Bullard thought that the single most important quality an officer should develop was the ability to lead citizen-soldiers. The regular officers' obsession with promotion policies, weaponry, and European military techniques had obscured the need to learn how to command America's wartime volunteers. "We seem to want to study and discuss every condition except the one we will have to face, every way except our own of getting soldiers in wartime. We persist in assuming a beautiful German-like trained soldier. . . . we know and never cease to talk about German or Japanese methods in war." His own experience and his study of the methods of the great captains of history convinced him that inspirational leadership produced the best results in warfare. Unfortunately, career officers generally followed the irrational and inefficient practice of applying the most authoritarian discipline to American soldiers. Bullard thought that this custom rested on several personal and institutional factors. Most officers believed only punitive discipline could counteract the egalitarianism of civil life. Many hid their own insecurity and lack of confidence behind the facade of formal discipline. Others used it as a means of personal gratification, relishing their naked power over others' lives. Rather than see that humane consideration and mutual self-respect created effective units, army officers believed punitive discipline was the only road to military efficiency. In the American context, Bullard wrote, they were dangerously wrong. Since career officers would be the core of America's wartime armies, they could best prepare themselves for their role by studying the methods of inspiring volunteers. Such skills were more important than learning the fine points of administration, army regulations, supply, and tactics. Without the ability to lead citizen-soldiers, the army officer was a menace to America's national defense.[32]

Such were Colonel Bullard's conclusions by 1910. While he did not stop his intellectual probing or his writing, he returned from Cuba convinced that he had identified, understood, and developed a personal position on the fundamental issues facing the new army. His career and his nation's history in the next decade eventually proved how right he was.

NOTES

[1]Notebook 5, entry, July 5, 1904, BP.

[2] Diarybook 3, entries, September 9, 1904 to March 25, 1906; Bullard autobiography, pp. 68-69, BP; Returns of the Twenty-Eighth Infantry Regiment, 1904-1905, reel 274, "Returns from Regular Army Infantry Regiments, June 1821-December, 1916," Microcopy 665, National Archives.

[3]Diarybook 3, entries, September 9, 1904 to March, 1906, BP; Maj. R. L. Bullard to Maj. Gen. L. Wood, December 7, 1904, Wood Papers; "Efficiency Record of Bullard, Robert L., 1906," in Bullard 201 File.

[4]Quote from Diarybook 3, entry, August 14, 1906. The conditions at the joint maneuvers are from Diarybook 3, entries, March 31, July 10, and August 26, 1906; Notebook 8, entries, August 18 and September 3, 1906, all BP.

[5]Notebook 5, entry, July 28, 1904, BP.

[6]Notebook 7, entry, January 27, 1906; Notebook 6, entry, November 27, 1904; Notebook 6, entry, May 23, 1905; Notebook 4, entry, July 4, 1904; Notebook 4, entry, January 6, 1904, all BP.

[7]Notebook 4, entry, March 25, 1904; Notebook 7, entry, January 27, 1906, BP.

[8]Notebook 4, entries, March 20 and April 7, 1904; Notebook 5, entry, July 21, 1904; Notebook 6, entries, April 11, 1905; Notebook 7, entry, April 9, 1906, BP.

[9]Notebook 4, entry, July 4, 1904; Notebook 6, entries, February 8, 1905; Notebook 8, entry, July 28, 1906, BP; Maj. Robert L. Bullard, "Cardinal Vices of the American Soldier," *JMSI* 36 (January-February 1905), pp. 104-114; Maj. Robert L. Bullard, "What is the Matter with Army Athletics?" *mss*, November 1905, all BP. See also Lt. Col. Alfred Reynolds, IG, *The Life of the Enlisted Soldier in the United States Army* (Washington: Government Printing Office, 1904).

[10]Notebook 7, entries, October 1905, BP; Maj. Robert L. Bullard, "Small Maneuvers," *Journal of the United States Infantry Association* 2 (April 1906), pp. 57-67.

[11]Notebook 5, entries, October 1905; Notebook 8, entries, July-August 1906, BP; Maj. Robert L. Bullard, "At Field Training and Maneuvers," *JMSI* 41 (March 1907), pp. 221-226.

[12]For background on the second intervention, see Allan R. Millett, *The Politics of Intervention: The Military Occupation of Cuba, 1906-1909* (Columbus, O.: Ohio State University Press, 1968), and Herminio Portell Vilá, *Historia de Cuba en sus relaciones con los Estados Unidos y España*, 4 vols. (Havana: J. Montero, 1938-1941), IV.

[13]Diarybook 3, entries, October 8 and 10, 1906; Notebook 9, entry, March 19, 1907, BP.

[14]Diarybook 3, entry, November 10, 1906; Bullard autobiography, pp. 70-71, BP; Capt. F. R. McCoy to Maj. Gen. L. Wood, October 18, 1906, and memorandum, "American Army Officers Who Were on Duty in Cuba," September 27, 1906, both Frank R. McCoy Papers, Manuscript Division, Library of Congress.

[15]Bullard autobiography, pp. 70-73; Diarybrook 3, entry, December 3, 1906; Notebook 8, entries, October 12 and 25, November 4 and 6, 1906; Notebook 9, entries, December 22, 1906, and January 10, 15, and 16, 1907, BP; Lt. Col. R. L. Bullard to the Provisional Governor, December 7 and 21, 1906, Files 015 and 033, "Confidential Correspondence of the Provisional Governor of Cuba," Records of the Provisional Government of Cuba, 1906-1909, Record Group 199, National Archives.

[16]Diarybook 3, entry, December 3, 1906; Notebook 10, entry, March 22, 1907, BP. Lt. Col. Robert L. Bullard, "The Army in Cuba," *JMSI* 41 (September 1907), pp. 152-157.

[17]Notebook 10, entry, November 30, 1907, BP.; Lt. Col. Robert L. Bullard, "Cubans," *Army and Navy Life* 11 (October 1907), pp. 361-365; Lt. Col. Robert L. Bullard, "How Cubans Differ from Us," *North American Review* 186 (November 11, 1907), pp. 416-421.

[18]Notebook 12, entry, May 18, 1908, BP; Lt. Col. Robert L. Bullard, "The Cuban Negro," *North American Review* 186 (March 15, 1907), pp. 623-630.

[19]Diarybook 4, entries, October 29 and November 5-9, 1907, and February 9, 1908, CP.

[20]Diarybook 4, entries, March-May, 1908, BP.

[21]Diarybook 4, entries, July 19-November 18, 1908, BP; Lt. Col. Robert L. Bullard, "Education in Cuba," *Educational Review* 39 (April 1910), pp. 378-384; Lt. Col. E. J. Greble to J. H. Wilson, August 21, 1908, James H. Wilson Papers, Manuscript Division, Library of Congress.

[22]Diarybook 4, entries, January 22 and February 13, 1909, and Notebook 12, entries, December 1908, BP.

[23]Notebook 13, entry, October 1908, BP.

[24]Notebook 13, entry, October 1908; Notebook 16, entries, March 31, April 3, and June 2, 1909; Notebook 17, entry, July 8, 1910, BP.

[25]Notebook 17, July 2, 1910, BP.

[26]Notebook 5, entry, July 28, 1904; Notebook 6, entry, February 4, 1905; Notebook 9, entry, July 22, 1907, BP.

[27]Notebook 12, entry, May 18, 1908, BP.

[28]Notebook 9, entries, June and July 1907, BP.

[29]Notebook 5, entry, October 17, 1904, BP.

[30]Notebook 7, entries, March 25 and 31, 1906; Notebook 13, October 1908, BP.

[31]Maj. Robert L. Bullard, "In Times of Peace," *Overland Monthly* 47 (February 1906), pp. 101-113; Lt. Col. Robert L. Bullard, "The Hard-Pressed Regular Army," *The*

National Guard Magazine (October 1907), pp. 214-215; Lt. Col. Robert L. Bullard, ''Popular Views and a Standing Army,'' *The National Guard Magazine* (March 1910), pp. 215-219; Maj. Robert L. Bullard, ''The Citizen Soldier, The Volunteer,'' *JMSI* 39 (September-October 1906), pp. 153-167; also Lt. Col. Robert Bullard, ''An Exiled Army,'' *Army and Navy Life* (1909), pp. 608-610, *mss* in BP.

³²Notebook 5, entry, October 29, 1904; Notebook 16, entry, December 22, 1909, BP; Lt. Col. Robert L. Bullard, ''When War Comes: A Mental Preparation,'' *Journal of the United States Infantry Association* 5 (September 1908), pp. 198-204.

12

California and

Mexico

1909-1911

By the time he returned to the United States in the spring of 1909, Colonel Bullard could see how little the army had changed since the War with Spain. An officer who, like Bullard, had joined his first garrison post in the 1880s would have found its essential character not very different thirty years later.

In the continental United States, the army, although it had run out of Indians to police, performed tasks it had done for years: fight forest fires and earthquakes, quell labor troubles, stage military competitions for fairs and pageants, build public works, and conduct its routine training. While it had been permanently enlarged in 1901, it was an army whose loyalties and identities still rested with the regiment. At 4,300 officers and 67,459 enlisted men, it was 9 percent below its authorized peacetime strength. The manpower shortage did not reflect the nation's antimilitarism as much as it did the War Department's recruiting standards. In 1910, for example, the army accepted only 15,000 of the 93,000 men who tried to enlist.

Its high degree of continuity did not mean that the army was not changing, but for most soldiers the change was glacial, accumulative, and unconscious. The visionary officer, like Leonard Wood, might see the significance of the new General Staff or of the army's flourishing school system, but these innovations held greater promise for the future than they had influence on the present. In terms of national strategy, an officer could see new military responsibilities and the possibility of war with potential enemies like Japan. But the schemes for creating a mass army and the theoretical threats from other nations were for most officers as ephemeral as the cigar smoke on the officers' club ceiling. More likely topics of conversation were adventures in the Philippines and China, the readjustment of rank for officers discriminated against by the system of regimental promotion before 1891, the latest changes in the *Army Regulations* and the *Army Register*, and the possibility of a pay increase.

Having assimilated the three-fold increase in the officer corps after 1901, the army's officers performed their duties in a stable fraternity. There were certainly more of them than in 1898, but not that many. There were only 3,000 officers in the army's Line, infantry, cavalry and artillery (coast and field), half of whom were infantry. The turnover in the officer corps was minimal. In fiscal year 1910, only 149 left the army, 80 retiring, 46 resigning, 18 dying, 5 being dismissed, and 2 failing their promotion exams for the second time. In the same period, 311 new lieutenants joined the army, 182 of them Academy graduates, 26 commissioned from the ranks, and 102 appointed from civil life, the latter most often graduates of military schools, university cadet corps, or the National Guard. When dressed in their new blue dress uniforms, the lieutenants looked little different from Bullard's classmates except that they stayed clean shaven.

Infantry officers found much about their condition which was agreeable when compared with the army of the 1890s. Weapons and field equipment continued to improve; the Springfield rifle model 1903 had all the stopping power and accuracy the troops needed. In addition, each regiment now had a machine gun platoon. The accretion of firepower sounds more impressive than it was, for each platoon had only two Vickers-Maxim machine guns which were used for long-range, overhead fire, little more help to the attacking soldier than John Henry Parker's Gatlings. Such mechanical devices as the airplane, the auto and truck, and the wireless promised to reshape tactics, but had little influence by 1910.

In the army of 1909, the Eighth Infantry was a typical regiment. It had served in the Philippines, but, like all but 10,000 soldiers, it now lived in a continental garrison. Most of its 12 companies called the Presidio of Monterey, California, home. It had 49 officers on its rolls, but was lucky to have 30 available for duty. It had 750 enlisted men, all volunteers who signed for 5 years in the ranks. They could shoot; they could drill; they could hike. Three percent of them deserted yearly, but every month as many as 20 privates reenlisted, continuing their "honest and faithful service." The men's health was good, for army hygiene stopped epidemic disease in the ranks. One can wax lyrical about the "semi-cloistered" life of an army garrison in 1909, but it cannot have been too isolated since an average of 16 percent of every regiment was ineffective with venereal disease and alcoholism.

Certainly the Eighth Infantry, even given the peculiar tenor of regimental life which separated it from civilians, was not physically isolated, for the Presidio of Monterey was a 360-acre reservation bordered on two sides by the scenic town of Monterey. Built between the bay of Monterey and the pine-clad foothills of the Big Sur mountains, the post was comfortable, undeniably beautiful, and close to all the attractions and temptations of civilian life. The officers and their wives spent ample time at Pacific Grove, Carmel, the Del Monte Hotel, Pebble Beach, and Cyprus Point. Since the garrison routine seldom took a full day, the Eighth Infantry's officers developed a wide range of skills as swimmers, hunters, golfers, picnickers, sightseers, gardeners, automobile drivers, and bridge players. When one considers the traditional rounds of dinner parties, musicales, calls paid and received, walks, Retreat Parades, and hops, duty at Monterey had as many

diversions as any urban middle-class community. For the anonymous correspondent who submitted post news to the *Army and Navy Journal,* the fact that the
Eighth Infantry went out for a hike and three nights in the field was more novel than
that Mrs. Major Wright and Mrs. Captain Smedberg continued to entertain
"indefatigably."[1]

1.

When he returned to the United States and his family in the spring of 1909,
Bullard was ready for more challenging service than duty with the Eighth Infantry.
For two years he had no choice but to fill as amiably as possible the role of
regimental lieutenant colonel. It was a role he was well prepared to play and a
necessary one if he was to continue to understand the life of regular officers serving
with troops. Physically, he was a model field grade officer, more impressive, in
fact, than many of his overweight, jowly, mustachioed contemporaries. Slender,
clean-shaven, gray-haired, his patrician face appropriately lined around the eyes
and mouth, Bullard had the right mixture of vigor, serenity, poise, and affability to
impress junior officers and visiting civilians. He looked younger than his forty-
eight years. While he and Rose did not participate in the officers' more vigorous
social activities, they held their share of dinner parties on the post, attended
musicales and dances, and played bridge. They opened the 1911 social season
New Year's Day with a "brilliant reception" in their quarters—"a perfect fairy-
land of palms, ferns and cut flowers"—plying the garrison's officers and wives
with coffee, punch, ices, and music by the Eighth Infantry band. Their life was
orderly, restrained, and frugal, since, even though quarters were provided, a
lieutenant colonel's salary of $2,600 did not allow much extravagance. Yet they
traveled together to San Francisco and quietly pursued their own interests, Bullard
by taking hunting and fishing trips, Rose by going on religious retreats to a Menlo
Park convent.[2]

Bullard's duties at the Presidio were routine, the endless rounds of boards,
courts-martial, correspondence, inspections, parades, and formal classes that
were the fabric of garrison life. Colonel Charles W. Mason, the regiment's
commander and a veteran of thirty four years service, ran the Eighth Infantry and
the post, and there was little of consequence for his lieutenant colonel to do.
Bullard seldom spent more than half a day on his military duties. To fill the extra
hours, he worked around his quarters, but his children had grown beyond his
capacity to get much direct satisfaction from being a patriarch. Rose, always in
marginal health, had had an operation in February 1909 and had subsequently
become more withdrawn than ever. Lee, much to his father's surprise, passed a
competitive examination and entered West Point in June 1909, but was "found"
academically by the end of the year and stayed in the East. Cleary and young Rose
were both in boarding schools in Washington; their academic work pleased the
colonel, but the cost of their education was worrisome. Only four-year-old Keith
lived at home. As always, domestic life made the colonel restless. When his

military duties offered little challenge as well and his rank made it difficult to associate in informal terms with the officers of similar interests, his morale faltered: "I very much fear that I shall never be able to recover in full from the Spanish-American war and the 'hustle' it brought to me. I am always looking out for something blood stirring. I am Rooseveltian in my love of moving things, stirring, exciting things. I never have enough of them. I am forever looking for more."[3]

As he had always done when duty slackened, Bullard escaped his military and family routine with exercise and study. At Monterey he translated in Spanish and French, scanned the military journals, and read a potpourri of books: biographies of Confederate generals, McDougall's *Psychology,* and histories of Canada, Mexico, and Germany, a triad of possible belligerents. He was most impressed by General Colmar von der Goltz's study, *The Conduct of War,* which he admired for its analysis of the interrelationship of politics and strategy and for its description of "the science and organization" necessary at the highest levels of command. Even more pleasing was his discovery in von der Goltz that individual inspiration and character still could influence the largest military operations.[4]

Thought, study, and his own continuous article-writing, however, were still too solitary to please Bullard, so he cultivated Monterey's civil community for personal and professional reasons. Convinced that his own future and the army's mission rested on understanding American society, he actively sought civilian contacts. Part of his motive was personal publicity. He wrote letters to Alabamans in behalf of Senator Bankhead's reelection. He joined the Knights of Columbus. When four congressmen visited the Presidio he assumed the role of host for the reluctant Colonel Mason and made "the cleverest speech" at a Chamber of Commerce luncheon for the visiting politicians. His talk was a sermon on preparedness on the theme "When a strong man armed keepeth his palace, his goods are at peace." He then showed the visitors, who included Julius Kahn, ranking Democratic member of the House Committee on Military Affairs, around the Presidio. His major community activity, however, was to organize a Boy Scout troop for the Monterey area in the summer of 1910. Speaking that summer to the California Chautauqua, he stressed the spiritual benefits of the Scouting movement: character-building, self-discipline, physical fitness, diligence in school work, and obedience, all qualities he thought lacking in middle-class urban life. He urged the War Department to sponsor Boy Scouts, probably to the horror of both civilian Scouters and many officers. Bullard recognized, in fact, that most of his sorties in civilian politics and social movements were viewed by the army as unprofessional.[5]

Aside from whatever personal satisfaction he got from organizing a Liliputian version of his old Volunteers and from keeping his name in the papers, Bullard saw his community activities as essential education in the business of leading Americans in war. He continued to worry that most army officers ignored the basic fact of their profession, that they would have to lead citizen-soldiers in wartime. With no other system of obtaining a mass army except that of raising wartime volunteers, army officers had to prepare themselves for the shock of seeing the army assimilate thousands of unsoldierly Americans. By studying the behavior and attitudes of civilians, the army officer could "accustom himself to learn, to expect and to prepare for that national rush so that he will not be so upset thereby that he will be unable to accomplish anything." He might learn that politics and war-making are inseparable; if he did not, he would not be prepared "to play the game *the way it is played.*" Therefore, the successful officer would have to master the same skills as the popular politician, to "persuade, coddle, cajole" people into accepting his ideas and decisions. Without skill in the arts of building consensus, wartime leaders, civil or military, would find themselves powerless. "One of the serious failures," Bullard wrote, "with U.S. Army officers is their failure to recognize this, being content with military knowledge alone, neglecting the means of making it useful to their country and profitable to themselves in case of war. They neglect, forget their association, sympathy and relation with their countrymen. They fail to recognize popular leadership as necessary to make useful and give opportunity for military leadership. They attend only to bald military knowledge and training. They have a profession but no leadership. Both are necessary."[6]

Contemplating the role of the officer as social psychologist, Bullard thought that modern industrial society had made leadership especially difficult because it produced "a common lack of manly honor and self-respect" among soldiers by its impersonality and its materialistic value system. The industrial state produced weaponry whose battlefield destructiveness seemed to increase in an inverse ratio to modern man's ability to cope with hard labor and danger. "The straining life of highly organized society has undoubtedly made men more nervous, more hysterical and less able to face danger, suffering and death. The growth of peace and civilization with their relief from hardships and the frequent necessity of defense of self and rights, have made them more than ever loth *[sic]* to risk their lives in war and battle." Such conditions placed a great premium on realistic training, psychological preparation for battle, and the need to match physical dispersion in combat with effective, decentralized leadership and individual initiative. Most army officers, Bullard thought, were so hyperprofessional that they ignored the power of leadership by example and the effectiveness of emotional appeals to men's basic but dormant values: ambition, honor, patriotism, and skill. Only this type of leadership could overcome the indiscipline, irresponsibility, and irreverence for authority that marked modern American society.[7]

The point at which Bullard's writing and military duties merged in 1910 was in his duties as an instructor for the National Guard. After the war with Spain, the War Department had shown greater official interest in joint army-militia training. Impressive though the size of the joint maneuvers was by 1910, the training was plagued by numerous problems. One was the high degree of absenteeism among enlisted Guardsmen, who saw a week or ten days of summer camp as an economic loss or inconvenience; in the joint maneuvers held in California in 1910, National Guard units from California, New Mexico, and Arizona had absentee rates from

29 to 65 per cent. Given the purpose of the "maneuver camps" to give the army and National Guard officers experience in handling large formations in simulated combat, the National Guard's weaknesses in personnel and training limited the encampments' value. In 1910 Brigadier General Tasker H. Bliss, commander of the Department of California and an enthusiast for the army's role as a school for citizen-soldiers, was distressed by the National Guard's inability to benefit from its summer training with the regulars. For his own troops the field training had some value, but joint training did not justify the time, cost, and effort it took to assemble the regulars. Clearly, despite the enthusiasm for joint maneuvers shared by the upper echelons of the War Department, the state adjutant-generals, and many governors, the army-National Guard relationship had to expand beyond its legal base and its brief summer outings. One suggested reform was federal pay for summer training. Another was to create a training association outside of the maneuver camps.[8]

Consistent with his faith in the potential of the American citizen-soldier, Bullard volunteered to instruct the California National Guard in its own encampments. In the summer of 1909 he, three officers, four sergeants and two cooks trained the Seventh Infantry Regiment, California National Guard, at its Bay City camp. Bullard found the Guardsmen serious and interested in his course in individual and small unit tactics. The Guardsmen were well-equipped and their camp was neat and orderly; drinking and carousing were minimal. Beyond the Guardsmen's military prowess, however limited, Bullard recognized an even more important asset: that the National Guard contained men with skills as necessary to a wartime army as to civil society. The regiment he trained had engineers, carpenters, plumbers, electricians, telegraphers, accountants, railroad men, draftsmen, businessmen, and lawyers. Guardsmen spoke five different foreign languages. In all, Bullard approved of the closer bond being forged between regulars and Guardsmen, the joint training, the increasing federal subsidies, the creation of state constabularies to relieve the National Guard of peacekeeping duties, and the growing insistence that the National Guard meet War Department standards in organization, regulations, and equipment in order to qualify for federal funds. His only caveat was an article of faith in the United States Army: there should be no National Guard commanders and staffs above the regimental level.[9]

In California, as in other states, a major problem in the National Guard was the company grade officers' lack of professional skill. Since the National Guard captains and lieutenants bore the burden of military instruction in their units, this limitation seriously hindered armory and field training. To attack this problem, General Bliss in 1910 established a special encampment at Monterey for eighty-eight National Guard infantry officers. Bullard, much to his pleasure, was assigned as camp commander and chief instructor. The training, in which other Eighth Infantry officers participated, again stressed fundamental military skills: map-reading, small-unit tactics, and the duties of officers in camp and field. Though he thought one week's training was too short, Bullard was satisfied with the class's performance. So was Bliss, for he arranged for Bullard to set up the same course of instruction in Honolulu in September for Hawaii's National Guard officers.[10]

Bullard enjoyed the Honolulu assignment even more than working with the California National Guard. Again his students were infantry officers, 80 percent of them of mixed blood, a fact which did not lessen Bullard's esteem for them. He returned from Hawaii impressed by the Guardsmen's enthusiasm, the climate and scenery, and the possibilities for important service a regular officer might find in the islands. He thought Hawaii would be caught in the middle if the United States had a war with Japan. If a regular officer trained the National Guard in peacetime, if he cultivated the islanders correctly, he could easily be the Hawaiian National Guard's wartime commander.[11]

Bullard had reason to be satisfied with his missionary work for military training, for he had never been more candid and hard-hitting in assessing the essential qualities of officership. In a talk on "military deportment," the colonel stressed that self-imposed discipline, the subordination of individual comfort to group needs, was basic both to a military unit and urban society. Bullard did not suggest a harsh, authoritarian system of privilege and coerced deferrence. Rather, he stressed the individual emotional satisfaction that order, trained competence, gentlemanly bearing, and due consideration for authority offered the individual. It was an officer's central obligation to foster this type of morale.[12]

Speaking on "field service," Bullard, with a deft combination of self-criticism and good humor, described the realities of compaigning. Bullard said bluntly that all infantry work could be summed up in three words: hike, dig, and shoot. Citizen-officers shouldn't let the involved terminology of army manuals obscure this fact. In equally precise language, the colonel warned the officers that the greatest weakness he had seen in the army was the officers' inability to adjust to war as it *was*, not as they thought it should be. Part of this adjustment had universal characteristics. The most important of these was the need to act. Uncertainty and confusion, he had found, were the essence of war, but the officer who acted on his instincts generally was more effective than one paralyzed by doubt.

Another misconception in American war-making was that soldiers needed equipment for every eventuality. Because the American supply system could procure almost unlimited quantities of equipment, the officer's temptation was to ask for more of everything and to load his soldiers like pack mules. Actually, the men could survive and fight on very little, and the lighter their load, the better they fought. Bullard also pointed out another eternal truth, that, given the affluence of the United States Army, in war there was never enough transportation to carry all the supplies that could be requisitioned. He warned the citizen-officers that they had better be prepared to be their own transport quartermasters and their own engineers and signal officers as well. While he was sure that new technology would change warfare as the aeroplane, automobile, and wireless were developed for military purposes, he cautioned the Hawaiian officers that no man knew the exact shape of the next war. Every officer from general to lieutenant would have to learn the character of the enemy, terrain, and climate of the future battlefield together. Those who did not make the intellectual effort would fail. Every officer would have to apply his individual intelligence to his special problems, applying his past experience, his theoretical knowledge, and his understanding of the realities of this particular future conflict.

Lastly, Bullard discussed the roots of troop psychology. He warned his audience that the biggest burden of war was waiting, that the combination of fear, anticipation, and inaction could be more deadly to troop morale than the most withering fire. The effective officer kept wasted motion to a minimum and prepared his men for extended periods of waiting. Other crucial matters were food and rest. Bullard had learned that soldiers in an active campaign needed even more food and rest than they got in garrison, but that officers seemed to think that they needed less. In all, Bullard's commentary on the *Field Service Regulations* was an intelligent and timeless bit of wisdom on the business of leading infantrymen in war. Many other officers have said what he said, but few said it better, and fewer still have had the chance to apply it so often over a forty-year career.[13]

What impact Bullard's sermons to the Guardsmen had is difficult to measure, but his speeches and articles further polished his reputation as an effective commander. By 1910 it was a reputation that may have had more impact among civilians then among his fellow officers. In the fall of 1910, for example, a Mr. Bailey Millard, a muckracking journalist for *Cosmopolitan* magazine, did a series of articles on the army's desertion problem and the harsh treatment some officers meted out to enlisted men. Millard's articles opened a war-of-the-letters in the *Army and Navy Journal* with Millard the loser, if victory goes to the side that unleashes the largest number of impassioned words. But Millard fired one interesting salvo. Though he admitted that he had been extremely critical of some army officers' conduct and of the false appeals of the army's recruiting system, he did not mean to imply that character-destroying punishment was the army's only form of discipline. In his research he had discovered another form of leadership, "the humane, I might say fatherly treatment" Lieutenant Colonel Robert L. Bullard gave enlisted men "under him in war time and time of peace." Millard thought that Bullard's professional success demonstrated the effectiveness of his brand of leadership. "I would recommend his example to all Army officers as a model and a provedly successful one."[14] Millard's favor, no doubt, was more than matched by a string of disgusted remarks when other officers read his letter. But in subsequent issues of the *Army and Navy Journal* no one contradicted Millard's characterization of Bullard. Being a lieutenant colonel perhaps had its own rewards.

2.

With a rapidity which startled Americans, the authoritarian regime of Mexican president Porfírio Díaz began to crumble in 1910. For a generation Don Porfírio had ruled Mexico with ruthless firmness. Unabashedly repressive, the Mexican government placed great emphasis on the type of "modernization" that means economic growth and industrialization but places little value on the distribution of wealth and civil liberties. While there had been periodic protests and rebellions against the regime before 1910, Don Porfírio, ruling through a network of *jefes político-militar* and the trigger-happy *Guardia Rural*, easily crushed the cliques of liberal intellectuals and rural leaders who dared to suggest that the heir of Benito Juárez was not ruling Mexico for the majority of the Mexicans. Lulled by Díaz's ability to keep order, American businesses had by 1910 invested $1 billion in Mexico, and 40,000 Americans were living there.[15]

Despite their notable factionalism and lack of organizational and military skills, the anti-Díaz groups became bold enough to contest Díaz's reelection in 1910. That Díaz had promised a journalist that he would retire raised his opponents' ire. Díaz's rigged reelection rallied the opposition coalition around Francisco I. Madero, the exiled loser. Raiding across the American border, conspiring throughout Mexico, bombarding the people with innumerable *plans* and *pronunciamientos*, shooting isolated *federales*, and confiscating property, the oppositionists started the revolt in the winter of 1910 which brought down Don Porfírio and started the cataclysmic Mexican Revolution.

Among these rebels was an exiled journalist named Ricardo Flores Magón. In 1910 Flores Magón had established a junta in Los Angeles, where he published the radical paper *La Regeneración* and attempted to start a guerrilla war in northern Sonora and Baja California. He, too, had a *plan*, which stressed improved wages and working conditions for the laboring class, but his fundamental bent was more anarchist than reformist. What made Flores Magón dangerous was not his newspaper but his alliance with the International Workers of the World and his contacts with military adventurers along the California-Mexico border.[16]

The first reaction of the Taft Administration to the revolt against Díaz in 1910 was smug certainty that Don Porfírio, an admirable Latin strongman, would weather this latest challenge. But there were certain conditions which made the State Department pay special attention to the Flores Magón movement. In January 1911 the *magonistas* managed to seize a base inside Mexico, the town of Mexicali. Mexicali lay at the foot of the Imperial Valley and was separated from the American town of Calexico by only a four-foot-wide irrigation ditch. In their fight to bring down Yanqui capitalism, the *magonistas* selected a sensitive target, for such American developers as the Southern Pacific railroad, the California Development Corporation, and Harrison Gray Otis' Colorado River Land and Water Company were in the process of turning the Imperial Valley on both sides of the border into a paradise for ranchers, mining companies, and truck farmers. At a time when the Taft Administration was still playing "wait and see" about American lives and property in strife-torn Mexico, it was asking Díaz to get his troops up to the border to guard the Colorado river basin from the *magonistas*.

In the meantime, the Taft Administration found its border difficulties multiplying, for the oppositionists were running men and guns from Matamoros on the Gulf to Tijuana on the Pacific, and rebels and *federales* clashed often enough along the border to send bullets into American towns. To support the Díaz regime and to behave like a proper neutral government, the Taft Administration invoked the

United States' neutrality laws and attempted to police the border with a confused host of immigration officers, marshals, secret service agents, customs agents, consuls, Justice Department officials, and cavalry detachments. The effort was not noticeably effective. Aside from the bureaucratic snarls and the physical impossibility of barring shallow streams and open desert to guerrillas, the neutrality laws themselves were so rigidly drawn and interpreted that their enforcement gave Díaz little aid. An additional reality was that many American citizens, Anglo-Americans and Mexicans, were sympathetic to the revolutionaries and uncooperative in their contacts with federal officials. Such conditions prevailed in California as well as Arizona, New Mexico, and Texas.[17]

Sustained by arms and recruits sent by the Los Angeles junta, the *magonistas* in Mexicali successfully defied both the American neutrality patrols and the Mexican army. The Díaz regime proved quickly that it could neither destroy the *magonistas* nor guard the Colorado River project. In late February 1911 General Bliss himself toured the border area to weigh the situation. He brought to the job a keen intelligence sharpened by years of study and service in Cuba and the Philippines. He had a flair for diplomacy, based on his Olympian view of human history and behavior, which eventually placed him on the Allied Supreme War Council. He was no alarmist nor was he especially friendly with the Imperial Valley developers, though he was acquainted with Otis, publisher of the conservative *Los Angeles Times* and sometime Volunteer general. But Bliss found conditions alarming enough. While he saw little evidence that the *magonistas* were either creating a separatist Mexican state or wantonly destroying American property, he called southern California "a seething mass of socialism. . . . the American border is sympathetic with the so-called revolutionaries." The IWW alliance with the Flores Magón movement meant that Anglo-American filibusterers might drive the Mexican revolutionaries to more radical measures, including separatism and the destruction of private property and the dams. Americans south of the border feared such consequences from the seizure of Mexicali, and Bliss shared their concern, for neither the Mexican government nor American civil officials appeared able to cope with the insurrectionists.[18]

Bliss's observations were only part of the bad news which the Taft Administration had to evaluate. In early March Ambassador to Mexico, Henry Lane Wilson, told the president that the United States would have to shut off the border if Díaz was to survive. Wilson, an ardent supporter of Díaz and American business interests, drew a stark picture of conditions in Mexico: 90 percent of the people were against the government and were virulently anti-Yanqui as well. It was quite possible that the next news would be that foreigners in Mexico were being massacred. When Wilson talked, the cabinet could see pyres of smoke boiling up from that $1 billion of American property. Although still reluctant to do anything more than seal the border, Taft on March 8, 1911, ordered Chief of Staff Leonard Wood to strengthen the army on the Mexican border. The concentration of troops would be a major mobilization which, it was hoped, would bolster the Díaz regime, deter border raids, and prevent the abuse of American lives and property.

The army was to carry out maneuvers, avoid antagonizing border Americans, stay healthy, and patrol the border. Unspoken was another possibility: that the United States Army would again cross the line for war in Mexico. Sixteen thousand troops began to entrain for the border.[19]

The Eighth Infantry mobilized to be part of a provisional brigade commanded by Bliss. The newspapers told the public that Bliss was simply holding additional maneuvers near San Diego, a ploy which hardly fooled anyone, since Bliss was stripping the rest of the Department of California to form a force of 1,700 men. Two companies went to Calexico on March 5. Three days later the rest of the regiment boarded trains and headed south for San Diego. On March 11 the Eighth Infantry reassembled at San Diego—25 officers, 579 enlisted men, 2 medical officers, 13 hospital corpsmen, 23 teamsters, 2 wagon masters, 1 blacksmith, 40 horses, 107 mules, 20 escort wagons, 4 ambulances, and 2 machine guns. Except for the machine guns, the Eighth Infantry might have been a Civil War regiment dressed in khaki.[20]

Lieutenant Colonel Bullard of the Eighth Infantry missed the big mobilization at San Diego, for he was attending a course for field grade officers at the Army School of the Line at Fort Leavenworth. When he finished the course, he rejoined his regiment in late March. He found the Provisional Brigade reasonably comfortable in its extemporized encampment. No one, however, was very happy about the mobilization. It had changed the training schedule, forced some officers to leave some of their uniforms at home, and did not promise to become a war. Bliss put only five companies along the border from the Colorado River to the Pacific. On War Department orders he held the rest of his brigade near San Diego. No significant change was made in American neutrality. Bliss' soldiers were bound by the same orders as civil officials: no soldier would cross the border, only armed Mexicans who crossed to the American side would be disarmed, and if bullets started to fly, the only action permissible was to get American civilians under cover. Within these instructions, Bliss truthfully reported that he could do nothing to stop the *magonistas*. At the same time, the Mexican army had not dislodged the *magonistas* from Mexicali, and danger to the Colorado River dams remained. Bliss suggested martial law, but Washington rejected the idea. The Provisional Brigade camped, trained, and waited and waited and waited.[21]

Nothing happened. The troops held field exercises, with the officers in pettish temper. Bullard went for some rides and helped Colonel Mason run the Eighth Infantry, much to Mason's satisfaction. Even the national news magazines ignored Bliss' brigade, visiting instead the Maneuver Division assembled near San Antonio, the force to which the War Department itself paid the most attention. The Eighth Infantry watched the Mexican Revolution go its tortuous and bloody way.[22]

3.

One thing that the United States Army caught along the border was rumors. As the revolution raged back and forth over Mexico, it swept a circus of refugees toward the northern border with the United States. Many of the dispossessed were Americans who had sought some sort of economic or psychological paradise south of the border. Many of the refugees were men who had traveled in Central America, and they assumed that their physical presence in the area made them experts in Latin affairs and especially in Mexican politics. Considering the vast ignorance of Americans about Mexico and the State Department's limited sources of information (which it seldom shared with the War Department), the travelers may have been a better source than they now appear. At any rate, the War Department was interested in almost any news out of Mexico. In such a process, the army picked up a lot of strange stories. Most were rumors. Some of the stories, however, if true, held information of the most significant sort. One such rumor sent Lieutenant Colonel Bullard from San Diego deep into Mexico as a spy.

On April 24, 1911, Bliss called Bullard to his headquarters and asked him if he spoke Spanish and knew anything about Mexico. Bullard replied yes. Bliss then told him that the War Department had recently received a report from one Dr. Ernest Forbes, a reliable and experienced traveler in Mexico, that Japan had made a secret treaty with the Díaz government to purchase coaling stations along Mexico's Pacific coast. If true, this treaty represented a military and diplomatic crisis. Much to his pleasure, Bullard accepted Bliss's suggestion that he go to San Francisco and talk to Forbes. Borrowing a headquarters automobile, Bullard left the maneuver camp for the train north. Covering in three hours ground it had taken three days to cover on horseback was enlightening: "A horse is a waste of time, henceforth, at least wherever a car can be used."[23]

By the end of April, Bullard had held several talks with Forbes, whom he found an articulate and impressive witness. Forbes's story was disturbing: a high official in the Mexican State Department had told him that Mexico would lease the Tres Marías Islands off the coast of the state of Nayarit to the Japanese as a coaling station for the Mitsui Company. The arrangement, which included additional coaling sites for the Japanese Navy at Acapulco and Manzanillo, would not go into effect, however, until the Díaz regime ended the insurrection. In exchange for the coaling stations, Japan would protect Mexico from American invasion. As yet, Forbes thought, there was no coal on the Tres Marías, but he had heard that coal had been stored for Japanese use at several Mexican ports. Forbes said that he had gotten essentially the same story from a member of the Japanese legation in Mexico City and from a representative of the Mitsui Company. Listening to Forbes, Bullard thought that some of his statements were dubious, but the doctor seemed to have sufficient knowledge and contacts in Mexico "to make me think that his Japanese coal report, perhaps, merits further investigation." Bullard reported to Bliss that he was ready to go to Mexico himself to check Forbes's story. Excited by the prospect of amateur spying, Bullard congratulated himself for having studied Spanish and Mexican history, and walked about San Francisco estimating the size of coalpiles while he waited for Bliss to approve the secret mission.[24]

With Bliss's good wishes and under orders to report his findings directly to the

General Staff, Bullard practiced lying to his wife Rose aoout his assignment and, posing as merchant "L. Mizelle" from Alabama, entrained for Nogales, Arizona. On May 8, with a pistol in his moneybelt and bullets in his shoes ("raising corns and blisters"), he passed through customs into Nogales, Mexico. The next day he was in Guaymas on the Gulf of California, talking with both Mexicans and Americans about their neighborhood coal supply. He was enjoying every moment, as he discovered that he had a talent for intrigue, duplicity, and dissimulation. In more sober moments, he learned that many Americans were fleeing Mexico and that the citizens of Guaymas were *maderistas* to the core. The only talk of Japanese influence he heard was a local rumor that five hundred Japanese farmers were going to start a colony near Guaymas.[25]

According to plan, Bullard caught a coastal steamer at Guaymas and headed south down the Pacific coast. For the next two weeks he moved from steamer to town to steamer through a string of ports: LaPaz in Baja California, Altata, Mazatlan, San Blas, Manzanillo, Acapulco (a "miserable little town"), Minizio, Puerto Angel, and Salina Cruz on the isthmus of Tehauantepec. Most of the towns were partially deserted and lifeless, in limbo between two rulers. He could find no signs of great coal stores or the Japanese Navy, although an occasional American refugee told him that there were both at the Tres Marías. Once, at Salina Cruz, he was held by a *federal* army officer, who thought the Yanqui too inquisitive about some local warehouses, but he managed to convince his captor that he was a harmless *norteamericano* salesman.[26]

Despite his scare in Salina Cruz and the questionable tales about the Tres Marías coaling station, Bullard decided to make one more attempt to collect information on the Pacific Coast before returning to California. On May 24 he rode across the isthmus of Tehuantepec to Vera Cruz on the Gulf, then caught a train to Puebla and Mexico City. In Vera Cruz he learned that rioting and street fighting had broken out in the capital and that Díaz had resigned. Trains with desperate *federales* began to jam Vera Cruz, but Bullard's train left on schedule on May 26. The thought of getting to a fight, even as an observer, excited the travel-weary spy:

> The Thrills! Turn back? Not much. It's the first real running of the blood I've felt since the Moro days seven years ago. I was scared, but I was grinning, joyful, jubilant. I cannot describe my feelings. I can only say that if I had seen death sure ahead, with that feeling of elation, ecstacy, I would have gone straight on to it. It was not bravery, nor moral courage; but a sort of drunken ecstasy; nothing else describes the feeling.

Along the uphill grade to the Valley of Mexico, the train suddenly pulled off onto a siding. Terrified passengers leaped from the train, including the conductor. Suddenly another train screeched by. Aboard was Porfírio Díaz, bound for exile in Paris. Underway again, Bullard's train was stopped short of the city by peasant-soldiers in *traje blanco*, bandoleers, and sombreros. Aboard the train the Mexican soldiers began to forage in the passengers' pockets, but Bullard escaped ruffling by giving his fieldglasses to the rebel *commandante*. (What did "L. Mizelle," merchant, use fieldglasses for?) The train finally reached Mexico City the next day without further incident.[27]

Fleeing the army of porters, cafe-owners, and coachmen who pursued his patronage with revolutionary fervor, Bullard gave up sightseeing in Mexico City and headed west by rail to Guadalajara and Manzanillo. He enjoyed the scenery, but his mind was still on the Tres Marías and the Japanese. In Manzanillo he caught a steamer north to San Blas, opposite the suspect islands. He learned that Japanese warships had indeed bought coal there, but from private Mexican sources. For three days he nosed around San Blas, trying to hire a boat for the Tres Marías. No one was interested in gold when it meant cruising about a Mexican penal colony still run by Díaz henchmen. Disappointed but reasonably satisfied that Forbes' story was a fantasy, Bullard worked his way back to the border and on June 16 was giving his report to Bliss.[28]

The general was glad to have his erstwhile agent back from darkest Mexico, since he had heard nothing from Bullard for two weeks. He was satisfied, as was Chief of Staff Leonard Wood, that Bullard's journey had been thorough and valuable. Díaz' collapse, of course, made his treaty with Japan moot, if it had ever existed. Wood apparently was impressed by the ease with which Bullard toured Mexico and with the fullness of his report, because four months later he again sent army officers on espionage missions in Mexico. This time the agents were two General Staff captains. Unlike Bullard's limited assignment, their instructions were to gather political information and weigh the possibility of American intervention. But here, too, Bullard had already submitted his impressions in June 1911. Analyzing his experiences, he was dismayed that his ideas about Mexico (ideas he recognized as commonplace in the United States) were so wrong. He thought that Mexico was thoroughly Hispanicized, but found it largely Indian. He had heard much about "progress" under Díaz, but found it a hoax. He had found a culture so different from that of the United States and a clash of American interests and Mexican national pride that was so intense, that friction, perhaps war, was inevitable. He thought it likely that "the U.S. will inevitably dominate Mexico." And he was sure that the fall of Díaz did not mark the end of the army's involvement in the Mexican Revolution.[29]

NOTES

[1]The sketch of the Army *circa* 1909 and of the Eighth Infantry is based upon "Report of the Secretary of War" and "Report of the Chief-of-Staff," *Annual Reports of the War Department, 1910* (Washington: Government Printing Office, 1910), I, pp. 7-144; "Report of the Department of California," Ibid., *1910,* III, pp. 133-151; Returns of the Eighth Infantry, February, 1909, to May, 1911, reels 99 and 100, "Returns from Regular Army Infantry Regiments, June, 1821-December, 1916," Microcopy 665, National Archives; *Army and Navy Journal*, July 1909-May, 1911. See also "What Is the Matter

with Our Army,'' U.S. Congress, 62d Congress, 2d Session, Senate Document 621; this publication is a series of articles printed in *Independent* magazine, February -April 1912.

[2]The Bullards' social life is reconstructed from the Bullard autobiography, pp. 74-75, BP, and the ''Army News'' letters from the Presidio of Monterey, *Army and Navy Journal*, June 1909-January 1911.

[3]Diarybook 4, entries April-July 1909, and Diarybook 5, entry, August 7, 1910, Bullard autobiography, pp. 76-77, BP.

[4]Notebook 16, entries for 1910; Scrapbook 28, entries for 1910, BP.

[5]Bullard autobiography, pp. 76-77; Diarybook 5, entries, May-June 1910, both BP; *Army and Navy Journal*, June 25, September 10 and 17, and November 26, all 1910.

[6]Notebooks 16 and 17, entries, February 19, March 21, April 16, and May 1910, BP.

[7]Lt. Col. Robert L. Bullard. ''A Moral Preparation of the Soldier for Service and War,'' *mss* (1910), BP.

[8]''Report of the Department of California,'' *Annual Reports of the War Department, 1910*, previously cited, and ''Report of the Department of California,'' *Annual Reports of the War Department, 1911*, (Washington: Government Printing Office, 1912), III, pp. 133-166; Bliss Diaries, September 14, 1910-March 26, 1911, Vol. 52, Tasker H. Bliss Papers, Manuscript Division, Library of Congress.

For background on the National Guard, see Louis Cantor, ''The Creation of the Modern National Guard: The Dick Militia Act of 1903'' (unpublished PhD. dissertation, Duke University, 1963), and James J. Hudson, ''The California National Guard, 1903-1940,'' (Unpublished Ph.D. dissertation, University of California, Berkeley, 1952).

[9]Lt. Col. Robert L. Bullard, ''A Regular's Visit to a National Guard Encampment,'' *The National Guard Magazine* (December 1909), pp. 519-521, and ''From a Look at the National Guard,'' *Arms and the Man* 47 (March 17, 1910), pp. 491-492.

[10]Diarybook 5, entries, May 5 and June 23, 1910; BP: ''Report of the Department of California,'' *Annual Reports of the War Department, 1911*, previously cited: *Army and Navy Journal*, September 10, 1910.

[11]Diarybook 5, entry, September 24, 1910, BP; W. S. Schuyler journal, entry, September 22, 1910, Walter S. Schuyler Papers, Henry E. Huntington Library.

[12]Lt. Col. Robert L. Bullard, ''Military Deportment,'' *The National Guard Magazine* (March 1912), pp. 117-119.

[13]Lt. Col. R. L. Bullard,'' Field Service,'' *JMSI* 169 (January-February 1911), pp. 67-75.

[14]Mr. Bailey Millard to Editor, *Army and Navy Journal*, December 23, 1910, reprinted in the *Army and Navy Journal*, December 31, 1910.

[15]For background, see Charles C. Cumberland, *Mexican Revolution: Genesis under Madero* (Austin, Texas: University of Texas Press, 1952), and Howard Cline, *The United States and Mexico*, Rev. ed. (Cambridge, Mass.: Harvard University Press, 1963).

[16]See Lowell L. Blaisdell, *The Desert Revolution* (Madison, Wisc.: University of Wisconsin Press, 1962).

[17]In addition to sources previously cited, see Henry F. Pringle, *The Life and Times of William Howard Taft* (New York: Farrar & Rinehart, 1939), pp. 700-715, and Edward J. Berbusse, ''Neutrality-Diplomacy of the United States and Mexico,'' *The Americas* 12 (January 1956), pp. 265-283.

[18]Brig. Gen. T. H. Bliss to Adj. Gen., February 24, 1911, copy in Vol. 105; Brig. Gen. T. H. Bliss to Brig. Gen. W. W. Wotherspoon, February 23, 1910, Vol. 105, both Bliss Papers.

[19]W. H. Taft to Maj. Gen. L. Wood, March 12, 1911, Wood Papers. See also Clarence C. Clendenen, *Blood on the Border: The United States Army and the Mexican Irregulars* (New York: Macmillan, 1969), pp. 116-151.

[20]Bliss diaries, September 14, 1910-March 26, 1911, Vol. 52, Bliss Papers; "Report of the Department of California," *Annual Reports of the War Department, 1911*, III, pp. 133-366; *Army and Navy Journal*, March 18 and April 1, 1911.

[21]Brig. Gen. T. H. Bliss to H. G. Otis, April 18, 1911; Bliss to All Commanders, April 18, 1911; Brig. Gen. T. H. Bliss to Brig. Gen. E. H. Crowder, April 30, 1911; Brig. Gen. T. H. Bliss to Adj. Gen., April 30, 1911, all Vol. 105, Bliss Papers; *Army and Navy Journal*, April 8, 1911.

[22]Diarybook 5, entry, April 18, 1911 and Notebook 18, entry, April 15, 1911, BP; Bliss Diary, March 27-October 22, 1911, Vol. 53, Bliss Papers; "Report of the Secretary of War," and "Report of the Chief-of-Staff," *Annual Reports of the War Department, 1911*, I, 7-178; Reports by Col. C. W. Mason for 1909 and 1910, Bullard 201 File.

[23]Supplementary Diarybook 1, entry, April 24, 1911, BP; Bliss Diary, entries, April 24 and May 1, 1911, Vol. 53, Bliss Papers. Bullard's autobiography contains a detailed account (pp. 79-97) of the secret mission, based on the diary Bullard kept during his travels.

[24]Lt. Col. R. L. Bullard to Brig. Gen. T. H. Bliss, April 30, 1911, Vol. 109, Bliss Papers.

[25]Supplementary Diarybook 1, entries, May 7-9, 1911, BP; Supplementary Diarybook 2, entry, May 10, 1911, BP; Brig. Gen. T. H. Bliss to Lt. Col. R. L. Bullard, April 30 and May 4, 1911, Vol. 106, Bliss Papers.

[26]Supplementary Diarybook 2, entries, May 14-24, 1911, BP.

[27]Supplementary Diarybook 3, entry, May 26, 1911, BP.

[28]Supplementary Diarybook 4, entries, June 1-7, 1911, BP.

[29]Supplementary Diarybook 4, entry, June 16, 1911, BP; Bliss Diary, entries, May 28, June 17 and 24, 1911, Vol. 53, Bliss Papers; Brig. Gen. T. H. Bliss to Mrs. R. L. Bullard, June 8, 1911, Vol. 107, Bliss Papers; Brig. Gen. T. H. Bliss to Maj. Gen. L. Wood, May 28, 1911, Leonard Wood Papers, Manuscript Division, Library of Congress; Brig. Gen. T. H. Bliss to Maj. Gen. L. Wood, June 16, 1911, Vol. 110, Bliss Papers; Maj. Gen. L. Wood to Brig. Gen. T. H. Bliss, June 22, 1911, Wood Papers.

See also Eugene Keith Chamberlin, "The Japanese Scare at Magdalena Bay," *Pacific Historical Review* 24 (November 1955), pp. 345-360.

13

The Army
War College
1911-1912

One thought that came to Brigadier General P.J.A. Cleary, formerly of the Medical Department of the United States Army, was that army life had been unduly harsh on his stepdaughter, Rose Bullard. Her husband had been to the Philippines, Cuba, the Mexican border, and she now had lost her two oldest sons and her daughter to West Point and Washington boarding schools. To Cleary there was one solution to the Bullard family's separation. Writing to an acquaintance, Congressman John A. Moon of Tennessee, he asked that Bullard be ordered to Washington for duty on the General Staff or for schooling at the Army War College. He assured Congressman Moon that Bullard did not know of his letter.[1]

Cleary's request, presented dutifully by Congressman Moon to the War Department, received favorable attention. Major General J. Franklin Bell, Chief of Staff of the army in 1909 when Bullard's assignment to Washington was proposed, remembered the colonel from the Philippines. Bullard, Bell knew, was "an excellent and most efficient officer. He is entirely qualified and fit for detail to the War College." Should Bullard apply through official channels, he would be so detailed. Secretary of War Jacob M. Dickinson pointed out to Congressman Moon that only a War College assignment was possible, for a board of officers made the selections for the General Staff and Bullard had not yet been recommended. He himself, however, could order Bullard to the Army War College, which he would be happy to do if Bullard made a formal application.[2]

Lieutenant Colonel Robert Lee Bullard, Eighth Infantry, was not an innocent party to his father-in-law's correspondence, for he had meditated upon the possibility of a Washington assignment ever since his return from Cuba. While he was pleased with the post life at Monterey, he could feel the ennui of garrison routine engulfing him, and he watched in horror the growing senility of his regimental commander. To remain intellectually alive Bullard participated in the map problems and tactical rides organized by some of his regiment's junior officers, a few of whom were ardent missionaries of the new "military science" taught at the School of the Line and Staff College at Fort Leavenworth. That theoretical education was high fashion in the army, Bullard had no doubt. Chief of Staff Bell openly advocated it, and his successor, the irrepressible Leonard Wood, had not only Bell's professionalism but the political power to reward the army's students. As Wood's appointment as Chief of Staff approached, Bullard noted that

Everybody is looking forward to increased professional activity under General Leonard Wood. . . . He will force out, they say, the backward, old and incompetent in the higher grades of the army. I doubt not that he will attempt it, but my observation is that even the President, much less the Chief of Staff, cannot do what he likes. However, in any case he'll not catch us unprepared.[3]

Reading the signs, he decided as "a matter of expediency (official and professional) to ask for the War College student detail." While he doubted that he would learn much, either at a compulsory field officers' course at Leavenworth or in Washington, he believed he needed the schooling much as a recruit needed drill. "I am finding it these days extremely hard to keep up my professional stroke. Army life seems always and only a preparation for something that never comes and it takes a god to maintain interest in his work under such conditions."[4] To throw himself, however reluctantly, into the competitive environment of the army's schools, he requested assignment to the War College in the fall of 1910. Wood, perhaps paying off old debts from Mindanao, immediately approved Bullard's assignment.[5]

Before he could enter the Army War College, Bullard had to complete a special three-month course for field grade officers at Fort Leavenworth. This abbreviated version of Leavenworth's rigorous curriculum for junior officers was called the "Get Rich Quick" course. The basic purpose of the "special course for tactical instruction" was to retrain the army's aging field grade officers, for both General Bell and his protégé, Lieutenant Colonel John F. Morrison, agreed that age did not necessarily prohibit learning. As Morrison put it: "Nearly all our officers can be trained to make good subordinate commanders and staff officers. This must be done." As chief instructor at the School of the Line, Morrison recognized that a Leavenworth education was not even an absolute, for the War Department's assignment policy denied formal training to many who would be "our best commanders in case of war." Even though they knew that the course material was not so difficult that an average officer could not master it, Morrison and Bell recognized that few officers would make the effort to learn outside the classroom. At Leavenworth they put the field grade officers through the same type of curriculum prepared for the regular students of the School of the Line and the Staff College: map maneuvers and terrain exercises designed to illuminate the "principles of war" extracted from German military theoreticians. Junior officers, exhilarated by the precision of the "military science" taught by Griepenkerl, Balck, von Alten, and Buddecke, believed their Leavenworth education made it possible to study military tactics and strategy with rationality and predictability. Bell and Morrison held a more conservative and realistic estimate of the value of a Leavenworth education: it forced officers to study waging war with forces of all the army's combat arms and it taught the commanders and staff officers of the future a common language and decision-making procedure.[6]

When Bullard arrived at Fort Leavenworth in January 1911, some twenty years after he first asked to be a student there, he had grave reservations about the army's theoretical training. His skepticism was rooted in experience and a personal defensiveness about his age and career.[7] Assessing his classmates, twenty colonels and lieutenant colonels from the army and Marine Corps, he sensed that he had been grouped with officers at the end of their careers. Yet the aggressiveness of his instructors, the challenge of his classmates, and "the hum, the spirit" of the Leavenworth schools goaded him into hard reading and diligent classroom performance. He got more motivation from one of his peers. One day an officer remarked to the class that in the German army no one could transfer to the Subsistence Department, get increased rank, and then return to the infantry with the rank intact. The class laughed. Furious, Bullard demanded an apology and got it, but without regret from the other officer or the class. He accepted their emnity as a "sign I am doing something" and concentrated on his studies.[8]

The course passed rapidly, and by the time it ended in March Bullard was convinced that he had profited from the schooling. The map problems and terrain exercises had made him a better judge of ground, a better map-reader, a more thoughtful tactician, and a more precise order writer. He also abandoned the notion that he was unusually talented and that his decisions could go without the constant scrutiny of other officers. Yet he had not embarrassed himself as had some of his classmates, especially the officers who admitted that they had never been in combat or a wargame. Comparing his work with that of his classmates, he felt no reason to regret or change his assignment to the Army War College.[9]

1.

In the summer of 1911, on the eve of his departure for Washington, Colonel Bullard had much with which to be pleased. For one thing, he was once again a full colonel, for the War Department had persuaded Congress to enlarge the officer corps by two hundred in order to meet the needs of the army's regiments and the growing demand for officers for detached service with the army's schools, the General Staff, colonial service, military schools, and the National Guard. The positions created by the Extra Officers Bill of 1911 were distributed proportionately by rank, and when the lineal lists were readjusted, Bullard became a colonel. Again his transfer in 1902 made the difference. Instead of being more than seventy numbers down the major's list of the infantry (where his West Point classmates rested) he was the seventh senior lieutenant colonel of infantry in the spring of 1911 and near enough the top of the list to be promoted in the officer expansion. At fifty, he had made colonel more than ten years before the average age. He also believed he still had the requisite youth and vigor to be an appealing candidate for brigadier general for army reformers like Wood and the new, progressive secretary of war, Henry L. Stimson.

In addition, Bullard was relatively pleased with the condition of his family. Rose's health was good at the moment and young Rose and Keith were flourishing. The two oldest boys were at West Point. Charming, irresponsible Lee had been reappointed by his father's old friend, Senator Joseph F. Johnston of Alabama. The studious, disciplined Peter Cleary had won an appointment by competitive examination. Two sons at the Military Academy was a fit condition for a colonel, and Bullard was pleased. Yet, as he and his family entrained for the east, he still had the feeling that he had accomplished "nothing that does me or anyone else or the world any good," and he thought that his own career had been unhappily narrow compared with those of the civilian men of affairs he talked with on the way to Washington.[10]

After a nostalgic visit to West Point, his first since 1885, Bullard found little encouragement in Washington. Lee had flunked out of the Military Academy for the second time, and the colonel feared that he would never be an army officer. He found his own status ambiguous when he visited the War Department's offices. He was pleased that Wood and Brigadier General Thomas H. Barry, Wood's able assistant on the General Staff, showed him "very considerable attention" and he wondered if his "treatment of late by such men . . . indicates anything as to the estimation in which I am held." But he also heard rumors that his "enemies," especially Charles Muir, had blocked his assignment to the General Staff. He had not sought such a detail, but "I'd like now to have it offered in order to decline, as I think would be advisable for me in such a case." Duty in Washington, the gossip, the interminable round of army parties and politics, had a suffocating effect. Before his War College class convened, Bullard fled the city with an old friend, Captain Andrew J. Dougherty, and motored to the Antietam and Gettysburg battlefields. He enjoyed the trip, lost some of his respect for Robert E. Lee's generalship, and did a reconnaissance of the battlefields which he knew his class would later visit as part of its instruction.[11]

The Army War College class of 1912 assembled, twenty-six strong, at the new War College building at Washington Barracks in early September. The composition of the class reflected the uncertainty about the War College's function and its relation to the General Staff: the student officers ranged from colonels in their late fifties to junior captains. The character of the class and the variety of its formal preparation for the course showed that the General Staff had compromised two points of view, that the War College Division (faculty and students) was the army's primary agency for contingency planning and that the War College was an educational institution to prepare the future high commanders and principal staff officers of divisions, corps, and armies. When the class of 1912 began its work, Brigadier General W. W. Wotherspoon, the college president, and Lieutenant Colonel Hunter Liggett, its senior director, had only begun to reshape the curriculum along Leavenworth lines. Yet the transition to a senior officer training school was not complete, for junior officers of great promise, many of them Leavenworth graduates, were still sent to the college to prepare for assignments on the General Staff. Thus in Bullard's class there were two colonels and three lieutenant colonels, but the bulk of the class was composed of majors and captains. Eight officers had attended the "Get Rich Quick" course, while ten were graduates of the Staff College or the Engineer or Coast Artillery schools. Bullard's position was, as usual, made more anomalous by his youthfulness in age and seniority in rank. While he was the second senior student officer, his West Point contemporaries at the college were majors. Were they officers with a General Staff future or reeducated oldsters? What was he himself? Rather than subject himself to the biting criticism of such classmates and his youthful instructors, Bullard wished he could rest on his rank and experience, but feared the professional contempt such an attitude would encourage among the General Staff's "military scientists." He had doubts that his War College tour would bring much benefit.[12]

The 1912 course began in September with a "preparatory" session of nineteen map problems and map maneuvers under the supervision of Major Guy Carleton, Captain Jens Bugge, and Captain Campbell King, all of the General Staff. While there were frequent conferences, the map work was done individually, and lectures were few and held to give the class the most recent description of the character of the army's various arms and services. The exercises themselves were focused on two contingencies, a British ("Red") invasion of New England and a mobilization for war with Mexico. As such problems went, the exercises were reasonably realistic, since they forced the students to cope with mobilizing militiamen and volunteers, to employ correctly all the arms and services of a field army, and to make detailed logistical arrangements. The students made estimates of the situation, drafted orders, and defended their solutions to the faculty and class. With the exceptions that the problems were based on General Staff plans and the scope of the problems focused on the corps and field army rather than the division, the work was much like Leavenworth training.[13]

The War College approach to strategic problem-solving and the classroom competition made Bullard defensive about his own abilities and critical of the curriculum. To one who prided himself on his intelligence and adaptability, the course outline was frightening and insulting. The Army War College, he learned, was not interested in increasing originality:

> It is not claimed that method develops genius or brilliancy. It may even be discouraging to an officer who imagines that the daring and unerring combinations of a Napoleon are now as possible as ever.
> The object is to develop a school of *safe leadership* for officers and not to encourage unusual and extraordinary methods.[14]

As he worked into October's problems, a war with Mexico "solely for the purpose of putting a stop to anarchy, and the establishment of stable government," he feared that the War College training was eroding the reputation he had so assiduously cultivated since 1898 and that he was losing confidence in his own judgment. He was distressed by his slowness to grasp the ''school solutions'' and by the academic nature of the work. He found the dependence on faculty and class approval a source of anxiety and concluded that his year's work would be of ''little profit'' if he concentrated only on his professional studies. His judgment was reinforced when he attended a Chief of Staff's reception and saw the army's generals and found *''not one who put his time on tactical studies which we are so emphasizing as the great essential.''* He did not believe that study had anything to do with leadership: ''It is the knowledge of men, not military instruction that constitutes the qualities of which generals and leaders are appointed and put in the lead.'' He decided to continue to trust his own judgment and cultivate the friendship of the army's generals. Otherwise, he feared, the War College's ''orthodoxy and regularity'' would destroy his future, homogenizing him along with the rest of the officer corps:

> After a year here, he [the officer] will do absolutely the same things as every one else that has been put through the same course as he; he will be orthodox, regular, common in all his methods. He will never be able thereafter to break away from the ordinary method of doing things. Would it not pay a fellow to take pains to resist this, not be cast into a mould *[sic]*, robbed of every original idea? I think it would. I shall try to find a way to avoid the regulation way of doing things here. I'm convinced the War College methods will ruin me.''[15]

Still restive about the value of ''school solutions'' and smarting from the criticism he received from the instructors and students when he presented unconventional views, Bullard tackled the November problems, all of them related to the defense of the Philippines, Alaska, Hawaii, the Canal Zone, and the West Coast against a Japanese (''Orange'') attack. As the problems became more taxing and the class worked as groups, the errors increased. The students faced real challenges: the optimum employment of all arms, the decisive use of their reserves, and the inherent difficulties of fighting with hastily raised armies of citizen-soldiers. In January the class turned to another General Staff contingency plan, that for a war with Great Britain in which the United States invaded Canada. By March the work centered upon ''military engineering,'' specifically the construction of a defended camp for training volunteers, raised to repel an invasion. In addition, the student officers studied harbor defense and the use of trenches and earthworks with the historical examples drawn from the Civil War, the Russo-Japanese War, and the Boer War.[16]

Bullard remained skeptical about the utility of much military theory, but he began to learn. Some of the education was in the course work; other lessons came from the classes' conduct. He learned that the General Staff was not really interested in the students' suggestions for changes in the contingency plans. He also relearned something he had experienced in the Philippines: that while senior officers paid lip service to the principle of initiative-taking by subordinates, they "want to direct everything." He guessed that this was a traditional American habit, for wartime generals, no matter how great the size of their command, did what they knew they could do—command regiments, battalions, and companies. Bullard thought that the detailed order-writing taught at Leavenworth and the War College sanctified this unfortunate tradition.[17] He had come to appreciate, however, the value of doing a detailed commander's "estimate of the situation," though he thought an experienced officer would quickly eliminate the irrelevant factors in any tactical situation. The major insight he got, though, was about the resistance any commander would face in his own army, the "obstruction and circumvention" of brother officers in wartime, expecially peers. Such officers could be as difficult as the enemy, for their envy and ambition could cripple the execution of the wisest plans. The gulf between the ideals and the reality of command was breathtaking, a condition whose study would be "a most instructive psychological one." Throughout his career, Bullard mused, the army had drilled officers in the ideals of obedience, duty, and honor, but not selflessness. The army's system of "rank and succession infallibly, *always* and surely engenders among officers rivalry, envy, jealousy that precludes all possibility of brotherliness except in the last danger and straits to all. This is its curse, its skeleton."[18] He had seen the clash of ambition, self-advertisement, and rivalry even in the War College's classrooms. What he did not see so clearly was that he was no different from his brother officers.

2.

Bullard's assignment to the Army War College brought him to Washington just in time to witness and then participate in a major crisis in the army's history. The crisis was over the legitimacy of the Chief of Staff and the General Staff as the ultimate professional authority on army policies, and it brought to a temporary halt arguments over the role of the General Staff which had plagued the War Department since the General Staff Act of 1903. For Bullard, the conflict had several dimensions. While he had no special loyalty to the concept of the General Staff or to the ambitious officers who filled its positions, he admired both the personality and policies of Leonard Wood. He, like Wood, favored shorter enlistments, the creation of a federal reserve force, the concentration of the army into tactical units, and the final ascendancy of line officers (through the General Staff) over the officers of the War Department's bureaus. But he also recognized that Wood had incomparable "pull," and he hoped to trade his support of the Chief of Staff into a promotion to brigadier general. For Colonel Robert Lee Bullard had no intention of leaving Washington without making a run for a set of stars.[19]

There were several reasons why Bullard, an able but not distinguished colonel, could honestly assume that his chances for becoming a general were excellent. The ultimate reason was the striking decision of two presidents, William McKinley and

Theodore Roosevelt, to abandon strict seniority in their selections. Rather than only honor long-service colonels with preretirement promotions, McKinley and Roosevelt changed the army's high command after 1898 by awarding brigadierships to relatively junior officers. These men, of whom Wood was the most famous, were to guide the reformed army into a state befitting America's world role. McKinley, however, with Elihu Root's approval, tended to appoint regular army brigadiers from among those who had been Volunteer generals between 1898 and 1901. McKinley's selections won their stars in the Civil War manner—by wartime performance as general officers.[20]

When Roosevelt became president, the promotion policy was even more radically changed. To McKinley and Root's criteria that generals win their stars in war or the colonial service and that some of them should be young enough to guide the army for years, Roosevelt added his own novel requirements: that the appointees be personal acquaintances of his, preferably from the Santiago campaign; that the candidate be physically vigorous; and that the candidate be relatively young, preferably (like the President) in his forties. Political influence was no disqualifier and made some attractive candidates, like John Pershing, irresistible. Recommendations from other generals, of course, were useful, but the examination of candidates' professional qualifications was anything but thorough. For officers, the most demoralizing thing was that the War Department had no systematic way of identifying all the possible candidates. The result of Roosevelt's personalism was that promotions not only were a matter of court politics, but that any ambitious officer with the right connections might win the general officer sweepstakes. Captains and majors, Line and Staff, even though they had not been generals in the Volunteer army, could entertain the idea that the president might reach down the lineal list and promote them.[21] When Roosevelt's policy was continued by the Taft Administration and with Bell and Wood doing some of the picking, Colonel Robert Lee Bullard decided to join the lobbying with a serious campaign of his own for promotion to brigadier general.

The political currents in Washington, both in the War Department and the Congress, encouraged Bullard to make his attempt. He assumed that his acquaintance with Wood would be a major factor. To emphasize his loyalty, he voluntarily appeared before hearings by the House Military Affairs Committee to support the Chief of Staff's position in Wood's clash with another general-politician, Adjutant General Fred C. Ainsworth. Bullard's appearance took some courage, for the committee chairman, James Hay, in league with Ainsworth, favored legislation which would disembowel the General Staff and remove Wood in one blow. Bullard, not realizing that President Taft was not Wood's ardent supporter, believed that his testimony improved his chances for promotion with Taft, Secretary of War Stimson, and Wood. When the Stimson-Wood coalition finally not only defeated Hay's legislation, but forced Ainsworth's retirement, Bullard rejoiced for the General Staff, the army, and himself.[22]

While attempting to convince Wood and the General Staff of his personal commitment to the army's reform, Bullard worked the halls of Congress for support. His most obvious targets were Southerners, whose influence was at a new high since the House had gone Democrat in the 1910 elections. In December 1911 the White House received pro-Bullard endorsements from some ten southern senators and representatives, including the faithful Senator Johnston. As one letter-writer put it, the message was: "Please urge as strongly as your good heart will let you with your influential friends of the President's family consideration of the claims of my great friend, Colonel Bullard.'"[23] Bullard reciprocated by escorting a Southern adjutant-general who had militia business to the War Department. Knowing Representative Oscar Underwood had presidential ambitions, Bullard asked that he present his case personally to the president in exchange for Bullard's active help in his campaign for the nomination. Underwood, Bullard suggested, should stress that Alabama had "for so long borne no name among the general officers of the regular army." Since Joseph Wheeler had for a short time been a regular brigadier and since the Civil War might have had something to do with this deplorable condition, Bullard's argument was not overpowering. But Underwood endorsed Bullard warmly. Bullard repaid the debt by offering his services to Underwood's sponsor, Senator John H. Bankhead of Alabama, and "warmed up my friends in the southern states as suggested by the senator. My best wishes and *efforts* will be for you [Underwood] to the end.'"[24]

Bullard reinforced his cultivation of Underwood with another tactic, getting the endorsement of America's two most progressive Catholic prelates, Cardinal Gibbons and Archbishop Ireland, both of whom had influence in Washington. Bullard thought that his Alabama background and conversion to Catholicism made him a strong candidate for Democratic politicians attempting to fuse a southern-urban immigrant coalition. The appeal was a simple one: "that Catholics are entitled to more representation among our generals." Although he did receive some vague promises of help, Bullard was disappointed that his clerical supporters did not do more.[25]

What amazed Bullard most was the indifference his civilian sponsors showed to his military qualifications: "In this B. G. fight I've been surprised, no impressed, with the fact that my record enters with influential men as a small thing or at least one of secondary consideration." This indifference worried him enough that he solicited some testimonials to his military efficiency. Turning to his record in the Philippines, he successfully lined up endorsements from Senator Elihu Root of New York, General George W. Davis, and the former officers of the Thirty-Ninth Volunteers.[26] He was also pleased to hear a rumor that if the United States intervened in Mexico, he would command a brigade. In all, Bullard felt confident that he would be a general.

While Bullard's lobbying for promotion was not wasted, it did not succeed. The basic flaw in his candidacy was that he was not quite senior enough to be honored by the president and too unschooled to be favored by the General Staff. It was not that his political and military credentials were not impressive; they were simply not impressive enough in combination. President Taft, approached by Senator Johnston and five Alabama congressmen, asked Wood about Bullard. The Chief of Staff replied dutifully but with mild enthusiasm: "Colonel Bullard is one of our most efficient infantry colonels, and is eligible for promotion."[27] Wood had his own ideas about forthcoming vacancies for brigadier general, and Bullard was not part of his planning. For one thing, he recognized that the army's elderly officers would have to be served, both to satisfy their congressional friends and to maintain the morale of the officer corps. He accepted the ploy developed by Secretary Root, filling the vacancies with officers on the verge of retirement before promoting a general of sufficient youth to give effective service. For the vacancy Bullard was eyeing, Wood favored promoting two elderly colonels, then moving to a younger man. When he asked for recommendations for the latter from the General Staff, he received a list of three colonels and three lieutenant colonels. Bullard was not one of the nominees, but neither was Wood's candidate, Lieutenant Colonel Morrison of the Leavenworth schools.[28]

Whatever Wood's desires, President Taft had the ultimate power to nominate a new brigadier. Members of one influential group that pressured Taft and Wood were the "bamboo" brigadiers of America's extemporized colonial service, the chief of the Bureau of Insular Affairs, Clarence R. Edwards, and the chief of the Philippine Constabulary, Henry H. Bandholtz. Personal friends of Taft's and already wearing brigadier's stars by virtue of their positions, Edwards and Bandholtz claimed permanent generalships in the army. Pushing their claims with unequaled fervor was an obscure captain of cavalry who was also a colonel in the Philippine Constabulary, James Guthrie Harbord. If Edwards or Bandholtz should be promoted into the Line, Harbord might slip into the vacant "bamboo" brigadiership.[29] Taft, however, postponed the decision by choosing a colonel near retirement. Bullard, he thought, was an excellent officer, but "there are others who are equally effective in the army." When the infantry vacancy appeared again in 1913, he rejected Wood's and the General Staff's candidates and selected the suave and obsequious Clarence Edwards.[30] Yet, blissfully ignorant of the depth of army court politics, Bullard plugged away for promotion and irritated his Army War College classmates with his politicking. One day some officers saw him talking to a Virginia farmer and asked him what office his friend held, since Bullard didn't talk to any civilians but politicians "of some future profit to me." Bullard "enjoyed the joke," but recognized the implied criticism. He thought the censure unjust.[31]

3.

With one eye on his promotion possibilities, Colonel Robert Lee Bullard struggled through the War College problems of March and April 1912, problems which, after number seventy-four, he found a bit repetitious. His restlessness made his criticisms of the "school solutions" even more caustic, and he became convinced that his candor had made more enemies on the General Staff.[32] On May 1, however, the class of 1912 abandoned the classroom and began a six-week staff ride over the Civil War battlefields of Virginia, Maryland, and Pennsylvania. For

Bullard it was a stimulating experience and convinced him of the value of formal theoretical training in the art of command and staff functioning. By the time the staff ride ended and his class graduated, he approved of the General Staff concept, but was equally sure that warfare still left sufficient room for his brand of leadership, the generalship that rested upon formal education, moral courage, flexibility of mind, intuitive assessments of situations, and inspirational appeals to one's soldiers. He finished the Army War College course intellectually renewed and convinced that the graduates of the army's schools of military science, whether on the General Staff or not, were the elite of the United States Army.[33]

Under a rainy sky, the class of 1912 assembled at Fredericksburg, Virginia, on May 1 along with a camp detachment of thirty-eight officers and men and fourteen wagons from Fort Myer. With Colonel Liggett and the War College staff guiding, the class rode around the battlefields of Fredericksburg, Chancellorsville, the Wilderness, and Spottsylvania and then turned south along the Army of the Potomac's line of march in 1864. Bullard was exhilarated by the experience. First, he was surprised that so few of his peers knew anything about the Civil War; at night in camp the other officers continually borrowed his copy of Matthew Steele's *American Campaigns*. As the class followed the Civil War fighting, he was repelled by his instructors' unthinking adulation of Lee and Jackson. He was nonplused when one "modern high brow" officer, gazing at some battlefield statuary, remarked: "There's been a lot of lying done about what these fellows did as soldiers. None of them have [sic] on the correct uniform."[34] The clash of opinions, which he himself did much to create, offered several insights. The one that most impressed him was how hard it was for a general to get his orders understood and executed by his subordinates. Clearly, General Staff experience and formal schooling helped ease this "friction of war." In the evenings, eating and chatting with his classmates, Bullard found himself winning converts to his view that leadership, for all the schooling, was still as much art as science. As the class rode south and east from Richmond to examine the battlefields of the Peninsula Campaign of 1862, Bullard felt confident that he still had the skill and energy for combat command or General Staff service.[35]

By late May the class had turned north in order to begin the formal staff rides. In the countryside around the battlefields at Manassas, Major Carleton organized the first of three problems based on Civil War situations. Under the faculty's supervision, the class of 1912 would assume the roles of chiefs-of-staff and staff officers for a field army of four divisions. For four days the class played out the exercises, writing every report and order required to move an army of thousands against an imaginary foe. Bullard, as a division adjutant, thought the problem extremely instructive. As a division supply officer in the second staff ride, he appreciated the difficulty of reconciling tactics and logistics, a dilemma some of his class underestimated. By the second ride he thought he had been forever spoiled and would actively seek a position on the General Staff. On the third and last ride, Bullard took the post of division chief-of-staff, and although he clashed with the exercise director, he thought he performed creditably. He thought this especially important, for Secretary of War Stimson and Brigadier General Albert L. Mills, the college's new president, had joined the class. Despite his disagreements with the exercise director, an officer of "less practical experience than myself," he ended the ride as self-confident as ever.[36]

By the end of his War College tour, Bullard saw the necessity for the army's new emphasis on advanced officer training. His private study since the Spanish-American War and his personal experience had convinced him that war was becoming more complex, primarily because of the growing size of armies and the influence of technology. This complexity demanded new forms of military management and a system for training future generals and the staffs which would assist them. The Army War College curriculum offered the sort of experience, short of actual war, which forced officers to think about the duties they would have to perform in a mass wartime army rather than in terms of peacetime routine. Bullard appreciated the value of this training, and he regretted that the War Department did not educate more younger officers and then spread them throughout the army to preach the gospel of cerebral soldiering. But he had his reservations about formal training. He did not think that the collective command represented by the General Staff system would replace the personal judgment and supervision of commanding generals. While he was convinced that the army had adapted the best methods of the German officer-training system, he still thought that the instructors themselves were too often "book soldiers" wedded to "abstract principles." His mistake had been "to wrangle with them about these things until it leaked in upon my intelligence that I could hear their teaching and yet not let it displace the teachings of my own experience." He was skeptical that the General Staff and his officer-instructors had monopolized all the army's talent for wartime command.[37]

As a student at the Army War College, Bullard increased his professional knowledge and stimulated his desire for further education, however informal. His formal training reinforced his self-confidence and gave him sharpened technical skills in the art of generalship. Furthermore, his War College training admitted him to the army's select minority of formally educated officers at a time when such education seemed the sine qua non for successful command or staff service in some future war. In 1917 less than 10 percent of the army's career officers had Staff College or War College schooling and fewer than half of those officers who became generals in World War I had any postgraduate education. With graduation from the War College, Bullard acquired a professional certification from the General Staff that outweighed the actual new knowledge he obtained. Evaluating his performance, the War College presidents judged him professionally alive and zealous. Colonel Bullard, they reported, was just the sort of officer Wood wanted, a mentally alert and physically active senior officer especially qualified to lead a brigade or division of citizen soldiers in wartime.[38]

4.

When he graduated from the Army War College in July 1912, Bullard was an officer without an assignment. What his next duties might be, he had no idea, although he knew he would not be a general. President Taft, he mused, was rewarding "old soldiers." The Chief of Staff's friendship remained constant as Wood suggested Bullard for a General Staff position or as an inspector-instructor with the National Guard. Bullard declined both assignments, which, he thought, angered Wood. There is little doubt that the Chief of Staff's sense of humor about officer assignments was limited, for his congressional foes had dealt his plans a blow by restricting his freedom to order line officers to detached duty. The "Manchu Law," an amendment to an army appropriation act, threw officer assignments into confusion by ordering many of Wood's reformers back to their regiments and reducing the General Staff. The law, however, did not restrict the Chief of Staff's power to order field grade officers on detached duty. Thus Bullard, relatively young, a progressive, and a Wood man, became an important appealing candidate for Wood's inner circle.[39] Unfortunately for the Chief of Staff, Bullard no longer wanted in. Although he found Washington duty exciting, he did not think that his reputation could survive the infighting of the General Staff corps. Instead he wanted the freedom of a personal command where he could apply his experience with some assurance of success. Without such a direct challenge, he feared he would lose his taste for action, the condition that "counts most in a soldier's life." Without a command, the gnawing thought came to him, he would quickly become not an old soldier, but an old man.[40]

The Chief of Staff did not have a regiment handy for Colonel Bullard, but he did have a couple of National Guard maneuvers which needed professional management. The first was the Anniston encampment of the Alabama National Guard, training shared as well by the Seventeenth Infantry. The training was a horror. The regular army department commander visited the camp, pronounced it a disaster and got orders for temporary duty. The colonel of the Seventeenth Infantry, his successor, paled at the lack of hygiene and discipline and turned the tactical instruction over to Bullard. He, too, was stunned by the National Guard's condition, for he had heard many stories about the improvements wrought by the Militia Acts of 1903 and 1908. To him the only thing that had changed since 1898 was that the officers were older. The troops' weapons were still dirty, their equipment lost, their toilet habits primitive, their camps noisy and squalid, and their respect for private property underdeveloped. When the troops tried a couple of field problems, the bungling was universal. Yet Bullard thought that he could still see real military value in the high-spirited citizen-soldiers. He believed that the War Department should pay the Guardsmen for their drills with federal funds. In return for the financial support, the War Department would put the Guardsmen under the direct control of regular army officers, and they would quickly improve.[41]

From his not-so-successful engagement at Anniston, Bullard drew orders to umpire a joint army-National Guard field exercise in Connecticut. Since the New England militia was supposed to be the nation's best and since the exercise was to be directed by Brigadier General Tasker Bliss, one of Wood's favorites, Bullard assumed the assignment would be educational. It was, in some unanticipated ways. The joint force of 2,300 regulars and 15,000 Guardsmen sparred for ten days, mismanaged its supply trains, and did $5,000 in property damage. The "battles" were not very realistic. Observing the problem, Bullard was impressed with the organizational difficulties of supply for large numbers of troops. Bliss' problem, however, struck him as stage-managed to please the Guardsmen so that Congress would appropriate more funds for joint maneuvers. In fact, he and Bliss argued when the general declared the mock war a draw between the Guardsmen and the regulars and then about Bullard's report of the "battle." Bullard openly criticized the New Englanders for being no better than the Alabama Guardsmen. Even Bliss, a Yankee and supporter of the citizen-soldiers, despaired. He accepted the idea that the army should be the school of the Guardsmen, but "for this purpose we have to lower ourselves to their standard." He, like Bullard, could see little good in joint maneuvers for the army's infantry regiments.[42]

As Bullard suffered through the summer encampments, he continued to hope for his own regiment. He had left Senator Johnston in charge of his fortunes at the War Department, and the senator had seen Wood about such an assignment. In August Wood discovered that he had a regiment that needed "some young energetic colonel." One of his friends had just been assigned to the Twenty-Sixth Infantry, stationed in Michigan. In the three years since this regiment had returned from Philippine service, it had turned from a combat unit into a rest home for underworked soldiers. Wood's friend, Lieutenant Colonel William H. Johnston, found the regiment low in military efficiency, discipline, and morale. The regimental commander went on hikes in a car or buckboard, attended by a dozen orderlies. In the field the men did not carry their full equipment, and exercises were promptly terminated in the early afternoon for guard mount and the troops' leisure. So many men were on detached duty that the regiment was a skeleton of demoralized officers and enlisted shirkers. The Twenty-Sixth had failed its last Inspector General's inspection with total unconcern. It took only four days for Wood to assign a new colonel, Robert Lee Bullard. Wood expected "to see great change for the better in the regiment." Senator Johnston thanked the Chief of Staff and congratulated him for his wisdom in assigning Bullard, "because I am sure that there is not a better man in the Army to be in command of troops in war or peace." The secretary of war approved of the assignment of Bullard, "tall, thin, energetic, said to have a great deal of drive and to have made a good record in the Moro country," to the Twenty-Sixth. And Colonel Bullard was pleased because he thought there might be a war with Mexico.[43]

NOTES

[1]Brig. Gen. P.J.A. Cleary to John A. Moon, March 29, 1909, Bullard AGO File.

[2]Maj. Gen. J. F. Bell to Secretary of War, April 1, 1909, and Secretary of War J. M. Dickinson to J. A. Moon, April 1, 1909, both Bullard AGO File.

[3]Diarybook 4, entry, December 31, 1909, BP. Bullard's reaction to the introduction of

theoretical study by map problems and terrain exercises is from his entries for March-May 1909 and January 22, 1910, in Diarybook 4.

⁴Diarybook 4, entry, March 24, 1910, BP.

⁵Diarybook 4, December 27, 1910, BP; Wood endorsement to letter, Lt. Col. R. L. Bullard to Secretary of War, September 4, 1910, Bullard AGO File.

⁶This assessment is based upon the following: Lt. Col. J. F. Morrison to Maj. Gen. L. Wood, September 12, 1912, Leonard Wood Papers; George Van Horn Moseley, "One Soldier's Journey" I, p. 86, George Van Horn Moseley Papers; John McA. Palmer, "Chapter Notes" IV, p. 92, and V, pp. 3-23, John McA. Palmer Papers; Beaumont Buck, *Memories of Peace and War* (San Antonio: Naylor Company, 1935), p. 119; Elvid Hunt, *History of Fort Leavenworth, 1827-1937,* 2d ed. (Fort Leavenworth, Ka.: General Service Press, 1937) pp. 131-155; Forrest Pogue, *George C. Marshall: Education of a General, 1880-1939* (New York: Viking, 1963), pp. 93-108; Edward M. Coffman, "The American Military Generation Gap in World War I: The Leavenworth Clique in the AEF," paper delivered at the Second Annual Military History Symposium, May 2, 1968, United States Air Force Academy, in *Command and Commanders in Modern Military History* (Washington: USAF Academy, 1971), pp. 35-43.

⁷Notebook 17, entry (?), 1910, BP.

⁸Diarybook 5, entries, January 11 and 22, February 5, 1911, BP.

⁹Diarybook 5, entries, March 19, 1911, and April 3, 1911; Notebook 18, entry, April 20, 1911; Scrapbook 28, entry, February 5, 1911, BP.

¹⁰Diarybook 5, entries, April 6, and July 31, 1911, BP.

¹¹Diarybook 5, entries, August 11, 18, 20, and 27, 1911, BP.

¹²Diarybook 5, September 4, 1911. To reconstruct the Army War College course for 1911-1912, I have relied on George S. Pappas, *"Prudens Futuri"*; *The U.S. Army War College, 1901-1967* (Carlisle, Pa.: Army War College, 1967), pp. 41-83; Moseley, "One Soldier's Journey," Vol. I, pp. 91-96; and the nine volume *Army War College Course, 1911-1912* at the USAMHRC, Carlisle Barracks, Pennsylvania. The latter is hereafter cited as *AWC Course, 1912.*

¹³*AWC Course, 1912,* Vol. I (September 1911).

¹⁴Maj. J. D. Leitch, GS, "Outline of Course of Instruction Army War College Session of 1911-1912," September 1, 1911, USAMHRC.

¹⁵The quote is from Diarybook 5, entry, November 10, 1911, and the other reactions from Diarybook 5, entries, September 15, October 27, and November 8, 1911, BP. The instruction is from *AWC Course, 1912,* Vol. II (October-November 1911).

¹⁶Diarybook 5, entry, November 20, 1911, BP; *AWC Course, 1912,* Vols. III-V (November 1911-April 1912), USAMHRC.

¹⁷Notebook 18, entries, February 25, 1912, BP.

¹⁸Notebook 18, entries, February 27, March 7 and 9, 1912, BP.

¹⁹Diarybook 5, entry, December 26, 1911, BP. For background to the Wood-Ainsworth controversy and War Department politics in the early days of the General Staff, I have used the following sources: Maj. Gen. William Harding Carter, "Creation of the American General Staff," U.S. Congress, Senate Document 119, 68th Congress, 1st Session (1924); Mabel E. Deutrich, *Struggle for Supremacy: The Career of General Fred C. Ainsworth* (Washington: Public Affairs Press, 1962); Henry L. Stimson Diary, "Personal Reminiscences, 1911-1912. Confidential," Vol. II, Henry L. Stimson Papers, Yale University Library: Jack C. Lane, "Leonard Wood and the Shaping of American Defense

Policy, 1900-1920'' (unpublished Ph.D. dissertation, University of Georgia, 1963); James W. Pohl, "The General Staff and American Military Policy: The Formative Period, 1898-1917'' (unpublished Ph.D. dissertation, University of Texas, 1967).

[20]AGO memo, "Appointments of General Officers, U.S. Army," November 10, 1899, General Correspondence, Elihu Root Papers; J. A. Porter to Gov. J. A. Tanner (Ill.), September 16, 1899, Vol. 149, Series 2, William McKinley Papers; Lt. Gen. S.B.M. Young to R. A. Alger, December 29, 1903, Wood Papers; E. Root to Sen. R. Proctor, November 18, 1903, Root Letterbooks, Vol. 177, Root Papers; Lt. Gen. N. A. Miles to E. Root, January 12, 1901, "Letters Sent by the Commanding General," Vol. XXXVIII, RG 108.

[21]T. Roosevelt to E. Root, November 15, 1901, in E. E. Morison, ed., *The Letters of Theodore Roosevelt,* 8 vols. (Cambridge, Mass.: Harvard University Press, 1951-54), III, pp. 197-198; E. Root to T. Roosevelt, July 22, 1903, Root Letterbooks, Vol. 176, Root Papers; E. Root to T. Roosevelt, July 16, 1903, *Ibid.*; Senator R. Proctor to T. Roosevelt, May 6 and 20, 1905, "Letters Received," Series 1, Theodore Roosevelt Papers; Acting Secretary of War R. S. Oliver to Chairman, Senate Committee on Military Affairs, April 11, 1904, Office of the Secretary of War, "Letters Sent, 1903-1913," Vol. VI, RG 107; Secretary of War W. H. Taft to Sen. F. E. Warren and T. Roosevelt, May 25, 1908, Office of the Secretary of War, "Letters Sent, 1903-1913," Vol. XXVII, RG 107; Col. C. R. Edwards to Col. (PC) J. G. Harbord, November 3, 1903, "Private Letters," Harbord Papers; Thomas Cruse, *Apache Days and After* (Caldwell, Ida.: Caxton Printers, 1941), pp. 306-308; Maj. Gen. J. F. Bell to Maj. Gen. H. L. Scott, July 28, 1915, Hugh L. Scott Papers; James Parker, *The Old Army: Memories, 1872-1918* (Philadelphia: Dorrance and Company, 1929), pp. 386-387; Adolphus W. Greely, *Reminiscences of Adventure and Service* (New York: Charles Scribner's Sons, 1927), pp. 276-277; Charles J. Crane, *Experiences of a Colonel of Infantry* (New York: Knickerbocker Press, 1923), pp. 414, 438.

[22]Diarybook 5, entries, January 31 and February 18, 1912, BP.

[23]T. H. McMaster to M. Durant, February 29, 1912, File 2870:1 "Col. Robert L. Bullard," Presidential Series 2, Taft Papers. This file contains most of Bullard's endorsements. See also Wood diary, January 12, 1912, Wood Papers.

[24]Col. R. L. Bullard to O. Underwood, March 10 and 12, 1912, Oscar Underwood Papers, Alabama Department of Archives and History.

[25]Diarybook 5, entries, December 26, 1911, and January 4 and February 10, 1912, BP.

[26]Diarybook 5, entries for March, 1912 and April 17 and 25, 1912, BP.

[27]C. D. Hilles (Taft's personal Secretary) to L. Wood, March 2, 1912, and L. Wood to C. D. Hilles, March 6, 1912, File 2870: "Col. Robert L. Bullard," Presidential Series 2, Taft Papers.

[28]Wood Diary, March 1, 1912, and Maj. Gen. L. Wood, "Memorandum for the Secretary of War," April 23, 1912, Wood Papers; Maj. J. McI. Carter, GS, "Memorandum for the Chief of Staff," May 2, 1912, Wood Papers.

[29]Col. (PC) J. G. Harbord to J. R. Harrison, January 26, 1909, "Personal Letters," Vol. III, Harbord Papers; Col. (PC) J. G. Harbord to Maj. Gen. L. Wood, September 6, 1910, "Personal Letters," Vol. III, Harbord Papers; Col. (PC) J. G. Harbord to W. H. Taft, October 3, 1911, "Personal Letters," Vol. III, Harbord Papers; Brig. Gen. C. R. Edwards to Col. (PC) J. G. Harbord, September 28, 1912, "Personal Letters," Vol. IV, Harbord Papers.

[30]W. H. Taft to Sen. J. F. Johnston, August 5, 1912, File 2870: "Col. Robert L.

Bullard," Presidential Series 2, Taft Papers; Brig. Gen. C. R. Edwards to W. H. Taft, October 24, 1912, Case File 65, Series 7, Taft Papers; Maj. Gen. L. Wood, "Memorandum for the Secretary of War," June 18, 1913, Wood Papers.

[31]Diarybook 6, entry, June 21, 1912, BP.

[32]Diarybook 5, entries, March 1-April 25, 1912, BP.

[33]Diarybook 6, entry, June 11, 1912; Notebook 18, entries January 28 and 30, 1915; Bullard autobiography, pp. 99-101, BP.

[34]Notebook 19, entry, June 12, 1912, BP.

[35]Diarybooks 5 and 6, entries, May 1 to June 12, 1912, BP; "Diary of Historical and Staff Rides," *AWC Course, 1912: Staff Ride No. 3,* Vol. II, USAMHRC.

[36]Diarybook 6, entry, May 31, 1912, BP; *AWC Course, 1912, Staff Ride No. 1* and *Staff Ride No. 2,* 2 vols., USAMHRC.

[37]Diarybook 6, entry, June 8, 1912; Notebook 19, entries, June 1, 1912; Bullard autobiography, pp. 99-101, BP.

[38]Brig. Gen. W. W. Wotherspoon and Brig. Gen. A. L. Mills, reports of February 21 and July (?), 1912, "Individual Service and Efficiency Report of Robert L. Bullard, Col., Inf," Bullard AGO File and Bullard 201 File; Memorandum for the Commandant, Army War College, "Study on the Results of the Army Educational System as Evidenced by the Records made by Officers in the World War," October 22, 1923, copy in "Book File," Pershing Papers.

[39]Office of the Chief of Staff, "Vacancies to be Filled in the General Staff, 1912" Wood Papers; Maj. Gen. L. Wood to Brig. Gen. W. W. Wotherspoon, July 3, 1912, Wood Papers; Diarybook 6, entry, June 30, 1912; and Bullard autobiography, p. 103, BP.

[40]Diarybook 6, entry, July 5, 1912, BP.

[41]Notebook 19, entries, July 5-August 21, 1912, BP.

[42]Brig. Gen. T. H. Bliss to Brig. Gen. J. J. Pershing, June 2, 1913, Vol. 168, Bliss Papers; Diarybook 6, entry, August 14, 1912, and notebook 19, entries, August 6-September 6, 1912, BP; Maj. W. W. Haan to Brig. Gen. T. H. Bliss, October 16, 1912, Major General William G. Haan Papers, Wisconsin Historical Society, Madison, Wisconsin; Brig. Gen. Tasker H. Bliss, *Report of Commander of Maneuvers and Chief Umpire, Connecticut Maneuver Campaign, August 10-20, 1912,* USAMHRC.

[43]Lt. Col. W. H. Johnston to Maj. Gen. L. Wood, August 25, 1912, Wood Papers; War Department General Staff, Report No. 9311, August 29, 1912, "Correspondence of the Office of the Chief of Staff, 1907-1916," RG 165; Maj. Gen. L. Wood to Sen. J. F. Johnston, August 29, 1912 and J. F. Johnston to Maj. Gen. L. Wood, September 2, 1912, both Wood Papers; H. L. Stimson to W. R. Pedigo, "Memorandum," September 19, 1912, Bullard AGO File and copy in the Stimson Papers; Diarybook 6, September 15, 1912, BP.

Robert Lee Bullard, 1885

Troops of the Third Alabama, Camp Shipp, Alabama, 1898

Officers of the Third Alabama Volunteers, 1898. RLB seated center.

Colonel Robert Lee Bullard, 39th
U. S. Volunteers, 1899

Major Robert Lee Bullard, Infantry, 1906

28th Infantry Assault with French Tanks, on Cantigny, May 28, 1918

Traffic Jam at Esnes, Meuse-Argonne, September 28-29, 1918

Pershing and Bullard Inspect Second Army Troops, Toul, France, April 11, 1919

IV   *WATCH ON THE RIO GRANDE 1912-1917*

A few days ago I made a memorandum to get out of my narrow military life, to get in touch more with outside things and people and turn my attention and efforts more upon things of real consequence. *Well, it's hard to do.*

Colonel Robert L. Bullard (1912).

14

The Second Division 1912-1915

General Leonard Wood, Chief of Staff of the United States Army, did not act like a visionary, but his concern in 1913 was the army-that-should-be, not the regulars scattered from the Canadian border to the Philippines. Wood longed to create a system of manpower mobilization which would provide a mass army in time of crisis. Like Upton and his disciples, Wood wanted the mass army of wartime to be raised and officered in accordance with the standards of the War Department alone, although he was friendly to the National Guard and to the concept that citizen-enlisted men could be trained rapidly to regular standards. Wood's difficulty was that he was not master of the War Department until he forced Adjutant General Fred C. Ainsworth into retirement in 1912. With Ainsworth out of uniform, Wood doubled his efforts to lay the legislative basis for a federal reserve and "to change the Army from a life occupation for the soldier to a training school for soldiers—to make it . . . a sort of feeder for the great volunteer armies of citizen soldiers upon which our country places its reliance for defense."[1] Neither the president nor the Congress responded.

When he turned to army reorganization, Wood exercised his powers to reshape the General Staff and to dictate those policy changes within his power to dictate for the regular army. His major concern was to give the army permanent tactical organization, to improve its readiness by concentrating units of all arms into cohesive brigades and divisions capable of immediate deployment. His conviction that such organization was necessary was reinforced in 1911 when it took nearly three months to create the single "maneuver division" in Texas. After this experience, Wood put the General Staff to work on the massive project of assigning all the line units stationed in the United States (the "mobile army") and the existing National Guard organizations to tactical divisions. Theoretically the preassigned units could be concentrated with a minimum of administrative turmoil since the General Staff and all the concerned commanders would know their assignments before a crisis occurred. In addition, Wood managed to stockpile some contingency supplies and to get the Congress and the War Department bureaus to accept the merger of the Quartermaster Department, Subsistence Department, and the Paymaster Department into a single Quartermaster Corps.[2]

In his fights for a federal reserve force, improved National Guard, supply merger, and tactical reorganization, Wood recognized that his reforms were more palatable to the Congress than to the "obstructionist type of officer" whom he estimated made up 90 percent of the officer corps. The Chief of Staff felt that the professional and personal hostility of the officer corps made internal reform as difficult as legislative change.[3] Conservative officers, for example, were those who favored old-style punitive discipline. Wood's ideal officer, however, was the persuasive leader who built morale by preserving the enlisted men's self-respect; such modern officers would create "a cheerful, willing, and highly efficient army."[4]

Secretary of War Stimson agreed that the Chief of Staff did indeed face a hostile officer corps. The secretary thought that the officer corps was the major barrier to change, not because of the merit of the reforms, but because change itself was agonizing for "such a conservative institution as the United States Army." Only Wood's identification and patronage of dedicated reform-officers promised to overcome the stand-pattism of the army.[5] Another of Wood's admirers and protégés, Major James G. Harbord, described Wood's dilemma:

> This is the age of trades unions, socialism, etc., and the Army does not escape. There is as strong a feeling in the Army against the officer who does anything beyond his routine, or to "acquire merit," to signalize himself above his fellows, as there is in the Bricklayer's Union against the wretch who would lay more than the 750 bricks or whatever the number is that the union thinks is a day's work. This is the real basis of the opposition to promotion by selection, not that promotions might be made on "pull" but that they might quite generally be made on merit, which would quicken the pace, "bust up" the routine, disturb siestas, and result generally in nullifying the Army's 750 brick attitude.[6]

Wood's sense of the officer corps' resistance to reform was based on more than his sensitivity to the criticisms of his own meteoric and highly political career. The urge to protect the army from change was as strong as ever in the bureaus and Line alike. Until Ainsworth's departure, the Adjutant General's Department stubbornly fought promotion by selection and detached service for line officers.[7] It was aided by another guardian of the status quo, General Enoch H. Crowder's Judge Advocate General's department, whose legal decisions ruined the use of the National Guard for expeditionary duty in 1912 and restricted Wood's ability to send reformers to the General Staff, service schools, and National Guard duty. Even generals like William Harding Carter and Thomas H. Barry, men whose careers soared with the Root reforms and the growth of the General Staff, complained of the growing impersonality of the officer corps, the erosion of the regimental tradition, the demoralizing effect of detached service on the officers and men of the Line, and the low caliber of officers in the "new army." Barry scolded Wood for encouraging Roosevelt and Taft to promote generals on any criterion but battlefield valor, while Carter worried that the standards of West Point and of America's educated elite were disappearing from the expanded officer corps. Thinking that long officer apprenticeship had disappeared with the frontier army (it had not), Barry and Carter feared that self-seeking and irresponsibility were characteristic of the "new army."[8]

While the Taft Administration was a burden to Wood and the army's progressives, Wood and the General Staff felt that at least a Republican administration would consider military matters with some seriousness and understanding. The same could not be said for the Democrats. Still soured by memories of the Civil War and Reconstruction or by fears of the army's use in labor violence, the general sentiment of the Democratic Party was antimilitary or at least antiarmy and antimilitary spending. In the case of Woodrow Wilson, doctor of philosophy in political science, president of Princeton, governor of New Jersey and president-elect of the United States, these traditional attitudes were fused with an abhorrence of the thought of war and of dealings with military men. Symptomatic of intellectuals of his era, Wilson seems to have regarded thinking of military affairs as a sinful activity. Moreover, Wilson and his inner circle were suspicious of all experts in government, both for their partisanship and their expertise. The Democrats' host of resident Republican devils to be exorcised after March 1913 included Wood and much of the General Staff and War Department bureaucracy.[9]

Though saddened and perplexed by the Taft-Roosevelt split in 1912 and the subsequent Democratic triumph, Stimson and Wood attempted to arrange a smooth transition for the War Department in meetings with Wilson's agents. They found the ignorance of the Democrats appalling and concluded that they must be either fools or pacifists, probably the latter. After a series of meetings which went on until the inaguration, Wilson finally selected Stimson's successor, a forty-nine-year-old New Jersey judge named Lindley M. Garrison. Methodical, conscientious, and uncompromising, Garrison proved a surprisingly happy replacement for Stimson, especially since he and the General Staff found that they could work amiably together. Certainly Garrison was more satisfactory to the army's officers, who considered themselves largely presidential Republicans, than the Democratic congressmen who were Wilson's self-proclaimed experts on military affairs.[10] The president-elect himself had no working knowledge or interest in the army. Knowing this, Colonel Hugh L. Scott, a friend of Wood and the brother of a Princeton professor, volunteered his services to Wilson as an adviser during the transition period. Although Scott was a life-long Republican, his integrity was well known, and the fact that his family were old Princeton residents convinced Wilson that he was trustworthy. Scott saw his chore as saving Wood for a full term as Chief of Staff and protecting Wilson from "the political element" of the army.[11] Such was the unsettled shape of military policy and the army's command structure when the Wilson Administration took office. Since there was still the possibility of military action with Mexico, the army watched the Democrats' advent with no little skepticism.

1.

Far from the madding War Department, Robert Lee Bullard, colonel of the Twenty-Sixth Infantry, savored his new command. After leaving Washington, he and his family had visited their relatives in Tennessee and Alabama, always an annoying and disconcerting business, made more so in 1912 by the increasing age of his kin. Realizing how little he had in common with his relatives, he, Rose, young Rose, and Keith fled to their new home, Fort Wayne, Michigan. Upon their arrival they found the garrison, two battalions of the Twenty-Sixth, turned out for a dress parade. Their quarters were clean and ready, and the regimental officers held a reception for them at the officers' club. Flattered and pleased, the new colonel, nevertheless, used the occasion to get a feel for his officers. While he knew that Lieutenant Colonel Johnston was able, he was convinced that he would have to change the regimental staff as the first step in tightening the regiment. Even before his family was settled and his leave ended, he inspected his other battalion which garrisoned Fort Brady at Sault Sainte Marie.[12]

Bullard's inspection of his new command revealed no surprises. The two posts were pre-Civil War fortifications to protect the key narrows along the Canadian border. Both still had earthworks and bastions, but had been changed into comfortable villages of high stone and brick buildings with wooden porticos and fences. Both posts were clean and livable, Brady's disadvantage being its distance from a city like Detroit.[13]

The Twenty-Sixth Infantry was neither any better nor worse than most of the army's infantry regiments. Its officers reflected the pattern of officer recruitment and army expansion since Bullard had been graduated from West Point. Lieutenant Colonel Johnston was Bullard's age, having been commissioned from civil life in 1883. His credentials were solid, and he was to become an excellent division commander in World War I. The Twenty-Sixth's three majors were all Academy graduates, but only one was with the regiment. The fifteen captains included five West Pointers (the five senior captains) and one ex-sergeant; all the others were commissioned during the War with Spain and the Philippine unpleasantness. The fifteen first lieutenants were of the same vintage, three being West Pointers and ten having been commissioned from the ranks. All twelve second lieutenants were commissioned after 1906 and ten of them were Academy graduates.[14] Of the regiment's forty-eight officers, thirty were available for duty. The regiment's enlisted men were the same sort of old soldiers and wandering youths Bullard had found in the Tenth Infantry, except that in 1912 there were more eastern and southern European names on the rolls. Duty must have been easy since there was not a single deserter, only one man sick, and but four in arrest when Bullard arrived. Of 811 men on its rolls, the Twenty-Sixth had 739 for duty with the regiment.[15]

Assessing his officers, Bullard found them suspicious and hostile to his policy changes, especially his decision to rotate battalions to and from the isolated Fort Brady. He also thought them reluctant to do their duty with more enthusiasm. "There'll be no changing them with breaking, smashing them. Well, they are going to change even if smashing has to be done to accomplish the change."[16] He clashed with Lieutenant Colonel Johnston, probably on the issue of the regimental staff. If so, Johnston proved persuasive, for the adjutant, quartermaster, and commissary held their jobs; nevertheless, each battalion filled its empty adjutant and quartermaster billets, presumably to increase the regiment's efficiency. The Twenty-Sixth probably needed just a change of colonels to make it soldier well, for Bullard, not an easy man to satisfy, was soon pleased with the regiment's condition. By December he judged the men's morale good and the officers willing. He concentrated on schooling his junior officers, knowing that the tightened discipline and accelerated training would extend to the ranks. By January he was writing: "A little hardship now borne together would meld it [the regiment] into one of the finest regiments ever seen."[17]

Before Christmas, Bullard felt that his family was well settled and his regiment responding, but he was discontented with the condition of his life. He had found disappointingly little challenge in his command, since the problems were easier than those he had faced with the Third Alabama and Thirty-Ninth Volunteers. He promised himself to get out among the Detroiters, "to get out of my narrow military life, get in touch more with outside things and people and turn my attention and efforts more upon things of real consequence. *Well, it's hard to do.*" A month later he still had not escaped the garrison's cloisters: "Got to make a start, somehow and will 'else I'll dry rot or die of narrowness."[18] But his routine duties held him and he had little time to cultivate friends. Occasionally, as he read the papers, he wondered about the Mexican situation and the continued speculation about American intervention. He thought that some sort of military action was inevitable, but that "we will probably in so doing move to it so piecemeal a way that intervention will be scatteringly done."[19]

At Fort Wayne, Mexico seemed far away. In January, groups of soldiers began the customary ski and snowshoe marches, while their comrades took apprentice training as cooks, bakers, clerks, shoemakers, butchers, telegraphers, and carpenters. Social life at Fort Wayne slowed down for the Lenten season, and the only stir was caused by the return of officers from detached duty cut short by the "Manchu Law." The winter was white and quiet along the Canadian border.[20]

2.

After ten days of sporadic shooting and intense conspiracy in Mexico City, General Victoriano Huerta seized the Mexican government from Francisco Madero on February 18, 1913. Before the end of the month the ex-president was executed by Huerta's officers. Although Huerta and his co-conspirator, General Felix Díaz, moved quickly to emasculate the Madero administration, they were immediately challenged by the "men of the North," the *maderistas* rallied by General Venustiano Carranza as the Constitutionalist movement. By March 1913, the Mexican Revolution had entered another of its violent phases.[21]

Huerta's *golpe de estado* caught the Taft Administration in its waning days, but Taft and his lame-ducks aroused themselves to handle the Mexican problem. Encouraged by the optimistic cables from the pro-Huerta ambassador, Henry Lane Wilson, the administration had every intention of recognizing Huerta's regime as soon as it demonstrated its capacity to preserve order, protect foreign interests, and settle some boundary and reparations matters with the United States. Army patrols and federal officials increased their efforts to keep the fighting south of the Rio Grande and to prevent the use of American territory as a sanctuary and firearms market. To these measures the administration added a naval deployment along both Mexican coasts, and, finally, decided to increase the number of soldiers available to the commander of the Southern Department, Brigadier General Tasker H. Bliss. The purpose of the partial mobilization was the same as it had been in 1911: to concentrate an expeditionary force capable of moving by sea to Vera Cruz or overland into northern Mexico in order to protect American lives and property. Weary and demoralized by their loss to the Democrats, the Taft cabinet was happy to let the Wilson Administration then decide what to do about Mexico and the troops sent to Texas.[22]

For the General Staff, the decision to assemble another expeditionary force in Texas provided a welcome opportunity to test the effectiveness of its latest contingency planning. Less than a month before Madero's fall, Stimson and Wood, in a conference with the Army War College planners and the generals stationed in the United States, had approved the final reorganization of the Line into tactical divisions. The "mobile army" would henceforth be organized as three infantry divisions and one cavalry division, with each division administered by one of the four new geographic departments. When asked to recreate an expeditionary division in Texas, Wood was able to order the General Staff to activate the Second Division and sent it to the Galveston area. Formed from regiments garrisoned in the north-central United States, the division was composed of ten regiments of infantry assigned to three brigades (Fourth, Fifth, and Sixth), the Sixth Cavalry, the Fourth Field Artillery, an engineer battalion, a Signal Corps company, an ambulance company, a field hospital, and assorted headquarters and service troops. The Second Division's effective strength was 11,000 men. Wood was pleased by the chance to test the General Staff and to gather a full division for combined arms training, regardless of whether the division was used in Mexico. He was under no illusion that the force would be adequate for anything more than the most limited of interventions; the General Staff calculated that a full-scale occupation would demand an army of several hundred thousand men and millions of dollars in military spending. Few in the Taft Administration thought Mexico worth such an effort, and the Democrats were supposed to be even less inclined to military intervention. Nevertheless, the Second Division was assembled in Texas.[23]

In the middle of an ordinary Friday, February 21, Bullard received a telegram from the War Department ordering him to prepare the Twenty-Sixth Infantry for a train trip to Galveston, Texas. On Sunday, the Chief of Staff ordered the regiment south. Admittedly surprised by the mobilization, Bullard packed and departed with the two Fort Wayne battalions. It was his fifth such crisis deployment since 1898. Arriving at Texas City on March 2, he found the Gulf Coast town in utter confusion, flooded by trains, soldiers, and piles of baggage and equipment. No one on the scene knew anything about an intervention, and he himself could hardly conceive of plunging into Mexico with such a "contemptible" force. It was, however, no time for reflection and bemusement, for he had seven hundred officers and men to house and train. Once more the challenge of disorder and the prospect of war fueled his enthusiasm for command.[24]

Bullard had an additional surprise in Texas City: he was made the acting commander of the Fourth Brigade until a brigadier general arrived. This assignment came strictly by chance because the colonels of the brigade's other regiments, the Twenty-Third and Twenty-Seventh Infantry, were his juniors by date of rank, though not by length of service. Both the other colonels were six years older than Bullard. Bullard was prepared for their hostility, accepted it, and commanded the brigade in spite of it. It was not a new experience, and it simply added another interesting challenge.[25]

Bullard's professional competitor became the Sixth Brigade's brigadier general, Clarence R. Edwards. Neither officer cared for the other. Tall, handsome, and charming in a florid way, an officer who curried the favor of his superiors and the affection of his subordinates with brilliant conversation and boundless energy, Edwards was Taft's Pershing, a relatively junior officer plucked from among his peers and made a permanent brigadier general of the Line. His most notable service had been behind a desk as the chief of the Bureau of Insular Affairs, and he was smarting from the army gossip that he was a desk soldier and political general. He knew that Bullard was one of his detractors, envied the Alabaman's field service record and his experience in troop training, and was peeved by Bullard's favored relationship with Wood.[26] Bullard reciprocated Edwards' distaste. Since Bullard's command was temporary, he ran the Fourth Brigade with his regimental headquarters. Edwards, on the other hand, established a large brigade staff, which made "a h—l of an impression." Bullard was convinced that a large and bustling headquarters would impress visitors, though it would not be more efficient. He conceded the social honors to the Sixth Brigade: "I suppose I shall always remain a fool about not putting up a proper show."[27] Nevertheless, he found the other officers responsive and deferential. "It is amusing but I can notice in many an increase in deference due no doubt to my increasing chances of a B. G." He certainly felt like a brigadier and thoroughly enjoyed pitting his troops against Edwards'.[28]

The first order of business at Texas City was to establish a camp. The initial site was a disaster, a nightmare of bad drainage and mosquitoes. The site was then moved nearer Galveston Bay where the drainage was better, though sand fleas joined the mosquitoes and the scenery was unimproved. When Wood visited Texas City, he found the countryside flat and uninteresting, recognized the mess the cold rains made of the camp, and predicted that during the summer "the dust and monotony will be very bad."[29] Setting up a permanent camp, however, was an army specialty, and floored tents, graveled walks, screened messhalls, and wooden latrines sprouted from the grasslands just outside Texas City. The Second Division settled in—for how long no one knew. The assumption was that the troops would stay at least through the summer.[30]

Having partially conquered the discomforts of Texas City, Bullard put the Fourth Brigade into the field for tactical training. Much to General Edwards' dismay, Bullard's field exercises pleased the division staff, and the slender colonel refused to contest the rigidly prescribed training established by the division. Bullard's headquarters was defective in arranging parties in Texas City, but it had the habit of getting its training schedules in on time.[31] Bullard himself enjoyed the opportunity to command a brigade and concentrated on the novel aspects of his command. He paid special attention to coordinating the fire support of his adequate artillery units and his inadequate Benet-Mercie machine guns. He worked carefully with his varied system of communications: motorcycle riders, radios, and field telephones. As always his special touch was in handling his men. He took special pains to see that all the troops were briefed on the purposes of the field problems, and he resisted the temptation to meddle in the handling of units below the regiment. When Bullard's brigade fought mock battles with the Sixth Brigade, Edwards was quick to claim that the Fourth was "practically annihilated" on two occasions, but the division commander, Major General William Harding Carter, was pleased with Bullard's performance and reported that he would be an excellent brigade commander in wartime. In the first three months in which he commanded the Fourth Brigade, Bullard got the reputation he wanted—he "played the game."[32]

Though his brigade training progressed to his satisfaction, Bullard found plenty of things with which to be irritated. One was his officers' tendency to plan attacks which put a premium on exotic envelopments and complex coordination. He diagnosed the disease as Leavenworthitis. Army officers, he mused, had learned so much tactical theory that they forgot that "somebody has to take the enemy head on . . . to go up against it—a sad but unavoidable fact that helps materially . . . to make war hell."[33] Another pet peeve was Edwards' blatant disregard for Carter's orders. Bullard agreed that Carter allowed too little discretion, but he could not understand why Edwards' consistent noncompliance was tolerated. Bullard also chafed under the mounting paper-work of his command, and he was annoyed by his officers' pleas for leave to visit their families or to settle them in Texas City. Totally absorbed in his work, he regarded families as the army's bane and his soldiers as natural shirkers. Day after day he was in the saddle watching the training, and at night he often fell asleep at his desk amid unsigned reports. He had seldom felt so extended and fulfilled.[34]

3.

Erect, slender, delicately handsome and gently graying, Colonel Bullard of the Fourth Brigade wanted not only a brigadier's command, but a brigadier's stars. As age and disability overtook the other colonels, his chances improved, although he began to realize that junior colonels and lieutenant colonels might now appear younger and more active. From his War College tour, however, he knew that his name at least was mentioned when selections were made. Early in 1913, two more brigadier generalships were vacant, and he once more hoped that he would be selected. He still had the mild support of Wood, who recommended John F. Morrison, Hunter Liggett, and Bullard, basing his nominations "only on fitness for future work." The General Staff's collective wisdom produced a neat compromise, for it nominated three elderly colonels of infantry and three more vigorous lieutenant colonels. Shortly before he left office, President Taft selected Hunter Liggett for the infantry generalship and chose Bullard's old friend James Parker, colonel of the crack Eleventh Cavalry, for the other vacancy. Though disappointed, Bullard approved of both promotions and waited for the next vacancy.[35]

Bullard thought his chances for promotion in 1913 were excellent, though he doubted that his performance as a brigade commander had much influence. The source of his optimism (and perhaps some of his courage in baiting Edwards) was the fact that his patron, Senator Johnston of Alabama, had just become chairman of the Senate Military Affairs Committee. His faith was not misplaced, for scarcely had Johnston taken his post in the reorganized Congress than he approached President Wilson in Bullard's behalf. Bullard should be the next brigadier, Johnston thought, because his personal merit and combat record justified it and because the South deserved more than one general of the Line.[36]

Secretary of War Garrison, however, had his own ideas about how generals should be selected and personal lobbying was not among them. Much to the army's surprise, Garrison closed the door on congressional influence and even upon the General Staff. He announced, instead, that all future vacancies would be filled only by colonels and would be based solely on the recommendations of the army's active general officers. Garrison's legal mind led him to a conclusion that flaunted tradition: only generals were competent to select other generals. Not only should Congress be cut from the selection process, but the president and the secretary of war should do no more than ratify the generals' choice. After more than a decade of having the proarmy Republicans treat promotions as a patronage matter, the supposedly antiarmy Democrats accepted the ultimate dictum of military professionalism: that only general officers were qualified to choose their own kind. It was a surprising reform.[37]

While he was stunned by the news that his congressional endorsements now endangered his candidacy, Bullard thought that he still had a chance. He learned from Wood, however, that only two generals had pushed his nomination, Major

General Carter and James Parker. Perhaps there were too many who remembered his transfer from the Subsistence Department, too many who resented his political lobbying. Garrison's new policy was a personal disaster. "In so far as Army men are concerned, I'm convinced that I must go it alone. . . . I have nothing to expect from the Army."[38] He knew that Edwards had not rated him highly, and Edwards knew that he knew, which did nothing for the relations between the Fourth and Sixth Brigades.[39] Bullard also sensed that Wood's influence was waning. When the selection for the next brigadier generalship was announced, Bullard was not surprised at the choice: Colonel Thomas F. Davis, sixty-year-old commander of the Eighteenth Infantry in Edwards' brigade. For Bullard his promotion was especially bitter, for Davis took over the Fourth Brigade. As a final blow, Senator Johnston died suddenly in August. Bullard bade farewell to his political influence, his chance for promotion, and his brigade command at the same time.[40]

4.

While the Second Division trained and its colonels lobbied, the Wilson Administration fiddled with its Mexican diplomacy. President Wilson took Madero's death personally, especially when he learned that the American ambassador was a *huertista*. Since he often confused politics with preaching, his first reaction was to condemn the *golpe* and deny the Huerta government diplomatic recognition, a Wilsonian "moral sanction" that angered Huerta and confused European governments. Not until May 1913 did Wilson suggest another step: the blood-stained Huerta should step down and allow the election of a constitutional government. Just how he might bring this about confused the president, but he was determined to bring Huerta down. Throughout the summer of 1913, Wilson dispatched a succession of private agents to Mexico. They studiously avoided encouraging the Constitutionalists, though support of the latest group of rebels would have allowed a proxy war on Huerta. American contact with the *carranzistas* was private and entrepreneurial; the border, despite army patrols, was a gunrunner's paradise.[41]

From his headquarters in San Antonio, Brigadier General Tasker H. Bliss watched the Mexican Revolution with equal confusion. As he had in 1911, Bliss correctly recognized the depth of Mexican upheaval, but he could not predict its twists and turns for the War Department. For American policy, he saw only two alternatives. The United States might act in the spirit of the Monroe Doctrine, intervening to preserve foreign businesses and to forestall European interference. This could be done only by massive military occupation. The wiser course, he thought, would be to cross the northern border and establish a buffer territory between the warring factions and the vulnerable American communities along the Rio Grande. Then the revolution might go on without immediately endangering American lives and property.

Bliss approved of protecting American citizens and their property in Mexico, but it seemed that this matter played no major role in American diplomacy.

Moreover, Bliss was supposed to prevent accidental death to Americans on the border, but without martial law or permission for cross-border reprisals. If he could not carry on the most innocuous policing activities on the Rio Grande, he wrote Wood, he wondered what the administration wanted with the Second Division.[42] The question was a pertinent one. The War Department's position was that the division was the lead element in a grand march from Vera Cruz to Mexico City. For the time being, it was a symbol of the administration's concern and reassurance to the people of Texas. Immediate military action was remote.[43]

In the Second Division the training went on. The brigades spent nearly every day in the field, but by June the sense of urgency in the command gave way to a more relaxed training schedule. Both Wood and Carter regarded the division as combat-ready, and both worried about the primitiveness of the Texas City camp and the plunge in reenlistments.[44] Carter decided that the answer to repetitious training and rough camp life was to reduce the field work, which pleased his apathetic officers and men. To his supporters, he was the commanding general who "put forth his hand and curbed and restrained the super-activities of inferior organization commanders when he saw them inclined too much to the strenuous life in the matter of drills, exercises, and hard field maneuvers."[45] Among the Fourth Brigade's colonels, Carter's appeasement policy was interpreted as a disaster. Bullard thought that Carter had an irrational fear of field training and the threat of heat casualties; he himself thought that the army would be better off to train a full day and cut enlistments in half. Bullard, however, recognized that the troops might be a little stale, and he had no desire to fight Carter directly on the issue.

Bullard grudgingly followed Carter's orders to cut military training and to begin a sports program of boxing, baseball, surf swimming, and fishing. He himself took up polo and was addicted to the sport. He overlooked no opportunity however, to obey his orders only superficially and follow his own ideas on training. He also vowed that he himself would always see that *his* orders were obeyed, and he would never assume that his subordinates would automatically do a task if it was the least bit discomforting. He remained convinced that the army's fundamental weakness was its distaste for military training and its passion for housekeeping, a vestige of its frontier days. In Japan he had seen one man trimming a lawn while a brigade trained; when he came to the Twenty-Sixth Infantry he found a battalion cutting the grass and a squad drilling. Internal esprit was directly proportionate to the intensity of a unit's military training, not its prowess in baseball or group gymnastics. Moreover, the public properly recognized and resented soldiers' idleness, and the army would never win support for its reserve training schemes until it proved that its regulars trained.[47] *"What's the matter with the Army?—* Answer. It doesn't work."[48]

In July Carter ordered the Fourth Brigade to march to Galveston for some big city recreation. Bullard used the occasion to present a military spectacular for the civilians of Galveston, having his troops perform mock battles, wall-scaling, trick drill, and full-scale parades. That his men trained and got publicity pleased Bullard, especially when he leaned that Edwards was miffed.[49] Back in Texas City he found his command still infected with apathy. Some strange consensus had swept the camp: intervention was impossible and the troops were all going home. Bullard saw there was no basis but "auto-persuasion" for the soldiers' faith. Its grip on his men was a distressing reality, and he took what little comfort he could from the fact that his men behaved well in Texas City and were tiring of its saloons, movie houses, and "filthy . . . disgusting Negro whorehouses." Only a handful really enjoyed the athletics, but the rest were at least passive, most going to camp movies and the YMCA reading tent. Finally the great consensus collapsed when Secretary Garrison announced that the division would stay in Texas indefinitely. The troops steadied, shirking and sick reports decreased, and the men again trained with some verve.[50]

The training, however, never regained the intensity of March and April, for the weather turned cool and rainy, and Carter again ordered a stand-down. Instead of holding field exercises in the rain, Carter ordered each company to take familiarization trips to the division bakery, butcher shop, quartermaster depot, and hospital. "Similarly all officers and men will visit the manure dump and observe the method of piling it in small windrows, and the method of applying the oil on the windward side near bottom before firing."[51] Although Carter was sure that the division was in fine spirits and peak form, General Bliss found the troops listless from tent-living and ennui. Bliss recommended breaking up the brigades and sending the regiments to permanent posts in Texas.[52] The other alternative was to change the division's leadership.

Of the Second Division's high commanders, Colonel Bullard ended 1913 in high esteem at the War Department, partially because of his actual performance, partially because he was once again only a regimental commander when Wood transferred the division's general officers. Bullard's brigade commander, General Thomas F. Davis, was shifted to the Sixth Brigade, and the Fifth Brigade commander retired.[53] Before his transfer, Davis sent another complimentary efficiency report in for Bullard.[54] While he was ready for a new start for the Second Division, Bullard had no regrets about his performance in 1913.

5.

As the Second Division hung in strategic limbo, Bullard inadvertently escaped Texas City and his command. From a psychological standpoint, it was a useful interlude, for he had become querulous and unpleasant. On August 27 his horse stepped on his right foot during an inspection. Always sensitive about his health, particularly his nervous stomach, Bullard immediately checked into the division hospital, convinced that his foot was broken. The doctors diagnosed his injury as a severe bruise. Barely able to hobble, he remained at the hospital. He was a difficult patient. He thought that the doctors were incompetent, and he was sure that they were miserable administrators. He thought their hospital a pesthole.

After carrying on his personal inspection of the hospital's deficiencies and writing a report, Bullard complained to the division surgeon and division quartermaster. They ignored him. He complained more loudly and a week later noted that "for some days past I've been hearing from the new C. O. of this hospital talk of moving the hospital to a new site. . . ."[55] His foot remained inflamed, and he worried about the possibility of retirement, but the conditions in the hospital still monopolized his interest. Finally he got the intervention he wanted: on October 22 a heavy storm inundated the hospital. Lying in his cot, Bullard measured the water as it rose above the tent floor and noted the depth for another memo to the division surgeon. The storm, however, did his work for him, and the hospital was moved to Texas City. Bullard did not go with it, moving back to his regimental tent even though his foot was still painfully swollen nearly two months after the injury.[56]

In November he took sick leave and returned to Fort Wayne to see his family, hoping that the change would improve his disposition and his foot. He first made sure that Wood understood that his foot was better and that the Twenty-Sixth did not need a new colonel.[57] He still believed that the Wilson Administration would be forced to occupy Mexico if it was serious about influencing events there, and he wanted to be included in the occupying army. Yet the enormity of the force necessary to bring peace to Mexico might very well preclude an American intervention. Because the United States could not organize an effective force of that size in anything less than a year, it would have to intervene with European allies, as it did in China in 1900. Prohibiting European intervention, however, was supposed to be part of the rationale of an American occupation. He knew that the European powers would not commit troops without receiving economic and military concessions in Mexico, precisely the thing the United States did not want. He then reasoned, circuitously but correctly, that the Wilson Administration would continue to limit its diplomacy to moral pronouncements and avoid war at all costs. The whole business was another distressing example of America's diplomacy-by-talk.[58]

His foot still throbbing, Bullard left Fort Wayne and admitted himself to Walter Reed Army Hospital in Washington for specialized care. Again the doctors examined his foot and could find no broken bones, prescribing bedrest and some physical therapy. Once more bedridden, the colonel turned philosophical: "Here, at least tonight, I have the feeling of being very much further from the Mexican question. For the U.S. Army and for me in my day I am becoming more convinced that there is nothing more of military attainment." He thought about looking for a civil post or a "snap" army detail.[59] In the meantime, he amused himself by writing letters to friends in the army and in Alabama, urging them to support the candidacy of Oscar Underwood for a Senate seat.[60]

Bullard's hospitalization provided the leisure for him to express his increasing conservatism. Following events in Mexico and the Progressive movement at home, he was convinced that the critics of American society based their criticisms "generally . . . upon the experience of a single life (of self)." But the prevailing social order was "always the result of experiences of countless lives, of generation after generation of men and cannot be lightly abandoned with safety." The radical always assumed that his own reforms, brilliant in their simplicity, were original, seldom realizing that most grand schemes had "already been tried and found wanting by men who have gone long before him. Many such plans have been. The world and the laws and customs that rule it were not made on the experience of today."[61] Life seemed more mysterious and man's assumption of omniscience and omnipotence the most arrogant human intellectual trait possible. Americans especially, a people with no sense of the past, were a people of mindless "brag," deluded by the idea that material progress and wealth would bring happiness.[62]

His own future remained obscure, but he was puzzled by two dreams he had at Walter Reed. In the first, he found himself in a museum standing before a long line of glass caskets. In the caskets he could make out the mouldering faces and forms of famous Union generals, including Grant and Sherman. Before his eyes, Sherman stirred and began to climb from his casket. Grant moved also. Suddenly an attendant came and scuffled with Sherman, attempting to push him back in the casket. The dead general shook off the attendant, the dust, and the ashes, and laughed. He climbed from the casket. The other generals began to move, and Bullard fled. In the other dream, Bullard was riding with two other officers down a Texas road. Suddenly a Mexican rode by, but fell from his horse in front of them. They hurried to help him. The Mexican drew a pistol and threatened him. Bullard and another officer bluffed him with their own weapons, which were inexplicably unloaded, and disarmed him. The dream faded.[63] What did the dreams mean? Perhaps they were a reminder that "a characteristic of greatness is unrelenting, unforgiving, unforgetting to whomsoever has opposed their (strong men's) ideas and plans."[64] Perhaps he still had some great destiny to fulfill. His foot feeling much better, he left Walter Reed on December 18. Spending Christmas and the month of January 1914 with his family in Michigan, he returned to the Fourth Brigade, ready for more service.

6.

During Bullard's service with the Second Division, the War Department attempted to find a standard procedure for the selection of general officers. In the fall of 1913 Garrison appointed a General Staff committee, headed by Brigadier General Hunter Liggett, president of the Army War College, to recommend a policy to make the officer corps more effective. The secretary of war already had a system in mind: promotion by selection rather than by seniority.

Influenced by the secretary's and chief of staff's known views on the subject, the General Staff committee recommended that the officer corps be made more competitive "by natural selection." The selection process would not be left to Nature, of course, but to boards of officers who would recommend promotions based on the following criteria: personality, military record, length of army service, and time in grade. The candidates for promotion would come only from the next lowest rank, a compromise between seniority and the captain-to-general days of the McKinley and Roosevelt administrations. The technical process by which future promotions would be made was easy enough to describe. The criteria promotion boards would apply were not. The Liggett Committee recognized at least three equally reasonable standards: promotions of officers best suited for command in the peacetime regular army; promotions of noncommand specialists; and promotions of officers "not among the most desirable, yet considered to have the qualifications which would make them useful officers in the case of mobilization of large bodies of volunteers." The committee could not agree on a satisfactory way to solve the problem of selection of criteria, although it proposed several schemes. Other officers did the same, but the War Department could find no common ground.[65]

Captain George Van Horn Moseley, whose intellectual acuity would eventually place him in the headquarters of the American Expeditionary Force (AEF) and make him Douglas MacArthur's deputy Chief of Staff, identified the crucial problem: the officer corps itself had no single criterion for expertise. In the past, when the strict seniority principle was modified, as it was in the promotion of generals, army officers suggested a bewildering range of ideal qualifications for promotion: length of service, participation in the Civil War, number of brevets, accomplishment as an author and teacher, excellence as an explorer and canal-builder, and, above all, administrative efficiency. These qualifications had been used by both the president and the Congress as well. The army could not complain about civilian intervention based on these criteria since they were not uniquely military. Moseley, however, believed that the army was approaching a single criterion: fitness to exercise command in the wartime army. The change, nurtured by the "progressive element of the army" and aided "here and there by a progressive officer of rank who was in close touch with his profession," was evolutionary. Once the officer corps accepted formal schooling and demonstrated performance in the "mobile army" as the basis for advancement, promotion by selection would be acceptable to the officer corps. That time had not yet arrived.[66]

Secretary of War Garrison accepted the judgment that neither the officer corps nor Congress was ready for promotion by selection. In the selection of line generals, however, he was disposed to accept the recommendations of his general officers. His major caveat was that he would not promote officers who had strong political ties with the Congress or the Republican party.[67] President Wilson shared the same bias, and extended it to army officers making speeches, testifying to congressional committees, and lampooning public officials in skits and songs. Wilson was so suspicious of army generals, particularly Wood, that he chose Hugh L. Scott for Chief of Staff on the basis that he could not find a more dutiful and silent general than Scott. Wilson's appointment as assistant chief of staff, a choice more popular with both Garrison and the officer corps, was the cerebral Tasker H. Bliss. Bliss shared the desire to promote generals solely for their value on active duty:

I should think that a dead brigadier general, dead doing his duty and as the Result of doing it, would be a sight pleasing to both gods and men. It would be well to make a mummy of him and stick him up in a glass case along with the dead Pharohs of Eygpt in the National Museum that travelers might come from afar to look at him. Certainly he would be just as instructive a sight— perhaps more so. . . . We would have a cheaper . . . and . . . a better Army if we killed more men on the active list instead of trying to make them live forever on the retired list.[68]

In practice, the War Department could find no alternative to seniority and professional anonymity. The only major decision the Liggett Committee recommended was procedural and designed to satisfy the officer corps' notions of equity: brigadier generalships would be awarded to infantry, cavalry, field artillery and coast artillery officers in proportion to the size of each arm of the Line. While the "quota system" had been followed informally in the Taft Administration, Garrison made it official and had the Army War College Division compile elaborate charts and ratios to guide the selection process. Beyond this manner of narrowing the nominees, the secretary's preference ran to nonentities.[69]

Even the General Staff had a hard time applying any other criterion than seniority. In the spring of 1914, during the Vera Cruz crisis and the waning days of Wood's tenure as Chief of Staff, Wood asked Liggett's committee for a list of colonels and lieutenant-colonels most suited for the high command in the National Guard and Volunteer army in the event of war with Mexico. His own choices were John F. Morrison, Edwin F. Glenn, Charles G. Morton, and Bullard. The General Staff's selections, done by seniority, were "very unsatisfactory" to the Chief of Staff.[70] Bullard's name was not on the committee's list, perhaps because of ability, but more likely because of his relative youthfulness and the residual animosity to his retransfer to the infantry in 1902.

Secretary Garrison and the General Staff could not agree upon the selection of brigadiers, but the secretary of war by the end of 1914 had made his position on lobbying clear. One colonel told a fellow officer that it would be fatal to his chances "to let it get to the Secretary" that he wanted to be considered for selection and suggested approaching President Wilson directly through Oscar Underwood.[71] General Scott himself made it clear to another colonel that the secretary decided the brigadier nominations and that he had one goal in the matter ". . . that one of the things he hopes before he leaves the Cabinet, is to create such a feeling in the army in regard to asking for promotion, that it would be regarded very much as if it were a case almost of cheating at cards; that is, that the person so convicted of it would be ostracised by the rest of the service."[72] For an officer like Colonel Bullard of the Twenty-Sixth Infantry, that was a difficult proposition.

7.

By the early months of 1914 the Wilson Administration's anti-Huerta diplomacy had taken some new twists which again increased the possibility of American intervention. The policy of nonrecognition continued, much to the consternation of the European governments. With good reason the European diplomats argued that American policy was abetting the disorder which threatened the lives and property of their nationals in Mexico. The State Department assured the Europeans that the United States would assume the responsibility of protecting all foreign interests and then, in a bit of dazzling peace-keeping, lifted the arms embargo upon the Mexicans. The Constitutionalists drew quickly upon the American arms markets, since they controlled much of the border. By the end of February 1914 the Constitutionalist cause, fueled with American munitions and the dramatic general-ship of Francisco "Pancho" Villa, rallied against Huerta's armies. Only his American naval presence along the Gulf Coast protected foreign investments and frustrated both the federal army and the Constitutionalist attackers. Navy ships with marines embarked lay in Mexican ports or hovered off the coast, and it seemed only a matter of time until some incident set off a Mexican-American clash. Whether such an incident became a casus belli depended upon the Wilson Administration.[73]

Bullard returned to Texas City to find the Second Division under a new commander, Brigadier General Frederick Funston, and training hard. Despite chill rains and the uncomfortable camp, the troops were in the field, preparing for a series of divisional exercises. Funston, the spade-bearded bantam who had captured Aguinaldo and become a regular general officer in 1901, was nothing if not energetic. Though an able soldier, Funston was not a school-trained, European-model officer. As the commander of the Second Division, however, he brought new drive to General Carter's lethargic command. Throughout March, Funston kept his units in the field. Assessing the division maneuvers, he thought that the soldiers' state of readiness was excellent, but that the Second Division's communications and supply system needed reform. He reported to Wood that he was satisfied with General Davis and Colonel Bullard as his brigade commanders. His only criticism of Bullard was that he had taken the time to issue a complete written order before conducting a retirement, but Bullard "showed great energy in handling his command."[74] Funston then organized a long division march to Houston, eighty miles distant, touting the expedition as the largest and longest troop movement since the Civil War. While the division was trudging northward, however, the Mexican situation broke wide open.[75]

On April 21, piqued by a minor incident between American sailors and federal troops at Tampico and irritated by a report that a German vessel was bringing munitions to the despicable Huerta, Woodrow Wilson ordered occupation of the port of Vera Cruz. Apparently he believed that the Mexicans would not resist and that the American military action would topple Huerta. In the ten days of diploma-tic exchanges and cabinet meetings which preceeded the seizure of Vera Cruz, Wilson persuaded himself, his secretaries, and his congressional leaders that the United States' motives were pure and objectives limited.

On April 15, Wood reviewed with Secretary Garrison the plans for a full-scale war with Mexico. As drawn by the General Staff, the plans called for the dispatch of the entire "mobile army" to Vera Cruz. The campaign would then develop on the Vera Cruz-Mexico City axis, the same route followed by Winfield Scott in 1847. In the meantime, the National Guard would be federalized and sent to the border either to guard it or to mount a second advance into northern Mexico. Wood estimated that his advance force, the Second Division, could be in Vera Cruz a week after it received orders. It would be the navy's responsibility to seize the port.[76]

Garrison dutifully explained the army plan to the president on April 18, pointing out that the Second Division was ready to move, but that he would need ten days to assemble shipping for them at Galveston. It would take additional time to mobilize the southern states' National Guard and use them to replace the nine regiments of regulars patrolling the border. Eventually the regular army could assemble 43,000 troops in Vera Cruz, while the National Guard might muster as many as 85,000 men on the border.[77]

What Wilson really decided to do before April 21 is conjectural since the president was a secretive man. Wood, however, was convinced that he was bound for Mexico in his favorite role, pacifier of "inferior" peoples. Early in the morning of April 19, some twenty-four hours before Wilson ordered the navy's assault, Funston recalled the Fifth Brigade of his division from Houston. The same day, Secretary Garrison assured Wood that he would command the Mexican expedition and handed him his instructions:

I am directed by the President to designate you as Commander-in-Chief of the land forces of the United States operating in Mexico, and in addition to appoint you as Commanding General of the First Field Army, consisting of such troops as may be assigned to it. The base of operations of the First Field Army will be Vera Cruz.

Your mission is to establish order in Mexico.[78]

On April 20, as Funston gathered his expedition, a force he himself was to command, the diplomatic crisis manufactured by the Wilson Administration deepened. In a cabinet meeting that day, the president stunned his associates by stating that it was a "terrible responsibility" for him to take a course that might lead to war and he asked them to pray for guidance. The same day, Wilson's congressional leaders introduced a joint resolution authorizing the president to use the armed forces to "enforce demands made on Victoriano Huerta," although the Democrats rejected the commitment of forces solely to safeguard American lives and property. The resolution passed on April 22 by a vote of 337-37, after Vera Cruz was occupied and blood shed.

Late on April 20 the State Department received a cable from a consular officer in Vera Cruz that a German freighter with arms for Huerta would put in the next day. Hurriedly, Wilson ordered the navy to seize the customshouse at Vera Cruz. On the morning of April 21 navy and marine corps landing parties took Vera Cruz, but not without a battle which killed nineteen Americans, wounded forty-seven, and caused five hundred Mexican casualties. Two days later, the Fifth Brigade, reinforced by part of the Second Division's cavalry and all its artillery and service units, sailed for Mexico.

Secretary Garrison, in the meantime, was urging the open adoption of the General Staff's war plan for Mexico, since the Vera Cruz landing had set off anti-American violence all over Mexico. Wilson, however, stopped the Second Division's deployment on April 25 and arranged negotiations with the Huerta government through the diplomatic representatives of Argentina, Brazil, and Chile. Nevertheless, it seemed that the United States was still on the brink of a wider war, and the units of the Second Division which remained in Texas intensified their training with new enthusiasm and sense of purpose.[79]

In Vera Cruz and Texas City, the army acted as if the Vera Cruz affair was only the first step in a major military campaign. To command the Second Division, the War Department assigned Major General J. Franklin Bell, an officer high in the officer corps' esteem and affection and a general superior to Wood in every way except political power and physical energy. Bell, a Scot-Irish farmboy from Kentucky who had been graduated from West Point in 1878, was virtually unknown outside the army in 1914. Serving in the Philippines from 1899 until 1903, Bell's intellectual acuity and physical vigor made him a combat commander and colonial administrator without peer. He went to Manila a first lieutenant in the regular army. He returned a brigadier general with the Medal of Honor. After the war, Bell became a leader in the "new army," serving as the commandant of the Infantry and Cavalry School and on the General Staff. In 1906, at fifty, he became Chief of Staff. Stout and of medium height, Bell's normal aging had been complicated by diabetes, but by 1913 he had recovered some of his energy and had lost little mentally. Under his command, the Second Division was to reach its highest point of readiness, and its officers judged his training the most educational and rigorous they received in Texas.[80]

The Vera Cruz crisis also brought the Fourth Brigade a new commander, Brigadier General Hunter Liggett. In appearance, Liggett could not have been more different from Bullard. Well over six feet and weighing over two hundred pounds, still wearing the close-cropped mustache affected by army officers commissioned in the 1880s, Liggett dwarfed the thin commander of the Twenty-Sixth Infantry. Liggett was at peace with himself and the world, but below his genial, unexcitable public personality was an original military mind and driving will. As he told another general, he had no fat above his neck and his record proved it even before World War I. Liggett, raised in Reading, Pennsylvania, by his tailor-father, had graduated from West Point in 1879 and served with the Fifth Infantry on the frontier. Always a reader and a student, especially of military history, Liggett's rise was meteoric when the officer corps went academic after the war with Spain. Unlike some of his peers, however, he always remembered that the training in tactical theory was meant to be practiced and that generalship was more than devising a brilliant scheme of maneuver on a map. After his War College tour, Liggett had been ordered to command the Fourth Brigade, but he had then been assigned a temporary administrative post in Chicago. After Vera Cruz, however, he quickly got to Texas City and his brigade.[81]

Under Bell's direction and Liggett's command, the Fourth Brigade went through the most realistic and useful training Bullard had seen in the army. Bell and Liggett accepted the fact that the Texas City camp was uncomfortable and the terrain uninteresting, but they did not agonize about these circumstances. Instead they designed problems which they took from the Mexican contingency plan, forced their subordinates to conform to the terrain and the problem's assumptions, and arranged a series of night exercises which included digging trenches. Bullard was amazed at the regimental commanders' resistance to the training, especially since in all their problems they never had to cope with war's greatest burden on a commander, the care of his own casualties. Bullard was once more convinced that nine-tenths of the objections officers raised to any policy came from a fear of any change, not from criticism of the policy's merits.[82] He himself concentrated not on tactics, but the whole range of command problems. And he watched Liggett command the brigade and studied his methods. Before Liggett left Texas for the Philippines in August, the two officers had gained a solid appreciation for each other's abilities.[83]

Bell drove his troops with the sincere conviction that they would be needed in Mexico. He wrote to Brigadier General Pershing, poised with his brigade at El Paso, that he thought Pershing was wrong in thinking that the United States would not continue what it had begun at Vera Cruz. Bell thought that order had to be restored in Mexico and that the Mexicans could never do it themselves. "I say, NEVER! and I mean it!"[84] Yet hardly had Bell made his point than President Huerta fled into exile, the Constitutionalists paraded into Mexico City, and Carranza began soothing the Wilson Administration with talk of a democratic provisional government and free elections. The Vera Cruz crisis was over.

As suddenly as it had begun, the Second Division's training slackened and the demoralization of inaction once more seized the troops, including the colonel of the Twenty-Sixth Infantry. Liggett departed, and Bullard was again brigade commander, but he concentrated on his golf and polo rather than his command. He was depressed by the fact that of all the Volunteer colonels appointed in 1899, only he and one other officer were still active and still colonels. Ten of the others had become generals. Even the new war in Europe did not prod his interest. "I somehow feel no especial desire to see it. I suppose it is because I have not the means to go. Poor always, broke always. I've never been ready for such things."[85] The only thing he took real satisfaction in was the fact that his second son, Peter Cleary, graduated fifth in the Academy's class of 1914 as a second lieutenant of engineers, reported to the Second Division for duty and became his father's companion. Bullard wanted to take leave and go to Detroit, but there was new fighting in Mexico between Carranza's forces and the armies of his Con-stitutionalist rivals, Pancho Villa and Emiliano Zapata. Finally, he got away in November when Rose's stepfather died in Chattanooga, and he spent another visitor's Christmas with his family in Detroit.[86]

Even though the Fifth Brigade was withdrawn from Vera Cruz in November and the immediate prospect of intervention waned, Bell kept the Second Division on a demanding training schedule. Bullard found his brigade committed to a daily schedule of training and special schools organized by the division staff. For the first time in his career, he lived by a printed training schedule designed by someone else and then delivered to him fresh from the division's whirring mimeographs. It was a frightening experience: "One must carry his schedule with him at all times or he hopelessly wanders therefrom and is lost. You must hold it before you at all times as a mariner does his compass. . . . There is in all a terrible, strained, hunted look-of-the-schedule feeling that gives him no rest. All will be glad when it is over."[87] As the anniversary of his second year at Texas City came, Bullard was absorbed in Bell's accelerated training, in routine paperwork, in the division training section's battery of tests and special schools, and in athletics. For amusement he took up roller-skating and motorcycling, interesting sports for a fifty-three-year-old man. The Division again held realistic maneuvers, and Bullard grappled again with what he considered the important functions of brigade command: intelligence gathering, communications, supply, and transportation. Once more he concentrated on writing and carefully explaining his plans to his subordinates, being convinced that no time spent in planning and briefing was expendable. He enjoyed the challenge of handling his supporting units of cavalry, artillery, engineers, ambulances, supply wagons, and signal troops. Of all these concerns, he found supply matters the most critical and most neglected by his officers.[88]

An expeditionary force without an expedition, an advance guard without a main body, the Second Division lingered on in Texas through the summer of 1915. Bullard had long since accepted the idea that there would be no war with Mexico. He viewed his service with the division as an educational peacetime experience. In its two and a half years of existence, the division had trained, he estimated, more than a third of the officers in the Line. It had conducted all sorts of field exercises and had tested the army's experimental equipment. Bullard was now convinced that the army had overemphasized the tactical training of officers and ignored the critical problems of organizing, supplying, and moving large bodies of men. "In these things we are wholly unprepared for war." The Second Division itself had never been large enough to test the officer corps' capacity for organizing a mass army, but Bullard hoped that the War Department would keep it intact as a training unit.[89]

Bullard's own contributions to the Second Division's readiness in 1914 and 1915 were not underestimated by Bell. The division commander judged Bullard one of the two best infantry colonels he knew. Bullard was completely fit for the command of a brigade or division in wartime, as an instructor to the National Guard or army schools, as a member of the General Staff, or for any other highly responsible duty which demanded complete military knowledge and broad experience. Bell reported that Bullard had all the qualities of a general officer: energy, thoughtfulness, physical capacity, thorough professional knowledge, and a driving will. Again, Bullard had flourished in an assignment demanding energy, adaptability, and persistence.[90]

The Second Division's campsite had always been a burden, and two and a half years of occupation had not changed its rude and monotonous character. With every improvement, with every wooden building constructed, with every tent strong-backed, with every messhall screened, the War Department's reluctance to close the camp grew. Few thought the location attractive. Wood found the Second Division demoralized by the thought of another winter in Texas City when he visited the troops in 1915; even the rugged Wood thought the mud and flatlands depressing.[91] Bell made a special trip to Washington to get the General Staff to rotate other regiments into the division; he also proposed that service with the division count as an overseas tour for officers. He reported that some of his officers were begging to be sent to the Philippines to escape Texas City.[92]

Bullard had no love for the Second Division's tent camp or for the high cost of living in Texas City. Only in the summer of 1915, when Rose and young Rose came to visit him and Peter Cleary, did Bullard participate in the weekly dinner-dances and receptions arranged by the officers' wives. He preferred polo and duck hunting. As a senior colonel he could afford to be stand-offish, and his lack of sociability probably enhanced his reputation for self-discipline and love of duty. Unfortunately there seemed no way to get out of the place or arrange another station for his regiment, since, by the summer of 1915, most of the army was camped along the Mexican border.[93]

Nature solved the War Department's dilemma and eliminated the Texas City camp. On August 17, 1915, a violent Caribbean hurricane devastated the Galveston-Texas City area with high winds and tidal waves. The destruction left by the storm was appalling: ten soldiers dead, most personal belongings and uniforms gone, animals drowned, the wells polluted, camp buildings reduced to kindling, military equipment and supplies washed away or ruined. After the storm, the War Department's only decision was where to send the units of the Second Division and how fast they might be reorganized and moved.[94]

Only one regiment escaped the holocaust: Bullard's Twenty-Sixth Infantry. Only twenty hours before the hurricane visited Texas City, the Twenty-Sixth had entrained for posts in the lower valley of the Rio Grande, their tour with the Second Division ended. Behind them was the hurricane, ahead the military pacification of part of Texas.

NOTES

[1]Office of the Chief of Staff to Secretary of War Lindley M. Garrison, memorandum, "The Army as an Educator," June 1914, File 350, Office of the Secretary of War Decimal File, "Correspondence Received, 1913-1922," Record Group 107, National Archives.

[2]"Report of the Secretary of War," and "Report of the Chief of Staff," *Annual Reports of the War Department, 1913,* (Washington: Government Printing Office, 1913), I, pp. 3-193.

³Maj. Gen. L. Wood to H. L. Stimson, September 19, 1913, Leonard Wood Papers.

⁴Maj. Gen. L. Wood, "Memorandum for the Adjutant General," February 7, 1914, attached to Wood Diaries, Wood Papers.

⁵H. L. Stimson to Maj. Gen. L. Wood, March 1, 1913, Wood Papers.

⁶Maj. J. G. Harbord to Brig. Gen. F. MacIntyre, April 16, 1913, "Private Letters," V, James G. Harbord Papers.

⁷The Adjutant General's Office, "Memorandum on S. 10599, 61st Congress, 3d Session," February 7, 1911, File 6273, Office of the Chief of Staff Correspondence, 1907-1917, Record Group 165, National Archives.

⁸Maj. Gen. T. H. Barry to Maj. Gen. L. Wood, November 6, 1913, Wood Papers; Maj. Gen. William H. Carter, *The American Army* (Indianapolis: Bobbs-Merrill, 1915), pp. 219-243.

⁹Arthur S. Link, *Wilson: The New Freedom* (Princeton, N.J.: Princeton University Press, 1956), pp. 55-144; Edward H. Brooks, "The National Defense Policy of the Wilson Administration, 1913-1917" (unpublished Ph.D. dissertation, Stanford University, 1950), pp. 1-18.

¹⁰Henry L. Stimson Diary, "Personal Reminiscences, 1911-1912" II, supplementary section, pp. 12-14, Henry L. Stimson Papers.

¹¹Hugh L. Scott, *Some Memories of a Soldier* (New York: Century Company, 1928), pp. 469-470, 569.

¹²Diarybook 6, entries, October 10-23, 1912, BP.

¹³Lois Prance and James R. Irwin, "History of Fort Wayne," *Michigan History Magazine* 30 (January-March 1946), pp. 5-40; Wade Millis, "Fort Wayne, Michigan," *Michigan History Magazine* 20 (Winter 1936), pp. 21-30.

¹⁴The Adjutant General's Office *Official Army Register, 1913* (Washington: Government Printing Office, 1913), pp. 381-384.

¹⁵November and December 1912, Returns, Twenty-Sixth Infantry Regiment, reel 266, "Returns of Regular Army Infantry Regiments, June 1821 to December 1916," MC 665, National Archives.

¹⁶Diarybook 6, entry, November 21, 1912, BP.

¹⁷Diarybook 6, entries, December 11 and 15, 1912 and January 9, 1913, BP; Col. R. L. Bullard to Lt. Col. G. C. Lewis, October 28. 1912, Clarence R. Edwards Papers, Massachusetts Historical Society.

¹⁸Diarybook 6, entries, December 15, 1912 and January 13, 1913, BP.

¹⁹Diarybook 6, entry, January 27, 1913, BP.

²⁰*Army and Navy Journal*, February 22, 1913.

²¹For the diplomatic background, see Kenneth J. Grieb, *The United States and Huerta* (Lincoln, Neb.: University of Nebraska Press, 1969), and Clarence C. Clendenen, *The United States and Pancho Villa* (Ithaca, N. Y.: Cornell University Press, 1961).

²²Henry L. Stimson Diary, "Personal Reminiscences, 1911-1912" II, pp. 115-118, and supplementary section, pp. 1-5, Stimson Papers.

²³Wood Diary, entry, February 24, 1913, Wood Papers; *Army and Navy Journal*, February 8 and 15, 1913.

²⁴Diarybook 6, entry, March 2, 1913, BP; February 1913, Returns, Twenty-Sixth Infantry, reel 266, MC 665.

²⁵Diarybook 6, entry, March 2, 1913, BP.

²⁶Brig. Gen. C. R. Edwards to Brig. Gen. George Andrews, March 10, 1913, and to Col. C. G. Treat, March 10, 1913, both in the Edwards Papers.

[27]Diarybook 6, entry, March 7, 1913, BP.

[28]Diarybook 6, entry, Ma.ch 17, 1913, BP.

[29]Wood Diary, entry, April 12, 1913, Wood Papers.

[30]Maj. Gen. L. Wood to Maj. Gen. W. H. Carter, April 1, 1913, Wood Papers; "Sanitation, Second Division," in "Report of the Surgeon-General," *Annual Reports of the War Department, 1913*, I, pp. 483-485; *Army and Navy Journal,* March 15 and 22, 1913.

[31]Brig. Gen. C. R. Edwards to Brig. Gen. W. W. Wotherspoon, March 15, 1913, Edwards Papers.

[32]Notebook 20, entry, May 14, 1913, BP; Bullard Autobiography, pp. 105-107, BP; *Army and Navy Journal,* May 3 and July 12, 1913; "Efficiency Record of Bullard, Robert L.," report by Maj. Gen. W. H. Carter, 1913, Bullard 201 File.

[33]Notebook 20, entry, May 15, 1913, BP.

[34]Notebook 20, entries, May 12-15, 1913, BP.

[35]Wood diary, entry, January 4, 1913, Wood Papers; Maj. W. S. Graves, GS, memo to Gen. Wood, January 1913, Wood Papers; *Army and Navy Journal,* February 15, 1913; Diarybook 6, entry, March 26, 1913, BP.

[36]Diarybook 6, entry, March 26 and April 7, 1913, BP; Sen. J. F. Johnston to W. Wilson, April 17, 1913, Bullard AGO File.

[37]L. M. Garrison to Brig. Gen. T. H. Bliss, April 21, 1913, Col. 173, Tasker H. Bliss Papers; *Army and Navy Journal,* April 26, 1913.

[38]Diarybook 6, entries, April 24 and 28, 1913, BP.

[39]Diarybook 6, entry, May 18, 1913, BP; Brig. Gen. C. R. Edwards to L. M. Garrison, April 26, 1913, and Brig. Gen. C. R. Edwards to W. Pedigo, April 26, 1913, both Edwards Papers; Brig. Gen. C. R. Edwards to Maj. J. G. Harbord, May 7, 1913, "Private Letters" V, Harbord Papers.

[40]Diarybook 6, entry, August 12, 1913, BP.

[41]Link, *Wilson: The New Freedom,* pp. 347-416.

[42]Brig. Gen. T. H. Bliss to Brig. Gen. W. Crozier (President, AWC), May 12, 1913, Vol. 160, Bliss Papers; Brig. Gen. T. H. Bliss to Maj. Gen. L. Wood, May 14, 1913, Wood Papers.

[43]Memo, Secretary of War to Secretary of State, "Conditions on the Mexican Frontier," August 18, 1913, Vol. 173, Bliss Papers.

[44]Wood Diary, entry, July 21, 1913, Wood Papers; Brig. Gen. W. H. Carter, "Report of the Second Division," *Annual Reports of the War Department, 1913*, III, pp. 113-120.

[45]*Army and Navy Journal,* September 27, 1913.

[46]Col. E. F. Glenn to Maj. Gen. L. Wood, May 16 and June 16, 1913, Wood Papers; Notebook 20, entries, May 27 and June 11, 1913, BP.

[47]Diarybook 6, entries, June 1-July 10, 1913, BP; Col. R. L. Bullard, "Occupying United States Soldiers," *JMSI*, 174, (May 1914), pp. 388-397.

[48]Notebook 21, entry, August 1913, BP.

[49]Diarybook 6, entry, July 10, 1913, BP. The activities of the Brigade may be followed in May-August, 1913, Returns, Twenty-Sixth Infantry Regiment, reel 266, MC 665.

[50]Notebook 20, entry, July 31, 1913, and Notebook 21, entries, August 2 and 9, 1913, BP.

[51]*Army and Navy Journal,* September 20 and October 25, 1913.

[52]Brig. Gen. W. H. Carter to J. McG. Dickinson, November 24, 1913, Jacob McGavock

Dickinson Papers, Tennessee State Library and Archives; Brig. Gen. T. H. Bliss to Brig. Gen. H. L. Scott, September 25, 1913, Vol. 171, Bliss Papers.

⁵³Wood Diary, entry, January 27, 1914, and memo, "Assignment of Brigadier-Generals," 1913, both Wood Papers; Maj. Gen. W. W. Wotherspoon to Brig. Gen. T. H. Bliss, November 14, 1914, Vol. 176, Bliss Papers.

⁵⁴Brig. Gen. T. F. Davis, "Efficiency Record of Bullard, Robert L.," 1914, Bullard 201 File.

⁵⁵Notebook 21, entry, October 14, 1913, BP.

⁵⁶The account of his hospitalization is from Diarybook 7, entries for October 1913, and Notebook 21, entries, October 10-November 7, 1913, BP; TAGO, "Statement of Medical Record in the Case of Maj. Gen. Robert L. Bullard, USA," February 23, 1922, Bullard 201 File.

⁵⁷Maj. Gen. L. Wood to Lt. Col. W. H. Johnston, November 20, 1913, Wood Papers.

⁵⁸Col. R. L. Bullard to Capt. G. H. McMaster, November 2, 1913, BP; Notebook 21, entries, October 29 and November 3, 1913, BP.

⁵⁹Diarybook 7, entry, November 30, 1913, BP.

⁶⁰Diarybook 7, entry, December 4, 1913, BP.

⁶¹Notebook 21, entry, September 12, 1913, BP.

⁶²Notebook 21, entry, December 9, 1913, BP.

⁶³Diarybook 7, entry, November 20, 1913, BP.

⁶⁴Notebook 21, December 9, 1913, BP.

⁶⁵War Department General Staff Report No. 10670 with appendices, September 29, 1913, Office of the Chief of Staff, "General Correspondence, 1907-1917," and "Appointment to Grade of Brigadier General, U.S. Army," File 7890, AWC Division General Correspondence, 1903-1919, both RG 165.

⁶⁶Captain George Van Horn Moseley, GS, "Commissioned Personnel of the Army," February 22, 1914, appended to WDGS Report No. 10670.

⁶⁷Maj. Gen. W. W. Wotherspoon to Brig. Gen. J. J. Pershing, May 13 and October 28, 1914, General Correspondence, John J. Pershing Papers; Brig. Gen. E. H. Crowder to Brig. Gen. T. H. Bliss, January 7, 1914, Vol. 188, Bliss Papers; Brig. Gen. T. H. Bliss to Col. C. J. Crane, May 22, 1915, Vol. 190, Bliss Papers.

⁶⁸Brig. Gen. T. H. Bliss to Maj. Gen. W. W. Wotherspoon, April 27, 1914, Vol. 162, Bliss Papers.

⁶⁹Brig. Gen. T. H. Bliss to L. M. Garrison, October 16, 1914, Vol. 165, Bliss Papers.

⁷⁰Wood Diary, entries, March 12 and June 15, Wood Papers; Leonard Wood, memo for the Adjutant General, "List of Officers Qualified for Appointment Brigadier Generals of Volunteers," June 9, 1914, Wood Papers.

⁷¹Lt. Col. M. W. Ireland to Lt. Col. J. R. Kean, June 9, 1914, Correspondence, 1890-1950, Jefferson Randolph Kean Papers, University of Virginia Library.

⁷²Brig. Gen. H. L. Scott to Col. C. J. Crane, December 5, 1914, Scott Papers.

⁷³In addition to the sources already cited, see Robert E. Quirk, *An Affair of Honor: Woodrow Wilson and the Occupation of Vera Cruz* (Lexington, Ky.: University of Kentucky Press, 1962).

⁷⁴Brig. Gen. F. Funston to Maj. Gen. L. Wood, March 23 and 31, 1914, Wood Papers; *Army and Nayy Journal,* December 27, 1913 and February 7, 1914.

⁷⁵Brig. Gen. F. Funston to Maj. Gen. L. Wood, April 15, 1914; April 1914, Returns, Twenty-Sixth Infantry, reel 266, MC 665.

[76]Maj. Gen. Leonard Wood, "Memorandum for the Secretary of War," April 15, 1914, appended to Wood Diary, Wood Papers.

[77]L. M. Garrison to Woodrow Wilson, April 18, 1914, appended to Wood Diary, Wood Papers.

[78]Wood Diary, entry, April 20, 1914, with appended order, Secretary of War to Maj. Gen. L. Wood, Wood Papers.

[79]Link, *Wilson: The New Freedom,* pp. 392-394, 395-405; *Army and Navy Journal,* April 25, 1914.

[80]"James Franklin Bell," *Dictionary of American Biography: Supplement One* (New York: Charles Scribner's Sons, 1944), XXI, pp. 67-68; Allen D. Albert, Jr., "The Roosevelt of the Army," *Munsey's Magazine* 36 (October 1906), pp. 52-60; Maj. Gen. J. F. Bell to J. McG. Dickinson, April 25, 1910, Dickinson Papers; T. Roosevelt to C. W. Eliot, September 22, 1906, Roosevelt Papers; Maj. Gen. L. Wood to Maj. Gen. H. L. Scott, March 26, 1915, Scott Papers.

[81]"Hunter Liggett," *Dictionary of American Biography: Supplement One,* XXI, pp. 494-495; B. H. Liddell Hart, *Reputations: Ten Years After* (Boston: Little, Brown, 1928). pp. 261-286.

[82]Notebook 23, entries, May 9 and 10, 1914, BP.

[83]On the Second Division's training, see Col. R. L. Bullard, "Impressions of Service with the 2d Division in Texas," *Infantry Journal* 11 (November-December 1914), pp. 353-359, and the draft manuscript "Some Impressions of a Year and a Half of Camp and Maneuver," 1914, BP; "Report of the Chief of Staff," *Annual Reports of the War Department, 1914* (Washington: Government Printing Office, 1914), I, pp 75-137; *Army and Navy Journal,* August 8, 1914; Maj. Gen. J. F. Bell to Brig. Gen. J. J. Pershing, June 20, 1914, General Correspondence, Pershing Papers; Hunter Liggett, *Commanding an American Army,* (Boston: Houghton Mifflin, 1925), pp. 1-3.
On Liggett and Bullard, see quote by Liggett in Bullard Autobiography, p. A-1-4, and pp. 105-106, and Diarybook 7, entries, June, 1914, BP.

[84]Maj. Gen. J. F. Bell to Brig. Gen. J. J. Pershing, August 1, 1914, General Correspondence, Pershing Papers.

[85]Diarybook 7, August 8, 1914, BP.

[86]Diarybook 7, entries, September-December, 1914, BP; August-December 1914, Returns, Twenty-Sixth Infantry, reel 266, MC 665.

[87]Notebook 23, entry, February 5, 1915, BP; Maj. Gen. J. F. Bell to Brig. Gen. J. J. Pershing, December 8, 1914, General Correspondence, Pershing Papers.

[88]Diarybook 7, entries, February-August 1915, BP; Notebook 23, entry, May 25, 1915, BP; Col. R. L. Bullard, "Impressions of Service with the 2nd Division in Texas," *Infantry Journal* 12 (July-August 1915), pp. 32-37, and "Tactical Instruction in the Brigade," *mss* (1917), BP.

[89]Notebook 23, entries, February 6 and May 28, 1915, BP.

[90]Reports of Major General Bell, "Efficiency Record of Bullard, Robert L.," 1914 and 1915, Bullard 201 File.

[91]Maj. Gen. L. Wood to Maj. Gen. H. L. Scott, March 26, 1915, Scott Papers.

[92]*Army and Navy Journal,* June 5, 1915.

[93]Diarybook 7, entries, July 1915, BP: *Army and Navy Journal,* July 17 and August 21, 1915; Mrs. William Paulding memoir, pp. 147-148, USAMHRC.

[94]*Army and Navy Journal,* August 21, 1915.

15

Pacification in the Lower Valley of the Rio Grande 1915-1917

Although it had its share of violence, the lower valley of the Rio Grande failed to prosper before the twentieth century because it lacked money, water, and a transportation system.[1] The potential of the area, now the Texas counties of Cameron, Willacy, Hidalgo, and Starr, was recognized by Spanish settlers who came there to raise horses, sheep, and cattle. Around their ranches and the banks of the Rio Grande, Mexican drovers and farmers settled to ride for the *hacendados* or to work the land along the river. By the Civil War, Anglo-American settlers had superimposed themselves upon the resident Mexican culture in two basic activities, commerce and ranching. Brownsville, across the river from Matamoros in the Mexican state of Tamaulipas, served the army garrison at Fort Brown and served as an entrepôt for American goods brought by sea and transshipped through Matamoros into Mexico. Brownsville also served the Anglo-owned ranches to the north and west. For the rest of the nineteenth century, ranching and the commercial life of Brownsville dominated the social and economic life of the Anglo settlers.

From the War for Texas Independence (1836) until the rise of Porfirio Díaz, the lower valley was plagued by race war and banditry. It was often hard to tell which was which. Anglo sheriffs and constables were scarce; the state of Texas occasionally provided Texas Rangers, pick-up squads of frontier toughs whose courage was matched only by their love of *ley fuga* when dealing with Mexicans. Peace-keeping remained a citizens' affair, bordering on vigilantism, and the big American ranchers hired their own guards to patrol their herds. In 1859 the civil law enforcement, which had managed to produce little better than an armed truce between the Anglos and Mexicans, broke down, and the lower valley was scourged by Mexican guerrillas led by Juan Cortina, a xenophobic rancher. Cortina's "war" was finally quashed by a punitive expedition of army troops, Texas Rangers, and Texas volunteers.[2]

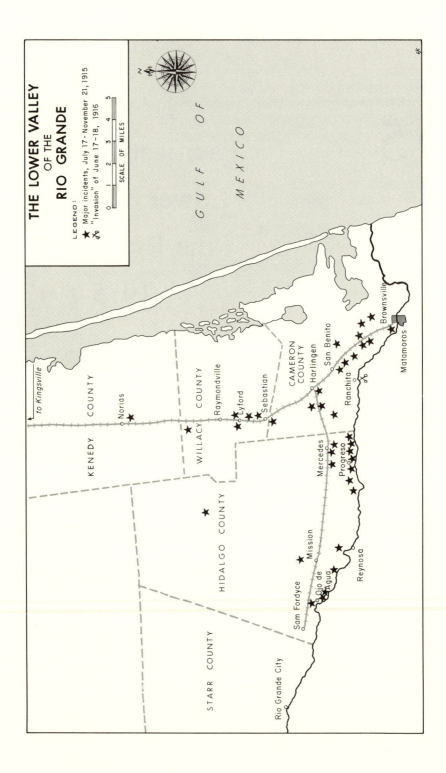

THE LOWER VALLEY
OF THE
RIO GRANDE

LEGEND:

★ Major incidents, July 17 - November 21, 1915

⚔ "Invasion" of June 17–18, 1916

SCALE OF MILES

0   1   2   3   4   5

GULF OF MEXICO

Brownsville

Matamoros

San Benito

Harlingen

Ranchita

CAMERON COUNTY

Raymondville

Lyford

Sebastian

WILLACY COUNTY

Norias

KENEDY COUNTY

to Kingsville

Mercedes

Progreso

Reynosa

HIDALGO COUNTY

Mission

Sam Fordyce

Ojo de Agua

STARR COUNTY

Rio Grande City

In the first decade of the twentieth century, the character of the lower valley began to change. After several decades of failure, the Anglo first families of the lower valley succeeded in raising the capital necessary to build the economic foundations for sustained growth: a railroad and the beginnings of a vast irrigation system. Plagued by financial and engineering false starts, the St. Louis, Brownsville, and Mexico Railroad was completed between Brownsville and Corpus Christi in 1904, and by 1905 a western branch had been built to Sam Fordyce with spurs both north and south. Along both the main road to Corpus Christi and the Sam Fordyce branch, new towns were created and settled, including, on the north-south line, San Benito, Harlingen, Lyford, Raymondville, and Kingsville. On the Sam Fordyce branch, which joined the main road at Harlingen, the Anglo first families incorporated a string of towns, among them Mercedes, Donna, Pharr, McAllen, and Mission. Where there had been only crossroads stores in 1900, there were in 1910 communities of new inhabitants.

The drawing power of the railroad and new towns was farming. The problem was getting credit to finance an irrigation system capable of sustaining orchards and truck gardens. With limited capital, the citizens of Brownsville created enough ditches to irrigate 500 acres by 1900. This success established their credit and attracted outside financing. By 1911 over 53,000 irrigated acres were under cultivation, growing vegetables, fruits, and nuts for commercial markets. The semi-tropical lower valley was well on its way to becoming an Eden along the Rio Grande by 1915. The population jumped from 34,401 in 1900 to 54,037 in 1910, a rate of increase unmatched since the Civil War. The development of the lower valley was a Chamber of Commerce's dream.

The outbreak of the Mexican Revolution in 1910 did not immediately affect the lower valley. The border itself had been fairly peaceful since the 1880s. The revolution came to the lower valley in 1913 when the garrison at Matamoros joined Huerta and was shortly beseiged and captured by a *carranzista* force. Mexicans of American citizenship died south of the Rio Grande and *huertista* refugees sought asylum across the river. American citizens, Anglo and Mexican, lost lands and property in Tamaulipas.

The responsibility of keeping the revolution south of the Rio Grande belonged in part to the United States Army. The army's main task was to prevent the organized battles for the Mexican border towns from including the neighboring American towns. Since American troops were ordered not to cross the border and not to fire across the border unless the Mexicans intentionally shot into the American onlookers and their property, the mission was frustrating. The army could do little more than make formal protests and try to control the movement of civilians north of the border. As General Bliss pointed out in 1913, he could not guarantee anyone's safety until either the Mexicans stopped fighting or he occupied the Mexican border towns and created a buffer zone south of the Rio Grande.[3] The other phase of the army's duties, preventing battles north of the border, was even more thankless. The traditional Anglo-Mexican hostility among the border citizens was stimulated by the revolution and complicated by the fact that some Anglo and Mexican groups wanted either to provoke a military intervention or to aid one or another of the revolutionary factions. Ordinary crimes masqueraded as revolutionary activity. Civilian law enforcement was confused and often ineffective, since Anglo peace officers became increasingly trigger-happy, vigilantism flourished, and Mexican-American constables and judges were paralyzed by their fear of persecuting their *compañeros*. In 1914, in the wake of the Vera Cruz affair, the Anglo border citizens feared that they would be either raided or invaded in retaliation and called for reliable (Anglo) peace-keeping forces. Bliss was sure that the fear came from local race hatred: "The curious thing is that most communities that ask for troops couple their request with a statement that they are not afraid of Mexico but are afraid of their own Mexican residents and citizens."[4]

Bliss' preferred strategy remained the creation of a border neutral zone, but he recognized that this would probably mean war with Mexico and do little to solve the problem of Anglo-Mexican conflict within the United States. His most fervent hope was that the local peace officers, Texas Rangers, and the Texas National Guard might patrol the border towns, but he feared with reason that the anti-Mexican bias of these forces would simply increase violence. He concluded unhappily that the army would have to take a role in pacifying the Rio Grande frontier.[5] In the summer of 1914 the War Department, pressured by the governor of Texas and the Texas congressional delegation, transferred more units to Bliss' command for the border patrol.

The officer directly supervising the border patrols was Brigadier General James Parker, commander of the First Cavalry Brigade. Parker had mellowed not a bit with age and rank. He had his reasons. His three cavalry regiments were given a nine-hundred-mile border to patrol and protect, and he thought that the restrictions placed on his men were odious. Scattered into sixteen different posts and more than thirty outposts, his force could only react and chase, leaving the initiative to the bandits. Incensed, Parker went to Wshington to protest his restrictive orders, but made no headway with the General Staff. He was told that Bliss' conduct of the border patrols was governed by the president himself and that he would have to accept the restrictions.[6]

Initially, the lower valley was not one of Parker's prime headaches. Until the Vera Cruz affair, the biggest activity in the area was the shipment of arms to Matamoros for the use of the *carranzistas*; only the merchants at El Paso did a bigger volume business.[7] After Vera Cruz, however, an epidemic of insecurity hit the lower valley. The Anglos feared either an invasion or a Mexican-American uprising, while the Mexicans were terrified that they would be massacred or deported by the Anglos. The governor of Texas tried to quiet the area by sending a thousand National Guardsmen to Brownsville, an act that so troubled Bliss that he offered to replace the Guardsmen with his own soldiers. The Brownsville-Matamoros area, however, quieted down in the summer of 1914 and business on the American side returned to normal.[8] Rumors of bloodshed persisted, and the munitions kept flowing into Mexico. Even though the lower valley again subsided into a restless peace, few thought that the Mexican Revolution had left the Rio Grande frontier for good.[9]

1.

In January 1915 a deputy sheriff for Hidalgo County arrested one Brasilio Ramos, Jr., in McAllen, Texas, for illegal entry. In Ramos' possession were two letters and a copy of a revolutionary *pronunciamiento*, the Plan of San Diego. The Plan startled the Texas civil authorities who saw it: it called for the Mexican-Americans of the lower valley to seize all the lost territories of 1848 and to help American Negroes create a black national state in the midwest. In this great adventure the Mexicans and Negroes would enlist their brothers, the American Indians, in a crusade against Anglo-American tyranny and capitalism. The uprising was supposed to begin in February with raids, extortion, and massacres in the lower valley. The American authorities treated Ramos' documents as a hysterical fantasy.[10]

Learning of the Plan of San Diego, citizens' groups in the lower valley petitioned Governor James G. Ferguson for more protection and appealed for army troops as well as Texas Rangers, but Ferguson and Major General Frederick Funston, Bliss' successor at San Antonio, were unconvinced that the lower valley was in great peril. Undeniably, there was rustling, smuggling, and thievery, but these were problems to be handled by local peace officers. Nevertheless, Ferguson increased the Texas Ranger force in the lower valley and Funston kept the Third Cavalry (under Colonel A. P. Blocksom) stationed at Fort Brown and its environs. A squadron of the Twelfth Cavalry picked up the border patrol along the Sam Fordyce branch of the railroad. Funston was not enthusiastic about army peacekeeping, but he hoped that it would calm the civilians and he thought that his troopers would be more effective than the Texas militia the governor might send.[11]

In May 1915, however, the turmoil in the lower valley reached epidemic proportions, for civil authorities were receiving almost daily reports of a bandit gang robbing outlying farms and ranches of arms, horses, cows, equipment, and food. Led by two American citizens, Luis de la Rosa and Aniceto Pizano, the guerrillas, numbering between twenty-five and a hundred, were the self-appointed vanguard of the Plan of San Diego army. Since the guerrillas had terrorized their countrymen, it was difficult to learn much about them. Local authorities claimed they were Mexican invaders sponsored by Carranza; the army regarded them as outlaws motivated by money and revenge upon their Anglo neighbors.

Emboldened by their successes at equipping themselves and paralyzing the isolated ranchers, the guerrillas made attacks near lower valley towns in July 1915. They robbed two stores, burned a railway bridge, and on July 17 killed two men near the Willacy County line. The response to these incidents was no less alarming, particularly to the Mexican-American citizens of the lower valley.

Although unable to make contact with the guerrillas, local deputies, Texas Rangers, and private citizens killed two Mexican suspects in Mercedes, allowed another to be lynched, and generally terrorized the Mexican population.

On August 2 a mixed expedition of deputies, private citizens, and a squad of cavalrymen, investigating a report that the guerrillas were hiding at a ranch near San Benito, was ambushed. One soldier died and two civilians were wounded. The following day a force of Texas Rangers and deputies attacked another ranch, killing the Mexican rancher and his two sons, all suspected bandits. Perhaps in retaliation, the guerrillas executed two leaders of the Sebastian Law and Order League. There were sniping incidents at automobiles. The guerrillas also wounded a nightwatchman at a cotton gin near Lyford.[12]

Two days after the Sebastian killings, the lower valley was further alarmed by two major developments. On August 8 the guerrillas fought a pitched battle with seven civilians and eight troopers at a ranch near Norias on the main line of the railroad. The Mexicans pushed their charges with considerable ferocity, leaving five bodies and an equal number of wounded. The defenders had four wounded. Rescued by a force of Texas Rangers and deputies, the defenders found a flag inscribed "*Viva la Independencia de Texas.*" A number of documents described the guerrillas' association with the Plan of San Diego and named their contacts in the lower valley. The Rangers believed that they had sufficient evidence to track down the guerrillas and proclaimed the movement broken, but others were not so sure and telegrams sped to Austin asking for either the Texas National Guard or more army troops. The guerrillas also seemed to be getting help from Mexico. On the day after the Norias fight, American patrols near the Rio Grande exchanged shots with another band, and in the next week there were three more battles between the troopers and Mexicans along the river. Among the Mexicans were men in military uniforms, and on one occasion the ambushers had dug trenches. In the shooting two troopers died and two were wounded. The conclusion was that the local *carranzista* commander, General Emiliano Nafarrate, was supporting the guerrillas and perhaps had been their sponsor all along.

The reaction of the lower valley's Anglo population to the Sebastian killings, the Norias fight, and the riverbank skirmishing was hysterical. The hardware stores quickly sold out their firearms, vigilance committees were formed, and a reign of terror, led by the Texas Rangers and local peace officers, began against the Mexican-American population. Bullet-riddled bodies of Mexican men and boys appeared along the roads, and piles of "bandits" were photographed beside mass graves. Mexican refugees fled across the river into Tamaulipas, abandoning their property in Texas to Anglo confiscators. Before the lower valley quieted down months later, perhaps as many as one hundred and fifty Mexicans died, most shot either for being found with arms or for being identified as guerrilla sympathizers. Caught in the Anglo-Mexican vendetta, new settlers in the lower valley fled north. Perhaps as much as half of the lower valley's population of 70,000 became refugees. The major towns became armed camps, agitated by constant rumors of mass Mexican attacks and perhaps an invasion by the Mexican army. Although some of the Anglo citizens were contemptuous of the army's restrictions on killing Mexicans, others asked for more troops and a declaration of martial law.[13] Funston refused to accept the responsibility for governing the lower valley, but he dispatched two battalions of the Ninth Infantry to guard the towns along the railroad and to reinforce the garrison at Fort Brown. When Nafarrate, fearing an American invasion, also got reinforcements and Funston received more documents incriminating the Matamoros garrison in the guerrilla raids, Funston asked for additional troops. The War Department still regarded the war as a civil problem and better handled by civilian authorities, since the evidence of official Mexican intervention was negligible.[14] Nevertheless, Funston's request was granted, presumably to appease the Texans. Detached from the Second Division, the Twenty-Sixth Infantry entrained to join the pacification of the lower valley of the Rio Grande.

2.

Colonel Bullard and two battalions of the Twenty-Sixth Infantry arrived in Brownsville on August 15, prepared to defend Brownsville against General Nafarrate and the guerrillas. Another battalion was split up along the St. Louis, Brownsville, and Mexico's mainline at Kingsville and Harlingen and on the Sam Fordyce branch at Mercedes. Given command of the Brownsville Cavalry Patrol District, Bullard had his own regiment, three squadrons of cavalry, and two field artillery batteries, which he considered a fine command with which to pacify the border.[15] He quickly learned that the job would be no Sunday social.

Bullard's immediate concern was tactical, deciding how to deploy his regiment best. He accepted the advice of the Brownsville authorities and the cavalry officers of his command that the guerrillas were border-crossers. He stationed his own troops with the cavalry posts patrolling the fords and irrigation works along the Rio Grande. It was not a bad snap judgment, for the valley people had scared many of the guerrillas across the river along with their innocent countrymen. Some refugees, augmented by Mexican nationals from the Matamoros area, had increased the guerrillas forces. While the July and early August killings had happened well north of Brownsville, most of the incidents after Bullard's arrival occurred between the river and the Sam Fordyce branch of the railroad. In the first week of his command, Bullard's troops had four fights, three near Progreso and one farther west. One cavalryman was killed and two wounded, but the raiders did not get across the patrol cordon. The worrisome thing was that more raiders wore Mexican army uniforms, suggesting that Nafarrate accepted the border-crossers.[16]

Given an area one hundred miles along the Rio Grande and one hundred and fifty into the interior, Bullard's troops could not both patrol and protect all the towns. Despite the fact that both the Twenty-Sixth Infantry and the cavalry had small detachments scattered all over the lower valley and patrolled actively, some raiders punched through the cordon. On August 30 they burned a railroad bridge just north of Brownsville and two days later executed two men near an irrigation pumping station in the same area. These deaths were partially avenged the next day when the Hidalgo County sheriff's posse and a cavalry patrol killed eleven of a party which had looted the river hamlet of Ojo de Agua south of Mission. Again there was firing back and forth across the Rio Grande with what appeared to be a Mexican army unit.

After the Ojo de Agua clash, there was a week of quiet, but the lower valley was hardly peaceful. In San Antonio, Funston had asked for more troops and again got part of the Second Division. Within a week the Fourth Infantry and Sixth Cavalry arrived in the Brownsville Cavalry Patrol District, raising the number of troops in the lower valley to nearly four thousand. With the reinforcements came Colonel Blocksom of the Third Cavalry, who, being senior to Bullard, assumed command of the district. Bullard was miffed, thinking that General Parker had been forced to relieve him because his men had been too aggressive, but the change of command appears to have been routine. In fact, Parker favored his old friend by creating a "Twenty-Sixth Infantry District," which gave Bullard an independent command. It was not an inspired move, for Bullard recognized that the command arrangement incorrectly divided cavalry and infantry activities. He himself moved his head-quarters up the tracks to Harlingen and drew his troops back to Harlingen, San Benito, and Mercedes. His third battalion was split up between Lyford and Kingsville to the north. Another irritant was the fact that the Twenty-Sixth got a new lieutenant colonel, none other than Charles Muir, Bullard's classmate and professional detractor. Bullard gave him the San Benito command and avoided him as much as possible. Like the other pacification operations he had served in since 1885, the "battle" for the lower valley was getting more complicated.[17]

For Nafarrate in Matamoros, the guerrillas and Mexican refugees were a considerable embarrassment, since his soldiers sympathized with the insurgents. In an open letter to Bullard the Mexican commander pledged his neutrality and complained that his own troops could not patrol the riverbank without being fired upon. Nafarrate protested the treatment of Mexican nationals in Texas and expressed his grief over the massacre of Mexican-Americans. He hoped that he and American army officers could come to an agreement on the border-patrolling since he was under strict orders not to involve Mexico in the "Texas revolution." He also suggested that provocateurs might be trying to start a Mexican-American war.[18]

The valley people viewed Nafarrate's statements as hypocritical cant. Even Bullard took it skeptically, but he recognized after three weeks in the valley that Nafarrate was correct in charging the Anglos with widening the conflict with their massacres. When Bullard moved to Harlingen, he concentrated on quieting the civil population as well as chasing raiders.[19]

Traveling to the towns garrisoned by his men, Bullard tried to calm the citizens and get them to disband their vigilante groups. He also urged that the Texas peace-officers end their *ley fuga*, an appeal which included the suggestion that the local leaders ask for the recall of the Texas Rangers. He was conciliatory on the surface, but he seethed with contempt for the valley people. He learned that the authorities had capitulated to the most violent members of their towns and allowed the summary executions. He thought that the community leaders could hardly call themselves a government when they tolerated such measures.[20] Whatever his feelings, he was the soul of propriety, politely asking for cooperation with his patrols and for modified curfews in the towns.[21] In addition, he made a special effort to talk with newspaper reporters to explain his actions and quell the inevitable flood of rumors. He knew that the newspapers would print something and he preferred the truth, however depressing, because it was seldom as bad as speculation.[22] He also had practical reasons for cultivating the Anglo-American citizens. The Twenty-Sixth Infantry had left much of its property in Texas City where it was destroyed in the hurricane. Thus the well-being of his troops depended upon the peoples' generosity, and at least initially the Texans responded with food and shelter. Bullard also gave eager car-owners an active role as his ad hoc transportation corps. When possible, the Twenty-Sixth Infantry used private cars to carry messages, supplies, and casualties during its border service and often made its patrols by auto. Judging the success of his auto corps, Bullard could not understand why the army did not motorize more rapidly.[23]

Other army officers recognized the necessity of calming the Anglos and ending the vigilantism, but few worked as hard as Bullard at soothing the Mexican-American population. Being a Spanish-speaking Catholic helped. During his travels he assured them that his men would protect them too since that was their right as citizens. He was dismayed though unsurprised to learn that the Mexicans thought that the land was theirs, but not the government or laws. He had no doubt that such sentiments were the same as the guerrillas', and he knew that while there were real bandits in the area, he was fighting a revolutionary movement. By trying to protect the Mexicans from the guerrillas and from land-hungry Anglos who were threatening to "deport" the Mexican-Americans, he hoped he could calm the civilian population and get more information on the raiders from the rural population. He believed his goodwill efforts paid dividends, for he received increased reports of strange riders in his district.[24]

For all of the Twenty-Sixth Infantry's efforts and those of other regiments, the warfare along the Rio Grande continued through October 1915. In September there were six incidents, four involving cavalry patrols, which left three troopers dead and four wounded. Twenty-three Mexicans died as well. Significantly, only one civilian was wounded during the month and the raids were confined to the area near the river. In October there were four more incidents, two of them serious. On October 18 the guerrillas derailed a passenger train six miles north of Brownsville, killing two civilians and one trooper, wounding three others. The next day Texas Rangers captured seven suspects and shot four of them. On October 21 another raiding party struck a cavalry camp at Ojo de Agua on the river. The Third Cavalry troopers and Signal Corps detachment were surprised in their sleep; three died and eight were wounded, but the ambushers took fourteen casualties pressing the attack. In November, however, the raids dwindled and not an American died north of the river. In December there were no incidents.

North of the river the army, including Bullard, thought that its active patrolling had stopped the war, while the local peace-officers claimed that their summary executions had scared the Mexicans into passivity. Neither gave the other force much credit, Bullard concluded, and probably with reason.[25] As the raids slackened, the army officers and civilians were still arguing about vigilantism, the use of bloodhounds and Apache scouts, martial law, hot pursuit, and punitive expeditions into Mexico. The bitter debate went all the way to San Antonio and through General Funston to the War Department. The response was predictable— more troops. Before the raids ended both the Twenty-Eighth and Twenty-Third Infantry regiments came to the lower valley.

The key to peace was in Washington and Mexico City. In October 1915 the Wilson Administration finally conceded that Venustiano Carranza's government did indeed control Mexico. The policy again was noninvolvement. Carranza then relieved Nafarrate and replaced him with General Alfredo Ricaut, who took his orders to stop the raiding seriously. With his regulars and some Tamaulipas militia, Ricaut broke up the guerrilla camp across from Progreso and halted at least four expeditions. With their sanctuary destroyed, the guerrillas lapsed into inaction.[26]

Although the raids were over, detachments of the Twenty-Sixth Infantry patrolled the countryside and the tracks of the St. Louis, Brownsville, and Mexico Railway through the winter of 1915-1916. Bullard kept his headquarters, the small machine gun and supply companies, and three to five rifle companies at Harlingen. One company stayed at Mercedes, three in San Benito, one in Lyford, and two in Kingsville. From these main posts, squads were rotated to outlying hamlets, farm, and ranches. Bullard himself motored to and from his stations, checking on his troops' condition and the state of public opinion. He made a special effort to supervise the training of his recruits and urged the young privates not to desert until they had talked to him about their problems.[27] In late October he brought Rose, young Rose, and Keith to Harlingen. Bullard, however, lived in his tent camp and demanded that the rest of his officers do so. Despite its scattered condition, the regiment profited by the officers' attention, for in December a visiting inspector general could find little wrong with the Twenty-Sixth except that its officers needed new regulation hats and the company funds auditing.[28] Bullard found stimulation in deer hunting (he won the regimental contest) and dining with the city fathers of Harlingen and San Benito.[29] He and his family entertained the civilians and army officers in Harlingen, drove to Brownsville for sightseeing, swam in the Gulf, and played bridge. After the years in Texas City, the lower valley was a paradise, and the Twenty-Sixth Infantry was generally satisfied with its lot.

Bullard's winter vacation was disturbed only once. The War Department sent a more senior colonel, Lyman W. V. Kennon, to the Twenty-Sixth Infantry for attached service. Bullard immediately assumed that someone in the War Department wanted Kennon to have his regiment. He took leave and went to Washington, only to find out from Assistant Secretary of War Henry Breckridge and his old friend and West Point roommate, Henry McCain, the Adjutant

General, that his command was secure. He even found that he had a clique of fans in the Adjutant General's Department, a discovery that made the trip worthwhile. It was, in fact, Colonel Kennon who was in trouble with Secretary Garrison. For some obscure reason, probably lobbying for his own regiment, he had irritated the secretary of war and his punishment had been exiled service under a more junior colonel.[30]

On March 9, 1916, Pancho Villa and the remnants of his army struck Columbus, New Mexico, an attack that not only staggered Colonel Herbert J. Slocum's Thirteenth Cavalry, but sent shock waves along the entire border. Bowing to the public outcry over the seventeen American deaths in Columbus, Woodrow Wilson ordered Villa's decimated band pursued into Mexico. Intelligently, the War Department gave Brigadier General John J. Pershing, commander of the Punitive Expedition, orders to kill and disperse the *villistas*, a mission that Pershing accomplished. The president, the press, and the public, however, in their own romantic way assumed that Pershing's troopers were to hunt down Pancho himself, a task that heroes in dime novels could accomplish but live soldiers found impossible in Chihuahua's mountains. Wilson understood that he risked war with the Carranza government and that nothing would suit Villa more, but he felt compelled to allow Pershing to go deeper and deeper into Mexico in pursuit. Negotiating, moving troops, passing notes, reading reports, each day the American and Mexican governments jabbed and parried over the length and size and geographic limits of the Punitive Expedition.[31]

In the war-weary lower valley, the Villa raid and the pursuit of the Punitive Expedition caused a brief flurry of restlessness, but by the end of March the population on both sides of the border calmed. For Bullard the new crisis brought no new problems with one exception. The secretary of war banned public statements by army officers on the border, and Bullard had to recall an article ("wholly professional") he had written on the guerrilla campaign in the lower valley. He was irritated but not surprised, given the Wilson Administration's hypersensitivity.[32] For two more months he did his routine chores, read the papers about Pershing's difficulties, and hoped that the army might be enlarged. Even another Mexican raid into western Texas and a clash between Pershing's troopers and Mexican regulars at Parral, events that increased tension on both sides of the border, interested him very little.[33] His worst crisis was a fight with his wife. Listening to him complain about another officer who had a better command, Rose accused him of petty jealousy and meanness. Bullard was hurt: "I wonder if others regard me as despicable. No doubt they do and more so."[34]

By June 1916 the war scares and anti-American agitation in Mexico had sufficient urgency to bring changes to the lower valley. Parker concentrated his regiments into larger detachments, abandoning the duties of property guarding to the civilians themselves. Bullard fully approved of the change. The squad-sized guard details were "an absurdity, a deliberate device of our military authorities, probably exacted by our political administration, to prevent *anything* from being done—*anything*. I've never felt so outraged and tied up in all my experience." He assumed that General Parker had a new strategy, to lure Mexican raiders across the border and then use the attacks as a justification for his own punitive strikes. Bullard thought it a grand idea.[35] On June 10 Parker made his strategy clear. All units would be poised for "active" defense, not tied to guard posts. All raiders would be "hunted down and exterminated . . . wherever they go," including into Mexico. Infantry units should be prepared to react by automobile. Hearing that some of the San Diego irredentists had new attacks planned, Parker was ready to make a fight and even a war out of any raid.[36]

Parker's trap snapped on a band of twenty Mexican raiders on June 14. Crossing the river at Ranchita, nine miles west of Brownsville, the Mexicans were spotted by a cavalry patrol near San Benito. In the ensuing melee, one guerrilla died and the raiders fled. Parker then ordered Troop H, Third Cavalry, to intercept the raiders at the river and pursue them into Mexico. Early in the morning of June 17 the punitive expedition cut the raiders' trail on the river and followed it to a ranch a mile into Mexico. The troopers surprised the raiders, killing two. The same day, Parker sent another force of four cavalry troops, infantry, and Signal Corps wireless operators to the place where the raiders had originally crossed the Rio Grande. The cavalry, commanded by Major Edward A. Anderson, forded the river, leaving the infantry and wireless teams in defensive positions on the north bank. Anderson's column rode eastward down the south bank toward Matamoros looking for the guerrillas' camp, but found nothing but deserted homes. The force camped for the night without firing a shot. In the meantime, Parker had given Ricaut an ultimatum: capture the raiders and the American troops would leave. Incensed by the incursion, however, Ricaut mustered his own troops and marched toward Anderson's position, albeit cautiously.

Bullard could hardly have missed the action, but he got Parker's permission to participate before he left Harlingen. Leaving his garrison with three companies in a column of civilian automobiles, Bullard arrived at the Ranchita crossing at 4 A.M. on June 18. He deployed his troops with Anderson's infantry and then crossed the river with one squad to confer with the cavalry major. As senior officer present, he also assumed command of the entire operation. His orders, direct from General Funston in San Antonio, were to withdraw the force if Anderson had not been attacked, as he had not been. Reluctantly he ordered Anderson to retire by stages to the defended crossing, a movement skillfully done but without harassment. As the last troop, however, started to ford the river in the gathering dusk, some Mexican snipers fired a wild volley into the troopers. Bullard ordered the troop around and in a wild charge the cavalry rode down a Mexican army patrol, killing three. Bullard then completed the crossing, highly satisfied with the whole affair and unconcerned that Ricaut viewed his acts as murder. He guessed that Parker would be pleased (as he was) and that the Mexicans would feel chastened by the experience. Perhaps they were, for Ricaut did capture the remaining raiders. The whole affair, which scared Funston and the War Department enough to conduct an investigation, was for Bullard a source of infinite satisfaction after three years of frustrating training.[37]

3.

Aware that Mexican army units were concentrating along the border and the eastern flank of the Punitive Expedition, General Funston was worried that he did not have enough regulars to protect the border towns and reinforce Pershing. The War Department obliged him by sending eight more regiments to the Southwest and went one step further, persuading President Wilson to federalize the National Guard of Arizona, New Mexico, and Texas for the border patrol. This the president did on May 9, motivated most likely by the public outcry over the bandit raid on Glen Springs, Texas. The Texas National Guard, which had already seen some border service under a state call, mobilized 4,000 men, a third of them raw recruits. The Second and Third Infantry Regiments of the Texas Guard did not get to their posts in the lower valley until the last week in June. By that time they were sharing the dust and monotony with a multitude of fellow citizen-soldiers.[38]

As the possibility of war with Mexico increased in June 1916, Funston again asked for troops and again the War Department responded. Funston had definite ideas about what he wanted to do: cross the border and seize the Mexican border towns and occupy ports on both the Pacific and Gulf coasts, thus outflanking General Alvaro Obregón's armies, which were hemming Pershing. An ambitious and provocative plan, Funston's scheme was rejected by Wilson, but he got more troops to saturate the American border with armed men. On June 18, a day after the Mexican army delivered an ultimatum to Pershing to withdraw, the president called the rest of the National Guard to federal service with the exception of coast defense troops. His purpose was to seal the border, even authorizing Funston to take the border towns if war was officially declared, and quiet the public clamor for action. Predictably, the mobilization was interpreted differently. The Guardsmen thought that the president was sending them to war. For regular officers, the National Guard mobilization was interpreted as an administration attempt to test its readiness. They had little doubt that the National Guard's arrival on the border would decrease, not increase, the army's ability to fight. The War Department would have to supply and train the Guardsmen at the expense of the regular units not already in Mexico with the Punitive Expedition. Moreover, the regular officers could not believe that Wilson or Carranza would at last fight a real war after three years of crises. The gap between the National Guard's and army's ultimate views of their mission on the border could not have been wider.[39]

The immediate tasks of the mobilization joined the National Guard and War Department in concerted action. The early days of the mobilization were complicated by the fact that some Guardsmen had not taken the federal enlistment oath required by the newly passed National Defense Act of 1916. The War Department intended to exercise the president's power to call the National Guard to federal service without geographic restrictions and time limits.[40] Faced with the new terms of service, 10 percent of the veteran Guardsmen did not take the oath and left their units, but eager recruits took their place. The other difficulties were predictable after the 1898 mobilization. There were physical examinations to administer, muster rolls to prepare, equipment and arms to issue, families and friends to reassure and placate.[41] Considering the lack of plans, the National Guard's response was reasonably prompt, though few claimed the citizen-soldiers were ready for war. Half had never fired a rifle or been to summer camp; 63 percent had been enrolled three months or less.[42]

From the end of June to the end of July, National Guard units from throughout the country concentrated in the Southwest at Douglas on the Arizona-Mexico border, El Paso, San Antonio, and the lower valley of the Rio Grande. Over 100,000 Guardsmen made the trip in the first move; others came later to the border from their state camps. Some never left home at all. In Texas all the National Guard units had to be organized, for few came with staffs above the regiment and there were too few service and supply units, both National Guard and army, to support the massed manpower on the border. It was 1898 all over again with some important exceptions. The army's supply system responded with new rapidity and efficiency, and the health of the camps was excellent. The improved housekeeping, of course, was only the first step in making the Guardsmen fit for combat.

In the lower valley, the National Guard mobilization wiped out Parker's cross-border raiding. The incoming units threw themselves upon their army host units, absorbing officers, sergeants and technical experts to such a degree that regular units declined rapidly in efficiency. Captain Frank McCoy, Parker's chief of staff, saw the state troops "come pouring in ready for a picnic, not for war." McCoy, who shared Leonard Wood's faith in the potential of the citizen-soldier, recognized the Guardsmen's potential, but estimated that it would take three months to prepare them for war. He thought that they would get three months (since war seemed so absurd) and that the training would be worthwhile. He feared war with either Mexico or Germany was inevitable since Wilson's foreign policy was so "firmly idealistic, based on the Sermon on the Mount itself." For the moment, he knew that the regulars in the lower valley would have to persuade and cajole the National Guard into shape.[43]

In Harlingen, the Twenty-Sixth Infantry suddenly became hosts to the Second and Third Texas, and Bullard had to tear himself away from Bullard Polo Field to cope with the uproarious Guardsmen. He viewed the mobilization with deep skepticism. He feared the Guardsmen would become quickly disillusioned to find their service little different from summer camp and would leave their units as soon as they could. When some Texans burned out a Negro homesteader, he wondered who would have to pacify whom. He saw no gain in the mobilization for the regular army. The General Staff's guiding hand seemed absent from the mobilization, which meant that the planners had missed a chance to gain experience in handling the mass movement of men. As usual, a mobilization had destroyed the tactical units of the regular army. His own Twenty-Sixth promptly lost nine officers and over a hundred key enlisted men as cadre to the National Guard.[44]

On July 23 Parker turned over more of his "troublesome but interesting guests" to Bullard. It had become clear that, although the National Guard regiments belonged to "paper" divisions, Parker would have to extemporize a command system for his thirty-thousand-man force. He sent Bullard to San Benito and gave him command of a provisional brigade composed of the Twenty-Sixth Infantry, the First Louisiana Infantry, the Fourth South Dakota Infantry, and the First Oklahoma Infantry regiments, in all a force of 3,000 men. Just naming the command was a problem. At various times it was known as the Sixth Separate Provisional Brigade and the Oklahoma-Louisiana-South Dakota Brigade, shortened awkwardly to the "Oklasodak" Brigade. Reverting to Civil War custom, the men gave up and called themselves "Bullard's Brigade," which the colonel thought had a nice ring to it. None of the regiments had a reputation for military efficiency, even with the National Guard. Only half of the premobilization Guardsmen in Bullard's brigade went to drill and camp regularly; both the South Dakota and Oklahoma regiments were threatened with the loss of their federal subsidies. But the Guardsmen were eager and able, and appreciated getting a commander who knew soldiering. Bullard and his new students got along. (After the World War, the Oklahomans, whose ranks included a sizable number of Indians, made their former commander an honorary chief.) Bullard turned his own regiment over to its new lieutenant colonel, Wilson Chase, and went to work training his command.[45]

Bullard was none too enthusiastic about his job, for he knew that Parker's assignment might be cancelled by the War Department, and he could not help thinking that he was doing the same chore with the same rank he had in 1898. Nevertheless, he organized a brigade staff and training cadre from the ranks of the Twenty-Sixth and Twenty-Eighth Infantry and turned to the task.[46] The first four weeks were chaotic. As he suspected, Bullard found the Guardsmen unaccustomed to bivouac living. He was disgusted that they complained constantly about the food, the largest military ration in the world. The army, he thought, was wrong in pandering to them when they got "a little hysterical" about roughing it. He spent too much time "hushing up *sobs* and whimpering among a luxury-loving hysterical people whose sons have come to soldier a little away from the luxuries of home." He admitted, though, that the army supply system was niggardly. The quartermasters should issue first and tally later, since time was the prime commodity and the peacetime system always broke down anyway.[47] To quiet the Guardsmen, he kept them busy and tired with a hard program of hiking, tactics, and marksmanship. Gradually the brigade improved. On August 18, Bullard got an assist from the weather, for one of those hardy annuals, a Gulf hurricane, ripped up the lower valley. During the storm's crisis, the National Guard chain of command jelled, and although the camp was destroyed, the men saved themselves and much of their equipment with disciplined action. As the sheets of rain and wind ripped the tents, Bullard patrolled the campsite in hipboots, urging the men to deepen their drainage trenches and tighten their lines. Bullard and his charges emerged from the experience with new mutual respect. By the end of the month he felt the brigade was showing signs of real military proficiency.[48]

The next crisis was created by the War Department. As the National Guard regiments settled in Texas, General Funston organized the troops into brigades and divisions, most of them unlike those planned by the General Staff in 1913 and 1914. If individual states produced full divisions of Guardsmen, like New York and Pennsylvania, he did not replace their National Guard generals. Such a decision would have caused an uproar. Other states had sufficient regiments to form brigades and he left them alone, too. In the lower valley, for example, there was a Texas Brigade, Indiana Brigade, a Minnesota Brigade, and an Iowa Brigade. There were, however, several composite divisions and brigades in Texas, and the War Department quickly assigned regular brigadiers and colonels as their commanding officers.

Parker, commanding the composite division in the lower valley, had already assigned Bullard one such command and his sixth brigade, the North Dakota-Nebraska brigade, to Colonel Blocksom of the Third Cavalry. Blocksom's appointment was acceptable to the War Department, but Bullard's was not. The General Staff's selection for his command was Colonel Slocum, whose regiment had been surprised by Villa. Slocum's misfortune was caused by the ban on cross-border patrolling and he had been cleared of negligence, but his reputation suffered. Learning of their new commander, Bullard's National Guard colonels protested to their adjutants-general. Bullard did nothing to stop them and may have actively encouraged their lobbying. Parker also wired the War Department, requesting the cancellation of Slocum's orders. The War Department accepted Parker's recommendation that Bullard keep the brigade. Bullard's esteem for his command climbed.[49]

The National Guard units in the lower valley continued their training into the fall of 1916. In November General Parker staged a two-week field exercise for his entire division, and "Whites" and "Reds" hiked and banged away with blanks to their officers' satisfaction. Bullard's brigade acted as the advance guard of the "White" army, commanded by an Indiana National Guard brigadier. Bullard thought the problem interesting tactically, but again had reservations about its realism, for Parker had told his subordinates not to worry about handling casualties or supplies. When the problem ended, he was satisfied that his brigade was combat-worthy and he once again concluded that he would rather command Volunteers than regulars because they learned so quickly and performed so ardently.[50]

Despite the training, both the regulars and Guardsmen had the gnawing suspicion that the mobilization served no immediate strategic purpose. As early as July 1916 General Bliss, touring the National Guard camps, admitted to General Scott that there was no need for the Guardsmen and that if they had not been sent immediately to Texas "they probably never would have left their mobilization camps."[51] As the war scare with Mexico waned, the dissatisfaction with the National Guard's status grew. Bullard's brigade was not immune and one of his regiments, the First Louisiana, was ordered home in early September. His other two regiments began to hear the siren call of home. "The feeling grows that the militia will before long be ordered back to their states," Bullard wrote. "The feeling also grows that they are, per se, a failure as a national reliance."[52] By

December, with the Fourth South Dakota and First Oklahoma still at San Benito, he observed that the Guardsmens' morale was plummeting. Though they worked well in the field, the camps were increasingly messy and they would not do the expected housekeeping, feeling that such menial chores were beneath them. The saloons in San Benito and its shanty-town red light district roared on paydays, and only Bullard's crack extemporized military police kept order. One night, in fact, Bullard personally had to persuade a mob of drunken soldiers not to lynch a town constable who had struck a Guardsman.[53] The Guardsmen were increasingly outspoken in their contempt for their stay-at-home neighbors and groused about missed families and lost income. Their dissatisfaction was dramatized one night at a camp movie. The newsreel showed a group of Guardsmen being sworn into federal service. From the audience came a storm of catcalls and shouts of "No, no" and "Never again!"[54]

Bullard himself thought that the mobilization proved that the National Guard could not serve as the army's reserve. The basic problem was that it was useless unless trained, and it would not train itself. No one would take responsibility. No one would command for fear of displeasing his neighbors, business associates, and friends. The Guardsmen's camaraderie was based on civilian social relationships, not military respect. Given the Guardsmen's distaste for soldiering and their assumption that they had been sent on a fool's errand, Bullard feared that the National Guard would disintegrate as well as demobilize. He doubted that there would be a National Guard three months after it got home, a conclusion widespread in Parker's division.[55]

As Christmas approached and the Guardsmen got even more restless, Bullard hoped they would be sent home as soon as possible. Clearly there would be no war with Mexico. Clearly Wilson's peace policy was very popular, since he had been reelected. "This country will take anything provided only it can keep out of war and go on in its individualistic schemes."[56] He himself stayed busy with routine paperwork, informal inspections, hunting, and polo playing. As a polo player, he was rough and profane, much to the spectators' amusement. Polo was the most dangerous activity on the border, Bullard mused, for again a horse stepped on his foot, the third such accident in four years. He decided that his misfortune was a sign of carelessness born of age, a discomforting thought. He had other petty irritations. Just after he had written an article on the National Guard, he got another general order prohibiting officers from commenting on the mobilization. He blamed the autocratic Wilson: "One surely gives up his freedom when he becomes a soldier."[57] His brigade's morale worsened, the troops split between demanding harder training and immediate demobilization. He could hardly wait for demobilization, even as the United States and Germany edged toward war. Finally the First Oklahoma and Fourth Dakota were sent home in February. Bullard watched them depart with mixed emotions. He had never felt completely committed to the training, and he doubted that he had accomplished much. Unlike his days with the Thirty-Ninth Volunteers, he had made few friends with his citizen-officers. He had been aloof, impersonal. He feared this, too, was a sign of increasing age and detachment. He doubted that he could ever recover his zest for command.[58]

With his brigade dissolving, Bullard turned his attention back to the Twenty-Sixth Infantry. While he had worked with the Guardsmen, his old regiment had been broken up and deployed in small detachments throughout the lower valley. There had been many discharges and officer transfers. Twenty-one officers were absent on detached service; most of the companies were commanded by lieutenants. When an inspector-general visited the regiment in February 1917, he found it deficient in drill, bayonet exercises, and company administration. Nevertheless, the regiment passed the inspection, and Colonel Chase was commended for holding it together under trying circumstances.[59] As spring came, Bullard resumed command of the regiment and turned once more to training it for battles he doubted would ever come. Certainly there was no more war in the lower valley.[60]

4.

Throughout his lower valley service, Bullard never lost his ambition to be a brigadier general. When the National Defense Act of 1916 was passed, he was pleased that it added four major generalships and nineteen brigadier's billets, although these slots were not all to be filled at once. The act also restricted promotion to officers serving in the rank of full colonel, bringing army policy full swing back to pre-1898 custom.[61] Bullard approved of the legislation. When the War Department announced in September 1916 that the next two brigadiers would be chosen from among infantry colonels, Bullard made sure the War Department had not forgotten about him. At his urging six southern congressmen, the governors of Louisiana and South Dakota, and the city fathers of San Benito wrote the Secretary of War, praising Bullard's latest services.[62] He himself wrote directly to General Scott, wishing the Chief of Staff holiday wishes. "Allow me," he also said, "to ask you to look at the inclosed sheet," a resume of Bullard's service record. Bullard pointed out that his strongest claim was the amount of his field service, which now included more time in command of an infantry brigade than half the brigadier generals had. His only liability, he thought, was the residual antagonism in the infantry about his premature majority and his return to the Line in 1902. Now that his West Point classmates were being promoted to colonel, he hoped this issue was dead.[63]

Privately, he thought that he would never be promoted. He feared that he had too many enemies in the army. He knew that soliciting civilian testimonials was against War Department policy, but he went ahead on the faint hope that "political pull" might count for something. Having no confidence in the judgment of his superiors and pretending not to care whether he was promoted or not, he watched the War Department make its selections.[64] He was not one of them. Again the promotions were based more on seniority than on fitness for command. The only promotion that appeared to be clearly a matter of selection for future service was the elevation of Bullard's classmate, fifty-three-year-old Joseph E. Kuhn, an engineer. Kuhn's appointment was ominous, for he was one of the General Staff's experts on the German army and he had spent part of 1915 and 1916 as a military observor with the German General Headquarters. Upon his promotion in March 1917, he became chief of the Army War College Division of the General Staff, the army's contingency planners.

Despite his failure to be selected, Bullard's abilities were not unappreciated nor unreported. As usual his self-pity had clouded his judgment. His service in the lower valley as both pacifier and National Guard commander was recognized by both General Funston and General Parker. Parker, of course, had been one of his consistent supporters, but Funston was a new convert. Assessing Bullard's ability, both generals gave him all "excellents," the highest marks on the efficiency ratings. They thought him well qualified for duty in the infantry, Adjutant General's Department, or Inspector-General's Department. His special ability, they reported, was the command and instruction of Guardsmen and volunteers. Bullard was energetic, alert, physically fit, and professionally knowledgable beyond the expected standards. Both thought him particularly qualified to serve as a division commander in wartime.[65]

For all his own reservations about his status and the quality of his service in the lower valley, Bullard had not yet been dismissed as just another old colonel serving out his time.

5.

Like the distant thunder of a bright summer's day, the news of war in Europe rumbled indistinctly along the Rio Grande. For an army absorbed with training for a war with Mexico and perplexed by the Wilson Administration's diplomacy, the war was only another episode in Europe's "Great Power" rivalry. When President Wilson declared that the United States' position would be neutral, the policy of aloof detachment and nonintervention was as acceptable to the army as it was to the majority of American civilians.

For Colonel Robert Lee Bullard, the initial response to the World War was ironic amusement. Although he disagreed with the idea that wars were caused by arms races, he had concluded that the articulate elite of the American peace movement were correct in contending that modern industrial states were past using war to accomplish their goals. In January 1914 he wrote that the "Peace tendency is *unmistakable* and I believe *irresistible [sic]*. I mean the peace tendency of our time, the present day. I believe it is as *sure* and *irresistible*. . . . adapt to it."[66] After the war began, he was chastened and took comfort only in the fact that he had shared his foolishness with noteworthy company. The irony was that just as the idea of international peace had begun to affect the affairs of great nations, "the greatest war of all history broke out, the European war of 1914." The peace movement's explanation for the war was nonsense, a rationalization for its false dreams: "*that the world has reverted to barbarism.*" [67] Bullard thought this judgment as fatuous as the predictions that modern nations would never again fight one another.

Bullard was not surprised that the initial public reaction to the World War was a general condemnation of war itself. His reading convinced him that the American tendency was to picture all wars as villainous except those wars in which the United States itself was involved. Such wars, regardless of their causes and outcomes, were by their nature righteous wars because the United States participated in them. "The wickedness of the war is greater in proportion as it does not concern us, its course does not come near us or affect us. When it does, then war is right."[68]

With the World War a fact, Bullard attempted to learn something about it, and he waited to see whether the army would make any changes based on the newest European experiences. Civilian newspapers and professional military journals were flooded with war news, and the *Journal of the Military Service Institution*, the *Infantry Journal*, and the *Army and Navy Journal* printed not only American analyses of the fighting but reprinted European assessments as well. Army officers followed much of the fighting in *The Times* of London. Bullard and his peers recognized, however, that the type of information they received was either propaganda or trivia. Everyone talked about the war news, but for all the discussion, a career officer could not learn much because the talk was "almost entirely academic and unreal of application."[69] Bullard could see little officer interest in the war, anyway. "The great war in Europe is hardly affecting us in the army. We read the brief of the morning and afternoon news and dismiss the subject from our minds." Only in 1916 was Bullard able to draw some tentative conclusions:

> "*Wiped out by European War:*
> 1. Cavalry ??
> 2. Light field artillery?
> 3. Open country warfare??"

Yet the reports of the war were so colored by romantic journalists and misleading military commentators that Bullard thought the battles on the Western Front had brought back the bayonet as a weapon of decision, even though his own experience made him think this unlikely.[70]

Busy with his own military duties, Bullard gave little thought to the possibility of American participation in the European war. After the outbreak of the war, he was truly neutral, if not slightly pro-German. He thought that the German army would again demonstrate its military efficiency, and he was critical of the confusion of the Anglo-French mobilization and the hypocrisy of Allied reports on the "rape" of Belgium. As his initial curiosity about the war passed, he decided that "we have no part in the great things going on in Europe." He was sympathetic to Wilson's neutrality statements, although he doubted that the president understood that true neutrality could be bought only at the price of military strength. By 1916, after the recurring crises created by British maritime policing and German submarine warfare, Bullard had lost his limited respect for the Wilson Administration. Wilson was not really keeping America neutral, but was already engaged in a largely gratuitous intervention of words, a flood of rhetoric from diplomatic notes, peace missions, and public speeches. American neutrality was a strange thing,

> apparently largely undertaken in a spirit of paternal superiority; we would be the wise advisor of both the foolish peoples that went to war; we would furnish the wisdom and balance to bring them back to their senses and peace. Both sides treated us with scorn and contempt; our fool, smug conceit of superiority has been exploded in our faces and deservedly. Our great superior Mr. President Wilson who put forth and has sedulously followed up the mediative paternality-superiority assumption will never I hope get a chance to paternalize the belligerents in the great war.[71]

Watching the Wilson Administration wend its way through the tides of "Big Power" diplomacy, harried by German torpedoes and strident Americans of both the martial and pacifist persuasion, Bullard became more critical of Wilsonian peacemaking. In his dealings with Germany, the president, Bullard thought, had brought American indecisiveness, impotence, and moralistic rhetoric to new heights. "But I suppose I ought not even to think of our present policies. I have so little faith in them, so little patience with them that I cannot think of them or have them mentioned and preserve my temper." His disgust was not, however, complete. He generally approved of the president's efforts to negotiate with the Germans on the submarine issue. Since the United States' armed forces were limited and the public apathetic to military preparedness, he supposed Wilson was right to rely on pious mediation. Yet the nation's apathy to the destruction of American lives and property appalled Bullard. "What a record we are making for peace at any price!"[72]

In February 1917, with relations worsening with Germany and quieting with Mexico, Bullard more seriously considered the chances of American intervention in the European war. After witnessing seven years of vacillation towards Mexico, he found it hard to believe that the United States would fight in Europe. He was not surprised when Germany renewed unrestricted submarine warfare. How could the German government take threats of retaliation seriously when they were made by an American president? To think that the United States could hurt Germany with armed force was the sort of delusion one associated with civilians. The only imponderable was American public opinion, for Bullard recognized that he was out of touch with the people's mood. The only thing he was sure of was that the thought of another war made him weary.[73]

Busy with the demobilization of his National Guard brigade in March 1917, Bullard did not sense the rapid shift of public opinion on war with Germany. He thought that Wilson was still too proud (and weak-willed) to fight. When the Congress, buoyed by public belligerency, declared war on April 6, Bullard was nonplussed. He approved of the act, believing that Germany's arrogant disregard for the United States justified punitive action. The thought that the war was to preserve the balance of power in Europe, to save the American economy, to impose a just peace, and to make the world safe for democracy never entered his mind. Just how the United States would wage war on Germany perplexed him. The U-boat problem was the navy's responsibility. In any event, he seldom thought about naval matters. The most immediate impression he had after the declaration of war was that the government was doing nothing, not even repressing antiwar and seditious critics of Wilson's war decision. His biggest fear was that pro-German, pro-Mexican subversives would destroy the president's momentary, fragile political consensus, built as it was on public emotion over unrestricted submarine warfare. Bullard was pleased, however, when he learned that civilian prowar vigilantes were hounding German-Americans. He saw the repression as a quick cure for espionage, sabotage, and enemy propaganda. "It looks as though the great American public, by its own motion, without direction or authority from government, has forestalled any German treachery inside our own country. If so, it will be wonderful."[74] As the April days dragged by, he could see no other signs of wartime action. What were the War Department's plans? What would his part be? The colonel of the Twenty-Sixth Infantry continued his watch on the Rio Grande with little sense that his nation and his army were at war.

NOTES

[1] The background on the lower valley is from J. Lee Stambaugh and Lillian J. Stambaugh, *The Lower Rio Grande Valley of Texas* (San Antonio: The Naylor Company, 1954), and Frank C. Pierce, *Texas' Last Frontier: A Brief History of the Lower Rio Grande Valley* (Menasha, Wisc.: George Banta, 1917).

[2] Clarence C. Clendenen, *Blood on the Border, The United States Army and the Mexican Irregulars* (New York: Macmillan, 1969), pp. 16-44.

[3] Brig. Gen. T. H. Bliss to Brig. Gen. H. L. Scott, July 1, 1913, Hugh L. Scott Papers; Brig. Gen. T. H. Bliss to the Adj. Gen., April 19, 1913, Vol. 149, Tasker H. Bliss Papers.

[4] Brig. Gen. T. H. Bliss to Maj. Gen. L. Wood, March 17, 1914, Leonard Wood Papers; Brig. Gen. T. H. Bliss to Brig. Gen. H. L. Scott, April 27, 1914, Scott Papers.

[5] Brig. Gen. T. H. Bliss to the Adj. Gen., April 22, 1914, Vol. 162, Bliss Papers; Brig. Gen. T. H. Bliss to Maj. Gen. W. W. Wotherspoon, May 22, 1914, Vol. 163, Bliss Papers.

Conditions on the Texas border are described in Headquarters, Southern Department, "Weekly Reports on Border Conditions," Nos. 1-99 (March 22, 1913-January 30, 1915), Vols. 149-152, Bliss Papers.

[6] Maj. Gen. W. W. Wotherspoon to Brig. Gen. T. H. Bliss, May 12, 1914, Vol. 175, Bliss Papers.

For Parker's account of his trying command along the border from 1913 to 1917, see James Parker, *The Old Army: Memories,* 1872-1918 (Philadelphia: Dorrance, 1929), pp. 418-430.

[7] Brig. Gen. T. H. Bliss, Border Report No. 53, April 4, 1914, Vol. 150, Bliss Papers.

[8] Gov. O. B. Colquitt to Secretary of War L. M. Garrison, May 8, 1914, and L. M.

Garrison to O. B. Colquitt, April 25, 1914, Lindley M. Garrison Papers, Princeton University Library; CO, Brownsville District, to Commanding General, Southern Department, monthly reports, April 1914 to February 1915, Vols. 121-123, Bliss Papers.

[9]Maj. W. H. Hay, CS, Southern Department, to Brig. Gen. T. H. Bliss, March 22, 1915, Vol. 189, Bliss Papers.

[10]William M. Hager, "The Plan of San Diego: Unrest on the Texas Border in 1915," *Arizona and the West* (Winter 1963), pp 327-336. See also Senate Committee on Foreign Relations, Hearings, "Investigation of Mexican Affairs," 2 vols., 66th Congress, 2d Session, Senate Document 285 (Washington, 1920), pp. 1181-1184, 1199-1225, 1225-1323 (hereafter cited as "Investigation of Mexican Affairs.")

[11]Brig. Gen. T. H. Bliss to Maj. Gen. H. L. Scott, April 2, 1915, Vol. 190, Bliss Papers.

[12]For the account of the lower valley's "bandit troubles," I have relied primarily on Charles C. Cumberland, "Border Raids on the Lower Rio Grande Valley—1915," *Southwestern Historical Quarterly* 57 (January 1954), pp. 285-311.

[13]The description of the lower valley's vigilante movement is based on the testimony in the "Investigation of Mexican Affairs," previously cited: Stambaugh and Stambaugh, *The Lower Rio Grande Valley of Texas,* photographs and pp. 215-230; Pierce, *Texas' Last Frontier*, pp. 114-115; and local newspaper accounts in *Lyford Courant*, August 6, 13, and 20, 1915; *Mercedes Tribune*, August 12, 1915; C. H. Pease (a Raymondville banker and newspaper correspondent), articles in the *Delta Irrigation News* (Elsa, Texas), March 3 through April 7, 1926, and "U.S. Troops End the Bandit Raids of 1915," *Hidalgo County Independent*, June 6, 1930; Mary E. Lane, "Bloody, Dangerous Days in the Valley Weren't So Long Ago," *Valley Morning News* (McAllen, Texas), May 10, 1936.

[14]L. M. Garrison to Maj. Gen. F. Funston, August 11, 1915, Garrison Papers; Acting Secretary of War Henry Breckenridge to Senator Morris Sheppard (D-Tex.), August 9, 1915, Vol. 192, Bliss Papers; *Army and Navy Journal*, August 7, 1915.

[15]Bullard autobiography, pp. 107-112, BP. For the arrival of the Twenty-Sixth Infantry and Bullard's initial impressions, see Diarybook 8, entries, August 16-26, 1915 BP; August, 1915, Returns, Twenty-Sixth Infantry, reel 269, MC 665; *Mercedes Tribune,* August 19, 1915.

[16]Diarybook 8, entry, August 26, 1915; *Mercedes Tribune,* August 26, 1915.

[17]Diarybook 8, entries, September 1-15, 1915, BP; Notebook 23, entry 8, 1915, BP; *Army and Navy Journal,* September 4 and November 20, 1915; September, 1915, Returns, Twenty-Sixth Infantry, reel 269, MC 665; *Mercedes Tribune,* September 9, 1915.

[18]Reprint of General Nafarrate's statement in the *Mercedes Tribune,* September 9, 1915. See also Cumberland, "Border Raids on the Lower Rio Grande Valley—1915," pp. 297-298.

[19]Diarybook 8, entry, September 15, 1915, BP.

[20]Notebook 23, entry, September 19, 1915, BP.

[21]*Lyford Courant*, September 10 and 17, 1915; *Brownsville Herald*, September 14, 1915.

[22]Notebook 23, entry, September 18, 1915, BP.

[23]Notebook 23, entry, November 9, 1915, BP.

[24]Bullard autobiography, pp. 107-110; Notebook 23, entries, September 21-October 18, 1915, BP; Capt. F. R. McCoy to Mrs. McCoy, September (?), 1915, Family Correspondence, McCoy Papers.

[25]Notebook 23, entries, October 9 and 16, 1915, BP.

[26]Cumberland, "Border Raids on the Lower Rio Grande Valley," pp. 302-308; Arthur S. Link, *Wilson: The Struggle for Neutrality, 1914-1915* (Princeton, N. J.: Princeton University Press, 1960), pp. 629-644.

[27]Mr. Jesse M. Hughes, Hattiesburg, Mississippi, to the author, March 12, 1972. The regiment's activities are described in October 1915-May 1916, Returns, Twenty-Sixth Infantry, reel 269, MC 665.

[28]Maj. W. H. Simons, IG, to Commanding General, Southern Department, "Inspection of 26th Infantry," December 15, 1915, File 1916/175, Records of the Inspector-General, United States Army, RG 159, National Archives.

[29]Diarybook 8, entries, November 1915-February 1916, BP; *Army and Navy Journal,* December 11 and 18, 1915, February 19 and March 8, 1916.

[30]Diarybook 8, entries, January, 1916, BP; Col. L.W.V. Kennon to the Adj. Gen., USA, January 27, 1916, and Secretary of War Newton D. Baker to Col. L.W.V. Kennon, March 30, 1916, both L.W.V. Kennon Papers.

[31]Arthur Link, *Wilson: Confusions and Crises, 1915-1916* (Princeton, N. J.: Princeton University Press, 1964), pp. 194-221, 280-318; Clendenen, *Blood on the Border,* pp. 196-284.

[32]Diarybook 8, entry, March 17, 1916, BP.

[33]Diarybook 8, entries, April 1 and 30, 1916, BP.

[34]Diarybook 8, entry, May 9, 1916, BP.

[35]Diarybook 8, entry, June 1, 1916, BP.

[36]Headquarters, Brownsville District, General Order 7, June 10, 1916, and Memorandum 2, June 15, 1916, copies in Wood Papers.

[37]The account of Parker's punitive expedition is based upon the following sources: Diarybook 8, entry, June 19, 1916, BP; June 1916, Returns, Twenty-Sixth Infantry, reel 269, MC 665; Capt. F. R. McCoy to Mrs. McCoy, June 21, 1916, Family Correspondence, F. R. McCoy Papers; Statement of Lt. P. C. Raborg, June 18, 1916, Organized Files (1915-1916), McCoy Papers; Testimony of Lon C. Hill, "Investigation of Mexican Affairs," p. 1261; Brig. Gen. J. Parker to E. C. Forto, June 24, 1916, Organized Files (1915-1916), McCoy Papers.

[38]*Army and Navy Journal,* May 13 and 27, 1916; Pierce, *Texas' Last Frontier,* pp. 104-106.

[39]For the National Guard mobilization in 1916, see: Secretary of War Newton D. Baker, "Memorandum for the Adjutant General: Instructions for the Commanding General, Southern Department," June 22, 1916, Newton D. Baker Papers, Manuscript Division, Library of Congress; Elbridge Colby, "The National Guard of the United States," Chapter IV, *mss.* history in the library of the National Guard Association of the United States, Washington, D. C.; "Report of the Chief of the Militia Bureau," *Annual Reports of the War Department,* 1916 (Washington: Government Printing Office, 1916), I, pp. 893-947; "Report of the Secretary of War," *Annual Reports of the War Department, 1917* (Washington: Government Printing Office, 1918), I, pp. 9-10; "Report of the Chief of the Militia Bureau," *Annual Reports of the War Department, 1917,* I, pp. 847-854; Clendenen, *Blood on the Border,* pp. 285-298; and Militia Bureau, War Department, *Report on Mobilization of the Organized Militia and National Guard of the United States, 1916* (Washington: Government Printing Office, 1916).

[40]Judge-Advocate General E. H. Crowder to Col. W. G. Haan, April 17, 1916, W. G. Haan Papers, State Historical Society of Wisconsin: Memorandum, Chief of the Militia

Bureau to Adjutants General of the Several States, Territory of Hawaii and the District of Columbia, ''Oaths of Officers and Oaths and Contracts of the Enlisted Men, National Guard,'' June 16, 1916, File 9696, Army War College Correspondence File, 1903-1919, RG 165.

[41]For two excellent memoirs of the mobilization, see Irving Goss McCann, *With the National Guard on the Border* (St. Louis: C. V. Mosby, 1917) and Roger Batchelder, *Watching and Waiting on the Border* (Cambridge, Mass.: Harvard University Press, 1917).

[42]The traumas of the mobilization may be sampled on paper in File 9696, Army War College Correspondence File, previously cited.

[43]Capt. F. R. McCoy to Mrs. McCoy, July 11 and 17, 1916, Family Correspondence, McCoy Papers.

[44]Diarybook 8, entry, July 18, 1916 and Notebook 24, entries, July 9-August 1, 1916, BP; Returns, July 1916, Twenty-Sixth Infantry, reel 269, MC 665; *Army and Navy Journal,* June 24, 1916.

[45]''Report of the Chief of the Militia Bureau,'' *Annual Reports of the War Department,1916,* I, pp. 1020-1021; 1106-1107, and 1088-1089; Diarybook 8, entry, August 1, 1916, BP; Col. W. H. Johnston to Brig. Gen. E. H. Crowder, September 22, 1916, Crowder Papers; Parker, *The Old Army: Memories,* pp. 427-430.

The Guardsmen's point of view of their service in San Benito is from the following sources: *Historical Annual, National Guard of the State of Louisiana, 1938* (Baton Rouge: Army and Navy Publishing Co., 1938), p. 26; *Annual Report of the Adjutant General of the State of Louisiana, 1916* (Baton Rouge: Ramires-Jones, 1917), pp. 7-8; *Historical Annual, National Guard of the State of South Dakota,* 1938 (Baton Rouge: Army and Navy Publishing Co., 1938), pp. 17-18; *Historical Annual, National Guard of the State of Oklahoma* (Baton Rouge: Army and Navy Publishing Co., 1938), p. 13.

[46]Diarybook 8, entry, August 8, 1916, BP.

[47]Notebook 24, entries, August 1, 9 and 16, 1916, BP.

[48]Diarybook 8, entry, August 25, 1916, BP; Notebook 24, entry, September 7, 1916, BP; *Army and Navy Journal,* August 26, 1916; Brig. Gen. J. Parker, memorandum, ''Report of Instruction of National Guard Troops,'' January 24, 1917, copy in Edwards Papers; Col. R. L. Bullard to Maj. Gen. L. Wood, August 25, 1916, Wood Papers; Mr. Will G. Robinson, Pierre, South Dakota, former sergeant major, Fourth South Dakota Infantry Regiment, to the author, December 10, 1971.

[49]Bullard autobiography, p. 112; Diarybook 8, entry, August 30, 1916, BP. Brig. Gen. J. Parker to the Adj. Gen., August 28, 1916, and the Adj. Gen. to Brig. Gen. J. Parker, August 29, 1916, and the Adj. Gen. to Brig. Gen. J. Parker, August 29, 1916, both Bullard AGO File; *New Orleans American,* September 5, 1916.

The correspondence in Bullard's AGO file also includes letters from three adjutants general and two congressmen.

[50]Diarybook 8, November 28, 1916, BP; *Army and Navy Journal,* November 18 and 25, 1916.

[51]Brig. Gen. T. H. Bliss to Maj. Gen. H. L. Scott, July 24 and 26, 1916, Scott Papers.

[52]Diarybook 8, September 6, 1916, BP.

[53]Mr. Clifford H. Irion, Benton, Louisiana, to the author, January 15, 1972. Mr. Irion, a private in the First Oklahoma, was the cook for the brigade officers' mess.

[54]Notebook 25, entries, December 11 and 17, 1916, BP.

[55]Notebook 24, entries, September 12, 19, 22, 28 and October 16, 1916, BP; Capt. F. R. McCoy to Maj. Gen. L. Wood, November 3, 1916, and January 24, 1917: Wood Papers; "The Oklasodak" (San Benito, Texas), brigade newspaper.

[56]Diarybook 8, entries, December 1916, BP.

[57]Diarybook 8, entries, January 1-19, 1917, BP.

[58]Diarybook 8, entries, February 1-March 8, 1917, BP.

[59]December 1916, Returns, Twenty-Sixth Infantry, reel 269, MC 665; Lt. Col. E. A. Helmick, IG, to Commanding General, Southern Department, memorandum, "Inspection of the 26th Infantry," February 7, 1917 with endorsements, Records of the Office of the Inspector-General, RG 159.

[60]Brig. Gen. J. Parker to Capt. F. R. McCoy, January 23, 1917, McCoy Papers.

[61]"Appointment to Grade of Brigadier-General, U.S. Army," File 7890, Army War College Correspondence File, 1903-1919, RG 165.

[62]Representatives Oscar Underwood (D.-Ala.) to the Secretary of War, September 30, 1916; George Huddleson (D.-Ala.) to Secretary of War October 17, 1916; Henry B. Steagall (D.-Ala.) to Secretary of War, September 29, 1916; K. D. McKellar (D.-Tenn.) to Secretary of War, September 19, 1916; Rep. S. H. Dent. (D.-Ala.) to the president, August 31, 1916; J. T. Heflin (D.-Ala.) to Secretary of War, August 25, 1916, all in Bullard AGO File.

[63]Col. R. L. Bullard to Maj. Gen. H. L. Scott, December 20, 1916, Scott Papers.

[64]Diarybook 8, entry, October 16, 1916, BP.

[65]"Efficiency Report of Robert L. Bullard, Colonel, 26th Infantry," March 3, 1917, Bullard 201 File.

[66]Notebook 22, entries, January 25, 1913 and January 31, 1914, BP.

[67]Notebook 22, entries, October 30 and December 31, 1914, BP.

[68]Notebook 22, entry, January 12, 1915, BP.

[69]Diarybook 7, entry, December 30, 1914, BP.

[70]Diarybook 7, entry, October 7, 1914; Notebook 23, entries, April and May, 1916, BP.

[71]Notebook 23, entry, April 16, 1916, BP.

[72]Diarybook 8, entries, April 15 and 27, 1916, BP.

[73]Diarybook 8, entry, February 12, 1917, BP.

[74]Diarybook 8, entry, April 10, 1917, BP.

V   *THE WORLD WAR*
1917-1919

This war, if anything at all, will [in] its hardships and sacrifices make the general and the private equal.

Brigadier General Robert L. Bullard, diarybook entry, June 1, 1917.

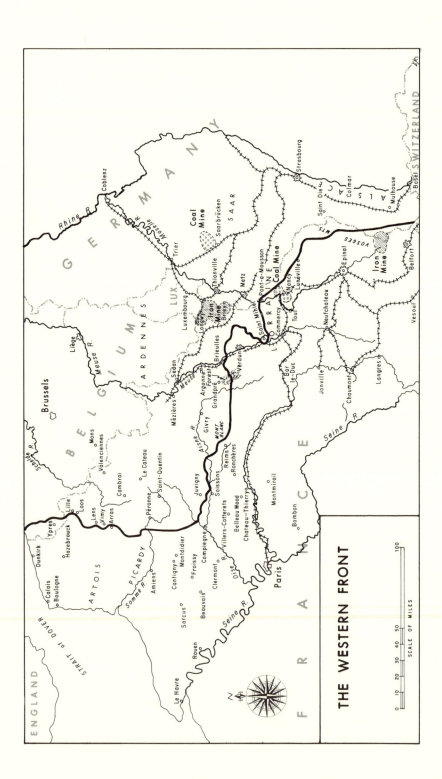

THE WESTERN FRONT

SCALE OF MILES

0 10 20 30 40 50   100

16   Joining the American

Expeditionary Force

1917

No American who had not seen it could quite appreciate how desperate World War I had become by the spring of 1917.[1] Anyone who could read the newspaper maps could see that the war's major theater was the Western Front in France, and students of the war knew that the belligerents had suffered enormous casualties without appreciable territorial gain. Because neither of the great warring coalitions had won a decisive victory, there was a great deal of talk of stalemate. But the war was anything but a stalemate except in geographic terms and then only in France.

Though staggered by casualties and growing economic weakness, the Central Powers still sought a clear-cut military decision in 1917. The German government believed it could turn the strategic balance with unrestricted submarine warfare on Great Britain and an increased effort against Russia. Even in 1917 the German military leaders had breath-taking territorial and economic concessions in mind as their sort of settlement. The German commanders recognized that unrestricted submarine warfare was likely to bring the United States into the war, but they gambled that Germany would have its peace before America could become a military threat. Since American industry and farms were already serving the Allied cause, the Germans thought that they had little to lose.

Despite the failures of their great Western Front offensives of 1915 and 1916, the British and French had not abandoned their own optimistic war aims, and they dragged Italy and Russia into a fourth year of fighting. The Allies were no more interested in a compromise peace than the Germans. Their goals were to topple the German and Austrian dynasties, eliminate the Central Powers' land and naval forces as a threat, push back Germany's borders to the Rhine, carve up the Austro-Hungarian and Ottoman Empires into national states, annex the Central Powers' overseas colonies, and force the enemy to make large reparations for the war damage done the Allies. To make such a peace, the Allies needed a decisive military victory over the German army on the Western Front, but by the summer of 1917 such a victory was beyond their capacity. The crucial problem was more troops, although the Allied generals had shown little sign that they would use reinforcements any more wisely than the armies they had sacrificed since 1914. The source of fresh troops was obvious—the United States.

As the United States entered the World War, the conflict's strategic contours were changing. Germany's submarine war was threatening the Anglo-French war effort, and then revolution ended czarist rule in Russia and took Russia out of the war within a year. The Russian Revolution meant that German troops could be redeployed to France and the Austro-Italian front, there to win victories before the Americans could create an army for the European war. Time was the crucial factor. The German and Austrian governments were aware that the Allied blockade and the war's demands on their resources were eating away the foundations of their societies. About all that kept the Central Powers and the Allies at war was the knowledge that all the belligerents were in similar straits, the optimism of the military commanders that one more offensive would win, and the deep emotional commitment that only a clear victory could even partially repay the great national sacrifices of three years of war.

Nowhere were those sacrifices more apparent than in France. For three years the French army had fought in vain to recover the countryside lost in 1914. Just as the United States entered the war, it tried again, commanded by an incurable optimist named General Robert Nivelle. In casualties the result was again disastrous. The Nivelle offensive ended with half the French infantry divisions in active mutiny or sullen noncooperation. Nivelle's successor, General Henri Pétain, restored the army as a reliable defensive force, but there could be no more general attacks until the Allied armies got better weaponry and American manpower.[2] Pétain passed the responsibility for offensives to the British Expeditionary Force (BEF) and the Italian army, which was preparing for its tenth campaign to break the Austrian front on the Isonzo River.

Comparatively, Great Britain was the strongest of the Allies, even with its merchant fleet imperiled, but it, too, had been badly damaged since 1914. Its manpower and economic losses were heavy enough to put severe limits upon the Lloyd George government. After several major campaigns in France, the BEF had not only lost men, but the government's confidence. The size of the BEF's casualties, the British government recognized, was eating away the foundations of British society. In 1917, although Field Marshal Sir Douglas Haig was planning another "big push" for Ypres, the British war effort was faltering. The hope for victory (outside of American intervention) was technological. The major technical developments of the war, the tank and the fighting airplane, promised to restore decisiveness to land warfare through firepower and mobility, but while the conceptions of armored warfare and strategic air war were real enough in 1917, the men and machinery to turn the ideas into decisive warfare were not. The BEF still fought with massive artillery barrages, infantry assaults, and limited success.

The Allies shared the German view that the United States could not intervene quickly on the Western Front, expecially if the Wilson Administration insisted upon creating a national army. As arrogant about their military skill as the

Germans, the British and French had little confidence that the United States could put an effective army into the field. Until the failure of the Nivelle offensive, the Allies were not even sure they wanted an American army, for they recognized that America's role in deciding peace terms would increase with each German killed by American arms. Moreover, they did not believe that the United States Army could provide sufficient officers to handle the complexities of warfare on the Western Front. The Allied preference was that American soldiers come to Europe as quickly as ships could be found to carry them; once in France they could be trained, equipped, and commanded in battle by Allied officers as part of either the French army or the BEF. The schemes for "amalgamation" varied; at one time or another the Allies asked for everything from companies to divisions to be integrated into their armies. But the meaning of the request was always the same: the United States Army officer corps was incapable of commanding its own countrymen on the Western Front. The ultimate fighting ability of the individual American soldier (properly trained, equipped, and seasoned) was not the heart of the issue, for only the Germans lapsed into blind chauvinism and declared that Americans were inherently inferior soldiers. The Allies wanted American soldiers. They did not want American generals.

1.

The initial shock of mobilization fell upon Secretary of War Newton D. Baker. In his first year in office, Baker had proved that he could work with Generals Scott and Bliss, and he supported the General Staff's authority to manage the army. He had done his best to make Wilson's Mexican policy palatable to the officer corps, and he had patched up the War Department's strained relations with the Congress. A short, slight man with the appearance and manner of a very efficient accountant, Baker admitted his ignorance of military affairs. His civilian admirers applauded his modesty and wisdom; the General Staff appreciated his self-deprecation but knew he was only telling the truth. Even after a year in office, Baker, like all of his recent predecessors except Henry Stimson, was still largely an innocent in army affairs. He knew few officers personally outside of the General Staff. He had formed strong opinions about only two generals outside Washington. Leonard Wood, he thought, was an untrustworthy, politically ambitious officer who lacked West Point training, in which the secretary of war put great store. The other general was the commander of the Punitive Expedition, John J. Pershing. Baker trusted Pershing because the fifty-six-year-old cavalryman looked like a soldier and took unpalatable orders from the War Department without public complaint. Since Baker was an avid student of Civil War history, expecially of the Army of Northern Virginia in which his father had fought, perhaps he saw something of Robert E. Lee in Pershing. If so, it was not an entirely accurate vision.

In the early days of America's war, Baker had more on his mind than generals. His major concerns were getting the Congress to pass the Selective Service Act, the legislative basis for the wartime draft, and to find the equipment for the newly raised army. Even with the loyal assistance of the General Staff and bureaus, the secretary of war had to rely heavily on the army's department commanders.[3]

On the eve of America's entry into the war, Pershing was a new major general and the commander of the Southern Department.[4] His second star and command came as a special reward for his service with the Punitive Expedition and because General Funston had collapsed and died from a heart attack. For Pershing, the promotion and assignment were welcome, but judged as no more than his due for duty performed and command responsibilities yet to come. General Pershing was a far more complex man than Baker knew. In appearance and public manner, Pershing was a model soldier, physically fit, vigorous, handsome, poised, plainspoken, and impeccably uniformed. As a soldier his public image was that of a simple cavalryman, a reputation cultivated by Theodore Roosevelt when the president explained Pershing's promotion to brigadier general in 1906. Roosevelt stressed Pershing's frontier service with the Sixth Cavalry, his coolness under fire at San Juan Hill, and his pacification of the Lake Lanao Moros. This image had been reinforced by Pershing's later Moro campaigns and his command of the Punitive Expedition. It was not a complete picture, either professionally or temperamentally.

In an officer corps rich with ambition, Pershing was a star performer. After the war with Spain, he had been chief of the Bureau of Insular Affairs and a member of the General Staff. He had arranged an assignment as a military observer during the Russo-Japanese War. Friendly with a host of politicians, he was an admitted Republican and married to the daughter of Senator Francis E. Warren, an influential member of the Senate Military Affairs Committee. His political footwork could be dazzling when necessary. During the Punitive Expedition, Pershing wrote Roosevelt that Wilson's Mexican diplomacy was contemptible; later he assured General Scott that rumors of his hostility to the president were false, that he had defended Wilson in his conversations with others, and that his attitude toward the president was one of "entire friendliness."[5] Pershing, however, was a real field general. As a brigade commander he had recognized the importance of artillery and machine gun fire to the success of infantry assaults. He appreciated the importance of new technology, motorizing his troops and supplies and employing the army's primitive airplanes. He paid close attention to his wire and radio communications, and he demanded thorough staff planning. He used officers impersonally, encouraging the most able and discarding without compunction those who made mistakes. He commanded as much by fear as he did by rapport with his subordinates.

Temperamentally, Pershing impressed people with his sang-froid. His public personality was interpreted by civilian acquaintances as the detached authority one associated with generals. His aloofness was much deeper than that. Pershing was a sensitive, passionate, melancholy man who walled himself off from all but his family and a few intimate friends. His reserve became almost a barrier to other human beings when his wife and three daughters died in a tragic fire in 1915. Close to emotional collapse after their deaths, he pushed all but the most superficial emotions deep within himself and controlled his grief and loneliness with a compulsive commitment to his military duties.

To his admirers, Pershing was an officer of heroic proportions, selfless with almost inhuman devotion. These admirers were primarily officers younger than Pershing who served him as staff officers and subordinate commanders; a few were his West Point classmates, like Avery D. Andrews. To his peers, officers of the West Point classes of the 1880s, Pershing was all that his admirers saw, but something more. He was not a man one could serve with comfortably. There was always the ambition, the air of moral superiority, the cold-bloodedness, the feeling that he would expend men like cartridges, the knowledge that he demanded an uncomfortable degree of personal loyalty and that he considered his own judgment nearly infallible. Few officers ever got close to Pershing, and few tried. Yet many served him well, and Robert Lee Bullard was one of them.

After their brief association on Mindanao in 1903, Pershing and Bullard did not serve together and had no reason to deepen their casual acquaintance. Pershing's associations were with the cavalry, Washington high society, the War Department, and the army school system; his sudden elevation to brigadier general separated him from line officers his own age. He was not a prolific writer for the military journals, and he was emotionally incapable of attaching his career to Leonard Wood and Wood's progressives, although he knew Wood and eventually used Wood's protégés to staff his expeditionary force headquarters. Bullard, of course, like many other officers, had followed Pershing's career, especially after 1906, and knew something of his formidable reputation. If Bullard had any strong feeling toward Pershing, it was probably envy. Though their careers had not been alike, Pershing and Bullard shared common strengths and weaknesses. Both were driven men who had given themselves with near totality to their army careers; both were thorough and demanding officers and spared no one, including themselves, in the performance of their duties. Both were students of their profession. They were also vain, suspicious men, often ungenerous and self-promoting among their peers. Both, however, recognized military talent and did not let their personal feelings interfere with army business, at least most of the time. The thing that separated them was that Pershing found Bullard's candor and loquaciousness distasteful. Bullard was self-disciplined, but his pleasure and disappointment with himself and others were usually apparent. Both men were basically introverts, but Bullard was much more sensitive to the social nuances of officership. He also enjoyed warm relationships with junior officers and enlisted men, a quality conspicuously absent in Pershing.

Pershing and Bullard crossed careers again in Texas before the war began. As commander of the Southern Department, Pershing had the responsibility of organizing Plattsburg-type volunteer training camps for the summer. Pershing consulted with his assistant chief-of-staff, Major Howard L. Laubach, the officer in charge of the department's civilian training and operations, about the assignment of a "specially selected commander" for one of these camps. He wanted the best field grade infantry officer in his department for the assignment.

Laubach told the general he could pick the man immediately, Colonel Bullard of the Twenty-Sixth Infantry. "Colonel Bullard is the best field officer you have." Since Laubach had supervised all the army and National Guard training in Texas in 1916, his opinion had weight.

"You consider Bullard a pretty good man, do you?" Pershing asked.

Laubach replied that he did and that he thought Bullard would "go far" if the United States entered the World War.[6]

One of the earliest programs the War Department started after America's entry into the war was the conversion of the Plattsburg camps into officer training courses, and the department commanders got the responsibility for executing the plan. On April 18, 1917, the War Department announced the creation of sixteen such camps and appealed for volunteers from among America's educated young men. In ninety days the War Department wanted thousands of company grade officers ready to lead troops in battle.[7] One of these camps was established at Fort Logan H. Roots near Little Rock, Arkansas, and Pershing selected Bullard to command it.

Bullard left San Benito for his new post in late April, feeling little regret in leaving the Twenty-Sixth Infantry and little enthusiasm for his training camp command. Arriving at Fort Sam Houston to receive his orders, he found the department headquarters a study of uncoordinated and ill-informed activity. Depressed by the confusion, Bullard went on to Little Rock where he was pleasantly surprised by the cordial welcome he received. With civilian assistance, War Department funds, and a small staff, he started to build the camp, but the candidates arrived before the construction was complete. Among the eager youths were his own son Lee, his nephew Dan Bullard, and his greatnephew R. M. Greene. Bullard also had his family with him and settled them in post quarters. His duties at Logan H. Roots were essentially administrative and supervision of the construction and housekeeping details. He thought that his assignment was a dead end, a sign of his lack of professional standing with the War Department. "I see no signs of any advancement for me here. I work pretty well and hard but I do not believe that it is of a nature to call attention to me at all. It is just duty, nothing more." Yet his camp was created and his training regiment was found to be in excellent condition when it was inspected.[8]

2.

In late April, as Bullard left San Benito, the Wilson Administration received some distinguished European visitors. Two special missions, one British, one French, had come to Washington to tell the Americans how to fight in the World War. The members of the British Mission were frankly shopping for American manpower to fill the depleted BEF as well as for more shipping and war loans. The French had similar interests, although their heads-of-mission, former premier Rene Viviani and Marshal Joseph Joffre, were more subtle in their public statements. In his conferences with Baker and the General Staff, Joffre was blunt.

He told the Americans that the French army was shrinking rapidly and was crying for more soldiers. Joffre's plea for men made an even greater impression when the marshal admitted the failure of the Nivelle offensive and the disaffection of the French enlisted men. He did not describe the French mutinies very frankly; if he had, the Americans would surely have been stunned. In addition, he abandoned his official proposal that American troops should be integrated into the French army. He urged instead that the United States quickly form its own national expeditionary force and send it to France for training and equipping. He urged that at least one division should be sent immediately to bolster French morale. Unspoken was the fact that American soldiers fighting and dying in France would unalterably commit the United States to a decision on the Western Front and galvanize American sentiment behind the Allied cause.[9]

On May 2 the War Department had President Wilson's approval to send one combat division and technical and service troops to France. How many more men would follow and how quickly was uncertain, but the General Staff was already thinking of an American expeditionary force of a million men. The same day, General Scott cabled Pershing to select one field artillery and four infantry regiments from his department for overseas service and to come to Washington himself. If the War Department's plans did not suddenly change, General Pershing would command at least this advance division and probably others to follow. Pershing selected for his infantry the Sixteenth, Eighteenth, Twenty-Sixth and Twenty-Eighth Infantry regiments. He then left for Washington, reporting to Secretary Baker on May 10. The American Expeditionary Force was in the making.[10]

Pershing's selection to command the expeditionary force was a relatively easy decision for Secretary Baker. If Pershing had not been the commander, it would have been startling. Of the six major generals, Scott, Bliss, Barry, and Bell were infirm and near retirement. The alternative to Pershing at that grade was Leonard Wood, the Wilson Administration's military nemesis and a man increasingly hobbled by nerve damage in one of his legs. Even Wood's army friends thought that physically, emotionally, and politically the former Chief of Staff was not the man he had once been. The officer corps' attention moved to Pershing even before he went to Washington, and he began to receive personal letters of fealty and requests for service. At least part of the officer corps had tacitly picked Pershing before Baker did, and their choice was supported by both Generals Scott and Bliss, despite their own ties with Wood. In a time of uncertainty, with careers to be made and rank won, with a large army building for the Western Front, there was every reason to look for a leader who symbolized the strictest professionalism and impersonality. The officer corps needed a man who represented the army's virtues—the "Duty, Honor, Country" of West Point—but who also had the force and grasp necessary to stop civilian interference with the affairs of the American Expeditionary Force. John Pershing was certainly that man.[11]

One of Pershing's tasks in Washington was to help select the army's newest general officers, presumably the men who would train and command his expeditionary force. It was not a task he took lightly, but he did not yet have the authority to make the selections alone. Instead, he shared the responsibility with Generals Bliss, Mann of the Militia Bureau, Kuhn of the War College Division and Adjutant General McCain. Secretary Baker promised to approve this board's recommendations, but only if there was unanimous agreement on the selections.

The generals had a limited field from which to choose. The original appointments had to be made in the Line of the regular army since no one knew what the size or organization of the wartime "National Army" would be. By law the candidates had to be selected from among colonels, and the board itself decided to follow the General Staff's system of proportional representation by branch. This meant that ten brigadiers would come from the infantry, three from the cavalry, two from the field artillery and three from the coast artillery. Even though the board recognized that they were selecting men for wartime command, they chose to favor seniority among colonels. Among the infantry colonels, for example, they went only halfway down the list of seventy-three candidates. The army's senior officers were themselves a select group; of the 1,081 commissioned from 1873 to 1889, only 234 were still in the service. Most of this group were Academy graduates. Except for Wood and the Surgeon General, every army general in 1917 was a West Pointer, though Academy graduates were a minority of the officer corps. Time and Pershing would make the American Expeditionary Force's high command a West Point affair.[12]

It took the board four days to make its selections. A preliminary list of candidates was drawn up by the War College Division, using the data collected for Wood's planned Mexican expeditionary force. Then the generals worked on the select list, but could not immediately make unanimous decisions. Pershing himself left Washington for France before the selections were made, having revised the infantry selections twice and complaining about the candidates' age and vitality. The board on May 30 presented its candidates to Baker, who approved their three selections to major general and eighteen to brigadier, all the promotions to be made in the regular army. Fourth on the infantry list was Robert Lee Bullard. Just whose candidate he was is difficult to judge; that he was the sort of colonel who would satisfy the board is clear enough. He was the most senior infantry colonel selected (fourth of seventy-three), a West Point graduate (like all but two of the selectees), a veteran commander and War College graduate, physically active and military in appearance, and at fifty-six as close to youthfulness as most officers on the combined list. Only three were younger and only Peyton C. March, a field artillery selectee, had graduated from West Point behind him. He had served several times with Bliss, Pershing knew him, and Kuhn and McCain were his West Point classmates. Seventeen years after he began to think of himself as a general, Bullard was to get a star. Yet, as the board recognized, time and the war also could allow any general the opportunity to turn the stars into a badge of incompetency and failure. As Bliss saw, the big promotions were yet to come and "in this war, as in others, the honors await those who do not go in first."[13]

3.

The large party of men which boarded the liner *Baltic* off Governors Island on May 28, 1917, could not have fooled an interested German spy. Most of them were dressed in civilian clothes, but looked uncomfortable enough to be mistaken for soldiers. It was also unusual to board a liner from Fort Jay, and even more unusual for a party of "civilians" to depart with the thunder of an artillery salute behind them. In any event the party's equipment had been lying about the Hoboken docks for several days; the boxes read "General Pershing's Headquarters." For all the comic opera secrecy, the general and his staff had a fair idea of their mission. Before Pershing left Washington, the president and secretary Baker gave him an assignment more formidable than the command of one expeditionary division. He was to organize and command in combat an independent American army in France, and in collaboration with the Allies he was to force a peace on Germany by destroying its army. Pershing's chief of staff, Major James G. Harbord, a bulky, balding cavalryman, caught the significance of the moment as the *Baltic* left New York harbor behind. Pershing's headquarters was a magnet which would draw millions of troops after it and bring "the end of an era in which America has preserved the traditional policy . . . of avoiding entangling alliances, and begin a new epoch in which our feet may travel roads now undreamed. Jason and his Argonauts, searching for the Golden Fleece, sailed on no more romantic errand than that which takes Pershing to France."[14]

A thousand miles west of the *Baltic's* wake, Colonel Robert L. Bullard, pleased with his camp's progress and expecting no other duty, received a telegram in the late evening of May 29. It was from the War Department. Interested, he opened the envelope and read the message: he was to proceed at once to Washington and report to the Chief of Staff. He was to travel "equipped for extended foreign service." The telegram began the worst night of Bullard's life, for he did not really want to leave his family and go to France. He himself was dazed by his assignment, and Rose was distraught. Worried by his wife's anxiety, Bullard summoned his son Lee from the camp and got him to agree to resign so that he could care for Rose, young Rose, and Keith while Bullard and Peter Cleary were in France. The next morning, just before he left, he decided that Lee should finish his service. The family would have to manage as best it could. Still in an unhappy frame of mind, Bullard reported to the War Department two days later. The flow of business at the War Department was not reassuring. He found no sense of urgency, much delayed business, and a General Staff which could not extract itself from its normal routine. Bullard was acutely aware that abnormal times had come to the army. He was not sure the General Staff and the bureaus realized it and predicted their imminent breakdown. He got his own assignment without emotion. He learned he was to command an infantry brigade and that he would probably be promoted to brigadier general. "I don't care three cents about it. This war, if anything at all, will [in] its hardships and sacrifices make the general and the private equal."[15]

Although it took four days to confirm, Bullard learned he was to command the Second Brigade of the First Provisional Division, the advance force sent to France to dramatize America's entry into the war. Before he left for Hoboken, Bullard knew his nomination for brigadier general had gone to the Senate for approval. Distressed by the War Department's ineffectiveness and the future challenges of his command, he was not particularly moved by his promotion. His only thought was that there were no better candidates and that the stars were long overdue. He left Washington convinced that the key to success in the war would be an officer's ability to expand his vision to fit the size of his mission and his command. As in the war with Spain and the Philippine Insurrection, he promised himself that he would not mire himself in bureaucratic routine or fret about inconsequential details others could handle. This resolution was strengthened by the conditions he found in Hoboken: transports unprepared, equipment and supplies scattered about the docks and railyards, troops bivouacked without order among the trains that had brought them from Texas, quartermaster officers and civilians rushing about on minor errands and little sense of overall direction and purpose. It was a grim but not unexpected beginning, and Bullard boarded the transport *San Jacinto* "feeling pretty somber about prospects."[16]

Bullard had a great deal to learn about the First Division. The units of the division were part of the standing army, but were "regular" only in name. The division commander was Major General William L. Sibert. Another Alabaman who had graduated from West Point in 1884, Sibert had served all but six years of his career as an engineer. He had performed with distinction in the Philippines as a staff officer and commander of an engineer battalion. He then became one of the organizers in the building of the Panama Canal, for which Congress promoted him to brigadier general in the Line in 1911. His line service was primarily administrative, although he had shown considerable drive and imagination in running summer training camps. A large man who showed his age, his broad face distinguished only by glasses and a salt-and-pepper mustache, Sibert was a thoroughly pleasant and hardworking officer whose gentlemanliness and balanced temperament won his talented staff's affection. His selection to command the division, a decision made by the General Staff, was somewhat mysterious since he had never led combat troops, was not a product of the Line's schools, and was little known to line officers except his immediate staff.[17]

Bullard's immediate interest was not his division commander, but his own brigade, composed of the Twenty-Sixth and Twenty-Eighth Infantry regiments. At least half the enlisted men were new recruits, enthusiastic volunteers from all over the United States, and the company grade officers were predominately newly commissioned "emergency" officers. The two regimental commanders, George B. Duncan and Beaumont Buck, he knew well. Duncan, an intelligent and aggressive Kentuckian, was from the class of 1886 and had had a varied and successful career as an infantry officer. Buck, a short, dogmatic, inflexible, and not very bright officer, was a classmate of Bullard, having been "set back" at the

Academy. His career had not been especially distinguished, but he had a reputation for being a driving infantry commander and strict disciplinarian.

Bullard's own small staff, extemporized from among the officers of his two regiments, was limited to an adjutant, quartermaster, and a handful of officer and enlisted assistants. His principal assistant was Captain Harold B. Fiske. Leavenworth-trained and a General Staff graduate, Fiske irritated Bullard with his air of intellectual superiority and admiration of the German army. Bullard regarded the latter as a sign of defeatism and disloyalty, for he was concerned about the patriotism of Americans in and out of uniform in the early days of the war. On board the *San Jacinto*, Bullard overheard Fiske and one of Fiske's Leavenworth friends, Captain Arthur L. Conger, discussing the AEF's prospects. Bullard thought that their army education in the German system had "so impressed them with the efficiency of the Germans as soldiers that they have plainly weakened their own courage in the face of the Germans. The impression that the average man derives from hearing them talk and from being with them is the hopelessness, the utter folly of our resisting or fighting the Germans at all."[18] Bullard, however, recognized Fiske's ability despite his personal distaste for the officer. So did General Pershing since Fiske, as a brigadier general, ended the war as one of the principal staff officers in the AEF headquarters; Conger became the AEF's primary expert on the German army.

On June 14 the convoy sailed for France. Despite the rumors of submarine attack and the newness of the navy crews, the voyage was easy, made in good weather and at a leisurely pace. Aboard the crowded *San Jacinto*, life was predictably confused. The soldiers talked themselves into exhaustion, filling the vessel with the nervous chatter of recruits at sea for the first time. They flooded the passageways with exploring parties, working parties, messlines, classes, physical drill parties, and squads of the seasick. Bullard won his men's esteem by replacing the ship's callous civilian cooks with veteran soldiers, but there was little else he could do for his troops' comfort. Bullard spent the voyage studying French, reading tactical studies, and holding training conferences with his staff. He had no illusions about the size of the task ahead. After one alarm in the submarine-infested waters of the Bay of Biscay, a midnight bacchanalia of sirens, gunfire, and depth-charging, the convoy reached St. Nazaire on the foggy morning of June 28. The next day Bullard and part of his brigade disembarked and took their first look at France.[19]

St. Nazaire was a peaceful old city on the Loire and its physical beauty was untouched by battle, but the Americans knew that they were in a country at war.[20] As they filed onto the quay, the ranks jostling while sergeants called the roll, quiet crowds of old men, women, cripples, and children gathered to watch the cheerful soldiers in the "cowboy" hats. The American officers were disturbed that the people seemed so hostile, but the crowd cheered with mild enthusiasm when the Twenty-Eighth Infantry band valiantly attempted *La Marseillaise*. The French civil and military authorities were cooperative, and the troops quickly marched to their temporary camp outside the city. The camp itself was crude, having been used to house German prisoners. Bullard's first contact with French civilization was to inquire in French where he could find a bank. Colonel Duncan respected his valor, since Bullard was among the handful of officers who tried to do business in French, but he was amused when Bullard was directed to a line of benches on the waterfront.[21] There was much for everyone to learn. To see that the First Division's ranking officers began their education immediately, General Pershing and his staff held a conference with them on June 29. Pershing was adamant: the American soldiers must be models in appearance and deportment; their training must begin immediately and stress drill and physical fitness; under no condition was anyone to discuss military matters.[22] The First Division had come to France to fight, not to sightsee and visit, though France's temptations were obvious.

The Second Brigade was not in St. Nazaire long, for AEF Headquarters wanted the division concentrated about the city of Gondrecourt in Lorraine. The division's infantry was to begin training with French units just behind the lines. Bullard loaded his troops aboard the small French boxcars ("Forty Men-Eight Horses") and rough coaches and rode to his new headquarters, the rural town of Trevaray. Bullard relished the trip: "It seemed like an entirely new start in life as it was all so different from all the things that I had theretofore been used to."[23] His curiosity was further stimulated in Trevaray. The villagers were hospitable and did not appear to resent billeting American troops; the population was not especially attractive, but hardworking, well-fed and dressed, and amiable. Bullard thought that they would be even friendlier after the troops were paid. He also witnessed a parade by a French infantry division fresh from the front. Their high state of appearance, morale, and discipline impressed him. Everywhere he looked he saw sacrifice, social discipline, and thrift. He was completely taken with the country and its people and was sure in his own mind that both were worth fighting for. With extra determination, he worked to settle his men and begin hard training. He was so busy and interested that he forgot to record his thoughts when he finally pinned a set of single stars to his blouse.[24]

4.

From the problems, plans, and policies which the General Headquarters, AEF, considered in the summer of 1917, certain ideas and attitudes about the American war effort in France emerged. In a sense, General Pershing and his staff were creating not only an army, but a distinct cultural milieu within which that army's soldiers were to function until 1919. To a large degree, Pershing himself created the AEF as a distinct society, impressing his wishes on his army in a way unknown to Americans since Robert E. Lee commanded the Army of Northern Virginia. That Pershing exercised such influence on an organization which came to number over two million men is powerful testimony to his force of character and driving will. It is not a judgment upon the wisdom of his decisions or the value of all his policies.[25]

General Pershing took seriously his mission of creating an independent American army in France, but he added nuances to that concept that the War Department had not foreseen. He believed not only in the political wisdom of the AEF, but also that it could break the geographic stalemate on the Western Front with its own strategic offensive. The first thing the AEF needed was a sector on the front. The selection of the American sector was dictated more by the interplay of diplomacy, the existing position of the BEF and the French army, and logistics than by strategy. Principally, the Americans had come to Europe to help France throw back an invader, not to become part of the BEF. Even if the BEF had offered part of its sector to Pershing, it is doubtful that taking it would have been politically acceptable in the United States. The AEF then was limited to finding a place along the French front. In 1917 the French army, standing on the defense, had concentrated along the front from Amiens to Verdun, guarding the approaches to Paris and its juncture with the BEF. Logistics played a formative role, for the Channel ports all the way to Cherbourg and the roads and rails inland were already supporting the BEF and the French. By the process of elimination the late-coming Americans had to settle for a sector in Lorraine.

Accepting all the these factors, General Pershing found strategic merit in taking a sector in Lorraine, and he put his staff to work creating a distinctly American approach for defeating the Germans. On what part of the Western Front was the German army most vulnerable? Where could it be attacked to force it backward from the lines it had seized and held since 1914, positions made frightfully strong with artillery, machine guns, barbed wire, and concrete? Pershing's eyes fixed on the St. Mihiel salient in the valley of the Meuse south of Verdun. His staff found the justifications.

By September 1917 Pershing's operations section had the AEF's independent strategy on paper.[26] Given the Lorraine sector, the best place to attack the German army was to drive for Metz, less than fifty miles from the existing front. To advance either north or south meant running into the Ardennes or the Vosges mountains, both easily defended and leading nowhere. Metz' principal importance was that it was a major terminus for the rail system which supplied the German army. Two major railroads ran into Metz, one from the north through Treves and Thionville, the other west from the Rhine at Strasbourg. From Metz running northeast through Sedan and Mézières, there was a single line which ran laterally behind the German front. It was the only source of supply south of the Ardennes. The AEF planners reasoned that the loss of this line would force the German army to retreat to the Rhine (at least south of the Ardennes) or stand and be destroyed in battle. As an added attraction, an offensive on the Metz-Thionville-Saarbrücken region would capture iron and coal mines crucial to the German industrial war effort.

To mount a drive on Metz, the planners knew that the AEF needed time and men. It was hoped that the British and French would buy the first by surviving the attack everyone feared the Germans would launch in 1918. For the AEF, the next year would be crucial, but Pershing's staff foresaw little alternative to reinforcing the French where they could. They hoped the AEF could take the offensive in 1918, but they planned only to reduce the St. Mihiel salient as a prelude to a great offensive on Metz in 1919. In terms of manpower, the AEF would need a minimum of half a million men in combat. A more desirable figure was 1.2 million. They thought that they could support the AEF with only one-third as many men in the logistical system as Pershing had on the battlefield, an estimate which proved hopelessly optimistic. In any case, the AEF's combat potential depended upon how rapidly troops could be trained and shipped to France. Presumably the Allies would furnish (as they had promised) the necessary arms and munitions until American sources could supply the AEF. Pershing accepted the plan and it remained the heart of the American solution to the Western Front.

Even before he reached France, Pershing had a more realistic conception of his need for a staff than did the War Department, and much of his first year in France was dominated by his concern for his headquarters and those of his subordinate corps and divisions. Once in Europe he gathered the staff officers he wanted, ruthlessly stripping incoming units, absorbing the War Department's own military missions, and even commissioning American businessmen he knew who had special skills. His obsession with creating an effective staff system was not misplaced, but it had other justifications besides military efficiency. Pershing knew that the professional reputation of the United States Army officer corps, symbolized in his own presence, was at stake in France. He knew that unless he could prove that his own system of command was effective in planning and managing large-scale offensive operations, an independent American army would not be justified. He recognized as well that his own headquarters would have to provide much of the professional authority he wanted. Around him he gathered the graduates of the Leavenworth schools and the General Staff. Almost immediately he made clear that his AEF headquarters staff, built around such able officers as Harbord, James McAndrew, John McAuley Palmer, Fox Conner, Dennis Nolan, Harold B. Fiske, George Van Horn Moseley, Frank McCoy, Malin Craig, and Hugh Drum, spoke with his voice. Their common training, experiences, and personal friendship made this group an impressive force. As Pershing's nervous system of command, they relished the commander-in-chief's authority. That they were self-confident and assertive, that they had little respect for the professional abilities of older, non-Leavenworth officers was a fact of life in the AEF. In the prewar army most of them, even though in their forties, had been only captains and majors. As brigadier generals and colonels, many of them lost what modesty and sense of fallibility they might have had. Part of the problem of their relationships with the AEF's tactical commanders was that the United States Army did not have a well-developed ethic for staff officer behavior. The relationship with Pershing was clear enough (advise, plan, and manage in the commander's name), but the AEF staff often acted and issued orders as if no other competent officer existed in France unless he worked or had worked at Pershing's headquarters at Chaumont. Even officers who rose in the AEF's command system, like Hunter Liggett and Bullard, feared the group others derisively labeled the "Leavenworth clique,"

"Chaumont crowd," or the "Cavalry Club." In any event, the AEF general staff wanted a tight, centrally controlled system of command, and they got it because Pershing replaced any officer who could not accept that system. After the war the surviving generals recognized that the AEF could not have functioned without the "Leavenworth clique." At the time they often felt that Pershing was a military Torquemada, his staff the Inquisition, and they the heretics. Unless a general got along with Pershing's staff, he did not hold "The Chief's" confidence and he might very well soon bid his command farewell.[27]

A major influence upon Pershing's commitment to an independent army, unilateral AEF strategy, and powerful general staff was his conviction that the Allies had little to teach the Americans about fighting. While he copied the French system of staff organization and accepted the necessity of using French weapons, he became progressively disillusioned with the Allies' military practices. He thought that both Allied armies were spiritually defeated, that they would never recover what he called the "offensive spirit" or their taste for "open warfare." Pershing was obsessed with the fact that the AEF's infantry must be trained for attacks in unfortified terrain. (Just how they would puncture the German lines is still unclear.) "Open warfare" became not just a tactical concept, but an "American" way of fighting and a symbol of the AEF's psychological fervor for battlefield victory.

Pershing's "open warfare" was not especially unique or effective. Built on the existing tactical doctrine of the United States Army infantry, "open warfare" emphasized the decisive role of the rifleman in the attack. While the AEF put more stress on the effectiveness of riflefire and small unit maneuver, the doctrine bore some similarity to French tactics of 1914, stressing the need for speed, the desire to close with the enemy, and the transcendent courage that accrues to the attacker. The practical result of this tactical doctrine in the AEF was that many infantry officers, especially those who took the doctrine literally, did not open their tactical formations and skillfully use their supporting arms. Except for the preplanned, set-timed barrages by both artillery and machine guns, the infantry did not get the sort of fire support it might have had, and it paid in casualties. Battlefield communications to supporting arms in 1918 were notoriously bad, depending on telephone wire, pigeons, flares, and messengers, but "open warfare" tactics as originally conceived did not place enough emphasis on the need for fire superiority. This need American officers soon recognized by working with the Allies or from their own experience, but for an officer to insist that the French infantry had some tactics worth copying was to risk being labeled a defeatist of the "trench warfare" school by the AEF general staff.[28]

Pershing viewed the issues of strategy, staff organization, and tactics not only as essential to the success of his independent American army, but a vindication of the army officer corps. He viewed the selection of American division commanders with the same perspective. In his early travels about the Allied front, Pershing was impressed by the youthfulness and energy of British division commanders. He came away convinced that he had to have general officers who were military looking (in the parade ground sense), physically very active, and mentally tough. He did not think that the War Department was going to provide him with such officers and urged it not to promote and send to France anyone "who is not strong and robust in every particular. . . . We have too much at stake to risk inefficiency through mental and physical defects."[29] Developing criteria for the selection of division commanders ("so important that it may truly be said that the success of this war depends on them") was not an easy task. As Colonel Harbord recognized, the key question was mental flexibility: could an officer readily adapt to the enormity of war on the Western Front? Could he wage war with equanimity while handling masses of men and equipment unheard-of in American military experience since the Civil War?[30] Pershing himself may have accepted Harbord's criterion, but he equated it with age and physical vigor. In 1917 he decided that his division and brigade commanders should be officers in their forties. Only such men would have the requisite ambition, confidence, and vigor to drive themselves and to win the respect of their younger subordinates. While they had to be professionally expert and adaptable, these officers must above all be energetic commanders, capable of long hours and much travel around their divisions' positions. Trying to define his idea of the perfect combat general, Pershing told a staff meeting that "no man who had arrived at the age of fifty without having had a command larger than a regiment would amount to anything in this war."[31] With the exception of Pershing himself and Leonard Wood, that excluded every other active general in the United States Army in the fall of 1917 and every colonel likely to be promoted by the War Department.[32]

Secretary of War Baker and the War Department were not so sure that Pershing had found the key to predicting successful combat leadership in division commanders, since no one (including Pershing) had any experience in "the sort of warfare now being waged." Worried that younger generals might lack "judgment and foresight" and sympathetic to the demands of senior officers to go to France as division commanders, Baker would not radically change the method of promoting generals. He did, however, make considerable concessions to Pershing. Prospective division commanders would be sent to France to inspect the Western Front, and Pershing could inspect them. If he felt they would not do, he could request that they be kept in the United States in training commands. Baker also thought that Pershing was correct in demanding physical fitness in his generals and promised that the War Department would convene a medical board to screen prospective division commanders carefully. The younger officers would have to wait until they had proved their own merit on the battlefield or the old officers disqualified themselves by physical disability or professional failures.[33]

AEF Headquarters seized on the physical fitness criterion and further refined it to mean that a general could not be obese or slow in movement and speech. Pershing would not accept officers who did not meet his physical qualifications, regardless of their past performance. He was unimpressed with the War Department's argument that the generals in their sixties and fifties deserved a chance since he believed officers of that age as a rule would not have the vigor to fight in France. He applied the rule of vigor ruthlessly. In Leonard Wood's case, he could not make his objections on medical grounds stick, but Wood was finally held in the United States because of his political ambitions and difficult personality; Pershing and Baker decided he was pathologically "insubordinate." In the case of Major General Franklin Bell, an officer whose expertise and devotion to his superiors had never been challenged, Pershing was equally obdurate.[34] Pershing and his staff held to their position on age and vigor, much to the consternation of the older officers and the pleasure of Pershing's friends. By 1918 AEF Headquarters policy was well established: a new generation of officers would command in France, a generation created by the trial of combat and the favor of John J. Pershing. To succeed, an American general had to meet both tests.[35]

5.

Crucial to Pershing's concept of an independent American army was the creation of an AEF school system. Pershing, himself a General Staff product, and his Leavenworth-trained staff wanted a centrally controlled school system managed directly by AEF Headquarters. Although he recognized that the French and British had mastered some new phases of war, particularly the use of whole families of new weapons, Pershing had no intention of letting Americans be educated in Allied methods unacceptable to AEF Headquarters. Pershing's staff also recognized that the American divisions were too busy, fragmented, and short of experienced instructors to establish schools of their own. Essentially, Pershing wanted an AEF version of the army's educational system in the United States, a system which would produce staff officers, infantry commanders, officer and enlisted experts in special weapons like trench mortars, gas, tanks, antiaircraft guns, and similar experts in engineering, communications, press relations, and sanitation. Only in artillery training was the AEF willing to trust the French, and then not completely.[36]

The challenge of creating the AEF school system provided Bullard with his first major assignment in France and suggested that Pershing valued his ability. It was his first big test before the AEF staff as well. His brigade settled, Bullard was ordered to report to Paris on detached duty. His assignment was to be commmanding general of the AEF schools, although his duties never became that elaborate. He himself approved of the concept of a central AEF school system, and he never questioned the immediate need for specialized training. After some exploratory conferences with the AEF General Staff's operations and training section, he toured the French army's specialist schools. In July and August he visited both the front and the schools at Remiremont, Nancy, and Belfort along with other American officers. The trip was extremely useful. Bullard got a sound grasp of the enormity of the war, a point driven home by his French officer guides who would not even visit major generals because they were so inconsequential. Bullard also got a sound appreciation of the complexity of the planning necessary to use all the Western Front's weaponry. While he was not especially excited about serving the

AEF as a superintendent of schools, he was pleased that his ability to speak French was rapidly improving, and he thought that his rapport with French officers might lead to more important assignments. His major impression, however, coincided with Pershing's: that the war still hung in the balance on the Western Front and it was up to the AEF to win it. The French army was too battle-weary, despite Pétain's reforms and the hopeful talk in Paris. "Nowhere do I find the spirit of the *offensive*; it does not show here; the French here have it *not*. We have in France heard much of winning the war. It will never be done with the unaggressive spirit prevailing here. I am concerned about it."[37]

After several more conferences in Paris, Pershing's staff drew up a plan for the initial school system. Bullard's assignment was to establish schools to train infantry officers as platoon commanders and weapons specialists. The schools had to be ready in two weeks to train two thousand officers coming from the United States. Within the AEF, Bullard's schools had to furnish trained infantry officers to three divisions in four weeks to replace lieutenants sent to other specialist schools. From his students he was also to create a corps of instructors, so that his limited number of American experts could be sent to tactical units and the Allied instructors replaced. Although Bullard could draw on existing French facilities and was urged to work closely with the French army, he was to avoid the uncritical acceptance of French tactics and the defeatism of trench warfare methods. He was also to continue the study of Allied infantry schools. He would not, however, have overall responsibility for the AEF school system, for Colonel James A. McAndrew was to establish the AEF Staff College at Langres and Pershing's staff would supervise both his and McAndrew's work. Bullard made no objection to the arrangement, a reaction that impressed Pershing's staff.[38]

Bullard accepted his assignment determined to meet Pershing's demands, although he knew that he would have to depend upon the French for instructors and material support. His optimism was boosted by the news that his son Lee had been commissioned as a first lieutenant of artillery and that he himself had just become a major general in the "National Army." He had no idea what the "National Army" was and had to find out that it was the War Department's name for the wartime American army raised by the draft. His promotion was automatic, for the War Department had made all the brigadiers of the regular army temporary major generals, intending them to command the new divisions. Bullard was too busy to get excited about his extra stars. With French assistance and unexpected aid from the American YMCA (which he thought more efficient than the army), Bullard set up schools at Lyon, Valreas, Valbonne, and Gondrecourt. While he appreciated that his schools would not exist without French help, he was nearly overwhelmed by their management practices. "I sometimes wonder if their defeat or near defeat by the Germans was not due to their 'Bureaucracy.'" He respected the French officers' attention to detail but criticized their lack of urgency. He was pleased with his relations with Pershing's staff, which he thought was able and determined. He shared its judgment that the AEF faced staggering organizational problems, while it appreciated his problems and was pleased with the progress of his infantry school system. He impressed one correspondent as "a veteran infantry officer" who had "a conviction that the proper time for men to stop work was when they dropped of exhaustion." By November he had his schools staffed and functioning to Pershing's satisfaction.[39]

Although he favored a clear military victory over Germany, Bullard was pessimistic about the Allies' chances and the AEF's ability to shift the military balance to the Allies' favor. When an Austro-German army shattered the Italians at Caporetto in late October, his hopes of victory plunged. The United States, he wrote, had entered the war too late. While the American intervention might save France from a "shameful peace, . . . we cannot beat Germany," which had defeated the Russians, had defeated the Italians, and still might starve England with submarine warfare. "*So far as we are concerned the war is practically lost; we will get nothing out of it, not even victory, barren.*" The most likely outcome was stalemate on the Western Front and a compromise peace, a bitter prospect. Bullard held Woodrow Wilson partly responsible for the Allies' probable defeat, but saw that the Allied military effort in France was the cause of France's war-weariness and internal unrest. The French, moreover, did not understand that it would take at least a year for the AEF to make its presence felt and blamed the Americans for the prospect of defeat. In his diary, he wrote a monotonous but understandable litany: "*too late, too late.*" Yet he was ready to continue the war:

> But after all we and they had better now fight this war to a defeat or a victory; otherwise there will be no end of war even in peace. I see indeed that one may as well be nothing daunted and go on. If defeated, one may as well be dead.

He had doubts about his own ability to meet the challenge, but he was fatalistic about his ability; either his continuous study and effort would be sufficient or it would not. He kept working. He worried, however, about his superiors. At the moment the president was carrying the American war effort with his fantastic military promises and dreams of world peace. "He is making us the sneer of the earth for talk." Pershing, Bullard thought, was not sufficiently determined to pull the AEF and the Allies together and fight. "He is in all his history a pacifist." He was sophisticated, wise, ambitious, and inspiring, but "*not a warrior.*"

In Pershing's case he hoped his opinion was mistaken, and he was encouraged when Pershing ordered American wives from the war zone, moved the AEF headquarters out of Paris to the simple barracks at Chaumont, and relieved two American commanders. Perhaps "The Chief" was the man to save France and the reputation of the United States Army. Bullard was glad he had put his doubts in his diary and not expressed them publicly. Poised and confident in all outward aspects, he went about his duties.[40]

It was fortunate that Bullard remained uncharacteristically silent, for even Pershing's own household was depressed and Pershing was aroused by the pessimistic talk of American officers. He was in no mood for anything but the staunchest confidence. And he was ready to tighten his grasp upon the AEF and the American war effort without sentiment.[41]

Despite his studied impersonality, Pershing had favorites, and in the AEF his favorite unit was the First Division.[42] He felt responsible for its formation and always thought of himself as its first commanding general, even though he had done nothing more than select its infantry and artillery regiments for service in France. He knew many of these regiments' career officers. He knew that the junior officers and enlisted men of the division were no more than recruits, but he thought of them as seasoned regulars and demanded perfection in appearance and attitude from them. In Pershing's eyes, the First Division always had a symbolic role. It represented both the "old army" and the military future of the AEF. It was the living promise to save France with American arms and to prove to Old Europe and its battle-weary soldiers that the United States would some day do what they had not—redeem the democracies and the profession of arms with victory on the Western Front. Pershing also expected the division to be a model which all future AEF divisions would follow, a model in organization, administration, discipline, tactics, and appearance. And he expected its commanding general to meet those standards and set them for every other man in the division. It was an impossible role, given Pershing's expectations in the fall of 1917.

With the exception of its artillery brigade (composed of the Fifth, Sixth, and Seventh Field Artillery Regiments, the First Trench Mortar Battery, and an ammunition train), the First Division settled into its billets in the villages around Gondrecourt. Like a mad amoeba, the division divided, amalgamated, absorbed, and divided as Pershing's staff played with their concepts of divisional tables of organization and equipment. Even as its organization changed, the division was stripped of officers and men to go to school and to fill billets in the AEF Headquarters, line of communications, and training establishment. In the two infantry brigades, the transformations were staggering. Each infantry company provided men for each regiment's expanded machine gun company and 37 mm. cannon platoon. Every company doubled to the new strength of two hundred and fifty-two officers and men. Similar turnovers went on in the division's other units: the First Engineer Regiment, the Second Field Signal Battalion, the headquarters troop, and various service and supply trains organized to support the division logistically. The infantry had other perplexing organizational problems, for its French instructors, officers, and sergeants from the Forty-Seventh Division (*Chasseurs Alpins*), insisted in organizing platoons on the French model of half grenadiers, half riflemen. For the American infantrymen, there were a host of new weapons to master: hand and rifle grenades, the complex Chauchat automatic rifle, and the Hotchkiss machine gun in all its variations.[43]

Pershing made the infantry brigades' tasks even more difficult because he expected the American infantrymen to reach West Point standards in dress and deportment, match "old army" proficiency with the rifle, give up alcohol and women, and be prepared to entertain AEF staffers and French political and military celebrities at a moment's notice. General Sibert and his division staff, all of them learning on the job, began with a difficult and thankless task, and Pershing gave them no rest and sympathy. Sibert particularly got off to a bad start with Pershing and his staff. He never recovered their confidence, although he worked manfully and had the loyalty and labor of an able staff led by Lieutenant Colonels Campbell King and George C. Marshall, Jr. Pershing's first visit to the infantry in the Gondrecourt area did not go well for the division and Sibert. Pershing found the troops zealous, comfortable in their billets, clean, and decently supplied, but unsatisfactory on all the things Pershing held dear—appearance, bearing, drill, discipline, and leadership habits.[44] Less than two weeks later, Pershing again visited the infantry brigades, accompanied by General Pétain and his staff, and saw no improvement. He could understand why the *Chasseurs Alpins* looked fine, but he was mortified that the attached Fifth Marine Regiment was up to French standards and his regulars were not. Sibert did not do much to impress "The Chief," becoming ill during a review, missing much of the tour, and recovering in time to complain that the AEF staff was stripping him of able officers. Pershing's staff came away convinced that Sibert did not understand Pershing's problems and that Pershing understood Sibert's only too well. In contrast, Bullard was with Pershing for all seventeen inspection stops.[45]

American civilian visitors to AEF Headquarters picked up Pershing's discontent with Sibert and reported it to friends at home. Felix Frankfurter wrote Newton Baker that Sibert was "too old to do the job" and said that Pershing thought that Sibert "cannot stand the gaff." Sibert, Frankfurter thought, could not get around to visit his troops and inspire them as a division commander should. "The contrast between his attitude to his men, the relation of the men to him, and the relation of the French officers to their men is striking beyond words. And in the simple words of an officer it all means death." Another amateur visitor, the editor of the *Boston Transcript*, wrote Leonard Wood that the First Division was suffering from a lack of experienced leadership, especially in its commanding general. Sibert and many of his troops showed no fighting spirit. General Bullard, however, was getting along well with the French, had impressed the AEF staff with his energy and stand for "the strictest sort of discipline," and was an acknowledged field soldier.[46]

The pressure on the First Division and on Sibert increased. In September they were visited by the French premier, who was critical of their readiness, much to Pershing's annoyance. Brigadier General André W. Brewster, the AEF inspector general, took another look at the infantry regiments and found a great deal wrong. The troops' appearance was improved, but their campaign hats were unsightly and their shoes muddy. Division training was much too Gallicized with not enough practical application and tactical decision-making. American officers did not look military, were undemanding instructors, and had bad "command voices." While the billets of the Second Brigade were decent, those of the First were not. The Sixteenth Infantry was a disaster in all respects. Brewster's total impression was that the division had good men, but bad commanders. It was not making much progress toward being physically and mentally ready for combat.[47] Pershing's headquarters bore down on the First Division and on Sibert. On October 3 a battalion of the Twenty-Sixth Infantry, led by Major Theodore Roosevelt, Jr., staged an elaborate trench warfare problem for Pershing at the division's training area. The problem went well, but Sibert fumbled the critique and Pershing upbraided him in front of his staff. Three days later the AEF training section sent the division an order which gave the division no latitude in its training schedule and stressed the use of American "open warfare" tactics and discipline.[48]

Sibert knew that Pershing was unhappy with the division and his command and tried to describe his problems that were real. His defense, however, only fed Pershing's desire to replace him, for Sibert's major point was that the division needed all the French assistance it could get for both staff work and infantry training. That was not the sort of news AEF Headquarters liked. Sibert pointed out that trench warfare required much planning. His division staff was inexperienced because of transfers, and the brigades and regiments had no staffs at all because the table of organization did not allow them. Sibert thought that the weapons training was going well, however, although work in tactics and communications lagged. But Pershing was unmoved by Sibert's explanation, though he admitted that the division was improving, and his staff began to scent the kill. Sibert, thought George Van Horn Moseley, was "a wonderful man," but saw the war as a great engineering problem, not as the leadership of men. Colonel Harbord learned that "The Chief" was thinking of relieving Sibert because he was not soldierly and had let the division "run down." Pershing was looking for a new division commander.[49]

On October 20 Pershing and Bullard conferred about the infantry schools, but Pershing was more interested in talking about his division commanders' failures. He told Bullard that he was going to relieve two of them and that he was thinking of making Bullard commanding general of the First Division. Bullard was sympathetic to both "The Chief" and the failing generals, one of whom had asked Bullard to serve with him. "So it goes. . . . a man can never judge himself." Pershing said no more, and the matter lapsed without elaboration.[50] Three days later, however, Pershing told the War Department he wanted to reassign Bullard. General Bliss replied that he wanted Bullard to come home and assume command of the Third Division and asked about his availability. Pershing let the matter slide but alerted Harbord that the Sibert-Bullard switch was still on his mind.[51]

Pershing had good reason to let the Sibert affair alone, for the infantry battalions of the First Division had just gone into the line with the French. One battalion of each regiment, reinforced by engineers, machine gunners, and communications troops, assumed a frontline sector under French command. The Sommerviller sector, northeast of Nancy, had been quiet since 1915, and the French thought that it was a good place to introduce the Americans to *les Boches*. With the French government and army watching the division so closely, it would have been impolitic to relieve its commanding general. Pershing waited and hoped his troops would do well. The artillery fired; a patrol captured a German prisoner; the machine gunners fired across No-Man's Land. In the meantime, Sibert was tightening his command. He relieved the colonel of the Sixteenth Infantry, the second of that regiment to lose his command, and obtained a replacement from Pershing's staff, Colonel John L. Hines. A veteran troop leader of forty-nine, "Birdie" Hines, a cheerful, buck-toothed giant, found his regiment "dazed or asleep. . . . They did not seem to realize that they were on the verge of a big war." As Sibert had told Pershing, the division's problem was junior officer leadership and the lack of any staff below the division level. Without a staff, the regimental commander was nothing but the "first sergeant of an enormous company." Hines immediately created a staff on the four section pattern the AEF had copied from the French. However, two days after he took command, the Germans raided his second battalion, then in the lines, and killed three, wounded twenty, and captured eleven. Hines thought that he would be relieved, but instead the burial of the three very ordinary, very dead men of the Sixteenth Infantry set off an orgy of French adulation and good feeling in AEF Headquarters. The French had their symbolic American dead and the AEF had real casualties to stiffen their troops. The division stayed in the lines until November 20, losing a total of eighty-three officers and men to snipers and shells. Pershing felt confident that they would now train more seriously.[52]

Bullard wondered why Pershing did not relieve Sibert, concluding that Pershing did not have the authority. Pershing himself may have wondered for not until he got a letter from Secretary Baker, reinforced by a cable from the War Department, was he certain he could replace division commanders. In the meantime, Bullard thought that he would get the Third Division.[53] But Pershing was only being circumspect, exhibiting all the guile which ruins his image as a "simple soldier." There were difficulties with relieving Sibert. One of them was also a very good reason for sending him home. Sibert was a major general in the regular army and the second ranking officer in France; the thought that he might replace Pershing was regarded by Pershing's staff as a "positive danger." His career also showed a considerable influence in Washington. Even if the secretary of war gave Pershing the general authority to relieve division commanders, could Sibert be removed without a crisis? Sibert was well known, an altogether pleasant man, and an excellent engineer. Pershing moved carefully. On the day the last First Division battalions left the Sommerviller sector, he talked with Bullard and told him he would replace Sibert. The arrangements, however, were not yet complete, so Pershing told Bullard to go to the front and look around. Bullard did and was staggered by the complexity of trench warfare. He also impressed his GHQ chauffeur by helping him change a flat tire and getting him a meal at an officers' mess. In the meantime Bullard heard rumors that Sibert was sick, which he took as a preparation for the First Division commander's relief.[54]

Pershing needed a stronger case against Sibert, and he built it while Bullard toured the lines. Pershing sent General Brewster, assisted by a team of skilled officers, to inspect the First Division again. Brewster's inspectors, future generals all, went over the division thoroughly and reported that the division's training and discipline were still unsatisfactory. Unlike earlier inspectors, they concentrated on criticizing the division's senior officers. Of all the regimental commanders, only Colonel Hines was satisfactory. General Sibert should go as well. The inspectors described Sibert as brave, conscientious, loyal, vigorous, and firm, since he had already relieved several regimental and battalion commanders. He simply was not an experienced line officer and lacked "keenness and initiative." The inspectors recommended that he be replaced "by a man of proved ability in these respects and [Sibert] should be transferred to work where his proved ability can be used to better advantage."[55]

Still Pershing did not act. On December 8 he again talked with Bullard. Pershing told him that he wanted Bullard in France. Pershing had so informed the War Department and there had been no objection. Pershing said that he was optimistic about the war, that he was confident the Americans had come in time and that the Allies would eventually triumph. He got his faith, he told Bullard, from President Wilson's example. ("He was always a good courtier," Bullard wrote that night.) Bullard politely agreed with the commander in chief, particularly since he thought that Pershing would not throw the AEF into battle until it was larger and better trained. Bullard went to his quarters uncertain about the interview.[56]

On December 13 Pershing's elliptical remarks became a little clearer. He issued a confidential memorandum to the senior officers of the AEF warning them against being pessimistic in thought and speech. Pershing wrote that he had heard reports that American generals had made critical remarks about the conditions the AEF faced. Too many had expressed a lack of confidence in the Allies and shown undue admiration for the Germans' skill and numbers. Such sentiments were intolerable. The commander in chief demanded positive attitudes, determination, and "conservative firmness and faith in our cause." Unless an officer fit that description, he would be relieved. This message was clear enough in the AEF, but few knew that the original memorandum had been addressed to Sibert personally.[57] On the same day, Pershing cabled the War Department that he expected his regular divisions to fight shortly, if only to bolster Allied morale. He thought it "highly essential" that the first American battles be successful in order to restore faith in the AEF and Allied victory. He expected the regular divisions to be on the line under American command in the spring and he wanted the best available leadership.[58]

The next day he relieved Sibert and appointed Major General Robert L. Bullard the commanding general of the First Division.

NOTES

[1]B. H. Liddell Hart, *The Real War, 1914-1918* (Boston: Little, Brown, 1930); pp. 54-320.

[2]Correlli Barnett, "General Henri Phillipe Benoni Omer Pétain," in *The Swordbearers* (New York: Morrow, 1964), pp. 193-265.

[3]Frederick Palmer, *Newton D. Baker*, 2 vols. (New York: Dodd, Mead, 1931, I, pp.

1-415, and Daniel R. Beaver, *Newton D. Baker and the American War Effort, 1917-1919* (Lincoln, Neb.: University of Nebraska Press, 1966), pp. 1-49.

⁴My description of Pershing is based on data from Don Smythe, "John J. Pershing: Soldier," previously cited, and Frederick Palmer, *John J. Pershing, General of the Armies* (Harrisburg, Pa.: Military Service Publishing Co., 1948). See also James G. Harbord, *Leaves from a War Diary* (New York: Dodd, Mead, 1931), and Charles G. Dawes, *A Journal of the Great War,* 2 vols. (Boston: Houghton Mifflin, 1921).

⁵Brig. Gen. J. J. Pershing to T. Roosevelt, May 24, 1916, General Correspondence, General John J. Pershing Papers, Manuscript Division, Library of Congress; Brig. Gen. J. J. Pershing to Maj. Gen. H. L. Scott, March 3, 1917, General Correspondence, Hugh L. Scott Papers.

⁶Brig. Gen. Howard L. Laubach, USA (ret.), manuscript review of Bullard, *American Soldiers Also Fought,* 1939, copy in Bullard Papers. Laubach's account is substantiated by a telegram, Maj. Gen. J. J. Pershing to Col. R. L. Bullard, March 3, 1917, which invited Bullard to San Antonio to discuss a special assignment. Copy in Box 36, General Correspondence, Pershing Papers.

⁷"Report of the Secretary of War," *Annual Reports of the War Department, 1917* (Washington: Government Printing Office, 1917), I, pp. 21-23.

⁸Diarybook 8, entries, May 1-20, 1917, BP; entry, June 30, 1917, Wood Diary, Wood Papers.

⁹Edward M. Coffman, *The War to End All Wars: The American Military Experience in World War I* (New York: Oxford University Press, 1968), pp. 20-53; Historical Section, Army War College, *The Genesis of the American First Army* (Washington: Government Printing Office, 1938), pp. 1-3.

¹⁰John J. Pershing, *My Experiences in the World War,* 2 vols. (New York: Frederick A. Stokes, 1931), I, pp. 1-3; Maj. Gen. T. H. Bliss to Maj. Gen. E. F. McGlachlin, November 14, 1921, reprinted in Frederick Palmer, *Bliss, Peacemaker* (New York: Dodd, Mead, 1934), pp. 169-170; Brig. Gen. Joseph E. Kuhn, memorandum for the Chief of Staff, "Plans for the Possible Expeditionary Force to France," May 12, 1917, copy in "Book File," Pershing Papers.

¹¹Palmer, *Newton D. Baker,* I, pp. 159-166, and *John J. Pershing,* pp. 72-81; Hermann Hagedorn, *Leonard Wood,* 2 vols. (New York: Harper and Brothers, 1931) II, pp. 204-223.

The transfer of allegiance is explicit in the following letters: Brig. C. R. Edwards to Maj. J. G. Harbord, June 18, 1917, and Col. J. G. Harbord to Brig. Gen. C. R. Edwards, July 6, 1917, "World War Military Activity," James G. Harbord Papers; Brig. Gen. F. R. McCoy to T. Roosevelt, January 1, 1919, Frank R. McCoy Papers; Lt. Col. R. Alexander to Maj. Gen. J. J. Pershing, April 23, 1917, and Maj. Gen. J. F. Bell to Maj. Gen. J. J. Pershing, April 3, 1917, Pershing Papers.

¹²Pershing Diary, entry, May 10, 1917, Pershing Papers; Palmer, *Newton D. Baker,* I, pp. 354-356; *Army and Navy Journal,* January 27 and February 3, 1917.

¹³The process of selection is described in Col. R. L. Michie, GS, "Memorandum for the Chief of Staff," April 26, 1917, in File 7928 ("Appointment of Officers of Organized Militia or Volunteers in Case of War with Mexico"), Army War College Correspondence File, RG 165; Memorandum, "List of Colonels Mentioned by the Secretary of War for Promotion," May 30, 1917, copies in Scott and Baker Papers; Palmer, *Bliss, Peacemaker,* pp. 173-176; Maj. Gen. H. L. Scott to Col. H. G. Sickle, August 20, 1917, and to Col. W.

C. Brown, August 17, 1917, and to Maj. Gen. E. H. Crowder, April 11, 1918, all Scott Papers; Maj. Gen. T. H. Bliss, memo to the Secretary of War, September 14, 1917, attached to WDGS Report 13949, Office of the Chief of Staff Correspondence File, Records of the War Department General Staff, 1907-1917, RG 165.

[14]Entry, May 29, 1917, in Harbord, *Leaves from a War Diary,* p. 3.

[15]Diarybook 8, entry, June 1, 1917, BP.

[16]Diarybook 8, entry, June 15, 1917; Bullard autobiography, pp. 118-120, both BP.

[17]Edward B. Clark, *William L. Sibert: The Army Engineer* (Philadelphia: Dorrance, 1930), pp. 39-158.

[18]Diarybook 8, entry, June 16, 1017, BP.

[19]Diarybook 8, entries, June 14-28, BP; Beaumont Buck, *Memories of War and Peace* (San Antonio: The Naylor Company, 1935), pp. 150-154; George B. Duncan, "Reminiscences of the World War," pp. 18-19, *mss* autobiography in the possession of Professor Edward M. Coffman, University of Wisconsin; The Society of the First Division, *History of the First Division during the World War, 1917-1919* (Philadelphia: Winston, 1922), pp. 6-7; Campbell King, "Tour in France," *mss* memoir (1919), Campbell King Papers, Manuscript Division, Duke University Library; Lt. Col. LaRoy Upton to his family, July 9, 1917, LaRoy Upton Papers; Maj. Gen. Joseph D. Patch, USA (Ret.), *A Soldier's War: The First Infantry Division, A.E.F.* (Corpus Christi, Texas: Joseph Dorst Patch, 1966), pp. 23-24.

Bullard's intervention in the messhall was recalled in Mr. Jesse M. Hughes to the author, March 12, 1972. Mr. Hughes became mess sergeant for the *San Jacinto.*

[20]Buck, *Memories of War and Peace,* p. 154; King, "Tour in Europe," p. 1; *History of the First Division,* pp. 7-8; Colonel Jacques Aldebert de Peneton Comte de Chambrun and Captain Charles de Marenches, *The American Army in the European Conflict* (New York: Macmillan, 1919), p. 117.

[21]Duncan, "Reminiscences of the World War," p. 22.

[22]Pershing Diary, entry, June 29, 1917, Pershing Papers.

[23]Diarybook 8, entry, July 18, 1917, BP.

[24]*Ibid.*

[25]Coffman, *The War to End All Wars,* pp. 125-126; Historical Section, Army War College, *The Genesis of the American First Army,* pp. 3-5; Pershing, *My Experiences in the World War,* I, pp. 124-179.

[26]Office of the Chief of Staff, Headquarters, AEF, "A Strategical Study on the Employment of the A.E.F. against the Imperial Government," September 25, 1917, copy in the Hugh A. Drum Papers.

[27]This discussion is based on the following sources, which emphasize the positive contributions of the AEF general staff, but which also recognize Pershing's demands for loyalty and the great power his staff wielded in his name: Edward M. Coffman, "The American Military Generation Gap in World War I," proceedings of the Second Military History Symposium, USAF Academy, 1968, *Command & Commanders in Modern Military History* (Washington: USAF Academy, 1971), pp. 35-43; Maj. Gen. J. G. Harbord, "Personalities and Relationships in the American Expeditionary Forces," Army War College lecture, April 29, 1933, copy in Drum Papers; Brig. Gen. F. R. McCoy to Senator J. W. Wadsworth, Jr., April 22, 1919, McCoy Papers; Brig. Gen. G. V. Moseley to Maj. Gen. C. C. Williams, May 10, 1928, and George Van Horn Moseley, "One Soldier's Journey," I, p. 160, Moseley Papers; Hunter Liggett, *Commanding an American Army* (Boston: Houghton Mifflin, 1925), p. 7; Duncan, "Reminiscences of the Great

War,'' p. 48; T. Bentley Mott, *Twenty Years as Military Attaché* (New York: Oxford University Press, 1937), pp. 285-286; Notebook 27, entry, February 1921, BP; and Bullard, *Personalities and Reminiscences,* pp. 59-63.

²⁸For a complete statement of the AEF position, see the cable, Pershing to C/S, USA, August 27, 1918, "AEF Confidential Cables Sent," Harbord Papers; Pershing, *My Experiences in the World War,* I, pp. 150-154.

For a professional assessment of World War I infantry combat, see Military History and Publication Section, The Infantry School, *Infantry in Battle* (Washington: Infantry Journal Press, 1934).

The "open warfare" issue divided the AEF from the War Department General Staff and agitated the officer corps. See Maj. Gen. Robert Alexander, *Memories of the World War: 1917-1918* (New York: Macmillan, 1931), pp. 2-3.

²⁹Cable, Pershing to AGWAR (Adjutant General, War Department), July 28, 1917, "AEF Confidential Cables Sent," Harbord Papers.

³⁰Entry, June 1, 1917, in Harbord, *Leaves from a War Diary,* p. 12.

³¹Diary entry, February, 1918, reprinted in Johnson Hagood, *The Services of Supply* (Boston: Houghton Mifflin, 1927), p. 137

³²Maj. Gen. J. J. Pershing to the Adjutant General, USA, September 9, 1917, reprinted in Historical Division, Department of the Army, *United States Army in the World War, 1917-1919,* 17 vols. (Washington: Government Printing Office, 1948), II, p. 39 (hereafter cited as USA/WW, 1917-1919); Gen. J. J. Pershing to N. D. Baker, October 4 and November 13, 1917, reprinted in Pershing, *My Experiences in the World War* I, pp. 189-192 and 227-230.

³³N. D. Baker to Maj. Gen. J. J. Pershing, September 10, 1917, reprinted in Pershing, *My Experiences in the World War* I, pp. 223-226; Cable, Acting Chief of Staff John Biddle to Pershing, November 13, 1917, "AEF Confidential Cables Received," Harbord Papers.

³⁴Maj. Gen. J. F. Bell to Gen. J. J. Pershing, June 25, 1918, General Correspondence, Pershing Papers. See also Donald Smythe, "Pershing and General J. Franklin Bell, 1917-1918," *Mid-America* 54 (January 1972), pp. 34-51.

³⁵In addition to the above sources, see the Pershing position in cable, Gen. J. J. Pershing to AGWAR, June 28, 1918, "AEF Confidential Cables Sent," Harbord Papers; Gen. J. J. Pershing to Maj. Gen. H. L. Scott, June 28, 1918, Scott Papers; Maj. Gen. J. G. Harbord to Maj. Gen. L. Wood, September 18, 1918, "Military War Activity," Harbord Papers; and Maj. Gen. H. T. Allen to Gen. J. J. Pershing, March 20, 1918, Pershing Papers. See Hunter Liggett, *A.E.F.: Ten Years Ago in France* (New York; Dodd, Mead, 1928), pp. 254-263, for the most perceptive critique of Pershing's criteria. See also Joseph Dickman, *The Great Crusade* (New York: Appleton, 1927), pp. 25, 163; Eben Swift autobiography, pp. 119-120, Eben Swift Papers, USMA Library; Maj. Gen. H. L. Scott to Maj. F. R. McCoy, January (?), 1918, McCoy Papers.

³⁶This section on the AEF schools in 1917 is drawn from the memo, "Army Schools of the American Expeditionary Force," n.d., "Schools File," G-5 (Training), AEF GHQ Organization Records, Records of the American Expeditionary Force, Record Group 120, National Archives (hereafter cited as RG 120). The entries for July 17-27, 1917, in the wartime diary of Hugh Drum, Drum Papers, were another valuable source.

³⁷Diarybook 8, entry, July 30, 1917, BP; Bullard autobiography, BP.

³⁸Diarybook 8, entries, August 1917, BP; entry, August 16, 1917, in "Chapter Notes" III, p. 38, and AGO, AEF, to Maj. Gen. R. L. Bullard, September 3, 1917, Chronological File 1917, both Palmer Papers; memorandum, AEF GHQ Operations and Training Section,

August 29, 1917, reprinted in "Army Schools of the American Expeditionary Forces," previously cited.

³⁹Diarybook 8, entries, September 18-October 20, 1917, BP; "Chapter Notes" VIII, pp. 107-108, and attached letter, and Col. J. McA. Palmer to Mrs. Palmer, November 13 and 17, 1917, Palmer Papers; Heywood Broun, *Our Army at the Front* (New York: Charles Scribner's, 1919), pp. 117-118.

⁴⁰Diarybook 8, entries, September 23-December 3, 1917, BP.

⁴¹General J. J. Pershing, memorandum for the Chief-of-Staff, AEF, October (?), 1917, Pershing-Harbord Correspondence, Harbord Papers; Diary entry, November 30, 1917, in Dawes, *A Journal of the Great War* I, p. 58-60; Diary entry, December 23, 1917, in Avery D. Andrews, *My Friend and Classmate John J. Pershing* (Harrisburg, Pa.: Military Service Publishing Company, 1939), p. 95.

⁴²Pershing, *My Experiences in the World War* I, pp. 87-88, 91-92; Harbord, *The American Army in France,* p. 99; "Chapter Notes," Vol. VII, pp. 39-46, Palmer Papers.

In addition to the First Division's official history, *History of the First Division,* previously cited, there are two basic sources for the division's service in France: Historical Section, Army War College, *Order of Battle of the United States Land Forces in the World War: American Expeditionary Force: Divisions* (Washington: Government Printing Office, 1931), and *World War Records, First Division, A.E.F., Regular,* 29 vols. (Washington: Society of the First Division, 1928-1930). The first is hereafter cited as *Order of Battle: AEF: Divisions,* and the second as *WWR/1st Div* with volume number (but without page numbers because it is unpaginated).

⁴³*History of the First Division,* pp. 9-27; entries, September 1-October 19, 1917, in "War Diaries HQ 1st Division, 1st Inf Brigade, 16th Infantry Regiment, 18th Infantry Regiment," *WWR/1st Div* XVI, and "War Diaries 2d Inf Brigade, 26th Infantry Regiment, 28th Infantry Regiment, 3rd MG Battalion," *WWR/1st Div* XVII.

⁴⁴AGO, AEF, to Commanding General, First Division, memo, "Inspection by the Commander-in-Chief," August 7, 1917, in *WWR/1st Div* XX.

⁴⁵Pershing Diary, entries, August 18-21, 1917, Pershing Papers; "Report of Official Journey August 18-21, 1917, and "Chapter Notes" VIII, pp. 41-43, Palmer Papers; General J. J. Pershing, "Memorandum for the Inspector General," August 25, 1917, File 745, Office of the Inspector General Correspondence, GHQ AEF Organization Records, RG 120.

⁴⁶F. Frankfurter to N. D. Baker, August 15, 1917, Correspondence, 1916-1921, Baker Papers; J. T. Williams to Maj. Gen. L. Wood, October 1, 1917, Wood Papers.

⁴⁷Brig. Gen. A. W. Brewster, IG, to AG, AEF, September 19, 1917, Office of the Inspector General Correspondence, GHQ AEF Organization Records, RG 120; Buck, *Memories of Peace and War,* pp. 163-166.

⁴⁸Pershing Diary, entries, October 6 and 7, 1917, Pershing Papers; G-5, GHQ, AEF, "Program of Training for the 1st Division, AEF," October 6, 1917, copy in Major General Harold B. Fiske Papers, National Archives; Forrest C. Pogue, *George C. Marshall: The Education of a General* (New York: Viking, 1963), pp. 145-156.

⁴⁹Pershing Diary, entry, October 15, 1917, Pershing Papers; Memo, Maj. Gen. W. L. Sibert to the C-in-C, AEF, October 8, 1917, *USA/WW, 1917-1919,* II, pp. 55-57; G. V. Moseley, entry, October 13, 1917, "War Notes" I, Moseley Papers; entry, December 18, 1917, in Harbord, *Leaves in a War Diary,* pp. 200-202.

⁵⁰Diarybook 9, entry, October 20, 1917, BP.

⁵¹Cable, Pershing to AGWAR, October 23, 1917, "AEF Confidential Cables Sent,"

Harbord Papers; memo for telegram, Gen. T. H. Bliss to Gen. J. J. Pershing, October 25, 1917, Bullard 201 File; memo, Pershing to Harbord, October 31, 1917, Pershing-Harbord Correspondence, Harbord Papers.

⁵²*History of the First Division*, pp. 27-35; Pershing, *My Experiences in the World War,* pp. 217-218.

Hines' experiences are taken from "Battle Command of a Regiment," speech to the District of Columbia chapter, Reserve Officers Association, June 19, 1923, and "Remarks to the General Staff College," speech in 1919, both in Hines Speeches, Vol. I, John L. Hines Papers, Manuscript Division, Library of Congress.

⁵³Diarybook 9, entry, November 11, 1917, BP; Cable, Acting Chief of Staff Biddle to Gen. J. J. Pershing, November 13, 1917, "AEF Confidential Cables Received," Harbord Papers.

⁵⁴Diarybook 9, entries, November 20 and 26, 1917, BP.

⁵⁵Memorandum, Inspector General to the Commander in Chief, "Tactical Inspection of the First Division on November 26, 27, and 28, 1917," December 4, 1917, File 745, Office of the Inspector General Correspondence, GHQ AEF Organization Records, Rg 120.

⁵⁶Diarybook 9, entry, December 8, 1917, BP.

⁵⁷Confidential memorandum HQ AEF, "Pessimism," December 13, 1917, copy in the Charles P. Summerall Papers, Manuscript Division, Library of Congress. A copy of the original draft, addressed to General Sibert, is in the Pershing-Harbord Correspondence, Harbord Papers.

⁵⁸Cable, Pershing to Chief of Staff, December 13, 1917, "AEF Confidential Cables Sent," Harbord Papers.

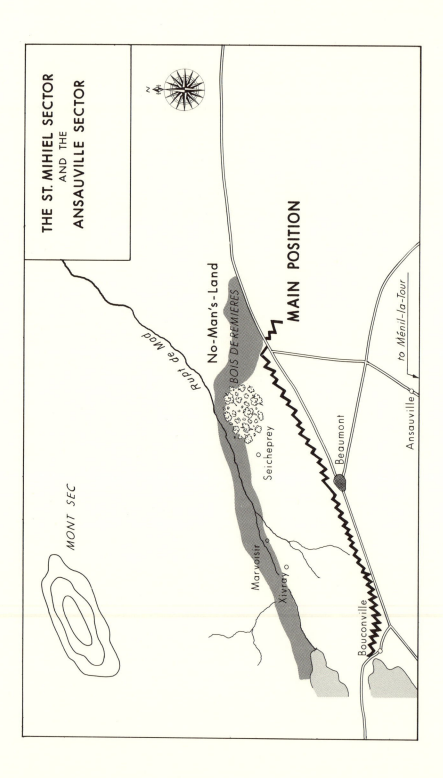

THE ST. MIHIEL SECTOR AND THE ANSAUVILLE SECTOR

MONT SEC

Rupt de Mad

No-Man's-Land

BOIS DE REMIERES

MAIN POSITION

Marvoisir

Xivray

Seicheprey

Beaumont

Bouconville

Ansauville

to Ménil-la-Tour

17

The First Division:

Introduction to War

1917-1918

General Pershing had reason to tighten the command of the First Division, for he was under increasing pressure from both the French and British high commands to commit his four-division AEF to battle. Anticipating a German offensive, Field Marshal Sir Douglas Haig was concerned that American manpower was not coming to France rapidly enough or becoming fit for combat with sufficient speed. The British urged President Wilson, the War Department, and Pershing to modify the concept of an independent American army and to rush infantry battalions and machine gunners to France. These fresh combatants would then be incorporated into the BEF and the French army for training and, by implication, battle. The British proposal was anathema at AEF Headquarters, but since the British promised to provide shipping and eventually to return the American troops to Pershing, he finally acquiesced. After two months of conferences, Pershing agreed to send six divisions (less artillery) to the BEF for training. The BEF would provide additional shipping for this force, keep the American units intact, and return them to AEF control around June, 1918, which meant that they would be in the BEF front during the period of the anticipated German offensive.

The French were equally insistent that Pershing put his soldiers under French command, knowing that the War Department had given Pershing the authority to do so if he thought it expedient. General Pétain, in a series of meetings with Pershing in December 1917 and January 1918, insisted that the AEF must get into the war to bolster French morale. Pershing, with characteristic stubbornness, rejected Pétain's proposals until the French general conceded that Franco-American military integration would be for training purposes only and that American artillery, support units, and division and corps staffs would also train at the front with their own troops.[1]

In their talks about the AEF's use, Pershing and Pétain discussed the commitment of the First Division. Just as the division had come to France as a symbolic gesture, it was now to go to the front for a similar purpose. Pétain stressed that French public morale would greatly improve with the First Division's appearance in the trenches. Since the French appeared more willing to compromise on the matter of an independent American army and held the sector Pershing wanted for his Metz offensive, "The Chief" was sympathetic to Pétain's proposals for temporary integration. He had Pétain agree that the division would go into the line along the St. Mihiel salient. In return, he assured the French that he would place American troops under French command if an emergency arose. Pershing thought that the French need was greater than the BEF's and he believed Pétain understood the political and professional imperatives which demanded an independent American army. On the other hand, he suspected that the British would use their shipping and diplomatic leverage to stall the creation of such a force.[2]

Part of Pershing's reluctance to commit even the First Division stemmed from his own and his staff's belief that the division was not ready for deployment as a division. Pershing had no intention of letting the First Division go to the front without an effective commander and division staff. Though the division head-quarters' responsibilities in the line would be limited, its failure could be used as proof of the AEF's inability to control large bodies of troops in combat. The French were still not enthusiastic about the Americans' ability to handle the complexities of modern trench warfare, although they were more willing than the British to accept the concept of an American army. Pershing's awareness that the competency of the Army officer corps was at stake no doubt confirmed his decision to replace Sibert. Certainly Pershing and his staff made it clear to the new division commander that he had little time to make the First Division combat-worthy. "The Chief" would accept no excuses for failure.[3]

1.

Taking command of the First Division on December 14, General Bullard imparted his own and Pershing's urgency to his subordinates and his troops. On his second day of command Bullard met with his division staff and the brigade and regimental commanders. His message was simple. First, the division's training "in all essentials" would conform to AEF Headquarters methods and expectations and to the United States Army's principles of training and warfare. Although the division would work cordially with the French, it must remember its own heritage and unique military character, learning and adopting from the Allies, but not aping their methods. In all matters it must become a model of military deportment and appearance, and the division staff would set the example. If his staff would not meet the standards of the Military Academy, Bullard himself would discipline them "as I must and will." All officers, from the division commander to the newest lieutenant, must supervise and direct training with greater con-scientiousness. Bullard made the point clear: "If we cannot do the job, we will be replaced." He made sure his officers understood that he himself would not be the first to be relieved. He also stressed that no officer or noncommissioned officer could command effectively if he did not exhibit more energy, knowledge, and determination than his men. As for the troops, Bullard was concerned that they were not mentally prepared to fight the Germans. To steel the troops for the fighting ahead, he wanted the division to develop "a deep spirit of hate, and offense against the enemy." To end the lackadaisical attitude of the division, Bullard promised more rigorous training:

> There is some talk about the men growing stale where so much is required. It is not a question of being or not being stale. It is a question of learning how [to] beat the Boche and to keep him from killing us. You must keep before your men this idea of hate and his [*sic*] watchword must be *kill, kill,* KILL the Boche.[4]

Upon departing from the Division PC (Post of Command), Bullard's officers had no doubts about his goals and his close relationship with Pershing. They knew his record as an aggressive officer. Whether the new division commander had the skill and determination for success remained to be seen.[5]

Bullard concentrated first on the system of command and the people within it. His experience in France, added to his service with the Second Division in Texas, had convinced him of the primary importance of organization in modern warfare, especially staff functioning. His goal in the First Division was to "create a machine that will work independently of the quality of the man that turns the crank."[6] Bullard started to build with his division chief-of-staff. When Sibert commanded the division, the chief-of-staff was Colonel Hanson E. Ely. Bullard thought Ely an unpleasant man, a large, heavy, humorless, overbearing officer who made every statement a threat. He had met Ely in the Philippines, and Ely had impressed him as "self-assertive, pugnacious, almost disrespectful in manner and tone."[7] Shortly before his relief, Sibert had given Ely command of the Twenty-Eighth Infantry, a change Bullard approved, but the staff had not yet recovered entirely from the anxieties of Ely's reign. The acting chief-of-staff, Campbell King, was an entirely different sort of officer. Colonel King, a South Carolinian of aristocratic lineage, had been educated at Harvard and in the family law firm, both of which he found depressing. Though a member of the bar of Georgia, he enlisted in the army as a private at the age of twenty-six to escape the monotony of law practice. Commissioned during the war with Spain, he had quickly established a reputation as one of the army's ablest staff officers, serving as a student and instructor at Leavenworth and the Army War College. In addition to King's excellence as a planner and staff manager, he was a personal friend of Pershing's brightest staff officers. His Leavenworth background had acquainted him with most of the army's promising mid-career officers. Bullard appreciated King's ability and contacts with AEF Headquarters and conceded that the First Division's success was as much King's accomplishment as anyone else's. King, in return, served Bullard brilliantly and deferentially.[8]

Before he became division chief-of-staff, King had shared responsibility for the division's operations and training section with a tall, diffident major of thirty-seven named George Catlett Marshall, Jr. Another Leavenworth man, Marshall had been one of Sibert's strongest supporters and resented Pershing's relief of his commanding general. Marshall had been acting chief-of-staff on the occasion when Pershing had embarrassed Sibert in front of his officers. Incensed, Marshall had talked back to ''The Chief'' with a candor that horrified the rest of the division staff. Marshall may have been a candidate for division chief-of-staff, but his outburst, however justified and courageous, cast some doubt on his relations with AEF Headquarters. Bullard, however, had the good judgment to keep Marshall as the division chief-of-operations, a decision he never had cause to regret.[9]

While King and Marshall served as the foundation of what became a model division staff, Bullard's personal staff was built around an improbable but indispensable doctor named Guy O. Shirey. Having served in the Texas National Guard, the tall, plump, moon-faced, good-humored Shirey had come to France with the division as a medical officer. Worried about his health, Bullard made Shirey his aide. Camouflaged as a captain of infantry, Shirey performed yeoman service as Bullard's private doctor and motorcycle driver. He treated his general without sending Bullard to the division surgeon (thus keeping Bullard officially healthy all but once) and whisked the division commander about the countryside in a motorcycle sidecar. Equally valuable was Bullard's French aide, Captain Henri Sechressee, an urbane reserve officer with wide acquaintances throughout France.[10]

Another part of the First Division ''machine'' that Bullard improved was its brigade and regimental command. With George Duncan and Beaumont Buck as infantry brigade commanders, Bullard was well served, but he was unhappy with the commander of the artillery brigade, Charles H. McKinstry. Bullard, however, had gotten one concession from Pershing, that the First Division could draw on AEF Headquarters for commanders. To replace McKinstry, Bullard asked Pershing for either William Lassiter or Charles P. Summerall, the same sober, beetle-browed artilleryman whose guns had led the Thirty-Ninth Volunteers down the road to Santo Tomás. Much to his pleasure Bullard got Brigadier General Summerall and thereafter worried neither about the handling of his guns nor about his artillery brigadier's drive and loyalty. Summerall, nicknamed ''Sitting Bull'' by his gunners, brought fire support for the infantry to a high art in the First Division. His artillery officers served in the trenches in liaison roles and his gun positions fired rapidly and accurately against the Germans without much regard for their own safety. If Bullard wanted to kill Germans, Summerall wanted to kill them faster and in greater numbers. What made him especially awesome was his own fearlessness, for Summerall's idea of excitement was strolling about in enemy shellfire and thus discomfiting weaker souls. Because the division eventually fought its most terrible battles under Summerall, it became ''his'' division.[11]

In Colonels John Hines, Hanson Ely, and Hamilton A. Smith, Bullard had infantry regimental commanders who were both aggressive and cooperative, and he was satisfied that their commands, the Sixteenth, Twenty-Eighth and Twenty-Sixth Infantry, were well managed. His headache was the colonel of the

Eighteenth Infantry, the short, pugnacious Ulysses Grant McAlexander. While he had no reservations about McAlexander's ability or love of regular army discipline, Bullard found him impervious to new techniques. McAlexander's contempt for the French army was embarrassing, and when he refused to visit a French unit to learn some special tactics, Bullard relieved him. Again he drew upon Pershing's headquarters. As in Summerall's case, his choice was another future commander of the First Division, Colonel Frank Parker. Parker was not only a widely experienced officer but also a former student of the *Ecole de Guerre*, spoke French fluently, and had been an observer with the French army before the American intervention. Anxious for a regiment to command, the slight, handsome Parker did not have to be persuaded to leave Chaumont. Generals Bullard and Duncan cordially welcomed him to the First Division, satisfied that they had just found as able a regimental commander as the army had in France. Parker was equally pleased to join the division's revived First Brigade.[12]

With division officers who included a host of future generals and three army chiefs-of-staff (Hines, Summerall, and Marshall), Bullard was blessed with outstanding talent. If he himself did not match their drive and brilliance, he had the wit to exploit their ability and weld them into a cohesive team. By providing decisive leadership and intelligent guidance, he gave the division a sense of direction it did not have under Sibert. His wisest decisions were to allow his subordinates to create adequate staffs and to give his commanders both full authority and responsibility for their units. Hiding his own fears that he needed as much education in modern warfare as any private in the division and knowing that General Pershing would give him less time to learn, Bullard quietly but forcefully pushed his officers to greater efforts. By the end of December he believed the division was "moving," an opinion shared by at least two of his subordinates, Duncan and Parker.[13]

It was fortunate that Bullard got the First Division's command system in order quickly, for he found that he not only had to deal with Pershing's AEF staff, but that of a corps commander as well. A month after Bullard took the First Division, Pershing's headquarters created the I Corps headquarters and gave it administrative control of the four divisions training in France. The corps commander was Major General Hunter Liggett, Bullard's former brigade commander in Texas. Because he was heavy, Liggett almost got a trip back to the United States after he brought his division to France. Only Liggett's exemplary reputation and a promise to diet stalled Pershing from sending him home as unfit for AEF command. With such insecure tenure, Liggett did not assert himself as corps commander. Instead, the driving force at I Corps headquarters was the corps chief-of-staff, Lieutenant Colonel Malin Craig. Craig, another prize student of warfare on the Leavenworth model, was a forceful and intelligent officer, but he unsettled division commanders with his quick decisions and his habit of giving orders in General Liggett's name. Like his friends at Pershing's headquarters, Craig was quick to censure older generals.

Bullard's own staff was somewhat more diplomatic, but the confused patterns of authority in the AEF made every commander's job more difficult. The general insecurity that Bullard and other division commanders felt made them very cautious, if not unduly defensive, about their division's activities and encouraged the staff officers of high headquarters to make further incursions into their commands. It was not an environment that encouraged trust and frankness among the different levels of command.[14]

2.

General Bullard's division was larger than the entire United States Army had been when he was commissioned. The American division of 1918 was the wonder of the Western Front. Unlike German, British, and French divisions, the AEF division emphasized large numbers of riflemen, although like Allied divisions, the AEF division's size swelled with attached service units. The very size of an AEF division challenged its commander and staff. By 1918 Pershing's headquarters had set its strength at 28,000 men, more than twice the size of comparable Allied divisions. The most publicized reason for the AEF division's numbers was that Pershing's staff favored "staying" ability on the battlefield; it assumed that there was a crucial relationship between numbers and combat effectiveness, a dubious conclusion as it turned out. There was another compelling reason to mass American troops: the AEF Headquarters doubted that the army could provide a sufficient number of effective commanders and staffs to handle a great number of divisions. The hypertrophy of the American division continued to cause problems, since the Allies were organized to transport, billet, equip, and deploy much different sized formations of their own. Combined with the American insistence that Americans must fight their own way, the room for Franco-American misunderstanding was great.

The fighting heart of the First Division was its two infantry brigades and artillery brigade. The basic infantry unit was the platoon of fifty men, organized on the French pattern into four sections of hand grenadiers, rifle grenadiers, riflemen, and automatic riflemen. All American infantrymen were supposed to be proficient riflemen first. Four platoons and a company headquarters made an infantry company of 258 officers and men, led by a captain. Four such companies made a battalion, commanded by a major who was assisted by three lieutenants (adjutant, intelligence officer, and gas officer) and fourteen enlisted men, mostly communicators. An infantry regiment (108 officers, 3,719 enlisted) had three battalions, a headquarters company, a supply company, and a machine gun company with twelve guns. For added fire power, the headquarters company included three 38-mm. tripod-mounted cannon for use against machine gun nests and six 3″ Stokes mortars for high-angle fire against trenches. Two regiments composed the infantry brigade. Each infantry brigade also had its own machine gun battalion of four companies, each having twelve guns. Normally, the brigade machine gunners were attached to regiments and battalions for employment. The weight and operating characteristics of the machine guns limited their use to direct and indirect long-range fire. Even in attack the machine gunners' role was primarily defensive. The gunners, either carrying their equipment or pulling it in two-wheeled carts (theoretically mule-powered), trudged along behind the riflemen to the objective where they would then defend the captured territory.[15]

Just as an AEF division put more riflemen and machine gunners on the line than its French counterpart, the First Division artillery brigade (roughly 9,000 officers and men) was more heavily gunned than French divisional artillery. The French had nine firing batteries of 75-mm. field guns and three of 58-mm. mortars. The First Division's artillery had twelve 75-mm. batteries, six of French 155-mm. howitzers, and the trench mortar battery. The artillery brigade also had attached communicators, range-finding teams, ordnance experts, ammunition handlers, and liaison teams, plus an elaborate headquarters to plan fire support.

Though the infantry and artillery brigades had more men than the War Department and AEF Headquarters anticipated in 1917, the AEF division's ballooning size came from the number of support and service units eventually added to the division. In May 1917 the American division had 25,000 men, but on Allied advice the War Department trimmed this to 17,000 men by cutting the number of infantry regiments from nine to four. The missing regiments were not replaced, but the strength went back to 25,000 men in August. Part of the increase came in the creation of machine gun battalions for each infantry brigade and a division machine gun battalion under the commanding general's direct control. The rest of the increase came by doubling the size of almost every service unit except the division engineer battalion. From beginning to end, the AEF division's key logistical problem was transportation. Originally the division was horse-powered, but the lack of horses in France was so critical that AEF divisions became progressively motorized. The transition, never complete, meant adding more service units to the division. For example, the last units to join the First Division in the early days of Bullard's command were truck machine shop units and the motorized portion of the division supply train.

The size and composition of the First Division caused serious management problems for the division commander and his subordinates that had little to do with tactics but influenced the division's ability to get itself into battle and sustain itself on the Western Front. Even with the increased manpower and some motorization, the division had a hard time distributing ammunition, food, and supplies, especially near the front lines. The primitive trucks were worthless off well maintained roads. The horses and mules in the division did heavy work, but broke down quickly without rest and proper fodder. The horse situation was exacerbated by another problem. To save shipping for American men, the French provided many horses to the AEF, most of them from the United States but worn out in the French service before being turned over to the AEF. Except for long trips by train and French trucks, the First Division did a lot of walking, which did little for the men's condition when they finally went into battle. Carrying the standard sixty-pound field pack did not help. The soldiers also carried the brunt of battlefield supply, and every tactical unit was weakened by the constant demand for carrying parties to bring supplies forward and evacuate casualties. The infantry even had to bury its own dead, which did little for morale. As Bullard and every other division commander learned, the AEF did not have enough service troops, even with the additional units. The engineers, numbering only 1,000, doubled as infantry. The result was that the infantrymen and artillerymen not only had to fortify their own frontline positions, but performed as labor troops when they were supposed to be resting in reserve. The "staying" power of a division often was reduced to replacing exhausted troops who had suffered casualties with exhausted troops who had not.

For a division commander, as Bullard had anticipated, war on the Western Front was an incredibly complex matter of training, planning, and coordination. The asymmetry between an American division and Allied divisions did not simplify the problems. Moreover, the dependence upon the French for transportation demanded close and harmonious relations with the French army despite AEF Headquarter's insistence upon the maximum self-sufficiency in tactics and logistics. Only at the very end of the war did the AEF even approach the sort of military independence Pershing wanted. Even then the AEF's divisions had transportation and labor troop shortages that seriously hampered their effectiveness. The only difference in the First Division's experience was that it had the problems earlier, but the lessons were learned the hard way by field training and combat.[16]

3.

Under the direction of its new commander, the First Division trained with urgency. In December 1917 the division finished its specialist and small-unit training and turned to regimental maneuvers as prescribed by AEF Headquarters. Although unable to prevent some cannibalization of his officer corps for schools and new jobs, Bullard decreased officer turnover and completed the organization of his machine gun battalions. The division also absorbed several thousand replacements from the United States. Their training was uneven, but their spirits were good. Despite some of the worst weather in modern European history, the division trained outdoors, the troops staggering through the problems in rain, mud, sleet, snow, and near-zero weather. Frostbite cases increased, but the training did not slow. There was a moment of festiveness at Christmas, with presents for the French children, big meals, and decorated trees. The troops held parties and shows and had a welcome day of rest. The next day the infantry, shaking in the cold, marched to their training areas before dawn. The training schedules now called for brigade exercises and, finally, a complete division problem in open warfare.[17]

The field exercises were absolute necessities for the division's high commanders, their staffs, and the headquarters and service troops, but they were a trial for the junior officers and men. Schooled as they were by the Allies, many of the junior officers believed that a division open-warfare problem was a fantastic anachronism and that they were being led by unreconstructed Indian fighters. Having as yet little appreciation of the intricacies of artillery-infantry coordination, staff functioning, battlefield communications, and the movement of service units, the infantry bitterly complained about the weather and their commanders. One lieutenant thought that the troops' remarks "almost amounted to mutiny" and a private wished that "we could get through educating our officers."[18] For the division's commanders, the exercises were severe tests and excellent learning experiences. King thought that the division staff only began to appreciate their task when they had to move the division (which covered nineteen miles of road space) and then deploy it on a front 2,000 meters wide and 3,000 meters deep. This they did on roads and fields glazed with sleet and snow. Hines and Parker worked themselves to near-exhaustion commanding their full regiments in the field. Both conceded that no commander could lead from his PC and run his regiment by telephone. While they sympathized with their troops' discomfort, they recognized that the suffering had just begun.[19]

Bullard personally supervised the regimental and brigade maneuvers, visited the men's billets, and commanded the division in its final exercise January 5-7, 1918. On Christmas day he visited the troop parties rather than celebrate with his staff and French hosts; at an ambulance company's dinner he made an impressive speech, quietly stating that there would be no peace on earth until the German army was destroyed. Wrapped in a shaggy wolfskin coat given him by his aides, the general became a familiar sight around the division as he prowled the billets and training areas. Bullard won the respect and affection of his junior officers for his informality and courteousness. The lieutenants were amused by the general in the "college boy coonskin coat," but they appreciated Bullard's obvious determination. Bullard's soldiers thought the general's high-pitched southern drawl was amusing, but they respected his folksy touch, his ability to speak French, and his presence in the field even when his health was not good. It became common knowledge that Bullard was being unofficially treated for stomach problems but would not stay in a hospital. Trudging through deep snow and driving sleet, a machine gun lieutenant saw Bullard talking with the troops about their good performance. The lieutenant thought that the division commander looked like a medieval knight, swathed in his nonregulation coat. Major Theodore Roosevelt, Jr., thought that Bullard's presence helped keep morale high in the worst conditions.[20]

The night of January 7 the division commander called his worn subordinates to his PC. Wolfskin coat or no, Bullard had developed a severe case of neuritis in his left shoulder and showed the strain. He admitted that the day had been the most trying in his thirty-five years of service. He had news, however, that distracted him from the pain: the division was going into the line. The First Brigade would go for two or three weeks, followed by the Second and supported by the entire division artillery and its service units. The position would be the Ansauville sector on the southern face of the St. Mihiel salient, northwest of Toul. The tour at the front would be the division's final test before it was certified by the French and AEF Headquarters for any combat mission. Bullard was grim. He told his officers that the troops must understand that only their own pride and their hatred for the

Germans would sustain them in the days ahead. The First Brigade would have a week to make its final preparations. In the meantime, the officers would visit the sector to make reconnaissances and plan the relief of lines with the French. Training could do no more. Now the division must fight, bleed, and kill Germans to become better soldiers.[21]

On January 15 the First Brigade set out for the Front. The troops were loaded in full field order, including two blankets, rations, a shelter-half, extra clothes, mess gear, entrenching tool, rifle, canteen, cartridge belt, bayonet, and a full load of ammunition. For the first time, they were issued steel helmets and two gas masks. The march began on bad roads in a rainstorm, and by midday the rain had turned to sleet and snow. Their packs and overcoats soaked, the men stumbled along the road to Sorcy, that night's bivouac. That day the brigade marched nearly twenty miles. At the last, the men had to rest fifteen minutes for every twenty they marched, but the brigade made its billets on schedule. For everyone, from General Duncan to the company cooks, the march was a nightmare, a horror of aching legs and pinched shoulders. The First Brigade had few doubts that night that they were at war.[22]

4.

Three days after the First Brigade and most of the supporting units of the First Division started the trek to the front, Bullard and his division headquarters left Gondrecourt and motored to their new PC at Ménil-la-Tour, a village ten miles south of the division's sector. Bullard thought the march north was the most trying he had ever made. The roads were so bad that often the division headquarters staff had to walk with the troops. Reflecting upon the course of the war as he rode to the front, Bullard was generally more optimistic about the Allied situation than he had been in November, primarily because the Allies seemed ready to settle for a compromise peace. He envied the German strategic situation. If the Germans pushed their offensive in Italy, they might easily bring the Allies to the peacetable in a position of weakness. Despite the discussion of a German offensive on the Western Front, Bullard thought that Hindenburg and Ludendorff would not be foolish enough to try it. If the offensive broke the BEF and French armies, it would be a magnificent victory, but the risks of defeat were equally great and the German army could not afford heavy casualties. Despite his reflections on strategy, Bullard could not really believe he was in a war. Though he heard and felt Allied artillery firing into the German positions, he supposed the emotional impact of fighting would not come until he saw some casualties.[23]

For the First Division's commanding general, the movement to the front marked the first serious test of his capacity to lead an AEF division in France. The success of his troops against the Germans in the style of war in a quiet sector— bombardments and trench raids—was but one part of the test. Much of his job was to keep Pershing and the AEF staff happy with affairs in the First Division, a problem he had already faced. The move into the Ansauville sector complicated command relations, however, for the First Division was under the tactical control of the French First Army. Until the French approved of the change, Bullard's headquarters would not command operations in the sector, such decisions remaining in the hands of the French Sixty-Ninth Division. The First Army commander, General Marie Eugène Debeney, established the conditions of the division's service. Debeney was an intimate of Pétain and an accomplished General Staff officer. He did not have a high opinion of American generals and their staffs, and Pershing's staff thought him hostile to the idea of using Americans under their own division and corps commanders. Bullard met Debeney at a planning conference early in January. The purpose of the conference was to work out an agreement on the First Division's use at the front. Debeney proved reluctant to let the First Division manage its own sector, as Pershing demanded. Only at dinner, when Bullard chatted with him in French, did the French Army commander change his mind. General Harbord thought Bullard's dinner-table diplomacy had won the day and congratulated him. Bullard and Debeney maintained their cordial relations, which set the tone for Bullard's generally excellent relations with other French high commanders. His praise of French generalship, in fact, eventually made his loyalty to the AEF suspect at Chaumont.[24]

Except that he approved of giving the First Division a position along the St. Mihiel salient, Debeney did the division no favors in selecting its sector. Although both the French and Germans considered the sector a rest home for battle-worn divisions, the terrain was inhospitable and the Allied lines were vulnerable to limited attacks. The front lines and No-Man's-Land were a maze of shallow, water-filled trenches and emplacements dug in a valley at the eastern edge of the Meuse plateau. Cut by streams and dotted with heavy woods, the valley was a muddy plain in which movement was easily observed. The Germans held the sector's most prominent terrain feature, a four-hundred-foot-high butte called Mont Sec. While the Germans held outposts in the valley, their main lines were in the woods and ravines on Mont Sec's slopes, which were pitted with machine gun nests and artillery observation posts.

On the Allied side, the major terrain feature was a low ridge which ran parallel with the front 2,000 yards behind the forward trenches. The ridge carried a highway linking the towns of Rambucourt and Beaumont along the main route between St. Dizier and Metz. This ridge was the French main line of resistance, but the sector's defenders were supposed to keep troops in the valley. The Allied position on the low ground was anchored to three fortified points built around the ruins of three farm towns: sector "F" on the right at Seicheprey, sector "H" in the center at Xivray-Marvoisin, and sector "I" at Bouconville. None of these positions was especially defensible, but sector "F" was the most vulnerable. The trenches curled around Seicheprey and the Bois de Remières to the east, forming a salient dangerously close to the German lines. Moreover, Seicheprey was easily observed from Mont Sec and the Germans controlled several woods and gullies that were avenues of approach to Seicheprey. Since the front had been stable in the Ansauville sector for years, German artillery had every observable terrain feature registered for fire. In all, the First Division's position was not very attractive. When one of Pershing's staff visited the sector, he was stunned by the condition of the trenches. "Poor fellows! Their life of real hardship now begins."[25]

The First Brigade, reinforced by machine gunners and engineers, did what it could to strengthen its positions forward of the Beaumont highway. Communicators strung miles of wire, carrying parties moved ammunition and supplies to forward dumps, and the firing batteries of the First Field Artillery Brigade deployed in French emplacements along the highway ridge and in defiles to its rear. The Germans harassed the troops with high explosive and gas shells; every day First Division stretcher-bearers struggled rearward with muddy, mangled soldiers or choking, crying victims of poison gas. Movement to the strongpoints was limited to carrying parties which staggered nearly two miles in the gluey communications trenches to reach the front at night. German and American sharpshooters and machine gunners sniped at one another every day. Water, warm food, and dry clothes were inconceivable luxuries, and no one got much sleep in the soggy dugouts. The most disconcerting feeling, however, was that the Germans on Mont Sec observed and enjoyed every American discomfort.[26]

Bullard prowled the positions along the Beaumont Road, easily recognizable in his wolfskin coat. He met often with General Duncan and Colonels Hines and Parker to discuss the tactical situation. He became a familiar sight at the artillery positions, chatting with General Summerall and the regimental commanders. His travels were more than *beaux gestes.* He took an active interest in the detailed work of the division and begrudged the time spent away from his self-education when working at his desk in Ménil-la-Tour. Bullard watched his officers carefully, judging the regulars as harshly as the "emergency" officers. He checked the French liaison personnel to ensure that their knowledge was used but not accepted as dogma. Bullard was not the only ranking officer touring the Ansauville sector. Debeney was a frequent visitor as were Generals Passaga (XXXII Corps) and Monroe (Sixty-Ninth Division), Bullard's immediate superiors. Bullard continued to soothe the French generals in their own language and felt that he had their confidence. The First Division had a host of American generals to entertain as well. Pershing sent his staff to the Ansauville sector often and made it a mandatory stop for visiting generals from the United States. Only after Colonel Fox Conner, Pershing's chief-of-operations, stopped a piece of shrapnel with his nose did the visiting slow down. Most of the American generals were shocked by the battlefield's devastation and the artillery fire's impersonal cruelty, but they were also impressed that the First Division's commanders were doing very well under the circumstances.[27]

Although he was pleased that his visitors thought that the First Division was doing well, Bullard was unhappy about several conditions in the Ansauville sector. He told both Hunter Liggett and Fox Conner that he thought his positions forward of the Beaumont highway were too vulnerable to raids, but that until Debeney gave him tactical control he could not alter his infantry's positions. Having gained some appreciation for the German artillery, he asked for more gas masks and medical units. Bullard continued to listen to the suggestions of the division's French liaison officers and the friendly advice of Generals Passaga and Monroe, but he did not think that French counsel was any substitute for his officers' planning and reconnaisances. Essentially, he wanted full control of the sector, which Liggett and Conner promised to press the French to give him. He himself worked on Debeney, and on February 5 the French put the Ansauville sector under American control.[28]

Bullard immediately changed the terms of the war in his sector. He thinned the strongpoints in the trenches north of the Beaumont Highway, leaving only two battalions (one from each regiment) to garrison the trenches and strongpoints. The other infantry battalion was drawn back to the main line-of-resistance. The frontline troops, however, were ordered to step up their raids and patrols. Bullard's first order set the new tone for the sector:

1. There are no orders which require us to wait for the enemy to fire on us before we fire on him; do not wait for him to fire first. Be active all over no-man's-land; do not leave its control to the enemy.

2. Front line commanders will immediately locate and report all places where there is a favorable opportunity for strong ambuscades and for raids on the enemy's lines and advance posts.[29]

Bullard also moved all of the First Field Artillery Brigade except two battalions into the sector, replacing some indifferent French batteries, and strengthened its telephone communications. Bullard insisted that his infantry not go into No-Man's-Land without making arrangements for artillery support. The tempo of the shelling increased, and the division's casualties climbed. Bullard, however, was satisfied that the Germans were losing men, too. As he intended, the First Division thought about killing Germans, not getting cold or wounded in its own trenches. His troops lost their amateur status rapidly. In less than a month, the infantrymen learned such nuances as not following the same route to and from their lines, of firing first, and of killing with artillery fire. They quit fighting as if war were a baseball game. Patrols were unit affairs, not groups of daring volunteers. Adequate plans were made, and American officers, not Frenchmen, ran the patrols. Bullard's confidence in his division increased.[30]

On February 16 Pershing and his staff visited the First Division to give it a searching inspection. "The Chief" and Liggett toured Bullard's units and talked with Debeney. The French army commander "was very pleased with General Bullard's administration of affairs." The inspectors found the men satisfied with their officers and complaining only about occasional shortages of food. They also learned that Bullard needed more engineer supplies, trucks, and horses, but was managing well with what he had. Infantry-artillery coordination was excellent, and the division staff now wanted air support of its own, for German planes were strafing and bombing the sector with relative impunity. Pershing and his staff left the front pleased with what they saw and told the French that the First Division was ready for any assignment. Pershing and Liggett, however, planned to keep the division where it was as the first step in preparing an offensive against the St. Mihiel salient.[31]

Bullard was not so sure that the First Division was ready for a more complicated assignment or that Pershing's headquarters was ready to manage an AEF offensive. In another conference with Liggett, he complained of Pershing's concern about every shelling and gassing the division received and "The Chief's" obsession with the troops' appearance. Without asking Bullard's opinion, Pershing had relieved an excellent artillery officer for having a sloppy unit. What AEF headquarters should be concerned about was the division's lack of air support. Without more air reconnaissance, the division could not deliver effective counterbattery fire. At the same time, German control of the air was a nuisance and made secret troop dispositions for raids impossible. Bullard also hoped that the division would have fewer high-ranking visitors to entertain. Liggett reassured him that the division was making good progress and that his own interest was friendly: "I don't have to come to see you, Bullard. It's the others I have to worry about."[32]

The visitors continued to pay as much attention to the division as the Germans. Late in February, Leonard Wood, fresh from a tour with the BEF, visited Ménil-la-Tour. Seething with resentment toward Pershing, Pershing's staff, and anyone in Pershing's favor, Wood could find little right. Like Bullard, he noted German air superiority. He also criticized the artillery positions for being too vulnerable to German fire: "when the time comes for its destruction it will be promptly wiped out." He thought the communications trenches and wire system inadequate. He criticized Bullard for having too few hand and rifle grenades and for failing to recognize the vulnerability of his position. He noted disparagingly that the artillery did not have sound- and range-finding equipment for counterbattery fire and deplored the absence of airborne spotters. Wood thought that the division high commanders were not well-versed in tactics and that Bullard "has grown much older and seems a little dazed in his present position." Wood left the division convinced that only he and Lieutenant Colonel Marshall ("a good man and very much alive to the situation") knew the First Division's peril.[33]

Bullard kept trying to improve the division's readiness. When replacing the two battalions forward of the Beaumont road, he ordered his own and subordinate PC's to displace forward to battle positions in order to test the division's communications. From their perch on Mont Sec, the Germans shelled the headquarters' personnel, causing casualties, but making the exercise especially realistic. One artillery colonel, thinking the losses senseless, called the division PC the next morning and reported that the Germans had taken Seicheprey in a surprise assault. Bullard was nonplussed. Because he "continually and always felt the lack of enough time to think," he had tried to imagine every possible tactical contingency in his sector. He was sure that this was the only way he kept his poise under pressure. The report that Seicheprey had fallen suddenly was so incredible that he was "terribly surprised and disconcerted." The officer who made the false report arrived at the division PC to find Bullard and Summerall in a state of anxiety. When he revealed the hoax, the generals were not amused, and the officer was reassigned.[34]

Bullard found the joke humorless because he was already aware that the Germans might be planning a raid against the Seicheprey strongpoint. On the day of Wood's visit, the Germans had gassed the positions of the Eighteenth Infantry and the First Trench Mortar Battery in the Bois de Remières. On that day and the next two, they had carefully registered on American batteries along the Beaumont road. French liaison officers feared that the Germans had special plans, an educated guess which convinced Colonel Marshall that the Eighteenth Infantry was in for a heavy raid. Marshall persuaded Bullard to order the front lines thinned down to only teams of automatic riflemen and artillery liaison personnel and to order the Eighteenth Infantry's rifle companies to occupy counterattack positions rather than the trenches at nightfall. Bullard thought that the retirement would damage the troops' morale, but Marshall convinced him that if he did not order the temporary withdrawal, more than morale would get hurt. Colonel Parker and his staff had reached similar conclusions and approved the move.

On the night of March 1, a reinforced company of German assault troops, protected by a devastating barrage, hit F-1. The courage of the frontline infantrymen kept them firing and, with artillery fire, the assault was broken. The Germans lost half the assault force and much of their demolitions equipment, mortars, and flamethrowers. The defenders, Company I of the Eighteenth Infantry, were long on bravery but short on tactical ability. Several officers manning an isolated PC were shot and the rest, responsible for organizing the counterattack, became casualties. American artillery responded slowly and wire communications went out under the German shellfire. The company's counterattack degenerated into a wild melee. Although the company took some prisoners, it suffered fifty-four casualties in the affair. Nevertheless, it was a tactical victory of sorts in the first serious fight with the Germans. The French quickly cited the Eighteenth Infantry for gallantry in action and awarded *Croix de Guerre* to several of the outpost defenders who had stopped the assault. Bullard personally congratulated the men and endeared himself to General Duncan and Colonel Parker by not hectoring them for reports when they didn't have any information from the front. It was another step in making the generals and privates veterans.[35]

The First Division planned its own retaliatory trench raids. Though the raiding parties were only platoon-size, Colonel Marshall wrote the orders and had his section supervise the operations. Bullard looked over Marshall's shoulder, and Pershing and his staff watched over his. The French were interested spectators, too. Despite elaborate preparations, the first large American raids, planned for night of March 3-4, were aborted. The two raiding parties cancelled their attacks when the engineer parties assigned to blow the wire got lost. When the engineers got straightened around, they discovered that their Bangalore torpedoes were defective. Pershing was irritated, Bullard embarrassed, and Debeney unconcerned, for he properly recognized the triviality of the matter and was pleased that the First Division was so aggressive. The raids were rescheduled for March 11. This time the planning and execution were superior. Unfortunately, the Germans had no intention of being raided. They had fallen back to another trench line and avoided the barrage. The American raiders found nothing to raid, returning to their lines safely. The only pleased soldiers were Summerall's artillerymen, whose counterbattery fire had prevented the German guns from making the raids disasters. For Bullard, the experience was another lesson in how unforgiving both the Germans and Pershing could be in combat. The aborted raids had set off another wave of AEF general staff inspections and criticisms, and at Liggett's headquarters the talk was that Bullard was covering up for his French superiors.[36]

On March 9 the Second Infantry Brigade replaced the First in the Ansauville sector (the raiders were left behind), and the education of the Twenty-Sixth and Twenty-Eighth Infantry began where their sister regiments' ended. At the front, the fresh infantry was gassed, shelled, and harassed by lice. Most of the Second Brigade's raids went well enough, but captured few of the careful German outposts. The infantry's skill in movement and the artillery's growing efficiency, however, kept American casualties down as well. During the Second Brigade's tour in the Ansauville sector, in fact, the artillery positions and supporting units drew most of the Germans' attention. The division's battery positions, communications trenches, and dugouts were harassed with high explosives and gas throughout the day and night. The Americans fired back and dug their holes deeper. The daily problems of trench foot, respiratory sicknesses, weak horses, faulty communications, gas-poisoned equipment, and the mundane but essential provisioning of food and supplies kept the division busy. Worst of all were the mud and the constant digging and rebuilding of dugouts and shelters. The cannoneers moved their guns and fired missions at night and stood inspections in the morning. There were always working parties, as well, to pick up salvage or repair camouflage nets. Like their British and French comrades, the men of the First Division were gradually sinking into the ground under the German shelling.[37]

At the division headquarters, the staff cars came and went with a stream of visitors. On March 20 the distinguished guest was Secretary of War Baker. He talked briefly with the officers of the First Brigade, telling them that the nation was behind them and that they should work with the French in the common cause of democracy and liberty. The war, Baker said, must be fought through to victory, "as this is the last time in world affairs it will have to be done."[38] Colonel Parker was impressed with the unprepossessing secretary's intelligence and articulateness, but could not recall what he said.[39] Hunter Liggett was also a frequent visitor. The portly corps commander had developed a fixation about the First Division's pitiable horses. Bullard admitted his animals were in poor condition, but wondered where they would get the rest and improved fodder they needed. At Liggett's insistence, he established a more stringent inspection system to make sure the horses were properly cared for, and there was some improvement in their condition.[40] Bullard shared his thoughts with Liggett on the division's experience in the Ansauville sector. His biggest worries had been logistical planning, especially the economical use of his horse-drawn wagons and trucks. Keeping the roads open was a critical task, and he needed a two-thousand-man labor force to do the work adequately. The division had had a battalion of Negro engineers attached to it for road work; and Bullard thought them outstanding. Bullard also worried about the quality of his junior officers, suggesting that perhaps French and British veterans might be assigned temporarily as troop leaders in American battalions. Such an opinion was heresy in the AEF, and Liggett and his staff were horrified at Bullard's indiscretion.[41] In his own notes, Bullard reflected that "war is labor." He had given most attention to staff functioning, supply, security, and communications rather than to tactics. Sometimes it was hard to remember the enemy. He had other heretical thoughts about the meaning of modern firepower, musing that artillery now did the killing and the infantry the dying and walking. He thought an American division should have more machine guns, artillery, and its own tanks. As for command, he still believed in getting out among the troops, but to have an efficient command system he borrowed a leaf from Pershing: "Make men fear you."[42] He concluded that his division had done a great deal of digging, a fair amount of shooting, a little killing and dying, "raiding and being raided, gassing and being gassed," and had done well. He felt sure, however, that the experience in the Ansauville sector and the division's 550 casualties were only the prelude to greater battles.[43]

The French liaison officers with the First Division also believed it faced more serious warfare, but they had reservations about the division's commanders and internal management. Although Bullard worked well with his French counterparts, he had a tendency not to keep his staff informed of his decisions. Staff work at all levels was flawed by disorganization and poor communications. The division's personnel and supply administration was good, but operational planning was poor, which forced Bullard and Marshall to intervene too often. The crucial problem was that many of the older regular army officers did not grasp the tactical concepts of the Western Front and neglected detailed planning. These officers, "often rather limited mentally, have a strong tendency to draw upon their experiences on the Cuban expedition, the one to Manila, or in Mexico, which they think was waging war, and tend to reject advice as an insult to their national pride." Unless they changed, they would waste the lives of their enthusiastic junior officers and enlisted men. The French mission also feared that the size of the division made its management impossible. "The automobile traffic is fantastic," and the movement of trucks and wagons was triple that of a French sector. The division's appetite for scarce supplies was insatiable and supply discipline virtually nonexistent. In light of the First Division's problems, "the high command is not yet, in the area of directing operations, up to its responsibilities."[44]

Yet the First Division and its commanding general had run out of time to solve their problems in the relative quiet of the Ansauville sector, for the German army was again on the march.

NOTES

[1]Historical Section, Army War College, *The Genesis of the American First Army* (Washington: Government Printing Office, 1938), pp. 13-16.

[2]Resumé of interviews between General Pétain and General Pershing, December 23, 1917, and January 13, 1918, *USA/WW, 1917-1919,* II, pp. 105-107, 155-157; Pershing diary, entry, January 11, 1918, John J. Pershing Papers.

[3]Pershing diary, entries, December 21 and 27, 1917; G. V. Moseley, "War Notes" I, entry, January 9, 1918, George Van Horne Moseley Papers.

[4]Colonel John L. Hines, memo, "Meeting with the New Division Commander," December 15, 1918, Vol. II, Hines Speeches, John L. Hines Papers. A sanitized version of Bullard's speech is Maj. Gen. R. L. Bullard, memo, "Requirements of Our G. H. Q. in France," December 15, 1917, *WWR/1st Div.* XX.

[5]George B. Duncan, "Reminiscences of the Great War," pp. 49-50.

[6]Diarybook 9, entry, December 23, 1917, BP; Bullard autobiography, p. 126, BP.

[7]"Hanson Ely," in Robert L. Bullard, *Fighting Generals* (Ann Arbor, Mich.: Edwards, 1944), pp. 43-45.

[8]Maj. C. King to R. B. House, September 18, 1919; Brig. Gen. F. Conner to Brig. Gen. C. King, September 7, 1918; Maj. Gen. R. L. Bullard to Brig. Gen. C. King, October 30 and December 6, 1918, all in the Campbell King Papers.

[9]Forrest C. Pogue, *George C. Marshall: Education of a General* (New York: Viking, 1963), pp. 151-163.

[10]Commanding General, Second Army, to Adj. Gen., AEF, January 17, 1919, "Correspondence of the Commanding General, Second Army," AEF Organization Records, RG 120; Robert L. Bullard, *Personalities and Reminiscences of the War* (New York: Doubleday, Page, 1925), pp. 122-123.

[11]Brig. Gen. C. King to Maj. Gen. C. P. Summerall, June 22, 1921; Maj. Gen. R. L. Bullard to Maj. Gen, C. P. Summerall, June 25, 1921, both Summerall Papers; Bullard, *Personalities and Reminiscences,* pp. 110-114.

[12]"Ulysses Grant McAlexander," in Bullard, *Fighting Generals,* p. 130-133; Duncan, "Reminiscences of the World War," pp. 34-35; Maj. F. Parker to Adj. Gen., USA, April 9, 1917; Col. F. Parker to Mrs. Parker, December 30 and 31, 1917; Lt. Gen. R. L. Bullard to Maj. Gen. F. Parker, August 5, 1936, all in the Frank Parker Papers.

In addition to his considerable ability, Parker was an intimate of the Roosevelt family. See T. Roosevelt to Maj. F. Parker, April 13, 1917, Parker Papers, and Theodore Roosevelt, Jr., *Average Americans* (New York: G. P. Putnam's Sons, 1919), pp. 199-200.

[13]Diarybook 9, entry, December 28, 1917, BP; Duncan, "Reminiscences of the World War," pp. 36-39; Col. F. Parker to Mrs. Parker, February 27 and 28, 1918, Parker Papers.

[14]Maj. Gen. C. R. Edwards, January 29, 1918, Edwards Papers; Lt. Col. P. L. Stackpole, diary entries, February 1 and 6, 1918, Stackpole Diary, George C. Marshall Library, Lexington, Virginia. Colonel Stackpole was one of General Liggett's aides.

[15]The author is indebted for his understanding of First Division machine gun operations to Mr. H. H. Caswell of Ann Arbor, Michigan, who served as a lieutenant in the Third Machine Gun Battalion and who recorded his experiences in "The History of the 3rd Mach. Gun Bn, of the 1st Division AEF," *mss* written in 1919 with addenda, 1971.

[16]The discussion of the AEF division's structure is based on the following sources: *Order of Battle: AEF: Divisions,* pp. 446-447; *History of the First Division* (Philadelphia: Winston, 1922), pp. 9-13, Maj. Frank Parker, "The Infantry Division," March 30, 1917,

Parker Papers; James A. Houston, *The Sinews of War: Army Logistics, 1775-1953* (Washington: Government Printing Office, 1966), pp. 356-387; Lt. Col. Oliver L. Spaulding, "Tactics of the War with Germany," *Infantry Journal* 17 (September 1920), pp. 228-240.

In addition to the division history, see: "Regimental Chaplain," *The Story of the Sixteenth Infantry in France* (Frankfurt: Martin Flock, 1919); Ben H. Chastaine, *History of the 18th U.S. Infantry* (New York: Hymans Publishing Company, 1920); "Regimental Adjutant," *The Twenty-Sixth Infantry in France* (Frankfurt: n.p., 1919); *The Story of the Twenty-Eighth Infantry in the Great War* (Coblenz, 1919); Maj. T. F. Farrell *et. al., A History of the 1st U.S. Engineers, 1st U.S. Division* (Coblenz: n.p., 1919); *Brief History of the Fifth Field Artillery, 1st Division, American Expeditionary Forces, 1917-1918* (Nancy: Berger-Levrault, 1918); *History of the Sixth Field Artillery, 1798-1932* (Harrisburg, Pa.: HQ, 6th Field Artillery, 1933), pp. 153-283; *History of the Seventh Field Artillery (First Division, A.E.F.), World War, 1917-1919* (New York: J. L. Little and Ives, 1929).

[17]For the training period, see especially *History of the First Division,* pp. 35-41; "War Diaries, Headquarters First Division, June 9, 1917 to December 31, 1918," *WWR/1st Div.* XIV; memoranda and orders, *USA/WW, 1917-1919,* III, pp. 422-490; training schedules, Sixteenth Infantry Regiment, December, 1917, Hines Papers.

[18]Shipley Thomas, *The History of the A.E.F.* (New York: Doran, 1920), pp. 55-56; *History of the First Division,* p. 30; *History of the Sixth Field Artillery,* pp. 174-176; Edith and Marjorie Betts, comps., "An Argonne Cross" (the letters of First Lieutenant Elden Sprague Betts, First Division, May 15, 1917 to October 4, 1918), copy in the Parker Papers. Thomas was a captain in the First Division and participated in the January maneuvers as did Betts, who died in action.

[19]Campbell King, "Tour in France," p. 2, King Papers; John L. Hines diary, entries, December 1, 1917-January 4, 1918, Hines Papers; Col. F. Parker to Mrs. Parker, January 1-5, 1918, Parker Papers.

[20]On Bullard as division commander, see Roosevelt, *Average Americans,* pp. 101-104; Joseph D. Patch, *A Soldier's War: The First Infantry Division* (Corpus Christi, Tex.: Joseph Dorst Patch, 1966), pp. 35-37; Col. Carroll Gray (USA, Ret.), Asheville, North Carolina, to the author, December 6, 1971; James A. Edgar, New York, N.Y., to the author, February 25, 1972; George Dudley Bogert, *Let's Go!* (San Francisco: H. S. Crocker, 1927), pp. 41-65; Lowell Thomas, *This Side of Hell* (London: John Long, Ltd., 1933), pp. 127-131; Caswell, "History of the 3rd Mach. Gun Bn. of the list Division," pp. 36-37.

[21]Diarybook 9, entry, January 8, 1918, BP; Hines diary, entry, January 7, 1918, Hines Papers; Col. F. Parker to Mrs. Parker, January 7, 1918, Parker Papers.

[22]Duncan, "Reminiscences of the World War," p. 52; "Regimental Chaplain," *The Story of the Sixteenth Infantry in France,* pp. 16-17; Col. F. Parker to Mrs. Parker, January 15, 1918, Parker Papers; Chastaine, *History of the 18th U.S. Infantry,* p. 33.

[23]Diarybook 9, entry, January 18, 1918, BP; Bullard autobiography, p. 129, BP.

[24]Bullard, *Personalities and Reminiscences,* pp. 120-21, 129-31; Diary entry, February 1, 1918, in James G. Harbord, *Leaves from a War Diary* (New York: Dodd, Mead, 1931), pp. 221-224; T. Bentley Mott, *Twenty Years as Military Attaché* (New York: Oxford University Press, 1937), pp. 111, 221.

[25]Drum diary, entry, December 31, 1917, Drum Papers.

The description of the Ansauville sector is based on the following sources: Douglas W. Johnson, *Battlefields of the World War* (New York: Oxford University Press, 1921), pp

349-372; American Battle Monuments Commission, *American Armies and Battlefields in Europe* (Washington: Government Printing Office, 1938), pp. 115-131; Duncan, "Reminiscences of the World War," pp. 58-59; Campbell King, "Tour in Europe," p. 2; Thomas, *The History of the A.E.F.,* pp. 59-60; *History of the First Division,* pp. 42-48; map "Ansauville Sector," in *Map Records: WWR/1st Div.*

[26]Headquarters, First Division, AEF, G-3 Memorandum 1370, "Brief History of Operations of 1st Division," December 21, 1918, copy in Summerall Papers and reprinted in *WWR/1st Div.,* Vol. XII; *History of the First Division,* pp. 49-52; 1st Lt. Elden Betts to Edith and Marjorie Betts, January 19-March 6, 1918, reprinted in "An Argonne Cross," Parker Papers; "Regimental Chaplain," *The Story of the Sixteenth Infantry in France,* pp. 16-17.

[27]Diarybook 9, entries, January 23 and 27, 1918, BP; Col. F. Parker to Mrs. Parker, January 20-February 9, 1918, Parker Papers; Capt. T. F. Farrell to Maj. Gen. R. L. Bullard, January 11, 1925, BP; Duncan, "Reminiscences of the World War," p. 59; Col. R. R. McCormick, *The Army of 1918* (New York: Harcourt, Brace, and Howe, 1920), pp. 58-90; Mr. Ralph H. Hutchins, Maryville, California, to the author, May 4, 1971; Maj. Gen. Robert Alexander, *Memories of the World War* (New York: Macmillan, 1931), pp. 8-13; Maj. Gen. Henry T. Allen, diary entries, January 23-26, 1918, Allen Diary, Henry T. Allen Papers. (Sergeant Hutchins was a receptionist and guide at the Division PC.)

[28]P. L. Stackpole diary, entry, January 29, 1918, Marshall Library; memo, Col. Fox Conner, G-3, GHQ, AEF, to C/S, First Division, January 19, 1918, *WWR/1st Div.* I; Bullard, *Personalities and Reminiscences,* pp. 138-145.

[29]Instruction No. 1, February 5, 1918, reprinted in *History of the First Division,* p. 48.

[30]Diarybook 9, entry, February 10, 1918, BP; Bullard, *Personalities and Reminiscences,* pp. 146-152; P. L. Stackpole diary, February 5, 1918, Marshall Library; Drum diary, entry, February 10, 1918, Drum Papers.

[31]Pershing diary, entries, February 16 and 17, 1918, Pershing Papers; P. L. Stackpole diary, entry, February 17, 1918, Marshall Library; Col. F. Parker to Mrs. Parker, February 16, 1918, Parker Papers; memo, Col. G. V. Moseley, GS, to Gen. J. J. Pershing, "Report of Inspection, February 15-17, 1918," February 19, 1918, and Moseley "War Notes" I, entry, February 21, 1918, Moseley Papers; Col. Fox Conner, G-3, AEF, "Memorandum on Prospective Availability of Divisions and Other Troops," February 17, 1918, in *USA/WW, 1917-1919,* II, pp. 208-210.

[32]P. L. Stackpole diary, entry, February 22, 1918, Marshall Library; Duncan, "Reminiscences of the World War," pp. 64-65.

[33]Wood diary, entry, February 26, 1918, and Maj. Gen. Leonard Wood, "Observations on Visit to the English, French and American Fronts," memorandum to the Adjutant General, USA, March 19, 1918, both Leonard Wood Papers.

[34]Notebook 26, entry, December 2, 1919, BP; Duncan, "Reminiscences of the World War," pp. 70-71.

[35]History of the First Division, pp. 56-58; Duncan, "Reminiscences of the World War," pp. 72-73; Col. James L. Collins diary, entry, January 24, 1924, James L. Collins Papers, Center of Military History, Department of the Army; Pogue, *George C. Marshall: Education of a General,* pp. 160-161; Capt. Charles S. Coulter, "The Winning of the First D.S.C.'s," *Infantry Journal* 20 (March 1922), pp. 239-242.

[36]Pershing diary, entries, March 3-5, 1918, Pershing Papers; Avery D. Andrews, *My Friend and Classmate John J. Pershing* (Harrisburg, Pa.: Military Service Publishing Company, 1939), pp. 114-115; P. L. Stackpole diary, entry, March 5, 1918, Marshall

Library; Maj. Gen. R. L. Bullard to Brig. Gen. C. P. Summerall, March 11, 1918, Summerall Papers; John L. Hines diary, entry, March 4, 1918, Hines Papers; Col. F. Parker to Mrs. Parker, March 4, 1918, Parker Papers; Commanding General, First Division, to Commander-in-Chief, AEF, "Miscarriage of Two Raids Organized for the 1st Division, Night of March 3-4th, 1918," March 7, 1918, *WWR/1st Div.,* XII.

[37]*History of the First Division,* pp. 59-64; Roosevelt, *Average Americans,* pp. 108-119; H. H. Caswell, "History of the 3rd Machine Gun Bn. of the 1st Division AEF," pp. 3-5, 37-38; Bullard, *Personalities and Reminiscences,* pp. 153-163; Dr. M. M. Thompson, Cambridge, Ohio, to the author, May 26, 1971. Doctor Thompson was a communicator in Headquarters Company, Twenty-Sixth Infantry.

[38]P. L. Stackpole diary, entry, March 20, 1918, Marshall Library.

[39]Col. F. Parker to Mrs. Parker, March 20, 1918, Parker Papers.

[40]P. L. Stackpole diary, entries, March 15 and 20, 1918, Marshall Library.

[41]P. L. Stackpole diary, entries, March 24 and 25, 1918, Marshall Library; Hunter Liggett, *A.E.F.: Ten Years Ago in France* (New York: Dodd, Mead, 1928), p. 52.

[42]Maj. Gen. R. L. Bullard, "Military Notes," January 26-March 14, 1918, BP.

[43]Diarybook 9, Entry, April 30, 1918, BP.

[44]*"Rapport du Capitaine Seligman, Officier de Liaison pres la 1 Division Americaine,"* January 13, 1918, and *"Le Lt. Colonel Sezille des Essarts, Officier de Liaison, à Monsieur le Général Chef de la Mission Militaire Française pres 'Armée Americaine,"* March 9, 1918, both File 17 N 109-2, Archives of the French Military Mission with the American Army, *Service Historique de l'Armée de Terre, Vincennes, France,* hereafter cited by file and French Military Mission Archives [FMMA].

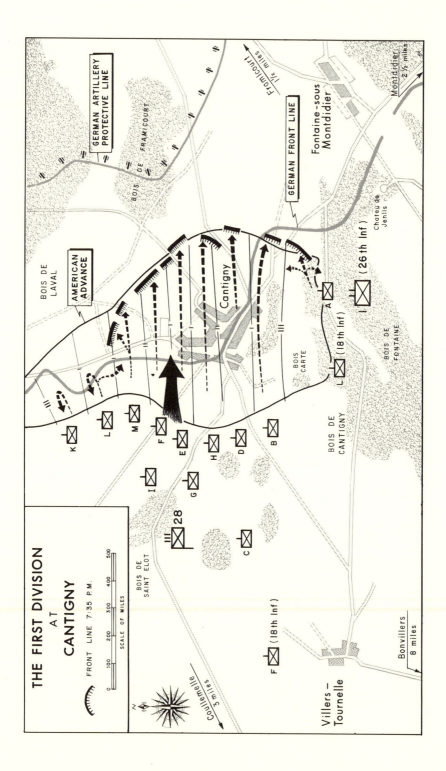

THE FIRST DIVISION
AT
CANTIGNY

FRONT LINE 7:35 P.M.

SCALE OF MILES
0   100   200   300   400   500

N

GERMAN ARTILLERY
PROTECTIVE LINE

BOIS DE FRAMICOURT

Framicourt
½ miles

GERMAN FRONT LINE

Fontaine-sous-
Montdidier

Montdidier
2½ miles

Château de
Jenlis

BOIS DE LAVAL

AMERICAN
ADVANCE

Cantigny

BOIS
CARTE

BOIS DE
FONTAINE

(26th Inf)

A

L   (18th Inf)

BOIS DE
CANTIGNY

K

L

M

F

E

H

D

B

I

G

III   28

C

BOIS DE
SAINT ELOT

Coullemelle
3 miles

F   (18th Inf)

Villers-
Tournelle

Bonvillers
8 miles

18

The First Division: Cantigny 1918

On the foggy morning of March 21, 1918, three German armies left their trenches. Leaning against a devastating barrage, the German infantry made a last dramatic effort to win the war on the Western Front. Planned by the de facto commander of the German army, General Erich Ludendorff, the great offensive involved 47 of the German army's 191 Western Front divisions and was executed with a tactical finesse unknown in France. Although British and French intelligence had strong hints of the time and size of the German offensive, nevertheless the place of the German effort, indicated by the massing of artillery and assault divisions, remained obscure. Field Marshal Haig and his staff could not quite accept the evidence that the blow would come against the British Fifth Army at the point where the BEF and the French army joined lines around Amiens. The British Fifth Army was not well deployed, and its fortifications were largely limited to its vulnerable frontline positions. General Pétain's general staff (*Grand Quartier General* or GQG) was prepared to backstop it, but with only six divisions and in four day's time. The vast majority of the French army's 99 divisions were deployed to protect the approaches to Paris in Champagne and to defend Lorraine. A blow against the seam between the BEF and the French would send the Allied armies backward on diverging axes, the British peeling back to protect the Channel ports and the French curling southward to defend Paris and its communications. As Ludendorff saw more clearly than his opponents, the most promising area for his assault was the valley of the Somme. That is where the March 21 assault struck.[1]

For two weeks the Germans hammered at the British Fifth and Third Armies, nearly destroying the former and knocking the latter backward. At Haig's urging, Pétain began committing not only the French Third Army which had been assigned the contingency mission of supporting the BEF's right flank, but other French divisions as well. From French army reserve units and even from quiet sectors of the front, GQG gathered divisions to seal the breach. The French build-up focused on the extreme right on the BEF's front where General von Hutier's Eighteenth

Army had made the most dramatic gains. The Allies hoped to hold the Germans along an axis running southeast from Amiens through Montdidier to Noyon on the Oise river. The hurried Allied defense got an assist from Ludendorff, who decided to support all three of his attacking armies rather than concentrate his reserves under von Hutier. In the crisis, however, the Allies very nearly gave the German army the total breakthrough it could not achieve on the battlefield. During the course of a conference on March 24, Haig and Pétain exposed their differing strategic priorities, to each other's consternation. Discussing the possibilities of further German advances and Allied withdrawals, Pétain made clear that his valuable reserves would not stand and die around Amiens, but would withdraw to cover Paris if heavily attacked. Moreover, he feared a German attack in Champagne and was reluctant to redeploy any of his divisions except those well south of Verdun, including those around the St. Mihiel salient. Haig, on the other hand, intended that the French fill in the front of the destroyed British Fifth Army and assume the responsibility for defending Amiens with twenty divisions while the BEF gathered divisions for a counterattack. Pétain would not make a firm commitment, but had already ordered Debeney's First Army (six divisions) to concentrate on the French Third Army's flank in the Montdidier-Noyon area. Fortunately for the Allies, Ludendorff gave them time to concentrate, for despite continued advances by the Eighteenth Army, the German high command decided to use more reserves for new but smaller offensives against the BEF north of Amiens, while continuing the original attacks.

Depressed by the German offensive and rightly worried about his own army's distaste for hard fighting in the open field, General Pétain approached Pershing on March 25 to ask for reinforcements. The French Third Army was not fighting with much determination, and Debeney's army was slow in concentrating. The picture Pétain painted for Pershing was of a strategic disaster which the French army faced without fresh reserves. Though not totally convinced by Pétain's description, Pershing alerted his staff that AEF divisions might be committed in the north. Weighing the benefits of using his troops as divisions with the French or as scattered help for the BEF, Pershing preferred the former. Three days later he dramatically pledged that ''all'' of the AEF could be used by the new Allied supreme commander, General Ferdinand Foch. ''All'' that Pershing had, by his staff's definition of first-class combat-preparedness, was the First Division.[2]

Following Pershing's meeting with Pétain, AEF Headquarters alerted Bullard that the First Division would be relieved from the Ansauville sector by Clarence Edwards' Twenty-Sixth Division of New England National Guardsmen. The division would concentrate near Toul, where it would get trains to its assembly area near Gisors, northwest of Paris. The First Division officers read the signs: Debeney's troops moving north, the reports of the British Fifth Army's demise, the lines on the intelligence maps that marked the German Eighteenth Army past Montdidier and Noyon. The division was going to Picardy to join the French army's desperate holding action.[3]

1.

The relief from the Ansauville sector started the greatest personal crisis in Bullard's command of the First Division. The enemy had nothing to do with it. About to lead his division into the AEF's first major fighting in France. Bullard almost became the victim of AEF staff prejudice, the self-serving acts of General Liggett and Colonel Malin Craig, his long-standing rivalry with Clarence Edwards, and his own ill-health. Bullard's difficulties with Pershing's staff centered on his overly enthusiastic attitude toward serving under French command. Since he was also part of the generation of officers which Pershing's staff wanted to eliminate from the command of combat divisions, he was doubly vulnerable. Yet his very ability to work happily with French generals made him at least a short-run asset for AEF Headquarters. Bullard had also developed a decent rapport with his citizen-soldiers without scrapping the disciplinary standards of the regular army, an achievement noted by both Pershing and the leaders of the Wood faction.[4]

The crisis began during the First Division's withdrawal from the Ansauville sector and the Twenty-Sixth Division's movement into Bullard's positions. Under the best of circumstances moving AEF divisions in and out of a constricted sector under harassing shellfire would have been trying, and the First Division was in a hurry. To complicate matters, Edwards was already suspect at AEF Headquarters for permitting casual discipline in his National Guard division and for criticizing Pershing's staff. Edwards was also disappointed that his division would fall under the control of General Augustin Gérard's French Eighth Army, not Debeney's First. Gérard, an uninspired commander, decided to change the conditions of the sector's defense, ordering that the positions forward of the Beaumont road be more heavily garrisoned. Edwards was unhappy with the changes and rightly so. He was so acrimonious in his discussions with Bullard that Liggett's staff urged his removal. Liggett, however, defended Edwards and ordered the relief to continue as planned.

As the First Division withdrew from the Ansauville sector, Bullard assigned General Summerall and his staff the responsibility of handling the details of the relief. Although the First Division performed a considerable feat in clearing the area in three days (April 3-5), Liggett's staff was dissatisfied with the sector's state of police and salvage. Just who made the original complaints about the sector is unclear, but I Corps pursued the matter, ordering Edwards' staff to make a thorough investigation of the First Division's sloppiness. The investigation turned up eighty-nine live (but sick) animals, thirteen dead mules, some abandoned clothing and equipment, fifteen court-martial prisoners awaiting disposition, some cluttered billets, one straggler, and a stack of unburned classified documents in one infantry battalion's PC. On the basis of the Twenty-Sixth's investigation, Colonel Malin Craig, Liggett's chief-of-staff, recommended to Harbord that the First Division was guilty of "demoralization, lack of discipline, and failure to obey orders that is utterly unexplained and beyond the experiences of regular officers at these headquarters.'' He recommended general courts-martial for Summerall, the commander and supply officer of the Sixth Field Artillery, Lieutenant Colonel George K. Wilson of Bullard's administrative section, and the officers of the Twenty-Sixth Infantry who had not destroyed their classified papers. Acting on Craig's report, General Harbord informed Bullard of the charges, but told him that AEF Headquarters would straighten the matter out. He told Bullard, however, that there would be more investigations and that the First Division had better not repeat its errors. Eventually, Pershing's investigators absolved the First Division of negligence and Pershing himself told Bullard to forget the incident, but Bullard was incensed by the affair. He assumed erroneously that Clarence Edwards had pushed the charges. The Twenty-Sixth Division, in fact, was censured for botching its liaison with the First Division. At the time, however, it was the First Division's commanding general who bore the criticism created by Liggett and his staff.[5]

The final blow was that Bullard's health broke on the eve of his division's departure for northern France.[6] Plagued by failing health in February and March, he developed a severe case of neuritis in his right arm and shoulder. His right side virtually paralyzed and his mind dulled by the pain, Bullard was driven to the First Evacuation Hospital at Toul, where Pershing found him. No one had to tell Bullard how ''The Chief'' felt about infirm generals. In fact, he was admitted in Toul for an alleged injury caused by having a car door slammed on his right arm. The diagnosis was probably Captain Shirey's and Bullard's two stars made the AEF doctors accept it. In the meantime, the First Division, without its commanding general, boarded trains for Gisors. In the crisis, Bullard's division staff handled the movement. Bullard knew that his staff had ''saved'' him. ''It worked by itself without me as I had planned that it should.''[7] More than his staff saved Bullard. General Ferdinand Foch asked whether Pershing would name a new commander for the First Division. He wanted the division for the Montdidier sector immediately. Passing on the request to Pershing, General Tasker H. Bliss, the American representative on the Allied Supreme War Council, also added that Foch wanted a division commander ''thoroughly familiar with his troops and conditions existing with the Division before committing it to battle.'' That could mean Bullard, but also Generals Duncan, Summerall, and Buck. Bliss, knowing of Bullard's illness, came to his defense: ''I think Bullard is an excellent officer and I hope he is not going to be incapacitated at this juncture.'' Bliss stressed that the French army thought highly of Bullard, a valuable asset under the circumstances.[8]

Bullard needed little prompting to rejoin the First Division, and he left Toul on April 12. By his own admission, he ''jumped'' the hospital without having improvement in his arm. Swathing him in his wolfskin coat, his aides drove him from Toul to the division PC at Gondreville. The next day he was back on duty, supervising an ''open warfare'' exercise staged for the French and discussing the division with General Harbord, who lauded the command and asked for one of its brigades. On April 15 Pershing arrived to see the exercise. That evening ''The Chief,'' Bullard, and Harbord chatted in high spirits. Bullard's orderly saw the generals in their shirtsleeves sitting together on a couch before a roaring fire, perhaps reminiscing about the Philippines. The generals' laughter filled the glowing room well into the night, their comaraderie honest and obvious. In the crisis, Pershing had stalled Foch in order to let Bullard rejoin his division, an act that testified to "The Chief's" confidence. Bullard's esteem for Pershing grew accordingly.[9]

Pershing gathered the First Division's officers in a chateau courtyard at Chaumont-en-Vexin on the morning of April 16. On the eve of their departure to the Front, he wanted to say a few words about their mission. To Pershing's left stood Bullard in his fur coat, his face drawn and his right arm cradled in his left hand. Beside him were Generals Duncan and Buck and Colonel Marshall. Pershing's speech was short and reminded Colonel Hines of a football coach getting his team up for a championship game. Pershing pointed out that the First Division was the first AEF division to go into a serious fight. It was the division's duty to show the American people that the AEF was in the fight, to hearten the Allies, and to enter the battle to save Europe and preserve "the sacred principles of human liberty." He knew that the division was ready, that its morale was high. He was sure it would not fail him. When Pershing finished, Bullard said a few words, and the crowd of 900 officers dispersed. The First Division's officers were sobered by the seriousness of the moment and "The Chief's" recurring references to "the supreme sacrifice," but some lieutenants in the back row chuckled when a listening teamster asked them who the guy was who had made the speech.[10]

Well rested and fed, refreshed by the unscarred countryside and the balmy spring weather, the division started its march to the Montdidier sector the next day. Pershing's observers reported that the division's spirit and skill were evident in the movement and predicted that the French First Army would welcome the reinforcements without reservation. They were not so sure that General Bullard was as fit as his command. One of Pershing's liaison officers reported that Bullard lived indoors and out in his fur coat and stayed near roaring stoves and fireplaces when possible. "He told me yesterday that he is improving steadily but he does not look at all well to me." Bullard wasn't, for the neuritis persisted. General Harbord, worried that the division would lack firm leadership at the top when it needed it, suggested to Pershing that General Duncan replace Bullard. Bullard could be assigned a liaison post with GQG where his language proficiency and high repute would be valuable to the AEF. Harbord recommended that Bullard should be asked about his health and perhaps ordered before a medical board.[11]

Pershing had other worries, one of which was to affect the First Division profoundly. On April 20 3,000 German assault troops overwhelmed a Twenty-Sixth Division battalion in the Seicheprey-Bois de Remières strongpoint. It was the second such assault against the Twenty-Sixth Division, the first having been stopped cold by American artillery. This time the Germans took no chances, hammering both Edwards' artillery and infantry with a sudden, fierce barrage. The stunned and disorganized New Englanders fought back in the trenches, but the

Germans destroyed three companies and isolated Seicheprey with enveloping infantry, machine gunners, and mortar crews. A touch of panic hit the PCs from regiment to division, a counterattack was fumbled, and French officers took it upon themselves to take charge on the scene. German shellfire hammered the Beaumont road, and the storm troops herded away over a hundred American prisoners as the battle raged into the next day. The isolated and wounded battalion in Seicheprey was still fighting, and the "Yankee" Division survivors in the Bois de Remières cleared the kindling-forest of Germans without much direction or help. The Germans withdrew finally, having lost 600 men. The Twenty-Sixth's losses were the same. The New England infantrymen who lived were pleased with their performance, but the I Corps staff and Edwards' headquarters were dismayed by the affair. Pershing's staff shared their embarrassment, not fully understanding that the Twenty-Sixth Division's orders were to hold in place rather than withdraw before attacks as the First Division had done. General Passaga, Edwards' immediate superior, was not particularly upset by the battle, but AEF Headquarters interpreted the melee as a defeat for the division's commanders, if not their soldiers. In the AEF's heaviest engagement to date, the Germans had won the battle of tactical management. Someone would have to redeem the honor of the AEF officer corps.[12]

2.

Moving by long marches to its positions, the First Division found the Picardy countryside unscarred and unfortified. Their sector was new battlefield, a mosaic of farm villages, sunken country roads, wheat fields, vales, and woodlots where the German Eighteenth Army's advance had been checked by the French. Wedged between two cautious French divisions along two and a half miles of front, the division started moving into its holes on April 24, after a week of marching, reconnaissance, and liaison with the French. In a topographical sense, the First Division's sector was undramatic. The left half, occupied by the Eighteenth Infantry, was mostly open, rolling farmland opposite the town of Cantigny. Cantigny sat on the southern edge of a low plateau with a sharp ravine circling the town's side. The slope was more gradual to the west, and part of the Allied front lines were on the plateau itself; at several points the outposts were only 600 yards from the town. Between the front lines and the Allied main positions and lateral roads was a low swale, nicknamed "Death Valley." The right half of the sector was dominated by two heavy woods, the Bois de Cantigny and the Bois de Fontaine, both of which still had plenty of trees and German outposts. The lines ran through the forests and then emerged into more open fields at Belle Assize farm on the division's right flank.[13]

As the infantry moved into position, they were struck by the rawness of the front. There was little barbed wire, and the French defenses were little more than linked shell-holes. There were no decent trenches to the frontline outposts, making movement hazardous. French and German corpses littered No-Man's-Land, ripening in the warm spring sun. Unlike Ansauville, the ground was firm, well-drained, and easy to dig. The chalky subsoil, however, marked the edges of each new trench with a white border, an easy reference line for German artillery observers. The weather did little to soften the soldiers' lot. When the sun was not beating down on the trenches, spring thunderstorms soaked the troops. Morning arrived around 4 A.M. and it remained light until past 9 P.M., which meant that the hours of dark, the period in which the Americans could move about unobserved and work on their positions, were short. Gas hung in the woodlots and sunken roads. Plagued by German shelling and green smells, the Eighteenth and Sixteenth Infantry began to dig themselves into their new battleground.

The division's mission was to stop an anticipated German offensive northwest of Montdidier, and its first three weeks in the Cantigny sector were devoted to organizing its positions for a protracted defense. The First Brigade deployed two battalions in the frontline trenches, organized as outposts and strongpoints built around machine gun positions. The infantry dug better trenches and dugouts and strung new barbed wire and phone lines, doing the work at night to avoid observed artillery fire. During the long hours of daylight, carrying parties with food, water, tobacco, and equipment could not move to the front. Frontline troops got one cold meal a day; some men stripped French corpses for food. A quarter of a mile from the German outposts, it was not a *bon secteur*. The main defensive positions were established about a mile to the rear of the front, just out of range of the Germans' numerous light artillery batteries. Here there was also much digging and fortifying, for the Germans brought up heavier guns which ranged along the rear villages and roads with ease. Except that the main-position troops had freer access to the hospitals and supply depots, their life in their fortified cellars and dugouts was not much different from that of the frontline battalions. The heaviest casualties, for example, were inflicted upon a reserve battalion of the Eighteenth Infantry billeted with the regimental headquarters in a crossroads village. On the night of May 3-4 the Germans dumped 15,000 rounds of high explosives and mustard gas on the battalion. In the morning, more than 800 casualties, most of them gassed, were evacuated, their comrades treated to the sound of burned lungs and the sight of scorched skin and swollen groins. Other positions as far to the rear as the division PC at Mesnil-St.-Fermin (three miles from the front) were harassed by shellfire and aerial bombardment, and even service and supply units suffered losses.[14]

The First Division did more than dig and absorb German shells. Reinforced by the fire of attached French guns and Corps and Army batteries, Summerall's First Artillery Brigade pounded the German trenches and gun positions enthusiastically, seldom firing less than 10,000 rounds a day and often more. The division's parent French corps headquarters, first Duport's VI and then Vandenberg's X, were delighted to give Summerall's gunners all the shells they could shoot. From the forward positions, the infantry sallied forth at night to scout the German lines and take prisoners, a job they did with increasing proficiency. Even though the division's mission was defensive, Bullard wanted it to take the fight to the Germans in order to build its offensive spirit. He forbade any retirements and insisted upon heavy counterbombardments: "All Groups will fight to the finish."[15]

Bullard himself, still suffering from neuritis, shared the division's ordeal. His PC in the manor house of Mesnil-St.-Fermin, its stone walls reinforced with tons of sandbags, was shelled and bombed, and the division staff took to working and living in the stale, damp basement. During the day, Bullard worked with his staff, held conferences with Generals Debeney and Vandenberg, and catnapped in his fur coat. At night he often visited his artillery, consulting with Summerall about battery positions and camouflage. He also appeared in the front lines to visit the infantry. During one visit he caught lice, an unusual affliction for a major general. Concerned that his casualties were running higher than the neighboring French divisions', he ordered his troops to take cover and personally urged them to be careful. He told the enlisted men at the division PC that jumping into a hole was not cowardice, but good sense. The men needed little encouragement in finding cover, but they appreciated the fact that the division commander would chat with them and had been himself shelled.[16]

Bullard's French superiors were impressed with the First Division's growing competence and showed their esteem by providing not only more ammunition, but also artillery reinforcements and aerial observation balloons and planes. Bullard and his staff worked effectively with Vandenberg's corps staff and the numerous French liaison officers with the division, although the French never gave them all the air support they wanted or abandoned their patronizing attitude about the niceties of trench warfare. A measure of Bullard's rapport with Debeney and Vandenberg was the concern of Pershing's staff that the First Division was becoming too Gallicized in its tactical practices.[17]

3.

As the threat of a major German attack in the Montdidier sector waned, Generals Debeney and Vandenberg discussed a limited counteroffensive of their own to seize Cantigny ridge along the X Corps front. They initially thought of using the First Division and its two flanking French divisions in the attack. There was some tactical benefit to such an assault, for the possession of Cantigny ridge would eliminate a salient into the Allied position and make any later German attack more difficult. Cantigny was as much high ground as the sector had and its possession would hamper German artillery observation and, conversely, would give the Allies increased surveillance over the woods and roads north of Montdidier. Presumably, Cantigny's capture would give the X Corps a better line of departure and artillery positions should it be ordered to attack Montdidier in the future. Debeney liked the idea, urged by Vandenberg and Bullard and approved by Pershing, but decided against a corps attack. He agreed instead to a more limited venture, the capture of Cantigny by the First Division alone. While the assault still had some tactical merit, its value was primarily psychological. A successful large-scale American attack would impress the Germans and Allied public opinion. Implied was a question that concerned Debeney and Pershing: could an American division handle an offensive mission? In addition, for AEF Headquarters there was the fresh, smarting memory of the "defeat" at Seicheprey. The seizure of Cantigny, twice taken and then lost by the French, would be a dramatic demonstration of American valor and expertise in the difficult business of the attack.[18]

As far as human wit and the resources of the French First Army and the First Division could provide, there was nothing left to chance in planning the Cantigny operation. Bullard's division staff, dominated by King and Marshall, handled all the preparations in cooperation with French representatives from X Corps and First Army. The French contributions to the assault were impressive—386 guns and trench mortars from Corps and Army artillery and twelve Schneider tanks, large, lumbering vehicles with a 3″ bow gun and machine guns. The French also gave the First Division flame-thrower teams and aerial photos of the objective area. The artillery planning was especially elaborate. The preparatory barrages were designed to isolate and destroy the German positions around Cantigny and to neutralize the ninety enemy artillery batteries in range of the town. The infantry assault was to be preceded by a thunderous rolling barrage, the shells hitting 100 meters in front of the advancing infantry and moving on every two minutes. Between the artillery and tanks, the German machine guns should pose no problem. To supplement the artillery, the division would employ sixty-four machine guns to lay barrages along the flanks of the assault. The plan called for an attack by a full infantry regiment with three battalions abreast; each battalion would attack with three companies up and one in reserve. The left battalion would cover the ridge north of Cantigny and tie its flanks to the French; the center battalion, supported by the tanks, would clear the town itself and then defend the reverse slope east of the town; the right battalion would pass through the southern edge of Cantigny and defend its gains with one flank on the center battalion and the other on the First Battalion, Twenty-Sixth Infantry, in the Bois de Cantigny. To hold its ground, each battalion would have a machine gun company and engineers attached to it.[19]

The First Division staff got a substantial education in the complexities of planning an attack, and Bullard asked for and got a postponement of the attack from May 16 to 28. The artillery preparations were difficult enough to warrant postponement, but hardly exhausted the range of organizational problems the division faced. With the extra time, the division staff made the plan more elaborate than ever. Dummy trenches and PCs were built; additional frontline trenches were constructed for the line of departure; communications stations were built and their crews instructed; supplies were moved forward, and additional units (including two companies of the Eighteenth Infantry) were added to the attack. The regiment chosen for the attack was the Twenty-Eighth, which had relieved the Eighteenth in the division's left sector on May 14. The choice was routine since the Twenty-Eighth was fresh and responsible for the positions in front of Cantigny anyway. That the abrasive Hanson Ely commanded the assault force was incidental, although Bullard and his staff may have enjoyed the prospect of forcing the colonel of the Twenty-Eighth to demonstrate his self-proclaimed prowess in battle. In any event, the division staff gave Ely and General Buck, his brigadier, little room for any initiative. When Colonel Marshall and his assistants pulled the Twenty-Eighth out of the line for rehearsals, Ely found that Bullard and his staff had arranged sand-table and lantern slide briefings for all officers and key sergeants and constructed a rehearsal site similar to Cantigny. The division operations staff then actually walked through the attack and liaison problems with the reinforced regiment. Little was left for subordinates to decide. Buck was allowed only to choose the moment to commit the brigade reserve (the two companies of the Eighteenth); Ely could choose the men to carry long-handled shovels and to decide whether to conduct a follow-up raid on some nearby German batteries. As the morning of the attack approached, the division staff and the assault forces, impressed by the thoroughness of the preparations, were highly optimistic about the attack and their ability to hold Cantigny, the crucial problem which had defeated the French.[20]

The Germans, suspicious of the First Division's activity and eager to give the impression that they themselves were about to attack, were not very cooperative. They may have had spies behind the American lines; they certainly had adequate air and ground observation over the sector. In addition, the German 82d Reserve Division and 25th Reserve Division, each garrisoning the Cantigny sector, received orders to conduct raids on the First Division. The raids were to take prisoners and divert Allied attention from a new offensive planned for the Champagne region. Early in the morning of May 27, as units of the Twenty-Eighth Infantry were settling into the frontline trenches, special raiding troops from both German divisions hit the lines of both Twenty-Eighth and Twenty-Sixth Infantry. The defenders first sensed the raid when German artillery heavily shelled the American battery positions and main-position shelters. The German artillery also increased its fire on the front lines, methodically walking down trenches and dugouts with shattering precision, killing and burying American soldiers. In front of Cantigny, a box barrage enveloped Companies E and H of the Twenty-Eighth Infantry, and, covered by mortar and machine gun fire, the German infantry ran toward the isolated outposts. To the rear, the artillery had cut the phonelines and pinned everyone to his dugout, but the survivors at the front successfully met the Germans with rifle and machine gun fire. A platoon commander got off a Very flare to signal the American defensive barrage, and shells completed annihilating the German raiders. One American soldier surrendered to the raiders, but was shot by his own comrades, who thought he was a German spy. While the Twenty-Eighth Infantry took sixty casualties and had one platoon break for the rear, fewer than ten raiders returned unharmed to their own lines.

In the Twenty-Sixth Infantry sector, the raid was stopped in much the same way. The Germans, however, took three prisoners in an isolated outpost, but two of them were killed by American artillery fire before they could be herded back to Cantigny. The lone survivor, a private, proved of little value to German intelligence, but the First Division staff had a bad twenty-four hours, fearing that this man or some prisoner they did not know about would tell the Germans about the Cantigny attack. The single American prisoner probably knew nothing about the planned assault.[21]

Their preassault tension increased by the German raids, the troops of the Twenty-Eighth Infantry moved to the front. They wondered whether their attack would be much of a surprise when French villagers lined the roads to wave to their trucks and to shout *"bon chance!"* The harassing German artillery fire did nothing for their nerves, either. At the front, the fatalistic French captain commanding the tank battalion assured American officers that the artillery fire was routine: *"Courage, mes braves. Tout le artillerie est comme ça. C'est la guerre."* The infantry groped its way forward in the dark, and in the departure trenches the troops fell silent as flares popped and shells fell. While waiting in a quarry, an engineer platoon was wiped out by German artillery, but the other units were in position by daylight. Only when the American artillery started its preparatory fires did the troops' morale lift.[22]

4.

The Cantigny operation began at 4:45 on the morning of May 28 with Allied batteries firing their final adjustments. An hour later the artillery thundered down on the German battery positions with gas and high explosives. Other guns blasted the German infantry positions around Cantigny and in the town itself. The waiting infantry saw the Cantigny plateau lift into the air as a cloud of smoke, shattered stones, dust, debris, and mangled bodies. Soon the whole sector was blanketed with smoke and dust. Though the heavy guns continued the counterbattery fire, the 75 mm. batteries shifted at 6:45 A.M. to the rolling barrage. To scattered shouts and the blast of officers' whistles, the assault waves of the Twenty-Eighth Infantry and the French tanks plunged forward. As soon as the troops left the trenches, the three spaced waves bunched together behind the barrage. The infantry, breaking into squad groups by instinct, ran between shell-holes, but kept close to the rolling barrage. Behind them struggled the heavily loaded machine gunners, engineers, and carrying parties. When they reached the first German positions, the men found only craters, scattered bodies, and arms and legs sticking from fresh shellholes. The assault waves pushed into Cantigny.

The initial assault was as successful as the division had hoped. The attack found the German 82d Reserve Division conducting a relief of its two frontline battalions around Cantigny. The American artillery caught the fresh battalions before they were secure in their positions; many Germans of one battalion simply scattered for Cantigny's basements. The Twenty-Eighth Infantry swept past the town against light resistance. The French tanks found little to shoot at except running survivors, although the flame-thrower teams provided useful assistance in flushing out the Germans from their basement refuges. The attackers took a hundred prisoners, many of them demoralized and passive teen-agers, but some German machine gunners proved "unfair" by firing and then surrendering. American infantry shot a few such prisoners and enjoyed doing it. In about half an hour from jump-off, the Twenty-Eighth Infantry was past the town and digging in on its objectives.

In the flood of excited, victorious messages from the Twenty-Eighth Infantry, the tactical situation appeared much more secure than it really was. Colonel Ely, setting his PC in a ravine below the town, was not aware that both his flanks were in the air and that the Germans were not entirely out of Cantigny. On the left flank in the sector of his Third Battalion, the two companies on the extreme left (K and L) never got much beyond their own wire, being stopped by German machine gun fire from the Bois de Laval. Only Company M and some determined groups from Company L got to their positions, leaving a gap north of the town. In the Second Battalion's sector, all four companies had moved through the town and dug positions on the plateau's eastern edge. They had not, however, cleared the town of Germans, and two reserve platoons took more casualties than the attackers and had to fight door-to-door; three days later American infantry was still killing Germans inside Cantigny. The Second Battalion trenches, though rapidly constructed, were exposed and too crowded with troops, an appetizing target for mortars and artillery. During its consolidation, the battalion also lost its commander, who was mortally wounded by machine gun fire. On the right flank, the First Battalion's attack had gone smoothly, with two companies moving out with the Second Battalion through the town's south edge. On the extreme right, however, Company A, wheeling out of the Bois de Cantigny, was caught in the ravine by machine gun fire and lost all its officers. The survivors fell back either into the woods or bunched into the trenches of the other companies. The Twenty-Eighth Infantry's right flank was thus also open, although Ted Roosevelt's battalion of the Twenty-Sixth Infantry could and did cover it with fire. Still, with most of its companies in position and with a loss of less than a hundred men, Ely's regiment had made the division's plan work.[23]

As they waited for more reports, Bullard and his staff knew that the important phase of the operation, the consolidation and defense of the Twenty-Eighth's new positions, had just begun. They did their best to control their anxiety. Colonel Marshall simply went to the front and was in Cantigny at Ely's PC. The division commander, however, equally tense, could ill afford to abandon the phones at his headquarters. The day before the attack, Pershing had visited Mesnil-St.-Fermin to check the plans and was due to return the morning of May 28 for Bullard's analysis of the assault. "The Chief" was optimistic, although his French aide thought that the First Division was in for communications problems. Having learned of Cantigny's fall, Bullard had little to do but wait for the Germans and Pershing. Carrying a new English gas mask, he walked with his sergeant-orderly to a nearby apple orchard, put on the mask, and walked between the trees for an hour. Saying nothing, he then returned to the manor house, where Pershing shortly arrived. Pershing was elated by the attack and relished the sight of German prisoners heading to the rear. However, he was worried about holding Cantigny and he gave Bullard orally and in writing much gratuitous advice. It was "very important'' that Ely's defenses be "very complete,'' for the Germans would surely counterattack and should be taught "a second and probably more severe lesson.'' Cantigny must be held. "I need not suggest that you give this your personal attention, which I know you will do, of course, but am writing this note to show you that I am rather anxious about it.'' Pershing also left his inspector-general, André Brewster, to look over Bullard's shoulder.[24]

Pershing's concern was justified, for the Cantigny operation got less overwhelming with each hour. The basic problems were not created by the Twenty-Eighth Infantry, which was digging and wiring itself in and getting equipment and supplies forward as rapidly as the carrying parties could bring them. The Twenty-Eighth's difficulties were that neither of its flanks was secure and German artillery was cutting its phonelines, but it was still in good shape. The crisis was caused by the Germans in another sector. On the morning before the Cantigny assault, General Ludendorff had launched another great offensive against the French Sixth Army, ill-deployed along the Chemin des Dames ridges north of the Marne. Twenty-four hours later it was clear that the Germans had broken through to the approaches to Paris. For the First Division the French disaster had a serious impact. Just when it most needed counterbattery fire, the First Division lost its attached Corps and Army artillery.

As the French batteries reduced their fire and pulled out, the German artillery built up against the Twenty-Eighth Infantry and the artillery brigade's positions. Marshall reported from Ely's PC that "all [was] quiet,'' but Ely more knowingly felt a counterattack coming as shells fell on his position and heavy machine gun fire swept his three defensive lines. While his men had destroyed two weak probes in the morning, Ely feared a serious attack and the effect of the German artillery fire. At the positions around Cantigny, the infantry endured the mounting artillery and mortar fire. The troops' morale was tested by the day's heat, the lack of water, and the sight of huge mortar shells soaring into their trenches. Above them German aircraft flew spotting missions and occasionally swooped down on strafing runs. A single French plane was in the air, doing artillery spotting when it could avoid the Germans. The Twenty-Eighth Infantry's losses mounted. As they moved to the rear, the American casualties told stories of their own dead, not the Germans', an ominous sign. Other soldiers struggled forward with supplies only to fall in the barrages. Others faded to the rear and hid in Cantigny's cellars, enveloping Ely's PC with dead, groaning wounded, and demoralized shirkers.[25]

The first serious counterattacks by the German 272d Reserve Infantry Regiment and the 83rd Reserve Infantry Regiment hit Ely's front between 5 and 7 P.M., preceded by a heavy barrage. The German infantry fell before the Twenty-Eighth's rifles and machine guns and the division artillery, but German shelling thinned the defenders. Ely's two flank battalions curled backwards from their first positions, and part of the Second Battalion fell back on Cantigny in confusion. Both Ely and the division machine gun officer reported the front line lost. Ely phoned that "unless heavy artillery can give us support it will [be] necessary to withdraw for entire front line is battered to pieces with artillery.''[26] At 6:40 P.M.,

Ely's calls had a touch of panic, for he had learned that the Third Battalion had only two companies in position and that the First Battalion, hardest hit by the counterattack, wanted relief. Ely asked that the Eighteenth Infantry relieve his regiment and suggested that the line of departure trenches be reoccupied. After another artillery barrage around 8:30 P.M., Ely again asked for relief. Bullard reassured him that General Buck now had two battalions of the Eighteenth for counterattacks and had just ordered in his brigade reserve, two companies of the Eighteenth. Despite heavy casualties, Roosevelt's battalion was still protecting Ely's right flank from the Bois de Cantigny. Bullard ordered Ely to get his men back in the forward positions: "Ely, you must hold your position and not give any ground at all. The whole world is watching the Twenty-Eighth Infantry and we must continue to hold Cantigny at all costs."[27]

The Twenty-Eighth Infantry held on, throwing back two weak, mismanaged German assaults the next morning. In the afternoon of the second day, two battalions of the German 272d Reserve Infantry Regiment made another determined attack on Ely's left flank. Again the American infantry gave ground. Two more reinforcing companies of the Eighteenth, thinking they were counterattacking, were hard hit in the open before taking cover. American artillery finally broke the attack. The German barrage, however, further punished the defenders. Ely phoned Buck: "Front line pounded to hell and gone, and entire front line must be relieved tomorrow night and he would not be responsible." An aerial spotter, however, said that the German infantry was not advancing, so Bullard refused Ely's request and ordered again that he push his troops out of Cantigny into their defensive perimeter. He also instructed the Sixteenth Infantry to prepare to relieve the Twenty-Eighth during the nights of May 30-31 and May 31-June 1. Ely would have to hold one more day.[28]

No one now confused Cantigny with a parade ground maneuver. About the town were the swelling bodies of nearly 300 Germans, and the defenders could count at least that many in the open fields and along the fringes of the Bois de Laval to the north, the Bois de Framicourt to their front, and swales to the south along the Bois de Fontaine. Ely's losses were climbing to nearly a third of his original attack force. Losses among officers and noncommissioned officers had been especially high. Reinforcements from the Eighteenth Infantry and First Engineers helped fill the scarred and bloody holes, but the Americans were still uncertain how high a price the Germans were willing to pay for Cantigny. On the morning of May 30, that price still appeared high. At daylight, German shells crashed down on the fragmented Third Battalion and more assault troops swept out of the Bois de Laval. Once again First Division artillery and infantry weapons broke the attack, although it took more soldiers of the Eighteenth Infantry to shore up Ely's left flank.[29] Riflemen and machine gunners set up in the ruins of Cantigny cemetery north of the town. In the rubble of bone fragments, splintered headstones, and pulverized floral decorations, they dug in and fought the Germans to a standstill. This was the last German counterattack, for the commander of the German 26th Reserve Corps had decided that the First Division's assault was limited to Cantigny and was not the prelude to a larger attack on Montdidier. Satisfied that the Americans were contained and irritated by the ill-coordinated counterattacks of the German 82d Reserve Division and the 25th Reserve Division, he called the attacks to a halt. The German 272d Reserve Infantry Regiment alone had lost 1,000 men, and the entire 82d Reserve Division had only 2,500 battle-worthy infantrymen left. The less heavily engaged 25th Reserve Division, which had staged the attacks from the south against the Bois de Cantigny, was not as short-handed, but its officer losses had been prohibitive. If the Americans wanted Cantigny that badly, the German corps commander decided they could have it.

The First Division wanted Cantigny badly enough to pay forty-five officers and a thousand men to take and hold it. As he promised Ely, Bullard sent the Sixteenth Infantry in to continue the defense. Sober, sad, and numb with fatigue, the survivors of the Twenty-Eighth Infantry and its reinforcements withdrew during the night of May 30-31. For the Sixteenth Infantry, the relief was a trial. Ely had little idea of his positions, especially on the flanks, and liaison with the confused and scattered units of the Twenty-Eighth Infantry was difficult. On the still-vulnerable left flank, Bullard personally ordered a night attack to take the Third Battalion's original positions. The attackers found the Germans gone, but endured shelling to hold the new lines. Four days later they were still getting heavy shelling, and one company commander wondered what kind of army would send a runner through mortar fire to deliver the following message: ''You will report with the morning report this date the names of all men in your company who are graduate chemists.''[30] But for all the shelling and the digging, the First Division's first big fight was over.

Even in victory there were the inevitable disputes and postmortems. Colonel Ely was sour because he had lost the French artillery support and air observers, and he criticized the division headquarters for not relieving his regiment sooner.[31] The French were pleased that the First Division had taken and held Cantigny, but they were too concerned about the Germans' massive attack across the Chemin des Dames to get very excited about such a local success. Generals Debeney and Mangin, commander of the French Tenth Army, thought the First Division's staff and fighting men had performed very well and showed what spirited assault troops the Americans could produce.[32] No one was more pleased than General Pershing. His report of the Cantigny affair, in fact, exaggerated his own role and the simplicity of the operation, stressing the original assault, not the defense of Cantigny. He cabled the War Department that ''while relatively small the affair at Cantigny on the 28th was well planned and splendidly executed.'' The artillery was excellent, the infantry superb, the ''staff work was excellent,'' and ''liaison perfect.'' He added that ''under my personal direction additional troops of the 18th and 26th were at once brought up to support the line,'' an ambiguous description of his minor intervention at Bullard's PC on May 28. He assured the War Department that the Allies were greatly impressed with First Division. ''It is my firm opinion that our troops are the best in Europe and our staffs the equal of any.''[33] For Pershing, Cantigny was a welcome reinforcement for his arguments for an independent American army.

For the ailing division commander, the Cantigny attack was a satisfying operation because it demonstrated the steadiness and gallantry of his division. Bullard thanked his men for their performance, telling them that they had set a high standard for the rest of the AEF. The attack had not been especially crucial tactically, but the results held great value: ''The moral effects to flow from this proof of the reliability in battle of the American soldiers far outweigh the direct military importance of the actions themselves.''[34] As he must have realized, Bullard himself had passed another test that transcended the direct military importance of Cantigny. General Brewster, evaluating Bullard's performance, assured Pershing that the First Division commander had done well:

> I have observed this officer in command of a Division both in and out of the line. He is hard working, painstaking, I believe he has quite an amount of tactical ability, is very loyal and always deserious [*sic*] of carrying out the policies of the Commander-in-Chief, a valuable asset. If I had any criticism at all to make, I have thought it must be said that in the CANTIGNY fight, when there was a request to relieve assault troops after the occupation at that time, he was very firm and kept them there; to have relieved them would not have been a good tactical move and could only have been accomplished with severe losses.

> /s/ Major General Brewster[35]

5.

With the success and casualties of the Cantigny attack still fresh, the First Division switched once more to the defense. French divisions had been pulled from the French First Army and sent southward to stop the German drive toward Paris; one of these divisions came from the sector on the First Division's left flank. General Vandenberg split the departed division's sector and assigned the Americans an additional mile of front. To man this extension, Bullard put all four infantry regiments on line and redeployed his artillery and support troops. He moved his own PC west from Mesnil-St.-Fermin to the Chateau of Tartigny. There was some urgency to the changes, for French intelligence predicted a new offensive by von Hutier's Eighteenth Army somewhere in the Montdidier-Noyon area. To probe German intentions, the First Division raided the German lines for prisoners and patrolled No-Man's-Land nightly. Bullard, not wanting to lose the division's psychological edge over the Germans, kept the infantry and artillery busy in order to refine their teamwork and tactical skills.[36]

Bullard's major concern was his division's ability to cope with a major German offensive, for his troops were spread thin along the division's front. His dispositions were based on three lines of defense: four battalions in the forward trenches, two in an intermediate position, and six battalions in the main line of resistance. His division reserve was the six companies of the First Engineers.[37] The division was not prepared for tactical withdrawals. The First Division's commitment to defend in place produced a trivial incident that redounded to Bullard's personal advantage. By June 6 the French First Army was convinced that it would be attacked in three or four days, and it alerted its divisions. The French general commanding the division on Bullard's right made a routine call on the First Division PC to check defensive arrangements. The Frenchman asked Bullard what the First Division proposed to do "in case we fall back." As Bullard told an American editor the day after the incident: "I did not answer him, for I didn't know what to say. My orders are to hold this line and I'll do so even if annihilated."[38] The French general asked only that Bullard let him know if he should make a tactical withdrawal and he promised to reciprocate. Bullard simply replied that a retreat didn't enter into his plans—which was true enough. Bullard thought his division could hold, a moot point.[39]

On the morning of June 9, the Germans heavily shelled the First Division and the French division on the right, which, according to the current French defensive doctrine, withdrew its infantry less than a mile to prepare to repulse the German infantry. Von Hutier's army was attacking, but against French divisions to the southeast, not northwest of Montdidier. In the X Corps sector, the German attack consisted only of four days of heavy shelling, which caused locally severe casualties. Bullard's right flank regiment, the Twenty-Sixth Infantry, was especially hard hit and lost contact with the French. What Bullard may have said or done in this small crisis is unrecorded, but the division stayed in place, much to Vandenberg's pleasure. Since Bullard and the division staff were confident the division could repulse an infantry assault, they did not claim to be seriously threatened.[40] On June 13 the Germans were halted and the shelling subsided.

Six months later American newspapers had so distorted Bullard's routine remarks to the French general that he was being called "No Retreat" Bullard and was credited with saying that "Americans never withdraw." For once the publicity embarrassed him, for the accounts were patently ridiculous. By the time romantic American newspapermen finished with the tale (spread by American civilian visitors to France), what Bullard had said originally was unrecognizable:

> He is credited with having sent word to a French commander that Americans were unused to seeing their colors in retreat, and that hence he would have to disregard the French strategic retreat plans. Indeed he gave orders that the Americans advance, and it was this spirit which saved the day at a time when it looked as if the German would succeed in his plan of taking Paris.[41]

Even without journalistic exaggerations, Bullard and his division were in high spirits in June 1918. Life in the frontline positions did not improve, but the shelling and bombing of reserve positions lessened and the men had adjusted to it as well. The artillery brigade led the division in stimulating morale, publishing its own newspaper, holding horse shows, and giving prizes for the most beautifully decorated gun positions. More important, the ripening fields provided abundant forage for the division's horses.

The division commander himself reflected the general sense of well-being. Bullard's staff and household functioned quietly and efficiently, receiving and briefing visitors with aplomb. Bullard himself impressed one American as a "tall, handsome, wiry" man with a "bronzed leathery complexion . . . a more agreeable man on first acquaintance it has seldom been my privilege to meet." Bullard appeared fit and vigorous, and the journalist thought he represented a new breed of American general—the commander without a walrus mustache and pot belly.[42]

Inspection parties visited Bullard from I Corps and AEF Headquarters. On June 30 Pershing came to award the first Distinguished Service Cross, a new American decoration for valor. "The Chief" praised the division, telling it that it had heartened the American people and the Allies and had done everything he had hoped. Inspecting equipment and billets, Pershing was delighted by the order and neatness. Members of his party from the AEF's Services of Supply were equally impressed by the division's efficiency.[43] Hunter Liggett and his staff also inspected the First Division. They thought Bullard looked tired, but were impressed with the division's condition and morale. Liggett, however, was disturbed to find that Bullard had company commanders who were lieutenants while platoons were led by "unsatisfactory" captains. He told Bullard to pay more attention to seniority in assignments. Bullard replied sharply that rank system should be made flexible enough to give people the rank they rated on the basis of proven battlefield competence. Liggett abandoned the subject.[44]

As the Fourth of July approached, the division sensed that it was in a time of change. It had taken heavy casualties—238 officers and 5,593 men in the Cantigny area—but replacements kept pouring in to fill the ranks. Wounded returned, men were promoted, equipment was repaired and replaced. Warned that the division would leave Picardy, Bullard put his affairs in order. He wrote Pershing to recommend that the First Division's senior officers be promoted and assigned larger commands. He suggested that all the brigadiers get divisions and that all four infantry regimental commanders become brigadiers, He also recommended that Campbell King and Lucius Holbrook, an artillery colonel, be made brigadier generals. Among his recommendations for regimental command were George Marshall, George K. Wilson (his G-1), and Ted Roosevelt.[45] Bullard's own reputation with both the French and Pershing's headquarters was in excellent shape.[46] The First Division and its commanding general had reason to be proud of their performance, and their trust and affection for each another was justified by their experiences together in Lorraine and Picardy.

NOTES

[1]For a general description of the German 1918 offensive, see Correlli Barnett, "General Erich Ludendorff," in *The Swordbearers* (New York: Morrow, 1964), pp. 269-361.

[2]John J. Pershing, *My Experiences in the World War,* 2 vols. (New York: Frederick A. Stokes, 1931), II, pp. 353-366; Cable, Pershing to C/S, USA, March 29, 1918, "AEF Confidential Cables Sent," James G. Harbord Papers.

[3]*History of the First Division* (Philadelphia: Winston, 1922), pp. 64-66; Col. F. Parker to Mrs. Parker, March 30-April 4, 1918, Frank Parker Papers.

[4]Bullard-Allen conversation noted in diary entry, June 29, 1922, in Maj. Gen. Henry T. Allen, *My Rhineland Journal* (Boston: Houghton, Mifflin, 1923), p. 384; Col. J. G. Harbord, "Memorandum for the Commander-in-Chief," March 8, 1918, "Pershing-Harbord Correspondence," Harbord Papers; Brig. Gen. Samuel T. Ansell, "A Few Sidelight Reflections on the War," 1918, Enoch H. Crowder Papers; Maj. Paul H. Clark to Gen. J. J. Pershing, April 10, 1918, General John J. Pershing Papers, Record Group 316, National Archives. (Hereafter cited as Pershing Papers/NA to differentiate this collection from the Pershing Papers in the Manuscript Division of the Library of Congress.)

[5]The account of the relief of Ansauville is based upon the following sources: P. L. Stackpole diary, entry, March 31, 1918, George C. Marshall Library; Frank Sibley, *With the Yankee Division in France* (Boston: Little, Brown, 1919), pp. 85-86, 108; and Robert L. Bullard, *Personalities and Reminiscences of the War* (New York: Doubleday, Page, 1925), pp. 174-176. The basic documents were collected by General Summerall, who divined correctly that Liggett and Craig had used the affair to discredit the First Division. See Lt. Col. C. M. Dowell, IG, I Corps, to Lt. Col. H. P. Hobbs, IG, 26th Div., April 5, 1918; Lt. Col. Hobbs to CG, I Corps, April 13, 1918; Col. M. Craig to C/S, AEF, April 17, 1918; Col. J. G. Harbord to Maj. Gen. R. L. Bullard, April 19, 1918; JAG memo for C/S, AEF, "Conditions Attending the Departure of the First Division from Sector Early in April," April 21, 1918; Lt. Col. B. Winship, Assistant IG, I Corps to C/S, I Corps, memo "Investigation of Evacuation of Ansauville Sector by 1st Division," June (?), 1918, copies in the Charles P. Summerall Papers.

[6]Bullard, *Personalities and Reminiscences,* pp. 177-178; TAGO, "Statement of Medical History in the Case of Maj. Gen. Robert L. Bullard, USA," Bullard 201 File; Pershing diary, entry, April 7, 1918, Pershing Papers.

[7]Bullard autobiography, pp. 135-136.

[8]Bliss diary entries, April 12 and 13, reprinted in Frederick Palmer, *Bliss, Peacemaker* (New York: Harper and Row, 1934), pp. 258-259.

[9]Bullard, *Personalities and Reminiscences,* pp. 179-181; Gen. J. J. Pershing to Brig. Gen. J. G. Harbord, April 10, 1918, and Harbord to Pershing, April 13, 1918, "Pershing-Harbord Correspondence," Pershing Papers; C-in-C, AEF, to CG, 1st Div., April 12, 1918, *USA/WW, 1917-1919,* III, pp. 489-490; entries, April 8 and 21, 1918 in James G. Harbord, *Leaves from a War Diary* (New York: Dodd, Mead, 1925), pp. 253-270; Ralph H. Hutchins to the author, May 27, 1971.

[10]Pershing diary, entry, April 16, 1918, Pershing Papers; Diary entry, April 16, 1918, in Charles G. Dawes, *A Journal of the Great War,* 2 vols. (Boston: Houghton Mifflin, 1921), I, pp. 92-93; Duncan, "Reminiscences of the World War," p. 82; Hines diary, entry, April 16, 1918, John L. Hines Papers; H. H. Caswell, "History of the 3rd Machine Gun Bn. of

the 1st Division AEF," *mss.;* Joseph D. Patch, *A Soldier's War: The First Infantry Division,* (Corpus Christi, Tex.: Joseph Dorst Patch, 1966), p. 83.

[11]G. V. Moseley, "War Notes," I, entry, April 25, 1918, George Van Horn Moseley Papers; Frederick Palmer, "Notes of Observation with the First Division," April (?), 1918, Pershing Papers; Maj. R. H. Lewis to Col. F. Conner, April 22, 1918, *WWR/1st Div.,* XII.

[12]Pershing, *My Experiences in the World War* II, pp. 9, 16; P. L. Stackpole diary, entries, April 23 and 24, 1918, Marshall Library; Maj. Gen. C. R. Edwards, "Report on Enemy Raid on Troops of the 26th Division at Seicheprey," *USA/WW, 1917-1919,* III, pp. 613-617; Col. J. H. Parker to Col. J. McA. Palmer, April 22, 1924 in "Chapter Notes" XVIII, John McAuley Palmer Papers; Emerson G. Taylor, *New England in France: 1917-1919: A History of the Twenty-Sixth Division, U.S.A.* (Boston: Houghton, Mifflin, 1920), pp. 110-133.

[13]American Battle Monuments Commission, *Terrain Photographs: American World War Battlefields in Europe—1st Division: Cantigny and Montdidier-Noyon Defensive* (April 19-July 13, 1918), copy at the USAMHRC, Carlisle Barracks.

[14]The description of war in the Cantigny sector is based on: *History of the First Division,* pp. 69-77; Shipley Thomas, *The History of the A.E.F.* (New York: Doran, 1920), pp. 70-77; "Regimental Chaplain," *The Story of the Sixteenth Infantry* (Frankfurt: Martin Flock, 1919), pp. 22-29; Ben H. Chastaine, *History of the 18th U.S. Infantry* (New York: Hymans Publishing Company, 1920), pp. 45-48; Maj. T. F. Farrell *et al., A History of the 1st U.S. Engineers 1st U.S. Division* (Coblenz: n. p. 1919), pp. 19-22; George B. Duncan, Reminiscences of the World War," *mss.,* pp. 83-85; Caswell, "History of the 3rd Machine Gun Bn. of the 1st Division," *mss.,* pp. 6-14; Campbell King, "Tour in France," p. 2, Campbell King Papers; Theodore Roosevelt, Jr., *Average Americans* (New York: G. P. Putnam's Sons, 1919), PP. 120-161; and 1st Lt. Elden Sprague Betts to Edith and Marjorie Betts, April 26-June 6, 1918, in "An Argonne Cross," Parker Papers.

The most vivid battlefield descriptions are contained in a series of vignettes in Jeremiah M. Evarts, *Cantigny* (New York: Scribner's Press, 1938), written by a platoon commander in the Eighteenth Infantry.

[15]HQ, First Division, Instructions No. 17, April 27, 1918, in *USA/WW, 1917-1919,* IV, pp. 264-265.

[16]Bullard, *Personalities and Reminiscences,* pp. 186-191, and *American Soldiers Also Fought* (New York: Longmans, Green, 1938), p. 30; G-3, First Division, memorandum, May 8, 1918, in *USA/WW, 1917-1919,* IV, p. 266.

Bullard's activities are described in letters from Ralph H. Hutchins to the author, May 27, 1971; Mr. E. V. Ryall, Kenosha, Wisconsin, to the author, December 5, 1971; and Mr. Richard Major, Philadelphia, Pennsylvania, to the author, November 5, 1970.

[17]Maj. P. H. Clark to Gen. J. J. Pershing, April 26, May 1 and 17, 1918, Pershing Papers/NA; Lt. Col. H. A. Drum, G-3 memo, "Divisional Organization," May 18, 1918, in *USA/WW, 1917-1919,* II, pp. 406-412; Forrest C. Pogue, *George C. Marshall: Education of a General* (New York: Viking, 1963), pp. 163-165.

[18]Memo S230, CG, X Corps, to CG, First French Army, May 12, 1918, and CG, First French Army, to CG, X Corps, May 15, 1918, in *WWR/1st Div.* XXV; Thomas. *The History of the A.E.F.,* pp. 72-78; Pershing, *My Experiences in the World War* II, pp. 54-55.

[19]HQ, First Division, Field Order 18, May 20, 1918 in *WWR/1st Div.,* I.

[20]My account of the Cantigny operation is based on the following sources: the documents printed in Vol. XXV of *WWR/1st Div.*, and *USA/WW, 1917-1919,* IV, pp. 259-348; HQ, First Division, G-3 memo 1355, "Cantigny Operation, May 28-30," with eighteen enclosures, in *WWR/1st Div.* XIII, especially HQ, 28th Inf., "Report of Operations Against Cantigny, May 28-30;" and an excellent postwar study by Capt. Paul B. Carter, "The Battle of Cantigny," in The Class of 1923, Infantry School, *Monographs of the World War* (Ft. Benning, Ga.: n.p., 1923), pp. 336-347.

The German side is reconstructed from the war diaries and selected documents, May 27-June 5, 1918, of the Twenty-Sixth Reserve Corps, Eighty-Second Reserve Division, Twenty-Fifth Reserve Division, 270th Reserve Infantry Regiment, 272nd Reserve Infantry Regiment, and 83rd Reserve Regiment, reprinted in *WWR/1st Div.: German Documents* I. For the status of German divisions, see Military Intelligence Division, General Staff, United States Army, *Histories of Two Hundred and Fifty-One Divisions of the German Army which participated in the War* (1914-1918) (Washington: Government Printing Office, 1920).

The First Division after-action narratives are generally dependable but minimize personal and unit shortcomings. See *History of the First Division,* pp. 77-88; Lt. Col. H. E. Ely, "The Attack on Cantigny," *National Service* 7 (April 1920), pp. 201-208; Beaumont B. Buck, *Memories of War and Peace* (San Antonio: Naylor Publishing, 1935), pp. 171-182; Bullard, *Personalities and Reminiscences,* pp. 192-201; and "Statement of Major General C. P. Summerall, Commanding General, V Corps, American Expeditionary Forces," transcript of testimony before the House Military Affairs Committee, April 28, 1919, Summerall Papers.

For realistic detail, the following sources were especially useful: Capt. C. F. Butler, "Battle of Cantigny" (1925); Maj. Stuart G. Wilder, "Operations of Company M, 16th Infantry in the Cantigny Operations, May 28-June 6, 1918" (1930); and Capt. Welcome P. Waltz, "Operations of Company C, 3rd Machine Gun Battalion at Cantigny" (1929). These narratives were tactical monographs written by officers of the First Division who participated in the Cantigny attack and who interviewed other survivors. The monographs were part of the authors' assignments as students at the Infantry School, Fort Benning, Georgia, where the monographs are still retained in the Infantry School Library. Subsequent monographs are cited as IS monograph, ISL.

[21]Capt. Edward S. Johnston, "The Day before Cantigny" (1929), IS monograph, ISL. (Captain Johnston was commanding officer of Company E, Twenty-Eighth Infantry, the attacked American unit.)

[22]Johnston, "The Day before Cantigny," and Waltz, "Operations of Company C, 3rd Machine Gun Battalion at Cantigny."

[23]For the flow of the battle, see the following journal of messages and reports: HQ, 1st Artillery Brigade, "Journal of Cantigny Operations, May 28, 1918," copy in Summerall Papers. The details are from Butler, "Battle of Cantigny," and Waltz, "Operations of Company C, 3rd Machine Gun Battalion at Cantigny."

[24]Pershing diary, entries, May 27 and 28, 1918, Pershing Papers; Gen. J. J. Pershing to Maj. Gen. R. L. Bullard, May 28, 1918, Pershing Papers. Bullard's stroll in the orchard is recounted in a letter by the orderly, Ralph H. Hutchins, to the author, May 4, 1971.

[25]Butler, "Battle of Cantigny"; "Operations of Company C, 3rd Machine Gun Battalion

at Cantigny''; Caswell, "History of the 3rd Machine Gun. Bn. of the 1st Division," pp. 40-41; interviews taken by Hamilton Holt (editor, *The Independent*), quoted in "The Black Snakes: A Visit to Bullard's Boys at Cantigny," *The Independent* 95 (August 3, 1918), pp. 184-185, 197-198, 200.

[26]CO, 28th Inf. to HQ 2d Brigade at 5:45 P.M., May 28, 1918, in *USA/WW, 1917-1919,* IV, p. 307.

[27]CO, 28th Inf. to CG, 2d Brigade at 6:40 P.M., May 28, 1918, in *USA/WW, 1917-1919,* IV, p. 309; telcon, CG, 1st Div. to CO 28th Inf. at 9:15 P.M., May 28, 1918, in HQ, 1st Artillery Brigade, "Journal of Cantigny Operations," May 28, 1918, Summerall Papers; Mr. James A. Edgar to the author, February 25, 1972.

[28]CO, 28th Inf. to CG, 2d Brigade at 8:55 P.M., May 29, 1918, in *USA/WW, 1917-1919,* IV, p. 319; telcon, CG, 1st Div., to CG, 2d Brigade at 9:20 P.M., May 29, 1918, in HQ, 1st Artillery Brigade, "Journal of Cantigny Operations," May 29, 1918, Summerall Papers.

[29]Brig. Gen. B. Buck to Col. F. Parker, June 1, 1918; Sgt. James Finnegan to Col. F. Parker, January 3, 1922; and Capt. E. S. Johnston to CO, Twenty-Eighth Infantry, February 21, 1922, all in Parker Papers.

[30]Wilder, "Operations of Company M, 16th Infantry in the Cantigny Operations, May 28-June 6, 1918."

[31]CO, 28th Infantry, "Report of Capture of Cantigny and Consolidation of Position," June 2, 1918, in *USA/WW, 1917-1919,* IV, pp. 326-331.

[32]Maj. R. H. Lewis to Col. F. Conner, May, 29, 1918, in *WWR/1st Div.* XII; Major. P. H. Clark to Gen. J. J. Pershing, May 28, 1918, Pershing Papers/NA.

[33]Cable, Pershing to AGWAR, June 1, 1918, "AEF Confidential Cables Sent," Harbord Papers, reprinted *USA/WW, 1917-1919,* II, p. 434.

[34]HQ, First Division, AEF, Memorandum 8, June 2, 1918, copy in Parker Papers.

[35]Maj. Gen. A. W. Brewster, IG, AEF, to Commander-in-Chief, AEF, July 15, 1918, copy in Bullard 201 File.

[36]*History of the First Division,* pp. 88-98; documents and reports on First Division operations, Cantigny-Montdidier, June 1-July 8, 1918, in *USA/WW, 1917-1919,* IV, pp. 735-806; Thomas, *The History of the A.E.F.,* 98-100.

[37]HQ, First Division, Field Order 22, June 4, 1918, in *WWR/1st Div.* II.

[38]Quoted in Holt, "The Black Snakes: A Visit to Bullard's Boys at Cantigny," p. 198. Holt's interview took place on June 7.

[39]Pershing diary, entry, June 11, 1918, Pershing Papers.

[40]*Ibid.*

Bullard's account of this episode is in Diarybook 11, entires, March 29 and July 10, 1920, and Bullard autobiography, pp. 138-140,

[41]"Bullard," *World's Work* 37 (November 1918), p. 88.

[42]Holt, "The Black Snakes: A Visit to Bullard's Boys at Cantigny," pp. 184-185; Ralph H. Hutchins to the author, May 27, 1971.

[43]Pershing diary, entry, June 30, 1918, Pershing Papers; Diary entry, June 28, 1918, in Johnson Hagood, *The Services of Supply* (Boston: Houghton Mifflin, 1927,) pp. 204-205.

[44]P. L. Stackpole diary, entry, June 28, 1918, Marshall Library.

[45]Memorandum, Commanding General, First Division to Commander-in-Chief, AEF,

"Recommendations for Assignment to Command," July 4, 1918, copy in King Papers.

[46]Maj. P. H. Clark to Gen. J. J. Pershing, July 3, 1918, Pershing Papers/NA; Lt. Gen. H. Liggett to Adj. Gen., USA, September 2, 1919, on the service of Major General Bullard as Commanding General, First Division, Bullard 201 File.

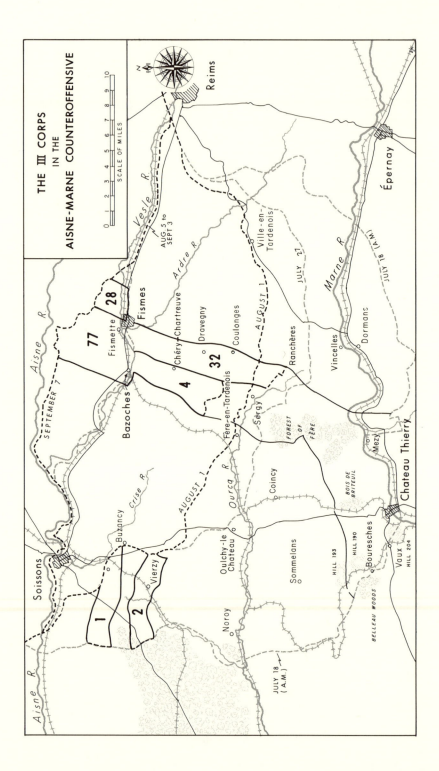

THE III CORPS
IN THE
AISNE-MARNE COUNTEROFFENSIVE

SCALE OF MILES
0 1 2 3 4 5 6 7 8 9 10

Reims

Épernay

Vesle R.

Ardre R.

Aisne R.

AUG. 5 to SEPT 3

Fismes

Fismette

28

77

Chéry-Chartreuve

Dravegny

Coulonges

Ville-en-Tardenois

Bazoches

4

32

Fère-en-Tardenois

Sergy

Rancheres

JULY 27

AUGUST 1

Vincelles

Dormans

JULY 18 (A.M.)

Marne R.

SEPTEMBER 7

Crise R.

AUGUST 1

Ourcq R.

Coincy

FOREST OF FÈRE

BOIS DE BRITEUIL

Mezy

Château Thierry

Soissons

Buzancy

Vierzy

1

2

Oulchy-le Château

Sommelans

Noroy

HILL 193

HILL 190

Bouresches

Vaux

HILL 204

BELLEAU WOODS

JULY 18 (A.M.)

Aisne R.

19

The III Corps: The Second Battle of the Marne 1918

The German offensive of 1918 nearly killed General Pershing's dream of an independent American army. Only his four best-trained divisions joined the embattled French armies, and Pershing had no intention of leaving them under French command any longer than necessary. In April and May, however, the Allies' pressure upon the War Department again altered Pershing's plans. Insisting that the Americans send only infantry and machine gunners to the Western Front, the Allies persuaded President Wilson and Secretary Baker to change the War Department's shipping schedules. The next divisions sent to France would not bring their artillery and service units unless additional shipping could be found. Four divisions (Third, Fifth, Seventy-Seventh, and Eighty-Second) came to Europe in April under this arrangement, although Pershing urged the War Department to find vessels for the artillery and trains as quickly as possible.

The Allies were not satisfied, for Pershing had also extracted additional promises from them and his own government that an independent army was still the goal of American military policy in France. In early June 1918 the Americans and the Allies further agreed that the United States should concentrate on sending infantry to France and increase the numbers of such troops shipped during the months of April, May, June, and July. The rate of troop arrivals were planned for 250,000 a month; the Allies would provide much of the shipping, equipment, and training for the reinforcements, which would go to both the BEF and French army in roughly equal numbers.[1]

While the troop-shipping agreements slowed Pershing's plans for an in-dependent army, the execution of the revised shipping plans rapidly expanded the number of American troops in France. Between April and the end of July, more than 600,000 troops sailed for France, expanding the AEF to more than a million men and twenty-four combat divisions. Though the divisions were slow in receiving their own artillery and service units and sometimes horrified AEF Headquarters by their state of training, the rapid American buildup not only heartened the Allies but gave Pershing the foundation for a field army of his own.

Pershing recognized that the BEF and the French army would be reluctant to part with their American divisions. Therefore, he extracted an agreement from Marshal Foch that the AEF should establish its own sector on the south face of the St. Mihiel salient and prepare for its 1918 offensive in that area. To strengthen its control of the American divisions and to quash Allied arguments that the AEF was not ready to command its own divisions, AEF Headquarters also accelerated the creation of corps headquarters, the intermediate echelon of command between the division and Pershing.

During its planning sessions in 1917, Pershing's staff had decided that AEF divisions should be permanently assigned to a particular corps. The planners specified that a corps should include four combat divisions, a depot division, and a replacement division. Like more than one AEF plan, however, the scheme for corps organization was seriously revised by the German spring offensive and the AEF's rapid expansion. With divisions scattered from Flanders to the Vosges, Pershing had to give up the idea of permanently assigning divisions to corps. He also had to provide corps headquarters for his new divisions or accept Allied corps commanders, not only for the tactical use of his troops, but their training and administration as well. Given his attitudes about Allied training, Pershing found such a prospect intolerable. On June 10 he announced the creation of three more corps headquarters: II, which was responsible for American divisions with the BEF; III, responsible for divisions with the French Seventh Army; and IV, controlling the divisions with the French Eighth Army. The latter two corps were to have administrative responsibility for the American troops deployed from the eastern edge of the St. Mihiel salient to the Swiss border. Liggett's I Corps would be responsible for American divisions deployed around the salient itself. Divisions themselves would be rotated from corps to corps as the tactical situation dictated.[2]

Although he ordered the creation of corps headquarters staffs before he formally activated each corps, Pershing was reluctant to assign general officers as corps commanders until he saw them in action with their divisions. Pershing's staff was unimpressed with most of the generals they saw, and few appeared ready for larger commands. Corps organization, however, would not wait. Pershing, therefore, followed the expedient course and chose commanders from among the general officers serving in the areas the new corps were to supervise.[3]

Unlike the I Corps in which the commanding general and chief-of-staff were assigned simultaneously, the chiefs-of-staff of the II, III, and IV Corps were selected weeks before a corps commander was chosen. The chief-of-staff for the III Corps was Lieutenant Colonel Alfred W. Bjornstad, who was serving as the director of the AEF General Staff School at Langres when he was assigned on March 30, 1918. Of all the bright and assertive officers of the "Leavenworth clique," Bjornstad was one of the most self-confident. A large, serious, handsome man, Bjornstad discovered in 1898 that the army promised more excitement than his native Minnesota. Serving as a captain in the Thirteenth Minnesota and the Forty-Second Volunteers in the Philippines, Bjornstad won a deserved reputation for physical courage and troop-leading skill. In 1901 he accepted a commission in the regular army as a first lieutenant, passing in seniority all the regular second lieutenants commissioned since 1898. This condition of his regular commission, provided by Congress to reward former Volunteers, did nothing to win him friends in the officer corps. Aloof, intolerant of slow thinkers, and meticulous, Bjornstad ignored his detractors. From 1908 until 1917, his career was shaped by his ambition and his demonstrated mastery of military science and staff procedures. In 1909 he graduated first in his class from the School of the Line with the highest grades Fort Leavenworth had yet recorded. Bjornstad then served on the General Staff and went to Germany as a military observer. When war came in 1917, Bjornstad's reputation for brilliant planning was so high that the War Department assigned him as chief-of-staff of the Thirtieth Division, despite the fact that he was only forty-three years old and had less than twenty years service. Only Douglas MacArthur got comparable advancement.[4]

Bjornstad joined Pershing's headquarters in the autumn of 1917 to train future AEF staff officers. Although his work as director of the General Staff School was characteristically energetic and brilliant, Bjornstad had his anxious moments. Once the War Department got confused and demoted him to major, an administrative error which did nothing for Bjornstad's slight sense of humor. The error was corrected, and in May 1918 he was promoted to temporary colonel, despite the reservations of General Harbord, who thought him too young and abrasive for such high rank.[5] Two months later, Bjornstad was promoted again— to brigadier general.

By nature intense and blunt, Bjornstad had little patience with AEF officers who did not match his energy and professional knowledge.[6] As chief-of-staff of the III Corps, Bjornstad was unforgiving and impatient with his staff's efforts. He allowed little personal initiative in any of the sections and ran the operations and training section himself. He let the staff do little tactical planning and often wrote entire operations orders. He slept with a phone on his bedpost and took incoming calls from other headquarters for the corps commander rather than trust a duty officer. He assumed that only he had the special staff skills necessary to run the corps; he viewed not just his staff as amateurs, but also the corps and division commanders as well. His successor as III Corps chief-of-staff, Brigadier General Campbell King, found the staff badly organized and demoralized by Bjornstad's autocratic style. King wondered why Bjornstad had not been relieved by his first corps commander. That corps commander himself called Bjornstad "as poor a chief-of-staff as I have ever seen; I mean in tact and loyalty. He had plenty of ability." The corps commander was Major General Robert Lee Bullard.[7]

For the first two months of its existence, the III Corps staff had little to do but observe others' operations and supervise the training of the newly arrived Third and Fifth Divisions. Plagued by officer transfers and confused by AEF Headquarters' changing definition of its function, the III Corps staff was not ready to direct combat operations when it left Langres for the French Seventh Army's zone. Under Bjornstad's direction, the III Corps staff shifted from sector to sector without sufficient personnel and without a mission.[8]

Like the AEF's altered shipping schedules, Pershing's plans for corps organization were shaped by the German offensive across the Chemin des Dames into the valley of the Marne. Behind a withering barrage, sixteen German divisions of General Max Von Boehn's Seventh Army shattered seven French and British divisions between Reims and Soissons. In the week between May 27 and June 4, the German Seventh Army pushed to the Marne, its forward units resting only fifty miles from Paris. From Paris the German advance—the opening stages of the Second Battle of the Marne—looked irresistible, and the French government made plans to flee south. While the tactical situation was serious, it was not as desperate as it seemed to the demoralized survivors of the French Sixth Army or to the Parisians, for French and British divisions were holding the corner of the salient at Reims and French reserves, mostly from the French Tenth Army, were gathering on the western corner of the salient. Moreover, Ludendorff had not planned great things for his third major offensive of 1918. The ease of the Seventh Army's advance, however, blurred Ludendorff's strategic vision, and he threw scarce reserves into his Marne salient, hoping for a dramatic victory at the gates of Paris. The Seventh Army, plagued by straggling and short supplies, was not, however, capable of an uninterrupted smash through the gathering Allied armies. Among its foes were new, large, and confident American divisions from the AEF.

Pressed by both Foch and Pétain, General Pershing gave the French the Second and Third Divisions for use against the German Seventh Army. Committed as an entire unit, the Second Division defended the sector west of Chateau-Thierry along the road to Paris and on June 1 handily stopped a German attack. Units of the Third Division defended the banks of the Marne in front and to the east of Chateau-Thierry. Temporarily halted, the German high command shifted its attacks westward to Champagne, striking June 8 between Montdidier and Soissons in an effort to enlarge the Marne salient. In June, however, Allied infantrymen became more numerous than the Germans on the Western Front for the first time in a year. And in the Marne salient, French and American units began limited counterattacks, the most impressive mounted by the Second Division against the tangle of Belleau Wood and the town of Vaux.

With the German third and fourth offensives halted by mid-June, Marshal Foch and General Pétain considered an Allied counterattack against the Marne salient, for they realized that the German Seventh Army's supply routes were especially vulnerable at the salient's western edge at Soissons. As soon as sufficient troops could be gathered, Foch wanted Pétain to strike the salient's western face with General Joseph Mangin's Tenth Army and its eastern corner with the French Fifth Army, while the French Sixth and Ninth armies held the Germans along the Marne. In this general redeployment, Pershing asked that his Second, Third, Forty-Second, and Twenty-Sixth Divisions be concentrated near Chateau-Thierry and given a corps sector. The French, however, intended to use both the First and Second Divisions as shock troops in the attack toward Soissons. They had no objection to forming an American corps in Mangin's army, and they also relinquished a sector west of Chateau-Thierry to Liggett's I Corps. Pershing, while not getting more than a small corps sector, was also promised that the First and Second Divisions would be placed under an American commander. On July 8 AEF Headquarters ordered Bjornstad to report to the First Division headquarters near Beauvais and informed Bullard that he had been assigned as the commanding general of the III Corps. His mission was to join the French Sixth Army, now also assigned an offensive role. Bullard was to prepare to direct the First and Second Divisions in the proposed attack against Soissons.[9]

1.

General Bullard left the First Division with some regret, but with little flurry or delay. Pershing selected Summerall, Bullard's personal choice, as his successor as division commander. The only unique feature of Bullard's departure was that he took not only his personal aides, but also some of the division general staff with him, particularly Lieutenant Colonel George K. Wilson, the skilled G-1. Bullard's act caused some resentment, although the general did it apologetically, for such transfers were new to the army.[10] The III Corps staff left the Vosges sector on July 12 and joined Bullard at the new corps PC at Meaux, where the III Corps headquarters was attached to the French Sixth Army. Bullard conferred with the army commander, General Jean Degoutte, a heavy, mustached, excitable burgher of Foch's school of the unrelenting offensive. Degoutte was expecting another German attack across the Marne, but told Bullard his army would repel it easily. Examining the Sixth Army's dispositions, Bullard was not so confident, being cheered only by the fact that half of Degoutte's 300,000 soldiers were fresh Americans.[11] Since both the First and Second Divisions were in reserve, Bullard was only a spectator at Degoutte's headquarters.

For an American general in the Sixth Army, it was a good time not to be in command. On July 15 Ludendorff launched his fifth and last offensive. The attacking force of forty-nine divisions struck between Chateau-Thierry and Reims and crossed the Marne in several places. Fortunately, in the nearby French Fifth Army, the defense was elastic and heavily gunned and halted the Germans without serious difficulty. The portion of Degoutte's army which absorbed the attack was not so well placed. French units along the Marne took the full force of the German barrages and crumbled, leaving American infantry from the Third and Twenty-Eighth Divisions to repulse the river-crossing. Only after a full day's serious fighting did the German assault troops end their attacks. It was the soldiers' victory, not the generals', and demonstrated Degoutte's tactical clumsiness and stubborn willingness to fight to the last American.[12]

Bullard's more immediate troubles were tied to Pershing's hurried effort to put his divisions under American corps commanders. The III Corps headquarters was inadequately staffed and equipped and had none of the corps artillery, communications, engineers, and aviation units AEF Headquarters deemed necessary. There was, additionally, the problem of General Omar Bundy, the Second Division's commander, who could not understand how a more junior major general could now be his corps commander. Bundy thought that his division was supposed to be in Liggett's I Corps, as did Liggett, and the staff wrangling did nothing but confuse Bullard and Liggett.[13] Pershing's staff issued the necessary orders to end the squabble and packed Bundy off to a corps command in a quiet sector. Major General James G. Harbord, who had handled the Marine brigade in Belleau Wood with the same aplomb he showed as Pershing's chief-of-staff, got the Second Division.

Despite the German attack of July 15, the French high command, hectored by Foch, continued its preparations for the counterattack against the Marne salient.[14] The planning of missions was hurried and confused, especially in the assignment of division boundaries and corps organization. Complicating the preparations was General Mangin's concern for tactical surprise in the Tenth Army sector. Instead of placing the assault divisions in the lines, he ordered them held in reserve and marched to the line of departure only in time to make the first attack. In addition, he abandoned the custom of long preparatory bombardments and planned a rolling barrage to precede the attacking infantry. While these decisions paid off handsomely, they also restricted preattack reconnaissances, artillery coordination, and supply arrangements by the attacking divisions. The III Corps, tossed about by changing French orders, experienced the general confusion. On July 16 Bullard and his handful of staff were transferred to the French Tenth Army. They established III Corps headquarters in a chateau at the edge of the vast Forêt de Retz, whose giant oaks screened the assembling divisions. With the attack scheduled for July 18, Bullard made a hard but wise decision. He recognized that III Corps was not ready to function and allowed the First and Second Divisions to be directed in the attack by the French XX Corps. Neither Summerall nor Harbord questioned his decision, since the confusion of orders and commanders was already frustrating. When Harbord went to III Corps headquarters for some enlightenment, he found Bullard and Bjornstad "with several stenographers, a mimeograph machine, and plenty of stationery," but little else. Bullard was eager to do what he could, loaning Harbord his mimeograph and arranging the only meaningful briefing Harbord got before the Soissons attack.[15]

In the early morning of July 18, Mangin's Tenth Army struck east toward the Soissons-Chateau-Thierry road with 10 divisions and nearly 350 tanks. For the first day the attack, especially in the sectors of the First and Second Divisions, was a stunning success, for the Germans were surprised by its timing and size. From various observation points behind the XX Corps sector, Bullard watched the offensive and was impressed by the weakness of the Germans' counterbarrage; he saw the horsemen of an entire French cavalry corps move eastward along open roads and fields. The German machine gunners, however, quickly responded and shot down the American infantry as it advanced in steady lines across the wheatfields. Bullard thought that Mangin should have thrown his cavalry against the Germans' sagging lines, but the one charge that was attempted was a massacre. Four days later, the XX Corps was astride the Soissons-Chateau-Thierry road, but the First and Second Divisions' infantry brigades were ruined by the attack. The advance of between 6 and 7 miles cost the American divisions over 12,000 casualties. Bullard saw his old regiment, the Twenty-Sixth Infantry, return from the front as a remnant of 200 men commanded by a captain, the highest ranking survivor. He regretted that his corps staff had not been ready to function, but he and Pershing, who visited him on July 20, were sure that the III Corps would have ample opportunity in the future. The Soissons counterattack, which began the German retreat from the Marne salient, was but the first of the Allied offensives. [16]

The success of the first day of the Soissons attack, measured in ground gained and prisoners and guns taken, exhilarated the French generals and forced Ludendorff to admit that the Marne salient was untenable. On July 20, learning of the first German withdrawals to the north bank of the Marne, Foch had Pétain expand the counteroffensive to the French armies holding the entire face of the salient. The counteroffensive committed more American divisions, most of them serving in Degoutte's Sixth Army, but involved only Liggett's I Corps head-quarters. Pershing's price for the expanded American participation in the Marne counteroffensive was a promise from Foch and Pétain that the bulk of the American divisions would be placed under his own corps commanders in adjacent sectors. Pershing himself would direct the American corps from his new First Army headquarters, managed by Colonel Hugh A. Drum, another Leavenworth staff expert. After July 18, Liggett's I Corps was continuously involved in the Marne counteroffensive, commanding both American and French divisions in its northerly attacks down the center of the salient. The natural place to establish another American corps was on Liggett's right; the two American corps would command at least six American divisions and whatever French divisions Pétain would assign. The second American corps headquarters to take tactical control in the Aisne-Marne operation was the III Corps. [17]

From a rest area behind the Soissons sector, Bullard's staff motored around the edges of the shrinking Marne salient and set up housekeeping with the French XXXVIII Corps at Mont St. Père. Arriving on July 31, Bullard was ordered to assume command of the three American divisions (Third, Twenty-Eighth, and Thirty-Second) on Degoutte's right flank on August 3. In the meantime, Pershing was sending him some American corps artillery and support units; the French, however, would provide the III Corps with the bulk of its corps troops. [18] While they waited to take active command, Bullard and Bjornstad visited Liggett's PC. The I Corps had committed the Forty-Second Division to a difficult assault against the German positions on the north banks of a stream named the Ourcq. Liggett, in fact, feared that he might be counterattacked, for the Germans had adequate reserves for such a maneuver. Degoutte, on the other hand, ordered renewed attacks. Bullard and Bjornstad were not welcome visitors in the crisis, especially since they proposed elaborate schemes of maneuver as soon as they took command in the adjacent sector. Liggett's aide noted that Bullard was in high spirits after the Soissons attack and "shot off a few views . . . on winning the war in general."[19]

As Bullard prepared to take over his own corps sector, the French XXXVIII Corps was using the Thirty-Second Division to push the Germans off the banks of the Ourcq. A determined division of Wisconsin and Michigan National Guardsmen, the Thirty-Second, commanded by Major General William G. Haan, had survived service as labor troops with their ardor intact. From July 29 to August 1 the Thirty-Second plunged against the fortified farms, deep woods, and defended ravines along the Ourcq. From woodlot to stonehouse to knoll, the Guardsmen shot and grenaded their way through the German positions, taking 4,000 casualties in the process and moving less than 2 miles.

On August 2 and 3 the German rearguards collapsed and both the I Corps and French XXXVIII Corps moved 7 miles to the heights south of the Vesle river. On August 3 a regiment of the Thirty-Second advanced into the valley of the Vesle to take the town of Fismes, but found that German infantry was still defending the southern bank of the river, supported by heavy machine gun fire and shelling from the bluffs north of the river. The Thirty-Second's casualties soared again as the American infantry fought its way into Fismes on August 4. The German infantry of the 200th and 216th divisions, relatively fresh troops, did not understand that the French General Staff had decided that the Germans were retreating back to their prepared defenses on the Aisne River. Accepting his optimistic intelligence estimates, Degoutte wanted the Vesle crossed and the general offensive continued. Along the Vesle, the Thirty-Second Division made an effort but could not even patrol the south bank without severe casualties. The regiment that secured Fismes left the battle with only 400 men.[20]

On the day the Thirty-Second Division took Fismes, Bullard took command of the French XXXVIII Corps sector along the Vesle. His self-confidence was diminished by conditions in his sector. All three of his divisions (Third, Twenty-Eighth, and Thirty-Second) were battle-worn and unhappy about their experiences in the French Sixth Army. The immediate tactical situation did not bolster their morale. The weather was hot and rainy, and the shattered villages and woods were alive with flies and rotting bodies. The terrain favored the German defenders, who commanded the Vesle valley from the ridges north of the river. The roads and American positions were observable from the north, and the Germans shelled the Americans in the valley and southern bluffs relentlessly. Americans moving to the front through sporadic machine gun fire and shelling passed a dismal rubbish of abandoned equipment, punctured food cans, splintered wagons, bloated animals, and mangled corpses. The nightly processions crawled on, bathed in the garish brilliance of flares and thermite shells. Conditions along the river were no better, for camouflaged German snipers and machine gunners made movement perilous. The Vesle itself, though only twenty or thirty yards wide, was unfordable. The bridges were destroyed, and German barbed wire twisted along both banks and in the stream bed. To the American officers, it was apparent that a successful crossing would require a coordinated, multidivision assault by both the I and III Corps, complete with massed artillery and substantial engineer support.

Nevertheless, Degoutte ordered the III Corps to "continue the pursuit" across the Vesle.[21] Bullard had the Thirty-Second Division try crossings for three days (August 4-6), but Haan's weary infantry could not seize and hold a bridgehead. The Thirty-Second Division's daily assaults had to fight to secure even the south bank. In the I Corps zone to the left, a battalion of the Fourth Division crossed the river and held on, but Liggett could not enlarge the position without prohibitive losses. On Bullard's right, the French Fourth Division made a gesture at attacking and fell back to its dugouts. Sixth Army headquarters regarded the failures as a lack of American will, and Degoutte complained that Bullard could not get the III Corps to move.

In this crisis, Bullard and Bjornstad had their first serious rift. Bullard allowed his chief-of-staff the same sort of freedom the First Division staff had had. Bjornstad interpreted Bullard's delegation of authority liberally, judging delicate matters of command as "details" within his purview. Bjornstad approached I Corps in an effort to stop the attacks and asked his friends in Pershing's headquarters to relieve General Haan. In the meantime, Bullard ordered Degoutte's attacks, but did not blame Haan for their failure because he recognized that the III Corps was not providing adequate artillery and engineer assistance. Bullard's irritation increased when he learned Bjornstad had seen Liggett about a joint attack and was complaining about Bullard and Haan to AEF Headquarters. He also began to appreciate his staff's insensitivity to the fighting troops' ordeal. When he met with his aviation advisors, he learned that the III Corps staff was not accepting the pilots' advice. The flyers were delighted when Bullard told them that he would accept and back their operational plans. He made a second hit when he refused to move a marking panel from a field near the corps headquarters. One of his colonels suggested that the Germans were ranging artillery in on the observation aircraft making message drops near the corps PC. Bullard turned to the officer: "Well, Colonel, if these young men will go out and get this information, I think that we can stay here and receive it." Yet for all his outward poise, Bullard was unhappy with the tactical situation, and his neuritis flamed with the tension. He had no regrets when Deboutte halted the attacks on August 7. Bullard used the pause to replace the Thirty-Second Division with the Twenty-Eighth.[22]

2.

At the time General Degoutte gave up the dream of a grand pursuit across the Vesle, the interest of the Allied high commanders was shifting to other sectors. On August 8, the BEF struck the Germans in front of Amiens and drove them back fifteen miles. This "black day" for the German army, as the shaken Ludendorff called it, started the German retreat to the Rhine. Field Marshal Haig, understandably, called for a greater Allied effort in the north, including American divisions. For Foch and Pétain, the place to concentrate the best French armies and Pershing's divisions was north and east of the Vesle where Mangin's Tenth Army was battering the Germans back across the Aisne. Foch's primary interest, other than his obsession with continuous offensives, was to deploy the French and American divisions where they could advance in concert with the British. General Pershing, however, clung stubbornly to his "independent" offensive to reduce the St. Mihiel salient, well to the southeast of the sectors which interested the Allied staffs. With the AEF still growing and gathering the full divisions and corps troops (plus aviation) for a complete field army, Pershing's plans could not be ignored. On August 10 the American First Army started serious preparations for the St. Mihiel assault, although Pershing reluctantly agreed to set limited objectives and restrict the offensive so that the First Army could join a grand Allied attack west of the Meuse river in late September. The result of the inter-Allied strategic bargaining was that Bullard's corps stayed on the Vesle as part of Degoutte's Sixth Army, while Liggett's I Corps departed with its divisions for the St. Mihiel salient and the American First Army sector. For more than a month Bullard and his two American divisions were orphaned by Pershing's strategy.

Degoutte did not surrender his plans to create bridgeheads on the north bank of the Vesle, although his army was supposed to be defending its gains of early August. The only such salient was the small enclave held by one Fourth Division battalion two miles west of Fismes. In the III Corps sector, a brigade from the Third Division held two footbridges across the river but hardly dared patrol across them. The French Fourth Division held nothing at all. The major effort was assigned the Twenty-Eighth Division, a solid force of veteran Pennsylvania National Guardsmen commanded by Bullard's rival, Major General Charles H. Muir. For once in their careers, Bullard and the balding, abrasive Muir did not clash; neither thought much of Degoutte's orders. For four days (August 7-10), the Pennsylvanians got their first taste of "Death Valley," as the Americans called the valley of the Vesle. One battalion got across the river and made contact with the Fourth Division's tiny "bridgehead." Another crossed the Vesle on the rubble of a stone bridge from Fismes into the neighboring hamlet of Fismette, but was shelled so badly that all but one company was withdrawn. Having infiltrated into Fismette at night, the Pennsylvanians needed two days to clear the village of German snipers and machine gunners, and their success was only temporary. The German defenders, stiffened by crack troops from the 4th Guard Division and a fresh machine gun battalion, filtered back into Fismette at night and counterattacked the Americans. Clouds of poison gas hung over the valley, mingling with the stench of charred buildings and mouldering flesh. During the day the Americans could do little more than hide in cellars, listen to their own artillery shell the far slopes, and endure the return German barrages. No one knew how many casualties the Twenty-Eighth Division had. At least 2,000 wounded passed through the evacuation hospitals, but the dead and missing were uncounted.[23]

General Pétain wanted the Sixth Army to advance to the Aisne, and Degoutte ordered it done. Thinking the German defeat of August 8 might have started a general withdrawal, Bullard ordered more attacks, although he had little confidence in Degoutte's judgment. The German counterattacks on Fismette convinced him that the Germans were not retreating, and on August 10 he ordered the Twenty-Eighth Division to stop trying to advance beyond Fismette. To satisfy Degoutte, he added that the existing enclaves would be defended to avoid "undue exposure" to enemy fire. To maintain the contact with Germans which the Sixth Army wanted, Bullard told Muir to send out patrols, but to give them close artillery support and limit their size to a company or less. Bullard defined close contact with the Germans to mean that if the Germans fired on the patrols, this indicated determined resistance. This interpretation of the Sixth Army orders departed from the spirit of the French instructions, which bristled with rear-echelon bellicosity.[24] Muir's patrols had no trouble drawing fire. On August 11 the Twenty-Eighth Division finally got an accurate count of its casualties, a stunning 6,000 men since it had entered combat on July 15.[25]

Throughout the bloody stalemate on the Vesle, Bullard had continued difficulty controlling his corps. While he got increased American and French artillery units to support his infantry, he had to cope with the growing traffic congestion the guns caused. Communications and supply management in the III Corps were not particularly impressive. Bullard's biggest frustration, however, remained his ill-organized corps headquarters and Bjornstad's inclination to run his own war. On August 13 the III Corps took over part of the departing I Corps' sector and received the Seventy-Seventh Division as reinforcement. The commander of the Seventy-Seventh, a division of aggressive but raw draftees from New York City, was Major General George B. Duncan, late of the First Division. Duncan was pleased to work again with Bullard, whom he considered a pragmatic and aggressive field commander. Duncan was appalled to learn that Bjornstad and his operations section often issued orders about which Bullard knew nothing. He thought that Bullard showed good judgment by telling him to ignore "damn fool" orders from III Corps until he had personally checked with Bullard. That Bullard had to give Duncan such instructions testified, however, to the tension between the corps commander and his chief-of-staff.[26]

After both his divisions had their patrols shot to pieces, Bullard called the patrolling to a halt on August 16. Degoutte, however, would not let him give up either bridgehead at Chateau du Diable or Fismette even though each division lost 200 men every day occupying the Vesle valley. On August 22 the Seventy-Seventh Division had to launch a major attack to recapture Chateau du Diable after its garrison there was forced out by a German assault. The situation in Fismette was even more desperate. The garrison, two companies of the One-Hundred Twelfth Infantry, could be supplied only at night across an improvised plank bridge, and the ruined village was pounded daily with artillery and machine gun fire. One German attack had already almost captured Fismette. The enclave was so vulnerable that General Muir and the regimental commander asked Bullard to withdraw their beleaguered men. Bullard agreed with their assessment and told them to pull the two companies out that night.

Upon returning from Fismes to his corps headquarters, Bullard found that Degoutte had visited his staff in his absence. Bjornstad had volunteered the information that the Fismette garrison was to be evacuated that night. Degoutte immediately countermanded Bullard's order and later phoned Bullard to censure him. The orders to Muir remained the same: hold Fismette. Early in the morning of August 27 the Germans struck the town with a crack assault battalion armed with demolitions and flamethrowers. In vicious house-to-house fighting, the Germans killed or captured all but thirty-nine of the garrison of two hundred. Degoutte acknowledged the tragedy by citing the Twenty-Eighth Division for breaking up a German counteroffensive, an imaginative interpretation of the raid on Fismette.[27]

Stung by what he considered the only disaster of his military career, Bullard wrote Pershing about the Fismette affair and complained bitterly to "The Chief" about the Pennsylvanians' needless sacrifices and about Degoutte and Bjornstad's complicty in their deaths. Equally upset, Pershing demanded to know why Bullard had obeyed Degoutte. Bullard had no answer since he knew Pershing needed no sermon on the necessity of obeying orders, even from French generals. Bullard, however, lacked the courage to do anything about Bjornstad, probably fearing his chief-of-staff's Leavenworth friends at AEF Headquarters.

3.

For the four German divisions of von Boehn's Seventh Army facing the III Corps along the Vesle, the defense of the "Blücher Position" throughout August had been trying, but successful.[28] The one German fear—that the Americans would bridge the Vesle and assault them with tanks—had not materialized. Generally, the German defenders had a much better understanding of the tactical situation, for their airplanes had the advantage in observation flights and they monitored American radios freely. Watching the highways on the Vesle's southern bluffs, they could see heavy artillery being emplaced and the roads jammed with wagons, trucks, and moving troops. In the patrol combats along the Vesle, the Germans seriously punished the aggressive but clumsy American infantry, but the German static defenses were severely shelled by the III Corps heavy artillery brigade, attached French batteries, and the divisions' artillery. Yet the German Seventh Army was confident that it could hold its positions, though von Boehn saw that the massed American corps to his front were preparing to force the river.

The fate of the German stand at the "Blücher Position" lay to the northwest where Mangin's French Tenth Army faced the German Ninth Army on the Aisne north of Soissons. In the last week of August, Mangin's army seized the Ninth Army's strongpoints. The Tenth Army's assault persuaded Ludendorff that the time had come to fall back to another series of prepared defenses. For von Boehn's Seventh Army the withdrawal meant that it was to abandon the Vesle and occupy new fortifications along the Aisne, some seven miles to the north. The Seventh Army had anticipated such a movement for about two weeks, and it had already begun to thin its defenses, destroy or move its supplies, burn the French villages in the sector, and evacuate the civilians. Skillfully covering its withdrawal with strafing airplanes, artillery, and infantry combat groups, the Seventh Army retreated from the ''Blücher Position'' between August 31 and September 5.

Degoutte was eager to press the Germans, and he ordered the III Corps to press the German Seventh Army outposts along the Vesle several days before its withdrawal actually began. The result was several severe German counterattacks and increased losses for both the Seventy-Seventh and Twenty-Eighth Divisions. Degoutte anticipated that the III Corps would lead the Sixth Army advance to the Aisne and he reinforced Bullard with artillery and French bridging engineers.[29] On the morning of September 4 American patrols and aerial observers found that the Germans had left their positions on the north bank of the Vesle. That afternoon Degoutte ordered the Sixth Army to make a general advance.

With only four hours' warning of the Sixth Army's attack, Bullard was rightfully unhappy about the lack of time he and his division commanders had to make liaison with their neighboring French divisions, but the advance, led by American combat patrols, went off as scheduled in midafternoon. The III Corps' movement was not well controlled and did little damage to the German rear guards. For the Seventy-Seventh Division, the advance with regiments abreast turned into a confused muddle. The Seventy-Seventh, commanded by Major General Robert Alexander, who had replaced the ailing Duncan, developed serious control problems when its eager infantry wandered into other sectors and mixed its own units. Bullard could not fault the division's aggressiveness, but its inability to locate itself on a map made supporting it with corps artillery and airplanes nearly impossible. On the night of September 5, however, the New Yorkers were on the hills overlooking the Aisne well in advance of the French on their left and the Pennsylvanians on their right. Alexander blamed his division's casualties and confusion on the III Corps' efforts to control the advance, Bullard's pandering to the reluctant French, and the failure of other divisions to take objectives on his flanks.[30] A better scapegoat was the German Seventh Army, whose stiffened resistance on September 6 and 7 cost the Seventy-Seventh about 900 casualties each day, many from mines and snipers. For the battle-weary Twenty-Eighth Division, the advance was slower and the resistance heavier, and it did not keep pace with the New Yorkers. After the division's experiences on the Vesle, Bullard did not expect much from it and he understood Muir's reluctance to expose his men to flanking fire. Nevertheless, the Twenty-Eighth took nearly as many casualties as the Seventy-Seventh, but fewer needless ones, indicating that the Germans were retreating more slowly on the III Corps' right flank.[31]

While he was not displeased with a six-mile advance on a six-mile front with two worn divisions, Bullard was under no illusion that the Germans were broken or that his corps had suddenly become tactically proficient. As he drove along the road between the Vesle and the Aisne, he worried about the number of straggling Americans and the havoc caused by bypassed German machine gunners. He admired in a grudging way the destruction the Germans had left the III Corps and the skill with which they shot American infantry. He was not surprised when the

German Seventh Army turned at the Aisne and stopped the Sixth Army's advance, since Degoutte had allowed little time to arrange for reserves or for the artillery to displace into range of the German defenses. On September 8 he received instructions to turn his sector over to a French corps commander and to move his corps headquarters to the town of Souilly, eastward on the Meuse. He was happy to leave the Marne counteroffensive and was not displeased to learn that Degoutte and his Sixth Army headquarters were being eliminated in a general consolidation of the French army command system. About all he could say for his Army commander was that he had been consistently aggressive. The III Corps was under orders to become part of the American First Army, a transfer Bullard gladly accepted.[32]

NOTES

[1]Historical Division, Army War College, *The Genesis of the American First Army* (Washington: Government Printing Office, 1938), pp. 20-37; John J. Pershing, *My Experiences in the World War*, 2 vols. (New York: Frederick A. Stokes, 1931), II, 1-70; Leonard P. Ayres, *The War with Germany: A Statistical Summary* (Washington: Government Printing Office, 1919), pp. 37-48, 101-105.

[2]Army War College, *The Genesis of the American First Army*, pp. 40-42.

[3]Gen. J. J. Pershing to Adj. Gen., USA, September 9, 1917, in *USA/WW, 1917-1919*, II, p. 39; Brig. Gen. H. B. Fiske to C/S, AEF, memorandum, "General Officers," July 27, 1918, Harold B. Fiske Papers.

[4]The major source of data on Bjornstad's personality and military career is U.S. Senate, Committee on Military Affairs, "Hearings on the Nomination of Col. Alfred W. Bjornstad, U.S. Army for Promotion to be a Brigadier General," January 9, 12, 13, and 14, 1925, 68th Congress, 2d Session (Washington, 1925) (hereafter cited as "Bjornstad Hearings").

Other assignments of his pre-1917 career are included in Capt. C. Cordier to Maj. Gen. L. Wood, October 31, 1916, and Maj. Gen. L. Wood to Capt. C. Cordier, November 1, 1916, Leonard Wood Papers; and Adj. Gen. USA to the Chief of Staff, August 3, 1917, File 7928, AWC Document File, Records of the War Department General Staff, RG 165; Mr. E. O. Nigel Cholmeley-Jones, Westport, Connecticut, to the author, January 11 and 31, 1972. (Mr. Cholmeley-Jones served as a lieutenant in the III Corps operations section and as General Bjornstad's aide.)

[5]Brig. Gen. J. G. Harbord to Col. J. McA. Palmer, January 19, 1918, "Chronological File, 1917-1919," John McAuley Palmer Papers.

[6]On Bjornstad's Leavenworth and General Staff experience, see Palmer, "Chapter Notes" V, pp. 13-14, and for his service at AEF Headquarters, see "Chapter Notes" IX, p. 142, and Col. J. McA. Palmer to Mrs. Palmer, February 5, 1918, in "Chronological File, 1917-1919," Palmer Papers.

[7]Diarybook 9, entry, October 31, 1918, BP; Campbell King, "Tour in France," pp. 6-7, Campbell King Papers; testimony of Maj. Gen. John L. Hines, Maj. Gen. Robert L. Bullard, Maj. Gen. George B. Duncan, Lt. Col. Francis W. Clark (III Corps G-3), and E. O. Nigel Cholmeley-Jones, in "Bjornstad Hearings," pp. 11-22, 81-97, 107-117, 180-194, 223-225.

[8]Army War College, *Order of Battle of the United States Land Forces in the World War:*

AEF: GHQ, Armies, Corps and SOS (Washington: Government Printing Office, 1931), pp. 237-267; Headquarters, Third Army Corps, "History of the Third Army Corps in Three Volumes, Volume I from April 1, 1918 to September 9, 1918," Miscellaneous Correspondence, John L. Hines Papers; messages and memoranda, *USA/WW, 1917-1919,* III, pp. 408-422; III Army Corps "War Diary" in AEF, Organization Records: War Diaries, Records of the American Expeditionary Force, RG 120.

⁹Maj. Gen. J. W. McAndrew to Maj. Gen. R. L. Bullard, July 8, 1918, in *USA/WW, 1917-1919,* III, pp. 415-416.

For the early French planning for the Marne counteroffensive, see General Foch to the Commander-in-Chief of the Armies of the North and Northwest, June 14, 1918; 3rd Section, General Staff, French Armies of the North and Northwest, to General Fayolle, June 27, 1918; 3rd Section, Armies of the North and Northeast, memorandum on the organization of an American sector, June 29, 1918; 3rd Section, General Staff, French Armies of the North and Northwest, to the Commanding Generals, Groups of Armies of Reserve and Armies of the Center, July 12, 1918, printed in *USA/WW, 1917-1918,* V, pp. 223-238.

¹⁰Beaumont B. Buck, *Memories of Peace and War,* (San Antonio: Naylor Company, 1935), pp. 213-214.

¹¹Entry, July 13, 1918, in Charles G. Dawes, *A Journal of the Great War,* 2 vols. (Boston: Houghton Mifflin, 1921), I, pp. 135-136; Robert L. Bullard, *Personalities and Reminiscences of the War* (New York: Doubleday, Page, 1925), pp. 212-213.

¹²United States Army General Service Schools, *The German Offensive of July 15, 1918* (Fort Leavenworth, Ka.: General Service Press, 1923); Edward M. Coffman, *The War to End All Wars* (New York: Oxford University Press, 1968), pp. 222-227.

¹³P. L. Stackpole diary, entries, July 13 and 14, 1918, Marshall Library.

¹⁴Telcon, General Foch to General Pétain, July 15, 1918; General Pétain to Headquarters, Group of Armies of the Reserve, July 15, 1918; General Foch to the General, Commander-in-Chief of the Armies of the North and Northwest, July 16, 1918; French Tenth Army Order No. 232, July 14, 1918; French XX Corps Orders Nos. 227-231, July 16, 1918, all reprinted in *USA/WW, 1917-1919,* V, pp. 242, 244, 276, 290-294.

¹⁵James G. Harbord, *The American Army in France* (Boston: Little, Brown, 1936), pp. 317-318.

¹⁶Bullard, *Personalities and Reminiscences,* pp. 218-224; Pershing, *My Experiences in the World War* II, pp. 156-168.

¹⁷3rd Section, General Staff, memorandum for the Commander of the Group of Armies of the Reserve, July 25, 1918; General F. Foch, memorandum of meeting with Generals Pétain and Pershing, July 24, 1918, reprinted in *USA/WW, 1917-1919,* V, pp. 261, 258-259.

¹⁸C/S, First Army, to the Commanding General, III Corps, July 29, 1918, and the G-3, GHQ, AEF, to the Commanding General, I Corps, July 29, 1918, reprinted in *USA/WW, 1917-1919,* V, pp. 267-268.

¹⁹P. L. Stackpole diary, entries, August 1 and 2, 1918, Marshall Library. For the I Corps situation, see the I Corps situation reports and field orders, July 29-August 3, 1918, in *USA/WW, 1917-1919,* V, pp. 458-471.

²⁰Maj. Gen. W. G. Haan, "Report on Operations of the Thirty-Second Division, July 29-August 7, 1918," August 24, 1918, copy in the Enoch H. Crowder Papers; Maj. Gen. W. G. Haan to Mrs. W. G. Haan, April 8-August 10, 1918, William G. Haan Papers; Maj. Gen. W. G. Haan to Maj. Gen. E. H. Crowder, August 8, 1918, Haan Papers; Captain Carl

Hanson for the Wisconsin War History Commission, *The 32nd Division in the World War, 1917-1919* (Madison, Wisc.: State Historical Society of Wisconsin, 1920), pp. 57-67.

[21]3rd Section, General Staff, French Group of Armies of the Reserve, "Instruction to the Sixth and Tenth Armies," August 2, 1918; C/S, First Army, to Maj. Gen. R. L. Bullard, August 2, 1918; 3rd Section, General Staff, French Armies of the North and Northeast, "Instructions to the Generals Commanding the Group of Armies of the Reserve and the Group of Armies of the Center," August 4, 1918; 3rd Section, General Staff, Sixth French Army, General Orders 3675, August 2, 1918; all of the above in *USA/WW, 1917-1919,* V, pp. 270-273, 389-393.

[22]For characteristics of the Fismes sector, see American Battle Monuments Commission, *American Armies and Battlefields in Europe* (Washington: Government Printing Office, 1938), pp. 77-82, and Haan, "Report of Operations of the Thirty-Second Division, July 29-August 7, 1918," previously cited.

For the French perspective on the Vesle attacks, I have relied on the following sources: 3rd Section, General Staff, Sixth French Army, General Orders 3700, warning orders and operations reports, August 5-7, 1918, in *USA/WW, 1917-1919,* V, pp. 394-398; Maj. P. H. Clark to Gen. J. J. Pershing, August 1-19, 1918, Pershing Papers/NA.

For the operations of the III Corps and the Thirty-Second Division, see III Corps field orders and operations reports, August 3-7, 1918, reprinted in *USA/WW, 1917-1919,* V, pp. 587-597; III Corps "War Diary, August 4-September 9, 1918," AEF Organization Records: War Diaries, RG 120; Haan, "Report on Operations of the Thirty-Second Division, July 29-August 7, 1918"; Thirty-Second Division operations reports, August 2-7, 1918 in *USA/WW, 1917-1919,* V, pp. 650-659.

Bullard's personal experiences are described in P. L. Stackpole diary, entries, August 5 and 7, 1918, Marshall Library, and Col. H. A. Drum to Col. F. Conner, August 7, 1918, File 120, G-3, HQ, First Army, AEF Organization Records, RG 120; Bullard, *Personalities and Reminiscences,* pp. 229-232; Mr. Harold F. Marshall, Palymra, N. J., to the author, April 10, 1972; Robert Alexander, *Some Memories of the World War* (New York: Macmillan, 1931), pp. 65-82; and the testimony of Major General Bullard and Colonel Bjornstad, "Bjornstad Hearings," pp. 81-97, 260-266.

[23]Entries, August 6-10, III Corps "War Diary, August 4-September 9, 1918," AEF Organization Records: War Diaries, RG 120; 3rd Section, General Staff, French Armies of the North and Northwest, "Instructions for the Generals Commanding the French Group of Armies of the Reserve and the French Group of Armies of the Center," August 8, 1918, *USA/WW, 1917-1919,* VI, pp. 5-6.

[24]For the French Sixth Army's orders, instructions, and operations reports, August 6-September 8, 1918, see *USA/WW, 1917-1919,* VI, pp. 59-76; memo, CG, III Corps, to CG, 28th Div.,August 10, 1918, *USA/WW, 1917-1919,* VI, pp. 118-19.

[25]Entry, August 11, 1918, III Corps "War Diary, August 4-September 9, 1918," AEF Organization Records: War Diaries, RG 120; *Le Chef d'Escadrons de Bertier de Sauvigny, Officier de Liaison près le 3e. C.A.U.S., "Compte-Rendu des Operations du 30 Juillet au 10 Aout 1918,"* August 14, 1918, File 17 N 102-4, FMMA.

The Twenty-Eighth Division's ordeal on the Vesle is vividly described in the division history: Edward Martin and E. S. Wallace, *The Twenty-Eighth Division in the World War,* 3 vols. (Philadelphia: 28th Division Publishing Company, 1923), I, pp. 81-100. Another invaluable personal description is Capt. Otto W. Freeborn, "Operations of Company A, 111th Infantry (28th Division), and on the Vesle River in the Aisne-Marne Offensive, August 4-September 7, 1918," 1932, IS monograph, ISL.

[26]George B. Duncan, "Reminiscences of the World War," p. 113; J. O. Adler, ed., *History of the Seventy-Seventh Division* (New York: Winthrop, Hollenbeck & Crawford, 1919), pp. 39-58; Bertier de Sauvigny, *"Note Confidentielle,"* August 12, 1918, File 17 N 102-4, FMMA.

[27]Entry, August 27, 1918, III Corps "War Diary, August 4-September 9, 1918," AEF Organization Records: War Diaries, RG 120; Martin and Wallace, *The Twenty-Eighth Division in the World War* III, pp. 103-126; James A. Murrin, *With the 112th in France* (Philadelphia: Lippincott, 1919), pp. 158-217; Bullard, *Personalities and Reminiscences,* pp. 234-238, including his letter, Maj. Gen. R. L. Bullard to Maj. Gen. J. A. McAndrew, C/S, AEF, *USA/WW, 1917-1919,* VI, pp. 96-97; and the testimony of Colonel Bjornstad, "Bjornstad Hearings," pp. 262-263.

[28]The German situation may be reconstructed from the orders and operations reports of the Ninth Army, Seventh Army and 4th Guard Division, August 7-September 7, 1918, printed in *USA/WW, 1917-1919,* VI, pp. 204-262.

[29]G-3, General Staff, French Sixth Army, Instruction 3827, August 29, 1918, *USA/WW, 1917-1919,* VI, pp. 68-70.

[30]Alexander, *Memories of the World War,* pp. 115-131; CG, 77th Div., to Adj. Gen., AEF, operation report of Oise-Aisne operations, November 11, 1918, in *USA/WW, 1917-1919,* VI, pp. 200-202.

[31]28th Division operations reports, September 5-7, 1918, *USA/WW, 1917-1919,* VI, pp. 131-134.

[32]Bullard, *Personalities and Reminiscences,* pp. 249-257; entries, August 29-September 9, 1918, III Corps "War Diary, August 4-September 9, 1918," AEF Organization Records: War Diaries, RG 120.

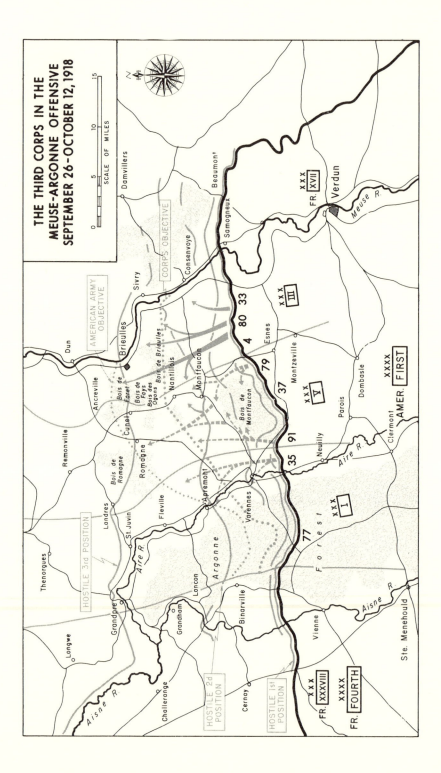

THE THIRD CORPS IN THE MEUSE-ARGONNE OFFENSIVE SEPTEMBER 26-OCTOBER 12, 1918

SCALE OF MILES

0   5   10   15

20

The III Corps:
The Meuse-Argonne
Offensive
1918

The BEF's successful offensives in the north and the happy conclusion of the Second Battle of the Marne sent a wave of optimism through the Allied high command. A victory in 1918, an impossible dream six months earlier, appeared a real possibility to Field Marshal Haig and Marshal Foch. While the fighting continued through August, Foch and Haig pressured Generals Pétain and Pershing to commit their armies to a grand Allied offensive along the entire northern half of the Western Front. Haig's strategic justification for this offensive was that the German lines from the Metz-Thionville region to the English Channel formed a large and vulnerable salient. Strong, converging Allied attacks eastward against the Germans in the BEF's sector and northward from Verdun in the zone of the Franco-American armies would force the Germans backward to the Rhine. An attractive objective would be to sever the Germans' major lateral supply line, the railroad which ran from Antwerp to Metz. This was the same railroad which Pershing's staff planned to cut at Metz; Haig wanted it broken farther to the northwest in the Mézières-Sedan region or south of Brussels. The Allied lines were closest to the railroad at these two points, and both attacks would present the Germans with difficult decisions on the use of their shrinking reserves.[1]

While the Allied Supreme Commander appreciated the British plan's geographic rationale, Foch was moved more by the prospect of handing the Germans a bloody defeat than of simply forcing them to withdraw to the Rhine. He envisioned the Allied armies smashing through the Germans' prepared defenses from Lille to Metz and then destroying their broken divisions in a vigorous pursuit. He was convinced that the Allies had the men, tanks, planes, and artillery to fashion such a decisive battle in the Napoleonic tradition. The BEF, revived by its own reinforcements and American divisions, would mount the eastward offensive, and the AEF would handle the drive north toward Mézières-Sedan. Between these attacks Pétain would deploy the bulk of the French army, which would place unrelenting pressure along the entire front between the British and the Americans.

For the Allied Supreme Commander, the major problem was getting Pershing's cooperation for an offensive which did not conform to the American's conception of winning the war. Despite fundamental changes in the situation on the Western Front, Pershing clung to his plan for a 1919 offensive against the Metz-Thionville region, preceded by the reduction of the St. Mihiel salient, the portal to the Woevre Plain. The Allied high commanders recognized that this offensive would probably produce considerable dislocation for the Germans, but they had little confidence that the Americans had the tactical skill or logistical capability to breach the German defenses (the "Michel Position") protecting Metz. Almost certainly the AEF (in the Allied view) would not have such capability before the spring of 1919, which was too long to wait for a decision on the Western Front.

Foch's view was that the AEF should be used in a sector between the Meuse River and the Argonne forest, formidable terrain made more lethal by German fortifications named the *Kriemhilde Stellung.* From Foch's point of view, the problem was that the increasing size and combat potential of the AEF gave Pershing increased freedom to follow his own strategic designs—as long as his government supported him. Foch wisely recognized, however, that Pershing was as interested in commanding an independent American army as he was in directing it against any particular objective. In a series of tense conferences in late August and early September, Foch and Pershing hammered out a complicated compromise on the use of the AEF in 1918. Foch allowed Pershing to go ahead with his offensive to reduce the St. Mihiel salient. Foch also agreed with Pershing that nearly all the American divisions should now fight under American command and that Pershing's First Army would have a sector of its own. Pershing's part of the bargain was that the St. Mihiel operation would reduce only the salient and free the Verdun-Nancy railroad. The American attack would be limited in time and size so that the American First Army could redeploy in the Meuse-Argonne region and be ready for its role in the great offensive, which Foch postponed until late September.[2]

In assigning the Meuse-Argonne sector to the American First Army, Foch had done Pershing no favors. Topographically, the American First Army's sector favored General Max von Gallwitz' Fifth Army even without considering the Germans' man-made fortifications. The sector was a combination of three parallel heights and two corridors, linked by lateral ridges. To the east of the Meuse River were high bluffs, garrisoned by the Germans. Observation posts and artillery positions east of the Meuse allowed the Germans to fire accurately into the Meuse valley and the ridges to the west; such shelling, fired laterally along the line of the American advance, could hardly fail to hit someone. West of the river, there was another long ridge running north and south. The southernmost tip of this ridge ended at the heights of Montfaucon, a German strongpoint built in the rubble of the

French town of Montfaucon. German artillery and machine guns at Montfaucon could also cover both the eastern and western corridors by fire. The third heights were those of the Aire River and the Argonne Forest, a wild tract of heavy trees, thick brush, and deep ravines, natural obstacles designed to punish attacking infantry and limit the effectiveness of artillery fire. Nature also provided the Germans with topographical advantages that prevented an easy advance up the two parallel corridors. On the western edge of the sector, the Aire River turned eastward between the Argonne and the Bois de Bourgogne, creating a natural barrier dominated by the German strongpoint at the town of Grandpré. A similar bend in the Meuse created a line of east-west ridges named for the towns of Romagne and Cunel. On the east-west line defined by Grandpré-Romagne-Cunel-Meuse River, the Germans had created a main defensive position ten miles behind the existing front and, therefore, out of range of the bulk of the Allied artillery.

The Germans, of course, fully exploited the region's topography. Recognizing the strategic possibilities of an attack toward Sedan, they had organized a standard six-echelon defensive position. The forward positions were lightly garrisoned with infantry outposts, machine guns, and light artillery, all well dug in. The second zone was more heavily manned and contained counterattack forces. The third line was the main defensive position, while the fourth, fifth, and sixth positions allowed staged withdrawals if necessary. All the positions were strung with barbed wire and were defended by entrenched infantry and machine gunners. The machine guns, mortars, and artillery of all varieties were assigned interlocking fields of fire. There was little to recommend the Meuse-Argonne sector for a major offensive.[3]

Following his meetings with Foch, Pershing had his First Army staff assess the AEF's resources for the Meuse-Argonne offensive. With much of his army committed to the St. Mihiel attack, which was eventually made on September 12, Pershing had only nine divisions and the III Corps headquarters available to deploy west of the Meuse. The nine divisions were not an impressive force. Three were worn from the Marne counteroffensive; five others were not battle-tested and lacked artillery. The only sound and veteran division was the Thirty-Third, Illinois National Guardsmen just returned from their successful initiation to combat with the BEF. Five divisions which were being held in reserve or training areas would be available only after the St. Mihiel offensive stabilized. Knowing that he had to take over his sector west of the Meuse, Pershing ordered Bullard's headquarters to join the French Second Army and assume command of the eastern part of the new sector's front line with the Thirty-Third Division. Other divisions and corps headquarters (the I and V) would join the III Corps in the two weeks preceding the Meuse-Argonne offensive.[4]

1.

As the highest American headquarters attached to the French Second Army, Bullard's III Corps was at the receiving end of train after train and convoy after convoy of American troops and supplies being concentrated for the great offensive. The AEF was alive with optimistic anticipation which was fed by the two-day victory in the St. Mihiel salient. That Pershing's attack had caught the Germans already withdrawing to the "Michel Position" did not dampen the elation of victory. The First Army staff tended to overlook the flaws in the operation: the confusion of orders and troop movements, the clogged roads, and the errors in infantry-artillery-air coordination. Certainly the press of the next campaign cut short the postmortems, and Pershing's assistants had to concentrate on moving their divisions and artillery trains to the new sector. At his headquarters at Rampont, Bullard faithfully coordinated the troops' arrival without fully understanding their purpose. The major movements were made only at night and without lights; telephone and radio traffic were restricted to increase the chance of tactical surprise. American units marched in from the south and west, and in a two-week period, nine different divisions joined and left the III Corps alone. The corps' task was to see that they and their supplies got to the assembly areas assigned by the First Army.[5]

While the troops marched to their front line positions or assembly areas, Pershing's First Army headquarters grappled with the task of creating a scheme of maneuver which offered some chance of rapid success. Estimating that the Germans would hold their first two defensive positions lightly (five understrength German divisions were so deployed), the First Army staff planned a nine-division attack which would breach the *Kriemhilde Stellung* west of the Meuse in the first day's attack. This meant a breathtaking advance of ten miles which would have to be supported over three weak roads. Much of the planners' optimism was born of desperation. If the First Army did not make such an advance the first day, the Germans could hurry perhaps as many as fifteen divisions into the sector in three days. Even though German divisions were a third the size of the AEF's and were badly disorganized and demoralized by their defeated attacks, they had already proven their skill as defenders to the AEF's satisfaction. The prospect of losing the race to the *Kriemhilde Stellung* was not very appealing. During the planning phase, however, General Hugh Drum and his staff apparently convinced themselves that their army not only would make the race but actually win it and avoid a bloody campaign against the German main position. Certainly Pershing believed it could be done, and his optimism spurred his staff to even grander predictions of success.

The First Army's American divisions would make the main effort west of the Meuse, supported by the three divisions of the French XVII Corps facing the heights east of the river. At the Americans' flank on the Meuse, the III Corps was to attack with three divisions (Thirty-Third, Eightieth, and Fourth) to clear the flank of the V Corps which was to make the crucial penetration along the axis Montfaucon-Romagne. Major General George H. Cameron's V Corps had three divisions for its attack, all fresh but not very experienced. On the American left flank, Hunter Liggett's I Corps received the unpleasant task of clearing the Argonne Forest and the Aire river valley as far as Grandpré, thus guarding the flank of the V Corps' penetration. Liggett had the worn Seventy-Seventh and Twenty-Eighth divisions to clear the forest and the green Thirty-Fifth Division to attack up the corridor between the Aire and Montfaucon. Since the First Army's frontage was not great for the number of divisions it had, the attack would have irresistible momentum as fresh troops moved forward. This concept underestimated the control, artillery coordination, and supply problems created by passages of lines. The First Army staff ordered that the most difficult terrain features on the way to the *Kriemhilde Stellung* be enveloped. These terrain features were the Bois de Montfaucon, Montfaucon itself and the entire Argonne Forest in the I Corps sector.[6]

The act of faith embodied in the First Army plan was that the Germans would be fooled about the weight and direction of the attack and that the local German resistance would be overwhelmed by the concentrated application of American infantry, aviation, artillery, and the newborn tank force. The First Army planned to crush the Germans with the fire of nearly 4,000 guns, which would deluge the enemy with high explosives and gas. The artillery preparation would come only three hours before the infantry attacked, thereby surprising the Germans. The Germans could reply with less than 1,000 guns. The difficulty was that even the longest-range First Army guns could not smother the *Kriemhilde Stellung*. Continuous local fire superiority meant that divisional and corps batteries would have to displace forward quickly, a feat that the First Army had not yet mastered. Allied airplanes would, it was hoped, provide some long-range firepower, and American and French tanks would discourage the German machine gunners in the line of combat outposts. The AEF had not surrendered its faith in the deadeye American infantryman, but it had recognized that he needed help. Whether the First Army had arranged enough support remained to be seen.[7]

The First Army's order for the Meuse-Argonne campaign was more than optimistic. It was also confusing. Part of the III Corps mission read: ''By promptly penetrating the hostile second position it will turn Montfaucon and the section of the hostile second position within the zone of action of the V Corps, thereby assisting the capture of the hostile second position west of Montfaucon.'' Presumably this meant that the left flank division of the III Corps would assist the V Corps by taking the defenses east of Montfaucon and thus enfilading the heights and its approaches with its fire. Certainly neither Montfaucon nor the neighboring village of Nantillois to the north were in the III Corps zone of action. The First Army's order was very clear on that point. After the war, a colonel of the First Army operations section stated: ''Possibly there was a misunderstanding at times as to what these division lines meant. These lines were intended to show the Army conception of the maneuver and were not intended to act as barriers between corps and divisions and thus limit their operations and prevent lateral movement.''[8] After the AEF had been built on the concept of obedience to Pershing and his staff, this about-face was to cause problems. Another part of the First Army order was equally ambiguous: decisions on liaison and timing of advances to both the German second and third positions would be ''regulated by the corps commanders.'' From H-Hour until the time the First Army exploited the assumed breakthrough of the *Kriemhilde Stellung,* the corps commanders were on their own.

The flaws in the AEF's command practices compounded the vagueness of the attack order. In its planning phase, the Meuse-Argonne operation was the property of the Leavenworth graduates. Drum discussed the order with the corps chiefs-of-staff on September 16, and the next day Bjornstad explained it to his division chiefs-of-staff. When the First Army order was officially published on September 20, it was again issued through the chiefs-of-staff. Three days later, when the III Corps gave its own order, Bjornstad and the division chiefs-of-staff conferred, not Bullard and his division commanders. No doubt the latter discussed the corps operation order before September 26, the day of the attack, but misunderstanding between commanding generals and chiefs-of-staff was to cause much confusion and recrimination throughout the First Army.

For the III Corps, the First Army's instructions appeared relatively clear, though the execution of the corps mission demanded careful preparation. The Thirty-Third Division had to attack across a creek and low swamp and wheel eastwards to the bank of the Meuse; the Eightieth was to bypass the Bois de Forges with a double envelopment and advance northward before wheeling on line with the Thirty-Third on the Meuse; the Fourth Division was to plunge straight past the heights of Montfaucon to the German defenses on Hill 299, northeast of Cunel, in the *Kriemhilde Stellung.* The planning provided, however, that all three attacking divisions of the III Corps would hold up at an intermediate line (called the "Corps Objective") until all three corps were abreast. The First Army hoped the V Corps would get to this phaseline first, although, as it developed, the III Corps made it and the V Corps did not. The III Corps objective line ran from just north and east of Nantillois on a straight line to the Meuse, roughly five and a half miles from the line of departure.

Bullard had the best divisions the First Army had available for its initial attack. The Thirty-Third Division had been as professional as the prewar New York and Pennsylvania National Guard, had already fought in the BEF, and was commanded by Major General George Bell, Jr., a benign-looking oldster with a white goatee. His division was both competent and enthusiastic. The Eightieth Division was as yet untested, but its common soldiers, draftees from the mid-Atlantic states, were solid and its officers adequate. It was commanded by portly Adelbert Cronkhite, whom Bullard knew and respected. The Fourth Division, blooded in the Second Battle of the Marne, was undoubtedly the best in the First Army's assault. It entered the Meuse-Argonne campaign with a new division commander, Major General John L. Hines, the driving former commander of the Sixteenth Infantry and First Brigade of the First Division. Bullard was delighted to have Hines and the Fourth Division in his corps, and it was probably no accident that they got the difficult task of paralleling the V Corps attack past Montfaucon.[9] The experienced Third Division was the corps reserve. Though the III Corps had no tanks, Bullard could support the infantry with the division artillery brigades and 374 guns and mortars from his French corps artillery.

In the shell-pitted woods and marshes to the III Corps' front, the German outpost line was manned by 117th Division and 7th Reserve Division. Both had already seen hard service in 1918. Casualties had forced companies and regiments to consolidate, damaging morale by introducing new, unproven officers and sergeants and destroying the regional-community homogeneity of the German units. At the same time, the most skilled soldiers had been pulled from the ranks to form the special assault teams which had spearheaded Ludendorff's attacks. Before September 26, there was little evidence that the German defenders suspected a major assault; German patrolling was light and garrison routine normal. The only enemy movements in the area were due to batteries moving east of the Meuse and to horse-carts tending to the normal distribution of food and ammunition. Except for an occasional shell, the German artillery did not bother the massed units and batteries of the III Corps, most of which went into French positions well known to the Germans.[10]

As the First Army prepared its attack, Pershing toured the corps PCs and sent his First Army staff officers to check the progress of the planning. His staff officers, nicknamed "periscopes" or "crocodiles" because they appeared so suddenly, lurked in the corners of PCs, observing the grasp, energy, and optimism of the division and brigade commanders.[11] On the eve of the offensive, "The Chief" exuded confidence about his army and the Allied cause and was pleased that the Germans expected attacks to east of the Meuse rather than in the Meuse-Argonne sector. Despite dire French predictions that the First Army would not reach its first day's objectives for months, Pershing was satisfied that his divisions would turn his plan into victory. When he visited the III Corps headquarters, his bouyant optimism impressed Bullard as "The Chief" expressed his pleasure with the state of the III Corps preparations.[12] Pershing's subordinates had no illusions that "The Chief" would tolerate a general in whom he had lost confidence. Pershing's corps commanders had already seen "The Chief" reach down through the chain of command to relieve division, brigade, and regimental commanders, often without explanation.[13] On the eve of the offensive, however, glowing with the St. Mihiel victory, Pershing was poised and satisfied when he chatted with visiting Secretary of War Baker.[14] After all his frustrations and compromises, Pershing had his army and his major offensive.

2.

It had rained intermittently for four days. The morning of September 26 began with heavy mists swirling through the swampy woods and ravines in the valley of the Meuse. The night had been dark, but as the American troops, trucks, and wagons moved to their attack positions, the Germans fired no more than routine harassing artillery missions. Even without heavy shelling, the movement was difficult, for the muddy, crumbling roads were jammed with marching men and carts. Shortly after midnight, the First Army artillery began its preparatory barrages, although it did not fire with full force until 2:30 A.M. Then the entire American front exploded with the flashes of field guns as the shells crashed down on the German positions and roads to the north. At 5:30 A.M., the artillery began its rolling barrage, a curtain of fire starting 100 meters in front of the line of departure and moving on 100 meters every four minutes. Behind the barrage the infantry swarmed from their trenches with whistle blasts and shouts and deployed in lines of skirmishers, wedges, and squad columns. They plunged forward into the scarred fields and pitted woods against weak machine gun fire and an occasional mortar shell, stumbling through barbed wire into the German outpost line. The great offensive had begun.

The III Corps attack went surprisingly well. The Thirty-Third Division struck out across Forges Brook to its front. German resistance was smothered by the artillery, and the assault battalions met only scattered machinegun fire and snipers. In five hours, the division completed its right wheel, advanced six miles with negligible casualties, and held its objectives overlooking the Meuse. By midafternoon, however, the Thirty-Third Division was receiving growing artillery fire, and with only one infantry brigade holding five miles of front, it was spread thin.

The Eightieth Division's attack reflected the division's inexperience, but it, too, met little resistance. Forced to detour around swamps and deep spots in Forges Brook and wrapped in smoke, its assault battalions wandered into neighbors' zones of action. Yet the Eightieth Division's attacking brigade chased the Germans from the Bois de Forges and was on the Corps objective on the Thirty-Third's left in the early afternoon of September 26. It had been delayed more by the terrain and its own traffic congestion than by the outposts of the German 7th Reserve Division, but it also took casualties from German artillery east of the Meuse.

On the III Corps' left flank, where the Fourth Division was supposed to parallel the Seventy-Ninth Division's envelopment of Montfaucon, the advances went well until noon. The veteran Fourth, rested and at full strength, regarded the attack as little more than a dangerous hike. The hardest work was done by the reserve brigade, which assisted the engineers in building a new road from Esnes to Cuisy, a task completed by midafternoon. The Fourth Division's attacking brigade was also on the Corps objective around noon and stopped according to its instructions. The Fourth Division's officers, however, sensed that the attack was rapidly becoming more than a long day's walk. The division received heavier machine gun and light artillery fire from the heights of Montfaucon to its left, and the troops had to dig in. One battalion which had wandered into the V Corps zone returned badly mauled. The signs were that the attack was not going well for the V Corps, and the Fourth Division could see German reinforcements hurrying along the Montfaucon-Nantillois road. Unlike the German infantry in the III Corps zone, these troops were hurrying into the fight, not out of it. Similar parties of riflemen and machine gunners were also infiltrating the wooded hills to the Fourth Division's left front.[15]

In the V Corps' zone, the attack had not developed as planned, for the Thirty-Seventh and Seventy-Ninth Divisions could not envelop Montfaucon through the machine gun and artillery fire directed from the heights. The tank and artillery support was not well handled, and the disorganized assaulting infantry made its efforts in insufficient numbers to storm the hill. The V Corps' "deep penetration" went the way of most eager operations plans, and in the early afternoon General Drum ordered the I and III Corps to go on to the Army objective without waiting for the V Corps. Drum's instructions to the III Corps emphasized the need to guard the front along the Meuse and did not mention any new missions affecting the situation around Montfaucon.[16] In fact, the First Army headquarters, aware that the V Corps was in trouble at Montfaucon, was satisfied that the III Corps was doing well and was enjoying tallying the prisoners captured, guns seized, and ground gained. Pershing's major concern was the swelling traffic congestion between the line of departure and the front; having to cope with narrow roads ruined by artillery fire, the guns and trains of the nine assault divisions were only inching forward. The attacking infantry was out of range of all but the heaviest cannon, and the German artillery east of the Meuse and in the Argonne Forest began to register on the columns of vehicles and troops moving up the corridors east and west of Montfaucon. There were also problems in the I Corps zone, where the attack up the Aire valley and in the Argonne Forest had not gone well. The First Army, however, did little more than order each corps to advance independently to the Army objective when it issued a revised attack order on the evening of September 26.[17]

From its PC in Rampont, the III Corps headquarters followed the attack through continuous phone calls and the grease-pencilled arrows on the operations map. As the morning progressed, Bullard and Bjornstad watched the blue military symbols march steadily up the map; it was hard to realize that the neat lines and boxes were infantrymen struggling through bogs, sweating inside their gasmasks and peppered by machine gun fire from hidden emplacements. Bjornstad controlled the troop movements himself, but checked with Bullard before the orders went out over the phones. Bullard occasionally intervened, most often to talk personally with the division commanders about their progress and to encourage them to push the attack. Isolated from the front, he felt ill at ease, for only the map, phone calls, and drumming of the artillery fire told him of the battle going on beyond his sight.[18]

During the afternoon of September 26, Bullard went forward to visit his division commanders and weigh the progress of the III Corps attack. He found the Thirty-Third holding its portion of the Army objective and the Eightieth also well deployed, although he erroneously reported that it, too, held all of the Army objective in its sector. The Fourth Division was still short of the second German defense line, being hit by machine gun fire and artillery on its left and left front from positions at Nantillois in the V Corps zone and Cuisy in its own zone. Making his report by telephone at 8 P.M. to Drum, Bullard said his only problem at the moment was getting his artillery forward.[19] He was probably unaware that some confusion was building over the capture of Montfaucon, although during his visit with General Hines, he had approved a plan Hines had worked out with Bjornstad to shift his reserve brigade westward.[20]

The V Corps' failure to take Montfaucon produced a crisis that clearly exposed the tension within the First Army's command. For the V Corps, the episode led to the relief of the corps commander, Major General George H. Cameron. In the III Corps, the Montfaucon episode further poisoned the relationship between Bullard and Bjornstad, angered Hines, and disgusted the officers of the Fourth Division. It may even have had some bearing on the pattern of the battle in the III Corps area, although this is not so clear. It did nothing, either, for Bullard's relationship with Pershing's staff. The difficulty arose from the wording of the First Army order for the attack. When the Fourth Division received the part of the III Corps mission that supported the V Corps, Hines asked Bjornstad whether this meant that the Fourth Division was to move physically into the V Corps zone, especially to seize Nantillois north of Montfaucon. The III Corps chief-of-staff said it did, if necessary. The Corps order, however, did not give the Fourth Division this mission, even on a contingency basis. The mission was to get the corps objective within the corps area—a forward advance, not an envelopment. In his meetings with Colonel Christian Bach, the Fourth Division chief-of-staff, Bjornstad stressed the importance of penetrating the German second position, not enveloping Montfaucon. The Fourth Division was to head for Cuisy, a town in the III Corps area, not Montfaucon or Nantillois.[21]

Harassed from his left flank during the morning of September 26, Hines proposed to Bullard and Bjornstad that he move his reserve brigade on line with his leading brigade, a move that would take him into the V Corps area and allow him to take Nantillois, a growing German strongpoint, on the morning of September 27. Bullard approved the plan at Hines' PC. When Hines phoned Bjornstad, the III Corps chief-of-staff approved the following mission: "The division on your left is held up by MONTFAUCON. Therefore, in order to assist their progression, you will send out strong patrols to the west to seize strong points in that division's area, and will outpost tonight not only your own front but also well over to your left. You will push up your reserve in order to do this, and to replace your supports, thus needed."[22] Bjornstad's response suggests that he did not approvs of taking Nantillois or at least would not assume the responsibility for such an attack. Hines, however, went ahead with his plan, ordering Brigadier General Ewing E. Booth to swing his brigade into line and attack Nantillois. Booth was quite properly reluctant to make the move without some assurance that the V Corps would not shell his men; he was also worried about the need to coordinate his movement with the III Corps artillery. Hines assured him that III Corps approved the attack and wculd handle the coordination with V Corps. Booth began to move his two regiments across the corps boundary into the gathering dark.[23]

Before the Fourth Division's attack was far along, Hines got a message from III Corps headquarters cancelling it. Bullard's explanation was that the First Army had disapproved of the attack, although it is unlikely that Drum knew the details of Hines' move. What the Army had done was to order the I and III Corps not to wait for the V Corps, but to go on to the *Kriemhilde Stellung*. The III Corps told Hines that "the Army Commander directs that without waiting for advance of 5th Corps on left of 3rd Corps you at once press advance towards Army Objective. You will have good strong advance guard to proceed your advance and will guard your left. . . . BULLARD."[24] At the time III Corps issued these instructions, Bullard and Bjornstad thought that the V Corps had finally taken Montfaucon because V Corps headquarters had so announced. Not until after Hines halted did they learn differently.[25] No doubt they then regretted their understandable caution in staying inside their own boundaries, a regret that grew when Pershing and Drum unfairly blamed the III Corps for not making the Nantillois attack. Bullard's defense was that the First Army's order to advance cancelled the attack by implication. General Drum's ingenuous defense of Army headquarters was that the III Corps should have understood that it had the freedom to cross corps boundaries without Army approval. Such a response from Drum was self-serving, for he had insisted in practice on a high degree of Army control over the corps' movements. It was not the first or last time he and Pershing disassociated themselves from schemes of maneuver that had turned sour.[26]

The immediate tactical implication of the Fourth Division's halt on the corps objective was that Montfaucon did not fall until the next day. The entire episode was symptomatic of the First Army's reluctance to accept the fact that its plans were too ambitious and that it not only had lost the race to the *Kriemhilde Stellung*, but had not even taken the second German positions screening the main line of resistance. Certainly the guns of Montfaucon ruined the First Army's timetable. So, too, did the shelling from the unassaulted heights east of the Meuse and the positions on the eastern edge of the Argonne Forest, where Liggett's I Corps had made even shorter advances than the V and III Corps. In the III Corps zone alone, fresh reserves from the German 5th Bavarian Reserve Division were already hammering Hines' right flank regiment and the Eightieth Division, neither of which was involved in "turning" Montfaucon. The Meuse-Argonne campaign in twenty-four hours had turned from a sprint to a slugging match, with or without the seizure of Nantillois by the Fourth Division.

For the next four days (September 27-30), the First Army's assault divisions hammered away at the German second position with scant success and declining effectiveness. In the III Corps sector, the Fourth and Eightieth Divisions fought back and forth across two heavy, broken woods (the Bois de Septsarges and the Bois de Brieulles) and a couple of knolls between the heights of Romagne and the Meuse. The German defenders, reinforced by units from four more divisions, fought with skill and persistence. Assessing the character of the American attacks, the Germans admired the courage of the First Army's infantrymen, but ridiculed their bunched formations and their dependence on rifle fire and the bayonet.[27] Where small groups of Americans penetrated the German positions, infantry counterattacks drove back the isolated units. The III Corps was also harassed by

German artillery firing from east of the Meuse; timely barrages into assembly areas of both the Fourth and Eightieth Divisions broke a couple of attacks and demoralized the Americans, who thought that the shells were coming from their own guns.

The III Corps' major problem was the lack of friendly artillery support. The Fourth Division began its attacks on September 27 with only a third of its divisional guns; the Eightieth was no better supported. Ammunition expenditure within the III Corps reflected the drop in artillery action; after firing 90,000 rounds on September 26, the division and corps 75-mm batteries fired only 27,000 rounds during the next four days. The trend in ammunition expenditure for the 105-mm and 155-mm guns was the same.[28] Part of the problem was the rude state of communications from the front to the firing batteries. The major difficulty, however, was that the artillery could not move to positions within range of the Germans for the one major road in the III Corps area was both nearly impassable and clogged with traffic.

In its desperate effort to move artillery forward, every corps in the First Army experienced the same problems that all attacking armies on the Western Front faced. As long as friendly artillery was firing from prepared positions behind long-stabilized lins, it could deliver the massed fire necessary to pulverize a fortified defender. Of course, the shells also tore up the roads over which the guns eventually had to displace. The weather seldom cooperated, and, in the Meuse-Argonne area, rain turned the roads into quagmires. In the III Corps sector, where the traffic congestion was no worse than anywhere else in the First Army, heavy artillery pieces slid off the road and jammed it. Of course, the divisions could hardly get along without ammunition wagons, rolling kitchens, ambulances, and essential supplies, and their transport added to the congestion. At one time the traffic in the III Corps area was tailgate to tailgate for six miles. Casualties moving from the front took twenty-eight hours to get to field hospitals. It took a whole week for the III Corps to move all its guns into new positions. If the Germans had systematically shelled the III Corps' single road, the crisis would have been even worse, but the enemy guns concentrated primarily on the attacking infantry. Bullard was amazed that the Germans did not pound his supply line, but the wrecked trucks and wagons, the bloating horses and mangled men piled in the ditches along the Esnes-Montzeville-Cuisy road warned travelers that the Germans were not neglecting the American specialty, the traffic jam.[29]

Despite his orders to continue the attack, Pershing watched his offensive slow with increasing frustration. Although he recognized the relationship between the traffic jams and the stalled advance, he was obsessed by the idea that his corps, division, and brigade commanders had failed him. He wrote in his diary that "I gave orders for the advance to be resumed, and certainly have done all in my power to instill an aggressive spirit in the different corps headquarters." He was most worried about the skepticism he found in the I and V headquarters.[30] He expressed his concern about the First Army's leadership:

Division and brigade commanders will place themselves as far toward the front of the advance of their respective units as may be necessary to direct their movements with energy and rapidity in the attack. The enemy is in retreat or holding lightly in places, and advance elements of several divisions are already on the First Army Objective and there should be no delay or hesitation in going forward. . . . All officers will push their units forward with all possible energy. Corps and division commanders will not hesitate to relieve on the spot any officer of whatever rank who fails to show in this emergency those qualities of leadership required to accomplish the task that confronts us.[31]

To help the corps commanders do their jobs, Pershing ordered them to move their PCs closer to the front. The III Corps headquarters moved to Montzeville, about six miles from the front, over the corps' single highway.

In the slowed First Army attack, Bullard's corps produced the best news Pershing received. Much of the optimism in the III Corps' reports were justified, for the corps was closer to its objectives than the V and I Corps. As long as the First Army staff was most concerned about the flank on the Meuse, where the Thirty-Third Division stood guard, the III Corps looked good. The few things Bullard and Bjornstad had in common were aggressiveness, optimism, and a desire to please the First Army headquarters. Their reports emphasized success and softened failure. After the fighting of September 27, a day in which both the Fourth and Eightieth Divisions made ill-managed and costly assaults that gained little ground, Bullard reported "everything progressing well. We are really on the Army objective, except on the left which has been held back."[32] Assessing the day's activities on September 28, the III Corps admitted that the Fourth Division had taken at least 800 casualties and gained only a kilometer, but had gone beyond Nantillois, which had been abandoned by the Germans. So optimistic were Bullard's reports that First Army extended the III Corps boundary westward and reassigned the corps reserve, the Third Division, to the V Corps. In exchange, Bullard got the worn Seventy-Ninth Division from Cameron's corps. Compared with the I and V Corps, Bullard's divisions were pressing forward, but by September 30 even limited local attacks were not moving, and the III Corps admitted it. When Pershing called off the corps attacks, Bullard's divisions had taken the German second position but little else, and needed a rest. Yet, contrasted with the advances of the I and V Corps, Bullard's command emerged from the first phase of the Meuse-Argonne campaign as the First Army's most dependable corps.[33]

3.

The First Army's failure to crack the *Kriemhilde Stellung* by October 1 produced another crisis in Franco-American military relations, a crisis that forced

Pershing to attack the German third position with desperate determination. In part, the trouble arose from the Allied successes in other sectors, particularly the BEF's dramatically successful attack of September 29. Even before any German reserves were shifted south against the Americans, the British Fourth Army broke through the Germans' main defensive positions. The northern wing of the great Allied double envelopment was developing as planned, but the First Army was stuck fast between the Meuse and the Argonne Forest. In the meantime, the two French armies between the BEF and the First Army had also launched attacks. Moving against the German defenses west of the Argonne, the French army wanted more American divisions to lead its attacks. The French argument was that the American divisions packed in Pershing's sector could be more wisely used west of the Argonne under a French army commander. Those pressuring Pershing included not only Marshal Foch and General Pétain, but French Premier Georges Clemenceau, who was ready to do more about Pershing's command than hold polite conferences.

On September 29, Clemenceau visited the First Army's zone in order to make a victory visit to Montfaucon. Caught in the immense traffic jam in the valley of the Aire, he was angry enough to press Foch to do something about the First Army. Foch's proposal, made to Pershing on October 1, was that the First Army should place the divisions of Liggett's I Corps under French army command; the new Franco-American army would then flank the Argonne Forest from both east and west. The implication was that these divisions were being wasted by the First Army and that Pershing and his generals were not up to the demands of breaking the *Kriemhilde Stellung*. Clemenceau was even prepared to act to remove the major barrier to the redeployment of American divisions from the First Army. He was ready to ask President Wilson to relieve Pershing. And Pershing knew what Clemenceau had in mind.[34]

The First Army had no intention of either halting its offensive or releasing its divisions to the Allies. The halt of September 30 had one purpose: to prepare another full assault on the *Kriemhilde Stellung*. All three attacking corps had three days to improve their supply lines, move up their artillery, and organize their assaults. In the III Corps area, Bullard had the Thirty-Third still holding the bank of the Meuse; the Illinois Guardsmen were patrolling the river for crossing places and taking German shells daily. Bullard's assault, which was supposed to break the *Kriemhilde Stellung* from Cunel heights to the Meuse, would be mounted by the Eightieth and Fourth Divisions. These divisions had switched places, since the earlier advance had pinched out the Eightieth's sector. In the III Corps zone, the Eightieth Division was on the left, joining the V Corps along the Nantillois-Cunel road, and the Fourth was on the right, facing the German third defensive position in the Bois de Fays.

The III Corps attack covered only half of the corps sector, for the corps' mission was to parallel the V Corps' main thrust against the defended ridge between Romagne and Cunel. Therefore, the III Corps attack swung west of the town of Brieulles on the Meuse and the marshy valley which guarded it. To have advanced along the entire corps sector would have served little purpose, for the Brieulles valley was vulnerable to fire from the north and east and the terrain was too open and swampy for a successful attack. For an attacker, the terrain in the rest of the zone was not much better. Between the III Corps front and the Cunel-Brieulles road (a distance of about two miles) lay three heavy woods and the main trace of the *Kriemhilde Stellung*. Within the same area, there were six separate ridges running across the line of advance, all of them heavily defended by wire, machine gun positions, and entrenched infantry. The German defenders, the tired but skilled 5th Bavarian Reserve Division and the fresh 263th Division, used all the advantages provided by the terrain. Beyond the Cunel-Brieulles road there was an even more forminable barrier, a heavily wooded plateau named the Bois de Forêt. The *Kriemhilde Stellung* ran below this plateau, creating a clever combination of man-made and natural defenses. The entire area was covered by German artillery north of the *Kriemhilde Stellung* and by German guns east of the Meuse.

The First Army attack order called for a simultaneous attack by all three corps against the *Kriemhilde Stellung*. Since Pershing had ordered another forward plunge with better artillery support, the orders needed little explanation. For the III Corps, however, the First Army complicated the operation by ordering the Thirty-Third Division to prepare an attack eastward across the Meuse.[35] The III Corps also ran into problems with the First Army's staff about the boundary with the V Corps along the Nantillois-Cunel road and about the artillery rate of fire in the rolling barrages. In the Fourth Division, General Hines and Colonel Bach saw to it that their planning did not wait upon the III Corps attack order, but in General Cronkhite's Eightieth, the preparations were confused by the dispute with the V Corps over boundaries and objectives and the fumblings of a green division staff. The Eightieth did not receive the corps order until 5 P.M. the day before the assault, and the attacking regimental commanders did not know their missions until 11 P.M. Reconnaissance and liaison with the artillery and the flanking Third Division of the V Corps suffered.

On the morning of October 4, the First Army resumed its offensive. The assault battalions of the Fourth Division, hugging the barrage, quickly crossed an open field and got into the Bois de Fays. There, the infantrymen in small groups infiltrated through the woods; avoiding clearings and searching out unguarded paths, they battled with snipers and German machine gun nests. Tired, short of water, gassed and shelled in the dripping woods, the Fourth Division inched forward with soaring casualties. On the III Corps' left flank, the Eightieth Division's attack was stopped short of the Bois de Ogons. Cronkhite's infantry was game, but showed their inexperience by losing the rolling barrage. While they were still crossing the open fields south of the wood, the German machine gunners crawled from their holes and stopped the assault. The Eightieth Division's infantry entrenched where they lay and waited for orders as the Germans shelled their exposed positions. The next day the Eightieth attack reached the Bois de Ogons and held the woods' forward edge, but the Third Division attack on the left flank, despite the use of tanks, did not keep pace. With isolated units of both divisions receiving fire from three sides and communication and resupply made difficult by the shelling, the III Corps attack did not prosper. On October 6 Bullard, on the advice of his staff, stopped the attacks in order to feed and rest his troops and increase his artillery fire against Brieulles and east of the Meuse. Pershing's headquarters approved the halt, for the V and I Corps were in even graver difficulty. In three days of hard fighting, the corps casualties had increased from some two thousand men (September 26-October 3) to somewhere between eight and nine thousand. No one knew with any certainty how many had fallen, and the only consolation was that the straggling had not been bad.[36]

During the attacks of October 4-6, Bullard spent most of his time in the Eightieth and Fourth Division PCs. At Hines' urging, he wrote a citation commending the Fourth Division for its attacks and had an airplane drop an order in leaflet form to the frontline troops. The infantry thought the message amusing: "You are there. Hold." Though Bullard was satisfied with the Fourth Division's performance, he was concerned that Cronkhite and his subordinates were offering too many excuses for themselves and their troops. He himself recognized that the Eightieth's tactical deficiencies were hurting, but he could not stop the attack to provide training on troop dispersion and artillery liaison. The Eightieth would have to learn the hard way, and he ordered more assaults. Bullard was in no mood to be sympathetic. His touchy stomach and neuritis had flared up, and Pershing was making no effort to conceal his own anger about the First Army's lack of progress. Pershing hinted that, if the renewed attacks did not produce breaks in the *Kriemhilde Stellung,* some generals were going to lose their jobs.[37]

The First Army's general offensive started again on the morning of October 9. In the III Corps zone the Fourth Division pushed on through the Bois de Fays into another heavy wood, making costly progress against units of a new German division. On its left, the Eightieth crossed into the fields beyond the Bois de Ogons, but was stopped by artillery and machine gun fire from the Germans holding Cunel. The III Corps attack had reached the point of crisis, for neither Cronkhite nor Hines was very enthusiastic about continuing the assaults. Even Bullard, whose official state of mind bordered on euphoria, showed the strain by agreeing with his subordinates that the Germans showed no signs of giving. He was unmoved, however, by pleas that the infantry was exhausted, and he relieved one brigadier in the Eightieth Division whom he thought insufficiently vigorous and optimistic. He ordered the brigade and regimental commanders in both divisions to move their headquarters closer to the lines and threatened to relieve Cronkhite if he did not push his division with more firmness, regardless of its losses and fatigue.[38]

Bullard, much to his satisfaction, had correctly gauged Pershing's vanished patience, for "The Chief" was convinced that the First Army's generals had failed him. On October 10 he issued another warning that he would not tolerate any commander who could not find the will or skill to take machine gun nests by storm. He ordered all commanding officers to displace closer to the front lines. That included corps commanders. Bullard promptly phoned Drum that he had already issued such orders to his division commanders and was moving his own PC forward.[39] On the same morning, Bullard was in the Fourth Division PC, supervising another attack by Brigadier General Benjamin Poore's Seventh Brigade. Despite heavy fire and infantry counterattacks, Poore's infantry got across the Cunel-Brieulles road and held on at the base of the Bois de Forêt. In the Eightieth Division zone, the attack went badly, and almost an entire battalion was wiped out at the line of departure by artillery fire. The next day, however, after Bullard had warned Cronkhite that he had one more day to be a division commander, the Eightieth also captured a foothold across the highway as the Fourth Division pushed into the Bois de Forêt. There was still no sign of a German collapse (which the First Army kept predicting), but the III Corps was at last through the worst of the *Kriemhilde Stellung* and holding part of the Army objective.[40]

Again, the First Army attack had not made much headway in the I and V Corps sectors, where the terrain and defenders were even more stubborn than those in the III Corps sector. Most of the *Kriemhilde Stellung* was still not only uncaptured but its outposts were also in German hands. There had been a great deal wrong with the First Army's offensive, from the tactics of its rifle platoons to the Army scheme of maneuver, but Pershing, having committed his army, his nation's honor, and his reputation to battle, would not halt the offensive. If he had done so, it would have been admission that his dream of an independent American army playing a decisive role in the defeat of Germany was nothing more than another delusion of the Great War. He would have had no answers for either his own government or the Allies when they asked why more American divisions could not be placed under French and British commanders. Pershing was keenly aware that the BEF was making more impressive gains in the north. He and his staff argued that the First Army assault made Haig's advance possible by drawing off German reserves. It was an improvised justification for the continuation of the Meuse-Argonne offensive, although eventually the First Army did pull more German divisions to its front. In any event. Pershing needed good news, and the III Corps gave him some on October 12—at the cost of nearly ten thousand casualties in its two assault divisions. There had been little finesse in the III Corps' successive attacks. Seldom did the First Army allow sufficient time, means, and maneuvering room for a corps commander to show much tactical skill. In such an environment, it did little good to argue with Pershing that a particular mission could not be accomplished. One corps commander and three division commanders who did so lost their jobs before the end of October. In Pershing's army, the better part of wisdom was to keep smiling and keep attacking. Between September 26 and October 12, Major General Robert Lee Bullard had done both.[41]

NOTES

¹B. H. Liddell Hart, *The Real War, 1914-1918* (Boston: Little, Brown, 1930), pp. 449-455.

²Historical Division, Army War College, *The Genesis of the American First Army* (Washington: Government Printing Office, 1938), pp. 50-58; John J. Pershing, *My Experiences in the World War,* 2 vols. (New York: Frederick A. Stokes, 1931), II, pp. 241-258.

³American Battle Monuments Commission, *American Armies and Battlefields in Europe* (Washington: Government Printing Office, 1938), pp. 167-328; Douglas W. Johnson, *Battlefields of the World War* (New York: Oxford University Press, 1921), pp. 316-349. I also used the collections of photographs compiled for the Fourth, Eightieth, and Thirty-Third Divisions in the series American Battle Monuments Commission, *Terrain Photographs: American World War Battlefields in Europe: Meuse-Argonne Offensive,* copies at USAMHRC, Carlisle Barracks.

⁴G-3, First Army, memorandum, September 4, 1918, in *USA/WW, 1917-1919,* IX, pp. 3-4; First Army memoranda and orders, September 12-17, 1918 *USA/WW, 1917-1919,* IX, pp. 7-27.

For the planning phase of the Meuse-Argonne campaign, see G-3, General Staff, First Army, AEF, *Special Operations Report: Part C: Meuse-Argonne Operations,* January 5, 1919, in File 110.1 (G-3, First Army, Reports), AEF "Historical File," Records of the American Expeditionary Force, RG 120; Col. R. T. Ward, Assistant G-3, First Army, "Explanation and Execution of Plans of Operation, 1st American Army for Argonne-Meuse Operation," December 18, 1918, and Maj. Gen. W. S. McNair, Chief of Artillery, First Army, "Explanation and Execution of Plans for Artillery for St. Mihiel Operation and Argonne-Meuse Operations," December 23, 1918, copies of lectures in the Clarence R. Edwards Papers; Pershing, *My Experiences in the World War* II, pp. 276-294.

⁵For the III Corps role in the Meuse-Argonne campaign, I have relied on: CG, III Corps, AEF to CG, First Army, AEF, "Report of Operations, Sept. 9 to Nov. 11, 1918," December 1, 1918, copy in First Army, AEF "Historical File," RG 120.

Bullard described his own activities first in an entry, October 7, 1918, Diarybook 9, BP, and elaborated on this account in *Personalities and Reminiscences of the War* (New York: Doubleday, Page, 1925), pp. 258-291, and in his manuscript autobiography, pp. 149-153, BP.

⁶First Army, AEF, Field Order 20, September 20, 1918, with annexes, appendices, and maps in File 112.08 (First Army Field Orders), First Army, AEF "Historical File," RG 120.

⁷Annexes 1 and 2 (Employment of Army Artillery) to First Army, AEF, Field Order 20, September 20, 1918, cited above.

⁸Col. R. T. Ward, "Explanation and Execution of Plans of Operation, 1st American Army for Argonne-Meuse Operation to November 11, 1918," previously cited.

⁹Bullard autobiography, p. 150, BP; Bullard, *Personalities and Reminiscences,* pp. 267-268. The service of these three divisions in the Meuse-Argonne campaign is ably described in Christian A. Bach and Henry Noble Hall, *The Fourth Division* (Garden City, N.Y.: Country Life Press, 1920), pp. 152-201; Frederic L. Huidekoper, *The History of the 33rd Division. A.E.F.,* 3 vols. (Springfield, Ill.: Illinois State Historical Library, 1921), I, pp. 56-103; and Maj. Gen. S. D. Sturgis, "Operations of the 80th Division," February 11, 1919, copy of lecture in the Edwards Papers.

[10]The German situation is drawn from Intelligence Section (G-2), First Army, *Summaries of Intelligence, First Army, American Expeditionary Force,* in two parts (August 29, 1918 to September 19, 1918, and September 20, 1918 to November 11, 1918), in File 203 (G-2 Reports), AEF "Historical File," RG 120; Headquarters, III Corps, Intelligence Summaries, Nos. 1-58, September 14-November 11, 1918, Hines Papers; The General Staff, AEF, *The German and American Combined Daily Order of Battle (25 September, 1918 to 11 November, 1918),* including the Meuse-Argonne Campaign (Chaumont, France, 1919), copy in "Book File," Pershing Papers; MID, USA, *Histories of Two Hundred and Fifty-One Divisions of the German Army* (Washington: Government Printing Office, 1920), pp. 149-152, 609-611.

[11]Entry, September 16, 1918, in Maj. Gen. Charles D. Rhodes, "Diary of the World War, 1918," Charles D. Rhodes Papers, USMA Library.

[12]Pershing diary, entry, September 21, 1918, Pershing Papers; Bullard, *Personalities and Reminiscences,* pp. 266-267.

[13]Bullard, *Personalities and Reminiscences,* p. 267; Joseph T. Dickman, *The Great Crusade* (New York: Appleton, 1927), p. 163; Maj. Gen. H. Liggett to Maj. Gen. C. R. Edwards, October 25, 1918, Edwards Papers; Maj. Gen. W. H. Johnston to Maj. Gen. C. R. Edwards, October 10, 1929, Edwards Papers; Brig. Gen. Benjamin Poore, "My Experiences in the American Expeditionary Force, 1918-1919," p. 7, memoir in the possession of Gen. C. L. Bolté, USA (ret.).

[14]Entries, September 23 and 25, 1918, journal of Secretary of War Newton Baker's second European trip, copy in the Newton D. Baker Papers, Case Western Reserve University Library (hereafter cited as Baker Papers/CWR).

[15]In addition to the division histories and III Corps reports and war diaries previously cited, I have used the following basic source for the Meuse-Argonne campaign: G-3, First Army, "Messages Received," File 107 (G-3 Reports), in First Army, AEF "Historical File," RG 120 (hereafter cited as First Army "Messages Received").

The German side of the fighting is described in Major Herman von Giehrl, "Battle of the Meuse-Argonne," *Infantry Journal* 19 (August-December 1921), pp. 131-138, 264-270, 377-384, 534-540. Von Giehrl was chief-of-staff of the German Sixteenth Corps during the battle.

[16]G-3, GHQ, AEF Report File 113.0, telephonic order by Chief-of-Staff to V and III Corps, September 26, 1918, in *USA/WW, 1917-1919,* IX, p. 135.

[17]Pershing diary, entry, September 26, 1918, Pershing Papers; C/S, First Army, to C/S, III Corps, telcon 8:30 A.M., September 27, 1918, in G-3, First Army, "Messages Received," RG 120; First Army Field Order 25, September 26, 1918, in *USA/WW, 1917-1919,* X, pp. 136-137.

[18]Bullard, *Personalities and Reminiscences,* pp. 264-269; E. O. Nigel Cholmeley-Jones to the author, January 11, 1972.

[19]CG, III Corps, telcon with C/S, First Army, 8:15 P.M., September 26, 1918, in G-3, First Army "Messages Received," RG 120.

[20]Entry, September 26, 1918, journal of Secretary of War Baker's second European trip, Baker Papers/CWR; Maj. Gen. J. L. Hines to Col. E. E. Booth, December 30, 1920, John L. Hines Papers; Col. H. A. Parker to Col. E. E. Booth, December 26, 1920, Hines Papers.

[21]III Corps Field Order 56, September 23, 1918, attached to III Corps "War Diary," in GHQ, AEF "War Diaries," RG 120; III Army Corps, American Expeditionary Force, "The Argonne-Meuse Operations, from Sept. 9 to Nov. 11," previously cited; Col. A. W. Bjornstad to Col. C. A. Bach, December 24, 1924, Hines Papers; Col. C. A. Bach to Capt.

C. L. Bolté, June 25, 1922, Hines Papers; Col. C. A. Bach to Lt. Col. F. W. Clark (G-3, III Corps), November 18, 1922, Hines Papers; Lt. Col. F. W. Clark to Col. C. A. Bach, December (?), 1922, Hines Papers; Col. E. E. Booth to Brig. Gen. H. A. Drum, March 21, 1921, Hines Papers.

[22]C/S, III Corps, telcon with CG, 4th Div., 3:30 P.M., September 26, 1918, copy in Hines Papers; testimony of Colonel Alfred W. Bjornstad, "Bjornstad Hearings," pp. 261-262.

[23]Narrative of Col. E. E. Booth, December 9, 1920, Hines Papers; Maj. Gen. E. E. Booth, memo on 8th Brigade, October 7, 1939, Hugh A. Drum Papers; Maj. Gen. E. E. Booth to Col. F. W. Clark, November 15, 1939, Drum Papers.

[24]CG, III Corps telcon to CG, 4th Div., (time unknown), September 26, 1918, copy in Hines Papers.

[25]CG, III Corps, messages to C/S, First Army at 8:15P.M., 10:15 P.M. and 10:40 P.M., September 26, 1918, in G-3, First Army, "Messages Received," RG 120.

[26]Brig. Gen. H. A. Drum to Maj. Gen. J. L. Hines, September 12, 1921, Drum Papers.

[27]General Commanding Reserve Corps, Army Corps Headquarters, Meuse Group East, "Lessons to be Drawn from Fighting on the West Bank of the Meuse," September 29, 1918, translated copy in the Hines Papers.

[28]G-4, First Army, "Report of the Munitions Branch, 4th Section, General Staff, Argonne-Meuse Operation," especially appendix 11 ("Daily Expenditures Artillery Ammunition"), in File 402.02, First Army, AEF, "Historical File," RG 120.

[29]Maj. Gen. W. S. McNair, "Explanations and Execution of Plans for Artillery for St. Mihiel Operation and Argonne-Meuse Operations to November 11, 1918," previously cited; Maj. C. H. Rice, memorandum, "Observations Third Corps 30 Sept. 1918," September 30, 1918, in File 120.01 (G-3 Reports), in First Army, AEF, "Historical File," RG 120; Bullard, *Personalities and Reminiscences of the War,* pp. 270-272; Capt. G. O. Shirey to Brig. Gen. C. King, October 7, 1918, King Papers; entry, September 28, 1918, John L. Hines diary in the possession of Gen. C. L. Bolté, USA (Ret.).

[30]Pershing diary, entries, September 27 and 28, 1918, Pershing Papers.

[31]C/S, First Army, to the CGs, I, III, IV, and V Corps, A.E.F., September 27, 1918, in *USA/WW, 1917-1919,* IX, pp. 138-140.

[32]CG, III Corps telcon to C/S, First Army, 10:15 P.M., September 27, 1918, G-3, First Army, "Messages Received," RG 120.

[33]This assessment is based on the following III Corps operations reports in G-3, First Army, "Messages Received" for September 26-27 (msg 1217), September 27-28 (msg 1274), September 28 (msg 1335), September 29 (msgs 1420 and 1529), September 30 (msg 1646).

[34]Pershing diary, entry, October 2, 1918, Pershing Papers.

[35]First Army, AEF, Field Orders 33, October 1, 1918, in *USA/WW, 1917-1918,* IX, pp. 191-192; CG, First Army, msg to CG, III Corps, October 1, 1918, in *USA/WW, 1917-1919,* IX, p. 193.

[36]Col. G. H. Master, memo, to the Commanding General, III Corps, "Report on Conditions," October 6, 1918, in File 120.01 (Correspondence and Inspectors' Reports, Meuse-Argonne Operation), in G-3, First Army, "Historical File," RG 120; Diarybook 9, entry, October 7, 1918, BP; III Corps messages and operations reports to First Army in G-3, First Army, "Messages Received": October 1, 1918 (msg 1646); October 4, 1918 (msgs 1890, 1948, 1973, 2051); October 5 (msgs 2067, 2109, 2122, 2184).

[37]Entries, October 4 and 5, 1918, Hines diary in the possession of Gen. C. L. Bolté, USA (Ret.); Bullard autobiography, pp. 149-153, BP; William Mitchell, *Memoirs of World*

War I (New York: Random House, 1960), pp. 265-267; Pershing diary, entries, October 7-9, 1918, Pershing Papers.

[38]Diarybook 9, entry, October 10, 1918, BP; Lt. Gen. R. L. Bullard to Maj. Gen. A. Cronkhite, May 12, 1919, Bullard 201 File; Bullard, *Personalities and Reminiscences,* p. 276; entry, October 10, 1918, Hines diary in the possession of Gen. C. L. Bolté, USA (Ret.).

[39]Pershing diary, entry, October 10, 1918, Pershing Papers; CG, III Corps telcon to C/S, First Army, 10:20 P.M., October 10, 1918 (msg 2826), in G-3, First Army, "Messages Received," RG 120.

[40]III Corps operations reports for October 9-12, 1918 (msgs 2832, 2942, 2990, and 3022), G-3, First Army, "Messages Received," RG 120; Brig. Gen. Benjamin Poore, "My Experiences in the American Expeditionary Force, 1918-1919," p. 23.

[41]Gen. J. J. Pershing to the Adj. Gen., USA, October 27, 1919, Bullard 201 File. Pershing reported that Bullard as commanding general, III Corps, had been an exceptionally loyal and able subordinate. "This officer possesses exceptional ability as a soldier in command of troops. He has excellent judgment and is very efficient."

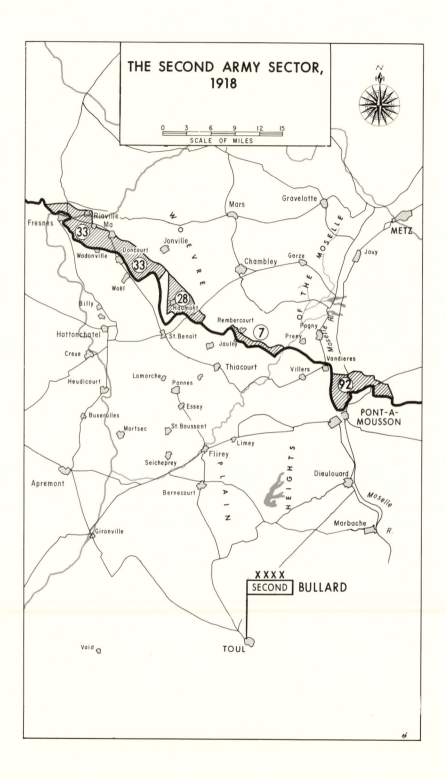

THE SECOND ARMY SECTOR,
1918

SCALE OF MILES

0   3   6   9   12   15

Fresnes
Riaville
Ma
Jonville
Wadonville
Doncourt
Woël
Billy
Hattonchatel
Creue
Haumont
St. Benoit
Rembercourt
Jaulny
Preny
Pagny
Heudicourt
Lamarche
Pannes
Thiacourt
Villers
Vandieres
Buxerulles
Essey
Mortsec
St. Baussant
Seicheprey
Limey
Flirey
Dieulouard
Apremont
Bernecourt
Marbache
Gironville
Void
TOUL

Mars
Gravelotte
METZ
Chambley
Gorze
Jouy

W O E V R E

H E I G H T S
O F   T H E   M O S E L L E

Moselle R.

P L A I N

Moselle
R.

PONT-A-
MOUSSON

33
33
28
7
92

XXXX
SECOND BULLARD

21　The Second Army
1918-1919

Throughout the German offensive of 1918 and the Allied counterattacks that began in July, Pershing and his staff saved their plan for an American offensive toward Metz. The strategic situation on the Western Front had undergone striking changes since Pershing's staff had first proposed this "independent" American offensive, but Pershing never surrendered the concept. He insisted that his army hold its sector in Lorraine, southeast of Verdun. This sector included the ground seized in the St. Mihiel attack. Even before that offensive he established an Army staff as the nucleus for the force which he hoped to use in the attack on Metz. On September 9, 1918, he announced the creation of the Second Army, with head-quarters at Toul. Although he was the commanding general of the Second Army, he gave Colonel Stuart Heintzelman, the chief-of-staff, the responsibility of organizing its sector. A West Pointer (1899) and the third generation of his family to serve with distinction in the United States Army, Heintzelman was another brilliant member of the Leavenworth clique. Unlike some of his contemporaries, Heintzelman worked without friction with the older generals of the AEF, and Pershing's staff thought "The Chief" could not have selected a better chief-of-staff for the Second Army.[1]

Until October 10, the Second Army was no more than a headquarters nucleus at Toul, although its sector was full of American support and service troops, new divisions getting their first taste of the war in a quiet sector, and divisions released from the Meuse-Argonne fighting to recuperate. As yet the Second Army had no mission or troops. And it had no commanding general of its own.

Angered by Allied criticism of his First Army staff's management of the campaign and by the rear-area conduct of his soldiers, Pershing was reluctant to give up personal command of his frontline divisions. Finally, he decided to turn over the First Army to Hunter Liggett and direct his fulltime attention to the entire AEF. He had the new Second Army and its future between the Meuse and Moselle to consider. Since it was common speculation that the Second Army would get a permanent commander and that commander a third star, Pershing may have used the vacancy to prod his corps commanders.

On October 7, as the III Corps prepared for its second serious assault at the

Kriemhilde Stellung, Robert Lee Bullard met with Pershing at the latter's headquarters at Souilly. At the end of their conference, Pershing told Bullard that he was to command "an American Army." Bullard was literally speechless. "I was greatly moved, couldn't talk, couldn't say a word, but offered Gen. Pershing my hand which he took and pressed. I saluted and withdrew. That was all the thanks I could give him, but he understood." Not knowing that Pershing had not really made up his mind, Bullard returned to his corps and spurred his division commanders to drive their troops through the German defensives. On October 10 the *Kriemhilde Stellung* was punctured, and the First Army paused again to reorganize. The next day Pershing and his most trusted aides, Brigadier Generals McAndrew, Conner, and Drum, discussed the AEF's general officers. They were discouraged that so many generals had not shown the energy, loyalty, and aggressiveness that Pershing required. Before the next major attack began, they agreed, the First Army "team" had to be straightened out and the Second Army established as an operational command. Six generals would lose their commands and return to the United States. Hunter Liggett's First Army would get new, seasoned corps commanders: Hines, Dickman, and Summerall. The Second Army's commander would be Bullard.[2]

1.

Bullard learned that he had been reassigned on October 11, but he was not sure what his new command would be when he met Pershing the next day at Souilly. Bullard's departure from the III Corps was undramatic. Feeling slightly guilty about leaving his command on the eve of another attack, he gathered his modest household staff and left without more than words of thanks to his corps staff. Besides the indispensable Shirey and Henri Secheresse, he took with him only Lieutenant Colonel Wilson, the corps G-1 who had so ably handled traffic and straggler control and other difficult administrative matters for him. In a discussion with Pershing on October 12, he finally learned that Liggett would take command of the First Army and he would have the Second. Bullard also learned that "The Chief" expected him to get the Second Army ready for a major offensive on both sides of the Moselle in the direction of Metz. Pershing briefed him on the status of peace negotiations with Germany, but insisted that the Allies must keep up the attack even though peace seemed near. Bullard was surprised at Pershing's optimism; the III Corps had faced few Germans who had seemed ready to quit. In response, Bullard thanked Pershing for his confidence and motored off to Toul.[3]

Settling into his headquarters, Bullard studied his newly created Army. He started with his Army staff, which he found well organized and functioning. After his difficulties with Bjornstad, he was delighted to have Stuart Heintzelman, elevated to brigadier general, as his chief-of-staff. He had known Heintzelman before the war and respected his professional reputation and character. He was "a better soldier and a more disciplined and straighter man altogether" than Bjornstad. He worried about his Army chief of artillery and Army chief of air service, indicating his understanding of the importance of fire support. He asked for and got two of the best men in the AEF for his staff, Major General William Lassiter for the artillery and Colonel Frank P. Lahm for the aviation units. Both pleased Bullard completely. For corps commander, Bullard had some choice. One of his corps, the French II Colonial, was commanded by an able French general. Bullard's other corps, the IV, became Charles Muir's command. Muir owed his new assignment to Bullard's recommendation to Pershing. Burying their animosity with the dead of the Twenty-Eighth Division along the Vesle, Bullard and Muir found they could work together. Bullard told Pershing during their October 12 meeting that he thought Muir would make a fine corps commander. Pershing approved Muir's elevation to corps command, but kept him in Bullard's Second Army. Bullard did not regret interceding for his longtime professional rival.[4]

Convinced that Pershing would give the Second Army little time to prepare its offensive, Bullard also worried about organizing his artillery and air support and his logistical system. He was satisfied with his staff, although he put pressure on them to perform more effectively with fewer officers than the First Army's headquarters. Only Lassiter's artillery staff met the challenge, but Bullard conceded that an Army was a complex organization to run even with a staff six times larger than III Corps'. While he needed no urging from Pershing to take personal interest in all the planning and to exercise his own judgment, he knew that the huge French staffs which had horrified him a year before were now a practical necessity. He accepted the fact that his working day, unless he was making inspection tours, was just one continuous staff conference.[5]

As he attended briefings and visited his units, Bullard was progressively astounded by the complexity of the logistical arrangements necessary to support an American Army. He was annoyed that it would take at least a month to ready his artillery, air, and service commands for an offensive. He found his subordinates full of promises for the future. He labeled this false optimism "the great American error" and admitted that it characterized the entire American war effort. Everywhere he visited he found serious shortages of skilled personnel and equipment in his specialized units. Only one aspect of his logistical system pleased Bullard. He had inherited the communications network, supply dumps, and facilities created to support the St. Mihiel offensive. His biggest liability was transportation. As long as his troops remained on the defensive, they could be supplied, since the sector was quiet. But if his Army attacked and supply and munitions requirements soared, his Army would be hard-pressed to support the attacking divisions. Accordingly, Bullard stressed the perfection of the Second Army's transportation network, hectoring horse-drawn trains to get their animals in better shape, truck battalions to improve the condition of their vehicles, and railroad units to expand their services. His G-4, Colonel George. P. Tyner, was never satisfied with his truck and horse-drawn transportation, but thought that the Second Army had made a major success by reducing the number of depots between the Army supply sources and the troops by better management. In any event, the Second Army's logistical system was never really tested.[6]

Bullard understood the enormity of a modern army's logistical base, but having his own army brought home modern war's complexity in a staggering way. As he toured his installations, he saw specialized support units and tons of equipment which would have confounded the officers of the Indian-fighting army. When Bullard joined the Army in 1885, there was one small engineer battalion; in the Second Army he had two labor battalions, five railway units, ten service battalions, and elements of eighteen engineer regiments specializing in map-making, mining, quarrying, forestry, electronics and mechanics, highway construction, searchlight use, camouflage, and bridge-building. He had four units whose sole duty was supplying fresh water. For communications he had more than five battalions, including twenty messenger pigeon "loft" units. The Second Army also contained postal units, ordnance repair shops, laundry companies, bath companies, butcher companies, motor maintenance companies, remount units, and dozens of truck and horse transportation units. For medical care, the Army had eight field and evacuation hospitals, six base hospitals, a score of ambulance companies, veterinary units, and mobile surgical units. To collect the Germans' hits and the doctors' misses, there were three graves registration units. Counting his Army artillery units and air service, Bullard had 17,000 Second Army troops under his direct supervision.[7]

For the direct fire support of his infantry, Bullard collected American coast artillery units and French field artillery batteries as his Second Army artillery force. Each corps and division also had its own artillery units, but Bullard never felt that he had sufficient guns for a major drive. His air service was also limited. While he was pleased with Lahm's management of the Second Army's air effort, Bullard had only thirteen American squadrons and four French aircraft and balloon squadrons. There was little American air activity except leaflet dropping and photo reconnaissance, though the American pursuit groups flew combat missions on the last two days of the war. Bullard eventually judged the artillery effort satisfactory and the air support less so, although he appreciated the possibilities of the latter.[8]

The Second Army put together enough of an artillery, air, and logistical organization to make Pershing's Metz offensive, but its capacity for combat ultimately depended upon its infantry. Bullard lacked fighting soldiers. When he took command, he found two small French divisions (both of which left before any serious fighting) and five American divisions. The latter included the Seventh, completing its training after coming to France in August. The other American divisions were battle-weary and understrength survivors of the Meuse-Argonne: the Seventy-Ninth, the Thirty-Seventh, and the all-Negro Ninety-Second. Bullard's lone reserve division was the Twenty-Eighth, worn and thinned by both the Aisne-Marne offensive and the Meuse-Argonne attack. Until the Second Army's divisions had some rest and replacements and got some reinforcements, Bullard was not going to send them anywhere except to man the front and conduct patrols. The help was slow in coming, and Bullard's force was never larger than six divisions. The major changes in assignment to the Second Army did little to increase the army's effectiveness. The French divisions and the Seventy-Ninth were transferred, and in their place Bullard received the expert but weary Fourth, the veteran Thirty-Third, and the demoralized and thinned Thirty-Fifth. Only on the last two days of the war did Bullard get a fresh division, the Eighty-Eighth, a latecomer to France. Although the Second Army had 180,000 men when the war ended, it was short of battle-ready infantry.

2.

As he readied his army for its maiden offensive, Bullard felt not only a little staggered by his command but also uplifted by it. By his elevation to commanding general of the Second Army, he shared with Hunter Liggett the distinction of being the AEF's senior combat leader. Two weeks after arriving in Toul, he learned from a newspaper that he had been appointed a temporary lieutenant general. The promotion came as a mild surprise, since Pershing had been vague about rank in their conversations. On November 1 he pinned on a third star; he and Liggett were the first active officers to hold the rank of lieutenant general since 1906. Like a feudal chieftain, he was spared the annoyance of arranging for his housekeeping and transportation. Around him were his faithful liegemen, all duly rewarded for their loyalty and energy with increased rank. Guy Shirey jumped from captain to lieutenant colonel in about a month. Joining Bullard's personal staff was a reminder of the "old army," Lieutenant Colonel Wesson Seyburn, the son of his friend of Tenth Infantry days, Stephen Seyburn. Bullard had reasons for satisfaction besides having good company and professional advisers. By November he had fully recovered from the neuritis in his arm and his nervous stomach had subsided. When he took command of the Second Army, he had feared that his health would crack with the new responsibility, but he had rallied physically. His optimism about his own performance increased proportionately.[9]

As commanding general of the Second Army, Bullard assumed an outer serenity he had not before shown in France. Before coming to Toul, he had been one of several corps commanders, subject to Pershing's hectoring, AEF General Staff condescension, and his peers' envy. As a lieutenant general and Army commander, he became a public figure and symbol of the AEF. Though he still got patronizing letters from Pershing about how to be an Army commander, he no longer feared AEF Headquarters as he had when he was a division and corps commander. Rather, he enjoyed his new role as "hero" of the AEF and in receiving personal notes from the secretary of war: "I hope . . . the inspiration of these stirring times will sustain you until you and your boys can safely return to your grateful country with your high mission fully accomplished." Bullard feared such flattery was making him fatuous and punished himself for allowing his driver to wreck his car against his orders. "I have not sufficient force to make people do their duty. I'll learn a lesson from this and no doubt I shall be doing pretty well by the time I'm a thousand or two years old."[10] Yet most of the time the general was gracious and poised. A visiting portrait painter thought Bullard had the most patrician looks he had ever seen in the army and was thoroughly captivated by the general's courtesy and soft-spoken candor.[11]

Bullard could afford to relax some because he was convinced that the war was nearly over. He never doubted that Germany deserved its defeat, for he had little respect for German strategy. He concluded that the German 1918 offensive was the major military blunder of the war and that Generals Hindenburg and Ludendorff deserved their present difficulty. He thought that if the Germans had stayed in their defensive lines for another year, the Allies would have sued for peace on German terms. He knew that the German government had changed and that, despite the verbal bellicosity of the French and British generals, the Allied political leaders might accept less than a German unconditional surrender. His intelligence officers told him that the German army was demoralized and weak in trained soldiers, but he saw few signs of a complete enemy collapse. He was ready to send the Second Army's thin divisions against the Hindenburg Line if Pershing thought the blow must be struck.[12]

3.

As Pershing's planners had concluded in 1917, the Woevre Plain between the Meuse and the Moselle was admirable open warfare country. Bullard's lines, resting on the eastern slope of the Heights of the Meuse, overlooked rolling countryside, only slightly broken by low hills, ponds, and scattered woods. Unlike the Meuse-Argonne, here the Germans had no special terrain advantages. While Bullard's front was a bit long (30 miles) for his four front line divisions to cover, it was a *bon secteur*. His left flank was anchored at the village of Fresnes-en-Woevre along the major road between Verdun and Metz. From the left, the Second Army's front ran southeast across Woevre Plain to the Moselle valley and the high ground east of the Moselle above Pont-a-Mousson. Major highways and railroads ran up the Moselle valley on both sides of the river to Metz, while another road split the sector, running to the village of Chambley before forking north to the Verdun-Metz highway and south to the Moselle river. For a staff planning an offensive, the Woevre Plain posed no special challenges.[13]

The German Army was still very much a problem. Abandoning the St. Mihiel salient in September, the Germans had fallen back to a belt of wire, trenches, and fortified strongpoints five miles deep. Having occupied the area for four years and having been backed by the French-built defenses around Metz, the German soldiers were well placed to stop a weak-willed or clumsy attacker. As always, the Germans had skillfully placed their machine guns and sited their artillery to bring the optimum amount of fire upon advancing infantry; the stone farmhouses and small woods became fortified positions protected by masses of wire and infantry outposts. The German troops on the Second Army front were not especially fearsome. In front of Bullard's divisions were eleven German divisions, but only three were rated firstline troops and all the units were worn by the hard fighting since March. Since Bullard's divisions were nearly as spent, the front lines had changed little since the end of the St. Mihiel offensive on September 17.[14]

Knowing that AEF Headquarters was planning a "big push" toward Metz, Bullard let his tired divisions rest only until October 21. The units from his frontline divisions started raiding and patrolling to harass the German outposts and collect intelligence. In two weeks, soldiers from the Second Army conducted 300 raids and patrols, capturing 300 prisoners. In part, the increased fighting was designed to restore the Second Army's combativeness. Bullard was concerned that service on a quiet sector and the peace talks would demoralize his soldiers. In a general order to the army, he stressed that the German army's withdrawal was caused by its battlefield defeats, not by talk. "The moment we stop fighting he will stop going. . . . Leave all expectation and talk of peace. Keep up your training, your vigilance, and your activity. No statement of reasons should be necessary to intelligent men."[15] Until Pershing ordered otherwise, however, there was no general advance. Until November 1, when some German reserves were displaced toward the Rhine, the Second Army was deployed primarily for defense astride the Moselle valley. Learning from the AEF general staff that German units were leaving Metz, Bullard displaced his artillery and reserves forward in anticipation of a general offensive.[16]

The Second Army awaited instructions from the commander-in-chief. The guidance it received was vague, for false optimism had seized AEF Headquarters. In the Meuse-Argonne, Liggett's First Army had finally punctured the last defenses in front of Sedan and was shelling the German roads and rail lines north of the Meuse. North and west of the First Army's sector, the Allies were still pushing the Germans back through Belgium. Pershing himself was exhilarated by the First Army's final victory in the Meuse-Argonne and was already thinking of extending the American offensive southeast of Verdun by ordering the right flank corps of the First Army and the Second Army to attack the German positions between the Meuse and the Moselle. This attack, bypassing Metz to the northwest, would sever the lateral railroad in a second place and threaten the Briey-Longwy mines. Since Austria-Hungry had accepted Allied armistice terms on November 4, Pershing assumed that the withdrawal of Austrian divisions would cripple the Metz defenses.

On November 5 Pershing gave Bullard orders to make limited attacks in preparation for a major offensive. "The Chief's" instructions were more exhortation than tactical guidance. He wrote that victory in the Meuse-Argonne had compromised the entire German situation west of the Moselle, a condition that demanded "boldness and most energetic action by both the First and Second Armies." Pershing wanted open warfare methods and active pursuit aimed at "the complete destruction of the enemy's armed forces." For the moment, the Second Army should conduct raids and advance on the axis Chambley-Gorze. This pointed Bullard's army toward Metz with his center corps, the IV, leading the way with its one frontline division, the Twenty-Eighth, in the attack.[17]

Bullard responded to Pershing's instructions by increasing his raids and planning a general advance west of Metz, the latter operation to be launched if the Germans began a large-scale withdrawal across the Woevre Plain. Bullard's soldiers found little sign of German collapse. Their patrols encountered machine gun fire, shelling, and stubborn infantry outposts, although they also found some abandoned fortifications. Pershing, however, visiting Toul on November 7, "found indications of withdrawal on that front," probably aerial reports of wagons headed to Metz. He ordered a general advance by the Second Army for November 11. Later the same day he had Fox Conner write Bullard to warn him that Foch might demand six American divisions for another offensive. Foch wanted Bullard to envelop Metz from the southeast while the French Eighth Army attacked east of the Moselle into Alsace. Additional divisions moved into Bullard's sector: the weary Thirty-Fifth and fresh Eighty-Eighth. The target date for the joint offensive was set at November 14. To further complicate Bullard's decisions, the commander-in-chief phoned the next day that Foch thought an armistice was imminent, but that the attacks must continue.[18]

Uncertain about the direction in which Pershing would eventually order the Second Army's main effort, Bullard ordered all four of his frontline divisions to make limited attacks on November 10. On his left, the Thirty-Third Division was to advance in a northeasterly direction beside the First Army's Eighty-First Division. Bullard's two center divisions were to make the Chambley-Gorze advance west of the Moselle. On the east bank of the Moselle the Ninety-Second Division was supposed to start up the east side of the Moselle in anticipation of the November 14 assault. While Bullard ordered all four divisions to jump off at first light on November 10, he allowed the corps and division commanders to establish limited objectives, for the tactical situation was much too uncertain. He knew that there had been some German withdrawals, but he was not as certain as Pershing that the German army to his front was in collapse. Shortly after issuing his own order, Bullard received more instructions from Pershing, this time to make a general advance on November 10 in pursuit of the withdrawing Germans. While he was again pleased that he had anticipated "The Chief's" orders, he was by no means confident that his divisions would make major gains against the Hindenburg Line. If his Army were to mount the November 14 attack east of the Moselle, he had no desire to be overcommitted west of the river.[19]

As Bullard had anticipated, the November 10 attacks were not very impressive in terms of ground gained or enemy destroyed. The day came wet and foggy, limiting air support and artillery observation. All four divisions drove in the German outposts and took some manned strongpoints, but were halted by long-range machine gun fire and artillery fire. As Colonel William N. Haskell, Bullard's G-3, noted: "The operations established definitely that the enemy was holding his position of resistance in force and defending it with the utmost determination." Bullard was not especially disappointed by the day's action, but ordered another attack for the next morning.

On the morning of the 11th the Second Army attacked, again with only modest success. Of the four committed divisions, only the Thirty-Third pressed its attack, losing 1,500 men in the two-day offensive. With rumors of an impending armistice sweeping the troops and with Bullard's instructions to press only where the Germans were retreating, the small gains are understandable. At 6:30 on the morning of November 11, Bullard learned from AEF headquarters that an armistice would begin at 11 and that his troops should halt in place at that time. Pershing did nothing to stop the morning attacks, and there is no evidence that Bullard suggested a halt. When he learned of the armistice, Bullard had his staff inform the corps commanders and then left his forward command post for the front. There he saw "the last of it" and listened to "the crack of the last guns in the greatest war of all ages."[20] He watched his troops, unbelieving, emerge cautiously from their trenches. Like his men, Bullard was stunned by the sudden silence. He was happy to see the Great War end.

4.

Among Bullard's problems during the short life of the Second Army was the Ninety-Second Division, the AEF's single complete Negro division. If the Ninety-Second absorbed more of Bullard's time than any other unit in his Army, it was because he himself took special interest in the organization. He emerged from the experience embittered by the War Department's policies on racial units in the AEF and, because of his rank and experience, he subsequently had some influence on the War Department's decision not to create another black combat division in any future war. When Bullard described his problems with the Ninety-Second in his postwar memoirs, he was assaulted by the Negro press as the worst sort of virulent Southern racist. While he was undoubtedly a white supremacist of the paternalistic sort, Bullard's attitudes and experiences with the Ninety-Second were not as simplistically doctrinaire or hopelessly racist as his critics or even he himself assumed after the war.[21]

Pressured by the National Association for the Advancement of Colored People and by other white and black racial egalitarians, the War Department had reluctantly agreed to create two Negro divisions in the AEF. It would have preferred to use all its black soldiers as labor troops, fearing that undertrained and poorly led black infantry would be ineffective and casualty-prone. Nevertheless, Newton D. Baker ordered two black divisions formed, the Ninety-Second and the Ninety-Third. The latter organization never fought as a division, but its infantry regiments, brigaded with the French, fought well in Europe.

From its arrival in France in June 1918, the Ninety-Second was an AEF problem child. The reasons were more complicated than the racial hostility between white and black troops and the exaggerated fears of AEF Headquarters that French and Negro fraternization would spark racial clashes. The division's very existence stirred deep emotions and prejudices, for its supporters regarded it as a blow against racial discrimination in the army and American society. The division's generals and colonels were army officers with considerable experience with black troops. Two, the division commander, Major General Charles C. Ballou, and the chief-of-staff, Colonel Allen J. Greer, were deeply involved in a professional and emotional sense with their command. Ballou, a classmate of Pershing and a colonel in the regular army, had served for four years as major and lieutenant colonel of the Twenty-Fourth Infantry. He had willingly established and commanded the first training camp for black officers in 1917. On one point Ballou was a racial radical in the United States Army: he believed that black troops should have black officers, at least at the company level. He recognized that to make allowances for his black officers was a kind of racism (however well-meaning), but he feared that if he applied a single standard for officer performance, the black officers would fail completely and the division's enemies would disband it. Ballou antagonized both whites and blacks with his vacillation and his ambiguous egalitarianism. Professionally, Greer was a more impressive officer. At forty, he had had a distinguished military career, winning the Medal of Honor in the Philippines. He was an honor graduate of the School of the Line and Staff College. A graduate of the University of Tennessee, he also had a law degree from the University of Minnesota.

The infantry brigade commanders were both excellent career officers. The regimental commanders were also able men, as ambitious as their peers and aware that they were risking their reputations with the Ninety-Second. They were not so eager (at least after the fact) as Ballou to have black officers, although they had reasonable confidence in their enlisted men, based on the regular army's post-Civil War experience with black regiments, both regulars and Volunteers. Proportionately, there were more regulars among the white officers in the Ninety-Second than the rest of the AEF's divisions. Perhaps because they were regulars, their expectations were too high, their careers too important, and their disappointments too keen for their own and the division's good.

The key to the division's difficulties was the relationship of the white and black officers, a friction built no doubt on reciprocated prejudice, but fed by the strains of training and leading the division in combat. In the regular army, it had been axiomatic that an officer of black troops had to take more interest in his mens' well-being and training than was necessary with white troops. This was a concept of leadership that some of the division's newly commissioned black lieutenants would not accept, apparently feeling that they should have all the prerogatives of officership in billeting, messing, relaxing, and avoiding danger. Their vision of officership as a social privilege was common in the AEF and demoralized white troops as well as black. The group of black officers who took such a casual attitude to their duties and military self-education was largely from the college-educated Negro middle class, the vanguard of the civil rights movement. They were especially sensitive to discrimination and white patronizing. They also did not get along well with black officers who had been sergeants in the regular army. The middle-class black lieutenants regarded the former noncommissioned officers, most of whom became their company commanders, as insufficiently militant on racial issues and too anxious to follow army ways in their relations with white officers.

The animosity among the Ninety-Second's officers was particularly dangerous, for the enlisted men of the division were largely rural blacks of very limited education and low self-esteem. Unlike the black infantry regiments of the Ninety-Third Division, the regiments of the Ninety-Second had no roots in the black communities of northern cities and little of the social cohesiveness that encouraged the black National Guardsmen. Unlike the white divisions and the Ninety-Third, the Ninety-Second never had enough self-motivated noncommissioned officers and privates whose bravery and initiative filled the leadership vacuum when officers fell or failed.[22]

After its arrival in France, the Ninety-Second Division had its problems with equipment, training, and officer turnover, but no more than other AEF divisions. It could afford them less. Before he came to France, General Ballou was sure that his black officers would make up with their dedication and inspiration whatever deficiencies the division had, but they turned out to be his biggest disappointment. He had written Pershing that the Ninety-Second "will prove the best close in fighters in your Army, which means the best in the world." But after the division's initial experiences on a quiet front, Pershing decided that the Ninety-Second was a disaster. The problem was its company officers, whose derelictions were so flagrant that even the French army wanted no part of the division. Moreover, the white officers wanted to get rid of the worst black officers. Ballou would not remove incompetents, although Greer pressed him on the issue.[23]

The division was moved into reserve and used as labor troops during the Meuse-Argonne campaign, which did nothing for its self-esteem. The one regiment that saw combat might as well not have been committed. While its liaison mission on the flank of the First Army was difficult and ill-organized, two of its battalions faded away under sporadic shelling and machine gun fire and its third advanced only when the battalion commander kept his officers at their posts with a drawn pistol.[24] After this debacle, the division was sent south astride the Moselle as part of the French Eighth Army.

Bullard inherited the Ninety-Second Division and all its problems when the Second Army was created, for the division was already holding the right flank of his new sector. He knew little about the division, except that it was deemed not battle-worthy by Pershing's headquarters. Yet he had considerable interest in its plight. He remembered the trials of the Third Alabama Volunteers vividly and he had solid military reasons for trying to resurrect the division, since it was the largest in his army. At least since 1899 he had thought often about the question of racial prejudice and recognized his own bias. Race prejudice could not be reasoned with, but "it cannot be ignored or denied, for that would be to attempt to neglect conditions and a problem must be solved upon its conditions, not on theory." He believed racial prejudice had to be faced and dealt with, but not by coercion, for that only spurred increased resistance to change. "Race prejudice anywhere . . .

can be softened by no positive measures of man but only by a policy of let alone, of leaving time and association—in no other way.''[25] Although such a view hardly qualified Bullard as an integrationist, his attitudes were not those of a reflexive bigot.

In his first contact with the Ninety-Second's problems, Bullard was distressed to learn that Ballou had just requested that thirty officers be dismissed for cowardice. Ballou avoided courts-martial only because he was convinced that no black officer would testify against another because they had all fled. Nevertheless, five had been court-martialed for cowardice in the face of the enemy before Bullard knew of the matter. The other twenty-five officers were before dismissal boards. Both the courts-martial and dismissal boards were made up entirely of white officers. Bullard could not decide whether Ballou's actions were unjust or impolitic, but he certainly thought them stupid. ''The justice of the white man is injustice to the Negro,'' he wrote, also noting that ''the 'all white' will cast doubt upon their recommendations should those recommendations be adverse to the Negroes and the partisans of the Negroes will howl.'' In cases in which hearings had not yet begun, Bullard ordered a halt in the proceedings. ''An error, slip in treatment of the Negro in the Army means ruin to the man who makes it.''[26]

Bullard then talked with both the white and black officers about the division's demoralization and tactical failures. He found the whites totally discouraged and the black officers much too forgiving. He continued his talks with the black officers, asking their opinion about the courts-martial. He got no complaints about the trials' fairness, but the black officers protested their lack of representation on the dismissal boards. Bullard ordered Ballou to appoint black officers to the boards.[27]

Worried about the cowardice courts-martial, Bullard let them continue, but attempted to get the sentences modified, since four officers had been sentenced to death. While he could not get the AEF Judge Advocate General to find technicalities for dismissing the cases, he recommended that the sentences be suspended and the officers dismissed. The War Department eventually followed his recommendation.[28]

He could do nothing about the low morale and battle-shy attitude of the Ninety-Second, a fact that shook his own self-esteem. By November 1 he had concluded that the Ninety-Second's men were ''really inferior soldiers,'' though he attributed it to the division's uninspired leadership. Its soldiers were ''hopelessly inferior'' and admitted it, an attitude that showed they had no pride or motivation. Everyone had told them they were no good, and they believed it, which ''shows their general inferiority.'' Just before the Second Army's brief offensive, Bullard concluded that the Ninety-Second would never be battle-worthy, but that perhaps a change of commanding generals would help. When the division's attacks did not gain much ground on November 10 and 11, he saw it as further proof of the division's demoralization, but also concluded that the division's ineptness was ''as much the fault of Gen. Ballou as of the Negroes.''[29]

Bullard was not entirely fair in assessing the Ninety-Second's performance on

10 and 11 November, for one infantry brigade did advance east of the Moselle, but on the west side of the river the other infantry brigade did not budge from its lines. Bullard admitted that this brigade's nonassault was in part a matter of command, for there had been insufficient coordination with the Seventh Division's flanking units. Whatever the reasons, he'd had enough of the Ninety-Second and Ballou. "I shall ask to be relieved of him or of them—I'd prefer that it be both." On November 14, he asked Pershing to relieve Ballou, which the commander-in-chief did four days later; the broken commander of the Ninety-Second returned to the United States and his permanent rank of colonel. Still not satisfied with the division's functioning, Bullard transferred Colonel Greer and replaced him with his trusted G-1, Colonel George K. Wilson. Both Ballou and Greer, their careers blighted, blamed Bullard's patronizing racism for the division's demoralization.[30]

The Armistice did not end Bullard's ambiguous relationship with the Ninety-Second Division. Concerned about indiscipline and fraternization in his army area, he wanted the Ninety-Second Division sent home. At the root of his request was his deep-seated distaste for black male—white female sex relations, which he tended to label as "rape," whatever the circumstances. Getting rid of the Ninety-Second, he thought, would ease the rising tension between all of his troops and the French villagers. Bullard had little trouble persuading Pershing to send the division home. He himself was convinced that he had saved the French population from mass rape by his blacks. "They are brutes."[31] Disgusted that the division had taken so much of his time with so little return in military effectiveness, he fell victim to the same emotionalism that had led Ballou to believe he would lead the hardest fighters in the AEF.

5.

Without a war to hold the Second Army together, Bullard let a couple of days of mild celebration seize his army and then prescribed "the most stringent and unrelenting discipline." He had no intention of commanding a mob under any circumstances, and there was the remote possibility his army might have to fight again or march into Germany. On November 19 he held a series of conferences to explain his approach to maintaining the discipline of the Second Army. While he did not ignore the need for authoritarian discipline, he stressed the need for constant training and counseling to preserve the honor, duty, and reputation of the American army. He insisted that the mission of the postarmistice Second Army must be explained down to the "last soldier." He was pleasantly surprised by his commanders' favorable response, especially since they were "regular officers who by their habit of live [*sic*] know practically but one way of securing discipline, namely, by force." Bullard's program for his Army was simple and thorough. To show Europeans that the American army was as excellent in garrison as in war, his organizations would provide better personnel administration, food, and services for the men and would demand in return the strictest military bearing and courtesy, a hard but varied work schedule, and flawless care of equipment and animals.

Bullard emphasized that commanding officers had better pay attention to all aspects of his program or lose their commands.[32]

Between their military training, athletics, and entertainment, the troops of the Second Army remained occupied, relatively continent, and sober. The AEF also formed a system of academic and vocational schools, which helped pass the time. Bullard thought that his men were keeping their spirits up beyond his expectations; he attributed it to the fact that the draft had brought a true cross section of America's young men instead of the misfits the regular army got. For the minority of the troops upon whom hard work and moral suasion didn't work, there were courts-martial. After the Armistice, Second Army court cases increased three-fold. Bullard, moreover, did not neglect his promise to sack any commander whose troops showed signs of inattention and demoralization; in the first month of the peace, he relieved two brigadiers. He recognized that it was difficult for any regular officer to be as interested in peacetime duties as in wartime command. Already he saw scores of regular officers relaxing into peacetime lethargy. If general officers could not maintain satisfactory standards of performance, how could they expect their subordinates to work at their duties? Starting with the brigadiers, Bullard had his division commanders purge the incompetents from their units.[33]

Next to his army's state of training and discipline, Bullard worried most about relations with the French population in his area. The part of Lorraine which the Second Army occupied had been badly scarred by the war, the scenery running heavily to splintered trees, fallow fields, and rubble-filled shells of villages. The trash of armies lined its roads. Bullard spent much of his time coping with the problems created by an army of seven combat divisions billeted among civilians who no longer saw them as saviors. In February 1919 the Second Army area was expanded to include all of Luxembourg, which did nothing to simplify its civil affairs problems. Both French civil and military officials demanded the release of facilities, high prices for services, and reduced American use of the rail system. At the same time, the French were irritated by the fraternization of the American and German soldiers who policed up the battlefield and collected German salvage. To do what he could to reduce the tension, Bullard worked closely with the French army, made many visits to civil authorities, and occupied his troops with work. He felt confident that his relations with the Lorrainers were satisfactory, but less so with the Luxembourgers. He wrote General Summerall that occupations were always difficult. "If it were Philippinos, Moros or Cubans I could make it all right, but the Luxembourgers have got me stumped. I have no doubt but that it will come out all right after a little more study."[34]

When he toured the occupied Rhineland and the American enclave at Coblenz, Bullard was struck by the relative order and affluence of the German population. He got his first surprise in Metz. French officials had reported that the city's population had been starved and brutalized by the Germans, but Bullard thought them better fed, clothed, and housed than the French in Toul. It began to occur to him that perhaps Germany was not so downtrodden, that heavy reparations might be in order. As he visited American headquarters, he was amazed to find the American generals and their staffs living in splendid castles, waited upon by German servants and wooed by German civil officials. He thought that the Germans were just as clever as the Filipinos and Cubans he had known, since they were encouraging lenient treatment by telling the gullible Americans how much nicer they were than the French. Bullard hoped he and his troops could get home as quickly as possible.[35]

As a prominent general, Bullard shared the military honors that came to the AEF generals who ended the war in Pershing's esteem. From the War Department in early December came the notification that he was now a permanent major general in the United States Army, jumping seven more senior brigadiers. From Pershing's headquarters came the award of a Distinguished Service Medal for his service in the AEF. "The Chief" himself decorated Bullard. Bullard thanked Pershing for all the duties and honors he had been given and pledged "the sincerest loyalty of which I am capable, for all things present and to come." Among the things to come were a wave of foreign decorations. The French government awarded him a *Croix de Guerre* with palm and made him a commander of the *Legion d'Honneur*. The Belgians made him a grand officer of the Order of Leopold and the Italian government gave him the Crosses of Saint Maurice and Saint Lazarus. As his honors pyramided, Bullard was swamped with congratulatory telegrams and cables. While he appreciated the notes from old comrades, he was amused by how many new friends he had in the officer corps, especially men with whom he had never gotten along. These were spoils of war he could understand and appreciate.[36]

On Christmas Eve, 1918, Bullard reflected on all that had happened in the past year. Only twelve months before he had been at the First Division headquarters at nearby Gondrecourt, a determined but bewildered division commander. He now felt less burdened commanding an army many times larger than that division. Considering the historic expendability of wartime American generals, he had at the time hoped to survive just six months as a division commander:

> My thought was that my country, the government, our authorities would act toward me as I've seen them act toward other commanders who have failed through no fault or rather lack of our military system; I was prepared to be sacrificed for the public's failure to have a military system. But I was not sacrificed: the public did not demand it, I don't know exactly why, perhaps the public realized how serious was the situation, perhaps because the President of the U.S. knows there was no military system and smothered its failures. Certainly there were many great failures and certainly there have been no demands for victims.[37]

Lieutenant General Robert Lee Bullard could not really believe his good fortune and the new prestige of the career officer corps. He was not confident that it would last.

Pershing and his staff shared some of Bullard's amazement that they had made a significant contribution to the Allied victory. They steeled themselves for the recriminations they felt would follow the Armistice. The AEF's worries centered on two internal army matters. One was Pershing's relationship with the War Department, particularly General Peyton C. March and the General Staff. The other central worry was the Pershing clique's fear that disgruntled generals and National Guard officers would stir public animosity and demand a congressional investigation of Pershing's handling of his National Guard divisions, especially Clarence Edwards' Twenty-Sixth and the Thirty-Fifth. Before Pershing returned to the United States, General Harbord proposed that Pershing tell his story of the AEF's accomplishments in a popular book and thus head off his critics. "The Chief" was impressed by Harbord's suggestion and continued gauging the loyalty of his staff and major subordinates.[38]

Bullard felt the growing conservatism at Chaumont. Until the war ended, he did not appreciate the extent of Pershing's disagreements with General March, but he noticed the AEF staff's reluctance to push any army-wide reforms. When he proposed creating a better awards and promotion system, his suggestions were ignored. His proposals for general staff reorganization, reforms which clarified the role of a chief-of-staff and gave the "Gs" a more functional division of responsibility, were shelved. Bullard was under no illusion that his ideas were especially novel, but he feared the army would not profit by its experiences in France. For the sake of internal peace and protection from public scrutiny, the army's high command was lapsing into the safe paths of bureaucracy and sloth. He admitted, however, that he had no stomach for an internal army or public fight about the AEF's performance.[39]

The winter days of ceremonies faded into the early days of planting in Lorraine. Though the peace conference at Paris dragged on and President Wilson came and went, Bullard felt there would be no more war for now. Turning away from his diminishing administrative duties, he and his aides traveled the length of the Western Front and southern France. They collected postcards, gaped at cathedrals, sipped aperitifs, and told funny stories of their days with the First Division. For Bullard, the travels were a pilgrimage in search of the war's meaning and his part in it. He was just beginning to understand how much the war had cost the Allies as he rode through one shattered town after another and saw the ruined fields that lacked the farmers and stock to restore them.

Of all the battlefields he saw, none affected him more than Flanders. He had had a vague respect for the British generals before his visit. After seeing the terrain around Ypres and the Somme, he wondered how any sane man could even plan an attack there, let alone make one. As his understanding of the war grew, his own sense of participation in it diminished. What had he done? Perhaps his French citation had the answer: "He has communicated his offensive spirit to his troops." Bullard considered that the highest compliment a combat officer could receive. He learned from friends that he was a "hero" of the Great War, the Indian-fighting Alabama country boy who had smashed the Hun and inspired the French. He replied that he thought that the newspapers had exaggerated his personal impact on the war. "Whatever I have done appeared to me at the time to be quite natural, simple and absolutely necessary. . . . I am not conscious of having done anything, but rather of having had something carry me along since I have been in France; and that something I believe has been just the American spirit and momentum. I simply went along with the soldiers."[40]

By early April 1919, Pershing was sure that the Second Army and its six combat divisions would not be needed. After the long winter of keeping the American army together, the orders were welcome. Bullard was in good spirits. He was pleased that Pershing had made the effort to show American reporters the battlefields and explain the AEF's achievements before the inevitable, sensational postwar scandals could begin at home. His respect for "The Chief" was as high as ever, although Pershing still impressed him as one of the most uninspiring great men he had ever met. Pershing's last inspection trip to Toul was cordial, and Bullard again thanked the general for his favor, a show of emotion that irritated "The Chief." Bullard thought that perhaps Pershing was the true "hero" of the war and that he might be a presidential candidate. He decided, however, that Pershing's diffidence would prevent him from being a popular candidate. That Pershing would hereafter dominate the army he had little doubt.[41]

With a half-dozen holdovers from his household staff, Bullard went to the embarkation port of Brest. He had his papers arranged and submitted with amusement to Pershing's mandatory venereal disease inspection. On May 14, 1919, he was aboard the transport *Kaiserin Augusta Victoria*; two years after leaving Hoboken, he was returning on another German liner. Aboard the ship he read American newspapers. There seemed to be civil turmoil and upheaval everywhere. The United States was "proceeding rapidly in the direction of abolishing capital" and desperately needed strong men to resist the "disorderly and revolutionary" labor unions. He wondered what kind of country he was going home to, but this was not his greatest concern. As the *Kaiserin Augusta Victoria* turned west across the Bay of Biscay, trailed by white waves and squalling gulls, Lieutenant General Robert Lee Bullard, DSM, wondered most about the army he would find in America and his place in it.[42]

NOTES

John J. Pershing, *My Experiences in the World War,* 2 vols. (New York: Frederick A. Stokes, 1931), II, pp. 335, 377-378; Brig. Gen. M. Craig to Maj. Gen. J. G. Harbord, September 16, 1918, "Personal War Letters," James G. Harbord Papers.

For the history of the Second Army, see "Second Army" in Army War College, *Order of Battle of the United States Land Forces in the World War: AEF;* GHQ, *Armies, Corps, SOS* (Washington: Government Printing Office, 1931), pp. 150-169; "Report of the Commanding General, 2d Army," March 2, 1919, with annexes, in General Headquarters, Second Army, "Reports," AEF Organization Records, Records of the American Expeditionary Force, RG 120; and AEF Organization Records: "War Diaries: Second

Army," October 12, 1918-April 15, 1919, RG 120. The latter includes all intelligence summaries, operations reports, field orders, and strength reports for the Second Army.

²Diarybook 9, entry, October 7, 1918, BP; Pershing diary, entry, October 11, 1918, John J. Pershing Papers; cables, Pershing to AGWAR, October 11 and 13, 1918, "AEF Confidential Cables Sent," Harbord Papers; Brig. Gen. J. McAndrew to Maj. Gen. J. G. Harbord, October 21, 1918, "Military War Activity," Harbord Papers.

Pershing's policy on the promotion of corps and army commanders is explicit in Gen. J. J. Pershing to Gen. P. C. March, July 27, 1918, General Correspondence, 1897-1930, General Peyton C. March Papers, Manuscript Division, Library of Congress.

³Diarybook 9, entry, October 14, 1918, BP.

⁴Diarybook 9, entry, October 14, 1918, BP; R. L. Bullard to J. G. Harbord, August 24, 1934, Harbord Papers/NY Historical Society.

⁵Diarybook 9, entry, October 15, 1918, BP. Bullard's activities may be verified in the "Correspondence of the Chief of Staff, 2d Army," GHQ Second Army, AEF Organization Records, RG 120. Bullard elaborated on his diary notes on his Second Army staff organization in *Personalities and Reminiscences of the War* (New York: Doubleday, Page, 1925), pp. 283-284.

⁶Diarybook 9, entries, October 15-28, 1918, BP; "Report of the Fourth Section, General Staff, Headquarters Second Army, American Expeditionary Force," January 1, 1919, annex 4 to "Report of the Commanding General, 2d Army," RG 120.

⁷For a resumé of the Second Army's logistical organization, see *Order of Battle of the United States Land Forces in the World War: AEF: GHQ, Armies, Corps, SOS,* p. 151.

⁸Bullard, autobiography, p. 8, BP; "Resume of Second Army Air Service Operations, Oct 12th-Dec. 31st, 1918," n.d., Annex 7 to "Report of the Commanding General, 2d Army," RG 120. See also Albert F. Simpson, ed., *The World War I Diary of Col. Frank P. Lahm, Air Service, A.E.F.* (Maxwell AFB, Ala.: Aerospace Studies Institute, 1970), pp. 141-179.

⁹Diarybook 9, entries, October 15-November 10, 1918, BP; Lt. Gen. R. L. Bullard to Brig. Gen. C. King, December 6, 1918, King Papers.

¹⁰Gen. J. J. Pershing to Lt. Gen. R. L. Bullard, November 1, 1918, General Correspondence, Pershing Papers; N. D. Baker to Lt. Gen. R. L. Bullard, October 16, 1918, BP; Diarybook 9, entry, October 26, 1918, BP.

¹¹Joseph Cummings Chase, *Soldiers All: Portraits and Sketches of the Men of the A.E.F.* (New York: George H. Doran, 1920), pp. 29-30.

¹²Diarybook 9, entries, October 17-November 3, 1918, BP.

¹³This topographical description is drawn from American Battle Monuments Commission, *American Armies and Battlefields in Europe* (Washington: Government Printing Office, 1938), pp. 105-166.

¹⁴Daily intelligence reports, October 12-November 1, 1918, in AEF Organization Records: "War Diaries: Second Army," RG 120.

¹⁵Headquarters, Second Army, General Order 7, October 24, 1918, in "Report of the Adjutant General," annex 18 to "Report of the Commanding General, 2d Army," RG 120.

¹⁶The discussion of the operations of the Second Army is based upon the "Report of the Assistant Chief of Staff, G-3," annex 3 to "Report of the Commanding General, 2d Army," RG 120. This report also contains basic orders and reports for the Second Army, some of which are also reprinted in *USA/WW, 1917-1919,* IX, pp. 415-469.

A detailed valuable study is Colonel James V. Heidt, "Operations of the 2d Army during the 3rd Phase of the Meuse-Argonne," 1923, IS monograph, ISL (Colonel Heidt was a regimental commander in the Seventh Division). See also Bullard, *Personalities and Reminiscences,* pp. 299-306.

[17]Commander-in-Chief to Commanding General, 2d Army, "Instructions for Future Operations," November 5, 1918, in annex 3 to "Report of the Commanding General, 2d Army, RG 120.

[18]Pershing diary, entries, November 5-10, 1918, Pershing Papers; Brig. Gen. F. Conner to Lt. Gen. R. L. Bullard, November 7, 1918, reprinted in Bullard, *Personalities and Reminiscences,* pp. 301-302; Gen. J. J. Pershing to Lt. Gen. R. L. Bullard, November 8, 1918, Pershing Papers.

[19]Diarybook 10, entry, November 9, 1918, BP.

[20]Diarybook 10, entry, November 11, 1918, BP; Pershing diary, entry, November 11, 1918, Pershing Papers; memo, CG, 2d Army to Commander-in-Chief, GHQ (G-3), "Special Report of Operations of Second Army, 10/11 November 1918," December 29, 1918, appended to "Report of the Commanding General, 2d Army," RG 120; Liggett, *The AEF,* pp. 234-236; Frederic L. Huidekoper, *The History of the 33rd Division, A. E. F.* 3 vols. (Springfield, Ill.: Illinois State Historical Library, 1921), I, pp. 173-234.

[21]Bullard autobiography, pp. 155-159, BP.

[22]The experience of the Ninety-Second Division is discussed in Arthur E. Barbeau, and Florette Henri, *The Unknown Soldiers: Black American Troops in World War I* (Philadelphia: Temple University Press, 1974) pp. 56-88, 137-163. The Army or "military efficiency" side of the argument is best presented in Office of the Chief of Staff, War Department, "An Analytical Study of the Ninety-Second (92nd) Division, Prepared by the Historical Section of the Army War College," copy in the USAMHRC, Carlisle Barracks, and the Historical Section, Army War College, "The Colored Soldier in the U.S. Army," May 1942, USAMHRC. The latter study is especially valuable, for it contains studies that date from 1924 on the Ninety-Second Division and extensive personal testimony collected by Ballou and Greer from the division's white officers (hereafter cited as "The Colored Soldier in the U.S. Army"). Col. A. J. Greer to Sen. K. D. McKellar, December 6, 1918, reprinted in *The Crisis,* 18 (May 1919), pp. 19-20.
  The Ninety-Second Division's black officers had their contemporary champions, most of them black journalists and historians associated with the civil rights movement. The important accounts are Emmett J. Scott, *The American Negro in the World War* (n.p., 1919), pp. 130-196; Charles H. Williams, *Sidelights on Negro Soldiers* (Boston: B. J. Brimmer, 1923), pp. 156-193; W.E.B. DuBois, "An Essay toward a History of the Black Man in the Great War," *The Crisis,* 18 (June 1919), pp. 78-86; Howard H. Long, "The Negro Soldier in the Army of the United States," and William H. Hastie, "Negro Officers in Two World Wars," in *Journal of Negro Education,* 12 (Summer 1943), pp. 307-323.

[23]Brig. Gen. C. C. Ballou to Gen. J. J. Pershing, October 20, 1917, General Correspondence, Pershing Papers; Pershing diary, entry, August 22, 1918, Pershing Papers; Pershing, *My Experiences in the World War* II, p. 228; Stackpole Diary, entry, October 3, 1918, George C. Marshall Library.

[24]Memo, Lt. Col. R. P. Harbold, Division Inspector, to CG, 92nd Division, "Investigation of the 368th Infantry," October 12, 1918, and memo, Maj. J. M. Merrill, Commanding Officer 1st Bn 368th Infantry to CO., 368th Infantry, "Operations of the Battalion, Officers and Men, during the period Sept. 26-30th," October 3, 1918, both appendices to "The Colored Soldier in the U.S. Army."

[25]Notebook 18, entry, October 12, 1910, BP.

[26]Diarybook, 9, entry, October 25, 1918, BP; memo, Maj. Gen. C. C. Ballou to

Commanding General, IV Corps, "Inefficient Officers," October 12, 1918, appended to "The Colored Soldier in the U.S. Army."

[27]Diarybook, 9 entries, October 26 and 27, 1918, BP.

[28]Bullard autobiography, pp. 155-159, BP; Diarybook 9, entries, November 1 and 7, 1918, BP.

[29]Diarybook 9, entries, November 1, 6, and 11, 1918, BP.

[30]Diarybook 10, entry, November 12, 1918; telegram, CG 2d Army to C-in-C, GHQ AEF, November 14, 1918, General Correspondence, Pershing Papers.

For Ballou and Greer on Bullard, see memo, Col. C. C. Ballou to Assistant Commandant, General Staff College, "Use to be Made of Negroes in the U.S. Military Service," March 14, 1920, appended to "The Colored Soldier in the U.S. Army": Col. A. J. Greer to Sen. K. D. McKellar, December 6, 1918, previously cited; memo, Lt. Col. Allen J. Greer to Assistant Commandant, General Staff College, "Use to be Made of Negroes in the U.S. Military Service," April 13, 1920, appended to "The Colored Soldier in the U.S. Army."

[31]Diarybook 10, entries, November 29 and December 6, 1918, BP.

[32]Diarybook 10, entries, November 14 and 19, 1918, BP; Commanding General, 2d Army, AEF, memorandum, November 19, 1918, BP.

[33]Diarybook 10, entries, November 19, 29, and 30, 1918, BP; "Report of the Judge Advocate," April 15, 1919, annex 21 to "Report of the Commanding General, 2d Army," RG 120.

[34]Lt. Gen. R. L. Bullard to Maj. Gen. C. P. Summerall, December 24, 1918, Charles P. Summerall Papers; Diarybook 10, entries, December 1, 1918-January 17, 1919, BP; Correspondence, December 1918 and January 1919, in "Correspondence of the Commanding General, 2d Army," AEF Organization Records, RG 120; Bullard, *Personalities and Reminiscences,* pp. 328-337.

[35]Diarybook 10, entry, December 8, 1918, and entries, January 1919, BP.

[36]Lt. Gen. R. L. Bullard to Gen. J. J. Pershing, December 7, 1918, Pershing Papers; Diarybook 10, entries, November 14 and December 12, 1918, BP; Lt. Gen. R. L. Bullard to Brig. Gen. F. Parker, December 29, 1918, Parker Papers; Lt. Gen. R. L. Bullard to Maj. Gen. C. P. Summerall, December 24, 1918, Summerall Papers.

[37]Diarybook 10, entry, December 24, 1918, BP.

[38]Maj. Gen. J. G. Harbord to Gen. J. J. Pershing, April 5, 1919, "Pershing-Harbord Correspondence," Harbord Papers.

[39]Diarybook 10, entries, February 16-May 15, 1919; memo, Lt. Gen. R. L. Bullard, CG Second Army, to Adj. Gen., AEF, December 18, 1918, Harold B. Fiske Papers, RG 316.

[40]Lt. Gen. R. L. Bullard to John Seyburn, January 3, 1919, and to W. H. Thomas, December 18, 1918, both in "Correspondence of the Commanding General, 2d Army," AEF Organizations Records, RG 120. Bullard's impressions of Europe are from Diarybook 10, entries, January-March 1919, BP.

[41]Diarybook 10, entries, April 1-15, 1919, BP.

[42]Diarybook 10, entries, April 20-May 14, 1919, BP.

VI *AFTER THE WAR*
1919-1947

I've learned that one must expect to lose one thing after another that he has had in life until only himself is left as he marches onward toward and into the grave without anything or anybody beside him.

Lt. Gen. R. L. Bullard,
U.S. Army (Retired),
age 73, in Diarybook 15,
July 12, 1934.

22

Major General,
United States Army
1919-1925

Like a doughboy buried in his dugout by a minenwerfer, the officer corps of the United States Army stumbled from the ruins of the mass citizen army they had led in France. Between the day the war ended and June 1920, the army shrank from 2.9 million officers and men to 201,918; the plunge in manpower did not halt for another two years, when the army mustered 131,000 regulars, approximately its prewar strength. In a year, the officer corps shrank from 200,000 to 17,726, who were predominantly regular officers not very experienced in handling peacetime duties. Half the regular officers had been commissioned after 1916. Even without assimilating the new weapons of World War I and adjusting to the army's many organizational changes, the prewar career officers had to rebuild their profession at the same time they bade good-bye to their citizen-soldiers.[1]

To restore some cohesion and order to the officer corps, Chief of Staff Peyton C. March reconstructed the army's officer schooling system as quickly as possible and tried to absorb the AEF's returning senior officers into the General Staff and other responsible positions appropriate to their rank. The number of such billets was limited, but March did his best to accommodate the AEF veterans. Most of the AEF's generals, however, wore only temporary stars, and more than one found himself back in his permanent rank of colonel with a handful of dazed regulars to command.

General March's efforts to restore the officer corps' morale and cohesiveness were also damaged by the rampant postwar inflation (which ate up the officers' fixed income) and growing civilian criticism of AEF disciplinary practices and discrimination against the National Guard divisions. Even without serious questions about the army's postwar structure and mission, the immediate postwar period was as difficult for those who stayed in the army as it was for those who peeled off their uniforms with relief.[2]

The postwar reconstruction of the regular army was slowed by internal rivalries and jealousies which split the officer corps. The most important split was between

439

Pershing and his AEF Headquarters and March and the General Staff. During the war, Pershing and March had had serious differences about officer promotions and assignments, the training program in the United States, shipping schedules, equipment deliveries, and management of the AEF's Services of Supply. By the time the war ended, the Army's senior officers realized that they were labelled (rightly or wrongly) Pershing men or March men, depending on the assignments they had held during the war. March attempted to scotch the assumption that an AEF clique and a War Department clique existed or could coexist in the officer corps, but Pershing made little effort to preach the unity of the officer corps. His immediate staff assumed that they were now at war with the War Department over control of the army. Since Pershing and March viewed their wartime rank and responsibilities as permanent and invaluable in the peace as well, the Pershing-March feud dragged on until 1921, when "The Chief" replaced March as Chief of Staff. For almost two years after the war, an army officer who made any policy recommendation ran the risk of alienating one or the other warring faction in the senior officer corps. The better part of valor was silence and noncommitment to the issues of army reorganization.[3]

With its World War experiences fresh and aware that the American military contribution had never matched the nation's potential, the War Department presented the Congress with reform legislation in January 1919. With a wealth of recent experience to draw upon, with anti-regular animosity running high in the National Guard, with the officer corps split into Pershing and March factions, and with the bureau-General Staff-line officer conflicts still simmering, the Congress had a field day probing the War Department's performance in the war and the army's future. When the National Defense Act finally passed in June 1920, it little resembled the plans proposed by either March's General Staff or Pershing's AEF Headquarters, but it set the mold for the regular army, the National Guard, and the army's scant reserves for the next twenty years.[4]

For the senior officers of the regular army, the heart of the postwar military policy debate was the question of manpower mobilization. Other issues impinged on the traditional arguments about manpower policies. Some, like the need for War Department planning for industrial mobilization and the arguments about autonomy for army aviation, made the congressional hearings more complex than usual, but the major issue still hinged on the interrelationship of the regular army and its citizen-soldier components, which together made the Army of the United States. March proposed that America's land forces be built around the standing combat divisions of the regular army. He recommended that the Congress establish a regular force of half a million men. The core of this army would be twenty divisions, but these divisions would not all be ready for immediate combat. Instead, they would serve as training organizations for America's nineteen-year-olds, who would enter the army annually for three months basic military training.

For antimilitary congressmen, March's plan smacked of European militarism, General Staff arrogance, and antidemocratic government. Even those congressmen sympathetic to the concept of greater military preparedness were not enthusiastic about the estimated cost of the plan or the political implications of peacetime conscription. Unconvinced that the United States faced any military threat so menacing as to justify peacetime conscription and high military costs, the Congress looked for an alternative army.

Pershing and his personal expert on manpower mobilization, Colonel John McAuley Palmer, offered the Congress the smaller and cheaper regular army it sought.[5] Palmer convinced the military affairs committees that the United States could get along admirably with about half the regulars March proposed. Palmer even thought a place for the National Guard could be found in America's land forces, a view hotly debated in Pershing's circle. He stressed, however, as did March, that America's next wartime army could be even more effective than the AEF if the nation's youth had a modicum of peacetime military training. In essence, Palmer and March agreed that three months training should suffice; both, in fact, agreed that the United States should have land forces of a million men. Palmer also hit a sympathetic congressional streak when he stressed that the army could provide a great national service in educating and acculturating the nation's youth. Although it rejected universal military training, the Congress did accept the concept of a voluntary reserve force, a force that would accommodate wartime officers who wanted a continued affiliation with the army, the graduates of the college Reserve Office Training Corps, and the summer citizen military training camps.

Having created a reserve system that, even without universal military training, was a reasonable structure for a citizen-army, the Congress refused to provide the appropriations that might have made the new Army of the United States a trained force. Annually paring the War Department budget after 1921, the Congress reflected public concern over federal fiscal policy and apathy about military preparedness. Between 1921 and 1925, the War Department's budget fell from $1.1 billion to $370 million. Much of this slender budget was spent on housekeeping and non-army matters. In 1923 Secretary of War John Weeks pointed out that the United States spent only 2.5 percent of its limited tax dollars on the army and had fewer soldiers in proportion to its wealth and population than any other modern nation. In contrast, the public spent six times as much on candy and soda pop as it did on its army.[6]

The National Defense Act of 1920, however, gave the War Department and the regular officer corps the theoretical framework for an Army of the United States. Until the 1930s, the War Department attempted to develop the sort of citizen army Pershing and Palmer promised the Congress. Both March and Pershing agreed that the new law required the regular army to become the training cadre for the citizen-soldier volunteers of the National Guard, Organized Reserves, ROTC, and citizen military training camps. General March estimated in 1920 that half the regular officer corps would be detailed to citizen components of the Army of the United States. Many other officers would be attending the army's formal schools to prepare themselves for high command and staff positions in wartime. At the risk of depriving regular army units of officers, the War Department planned to tie the officer corps to the civilian population that provided America's wartime soldiers.

The army, in fact, stressed its educational and social function for America's youth, not its combat readiness; the War Department wanted the public to view the regular army as a great vocational training school. By personal example, by public debate, by prudent and continuous publicity, the regular officers' primary function was to stimulate voluntary peacetime training and public interest in military preparedness.[7]

1.

Arriving in New York on May 24, 1919, Lieutenant General Robert Lee Bullard joined his reunited family. He could not understand everyone's excitement about the peace nor their happy chatter about going on to do important things now that the war was over. His reunion with his wife and children reeducated him to the fact "that it is easier to manage a large army than a small family." Within a week, the Bullards were living in a hotel in Washington, while the general reported to the War Department to learn what his next assignment might be.[8]

Bullard's meeting with March was a matter of some interest to Pershing's staff, which was still in France. Although Bullard noticed no discourtesy or hostility, General Harbord thought that Bullard, the AEF's first returning high commander, las being purposely slighted by the General Staff. Harbord thought that March had insulted Bullard by attaching him to the Office of the Chief of Staff instead of giving him an important assignment. In Washington, Bullard noticed no ill-treatment and appreciated the fact that March could not immediately find a suitable job for a temporary lieutenant general. Pershing himself was satisfied that the War Department understood Bullard's status: "The Chief" wanted his Second Army commander to have the permanent rank of lieutenant general as recognition of his service in France. Clarence Edwards and Leonard Wood, nursing their separate grudges against Pershing, had no doubts that Bullard would remain part of the army's inner circle, which was dominated by the AEF's senior officers.[9]

Bullard's initial assignment in March's office was to head a board screening infantry officers for retention in the regular army, but his major contribution was to support the Chief of Staff's recommendations for the postwar Army of the United States. Since Pershing had not yet taken a position and Colonel Palmer's views were influencing only the congressional committees, Bullard did not have to make a hard decision about disappointing March or Pershing. Testifying to the Senate Military Affairs Committee on August 14, Bullard supported March's plan for a half-million man regular army and universal military training. His testimony was cautious and confusing. Bullard told the senators that he believed it took three regulars to train a new recruit, primarily because a recruit learned best by training in the field with a standing unit, not by listening to lectures. Bullard thought that the 3:1 ratio was especially valid if the recruit was to have only three months training. If the recruit's initial training were extended to nine months, perhaps the army's manpower overhead could be reduced.

Although the senators pressed Bullard to admit that raw replacements in the AEF had been adequately trained without a large overhead of regulars, the general politely but firmly supported the Chief of Staff's program. He favored expansible regular divisions, not an elaborate system of skeletonized reserve divisions. Privately, he doubted that either version of the federally controlled force would be established. "I imagine that after much hearing the National Guard will move forward with some fake scheme of training that will claim to be cheap and will be given the work by Congress." When Bullard withdrew from the hearings, the senators thanked him for his candid views, but argued among themselves about what Bullard had really said.[10]

Although Bullard's debut as one of the army's senior policy advisers was not especially auspicious, the General Staff wanted to exploit his modest public fame. Bullard gloried in his new role as a leader of the AEF. When Pershing and his entourage arrived in New York City on September 7, Bullard was there to welcome "The Chief" back to the United States. On September 10, Pershing, his personal staff, a special AEF ceremonial regiment, and the First Division paraded for a tumultuous crowd of New Yorkers. Bullard watched the parade from the reviewing stand and marveled at the unrestrained applause for "The Chief" and his polished regulars. The victory parade coincided with the Boston police strike of 1919 and followed a summer of violent racial clashes, bombings, and labor strikes. Seeing Pershing greeted by the New York crowd with near-hysterical excitement, Bullard again wondered if Pershing might not be a presidential candidate. Certainly "The Chief" seemed to symbolize traditional authority and order. Bullard concluded that Pershing was only waiting for the proper moment to announce his candidacy, a conclusion shared by some of Pershing's staff.[11]

After a round of dinners and public appearances in New York, the AEF victory party moved to Washington for another parade. The capital seethed with Pershing-mania and "Pershing for president" rumors. On September 17, Pershing, riding with military majesty, led his symbolic command down Pennsylvania Avenue before 400,000 screaming people. Behind Pershing, Bullard rode with thirty-two other generals. Behind the officers marched the AEF ceremonial regiment and the entire First Division in full field order. Beneath an arch of American flags, bunting, and roses, the soldiers (". . . bronzed veterans and victors of battles that saved the world for liberty. . . ."), guns, and vehicles of the First Division filled five miles of pavement. After Pershing and his generals completed the parade route, they galloped back to the White House reviewing stand and joined Vice President Thomas Marshall, Newton D. Baker, and their guests. Watching the parade from the rank of generals behind "The Chief," Bullard did not resent Pershing's glory, but he wished he were still marching. When the Twenty-Sixth Infantry swept by the stand, he openly wept. For a moment he was tempted to leave the stand and march off with his old regiment, but he feared the disapproval of "my contemporaries and the high ranking officers present" at such an emotional display. As the moment passed, Bullard half-wished his sense of propriety had not been so strong. The First Division's Washington parade reminded him, as nothing yet had, that the war was over and with it the climax of his military career.[12]

Deep in the fight to create its vision of a postwar army, the General Staff did not allow Bullard to lapse into postwar reveries. Shortly after his assignment to the War Department, Bullard escorted a congressional party to Fort Bragg, North Carolina, and to Fort Benning, Georgia. The War Department wanted both camps preserved, and it asked its highest-ranking Southern general to explain their value. Bullard was so successful in his new role of army spokesman that he accompanied another congressional investigating party to army posts in Kentucky, Tennessee, Arkansas, Texas, Oklahoma, Kansas, and Illinois. During this junket Bullard thought that his greatest contribution was explaining the importance of the Leavenworth schools. He was amazed how little the congressmen knew about the army. In most cases, Bullard concluded, the congressmen's hostility to the army was based on their unfamiliarity with military matters. The general hoped that the congress would approve some sort of peacetime training program, for without it the army and civil society would again lose touch with each other. He feared that the American people would return to their apathy toward military matters and their antipathy to the regular army.[13]

During his travels, Bullard fretted about the Midwest's industrial unrest. In Chicago, he told General Wood, the department commander, that he completely approved of Wood's use of regulars to put down the steel strike in Gary, Indiana. The general thought that he noted a ground swell of popular antiunionism and disgust with the Wilson Administration. Perhaps "The Chief" could capitalize on the public's thirst for a military hero who symbolized the nation's traditional virtues:

> The country is much perturbed by socialistic, revolutionary labor strikes and demands. The Federal govt. seems too weak to deal with the question and nothing is being done to meet the conditions as there is no organized group to resist the organized labor party that seems determined to upset our entire social, industrial and political conditions. This is just what I feared last winter when I told Gen. Pershing that someone would have to be found strong enough to resist this thing and intimated that I expected him to be the man and that in [that] case I wished him to count upon my support. The conditions seem to be ripening for this. I shall try to see Pershing upon this.[14]

Bullard, who enjoyed his own speech-making in support of law and order, had his travels cut short when the War Department permanently assigned him as commanding general of the Eastern Department on October 28, 1919. This assignment prevented Bullard from accepting an invitation to participate in the newly formed American Legion's armistice day celebrations in Washington, but he appreciated the invitation and commended the veterans for their "steady and reliable line of conduct" in turbulent postwar America as well as in France. The veterans' support for the civil authority and the law "stands out as an example to be imitated by the whole country in these days of Bolshevik and disorderly agitation and unrest."[15] Although the nation's European enemies were defeated, Bullard had returned to find new foes at home.

2.

Built around nineteenth-century coastal fortifications on Governors Island in New York harbor, Fort Jay, headquarters of the Eastern Department, was a comfortable post. It had its own golf course, clubs, boating facilities, and athletic fields as well as the normal quarters, office buildings, and barracks. It was a well manicured and maintained post, much to the annoyance of the officers whose infantrymen did the housekeeping. In many ways, Fort Jay might have been on the frontier, although the ferry to New York ran continually. It had not changed much in decades, though the World War had brought new trophies to the parade ground.

An assignment to Governors Island was especially attractive, since it placed an officer near New York City and still kept him within the inner circle of army society. In more ways than geographically, Governors Island was between West Point and the War Department. For most commanders of the Eastern Department before the World War, the assignment had involved nothing more complicated than routine inspections of army installations and coast defenses and the processing of routine correspondence. Leonard Wood, however, had broken the pattern between 1914 and 1917 when he used his position to stimulate the Preparedness Movement. His experience and that of the War Department's during the war dramatized the fact that New York City was favorable to the regular army and military matters in general. After the war, the War Department officially encouraged what Leonard Wood had unofficially begun: the Eastern Department commander's primary duty was to cultivate proarmy public sympathy.[16]

Bullard was pleased by his assignment as Eastern Department commander. As a well-known AEF general, he relished the public's attention and the chance to meet "all the celebrities, foreign and domestic." He had no objection to his ceremonial duties, especially since he felt the army owed him public acclaim as a loyal and able officer, a World War hero, and a living symbol of the army officer corps.[17] It never occurred to him that he had much in common with the captured German cannon along the Fort Jay parade ground.

As he had in France, Bullard gave his staff officers great latitude in their duties. Bullard let his chief-of-staff, the genial, pudgy William Weigel (USMA, 1887), a former brigade and division commander, handle routine army matters. Instead of closeting himself in his headquarters and burying himself in regular army minutiae, Bullard sortied out into New York's clubs, associations, and patriotic societies to make speeches. He found, however, that talking about military preparedness in a general sense often encouraged antimilitary criticism and that discussing specific military legislation opened him to charges of political partisanship. "It is hard for an army officer to make a speech without getting into some sort of trouble about mixing in politics but I've managed thus far to do so, but at the expense of talking a great deal of foolishness—no other way to avoid trouble: you cannot make a serious speech."[18]

Nevertheless, he cultivated civilian groups because he knew it was War Department policy to "keep the Army in as close relation with civilians as possible." He also learned that he could use his own name for worthy causes, such as raising money for Alabama Polytechnic Institute and preaching brotherhood and isolationism to the national congress of Alpha Tau Omega. He was not unaware that his public appearances reminded his friends that he should be a permanent lieutenant general.[19]

In March 1920, with demobilization nearly complete and fundamental military legislation about to be passed by the Congress, Secretary of War Baker and Chief-of-Staff March called the department and division commanders to Washington for a conference on postwar army policies.[20] Bullard relished the opportunity to participate in a high-level general officers meeting, although he returned from Washington dismayed by the General Staff's word wars and office-bound life:

> The visit to Washington made me more contented than ever with my station at New York. Washington, I came to see, was a place of words, not action. If you say anything to one officer there, he turns and says the same thing to some other officer, and the whole thing is lost in circumlocution. I noticed also, return to same condition of bowel constipation and obstruction that seemed to exist among these officers at the outbreak of the war. They seem to have so little outdoor exercise and movement that they literally smell bad.[21]

Baker and March did not have the matter of the General Staff's regularity on their agenda. They were more concerned that War Department, territorial department, and General Staff-Line relations were as harmonious as possible. Major General William G. Haan, March's assistant, reviewed the army's command relationships. Although the War Department would determine army policy, the department commanders, who would have complete staffs of their own, would have the responsibility of executing that policy in their commands. Chiefs-of-arms and bureaus would work with department commanders. Bullard pointed out that in New York alone there were three independent commands: his own, the port of embarkation, and the quartermaster zone. One of General Haan's assistants said there would be a consolidation of commands and staffs to reduce personnel and concentrate authority, but that there was "a large twilight zone" in the army command system. Bullard quipped: "Yes, it is all twilight." The conferees laughed.

The General Staff's major interest, Bullard learned, was the morale of the regular army (especially the officer corps) and the manpower mobilization plans before Congress. During General Haan's initial briefing, Bullard, however, brought up the question of supply mobilization planning: "Have you a branch studying the matter of mobilization of the industries and the making of plans looking toward the provision of the necessary material in the case of any ordinary assumed war? We had the troops ready long before we had material in the last war. Has any study been made of that?" Haan replied that the General Staff was studying the question. Bullard thought that was inadequate. "Have you a plan to mobilize the industries and put them to work?" Not yet, Haan replied. The War Department would deal with the problem somehow. On the conference's fourth day, Bullard was more satisfied about economic mobilization planning when Bernard Baruch, former head of the War Industries Board, assured the generals that the matter of economic regulation would be part of the War Department's future responsibilities.[22]

The General Staff's real purpose was to involve the generals in preparing recommendations on the status of the career officer corps and the regular army ranks. Taking their lead from Major General Harbord, the conferees concluded that the army's morale was rock-bottom. For the officer corps, the generals recommended that all promotions and demotions in the near future be done on the basis of seniority. Everyone thought that the army's pay should be increased, since postwar inflation had eroded the officers' standard of living. Although the exchanges of opinion were spirited and touched with a renewed sense of determination to see the army through its hard times, the general officers adjourned without much sense of direction or purpose. Without any basic legislation to build upon, the army could only attend to its housekeeping and morale-building and wait for better days.

Until his retirement, Bullard periodically returned to Washington to serve on a series of War Department boards. He helped pick officers for retention in the regular army and to place officers on the "B" List, the General Staff's category of marginal officers to be severed from the army in the cutbacks that followed 1920. Bullard thought some of his peers were not "sufficiently exacting" in judging officers' value, while he fancied himself "hard-hearted." He also helped make the army's recommendations for the promotion of general officers. Composed of the senior officers of the AEF, the selection board favored Pershing's former combat commanders. Its recommendations, however, were not inviolate. Bullard concluded that army officers were gathering political endorsements with the most enthusiasm since the Roosevelt Administration. "Herein the Army has suffered a distinct loss and setback."[23]

Far from the officer corps' ignoble strife, Major General Bullard, sixth ranking officer of the United States Army, went about his duty, "a bit monotonous in its sameness and tameness."[24] After the passage of the National Defense Act of 1920, however, his command, redesignated the Second Corps Area, took more permanent form. Under his supervision was one regular army division (the First) stationed at Fort Dix, New Jersey, and commanded by his old comrade, Major General Summerall. The only other regular army combat troops in the Corps area were the coast artillery units of the Second Coast Artillery District. Under the provisions of the National Defense Act, Bullard also became the patron of the National Guard organizations of New York, New Jersey, and Delaware. Bullard made the required visits to drills and summer camp for all the Guard units, and he especially enjoyed the social functions of the New York City regiments. In addition to the National Guard component of the Army of the United States, the Second Corps Area commander had a second group of citizen-soldiers to supervise. Bullard's area included nearly six thousand reserve officers who had voluntarily held their wartime commissions or had received postwar commissions through the ROTC or citizen military training camps. Nearly half these officers were assigned to the skeleton headquarters of four reserve divisions. Finally, Bullard's headquarters was responsible for the corps area's citizen military training camp, held each summer at Plattsburg, and the college ROTC units in the corps area.[25]

Bullard's official duty was not only to supervise his portion of the Army of the United States but to stimulate public interest in military affairs. Bullard thought that only compulsory universal military training would solve the army's manpower shortages, and his speeches largely dealt with this issue. His headquarters handled army publicity with the New York City newspapers and published the newspaper *U.S. Army Recruiting News*. Bullard's public relations staff seldom missed a chance to feed copy to the press. Pershing, in fact, wondered if Bullard was not exaggerating his own importance in the army and the Second Corps' role in military affairs.[26]

As the senior regular army officer in the New York City area, Bullard was included in the social activities of the National Guard, patriotic societies, and veterans groups. He joined the American Legion, although its bonus demands "gagged him." He became a familiar figure in New York high society and made friends with the Vanderbilts and Rhinelanders. On a salary of $8,000, he could hardly have competed socially except for his military position; living costs in New York City had increased 80 percent since 1914, and a general's pay in the 1920s had about the same purchasing power of a captain's before the war. With the facilities of Fort Jay at his command, however, Bullard justified entertaining the civilian elite of the city as army public relations. Still animated and gregarious at sixty, Bullard was a favorite dinner guest and speaker, although some veterans found his rambling anecdotes tiresome. At Governors Island, the Bullards' army social life was limited. Their social activities were nearly as ceremonial at Fort Jay as in the city, for age and rank now cut the Bullards off from most of the garrison's officers except the senior colonels.[27]

The pall that fell about Bullard's official and social life was his wife's health. Soon after the general's assignment to Governors Island, Mrs. Bullard began to fail badly. In December 1921, Rose died of cancer. The general's grief was deep and sincere, for he understood the price Rose had paid as an army wife. Her death opened a void in his life that struck him with unanticipated force. For once his duty could not compensate for tragedy in his family, and he saw that the army could provide many things, but not the emotional companionship and comfort of his wife. The army, however, could bury Mrs. Bullard with dignity. After ceremonies in the post chapel, she was buried in the Cypress Hill national cemetery in Brooklyn. Fort Jay had buried its dead there since 1798. With military honors and the garrison's colonels for pallbearers, Rose Bullard finally found the peace her husband's career had denied her.[28]

3.

Bullard's contact with New York society, the first extended urban experience of his life, was not altogether comforting. Although Manhattan was only a fifteen-minute ferry ride from Governors Island, it was "a foreign country . . . not far to go."[29] Bullard feared that an urbanized, industrialized America would be a far different and less admirable nation than the country he had loved and served. Material luxury had induced weakness and moral paralysis in the people. Reflecting the uncertainty and apathy of the public, the government had capitulated to "socialistic, bolshevistic radicals" in "industrial matters." Bullard believed he could identify at least one symptom of the nation's growing impotence: voluntary organizations were relinquishing more and more functions to government. He thought the trend, the product of pernicious European influences, would breed paternalism. Worse yet, many Americans had no tradition of community solidarity and self-help. When added to the traditional individualism of native Americans, the lack of patriotic consciousness in the unassimilated, immigrant working class would produce national degeneration. Neither group recognized that individuality must be compromised for the public good and the stability of the government.[30] Democratic government was at best vulnerable, since it was the captive of vocal minorities and its own insistence on individual rights. The failure to enforce the law was typical; the rights of the criminal seemed to transcend those of society. Bullard concluded that:

Democracies cannot be Honest: Because they are so based on kindness and consideration to the individual citizen *who is still in all the world selfish*, that they, democracies, cannot refuse his selfish demands.[31]

Bullard's concern about American society was not the anxious imaginings of an unacculturated rural general, for he and his peers remembered the shocking findings of the wartime draft. Nearly half the draftees had had physical defects serious enough to disqualify them for service. Twenty-five percent were illiterate, and seventy-five percent had never participated in group sports. Many knew nothing of personal hygiene or public sanitation. Following War Department policy and his own conclusions, Bullard advocated universal military training for the rehabilitation of youths. Compulsory military training would not only prepare the Army of the United States for war but would allow the regular army to teach citizenship, honesty, integrity, "Americanism," the glories of hygiene and physical fitness, and a useful skill or two. In social terms, Bullard thought that the egalitarianizing and nationalizing experience that had characterized enlisted mens' service in the AEF should be extended to others. That the army's self-proclaimed role of teacher to American youth might be called militarism never occurred to him. He was only following the logic of his own experience and the policy of the War Department.[32]

For all the General Staff's emphasis upon the army's role as social reformer in peacetime America, Bullard saw universal military training as a military necessity. He correctly saw that the United States was entering another period of postwar, unilateral disarmament. His World War experiences had reinforced his belief that this policy was foolish romanticism.[33] Writing for the *Infantry Journal*, the general pictured disarmament as an invitation to disaster in a hostile world. As it had in the past, the United States would need arms and trained manpower. If it had neither, the nation risked its international influence and freedom of action. The nation's traditional lack of preparedness, Bullard believed, had seldom restrained policy-makers when the nation's fundamental interests had been threatened. Historically, military unpreparedness only meant shifting the costs of war to succeeding generations. Moreover, America's disarmed state had been either irrelevant or an invitation to war, not a deterrent. Certainly, no one had followed America's idealistic example. American notions of peace and justice were not universal, and no nation appreciated America's pacifism, which was a sometime thing anyway. To end war as a universal phenomenon was beyond America's capacity, and only armed vigilance would keep America out of more conflict.[34]

In May 1921 Bullard gave his pessimistic assessment of America's foreign and military policies to the annual meeting of the American Academy of Political and Social Science. Although flattered by the invitation to participate in the Academy's conference on the United States' relations with the League of Nations, the general said nothing to hearten his academic and generally liberal audience. He recognized that some of the audience held cherished American notions that the armed forces were too costly and that readiness only brought war. He himself could find no evidence for either assumption. The only true way to gain national security outside of military readiness was to enter into an international agreement to reduce military power. Such an agreement would have to include enforcement provisions, which would require an international armed force. Even under such conditions, Bullard was not optimistic that such a system would work for long. National interests would persist, and with them the will to fight. He pointed out that no nation had ever admitted that it had started a war. Nations always claimed that they had resorted to arms only as the last resort and in times of the gravest national peril. This persistent pattern of behavior reduced the chances for a lasting international peace.

In such a world, unilateral disarmament was at best misguided altruism or economic selfishness. Bullard hoped that, under the circumstances, the United

States would arm itself sufficiently to deter war, not follow the false advice of pacifists and special pleaders. Not to arm was to risk national disaster.[35]

4.

Numbed by his wife's death, Bullard went about his military duties with an efficiency based only on self-discipline and habit. He dabbled in the stock market and lost. He played polo, golf, and one day ran a mile to see whether it would kill him or not. It didn't. Despite his determination to follow his routine of work, study, and exercise, he felt stale. He turned to travel. He, daughter Rose, and son Keith took an army cruise to Puerto Rico and the Canal Zone, then visited relatives in Alabama. His wanderlust unsatiated, the general, Rose, and Keith then sailed for Europe in June 1922. For two months the Bullards toured the continent and the lands bordering the Mediterranean. Freed from the responsibilities of command, Bullard thoroughly enjoyed the trip. Although the Bullards did not return to Governors Island until late August, even then their travels were not ended. In September, Secretary of State Charles Evans Hughes invited Bullard to join the official American delegation to Brazil's centennial exposition in Rio de Janeiro. Accompanied by Rose, the general savored the excitement of new places and splendid military ceremonies. By the time the Bullards returned to their quarters, the holiday social season had begun at Fort Jay.[36]

His wife's death, his own advancing age, and his undemanding duties forced Bullard to consider the condition of his own and his children's emotional life. Lonely, reassured only by his daughter Rose's presence, the general thought he should remarry for companionship. He was depressed by his children's aimlessness. His oldest son Lee, living in Detroit, was an uninspired businessman. Peter, a captain in the postwar army, was also quarreling with his wife, the daughter of a French navy officer, who wanted to return to Europe. Rose, approaching thirty, was unmarried, and in the winter of 1922-23 she was hospitalized at Walter Reed. Fearing his daughter had cancer, Bullard wept sporadically for two days until he learned Rose was recovering. Only Keith, at eighteen, seemed unspoiled. Keith, however, was eager to go to West Point like his father and brothers, an ambition that Bullard tried to check. When he failed his physical, Keith was disappointed, but the general was thankful when his son enrolled at Columbia University.[37]

Bullard could afford to worry about his family, for the Second Corps headquarters had less and less to do. By 1923 the grandly conceived Army of the United States had withered as a result of public apathy and congressional economizing. The regular army's nine divisions shrank to skeletons of six; underequipped and plagued by officers' absence, the regulars vegetated. The National Guard showed scant signs of life. Instead of the authorized force of 450,000, the Guardsmen numbered only 176,000. The reserve division cadres limped along on sporadic training, much of it theoretical and uncompensated by the army. The only hopeful sign of public interest in military training was the demand to increase ROTC enrollments and summer civilian military training camps, but the War Department did not have the money to expand either program. A department budget of $256 million did not stretch far enough to provide for all the components of the Army of the United States.[38]

Bullard's duties in the Second Corps Area became primarily ceremonial. Although he occasionally visited the First Division and the forts of the Second Coast Artillery District to see firing exercises, he spent as much time having tea with the Daughters of the American Revolution, praising the cooperation of the YMCA and YMHA with the summer training camps, issuing public statements on army affairs, and speaking to reserve officer meetings. In 1924, Pennsylvania Military College made him a "Doctor of Military Science," much to his pleasure. Although Bullard enjoyed the attention and prestige his rank attracted, he found his public life a pale imitation of wartime command or even active service with troops of the regular army. He thought that the War Department's public relations campaign was barely keeping the army alive.[39]

Throughout his tour as Second Corps commander, Bullard's relations with Pershing and the War Department were untroubled. "The Chief" judged Bullard's performance of duty eminently satisfactory, rating him the fifth best of the army's twenty-one major generals. The rating matched his seniority. Pershing's efficiency reports had an antique ring when he reported that Bullard was fitted to command a corps or army in wartime. Pershing found Bullard's military knowledge and loyalty to superiors to be exceptional. He was "an officer of soldierly instincts, high character, and enthusiasm, which he inspires in his subordinates; able as a commander and loyal as a subordinate. . . . He deserves every consideration because of his distinguished services to his country in the World War. . . ."[40] Pershing knew that Bullard wanted his third star back, as did Hunter Liggett. Bullard himself found the ambition of younger officers tiresome and undignified. When he went to Washington to sit on a classification board which was still screening officers for involuntary retirement or discharge, he was annoyed by the number of "*political* recommendations" in officers' files.[41] With his own retirement imminent and officers reaching for any recognition they could to justify their continued careers, Bullard received many letters asking for World War decorations. Conveniently forgetting his own frantic lobbying, he complained about the pleas for favor:

> Of late I have been beset by officers begging for recommendations for Distinguished Service Medals and Distinguished Service Crosses in France. A very undignified performance. I'd see everybody a long way before I would make such a request upon anybody. The struggle for decorations has become disgraceful.[42]

Bullard, wearied by internal army politics and skeptical about the public's interest in preparedness, contemplated his retirement. On January 15, 1925, he would reach sixty-four, the army's age limit on active service. He worried about what he would do. He decided he would live in New York City if he could possibly afford it, for the city's social life and his civilian contacts were too pleasant to abandon. Pondering retirement demoralized the general, giving him an acute sense of diminished usefulness. "It has shown me how great has been the prestige of being on the active list and a man of high rank in the U.S. Army. That prestige is now fading and leaving me helpless. What would happen if my retired pay were lost? I don't believe I could take care of myself."[43] The future seemed to hold little beyond romantic memories and genteel poverty.[44]

The War Department helped remind Bullard that he would soon be leaving the army when it staged a special "Defense Test Day" to coincide with Pershing's retirement on September 12, 1924. The "Defense Test Day" was supposed to exercise the War Department's mobilization plans for the National Guard and reserves. In reality, the test was little more than a nationwide patriotic rally at army bases. Supported by patriotic societies and veterans groups, the War Department wanted to demonstrate that "every unit is part of its own community." For Bullard, on Governors Island, "Defense Test Day" was a farce. Since he thought that Pershing had been well rewarded for his World War services, Bullard was not especially sympathetic to all the gracious gestures "The Chief" received. He begrudged Pershing none of his glory, but he wished that President Coolidge had allowed at least one honest test mobilization before he himself left the army. The exercise ended, however, with Pershing talking by phone with his generals, thanking them for their loyal efforts in the AEF.[45]

As Bullard's sixty-fourth birthday approached, his routine public appearances became a succession of ceremonies in his honor. Still uncertain about his postarmy life, Bullard appreciated the round of special dinners and military reviews, most of them staged by the National Guard regiments in his area. The consideration of his army and civilian friends eased his growing sense of emptiness. Bullard also felt that his influence within the regular army, an influence he had had only since the World War, was slipping away. His political impotence at the War Department irked him since he had enjoyed it such a short time. More and more often, he talked not of contemporary army problems but of his memories of the war.[46]

On the evening of January 14, General Bullard was honored at a testimonial banquet at the Hotel Astor. Members of New York City's social elite and representatives of the city's patriotic and veterans' societies joined officers of the regular army, National Guard, and reserve to eulogize Bullard. The general was touched by the affection and genuine appreciation he received from "1700 of the best people of the land. . . ." He was pleased when General Harbord, now president of the Radio Corporation of America, and General Summerall, his successor as Second Corps commander, urged the Congress to restore Bullard's wartime rank of lieutenant general. (Their suggestion set off a series of mild newspaper criticism of the army's compulsory retirement system and the Congress' slavish reverence for Pershing.) In the main address, Bullard simply reviewed his military career in nostalgic, anecdotal fashion, though he intended the speech to be a plea for further peacetime citizen military training. He reviewed what he considered the major reforms during his years in the army: the creation of the General Staff, the increased efficiency of the National Guard, the foundations of citizen military training embodied in Wood's Plattsburg camps, and the recent development of the Organized Reserve. Predictably, Bullard warned that the nation's security was still not adequate and that further reform and military spending was essential. gafter his retirement, he found that his audience remembered little about his speech except that he had told an amusing off-color Negro-dialect joke.[47]

Bullard's last day of duty conformed to the unwritten army ritual for retiring a general officer. As enlisted men packed his books and souvenirs, Bullard briefed Summerall about his new command. Occasionally they posed for photographs. During the morning, Bullard received telegrams from the secretary of war and army Chief of Staff, John L. Hines, thanking him for his forty-four years of distinguished service. From army posts throughout the country came affectionate notes wishing him a happy birthday and pleasant retirement. At noon, Bullard's staff had a party in the general's quarters and presented him with a leather traveling bag and silver toilet articles. For Bullard there was but one last duty: publishing an order announcing his retirement in accordance with army regulations. Writing as if the Second Corps Area was a loyal infantry regiment instead of citizen-soldiers scattered over three states, the general expressed his appreciation for his command's obedience, loyalty, energy, and goodwill. The soldiers of his corps were "tried and true, imbued with those high and patriotic ideals which were the foundations of our splendid army. In years to come in retrospect I shall see passing in review my last command the Second Corps Area. I bid you farewell."[48]

At three o'clock, Major General Robert Lee Bullard, United States Army, Retired, walked with his staff from his quarters to the ferry. Lean and straight at sixty-four, the general marched between two lines of men of the Sixteenth Infantry, the troops at "present arms." As Bullard's party reached the ferry slip, the regimental band struck up "Auld Lang Syne." The Fort Jay saluting battery boomed thirteen times. Bullard returned the salute, then stepped aboard the ferry. Ahead was a new and puzzling life as a citizen of New York City. Behind him, he left the army that had been his very soul.

NOTES

[1]Russell F. Weigley, *History of the United States Army* (New York: Macmillan, 1967), pp. 395-420; and Oliver L. Spaulding, *The United States Army in War and Peace* (New York: Putnam, 1937), pp. 458-567.

[2]"Report of the Secretary of War," *War Department Annual Reports, 1920* (Washington: Government Printing Office, 1921), I, pp. 1-76.

[3]Edward M. Coffman, *The Hilt of the Sword: The Career of Peyton C. March* (Milwaukee: University of Wisconsin Press, 1966), pp. 152-230.

[4]For the passage of the National Defense Act of 1920, see Bernard L. Boylan, "Army Reorganization 1920: The Legislative Story," *Mid-America* 44 (April 1967), pp. 115-128;

U.S. Congress, Senate Committee on Military Affairs, Hearings: "Reorganization of the Army," 66th Congress, 1st and 2d Sessions, 2 vols. (Washington: Government Printing Office, 1920); U.S. Congress, House Committee on Military Affairs, Hearings: "Army Reorganization," 66th Congress, 1st Session, 2 vols. (Washington: Government Printing Office, 1919).

[5]Memorandum on universal military training, General Headquarters, American Expeditionary Force, December 23, 1918, Miscellaneous Papers, John L. Hines Papers; Brig. Gen. G. V. Moseley to Brig. Gen. R. E. Wood, March 3, 1919, George Van Horn Moseley Papers; Maj. Gen. C. R. Edwards to Senator J. W. Wadsworth, January 21, 1920, Clarence R. Edwards Papers.

[6]"Annual Report of the Secretary of War," *Report of the Secretary of War to the President, 1922,* (Washington: Government Printing Office, 1922), pp. 1-22; "Annual Report of the Secretary of War," *Report of the Secretary of War to the President, 1923,* (Washington: Government Printing Office, 1923), pp. 1-30; U.S. Congress, Senate Committee on Military Affairs, Hearings: "Army Appropriation Bill, 1922," 66th Congress, 3d Session (Washington: Government Printing Office, 1921).

[7]"Excerpts from Annual Report of the Chief of Staff," *Report of the Secretary of War to the President, 1922,* pp. 111-121; War Department, General Orders No. 56, September 14, 1920, copy in William G. Haan Papers; War Department Information Section, "General Pershing's Letter on Organization of the Army of the United States," July 15, 1921. copy in John McA. Palmer, "Chapter Notes" XVI, John McAuley Palmer Papers.

[8]Bullard autobiography, p. 166, BP; Lt. Gen. Robert L. Bullard, "Statement of Military Service," Bullard 201 File.

[9]Maj. Gen. J. G. Harbord to Gen. J. J. Pershing, June 14, 1919, with Pershing's marginal notes, Pershing-Harbord Correspondence, James G. Harbord Papers; Gen. J. J. Pershing to Adj. Gen., USA, July 15, 1919, Bullard 201 File; Maj. Gen. C. R. Edwards to Maj. Gen. L. Wood, December 21, 1919, Edwards Papers.

[10]Diarybook 10, entry, August 22, 1919, BP; "Testimony of Lieutenant General Robert L. Bullard, U.S.A.," August 14, 1919, in Senate Military Affairs Committee, Hearings: "Reorganization of the Army," I, pp. 111-128.

[11]Diarybook 10, entries, September 11-30, 1919, BP; *New York Times,* September 11, 1919; *Evening Post* (New York), September 10, 1919; *New York Herald,* September 11, 1919.

[12]Diarybook 11, entry, October 18, 1919, BP; Bullard autobiography, pp. 166-167, BP; *Washington Post,* September 15-18, 1919; *History of the First Division* (Philadelphia: Winston, 1922), pp. 259-261.

[13]Diarybook 11, entry, October 16, 1919, BP; Notebook 25, entries, October 17 and 18, 1919, BP.

[14]Diarybook 11, entry, October 26, 1919, BP; Bullard autobiography, pp. 168-169, BP.

[15]Diarybook 11, entry, October 28, 1919, BP.

[16]Bullard autobiography, pp. 170-176.

[17]Bullard autobiography, p. 176, BP; Col. W. Weigel to Maj. Gen. W. G. Haan, December 3, 1919, Haan Papers.

[18]Diarybook 11, entry, December 13, 1919, BP.

[19]Diarybook 11, entry, June 2, 1920, BP; Lt. Gen. R. L. Bullard to T. M. Owen (Director, Alabama Department of Archives and History), Bullard Papers/Alabama Department of Archives and History; Sen. K. M. McKellar to Mrs. M. B. Owen, Bullard Papers/Alabama Department of Archives and History; "Bullard on Brotherhood," *The*

Palm [Alpha Tau Omega], (February 1923), p. 16; *Philadelphia Public Ledger*, June 6, 1922.

[20]"Minutes of Conference of Department and Division Commanders," Washington, D. C., January 12-19-,—12-19, 1920, copies in the Edwards Papers.

[21]Diarybook 11, entry, January 26, 1920, BP.

[22]On the question of industrial mobilization planning in the interwar period, see Paul A. C. Koistinen, "The 'Industrial-Military' Complex in Historical Perspective: The InterWar Years," *Journal of American History* 55 (March 1970), pp. 819-839.

[23]Diarybook 11, entries, July 10, 1920, and April 4, 1921, BP; *Army and Navy Journal*, December 4, 1920; War Department Special Orders 138-0, June 12, 1920, Hines Papers.

[24]Diarybook 11, entry, October 3, 1921, BP.

[25]*Army and Navy Journal*, January 8 and 15 and June 17, 1921; August 19, 1922.

[26]Diarybook 11, entry, February 7, 1921, BP; Maj. Gen. R. L. Bullard to H. L. Stimson, May 3, 1923, Henry L. Stimson Papers; correspondence, Maj. Gen. R. L. Bullard and Gen. J. J. Pershing, February 3, 1922-April 25, 1924, John J. Pershing Papers; H. I. Brock, assistant editor of the *New York Times*, to Maj. Gen. R. L. Bullard, April 28, 1922, Bullard 201 File; *Army and Navy Journal,* April 30, 1921.

[27]Bullard analyzed his duties in Diarybook 11, entries, March, 1920, BP. See also the following issues of *Army and Navy Journal:* October 2, November 13, December 4, 1920; January 8 and 15, February 12, March 5, April 23, June 4, October 8 and December 17, 1921.

[28]Diarybook 11, entries, December 1920, and December 1921; *Army and Navy Journal*, December 17 and 24, 1921.

[29]Notebook 26, entry, January, 1920, BP.

[30]Notebook 25, entry, December 21, 1919; Notebook 26, entries, February 1920 BP; Scrapbook 27, entry, June 20, 1921, all BP.

[31]Scrapbook 27, entries, April 19, 1920, and January 1921, BP.

[32]Notebook 25, entry, February 17, 1920, and Notebook 26, entry, November 26, 1919, BP; Maj. Gen. Robert L. Bullard, "Physical Training in the Army," *U.S. Army Recruiting News,* 5 (August 1, 1923), pp. 3-4; Maj. Gen. Robert L Bullard, "Military Training—Its Effect on the Citizen," *Infantry Journal,* 19 (July 1921), pp. 7-11.

[33]Scrapbook 27, entries, January-February 1921, BP; Maj. Gen. Robert L. Bullard, "The Army in the Life of the Country," speech made to the Brooklyn Chamber of Commerce (n.d., but either 1924 or 1925), *mss.* BP.

[34]Maj. Gen. Robert L. Bullard, "Disarmament," *Infantry Journal*, 18 (May 1921), pp. 434-437, and "The U.S. Should Not Lead in Disarmament—Because," *Infantry Journal,* 18 (June 1921), pp. 558-560.

[35]Maj. Gen. Robert L. Bullard, "The Possibility of Disarmament by International Agreement," *Annals of the American Academy of Political and Social Science*, 96 (July 1921), pp. 49-52.

[36]Diarybook 11, entries, January-July 16, 1922, and Diarybook 12, entries, July 17-August 12, 1922, and Diarybook 13, entries, August 31-Ocotber 26, 1922, all BP; Lt. Gen. Robert L. Bullard, "Statement of Military Service," Bullard 201 File; *Army and Navy Journal*, February 18, March 4, August 26, October 28, 1922.

[37]Diarybook 13, entries, January-November, 1923, BP.

[38]"Report of the Secretary of War," in *War Department Annual Reports, 1924* (Washington: Government Printing Office, 1924), pp. 1-36, and *1925* (Washington: Government Printing Office, 1925), pp. 1-29.

[39]Diarybook 13, entries, April 14 and November, 1923, BP; *Army and Navy Journal,* November 25, 1922; January 20, May 12, June 9, June 30, July 28, September 1 and 15, 1923; July 5, August 23, and September 13, 1924.

[40]General of the Armies John J. Pershing, C/S, to the Adj. Gen., USA, memorandum, "Efficiency Report on General Officer," July 1, 1922 and June 30, 1923, Bullard 201 File.

[41]Diarybook 13, entry, October 14, 1924, BP; *Army and Navy Journal,* October 11, 1924.

[42]Diarybook 13, entry, February 27, 1913, BP.

[43]Diarybook 13, entry, December 15, 1923, BP.

[44]Diarybook 13, entries, January-February and September 1924, BP; Maj. Gen. R. L. Bullard to Brig. Gen. F. Parker, May 10, 1924, Parker Papers.

[45]Diarybook 13, entry, September 17, 1924; *Army and Navy Journal,* September 6 and 13, 1924.

[46]Diarybook 13, entry, January 11, 1925, BP; Brig. Gen. F. Parker to Maj. Gen. H. E. Ely, January 9, 1925, Parker Papers; *Army and Navy Journal,* December 20, 1924.

[47]Bullard autobiography, pp. 178-179, BP; *Army and Navy Journal,* January 10 and 17, 1925; "Two Gallant Soldiers," *Outlook,* 139 (January 28, 1925), pp. 125-126; "The Last of Our Great A.E.F. Generals Out," *Literary Digest,* 84 (February 7, 1925), pp. 36, 41-42; Herbert B. Mayer, "The Last of the Army's Big Four Goes," *The New York Times Magazine* (January 11, 1925), p. 3.

[48]Diarybook 13, entries, January 14-17, 1925, BP; *New York Times,* January 16, 1925; Secretary of War J. W. Weeks to Lt. Gen. R. L. Bullard, January 15, 1925, BP; Headquarters, Second Corps Area, Governors Island, N. Y. General Orders 2, January 15, 1925, Bullard 201 File.

23

Evening Parade
1925-1947

Accustomed to the tender attention of his aides and staff, having lived in spacious quarters maintained by the War Department, Bullard now had to contend with the expense and inconvenience of civilian city life. A thin, occasionally ill man of sixty-four without a job or sufficient income for the social life he had relished, he faced an adjustment as challenging as any of his army assignments. He knew he could not live on his pension in New York City and maintain his social contacts. Fortunately, some of his wealthy friends knew his army pension was small and, shortly after his retirement, they gave him $20,000. They also arranged for Columbia University to give him an honorary degree, a gesture the general appreciated.[1]

Bullard had no intention, however, of living on charity, and he looked for work. It was not a happy experience, for it dramatized the transitory nature of military fame in the United States. One man asked him to take a job leading circus parades in full uniform, mounted on a white horse, and an old family friend in Alabama offered him ten acres of cotton land. Some prohibitionists suggested he become president of the Anti-Saloon League, a job for which he had no taste. Bullard was also offered a position in Governor Alfred E. Smith's political organization. He felt the same way about this job as he did about the Anti-Saloon League position. In February 1925, he received an offer which he could accept with enthusiasm. Through the influence of his friends, Bullard was approached by the directors of a military preparedness and citizenship organization, the National Security League. Since the National Security League's purpose was to publicize the nation's needs for defense spending, compulsory military training, and patriotism education in the schools, Bullard thought that the League's presidency was a job that suited his interests and talents.

Organized in 1914 by New York lawyers and businessmen involved in the Preparedness Movement, the League had lobbied for universal military training, both for its military value and the social benefits of ''Americanization'' by military service. In 1918, however, the League turned its attention to the issue of ''100% Americanism'' and encouraged the witch hunts of the war and the ''Great Red Scare'' which followed. In 1918 the League, which had 85,000 members in twenty-two states, used its ample funds to defeat congressmen it deemed un-American. This intervention provoked Congress, which investigated the League and found that most of its money came from plutocratic New Yorkers. Its mass-movement image tattered, the League stumbled into the postwar decade unsure of its purpose and plagued by declining membership and contributions. The League turned to lobbying for compulsory citizenship education and military training in the nation's schools. The League also protested the extension of government bureaucracy and the pernicious belief that personal liberty could be separated from property rights. Its printed and broadcast propaganda urged Americans to force their leaders to return to nineteenth-century liberalism and "pure " Constitutionalism.[2]

Although he shared the League directors' social and economic prejudices, Bullard was primarily interested in publicizing military preparedness and the army and navy's needs. Under Bullard's direction, the League sponsored public speeches urging that the Congress spend more money on the army and navy and that the nation should avoid arms limitations agreements. Bullard himself addressed the League's members and the press, emphasizing that the Congress was rapidly reducing the army and navy to impotency. The League condemned the Kellogg-Briand Pact, urged closer War Department-industry ties, and advocated increased support for the citizen military-training camps. The League assumed, too, that a major factor in America's military decay was the influence of domestic radicals. It attempted to blacklist radical speakers in New York City, held patriotic rallies for school children, condemned the Soviet Union, set up studies of the Constitution for schools and by correspondence, and attacked domestic radicalism in the schools and the labor force.[3]

Bullard's duties as fund-raiser and publicist for the National Security League meshed nicely with his social life as a New York clubman, but for all his apparent social status, Bullard was not entirely happy with his civilian life. Bullard himself thought that his work had taught him a disconcerting lesson: "how tricky the average man is, how oblique and unreliable, how very different from the man that I've all my life known in the army."[4] He found his mind drifting more and more to his memories of the World War.

1.

Anxious about both his income and his reputation as a general of the AEF, Bullard started writing a personal memoir of the war shortly after his retirement. Some of the European politicians and generals had already rushed into print to continue the battle of reputations, and a handful of Americans had written instant histories of the AEF, but Bullard was the first well-known AEF general to publish. Writing from his diary entries of 1917 and 1918, he completed the manuscript in the summer of 1925. His memoir was first serialized in the Hearst chain's major New York newspaper, *The American*, and distributed to the twenty-one other Hearst papers throughout the United States. Bullard's memoir thus reached some three million readers. The complete manuscript, entitled *Personalities and Reminiscences of the War*, was then published in book form by Doubleday, Page and Company in the autumn of 1925.

Personalities and Reminiscences was full of strong opinions about American and Allied generals and free of romantic nonsense about the battlefield performance of American soldiers, but it caused very little sensation, either in the army or among the reading public. Although reviewers thought the book was charming, candid, and interesting, they tended to dismiss it as personal history. Some thought it indecent for a general to admit that he often found the war confusing, tiring, frustrating, frightening, and boring. A more telling criticism was that the book did not deal with the great issues of strategy and relations with the Allies. Most of the reviewers were disappointed that Bullard's account was not of more heroic proportions. The only strong reaction to the book came from the Negro press, which branded Bullard (the "Alabama bully") as the source of the Ninety-Second Division's troubles. The general anticipated such reaction and was untroubled by it.[5]

Bullard was unrepentant about anything else he had written in *Personalities and Reminiscences of the War*. His memoirs had proved a modest commercial success. He had established a reputation as a newspaper columnist and authority on the World War upon which he could later capitalize. His writing, however, was more important to him than his royalties. When he left the army, he had left the only society that gave him any sense of identity. Adrift from his profession in an unsympathetic civilian world, the general had restored his sense of worth by reestablishing his ties with the army in his writing. It was not, of course, the army of 1925, but the army of the World War. In writing *Personalities and Reminiscences of the War*, Bullard had not been concerned about being criticized or glorified. He was afraid that he would be forgotten. His World War memoir brought him the immortality he sought.

In 1930 Bullard again turned to the World War for the subject matter of two more books. Angered by Georges Clemenceau's claims that the AEF had made no significant contribution to the victory of 1918, he wrote a series of articles defending Pershing's position in the amalgamation issue and praising the AEF's contributions to the 1918 campaigns. As he had in his first book, Bullard did not disguise the AEF's shortcomings in command, tactics, and discipline, but he argued forcefully that it had performed well, if imperfectly. He was equally concerned that Americans would too soon forget the valor and sacrifices of the AEF's common soldiers, and he was afraid that General Pershing's much-publicized *My Experiences in the World War* was too long and stiff for the common reader. Therefore, Bullard wrote a brief history of the AEF in 1932 and revised it until its publication in 1936. Although *American Soldiers Also Fought* was not the popular and financial success Bullard hoped, he was satisfied that it was an honest history and adequately answered Allied criticisms of the American war effort. He also concluded that the Allies had perhaps not been worth saving.[6]

Bullard had made a gallant effort to assure the AEF's veterans that they and their families had no apologies to make for their service. As he worked on *American Soldiers Also Fought*, the general thought he would do something about the reputations of the AEF generals with whom he most identified—the division commanders. He decided to do a collective biography of the most "distinguished American leaders of the World War." His choices were little known outside the army. They were Henry T. Allen, Preston Brown, Hanson E. Ely, William G. Haan, Ulysses Grant McAlexander, Joseph T. Dickman, and the brilliant New York National Guardsman, John F. O'Ryan. Bullard had known all of these men for years and his treatments were candid and colorful. He did not gloss over his subjects' eccentricities or his own strained relations with some of them.

Despite his efforts, he could not find a publisher interested in producing a well written, profusely illustrated book about men the public did not know or care to remember. He had the same experience marketing his own autobiography. Profoundly unhappy with the ahistorical, profit-oriented New York publishing houses, Bullard turned away from writing of the World War. After *American Soldiers Also Fought* was finished, he gave his research materials to the New York Public Library and vowed that he would talk of the war only to those that understood—the men who had fought it. His historical writing had convinced him that the study of past wars was of no value either to active officers or to the public. There might be lessons to learn from the World War, but he was no longer confident that he knew what they were. Perhaps the rapid development of military technology, the revolutionary developments of weapons like the airplane and tank, had made his army's emphasis on character and courage irrelevant. It was as bitter a conclusion as he had ever reached.[7]

2.

Bullard attempted to construct a satisfactory new life, a task the general compared to learning to walk again, but he could not quite get used to the lack of form and ritual in civilian life: "In method and way civilian and soldier are as far apart as the antipodes."[8] In August 1927 the general wed Mrs. Ella Reiff Wall, a well-to-do widow with family ties in Philadelphia society. Even with his remarriage, Bullard was not happy. "Retirement from the active list of the army is retirement from life."[9]

Late in 1928 Bullard made a strange attempt to recapture his lost glory. He posed in full uniform for an advertisement for Lucky Strike cigarettes. His endorsement stated that Luckies helped get the AEF through the strain of battle and allowed weight-conscious soldiers to handle their tension without snacking. No sooner had the advertisement appeared in several national magazines than letters flooded the War Department. Public school teachers and administrators, doctors, veterans, mothers, National Guardsmen, and the P. Lorillard Company protested that the general had outraged their sensibilities, military and otherwise, with his cigarette endorsement. Pershing, living among his Washington worshippers, wrote James G. Harbord about the ad: "I am sending you herewith a leaf out of the

Army and Navy Journal in which one of our comrades appears in all his glory as an advertisement for Lucky Strike cigarettes."[10] Prodded by everyone from Pershing to outraged mothers, the War Department wrote Bullard to remind him that Paragraph 2.e (1) of Army Regulation 600-10 prohibited active or retired officers from giving endorsements or using their titles in commercial enterprises. The advertisement must be withdrawn, and the general must not do such a shocking thing again. Bullard took the War Department's censure lightly and found the affair amusing. He was not the least sorry he had posed for the ad, for it "pulled me out of the grave of retirement into life again before the country."[11]

Bullard was keenly aware of his growing anonymity. The thing that rankled him most was that the War Department and his army friends had forgotten him and the honor he most wanted, restoration of his wartime rank of lieutenant general. He could not forget or forgive Congress for showering Pershing with special rank (General of the Armies) and pension, while he and Hunter Liggett were forgotten. Bullard, however, had an ardent supporter in the Chief of Staff, his old friend General Summerall. Summerall and some Southern representatives persuaded Congress to restore Bullard and all other retired officers to their World War rank, but without any increase in their pensions. In Bullard's case, there would have been no increase anyway, for he was already drawing the highest regular pension. Bullard was mortified by his "shadow" honor, *"the dryest [sic] old bone that I've ever had thrown out to me."* He wished that the Congress had not bothered to raise his rank since it seemed that the government's act was more contemptuous than courteous. The incident simply dramatized the general's fall from grace since retirement. "I am impressed with the little of consequence that has been in my life in that time [1925-1930]. Truly we are nothing, can accomplish nothing no matter how hard we try and certainly I have tried. . . ."[12]

3.

Like the nation's economy, Bullard's sense of worth plummeted at the end of the 1920s, but unlike the Gross National Product, the general's morale began a slight upturn. In 1930 his daughter Rose finally married. Another encouraging aspect of his life was that the National Security League was solvent, buoyed by the contributions of its business-elite supporters. Bullard was concerned that the organization had no grassroots support, but he thought the League was more effective after the Depression began and as the threat of war increased after 1930. Bullard was pleased that the League's own budget was balanced after the League vowed to fight "COMMUNISM, GOVERNMENT RUNNING BUSINESS, AND THE DOLE."[13] The League's fight against Hooverian radicalism like the Reconstruction Finance Corporation brought Bullard additional personal publicity. In 1932 he began writing syndicated columns for the Hearst newspaper chain and articles for *Liberty* magazine, the property of his personal friend and League director, Bernarr Macfadden, the health faddist and publisher. After the Bonus March episode, Pershing finally broke his Olympian silence toward Bullard. "The Chief" approved of the League's work "in the suppression of crime and especially in chasing down Communists and Anarchists." He encouraged Bullard to keep up the good work and said he was willing to speak to private League gatherings. He would not, however, serve on the League's board of directors or make a League-sponsored broadcast against crime. Pershing wanted Bullard to keep the League in the fight against radicalism, although he himself wanted no active role.[14] Bullard was disappointed that the League could not draw on Pershing's prestige, but was not surprised that "The Chief" would jealously guard his reputation for being above politics.

Throughout the 1930s Bullard participated in the war of words against the New Deal. Initially encouraged by Roosevelt's call for national sacrifice and the action of the "Hundred Days," Bullard turned against the administration in 1934 as the promises of the National Industrial Recovery Act collapsed into class and bureaucratic conflict. Branding Roosevelt a demagogue pandering to the unemployed masses, Bullard thought that the United States was "headed for a communistic dictatorship." From 1935 until 1940 Bullard attacked the New Deal in columns in the Hearst newspapers. Although he was no apologist for Big Business and did not join the Liberty League, the general railed against welfare, deficit spending, and the urban unemployed, which he viewed as the germ of a revolutionary proletariat. He thought that the American compulsion to "bigness" and material achievement had ruined the country and that "big" government was a dangerous antidote for the nation's economic ills. Instead he urged a return to "rigidly limiting the power of government, protecting the individual against government and insuring to the common man more rights."[15]

Bullard saw the fine hand of radicals in both the New Deal and attacks upon the Reserve Officer Training Corps, one of the more useful vestiges of the National Defense Act of 1920. When peace groups struck American colleges in 1934 and 1935, Bullard rushed to the rhetorical barricades. He reminded his readers that the nation's enemies (whom he identified as Communists) hoped to ruin America's scant military establishment and delude the people that military establishments caused wars. He had no confidence that the nation had fought its last war.[16]

Rescued from obscurity by becoming a spokesman of the anti-New Deal, anti-Communist movement, Bullard found new meaning in his retirement. The Depression, the New Deal, and the radicals' vocal assault on traditional American institutions (including the army) convinced him that he could still play an important part in reconstructing American life around the nation's most hallowed values: patriotism, the Constitution, individual liberties, and the capitalistic system. He had no doubt that the 1930s marked a crucial turning point in the nation's history.

In the last fifty years the vast influx, intermixture and acceptance as citizens of the United States of foreigners and their enormous progeny, who differ widely from us and who know nothing of American democracy, have tremendously diluted the blood and changed the ideas about the functions of government of the men who founded and put this country on its course of its first 100 or 125 years. In those past fifty years we have proudly referred to our America as a "melting pot of the nations." It was, America included. . . . Today it is scarcely recognizable for what it was even a few years ago. But it was our system to accept immigrants as they came, give them citizenship; and it now looks as though we have got to take the consequences and make a new and another kind of America out of the molten changed mass. Certainly the small percent of all American ideas and blood left in the mass is too small to carry us back to be formed again into the Old America.[17]

The general never surrendered his faith that American democracy would prevail, despite "the hundreds of organizations and thousands of citizens" undermining the Constitution. Unfortunately, many Americans blamed the government "for social and economic conditions for which it is no way responsible." The nation's problems were rooted in "poverty, crime, physical or mental illness, laziness, thriftlessness." Yet he still had hope that, when the Depression passed, the American people would recover their self-confidence, take a greater interest in their nation's history, restore the strength of voluntary organizations and local government, improve public education, and assist the unemployed of all origins and races to find a place in the economic system. Bullard never quite surrendered his faith in democracy and American greatness, for to do so would have been to turn his back on forty-four years of service to a nation he did not quite understand but could not help loving.[18]

4.

As president of the National Security League and military columnist for the Hearst newspapers, Bullard could not easily renounce his interest in military preparedness. To deny that the continental United States needed protection was to deny the need for both the navy and army, and Bullard at seventy was not ready to abandon the philosophical cornerstone of a military career. In the autumn of 1933, Bullard did a series of articles on the army's current condition. Although he did not think that the United States was immediately menaced by the world's "suspicious and quarrelsome" nations, the general pointed out that the army lagged badly in mechanizing and motorizing its existing units. He predicted that the next war would be decided by mechanized and motorized forces which, carrying their supplies with them, would penetrate the enemy's lines and destroy the opposing army's command and supply system. He called the army's technological obsolesence a national scandal, particularly when the nation boasted that it was the most technologically advanced country in the world. Bullard criticized the Roosevelt Administration for its disregard for the army's needs, but admitted that the Congress and the War Department were equally responsible for the false economy which made the army impotent. He concluded that the army needed its own "New Deal."[19]

Prodded by friends still in the army, Bullard attended summer maneuvers in 1936 and 1937 to examine the army's first steps to improve its mobility and firepower. Initially impressed with the army's new aircraft, trucks, motorized artillery, and light tanks and scout cars, the general shortly recognized that less than 10 percent of the army and National Guard had adequate equipment. He had little doubt that the United States was far behind the European powers in developing modern forces for land warfare.[20]

By 1938 Bullard's pleas for rapid rearmament and equipment modernization were more insistent. For the first time, the general advocated military preparedness for a particular purpose—the defense of the United States in a world that appeared on the brink of war. He urged that the air forces be doubled, two full armored divisions be created, and all other divisions be fully motorized. For the first time, he stressed that the Army of the United States needed to be larger as well as better. He wanted the regular army increased to 200,000 and the National Guard to 300,000. He also proposed that 120,000 more reserve officers be trained immediately. In recruiting men, the army should stress mechanical aptitude.[21]

Bullard watched the Roosevelt Administration reluctantly rearm in the aftermath of the Munich Conference and supported the government's increased military budgets. He disagreed, however, with the administration's emphasis on the navy and on aircraft-building. He thought that the army needed its own share of "machine power and fire power" to be truly modern. When he reviewed the rearmament program in the summer of 1939, Bullard was disappointed at how little the administration had accomplished. Reflecting the War Department's official position, he advocated "balanced preparedness" or ground forces modernization. Having studied the First Army's maneuvers that summer, he was shocked that this force had only 15 percent of its authorized trucks. He concluded accurately that the United States had a 1918-vintage army with a handful of 1939-prototype weapons. He believed that it would no longer be possible for the United States to "bungle through" in a swift, modern war. For the first time, he also pointed out that the United States, if it became again involved in a general European war, should be prepared to carry that war far beyond its own shores. He knew that in 1939 the army did not have that capability.[22]

Although his interest focused on the army's ground forces, Bullard also investigated the condition of the Army Air Corps. In 1933 he wrote an old friend from Mindanao days, Major General Benjamin D. Foulois, chief of the Army Air Corps, about the General Staff's plans to assign all the army's squadrons to ground armies. Foulois responded that the Air Corps should mass its bombers for coast defense and its fighters for air defense. Although the General Staff prohibited Foulois from mailing his letter, it could not persuade Bullard to stop writing critical articles about army air policy.[23]

In his military affairs columns for the Hearst chain and *Liberty* magazine, Bullard gave the matter of air warfare increasing consideration. Like other prophets of air power, he believed that the lessons of war in the twentieth century were two-fold: war had become a national experience involving the total mobilization of a nation's human and material resources, and "the air plane has become the first and paramount weapon of war." There was no reason to assume that a future enemy would spare America's civilian population if he had the weapons to attack it. The only hope was that modern urban and industrial nations would so fear reprisal attacks by bombs and gas that war would be avoided.[24]

In 1934, after a series of investigations of the Air Corps' condition, the War Department authorized the formation of a central operational command, General Headquarters (GHQ) Air Force, to control the continent's air defense. GHQ Air Force's conception of its mission, however, was to emphasize strategic bombardment, not defense against bombers. Bullard watched Air Corps exercises with mounting concern. Basically, he accepted GHQ Air Force's analysis that pursuit planes could not halt the bombers. Bullard, however, concluded that the "lesson" of these exercises was that the United States should give highest priority to the development of pursuit planes, antiaircraft artillery, and civil defense programs. He feared that neither the Roosevelt Administration nor the War Department fully appreciated that the airplane was rapidly ending America's geographic isolation and safety from attack, but he could not yet envision American bombers attacking another nation's cities.[25]

Bullard's advocacy of preparedness grew from a conservative assessment of world politics and American foreign policy. He saw no value in the United States' leaguing itself with either international organizations or European allies for collective security. Even if weak in military strength, the United States should follow a unilateral course in its foreign relations and avoid commitments outside the Western Hemisphere. Bullard recognized that Europe (after the outbreak of the Spanish Civil War in 1936) was on the brink of another general conflict. His own antiradicalism, on the other hand, led him to describe the approaching European war as a struggle between the "Red" and "anti-Red" nations. If so, Europe and the Western Hemisphere would be bound in a "class war" of "unprecedented industrial disturbances and civil disorders."[26]

Bullard was mildly surprised when Nazi Germany invaded Poland in 1939. He had not thought that Germany would be so bold as to challenge both the French-British alliance in western Europe and the interests of the Soviet Union (the Germans' "natural" enemy) in eastern Europe. He was confused when Germany and Russia signed a nonagression pact and then partitioned Poland, since this alliance did not conform to his conception of the great class war. Bullard was no more accurate as a strategic analyst than he had been as an international affairs pundit. He assumed that the French and British would mount an offensive on Germany via the Moselle River valley, an attack Bullard believed would be successful.[27]

Bullard's major interest in the European war was in drawing the correct military lessons from the German conquest of Poland. Generally, he was satisfied that his prewar predictions on the efficacy of air power and armored warfare had been correct. The implications for the United States, an urbanized, industrial nation which depended upon overseas sources of raw materials and markets, were ominous. Bullard urged that the Roosevelt Administration immediately improve the nation's antiair and antisubmarine defenses.[28] Bullard did not ignore the lesson of the Polish campaign for the United States Army. The German armored *blitzkrieg* had made it obvious that the United States needed more tanks. The problem was more complicated than just buying more tanks and trucks. Bullard's concern was that the army's tactical doctrine had not adjusted to the increased mobility and firepower of mechanized forces. Bullard was not satisfied that the army really appreciated that armored forces and tactical aircraft now dominated the battlefield.[29]

When the German army demonstrated its tactical proficiency against the French army and the BEF in 1940, Bullard saw the Fall of France primarily in tactical terms. The campaign in France again suggested that the United States Army was too small, ill-equipped, and ill-organized to throw back a modern invader. Bullard witnessed army field exercises in New York, Wisconsin, Louisiana, and Texas in 1940 and came away depressed. Obviously, he wrote, the Roosevelt Administration still had no conception of the army's lack of modernization.[30] When he watched the army's large-scale maneuvers in the South in 1941, Bullard correctly saw that the army's mechanized forces had excellent mobility, but too little firepower and insufficient numbers. He saw much *blitz*, but too little *krieg*. He thought that the army's reconnaissance forces were good, and he saw hopeful progress in tactical defense doctrine and the use of parachute infantry, but he reported that the army's basic tank forces were badly undergunned and had too little tactical air support.[31]

Bullard did not ignore the fact that the existing army's manpower did not meet the War Department's contingency plans for continental defense, and he approved when the Congress passed the Selective Service Act of 1940. He saw the draft as the only way to raise an adequate army, but he worried about the quality of the conscripts and the cost of training the enlarged army. He agreed that the draft was the only democratic way to raise troops, since all citizens had an equal military responsibility, but he was pleased that the selective service system would take men whose departure for the army would not disrupt the reviving economy. If the draft in practice bore most heavily on young men from low income families, that was actually to the draftees' advantage. Bullard was sure that the draft would *"build better men"* physically, psychologically, and mentally.[32]

Bullard remained a diplomatic isolationist for all his advocacy of military preparedness. His rearmament proposals were not for overseas intervention but continental defense. He viewed the European war only as a useful case-study in the methods of modern warfare, although he agreed that the war endangered American security. He pessimistically concluded that democratic states could not match the war-making ability of dictatorships. The United States was powerless to halt totalitarianism "in the Old World" and was unprepared even to defend its own shores from invasion. Bullard concluded that "war overseas . . . would be suicidal." He had mixed emotions about the administration's support for embattled Great Britain and approved of naval cooperation and Lend-Lease only because the Royal Navy helped keep the Axis out of the Western Hemisphere while the United States slowly rearmed. Even as late as the summer of 1941, Bullard approved only of United States military intervention in the Americas to stop Axis expansionism. Bullard had no taste for entry into World War II as an active member of the strange Allied coalition.[33]

5.

A visitor to the National Security League's dilapidated, walk-up office on Forty-Fifth Street would have found it hard to believe that his host was a retired general of the United States Army. The old man working at his neat desk looked more like a misplaced smalltown editor preparing his weekly paper for his county's farmers. Thin, weak-looking, indifferently dressed in a rumpled suit that was too big for his shrinking body, the aged president of the National Security League greeted his guests while wearing a green eyeshade and the black half-sleeves of a clerk. Robert Lee Bullard, however fragile-looking and gray, still had zest for conversation, and he would invariably entertain his guest with delightful anecdotes. The general was also a good listener, enjoying good stories as well as telling them. His lined face still wrinkled in smiles, and his blue-gray eyes brightened easily. His manner and surroundings suggested a man well organized, mentally alert, and aware of the world about him despite the fact that he was nearing eighty.[34]

Masked by his unfailing politeness and good-humored loquaciousness, Bullard's fear of obscurity grew with his advancing age. The general was especially distressed that he had so little influence in the army. In 1939 he lobbied for a West Point appointment for Peter's son, Robert Lee Bullard III. Although he was pleased when his grandson won a competitive appointment, he was miffed that he himself had not had sufficient influence to get the appointment. Bullard did what he could to preserve his historical identity. He donated a portrait and bust to the Military Academy, his books to the New York Public Library, his uniforms and memorabilia to the New York Historical Society and the Alabama Department of Archives and History and Alabama Polytechnic, and personal photographs to his friends and family.

When the War Department began to recreate the Army of the United States, Bullard wrote General Marshall to suggest that the army call to active duty *"senior experienced retired officers competent and anxious to render such service."* He did not include himself in this category, being "too old and played-out even to think of further service." Marshall assured Bullard that the army had the authority to recall retired officers and was already doing so.[35]

Having watched the United States slide into a war he knew it was not prepared to fight and questioning the wisdom of intervention, Bullard followed World War II as best he could in the newspapers. As a new wave of war patriotism swept the country after Pearl Harbor, the general wondered why he remained such an obscure public figure. As one of the few surviving high commanders of the AEF, he thought that he might make some contribution to the war effort. The War Department never called. He thought that perhaps his religion and his activities for the National Security League had ruined his public reputation. He drew what consolation he could from letters from old army friends and occasional lunches with his cronies at the Army and Navy Club.[36]

America's entry into World War II, however, provided Bullard with new opportunities to write. In the summer of 1942, he lucidly described the significance of the reorganizations in the Army Ground Forces for the readers of *Think* magazine. Bullard was pleased to report that the wartime army was everything he had hoped for in the 1930s. The infantry and armored divisions were an effective combination of foot soldiers, mechanized firepower, and highly responsive artillery. Division commanders had better communications and more authority than the generals of the AEF. When one considered the added combat effect of tactical fighter-bombers, the new American divisions should be able to handle the best the Germans could field. Bullard particularly approved of the massive War Department investment in the Army Air Force and the new emphasis on teamwork within the army instead of coercive discipline.[37]

Bullard was not, however, happy with the public optimism on America's Home Front. Bullard recognized the significance of Germany's setbacks in Russia and the shifting balance of the naval war in the Pacific, but he thought that there would be more "self-denial, slaughter, black times" for America before the war was won. He feared that the public was not being conditioned for the costs of a victorious war effort. Both Germany and Japan would have to be defeated totally and their peoples subjugated. To end the Axis threat the Allies would have to wage "hard, tough war completely to defeat them *and dictate and enforce peace*" whatever the cost. This time there should be no armistice.[38]

The general's own interest was in the European theater, his attention on the enemy and terrain he knew best. For Bullard, the real American war effort began with the invasion of Normandy and the liberation of France in 1944. D-Day was personally satisfying as well as the army's greatest triumph. His nationalism and army loyalty undiminished, Bullard told the members of the Army and Navy Club after V-E Day that the Allied Expeditionary Force had brought the Third Reich down, not the Red Army. The final victory belonged to the great Anglo-American democracies, not the despotic Russians, who had depended on the Allies "in all their means of war except men." However misconceived Bullard's assessment of the victory, it was a comforting thought for an old general.[39]

His pension eaten away by wartime inflation, Bullard remained obsessed by the idea that the War Department had forgotten him. He pulled from his files a biographical sketch written in 1931 by his son Peter and wrote another resumé of his career. In a sense, Bullard was writing his own obituary. When he complained to a friend about the War Department "having let me down a good deal since I retired," the friend asked whether he had ever been reprimanded. Reading his diaries, the general found six episodes where a superior had reproved him; in each case his sin had been overaggressiveness in combat. Bullard was unrepentant and was satisfied that in each case the superior had later approved of the results of his actions.[40] He knew that he had never been officially reprimanded and was proud of his combat record. In preparing his appeal to the War Department, Bullard emphasized that he had made every effort to improve his professional knowledge, that he had educated himself and then taught others all he knew of the military trade. He had led by personal example and a considerate understanding of human nature. All his efforts, however, would have been worthless if they had not brought victory to American arms on the battlefield, whether that battlefield was the high grass of Mindanao or the *Kriemhilde Stellung*. Bullard did not want to be remembered as an army bureaucrat. He had "merely caromed in Washington. Never sought, always when allowed, declined service that tended to make [me] an office soldier." He claimed no special preferment for individual bravery, only for being a successful officer. "I must add . . . that I do not claim personally to be a fighter. My job as an officer was to make my men fight."[41]

Bullard wrote Pershing and Bernard Baruch to ask their help in getting his lieutenant general's pay "restored." He suggested that they write Senators Lister Hill and John Bankhead of Alabama and Kenneth McKellar of Tennessee on his behalf, stressing his long service and fine record. Pershing, bed-ridden and close to mental incompetency, was no help, but Baruch wrote an inquiry to the Adjutant General. The Adjutant General's formal reply was gentle: General Bullard had been carried on the retired list as a lieutenant general since 1931, and there was no difference in retired pay between major generals and lieutenant generals.[42]

On February 20, 1947, shortly after his eighty-sixth birthday, General Bullard slipped upon leaving the subway at the Wall Street Station. He broke his leg. He was taken to the army hospital at Governors Island, his leg was set, and he was given a thorough physical. The doctors discovered that he had generalized, severe arteriosclerosis, and on March 23 he had a cerebral vascular hemorrhage. He lingered on in the Fort Jay hospital throughout the summer. On September 11 he suffered a second cerebral hemorrhage and died peacefully. The *Army and Navy Journal* which carried his obituary also reported that the Air Force would soon test-fly the XB-47, that the Strategic Air Command would soon have more powerful nuclear bombs, that the navy had just organized its first jet carrier squadron, and that General Eisenhower wanted a larger army. Who remembered an old soldier whose military career had started with a campaign against the Apache Indians?[43]

With his death, General Robert Lee Bullard emerged from public obscurity. More important, he returned to the army. The New York City newspaper obituaries were long and rich in hyperbole. All lauded the general's fighting record; all commented upon Bullard's rise from rural Alabama roots to command of the Second Army; all lauded his retirement career as citizen of New York City and advocate of preparedness. Not one obituary in the New York newspapers got the facts of his military career correct.[44] The only accurate obituary appeared in *Assembly*, the magazine of the West Point graduates association. The *Assembly* eulogy emphasized that Bullard's reputation in the army was based on his long experience in troop command and his drive for success as a combat officer. There was little doubt that his career had been the fulfillment of his wishes. Yet Bullard's military achievements were not the sum of the man. Lieutenant General Hugh A. Drum recalled that Bullard (whom he had known from boyhood) "typified to me, as well as many others, the highest type of true Americanism, not only as a citizen but as a soldier also." As a soldier Bullard had "a strong, unwavering will to succeed. He created and endeavored to grasp every opportunity for success. Such characteristics, combined with a very fertile imagination and broad vision opened the way for his progressive spirit and nature." Bullard was an aggressive leader who always sought assignments in "the thick of things." Yet, General Drum continued, Bullard's ambition and aggressiveness never destroyed his charm and warmth:

> He loved people and they loved him. He captivated his associates by his personal characteristics as well as by his good fellowship and facility to teach and amuse by his good, timely and humorous stories. In all these years his friendship never wavered; it was bountiful and lasting. . . . Those associated with him absorbed some of his aggressive spirit and drive and thus succeeded through his influence which was wide and deep in our civil life as well as in the army.[45]

On Monday, September 15, after a short memorial service in the Fort Jay chapel, Bullard's remains were taken by a Military Police escort to the Church of St. Ignatius Loyola at the corner of Park Avenue and 84th Street for a low requiem mass. As the Fort Jay band played "Abide with Me," the general's coffin was carried by six sergeants into the church. Among the 500 mourners were his wife, three of his four children, and the general's army and civilian friends. The honorary pallbearers represented the continuities in Bullard's life: General Courtney Hodges and Admiral Monroe Kelley, the highest ranking military officers in the New York area; five retired generals and admirals, including Generals Drum and Dennis Nolan from the AEF; federal judge Francis G. Caffey, former lieutenant colonel of the Third Alabama Volunteers; Wesson Seyburn, Bullard's former aide and son of his first company commander in the Tenth Infantry; Bernarr Macfadden; and the general's friends from his New York clubs, the National Guard, and the National Security League. The mass was celebrated by the former post chaplain at Fort Jay.[46]

After the service, a five-car cortege drove north from the city along the Hudson River. The cortege, moving well-spaced and deliberately like an army convoy, reached its destination in the early afternoon. Moving through Highland Falls, it entered the south gate of the United States Military Academy and proceeded to the post cemetery. A battalion of cadets was formed at the gravesite along with the superintendent and commandant of cadets at the Academy. Again there were brief words of remembrance and farewell, the honor guard fired the prescribed volleys, and a bugler played taps. General Robert Lee Bullard had returned to the place where it had all begun so many years before.

NOTES

[1] Diarybook 13, entry, July 22, 1925, BP; Diarybook 14, entry, June 29, 1928, BP.

[2] Robert D. Ward, "The Origin and Activities of the National Security League, 1914-1919," *Mississippi Valley Historical Review* 47 (June 1960), pp. 51-65.

[3] New York Times, May 6, May 22, July 3, and July 11, 1926; July 7, July 13, July 26, September 12, and October 13, 1927.

[4] Diarybook 14, entry, December 4, 1926, BP.

[5] Reviews in the *Infantry Journal* 28 (January 1926), p. 78, and *Coast Artillery Journal* 44 (February 1926), p. 215; Henry E. Armstrong in *The New York Times Book Review* section, December 27, 1927, p. 7; *New York Tribune*, December 20, 1925; *The Outlook* 141 *(December 23, 1925), p. 642;* World's Work V (December 1925), pp. 162-168; Frank H. Simonds in *The Saturday Review of Literature* 2 (November 28, 1925), p. 337; "Bullard," *The Crisis* 30 (September 1925), pp. 218-220; the unfavorable reaction to Bullard's remarks on the Ninety-Second Division are reviewed and summarized in *Literary Digest* 85 (June 27, 1925), pp. 14-15.

[6] Bullard columns in the New York American, May 4, 11, and 18, 1930, BP; Diarybook 15, entries, 1935, BP; Robert Lee Bullard, *American Soldiers Also Fought* (New York and Toronto: Longmans, Green, 1936).

[7] Diarybook 15, entries, 1934-1935; manuscript drafts in Boxes 7 and 8; and Bullard's summary of his historical writing in Diarybook 15, entry, July 8, 1936, all BP.

[8] Bullard autobiography, p. 182, BP.

[9] Diarybook 14, entry, December 12, 1927, BP.

[10] J. J. Pershing to J. G. Harbord, January 24, 1929, James G. Harbord Papers/NY Historical Society.

[11] Bullard autobiography, p. 183, BP; Diarybook 14, entry, April 18, 1929, BP. Copies of the advertisement and the protest correspondence are in the Bullard 201 File.

[12] Diarybook 14, entry, July 5, 1930, BP; Maj. Gen. C. P. Summerall to Maj. Gen. J. L. Hines, (?) 1929, John L. Hines Papers.

[13] Diarybook 15, December 20, 1931, BP.

[14] J. J. Pershing to R. L. Bullard, July 30, 1932, John J. Pershing Papers; J. J. Pershing to R. L. Bullard, August 23, 1934, appended to Diarybook 15, BP.

[15] Diarybook 15, entries August 21, November 6 and 25, 1934, BP; Robert L Bullard, "New Personal Rights Established or Being Established," 1935, *mss*, BP; Robert L. Bullard, "America's Obsession for the Striking, the Sensational, the Colossal," 1934, *mss.* BP; Bullard column, New York *American*, September 16, 1934.

[16] Lt. Gen. Robert L. Bullard, "Communist-Pacifist Propaganda Aims to Cripple U.S.," *Scabbard and Blade* 19 (April 1935), pp. 2-3.

[17] Notes, July 18, 1938, Box 14, BP.

[18] Lt. Gen. Robert L. Bullard, "The Meaning of Citizenship," speech to the graduating

class of Castle Heights Military Academy (Lebanon, Tennessee), 1939, copy in BP.

[19]Bullard columns in the New York *American,* September 3, 10, and 17, 1933, BP.

[20]Diarybook 15, entry, August 25, 1936, BP; Diarybook 16, entries, January-February 1937, BP; Bullard column in the New York *American,* March 28, 1937, BP; *Army and Navy Journal,* August 8-29, 1936; Diarybook 16, entries, September-October, 1937, BP; *Army and Navy Journal,* September 11, 1937.

[21]Lt. Gen. Robert L. Bullard, "A Liberty Program for National Defense," *Liberty* (circa 1938), copy in BP.

[22]Lt. Gen. Robert L. Bullard, "Give Us an Army," *Liberty* (February 11, 1939), pp. 24-25, and *mss* on lack of army preparedness (circa 1939), copies in BP; Lt. Gen. Robert L. Bullard, "We Are Still Not Prepared," *Liberty* (August 26, 1939), reprint in BP.

[23]Maj. Gen. B. D. Foulois to R. L. Bullard, October 17, 1933, Bullard 201 File; Brig. Gen. Alfred T. Smith to Gen. D. MacArthur, November 23, 1933, Bullard 201 File; Benjamin D. Foulois, *From the Wright Brothers to the Astronauts: The Memoirs of Major General Benjamin D. Foulois* (New York: McGraw-Hill, 1968), p. 227.

[24]Lt. Gen. Robert L. Bullard, "Can Our Army Defend Us," *Liberty* (July 1934), pp. 16-21; Bullard column in the New York *Herald-Tribune,* November 10, 1935, BP.

[25]Robert L. Bullard, *mss* on defense against strategic bombardment, February 1936, BP; Bullard columns in New York *American,* February 16, 1936, BP, and in the Denver *Post,* February 27, 1936, copy in USAMHRC; Lt. Gen. Robert L. Bullard, "Why We Need 4,000 Airplanes Right Away," *Liberty* (October 15, 1938), pp. 11-12, BP.

[26]Lt. Gen. Robert L. Bullard, "The World Ready to Crack," *Liberty* (?, 1938), n.p., copy in BP.

[27]Bullard column in the New York *Journal and American,* September 10, 1939, BP.

[28]Bullard columns in the New York *Journal and American,* October 8, November 5, November 24, and December 2, 1939, BP.

[29]Bullard columns in the New York *Journal and American,* October 29 and November 19, 1939, BP.

[30]Robert L. Bullard, "That Blitzkreig Can Be Halted," *mss,* June 1940, BP; Lt. Gen. Robert L. Bullard, "We Have No Army," *Liberty* (June 1, 1940), pp. 7-8, BP.

[31]Robert L. Bullard, "Have Our War Manoeuvres Taught Us Anything," *mss,* October, 1941, BP.

[32]Lt. Gen. Robert L. Bullard, "Straight Talk to the Families of Drafted Men," *Liberty* (November 30, 1940), pp. 21-22, and "To Save Billions In Defense," *Liberty* (September 13, 1941), pp. 16-17.

[33]Lt. Gen. Robert L. Bullard, "A Program for National Defense," *Liberty* (August 17, 1940), pp. 7-9; article notes, July 22, 1941, Box 14, BP.

[34]Daniel W. Bender tape, March, 1969, in the author's possession.

[35]R. L. Bullard to Gen. G. C. Marshall, June 5, 1940; Gen. G. C. Marshall to R. L. Bullard, June 25, 1940, AGO File 325; R. L. Bullard to Gen. G. C. Marshall, December 18, 1940; Gen. G. C. Marshall to R. L. Bullard, December 27, 1940, AGO File 210.851, Records of The Adjutant General's Office, 1917-   , Record Group 407 National Archives.

[36]Diarybook 16, entries, January, 1942-December 1944, BP.

[37]Lt. Gen. Robert L. Bullard, "Our Streamlined Army," *Think* 8 (July 1942), pp. 12-13, 40-41.

[38]Lt. Gen. Robert L. Bullard, "Still Needed: An Adequate Public Concept of Our War and Our Enemies," *mss* written September 1942, and printed as "What We Are Up Against," *American Legion Magazine* 34 (January 1943), pp. 1, 42-43.

[39]Lt. Gen. R. L. Bullard speech to the Army and Navy Club, May (?), 1945, copy in BP.

[40]Diarybook 17, entry, January 25, 1946; P. C. Bullard, "General Bullard," 1931; "Brief of Service of Major-General Robert L. Bullard, Retired, *age 85 years,*" 1946, all BP.

[41]Diarybook 17, entry, January 25, 1946, BP.

[42]R. L. Bullard to J. J. Pershing and Bernard Baruch, October 1, 1945, Bullard 201 File.

[43]TAGO, "Statement of Medical History in the Case of Maj. Gen. Robert L. Bullard, USA," with addenda, 11 September 1947, Bullard 201 File; *Army and Navy Journal,* September 20, 1947.

[44]New York *Herald-Tribune,* September 12, 1947; New York *Tribune,* September 12, 1947; *Time,* September 22, 1947; *New York Times,* September 12, 1947; Robert R. McCormick's editorial in the *Chicago Tribune,* September 21, 1947.

[45]Irving J. Palmer, "Robert Lee Bullard," *Assembly* (July 1948), pp. 3-4.

[46]*New York Times,* September 15, 1947; New York *Sun,* September 15, 1947; New York *World-Telegram,* September 15, 1947.

Essay on Sources

Robert Lee Bullard

The Bullard Papers in the Manuscript Division, Library of Congress, Washington, D. C., are not large, filling only sixteen boxes. The quality of those papers General Bullard saved, however, was superb. The heart of this biography is Bullard's seventeen diarybooks (1899-1946), twenty-five military notebooks, his manuscript autobiography, and file copies of Bullard's own books and articles. The personal correspondence, particularly to his family, is thin, and some of it was probably destroyed by Bullard during his retirement. The general also saved some useful maps, photographs, books, and other memorabilia, most of which were related to his service in the Philippines and France. In addition to the Bullard Papers in Washington, I found a file of correspondence in the Department of History and Archives, State of Alabama, Montgomery, Alabama. For Bullard's boyhood and year of college in Alabama, I received memoirs, archival material, and court records from Mr. Alexander Nunn of the Lee County Historical Society; Mrs. Ruth Crump, Lanett, Alabama; Mrs. T. F. Yancey, Sr. of Opelika, Alabama; Mr. Charles W. Edwards of Auburn, Alabama; Mrs. C. W. Canon of Opelika, Alabama; Miss Marjorie Andrews of LaFayette, Alabama, and Mr. James Noel Baker of Opelika, Alabama. Mrs. Frances Honour of the Ralph Brown Draughon Library, Auburn University, provided materials from the Auburn University archives, and the national headquarters of Alpha Tau Omega, Chicago, Illinois, also had a file on Bullard.

Bullard's military records begin with the cadet records at the archives and manuscripts division of the United States Military Academy Library, West Point, New York. I found a personal file for Bullard in the Records of The Adjutant-General's Office, 1780s-1917, Record Group 94, National Archives of the United States, Washington, D. C. The file was "Bullard, Robert L.," File 4482 ACP 1885. During World War I, however, the army changed its personnel accounting system and created a second Bullard file. It is the Bullard 201 File, now held by the U.S. Army Administration Center, St. Louis, Missouri. It contained a detailed statement of military service, efficiency reports, medical records, and scattered correspondence.

Bullard wrote three books: *Personalities and Reminiscences of the War* (Garden City, N.Y.: Doubleday, Page, and Co., 1925); *American Soldiers Also*

Fought (New York and Toronto: Longmans, Green, and Co., 1936); and *Fighting Generals* (Ann Arbor, Michigan: J. W. Edwards, 1944). His many magazine articles are cited in the appropriate footnotes; most I read as file copies in the Bullard Papers, although there is also a file of retirement era writings on preparedness in the archives of The Hearst Corporation in the library of the University of Texas at Austin.

The Bullard photographs came from the Bullard Papers, the Audiovisual Records Division of the National Archives, and the United States Military Academy library.

The Officers of Bullard's Army

I found a great deal of continuity in the lives of army officers during Bullard's active career, but I also believe that the officers of 1885-1925 fall into three general categories: those who served in the Army of the Civil War and Reconstruction; those commissioned in the period 1870-1898, whom I considered Bullard's contemporaries for the basis of comparative biography; and the "emerging elite" of the AEF, predominately officers who entered the regular army after 1900. I used the materials on the Civil War vintage officers primarily to get some feel for military policy, 1800-1898, and for the quality of frontier service. The data on the "emerging elite" of World War I was most helpful for understanding the younger officers' views of the war and their generals' performance in it.

The Civil War Generation

I made no systematic effort to use the materials of this group of officers unless I thought they bore directly on army policy in the 1880s and 1890s or touched Bullard's career. The commanding generals of the army all left personal accounts. William T. Sherman wrote his *Memoirs of General William T. Sherman*, 2 vols. (New York: D. Appleton & Co., 1875) before his retirement, but followed with another edition in 1891 which included more on the postwar army. Sherman's successor, Philip H. Sheridan, died in office, and his *Personal Memoirs of P. H. Sheridan*, 2 vols. (New York: C. L. Webster & Co., 1892), show it. Lieutenant General John M. Schofield, *Forty-Six Years in the Army* (New York: The Century Company, 1897) is essential for the post-Civil War army and catches the first-rate intelligence of its author. Lieutenant General Nelson A. Miles, whose skill at personal publicity was highly developed, wrote two memoirs, *Personal Recollections and Observations of General Nelson A. Miles* (Chicago and New York: The Werner Company, 1897), and *Serving the Republic* (New York and London: Harper and Brothers, 1911). There are Sherman, Sheridan, Schofield, and Miles Papers in the Manuscript Division of the Library of Congress, but I consulted them only for references to Bullard.

The second Chief of Staff was a Civil War veteran who rose from private to lieutenant general, and his career is sympathetically told by one of his aides, Maj.

Gen. William H. Carter, *The Life of Lieutenant General Chaffee* (Chicago: University of Chicago Press, 1917). Like Adna Chaffee, other gallant young officers of the Civil War surfaced as the aging generals of the War with Spain, but still served with determination if not always energy and distinction. Generally they did better than the nation had a right to expect. Their experience is described in: Alice Blackwood Baldwin, *Memoirs of the Late Frank D. Baldwin, Major General, U.S.A.* (Los Angeles: Wetzel Publishing Co., Inc., 1929), the story of a two-time Medal of Honor winner; William Haymond Bisbee, *Through Four American Wars: The Impressions and Experiences of Brigadier General William Henry Bisbee* (Boston: Meador Publishing Co., 1931; and Merrill J. Mates, *Indians, Infants and Infantry: Andrew and Elizabeth Burt on the Frontier* (Denver, Colorado: The Old West Publishing Company, 1960).

An impressive officer of Civil War vintage to reemerge in 1898 was Major General James Harrison Wilson, who had been a major general of Volunteers before he was thirty. His meteoric rise was not accidental, as he demonstrated after resigning in 1870. He prospered as a businessman and Republican politician, returning to uniform in 1898 to serve in Puerto Rico, Cuba, the Philippines, and China. Wilson's voluminous papers (nineteen shelf-feet) are in the Manuscript Division of the Library of Congress. They were especially useful, for Wilson corresponded with many of the army's promising officers, fourteen of whom became generals. Wilson's autobiography is *Under the Old Flag,* 2 vols. (New York and London: D. Appleton and Company, 1912).

For careers in the Medical Department, see John M. Gibson, *Soldier in White: The Life of General George Miller Sternberg* (Durham, N.C.: Duke University Press, 1958), and Maria B. Kimball, *A Soldier-Doctor of Our Army: James P. Kimball* (Boston: Houghton Mifflin Company, 1917).

Other valuable sources for this generation of army officers include Martin F. Schmitt, ed., *General George Crook: His Autobiography* (Norman, Oklahoma: University of Oklahoma Press, 1960); Brig. Gen. A. W. Greely, *Reminiscences of Adventure and Service* (New York: C. Scribner's Sons, 1927); William Mitchell, *General Greely* (New York: G.P. Putnam's, 1936); Andrew Wallace, "Gen. August V. Kautz and the Southwestern Frontier," 1967, typescript biography in the U.S. Army Military History Research Collection; Anson Mills, *My Story* (Washington: Byron S. Adams, 1918); and Ernest S. Wallace, *Ranald S. Mackenzie on the Texas Frontier* (Lubbock, Texas: West Texas Museum Association, 1964).

The standard biography of Colonel Emory Upton, the army's St. Joan, is Stephen E. Ambrose, *Upton and the Army* (Baton Rouge: Louisiana State University Press, 1964).

Bullard's Generation

In designing the collective biography by which I tested General Bullard's typicality, I considered officers commissioned between 1870 and 1900 as

Bullard's contemporaries. I have reservations about identifying a "generation" of officers, for I believe that officers shared like experiences only with officers within five years (older and younger) of their own age and date of commissioning. However, this group shares some characteristics. They were not Civil War veterans. They reached positions of responsibility only in the War with Spain. Most became generals in World War I, although some, like Leonard Wood and John J. Pershing, were promoted "prematurely" for colonial service.

The Line

Major General Henry T. Allen (1859-1930), USMA, 1882, left the Manuscript Division of the Library of Congress some fifteen thousand items, the most useful of which are letters, diaries, military reports, and maps which cover his service as Alaskan explorer, cavalry officer, chief of the Philippine Constabulary, and commanding general of the Ninetieth Division and the U.S. forces on the Rhine. The latter experience he described in *My Rhineland Journal* (Boston: Houghton Mifflin, 1923). Allen corresponded with both MacArthurs, Theodore Roosevelt, Wood, March, Pershing, and Newton Baker. His biography is Heath Twichell, *Allen: The Biography of an Army Officer, 1859-1930* (New Brunswick, N.J.; Rutgers University Press, 1974).

Major General Harry H. Bandholtz (1864-1925), USMA, 1890, saved primarily his correspondence for the period he was an officer and chief of the Philippine Constabulary (1903-1913). His correspondents included other generals: Henry T. Allen, J. Franklin Bell, Frederick Funston, James G. Harbord, Mark Hersey, Leonard Wood, John J. Pershing, Albert L. Mills, and Harry S. Howland. The five boxes of Bandholtz Papers are in the Michigan Historical Collections, University of Michigan, Ann Arbor, Michigan.

Major General Thomas H. Barry (1855-1919), USMA, 1877, is described in Eugene Wildman, "From Bowery Boy to General," *The World To-Day* XVI (March 1909), pp. 281-285.

General Tasker H. Bliss (1853-1930), USMA, 1875, saved one hundred sixteen shelf-feet of papers, which now belong to the Manuscript Division of the Library of Congress. The bound volumes of correspondence, diaries, reports, memoranda, cables, and scrapbooks are concentrated in the period 1898-1919 and are especially good for the Mexican border troubles, 1911-1917, and World War I. A former acting Chief of Staff, Bliss was the American military representative on the Supreme War Council and was in close touch with General Headquarters, AEF. Bliss' career is fondly told in Frederick Palmer, *Bliss, Peacemaker: The Life and Letters of Tasker H. Bliss* (New York: Dodd, Mead & Company, 1934).

Brigadier General William Carey Brown (1854-1939), USMA, 1877, left scattered diary notes on frontier service, 1874-1875; service in the Philippines in 1900-1901; and for 1906-1907. His letters (1915-1939) deal with the Punitive Expedition and World War I. There are only three boxes of Brown Papers at the U.S. Army Military History Research Collection, but Francis F. Brimlow interviewed the general and others and wrote a detailed biography, *Cavalryman Out of the West: Life of General William Carey Brown* (Caldwell, Idaho: Caxton Printers, Ltd., 1944).

Major General Beaumont B. Buck (1860-1950), USMA, 1885, wrote a highly selective autobiography, *Memories of War and Peace* (San Antonio, Texas: The Naylor Company, 1935). The book is silent on the unpleasantness in Buck's career from his academic troubles at West Point to his relief in France. Nevertheless, the memoir covers his full career in useful detail.

Virginia Conner, wife of Major General Fox Conner (1874-1951), USMA, 1898, caught her husband's exceptional career and the army lifestyle in *What Father Forebad* (Philadelphia, Pa.: Dorrance and Company, Inc., 1951).

Colonel Charles J. Crane (1852-1928), USMA, 1877, recalled his service, primarily with Negro infantry regiments, in *The Experiences of a Colonel of Infantry* (New York: The Knickerbocker Press, 1923).

"Reminiscences, 1882-1905" and "Reminiscences of the World War" catch the formative years in the career of Major General George B. Duncan (1861-1950), USMA, 1886. Professor Edward M. Coffman of the University of Wisconsin at Madison lent me his copy, which I used with the permission of the general's son, Mr. Henry T. Duncan of Lexington, Kentucky. The Duncan memoirs are rich with anecdotes and descriptions of army life and personalities.

Major General Clarence R. Edwards (1859-1931), USMA, 1883, left twenty-seven boxes of correspondence and printed orders, memoranda, articles, and speeches to the Massachusetts Historical Society, Boston. Like most of his contemporaries, Edwards began to collect his papers during the War with Spain, and his manuscripts are best on his service in the Philippines, his long tour as chief of the Bureau of Insular Affairs, and tenure as a general officer, 1912-1922. The Edwards Papers are fair on World War I and the Twenty-Sixth Division. They are quite good on the postwar period.

Major General Frederick Funston (1865-1917), was appointed a brigadier general in the army in 1901 without a day's service as a regular officer, thus making his career the Horatio Alger story of the Philippine Insurrection. Before entering the regular army, he won a Medal of Honor and captured Aguinaldo, but died before World War I. He left five boxes of papers to the Kansas State Historical Society in Topeka, which I did not search because I could and did consult Thomas W. Crouch, "The Making of a Soldier: The Career of Frederick Funston, 1865-1902" (unpublished Ph.D. dissertation, University of Texas at Austin, 1969), and Funston's own *Memories of Two Wars; Cuban and Philippine Experiences* (New York: C. Scribner's Sons, 1911).

Brigadier General Charles Gerhardt (1863-1957), USMA, 1887, wrote a manuscript memoir which covers his infantry service in the West, Alaska, and Cuba and his experience in France with the AEF. His memoir is part of the U.S. Army Military History Research Collection.

Major General William G. Haan (1863-1924), USMA, 1889, left twelve boxes of papers to the State Historical Society of Wisconsin, Madison, Wisconsin, but the papers cover Haan's career unevenly. The correspondence covers 1898-1925. There are partial diaries for Haan's service in the Philippines (1898-1899) and Panama (1904). The manuscripts, however, are good on General Staff duties, artillery matters, and coast defenses before World War I; they also contain the general's letters to his wife from France, where he commanded the Thirty-Second Division. The postwar papers are excellent on army educational policies and reorganization.

Brigadier General Johnson Hagood (1873-1948), USMA, 1896, was one of the prime organizers of the AEF's logistical system. He continued his fight with Pershing's headquarters in *The Services of Supply: A Memoir of the Great War* (Boston: Houghton Mifflin, 1927), which includes autobiographical data on the rest of his military career, especially his prewar General Staff experiences.

Major General James Guthrie Harbord (1866-1947), commissioned from the ranks in 1891 after two years as a cavalry sergeant, managed to be an indispensable officer for both Leonard Wood and John J. Pershing. The bulk of Harbord's papers are held by the Manuscript Division of the Library of Congress, but the New York Historical Society, New York City, also has a Harbord collection, primarily Harbord's World War I diaries and correspondence with Charles Dawes, and postwar military papers until his retirement in 1923. The Washington collection is extensive, twelve shelf-feet. Harbord's correspondence is heaviest for World War I, but adequately covers his entire career. The World War I material is priceless: his own candid letters home, correspondence with Pershing and Newton D. Baker, and copies of the AEF's cable traffic with Washington. General Harbord wrote of his World War experiences in *Leaves from a War Diary* (New York: Dodd, Mead & Company, 1931), and *The American Army in France, 1917-1918* (Boston: Little, Brown and Company, 1936).

Lieutenant Colonel Otto Hein (1847-1933), USMA, 1870, was unknown outside the army, but he was an acute observer of army life, and his connections in Washington high society made his home a popular rendezvous with visiting officers. His autobiography is *Memories of Long Ago* (New York and London: G. P. Putnam's Sons, 1925).

The son of a distinguished officer, Major General Guy V. Henry, Jr. (1875-1967), USMA, 1898, recalled his career in a detailed manuscript autobiography, "Brief Narrative of the Life of Guy V. Henry, Jr.," written after his second retirement from active service in 1944-1946. It is part of the U.S. Army Military History Research Collection.

Major General John L. Hines (1868-1968), USMA, 1891, left seventy-two containers of papers to the Manuscript Division of the Library of Congress. Most of the papers deal with World War I and Hines' postwar career, which included a tour as Chief of Staff. The Hines Papers compose personal archives for the histories of the First and Fourth Divisions and III Corps of the AEF. The personal correspondence (six boxes) contains ample data on Hines' career before World War I; his correspondents included Malin Craig, Hugh Drum, Robert C. David,

Hanson E. Ely, James G. Harbord, Charles P. Summerall, John J. Pershing, George C. Marshall, and Douglas MacArthur. I also had access to General Hines' World War I diaries and journals, now in the possession of his former aide, General Charles L. Bolté, U.S. Army (Ret.) of Alexandria, Virginia.

Colonel Lyman W.V. Kennon (1863-1918), USMA, 1881, had assignments much like Bullard's until his untimely death in 1918. The Manuscript Division of the Duke University Library, Durham, North Carolina, has one box of Kennon papers. They are personal papers, letters to his wife, and scattered diaries. In addition to the Duke University collection, the U.S. Army Military History Collection holds a box of Kennon papers.

Major General Frank R. McCoy (1874-1954), USMA, 1897, was one of the most attractive officers of Bullard's army. An even-tempered, talented, and versatile officer, McCoy specialized in colonial affairs in the Caribbean and the Philippines, but was equally adept as a troop leader in France, General Staff officer, aide to Leonard Wood and Theodore Roosevelt, and diplomat. His letters to his mother, Mrs. Margaret McCoy, and his wife, Mrs. Frances McCoy, are rich in detail on the army's leap overseas after 1898. McCoy also kept organized subject files which are very useful. His correspondents included Robert C. Davis, Leonard Wood, Halstead Dorey, Hugh L. Scott, William D. Connor, James G. Harbord, Theodore Roosevelt, and William Howard Taft. The McCoy Papers (comprising ninety-five boxes with finding aids) are in the Manuscript Division of the Library of Congress; I searched them with the permission of Mrs. Frances McCoy.

General Peyton C. March (1864-1955), USMA, 1888, left his extensive papers to the Manuscript Division of the Library of Congress. I found most of them applied to World War I and March's career as Chief of Staff, although there was good coverage of March's experience as a military observer in the Russo-Japanese War. I found the twenty-two boxes of material helpful, but I reconstructed March's career with Edward M. Coffman, *The Hilt of the Sword: The Career of Peyton C. March* (Milwaukee, Wisconsin: University of Wisconsin Press, 1966), an admirable biography, and March's own *The Nation at War* (Garden City, N. Y.: Doubleday, Doran & Company, Inc., 1932).

Major General George Van Horn Moseley (1874-1960), USMA, 1899, wrote the most striking account of an army career I found, the two-volume "One Soldier's Journey," part of the Moseley collection in the Manuscript Division of the Library of Congress. There are plenty of manuscripts to supplement the autobiography, some seven thousand items which include correspondence, diaries, reports, memoranda, scrapbooks, speeches, and clippings. Moseley seemed to find the center of the action in the Philippine jungles, on the General Staff in France, and in Washington as Douglas MacArthur's assistant chief-of-staff.

Colonel T. Bentley Mott (1865-1952), USMA, 1886, did his army apprenticeship as an artillery officer. His mature years were spent as a General Staff officer and military attaché, and he was a linguist and expert on European armies. He tells his own story, including his friendship with Pershing and service in France during World War I, in *Twenty Years as Military Attaché* (New York, London, and Toronto: Oxford University Press, 1937).

Brigadier General John McAuley Palmer (1870-1955), USMA, 1892, was a key figure among the professionalizers, and his papers detail the debates on military policy from 1910 until 1945. He describes his own career in a two-volume typed memoir, "An Old Soldier's Memories," which covers his life from 1870 until 1906. He did not live to finish the work, but organized his notes, letters, memoranda, and diaries as twenty-one volumes of "Chapter Notes" for 1906-1945. Palmer also kept a correspondence file of nine boxes for 1886-1941. The Palmer collection was donated to the Manuscript Division of the Library of Congress, but was on loan to Professor I. B. Holley of Duke University, Palmer's biographer, when I searched it.

Major General Frank Parker (1872-1947), USMA, 1894, left ten shelf-feet of material to the Southern Historical Collection, University of North Carolina at Chapel Hill. Most of the material deals with World War I and Parker's postwar service until 1936. The one box of material on Parker's career before World War I is, however, very good on army life, cavalry training, colonial service, and genealogy.

Major General James ("Galloping Jim") Parker (1854-1934), USMA, 1876, was one of Bullard's close friends. He told his own story (without modesty and with some errors) in *The Old Army: Memories, 1872-1918* (Philadelphia: Dorrance & Company, 1929).

Colonel William Paulding (1852-1933), commissioned from civil life in 1873, wrote a 139-page memoir which covered all but his service as colonel of the black Twenty-Fourth Infantry, 1908-1913. He was a company officer in the Tenth Infantry and a field grade officer in other regiments his entire career, serving in Cuba, the Philippines, and Alaska. His wife Grace also wrote a memoir which begins in 1894 and covers Paulding's career through 1913; Mrs. Paulding is very good on army social life and the garrison duties of an officer's wife. The Paulding papers are in the U.S. Army Military History Research Collection.

Like everything else about General of the Armies John J. Pershing (1860-1948), USMA, 1886, the Pershing papers are awesome. There are 127,000 items in the Manuscript Division of the Library of Congress and another twenty-nine shelf-feet in Record Group 316 in the National Archives of the United States in Washington. I read Pershing's diaries and notebooks, which cover 1882-1923; they exhibit the general's professional thoroughness and analytic skill. I read sections of the General Correspondence, 1904-1948, which is alphabetically organized; most of the letters cover Pershing's career after 1914, although there are letters from his earlier tours in the Philippines. Even before he became commander of the AEF, Pershing knew the army's "Who's Who." I read the letters exchanged with forty other officers who were generals, presidents, and secretaries of war, and a platoon of senators and congressmen. The Pershing papers also include extensive subject files; I read those for 1900-1903 for Pershing's service on Mindanao. I also read the "Book Files," which contain the staff studies and memoranda Pershing consulted when he wrote *My Experiences in the World War,* 2 vols. (New York: Frederick A. Stokes Company, 1931). The Pershing Papers in the National Archives contain material from the Punitive Expedition and the World War; much of it deals with officers' performance and relief. This collection contains the letters of Colonel Paul H. Clark, who reported on the war from the Operations Section of the French General Staff. Pershing, of course, has ample biographers. Avery D. Andrews, *My Friend and Classmate John J. Pershing* (Harrisburg, Pa.: The Military Service Publishing Company, 1939), and Frederick Palmer, *John J. Pershing, General of the Armies* (Harrisburg, Pa.: The Military Service Publishing Company, 1948), give the view of intimate friends, but are also based on manuscript sources. The closest student of Pershing's career, however, is Professor Donald W. Smythe, S.J., of John Carroll University. I had the good fortune to read Professor Smythe's "John J. Pershing: Soldier," which covers the general's service through 1916; this manuscript has been published as *Guerrilla Warrior: The Early Life of John J. Pershing* (New York: Scribners, 1973). Professor Smythe is now working on a second Pershing volume and often sent me Bullard-related items during his own research.

Sometimes I found it easy to forget that not all army officers became generals. Therefore the following source was particularly good: Frank D. Reeve, ed., "Frederick E. Phelps: A Soldier's Memoirs," *New Mexico Historical Review* XXV (July-October 1950), pp. 37-57, 109-135, 187-221, and 305-327. Lieutenant Colonel Phelps (1847-1923), USMA, 1870, was a frontier cavalry officer who retired through disability in 1891, but returned to active duty as a recruiter and quartermaster for 1907-1919. His memoirs, however, cover only his frontier service in the Eighth Cavalry, 1870-1884.

Major General Charles D. Rhodes (1865-1948), USMA, 1889, left eleven boxes of diaries, letters, notebooks, and scrapbooks to the United States Military Academy Library. The collection is excellent, particularly the diaries, which span Rhodes' entire career. Rhodes' diaries dramatize the fact that pleasant officers can become generals without sacrificing their friends, family, and modesty.

Colonel Wirt Robinson (1865-1929), USMA, 1887, should destroy any stereotype about "typical" officers. Although he served more than ten years as a coast artillery officer, he spent most of his career as a professor of science at the Military Academy. His twenty-nine volumes of meticulously printed diaries are good on his Coast Artillery service, but lean more to birds than ballistics. They are good on army life, especially at West Point. The Robinson collection is in the Military Academy Library.

Colonel George B. Rodney (1872-1950), was a Delaware Volunteer officer of 1898 and integrated into the regular army in 1901. After retirement he wrote *As a Cavalryman Remembers* (Caldwell, Idaho: The Caxton Printers, Ltd., 1944), a good memoir by a man who was *not* part of the army's elite and seldom saw dramatic action.

Brigadier General Walter S. Schuyler (1849-1932), USMA, 1870, was another cavalryman whose lineage, like Rodney's, went back to America's colonial First Families. An aristocratic upstate New Yorker, Schuyler fought Indians with the Fifth Cavalry; commanded New York and federal Volunteers in 1898-1901 in Cuba, Puerto Rico, and the Philippines; went to Russia as a military attache and later observed the Russo-Japanese War; commanded the Fifth Cavalry; built Schofield Barracks in Hawaii, 1909-1910; and retired in 1913. I got to know General Schuyler through his journals, 1879-1913, which are part of the Schuyler collection in the Henry E. Huntington Library and Art Gallery, San Marino, California.

General Hugh L. Scott (1853-1934), USMA, 1876, was known in the army as "Good Old Scott," not as a good bet to be a general. He became Chief of Staff, primarily through his persistence, integrity, association with Leonard Wood, and family ties to Woodrow Wilson. General Scott's voluminous papers (thirty thousand items) are in the Library of Congress Manuscript Division. I read five boxes of family correspondence (1874-1933), forty boxes of general correspondence (1870-1934), selected subject files, and the rough drafts of the general's autobiography, *Some Memories of a Soldier* (New York and London: The Century Company, 1928). The Scott papers are excellent on frontier service, the first occupation of Cuba, Philippine service, and the Mexican border troubles. The general was past his peak when World War I came and it shows in his correspondence. His correspondents included Wood, McCoy, J. Franklin Bell, Bliss, Fred Ainsworth, Edward St. J. Greble, Herbert J. Slocum, Woodrow Wilson, and Newton D. Baker.

General Charles P. Summerall (1867-1955), USMA, 1892, also was a Chief of Staff. His papers, sixteen shelf-feet in the Library of Congress Manuscript Division, are best on World War I and the postwar army, but cover his full career. The three boxes of diaries and correspondence were disappointing, for Summerall was not an open or imaginative man. He did, however, collect excellent materials on World War I (much to glorify his own role) and the postwar army. His correspondents included Bullard, Pershing, MacArthur, Baker, Theodore Roosevelt, and others.

Major General George O. Squier (1865-1934), USMA, 1887, went from the Artillery to become Chief Signal Officer and designer of electrical equipment. His papers, 1884-1945, are part of the Michigan Historical Collections at the University of Michigan. They are slim, but offer excellent data on the relationship of military men and modern technology, including electronics and aviation. I was, however, particularly interested in Squier's own "Biographical Sketch of Major General George Owen Squier Chief Signal Officer of the Army" and his autobiographical notes written while a cadet at West Point.

Major General Eben Swift (1854-1938), USMA, 1876, was a frontier cavalryman and colonial commander of Volunteers. His manuscript autobiography, written in 1930, is excellent on army life. It is held by the Military Academy Library.

Brigadier General LaRoy S. Upton (1869-1927), USMA, 1891, was an infantry officer who described his life at West Point; his Cuban service (1899-1902); garrison life in the United States and Philippines (1902-1908); and his experience in the AEF, 1917-1919, in letters to his family. The small, but useful Upton collection is held by the Minnesota Historical Society in St. Paul.

Major General Leonard Wood (1860-1927), commissioned as a surgeon in 1886, had a career which boggles the imagination. So do his papers, all one hundred forty-six shelf-feet in the Manuscript Division of the Library of Congress. The coverage is even and complete for his entire career. I read his diaries, 1875-1919, which are sketchy for the period 1898-1902, but otherwise excellent. I also went through fifty-one boxes of personal correspondence, 1903-1918, and looked at assorted subject files; I did not pay much attention to the period 1919 to 1927, which marked the peak of Wood's political ambitions and Philippine service. As both a political power and army Chief-of-Staff, Wood had wide connections in the army and the federal government. He also had a Boswell, the journalist Hermann Hagedorn, whose *Leonard Wood: A Biography*, 2 vols. (New York and London: Harper and Brothers, 1931), is still the standard work. Hagedorn's excesses are corrected in Jack C. Lane, "Leonard Wood and the Shaping of American Defense Policy, 1900-1920" (unpublished Ph.D. dissertation, University of Georgia, 1963).

The Staff

The careers of line officers in Bullard's generation varied considerably, and the patterns of service in the staff departments show similar variations. In the Adjutant General's Department, the Quartermaster Department, the Subsistence Department, the Judge-Advocate General's office, and the Office of the Inspector General, the officers were former line officers. In the Paymaster General's department, the officers were a mix of former line officers and civilian appointees. The Corps of Engineers was formed by West Pointers who served their entire careers in the corps. The medical officers ("surgeons" and "assistant surgeons") of the Medical Department were physicians who entered from civil life and were seldom called anything but "doctor," regardless of their rank.

In the case of Major General Fred C. Ainsworth (1852-1934), commissioned in 1874, a doctor was more bureaucratic than the bureaucrats. Before he was forced into retirement in 1912, Ainsworth rose to Adjutant General. His career is skillfully told in Mabel E. Deutrich, *Struggle for Supremacy: The Career of General Fred C. Ainsworth* (Washington: Public Affairs Press, 1962).

Major General Enoch H. Crowder (1859-1932), USMA, 1881, spent fourteen years as a cavalry officer before he became a judge-advocate. He went to Manchuria as an observer of the Russo-Japanese War, served in the colonial administration in the Philippines and Cuba, and was appointed Judge Advocate General in 1911. In 1917 he was given the title Provost Marshal General and

placed in charge of the wartime draft. Crowder's papers (twelve boxes) are part of
the Western Historical Manuscripts Collection, housed in the library of the
University of Missouri at Columbia. There is also a good biography: David A.
Lockmiller, *Enoch H. Crowder: Soldier, Lawyer, Statesman* (Columbia, Mo.:
The University of Missouri Press, 1955).

Brigadier General Thomas Cruse (1857-1943), USMA, 1879, spent seventeen
years in the Sixth Cavalry and was still a first lieutenant. In 1896 he transferred to
the Quartermaster Department, serving with ability until 1918. He tells his own
story in *Apache Days and After* (Caldwell, Idaho: The Caxton Printers, Ltd.,
1941).

The Corps of Engineers is well represented in the 1870-1900 group of future
generals. Major General George W. Goethals' biography is eulogistic, but based
on private papers and family archives. It is Joseph B. Bishop and Farnham Bishop,
Goethals: Genius of the Panama Canal (New York and London: Harper and
Brothers, 1930). General Goethals (1858-1928), USMA, 1880, spent a full career
as an instructor at West Point and construction supervisor on canals, locks, and
river dredging projects before he took on the Big Ditch in Panama. He returned
from retirement to become the army's supply chief in World War I. Brigadier
General Jay Johnson Morrow (1870-1937), USMA, 1891, the brother of banker-
diplomat Dwight Morrow, had a less illustrious career, but reported it fully to his
father, 1887-1904, and to his mother, 1904-1918. Morrow's letters are part of the
Clara Johnson Morrow collection in the Manuscript Division of the Duke University Library. Major General William B. Sibert (1860-1935), USMA, 1884,
went in over his head with the First Division after a distinguished career as an
engineer; he recovered as chief of the Chemical Warfare Service. He is praised in
Edward B. Clark, *William L. Sibert: The Army Engineer* (Philadelphia: Dorrance
& Company, Inc., 1930), the sort of book that pleases families, but also contains
useful information.

Unlike Wood and Ainsworth, some doctors stayed in the Medical Department.
Those who made their mark usually did so as epidemiologists. Major General
William C. Gorgas (1854-1920), commissioned in 1880, is memorialized in Marie
D. Gorgas and Burton J. Hendrick, *William Crawford Gorgas: His Life and Work*
(Garden City, N.Y.: Doubleday, Page and Company, 1924), and John M. Gibson,
Physician to the World: The Life of General William C. Gorgas (Durham, North
Carolina: Duke University Press, 1950). Brigadier General Jefferson R. Kean
(1860-1950), commissioned in 1884, did not win any special fame, but did his part
in the fight against yellow fever in Cuba (1899-1902, 1906-1909) and in the AEF's
medical service. Both experiences are well covered in his papers, which are held in
the manuscript division of the University of Virginia Library, Charlottesville,
Virginia. L. N. Wood, *Walter Reed: Doctor in Uniform* (New York: Jullian
Messner, Inc., 1943), does not do justice to Major Reed (1851-1902) who
received his commission in 1875 and died of appendicitis after conquering yellow
fever.

Partial Accounts

Some of Bullard's most interesting contemporaries left only partial accounts of their service. Major General Robert Alexander (1863-1941), commissioned from the ranks in 1889, spent four years as an enlisted man in the infantry, but wrote only of his *Memories of the World War, 1917-1918* (New York: The Macmillan Company, 1931). Lieutenant General Joseph T. Dickman (1857-1927), USMA, 1881, did the same in *The Great Crusade: A Narrative of the World War* (New York: Appleton, 1927). Dickman, a cavalryman of wide accomplishment and great determination, at least got a sketch in Bullard's *Fighting Generals.* Lieutenant General Hunter Liggett (1857-1935), USMA, 1879, rates at least a memoir and several biographies, but we have little more than a sketch by B. H. Liddell Hart in *Reputations: Ten Years After* (Boston: Little, Brown and Company, 1928), pp. 261-285; Stephen A. Park, "Liggett, Hunter," *Dictionary of American Biography XXI: Supplement One* (New York: Charles Scribner's Sons, 1944), pp. 494-495; and his own *Commanding an American Army* (Boston: Houghton Mifflin, 1925) and *AEF: Ten Years Ago in France* (New York: Dodd, Mead, 1928). Major General Harold B. Fiske (1871-1960), USMA, 1897, left little more than World War I materials in the National Archives, although some of his correspondence goes back to 1911. The collection is only five shelf-feet and basically contains documents from the GHQ AEF G-5 section. Major General Campbell King (1871-1953), commissioned from the ranks in 1898, left excellent material on World War I, but little else from his distinguished career. His papers are in the Duke University Library and number only 259 items.

I also found some scattered materials in the West Point Library which were worked into the study where appropriate. Colonel Joseph H. Dorst (1855-1916), USMA, 1873, left a few letters on the frontier army. I also used the cadet letters of Colonel Charles F. Crain (1872-1956), USMA, 1894, and the letters of Brigadier General Hiram M. Chittenden (1858-1917), USMA, 1884. The Crain collection also had some letters on the frontier army.

The "Emerging Generation"

I made no systematic effort to study the careers of officers commissioned after 1900 unless their experiences somehow touched Bullard's service or their biographies were exceptional studies of the army. In both categories fall Forrest C. Pogue, *George C. Marshall: The Education of a General 1880-1939* (New York: The Viking Press, 1963); Martin Blumenson, *The Patton Papers, 1885-1940* (Boston: Houghton Mifflin, 1972); and D. Clayton James, *The Years of MacArthur, Vol. I: 1880-1941* (Boston: Houghton Mifflin, 1970); and Barbara W. Tuchman, *Stilwell and the American Experience in China, 1911-1945* (New York: The Macmillan Company, 1970). See also Brigadier General Hugh S. Johnson, *The Blue Eagle From Egg to Earth* (Garden City, N.Y.: Doubleday,

Doran & Company, 1935). For the aviators, there are Brigadier General William Mitchell, *Memoirs of World War I* (New York: Random House, 1960), and Major General Benjamin D. Foulois with Colonel C. V. Glines, USAF, *From the Wright Brothers to the Astronauts: The Memoirs of Major General Benjamin D. Foulois* (New York: McGraw-Hill Book Company, 1968).

I also found the following personal accounts useful: Charles G. Dawes, *A Journal of the Great War,* 2 vols. (Boston: Houghton Mifflin, 1921), the diary of Pershing's friend, the AEF purchasing agent, and future vice-president: John R. White, "Three Generals," personal memories of Wood, Pershing, and Harbord by a former officer of the Philippine Constabulary, in the special collections of the University of Oregon Library, Eugene, Oregon; and the letters of Captain John Leland Jordan, Thirty-Eighth U.S. Volunteers, 1898-1903, on his experiences in southern Luzon during the Philippine Insurrection. These letters, held by the Tennessee State Library and Archives, Nashville, Tennessee, are the best descriptive accounts of service in the Philippines I found.

In addition I used material from the papers of Lieutenant General Hugh A. Drum in the possession of Colonel Elliott H. Johnson, USAF.

The Army

The National Archives of the United States in Washington, D. C., and the Washington National Records Center, Suitland, Maryland, provided a variety of army records useful in this study. From the Records of the Headquarters of the Army, 1798-1903 (Record Group 108), I used the "Letters Sent" and "Letters Received" by the Commanding General of the Army for 1895-1903. I searched the Records of the Office of the Secretary of War, 1800-1942 (Record Group 107), for Bullard-related material in the "Correspondence File, 1890-1913," and found useful background information on army education, promotions, and training. I did the same for the "Decimal Correspondence File, 1913-1922." I paged the "Letters Sent" volumes for 1903-1913 and got tired of reading about War Department lands, bureau activities, and Corps of Engineers projects. In the Records of the Office of the Inspector-General, "Reports, 1814-1939," (Record Group 159), I found several reports on units Bullard commanded. I located Bullard-related letters in the Records of the Adjutant General's Office (Record Groups 94 and 407), as well as in the records of the U.S. Thirty-Ninth Volunteer Infantry Regiment. I found a variety of items in the Records of the War Department General Staff (Record Group 165). I searched the "General Correspondence, Chief of Staff" for 1903-1916 and 1917-1921 for files on officer promotions, military education, mobilization plans, reorganization of the infantry, manpower legislation, and National Guard matters. Most contained studies done by the Army War College Division of the General Staff. For background on the infantry units in which Bullard served and the posts where he lived, I used two National Archives microfilm collections: "Returns from Regular Army Infantry

Regiments, June, 1821-December 1916'' (Microcopy 665), and "Returns, U.S. Army Posts, 1800-1916'' (Microcopy 617). The Records of the American Expeditionary Force, 1917-1919 (Record Group 120), are massive. I generally sought materials which dealt directly with General Bullard's own commands and his superiors' headquarters. Searching Record Group 120 is simplified by the use of the "Historical Files" which each AEF command created. These files contain essential war diaries, operations reports, maps, orders, staff studies, intelligence analyses, logistical memoranda, and other related documents. I used the "Historical Files" of the GHQ AEF, First Army, and III Corps. I also searched the "Organization Records" (which contained the commanding general's correspondence) of the First Division, III Corps, and Second Army; the special files of AEF schools in the GHQ AEF "Organization Records"; and the pertinent files from the records of the office of the inspector-general of the AEF.

Of the printed original sources, the *Annual Reports of the War Department*, 1885-1925, were indispensable, as was the *Official Army Register*, printed annually by the Adjutant General in all but the World War I years. The *Annual Reports of the War Department* were multivolume publications done primarily for the Congress. They lean heavily to statistics, but until after World War I they are a mine of data. Discontinued during the height of the war, they were reintroduced in very abbreviated form (to save printing costs) in the 1920s. The *Official Army Register* is the basic source of officer career data. I also sampled the hearings of the Senate and House Military Affairs Committees and the *Congressional Record*, but only when I thought I could find Bullard-related data.

A semiofficial source for the careers of West Point graduates is Edward S. Holden and Wirt Robinson, eds., *General Cullum's Biographical Register of the Officers and Graduates of the U.S. Military Academy: Supplements, 1890-1900, 1900-1910, 1910-1920*, Vols. IV, V, VI (Cambridge, Mass.: Riverside Press 1901, and Saginaw, Michigan, Seeman and Peters, 1910 and 1921). "Cullum," as it is fondly called by army buffs, should be checked against the 1964 edition of the West Point Alumni Foundation, *Register of Graduates and Former Cadets of the United States Military Academy* (West Point, N.Y., 1964), and Francis B. Heitman, *Historical Dictionary and Register of the U.S. Army* (Washington: Government Printing Office, 1903).

Military journalism flourished and persisted in the United States for the first time after the Civil War. For news of the army, the weekly *Army and Navy Journal*, published in Washington, is essential. Except for two years during World War I it was published continuously during Bullard's career; it is now the *Journal of the Armed Forces*. In 1878 a group of army officers formed a professional study association, the Military Service Institution of the United States; their bi-monthly magazine, the *Journal of the Military Service Institution*, was the primary outlet for officer writing. It was published until World War I. the *JMSI* was shortly challenged by specialized magazines supported by line officers of the combat arms. The *Cavalry Journal* first appeared in 1888, the *Infantry Journal* in 1904, and the *Journal of the United States Artillery* in 1892. These journals were closely associated with the schools established by each of the combatant arms and published not only specialized articles, but general military items as well.

The histories of the post-Civil War army begin with descriptions of that antique curiosity, the frontier army, a melange of Washington bureaucrats and Indian fighters. They are captured in William Walton, *The Army and Navy of the United States,* 2 vols. (Boston: G. Barrie and Son, 1889-1895), and Rufus Zogbaum, *Horse, Foot, and Dragoon* (New York: Harper & Brothers, 1888). Zogbaum actually visited frontier posts, and while he never rivaled Frederick Remington and Charles Schreyvogel as an illustrator, his artwork is passable. In the 1890s, while the regular army was undergoing a collective identity crisis, the *Journal of the Military Service Institution* published a comprehensive set of histories of the line regiments and the staff bureaus, 1890-1895. These histories were collected and published as William L. Haskin and Thomas F. Rodenbaugh, *The Army of the United States* (New York: Maynard, Merrill & Co., 1896). The studies after 1898 tend to be preparedness polemics which advocate one form or another of a cadre-conscript system or enlarged regular force. Emory Upton, *Military Policy of the United States* (Washington, 1904), is of historical interest, since it was a Bible of sorts to the most rigid professionals. The best description of the army between San Juan Hill and the Meuse-Argonne is Major General William H. Carter, *The American Army* (Indianapolis: The Bobbs-Merrill Company, 1915). John Dickinson, *The Building of an Army* (New York: The Century Company, 1922), covers the land forces, legislation, Selective Service, and oddments from World War I in a competent discussion of manpower mobilization and the legal-constitutional questions of army organization. After World War I, the officer corps itself produced two dependable histories which are still valuable: Colonel William Addleman Ganoe, *The History of the United States Army* (New York: Appleton, 1924), and Colonel Oliver L. Spaulding, *The United States Army in War and Peace* (New York: G. P. Putnam's Sons, 1937). The colonels tend to see only the regular army, both in peace and war. Russell F. Weigley, *History of the United States Army* (New York: The Macmillan Company, 1967), is the best history to date, for it differentiates between the peacetime standing army and the wartime army swelled by militia, volunteers, or draftees and their accompanying citizen-officers.

The National Guard has not been as well served as the regular army in the writing of history, either in state studies or discussions of the National Guard as a national military institution. The most complete printed study is Jim Dan Hill, *The Minute Men in War and Peace: A History of the National Guard* (Harrisburg, Pa.: The Military Service Publishing Company, 1964). I am not sure what the antonym of "Uptonian" is (perhaps "Jacksonian"), but Jim Dan Hill's book is it, being militantly anti-War Department. I prefer Elbridge Colby, "The National Guard of the United States," an unpublished manuscript in the Edward Martin Library, National Headquarters of the National Guard Association of the United States, Washington, D. C.

For a visual impression of Bullard's army, see *Uniforms of the United States Army* (New York and London: Thomas Yoseloff, 1960), a two-volume collection of the plates of Henry Alexander Ogden with an introduction and text by Marvin Pakula.

INDEX

Ainsworth, Fred C., 179, 228, 247, 485

Alexander, Robert, 389, 487

Alger, Russell A., 82, 104, 111

American Expeditionary Force: Fismette incident, 386-88; formation of corps, 377-78; generals for, 307-8, 315-17, 378, 407, 418; headquarters staff of, 314-15; Montfaucon incident, 399, 403-5; occupation duties, 429-40; origins of, 301-3, 306-7; policy on black troops for, 425-29; postwar studies of, 432-33; schools for, 317-18; strategy for, 313, 331, 377-81, 395-97, 417; tactics of, 315

American Expeditionary Force Armies: First, 386, 395-411, 417, 423; Second, 417-33

American Expeditionary Force Corps: I, 355, 378, 381-86, 397-411; II, 378; 111, 378-89, 397-411; III, 378-89, 397-411; IV, 378, 419, 423; V, 397-411

American Expeditionary Force Divisions: Second, 380-83; Third, 322, 377, 380-81, 384, 400, 409; Fourth, 386-411; Fifth, 377; Twenty-sixth, 354-58, 380; Twenty-eighth, 381, 384-90, 420, 423; Thirty-second, 384; Thirty-third, 397-98, 400-411, 421, 424; Thirty-fifth, 421, 424; Thirty-seventh, 403, 420; Forty-second, 380; Seventy-seventh, 377, 387, 389; Eightieth, 398, 400-411; Eighty-second, 377; Eighty-eighth, 421, 424; Ninety-second, 420, 424, 425-29. *See also* American Expeditionary Force First Division

American Expeditionary Force First Division: in Ansauville sector, 340-47; capture of Cantigny, 360-68; early training of, 312, 320-24; in Montdidier sector, 354-70; organization of, 307; at Soissons, 381-83; as tactical organization, 336-38; use of in early 1918, 331-32, 338; victory parade, 443; voyage to France, 311

Anderson, George S., 128-29, 131

Andrews, Avery D., 305

Apaches, campaigns against, 53-60

Army War College, 224-32

Bach, Christian, 404, 409

Baker, Newton D., 303, 307-8, 316, 321, 346, 401, 443, 446

Baldwin, Frank D., 117, 168, 477

Ballou, Charles C., 426-29

Bandholtz, Harry H., 94, 230, 478

Barry, Thomas H., 81, 224, 248-49, 307, 478

Bates, John C., 124, 127, 131

Bell, George, Jr., 400

Bell, J. Franklin, 195, 221-22, 265-68, 307, 317

Bellinger, Rose Brabson Bullard, 77, 207, 224, 250, 268, 282, 309, 451, 462

Bjornstad, Alfred W., 378-83, 385-88, 400, 403-5, 407, 418

Bliss, Tasker H., 81, 154, 210, 214-18, 233-34, 252, 256-58, 261-62, 275-76, 288, 303, 307-8, 356, 478

Blocksom, A. P., 277, 280, 288

Booth, Ewing E., 404

Brewster, André W., 321, 323, 365, 368

Buck, Beaumont, 94, 310-11, 356-57, 362, 479

Bullard, Daniel (father), 19-21, 41

Bullard, Ella Reiff Wall (wife), 461

Bullard, Keith (son), 190, 207, 224, 250, 282, 309, 451

Bullard, Peter Cleary (son), 75, 207, 224, 266, 268, 309, 451, 468, 469

Bullard, Robert L.: as agent on secret mission to Mexico, 216-18; on American diplomacy, 289-90, 293, 450-51; on army organization, 192, 446-47; as brigade commander, Second Division, 1913-1915, 253-54, 263-68; as child and youth in East Alabama, 21-26; on citizen-soldiers, 155-56, 201; as colonel, Thirty-ninth U.S. Volunteer Infantry, 115-49; as colonel, Twenty-sixth Infantry, 1912-1917, 250-93; as commander and governor on Mindanao, P.I., 1902-1904, 168-83; as commander, Camp Logan H. Roots (Ark.), 306, 309; as commander, National Guard brigade, 287-89; as commanding general, First Division, AEF, 332-47, 353-70; as commanding general, Second Army, AEF, 418-33; as commanding general, Second Brigade, First Division, AEF, 309-10; as commanding general, III Corps, AEF, 379-89, 397-411; in

community and political activities, 190, 208; death and burial of, 470-71; family background of, 19-21; on garrison duty, 189; on General Staff, 224, 230-32; on leadership, 156, 192-93, 199, 208-9, 212, 227; as lieutenant colonel, Eighth Infantry, 207-18; as lieutenant, Tenth Infantry, on frontier, 52-64, 81-85; as lieutenant, Tenth Infantry, at Infantry and Cavalry School, 75-76, 80; lobbies for promotion to brigadier general, 227-30, 255-56, 290-91; on logistics, 156-57; as major and colonel, Alabama Volunteers, 95-107; as major, Twenty-eighth Infantry, 189-91; as military cadet, 32-44; on National Guard, 80, 201, 209-12, 233-34, 288-89, 443; on officer education, 221-23, 225-26; as officer in Provisional Government of Cuba, 194-98; as PMS&T, North Georgia Agricultural College (Dahlonega), 79-80; on postwar American society, 444-45, 449, 462, 463-64; on preparedness, 199-200, 259-60, 442, 450-51, 464-66; as president, National Security League, 458-69; relations with John J. Pershing, 305-6, 322-24, 355-58, 388, 410-11, 418, 443-44, 452-53, 461-63; relations with the Ninety-second Division, 425-29; seeks transfer to infantry, 154-162; seeks transfer to staff, 82-83; sources for, 475-76; as student at the Agricultural and Mechanical College of Alabama (Auburn), 25-26; as student, Army War College, 1911-1912, 221-32; summarizes career, 469-70; on training, 157, 194, 211-12, 254, 257, 266-67; on troop duty, 182; as unattached major general and commanding general,

Second Corps Area, 442-54; as vehicle for examining military professionalism, 3, 10-12; on war, 156, 198-99; on World War I, 291-92, 294, 318-19, 340, 421-22, 431-33, 459-61; on World War II, 466-69

Bullard, Robert L., Jr. (son), 75, 207, 224, 306, 309, 451

Bullard, Robert L., III (grandson), 468

Bullard, Rose (daughter). *See* Bellinger, Rose Brabson Bullard

Bullard, Rose Douglass Brabson (wife), 53, 62, 75-80, 161, 207, 224, 250, 268, 282-83, 309, 448-49

Bullard, Susan Mizell (mother), 19-21, 41

Bundy, Omar, 381

Caffey, Francis G., 99-100, 102, 103, 471

Cailles, Juan, 138-39, 141, 148

Calamba, Laguna Province, P.I., battles around, 123-26

Cameron, George H., 398, 404

Camp Shipp (Ala.), 104-6

Cantigny, battle of, 360-68

Carter, William H., 159, 248-49, 254-55, 257-58

Chaffee, Adna R., 167-68, 477

Cleary, Peter A. J., 53, 62, 158, 221, 266

Clemenceau, Georges, 408, 460

Conger, Arthur L., 311

Conner, Fox, 314, 342, 418, 424, 479

Corbin, Henry C., 81, 104, 112-15, 158-59, 167

Craig, Malin, 314, 335, 355-58

Crane, Charles J., 128, 479

Cronkhite, Adelbert, 400, 409-11

Crook, George, 54-55, 477

Crowder, Enoch H., 116, 197, 248, 486

Davis, George W., 167-71, 229

Davis, Thomas F., 256, 258, 263

Debeney, Marie E., 341-43, 345, 354, 360-61, 367

Degoutte, Jean, 381, 383-90

Dickinson, Jacob M., 221

Dickman, Joseph T., 418, 487

Divisions, U.S. Army, Second (1913-1915), 252-67

Dougherty, Andrew J., 195, 224

Douglass, Henry, 51, 62

Drum, Hugh A., 314, 383, 398, 400, 403, 405, 410, 418, 471, 488

Duncan, George B., 310, 335, 340, 342, 345, 356-57, 389, 479

Eastman, Frank F., 158-61

Edwards, Clarence R., 230, 253-54, 257, 354-58, 442, 479

Ely, Hanson E., 333-34, 361-68

Fiske, Harold B., 311, 314, 487

Foch, Ferdinand, 354, 356, 380, 395-97, 408, 424

Fort Jay (N.Y.), 445

Fort Leavenworth (Ka.), 63, 74-76, 222-23

Fort Marcy (N.M.), 63

Fort Sill (Okla.), 78

Fort Stanton (N.M.), 77

Fort Union (N.M.), 51-52, 61-64

Frankfurter, Felix, 321

Funston, Frederick, 11, 263, 277, 280, 282, 285, 291, 304, 479

Gardener, Cornelius, 129-31

Garrison, Lindley, 249, 255, 258, 260-61, 263-65

Gatewood, Charles B., 58-60

General Orders 100, as applied in Philippines, 145-48

Geronimo, 55-59

Godfrey, Edward S., 40

Grant, Ulysses S., 42

Greer, Allen J., 426-29

Haan, William G., 384-85, 446, 479-80

Haig, Sir Douglas, 302, 331, 353-54, 386, 395

Harbord, James G., 71-72, 230, 248, 309, 314, 316, 322, 341, 356, 379, 382, 442, 447, 453, 480

Haskell, William N., 424

Heintzelman, Stuart, 417-18

Hilton, Charles, 116, 146

Hines, John L., 323, 334-35, 339, 342, 357, 400, 404-5, 409-10, 418, 454, 480-81

Hughes, Robert P., 81

Infantry and Cavalry School, Fort Leavenworth, 63, 73-75

Johnston, Joseph F., 96-104, 224, 229, 234, 255-56

Johnston, William H., 234, 250-51

Kean, Jefferson R., 179, 486

Kennon, Lyman W. V., 94, 282-83, 481

King, Campbell, 321, 333, 339, 361, 370, 487

Kriemhilde Stellung, German defense of, 396-400, 405, 407-11

Kuhn, Joseph, 43, 291, 308

Lahm, Frank P., 419-20

Langhorne, George T., 116, 127-28, 130, 138, 142-43, 148-49, 170

Lassiter, William, 334, 419

Laubach, Howard L., 305-6

Lawton, Henry W., 56-60, 123-24

Liggett, Hunter, 82, 224, 231, 255, 260-62,

265-66, 314, 335, 342-44, 346, 355-58, 370, 378, 383-85, 398, 405, 408, 417-18, 421, 423, 452, 462, 487

Long, Frank S., 115, 126, 130

McAlexander, Ulysses G., 335

McAndrew, James, 314, 318, 418

MacArthur, Arthur, 81, 130, 141, 147

McCain, Henry, 42, 43, 118, 161, 282, 308

McCoy, Frank R., 178, 181, 195, 286, 314

Macfadden, Bernarr, 462, 471

McIntyre, Frank, 28

McKinley, William, 83, 111-15, 122, 130, 227-28

McKinstry, Charles H., 334

Magoon, Charles E., 195-98

Malvar, Miguel, 127, 130, 138, 141, 146, 148

Mann, W. A., 308

March, Peyton C., 308, 439-41, 446, 481

Marshall, George C., Jr., 321, 334-35, 344-45, 347, 357, 361-62, 364-65, 370, 468, 487

Merritt, Wesley, 44, 70

Mexican Revolution: American policy toward, 214, 251-52, 256, 262-65; in Baja California, 213-14; impact of on the lower valley of the Rio Grande, 275-79; origins of, 212

Miles, Nelson A., 55-60, 69, 71, 112-15, 158-59, 170, 476

Military Affairs Committee, U.S. House of Representatives, 228

Military Affairs Committee, U.S. Senate, 159-61, 179

Millard, Bailey, article on Bullard's leadership, 1910, 212

Mills, Anson, 69

Mindanao: Army posts on Iligan, 168-69; Camp Overton, 173; Camp Vicars, 168,

173, 179-82; Marahui, 168, 173, 178
Moros: of Jolo, 176-78; of Lake Llano,
    Mindanao, 165-67, 171-76, 178-82
Morrison, John F., 222, 230, 255, 262
Morrow, Jay Johnson, 169, 486
Moseley, George van Horn, 261, 314, 322,
    481
Mott, T. Bentley, 33, 481-82
Muir, Charles H., 42, 44, 129, 224, 280,
    386-89, 419
Mulford, Henry B., 116, 130, 138, 143
Murphy, William L., 116, 142

National Defense Act, 1920, 440-41
National Guard: missions of, 70; relations
    with War Department, 72
Noble, Charles H., 169-70
Nolan, Dennis, 314, 471

Officers, U.S. Army: assigned to
    Volunteers, 92-94, 113-15; attitude
    toward reform, 247-49; detached duty
    for, 78-79; French opinion on, 347; post
    World War I concerns, 440-41, 447, 452;
    staff transfers for, 81-82
Officership: in America, 9-10; historical
    development, 7-9; as a profession, 6-7
Otis, Elwell S., 112, 114, 122, 141

Palmer, John McAuley, 94, 201, 314, 441-
    42, 482
Parker, Frank, 335, 339, 342, 345, 346,
    482
Parker, James, 57-60, 125, 255-56, 276,
    280, 284, 286, 291, 482
Parker, John H., 116, 125, 135, 138, 140,
    146
Pershing, John J., 11, 43, 113, 168, 172-
    73, 177-79, 228, 266, 283, 286, 303-9,
    312-24, 331-36, 340-41, 343-45, 354-

58, 361, 364-65, 367-68, 370, 377-78,
    380-81, 386, 395-411, 417-25, 427, 429,
    431-33, 440-43, 452-53, 461-63, 482-83
Pétain, Henry P. B. O., 302, 331, 353-54,
    380, 386, 408
Pettus, Edmund W., 82-83, 98, 158-61,
    179
Philippine Insurrection (1899-1902):
    campaigns of 1899, 122-23; First
    Division, Eighth Corps, offensive, 1899-
    1900, 124-31; origins of, 121;
    pacification in southern Luzon, 1900-
    1902, 135-49
Poore, Benjamin, 411
Proctor, Redfield, 73, 160-61
Professions, attributes of, 3-6

Regiments, National Guard, Infantry: First
    Louisiana Infantry, 287-89; First
    Oklahoma Infantry, 287-89; Fourth
    South Dakota Infantry, 287-89; Second
    Texas Infantry, 285-86; Third Texas
    Infantry, 285-86
Regiments, U.S. Army, Artillery: Fifth
    Field Artillery, 320; Sixth Field
    Artillery, 320; Seventh Field Artillery,
    320
Regiments, U.S. Army, Cavalry: Third
    Cavalry, 277, 280, 284; Fourth Cavalry,
    56-59, 129; Sixth Cavalry, 62; Twelfth
    Cavalry, 277; Fifteenth Cavalry, 169,
    172-74
Regiments, U.S. Army, Engineers: First
    Engineers, 338, 366, 369
Regiments, U.S. Army, Infantry: Eighth
    Infantry, 206-7, 215; Tenth Infantry, 51,
    57, 60-64, 94-95, 169; Sixteenth
    Infantry, 307, 334, 366, 454; Eighteenth
    Infantry, 307, 335, 345, 358-59, 361-62,
    366; Twenty-first Infantry, 123; Twenty-

sixth Infantry, 234, 250-51, 279-84, 286-90, 322, 334, 346-47, 361-68, 383; Twenty-eighth Infantry, 168-78, 334, 346-47, 361-68

Regiments, U.S. Volunteers, Infantry: Thirtieth U.S. Volunteers, 129, 139; Thirty-seventh U.S. Volunteers, 127-29, 139; Thirty-eighth U.S. Volunteers, 128-30

Regiments, U.S. Volunteers, Infantry, Thirty-ninth U.S. Volunteers: campaigns in southern Luzon, 124-31; organization, 115-19; pacification operations in southern Luzon, 138-49

Regiments, U.S. Volunteers (State), Infantry, Third Alabama Volunteers: organization and service of, 101-7; origins of, 95-101

Roosevelt, Theodore, 115, 158-59, 179, 194, 228

Roosevelt, Theodore Jr., 322, 339, 364, 370

Root, Elihu, 114-15, 158-60, 228-29

Santo Tomás, Laguna Province, P.I., battles around, 127-31

Schofield, John M., 9, 70-71, 74, 476

Schwan, Theodore, 81, 124-30, 135, 149

Scott, Hugh L., 91, 176-79, 249, 261-62, 288, 304, 307, 484

Sechresse, Henri, 334, 418

Second Division Camp, Texas City, Texas (1913-1915), 253-54, 266-68

Schuyler, Walter S., 94, 484

Seyburn, Stephen Y., 53, 57, 63, 77, 82, 95, 421

Seyburn, Wesson (son), 421, 471

Sheridan, Philip H., 56, 476

Sherman, William T., 9, 10, 12, 32, 50, 71-74, 476

Shirey, Guy O., 334, 356, 418, 421

Sibert, William L., 28, 97, 101, 310, 321-24, 332-34, 486

Slocum, Herbert J., 283, 288

Smith, Hamilton A., 334

Steele, Matthew F., 97, 101, 231

Stimson, Henry L., 224, 228, 232, 248, 252, 303

Stretch, John F., 51, 53, 63, 75

Summerall, Charles P., 125-30, 334-35, 342, 346, 355-56, 359-60, 381-82, 418, 447, 453, 462, 484

Sumner, Edmund V., Jr., 63, 75

Sumner, Samuel, 63, 82, 169-70, 172

Taft, William H., 195, 228, 252, 255

Taylor, Wallace C., 116, 125, 127, 138-39

Thurston, Walter A., 83, 97

Trias, Mariano, 123, 127, 138, 148

Tyner, George P., 419

Underwood, Oscar W., 82, 262

Upton, Emory, 10, 12, 50, 72, 477

U.S. Army: controversy over missions, 1890s, 69-74; educational programs for, 73-74; Line-Staff conflict, 49-50, 71-73, 247-49; organization and functions, 1885, 47-51; organization and functions, 1909, 205-6; organization of tactical units, 1911-1913, 247-49; post World War changes in, 439-41; Quartermaster's Department, 81, 83, 93, 98; relations with the National Guard, 209-10, 248, 285-86, 439-40; Subsistence Department, 81, 83, 93, 98, 150, 154

U.S. Military Academy (West Point, N.Y.): appointment of cadets to, 26-29, 33-34; Class of 1885, 42-44; curriculum, 37-39; discipline, 34-37; faculty of, 33,

38; military socialization at, 39-43; policies, 32-34

U.S. War Department: organizes Volunteers, 1898, 93; plans for war with Spain, 91-93; policy on promotion to brigadier general, 260-62; raises troops for Philippine service, 111-15

Wagner, Arthur L., 10, 73, 77

Weigel, William, 445

Western Front (1918): Aisne-Marne campaign, 383-90; fighting, Cantigny sector, 358-70; fighting, Seicheprey, 341-47, 357-58; fighting, Vesle River, 384-89; German offensives, 353-54, 365-70, 380-82; Meuse-Argonne offensive, 395-411; second battle of the Marne, 380-81; Second Army offensive, 422-25

Weston, John F., 154, 157-58, 160

Wheaton, Lloyd S., 124, 128, 131

Wheeler, Joseph, 83, 97

Wilson, George K., 356, 370, 381, 418, 429

Wilson, Woodrow, 249, 255, 261

Wotherspoon, W. W., 224

Wood, Leonard, 10, 11, 56-60, 173-82, 195, 201, 205, 214, 218, 222, 227-34, 247-49, 252-53, 255, 261, 264, 286, 305, 307, 317, 321, 344, 442, 444-45, 485

ABOUT THE AUTHOR

Allan R. Millett is professor of history at Ohio State University and director of the Force and Polity Program of the Mershon Center. He was awarded his B.A. by De Pauw University and received his M.A. and Ph.D. from Ohio State University. Professor Millett's special interest is the history of American military policy and military institutions. His previous publications include *The Politics of Intervention: The Military Occupation of Cuba, 1906-1909,* several essays, and a number of journal articles.